The Logic of Language

Language From Within

In this ambitious two-volume work, Pieter Seuren seeks a theoretical unity that can bridge the chasms of modern linguistics as he sees them, bringing together the logical, the psychological, and the pragmatic; the empirical and the theoretical; the formalist and the empiricist; and situating it all in the context of two and a half millennia of language study.

Volume I: Language in Cognition
Volume II: The Logic of Language

The Logic of Language

PIETER A. M. SEUREN

OXFORD
UNIVERSITY PRESS

OXFORD
UNIVERSITY PRESS

Great Clarendon Street, Oxford, OX2 6DP,
United Kingdom

Oxford University Press is a department of the University of Oxford.
It furthers the University's objective of excellence in research, scholarship,
and education by publishing worldwide. Oxford is a registered trade mark of
Oxford University Press in the UK and in certain other countries

First published 2010

Published in the United States of America by Oxford University Press
198 Madison Avenue, New York, NY 10016, United States of America

British Library Cataloguing in Publication Data
Data available

Library of Congress Cataloging in Publication Data
Data available

ISBN 978–0–19–955948–0

to Pim Levelt
for his unfailing support, advice and friendship

Contents

Preface

This is the second and last volume of *Language from Within*. The first volume dealt with general methodology in the study of language (which is seen as an element in and product of human cognition), with the intrinsically intensional ontology that humans operate with when thinking and speaking, with the socially committing nature of linguistic utterances, with the mechanisms involved in the production and interpretation of utterances, with the notions of utterance meaning, sentence meaning, and lexical meaning, and, finally, with the difficulties encountered when one tries to capture lexical meanings in definitional terms. The present volume looks more closely at the logic inherent in natural language and at the ways in which utterance interpretation has to fall back on the context of discourse and on general knowledge. It deals extensively with the natural semantics of the operators that define human logic, both in its presumed innate form and in the forms it has taken as a result of cultural development. And it does so in the context of the history of logic, as it is assumed that this history mirrors the path followed in Western culture from 'primitive' logical (and mathematical) thinking to the rarified heights of perfection achieved in these areas of study over the past few centuries.

The overall and ultimate purpose of the whole work is to lay the foundations for a general theory of language, which integrates language into its ecological setting of cognition and society, given the physical conditions of human brain structure and general physiology and the physics of sound production and perception. This general theory should eventually provide an overall, maximally motivated, and maximally precise, even formal, interpretative framework for linguistic diversity, thus supporting typological studies with a more solid theoretical basis. The present work restricts itself to semantics and, to a lesser extent, also to grammar, which are more directly dependent on cognition and society, leaving aside phonology, which appears to find its motivational roots primarily in the physics and the psychology of sound production and perception, as well as in the input phonological systems receive from grammar.

The two volumes are not presented as a complete theory but rather as a prolegomena and, at the same time, as an actual start, in the overall and all-pervasive perspective of the cognitive and social embedding of language—a perspective that has been hesitantly present in modern language studies but has not so far been granted the central position it deserves. In this context, it has proved necessary, first of all, to break open the far too rigid and too narrow restrictions and dogmas that have dominated the study of language over the past half-century, which has either put formal completeness above the constraints imposed by cognition or, by way of contrast, rejected any kind of formal treatment and has tried to reduce the whole of language to intuition-based folk psychology.

The present, second, volume is, regrettably but unavoidably, much more technical than the first, owing to the intrinsic formal nature of the topics dealt with. Avoiding technicalities would have reduced the book either to utter triviality or to incomprehensibility, but I have done my best to be gentle with my readers, requiring no more than a basic ability (and willingness) to read formulaic text and presupposing an elementary knowledge of logic and set theory.

Again, as in the first volume, I wish to express my gratitude to those who have helped me along with their encouragement and criticisms. And again, I must start by mentioning my friend of forty years' standing Pim Levelt, to whom I have dedicated both volumes. He made it possible for me to work at the Max Planck Institute for Psycholinguistics at Nijmegen after my retirement from Nijmegen University and was a constant source of inspiration not only on account of the thoughts he shared with me but also because of his moral example. Then I must mention my friend and colleague Dany Jaspers of the University of Brussels, whose wide knowledge, well-formulated comments, and infectious enthusiasm were a constant source of inspiration. Ferdinando Cavaliere made many useful suggestions regarding predicate logic and its history. Finally, I want to thank Kyle Jasmin, whose combined kindness and computer savviness were indispensable to get the text right. The many others who have helped me carry on by giving their intellectual, moral, and personal support are too numerous to be mentioned individually. Yet my gratitude to them is none the less for that. Some, who will not be named, inspired me by their fierce opposition, which forced me to be as keen as they were at finding holes in my armour. I hope I have found and repaired them all.

P. A. M. S.
Nijmegen, December 2008.

Abbreviations and symbols

AAPC	Aristotelian-Abelardian predicate calculus
ABPC	Aristotelian-Boethian predicate calculus (=the Square of Opposition)
BNPC	basic-natural predicate calculus
BNST	basic-natural set theory
fprop	'flat' proposition without TCM
IP	incrementation procedure
modprop	proposition with TCM
M-partial	mutually partial
NPI	negative polarity item
NST	natural set theory
OSTA	Optimization of sense, truth and actuality
PEM	Principle of the Excluded Middle
PET	Principle of the Excluded Third
PNST	principle of natural set theory
PPI	positive polarity item
SA	semantic analysis
SMPC	standard modern predicate calculus
SNPC	strict-natural predicate calculus (=ABPC)
SNST	strict-natural set theory
SST	standard (constructed) set theory
SSV	Substitution *salva veritate*
TCM	topic–comment modulation
UEI	undue existential import

A	All *F* is *G*	ev	extreme value (∅ or **OBJ)**
I	Some *F* is *G*	iff	if and only if
N	No *F* is *G*	**L**_L	logical language
A*	All *F* is *not-G*	∀	the universal quantifier
I*	Some *F* is *not-G*	∃	the existential quantifier
N*	No *F* is *not-G*	N	the quantifier NO in BNPC
A!	All *G* is *F*	¬	standard bivalent negation
I!	Some *G* is *F*	X ∩ Y	set-theoretic intersection of *X* and *Y*
P ≡ Q	P and Q are equivalent	X ∪ Y	set-theoretic union of *X* and *Y*
P ⊢ Q	P logically entails Q	$\overline{X}$	the complement of set *X* in **OBJ**
P ⤬ Q	P and Q are contraries	**a** ∈ X	a is an element in the set *X*
P ⤲ Q	P and Q are subcontraries	X ∋ a	the set *X* contains the element a
P # Q	P and Q are contradictories	X ⊂ Y	*X* is properly included in *Y*
U	the set of all admissible situations	X ⊆ Y	*X* is included in or equal to *Y*
OBJ	the set of all objects	∅	the null set
VS	valuation space	[[F]]	the extension of predicate **F**
/P/	the VS of proposition P in **U**	X Ů Y	*X* and *Y* are in full union: X ∪ Y = **OBJ**
a = b	a is identical with b	X OO Y	*X* and *Y* are mutually exclusive:
|X|	the cardinality of set X		X ∩ Y = ∅; X,Y ≠ ∅ ≠ **OBJ**
Q ≫ P	Q presupposes P	X ⓪ Y	*X* M-partially intersects with *Y*: X ∩ Y ≠ ∅ ≠ X ≠ Y; X,Y ≠ **OBJ**
Q > P	Q invites the inference P		
ρ(a)	the reference value of term a		
@	'asinus': donkey pronoun		
•	basic-natural NEITHER–NOR		

1

Logic and entailment

1.1 What is a logic and why do we need one in the study of language?

The paramount reason why we need logic in the study of language is that logic is the formal theory of consistency and that consistency is an all-pervasive and essential semantic aspect of human linguistic interaction. This is true not only of single sentences but also, and in a much bigger way, of texts and discourses. And since presuppositions are, if you like, the cement that makes discourses consistent and since they are induced by the tens of thousands of lexical predicates in any language, it should be obvious that the logic of presuppositions is a prime necessity for natural language semantics. Yet so as not to drown the reader in a sea of injudiciously administered complexities, presuppositions (and its logical counterpart, presuppositional trivalent logic) are kept at bay till Chapter 10. Until then, we stay within the strict limits of bivalent predicate and propositional logic, though with occasional glances at multivalence and presuppositions. But the reader will discover that, even within these limits, there is plenty of room for innovative uncluttering.

A further reason why logic is important for the study of language lies in the fact that the syntax of the formulae of the various predicate-logic systems considered is essentially the same as that of the semantic analyses (SAs) that underlie sentences. And, as was shown in various works belonging to the tradition of Generative Semantics or Semantic Syntax (e.g. McCawley 1973; Seuren 1996), the hypothesis that SA-syntax is, in principle, the syntax of modern logical formulae has proved an exceptional tool for the charting of striking syntactic generalizations in all natural languages and thus for the setting up of a general theory of syntax of exceptional explanatory power.

Moreover, a closer investigation of the logic inherent in natural cognition and natural language will help clarify the hitherto opaque relation between logic on the one hand and language and cognition on the other. (Ask any logician what this relation amounts to and you will get a curiously strange gamut of replies, all of them unsatisfactory.) This is, in itself, surprising because language and logic have, from the very Aristotelian beginnings, been close, though uneasy, bedfellows, never able either to demarcate each other's territories or to sort out what unites them. The last century has seen a tremendous upsurge in both logic and linguistics, but there has not been a *rapprochement* worth speaking of. No logic is taught in the vast majority of linguistics departments or, to my knowledge, in any psychology department, simply because the relevance of logic for the study of language and mind has never been made clear.

All in all, therefore, it seems well worth our while to take a fresh look at logic in the context of the study of language. But, in doing so, we need an open and flexible mind, because the paradigm of modern logic has come to suffer from a significant degree of dogmatism, rigidity, and, it has to be said, intellectual arrogance. Until, say, 1950 it was common for philosophers and others to play around with logical systems and notations, but this, perhaps naïve, openness was suppressed by the developments that followed. The august status conferred upon logic once the period of foundational research was more or less brought to an end, which was, let us say, around 1950, has not encouraged investigators to deviate from what was, from then on, considered the norm in logical theory. Yet that norm is based on mathematics, in particular on standard Boolean set theory, whereas what is required for a proper understanding of the relations between logic, language, and thinking is a logic based on natural cognitive and linguistic intuitions. We are in need of a 'natural' logic of language and cognition drawn from the facts not of mathematics but of language. The first purpose of writing about logic in this book is, therefore, programmatic: an attempt is made at loosening up and generalizing the notion of logic and at showing to linguists, psychologists, semanticists, and pragmaticists why and how logic is relevant for their enquiries.

An obvious feature of the present book is the attention paid to history. The history of logic is looked at as much as its present state. This historical dimension is essential, for at least two reasons. First, there is a general reason, derived from the fact that the human sciences as well as logic are not CUMULATIVE the way the natural sciences are taken to be, where new results simply supersede existing knowledge and insight. In the human sciences and, as we shall see, also in logic, old insights keep cropping up and new results or insights all too often prove unacceptably restrictive or even faulty. Since the human sciences want to emulate the natural sciences, they have adopted the latter's convention that all relevant recent literature must be referred to or else the paper or book is considered lacking in quality. But they have forgotten or repressed the fact that they are not cumulative: literature and traditions from the more distant past are likely to be as relevant as the most recent literature and paths that have been followed in recent times may well turn out to be dead ends so that the steps must be retraced. Recognizing that means recognizing that the history of the subject is indispensable.

The second, more specific, reason is that the history of logic mirrors the cultural and educational progress that has led Western society from more 'primitive' ways of thinking to the unrivalled heights of formal precision achieved in modern logic and mathematics. This is important because, as is explained in Chapter 3, it seems that natural logical intuitions have only gone along so far in this development and have, at a given moment, detached themselves from the professional mathematical logicians, leaving them to their own devices. It is surmised in Chapters 3 and 4 that natural logical intuitions are a mixture of pristine 'primitive' intuitions and more sophisticated intuitions integrated into our thinking and our culture since the Aristotelian beginnings. It is this divide between what has been culturally integrated and what has been left to the closed chambers of mathematicians and logicians that has motivated the distinction, made in Chapter 3, between 'natural' logical intuitions on the one hand and 'constructed', no longer natural, notions in logic and mathematics on the other.

Historical insight makes us see that linguistic studies have, from the very start, been divided into two currents, FORMALISM and ECOLOGISM (see, for example, Seuren 1986a, 1998a: 23–7, 405–10). In present-day semantic studies, the formalists are represented by formal model-theoretic semantics, while modern ecologism is dominated by pragmatics. It hardly needs arguing that, on the one hand, formal semantics, based as it is on standard modern logic, badly fails to do justice to linguistic reality. Pragmatics, on the other hand, suffers from the same defect, though for the opposite reason. While formal semantics exaggerates formalisms and lacks the patience to delay formalization till more is known, pragmatics shies away from formal theories and lives by appeals to intuition. Either way, it seems to me, the actual facts of language remain unexplained. If this is so, there must be room for a more formal variety of ecologism, which is precisely what is proposed in the present book. One condition for achieving such a purpose is the loosening up of logic.

It may seem that logic is a great deal simpler and more straightforward than human language, being strictly formal by definition and so much more restricted in scope and coverage, and so much farther removed from the intricate and often confused realities of daily life that language has to cope with. Yet logic has its own fascinating depth and beauty, not only when studied from a strictly mathematical perspective but also, and perhaps even more so, when seen in the context of human language and cognition. In that context, the serene purity created by the mathematics of logic is drawn into the realm of the complexities of the human mind and the mundane needs served by human language. But before we embark upon an investigation of the complexities and the mundane needs, we will look at logic in the pure light of analytical necessity.

What is meant here by logic, or a logic, does not differ essentially from the current standard notion, shaped to a large extent by the formal and foundational progress made during the twentieth century. As far as it goes, the modern notion is clear and unambiguous, but it still lacks clarity with regard to its semantic basis. In the present chapter the semantic basis is looked at more closely, in connection with the notion of entailment as analytically necessary inference—that is, inference based on meanings. This is not in itself controversial, as few logicians nowadays will deny that logic is based on analytical necessity, but the full consequences of that fact have not been drawn (probably owing to the deep semantic neurosis that afflicted the twentieth century).

During the first half of the twentieth century, most logicians defended the view that logical derivations should be defined merely on grounds of the agreed FORMS of the L-propositions or logical formulae,[1] consisting of logical constants and typed variables in given syntactic structures. The derivation of entailments was thus reduced to a formal operation on strings of symbols, disregarding any semantic criterion. Soon, however, the view prevailed that the operations on logical form should be seen as driven by the semantic properties of the logical constants. I concur with this latter view, mainly because there is nothing analytically necessary in form, but there is in meaning. This position is supported by the fact that a meaning that is well-defined for the purpose of logic is itself a formal object, in the sense that it is representable as a structured object open to a formal interpretation in terms of a formal calculus such as logical computation.

In earlier centuries, the ideas of what constitutes logic have varied a great deal. In medieval scholastic philosophy, for example, a distinction was made between *logica maior*, or the philosophical critique of knowledge, and *logica*

---

[1] The notion of L-proposition is defined in Section 3.1.4 of Volume I as 'a type-level semantically explicit L-structure, which is transformed by the grammar module into a corresponding type-level surface structure, which can, in the end, be realized as a token utterance'. L-propositions form the language of SEMANTIC ANALYSIS (SA), whose expressions (L-propositions) equal logical formulae in some variety of predicate logic. It is important to note that L-propositions are *type-level* elements, whereas propositions are *token-level* mental occurrences. L-propositions are part of the linguistic machinery that turns propositional token occurrences into sentence-types of a given lexically and grammatically defined language system. See also Section 1.4.

minor, also called *dialectica*, which was the critical study and use of the logical apparatus of the day—that is, Aristotelian-Boethian predicate calculus and syllogistic. Logica maior is no longer reckoned to be part of logic but, rather, of general or 'first' philosophy. Logica minor corresponds more closely to the modern notion of logic. During the nineteenth century logic was considered to be the study of the principles of correct reasoning, as opposed to the processes actually involved in (good or bad) thinking, which were assigned to the discipline of psychology. The Oxford philosopher Thomas Fowler, for example, wrote (1892: 2–6):

> The more detailed consideration of [...] Thoughts or the results of Thinking becomes the subject of a science with a distinct name, Logic, which is thus a subordinate branch of the wider science, Psychology. [...] It is the province of Logic to distinguish correct from incorrect thoughts. [...] Logic may therefore be defined as the science of the conditions on which correct thoughts depend, and the art of attaining to correct and avoiding incorrect thoughts. [...] Logic is concerned with the *products* or results rather than with the *process* of thought, i.e. with *thoughts* rather than with *thinking*.

Similar statements are found in virtually all logic textbooks of that period. After 1900, however, changes are beginning to occur, slowly at first but then, especially after the 1920s, much faster, until the nineteenth-century view of logic fades away entirely during the 1960s, with Copi (1961) as one rare late representative.

But what do we, following the twentieth-century tradition in this respect, take logic to be? Since about 1900, logic has increasingly been seen as *the study of consistency through a formal calculus for the derivation of entailments*. In this view, which we adopt in principle, logic amounts to the study of how to derive L-propositions from other L-propositions *salva veritate*—that is, preserving truth. Such derivations must be purely formal and independent of intuition. According to some logicians, they are based exclusively on the structural properties of the expressions in the logical language adopted, but others, perhaps the majority, defend the view that the semantic properties of certain designated expressions, the LOGICAL CONSTANTS, co-determine logical derivations, provided these meanings are formally well-defined, which means in practice that they must be reducible to the operators of Boolean algebra (see Section 2.3.2 for a precise account). On either view, logic must be a CALCULUS—that is, a set of formally well-defined operations on strings of terms, driven only by the well-defined structural properties of the expressions in the logical language and the well-defined semantic properties of the logical constants.

When one accepts the dependency on the meanings of the logical constants involved, one may say that logic is an exercise in analytical necessity.

This basic adherence to the twentieth-century notion of what constitutes a logic is motivated not only by the fact that it is clear and well-defined but also by the consideration that it allows us to re-inspect the 'peasant roots' of logic, as found in the works of Aristotle and his ancient successors, from a novel point of view. Traditional logicians only had natural intuitions of necessary consequence and consistency to fall back on for the construction of their logical systems, lacking as they did the sophisticated framework of modern mathematical set theory. Yet this less sophisticated source of logical inspiration is precisely what we need for our enterprise, which aims at uncovering the logic people use in their daily dealings and their ordinary use of natural language. *Pace* Russell, we thus revert unashamedly to psychological logic.

Though Aristotle, the originator of logic, did not yet use the term *logic*, his writings, in particular *On Interpretation* and *Prior Analytics*, show that his starting point was the discovery that often two sentences are inconsistent with regard to each other in the sense that they cannot be true simultaneously. He coined the term CONTRARIES (enántiai) for such pairs (or sets) of sentences. When two sentences are contraries, the truth of the one entails the falsity of the other. He then worked out a logical system on the basis of contrariety and contradictoriness—and thus also of entailment—as systematic consequences of certain logical constants.

Of course, the question arises of what motivates the particular selection of the logical constants involved and of the operations they allow for, given their semantic definition. A good answer is that the choice of the relevant constants and of the operations on the expressions in which they occur is guided by the intuitive criterion of *consistency* of what is said on various occasions. Such consistency is of prime importance in linguistic interaction, since, as is argued in Chapter 4 of Volume I, speakers, when asserting a proposition, put themselves on the line with regard to the truth of what they assert. Inconsistency will thus make their commitment ineffective. When a set of predicates is seen to allow for a *formal calculus* of consistency, we have hit on a *logical system*, anchored in the syntax of the logical language employed and in the semantic definitions of the logical constants, whose meanings are specified in each language's lexicon. That being so, a not unimportant part of the semanticist's, more precisely the lexicographer's, brief consists in finding out how and to what extent natural language achieves informational consistency through its logical constants.

Consistency is directly dependent on truth and the preservation of truth through chains of entailments, also called logical derivations. The operations licensed by the logical constants must ensure that L-propositions, when interpreted as being true in relation to given states of affairs, yield L-propositions that are likewise true under the same interpretation. When they do that, it is said that the logical derivation is VALID. The validity of logical derivations should depend solely on the MEANING—that is, the SATISFACTION CONDITIONS—of the logical constants involved and by their syntactic position. This ensures that the validity of a sound logic is based on analytical necessity. It does not mean, however, that there can be only one valid logic, a misconception often found among interested laymen and even among professional logicians. In principle, there is an infinite array of possible logics, each defined by the choice of the logical constants and the meanings and syntax defined for them. But once the constants and their meanings have been fixed, logical derivations are analytically necessary.

It is now obvious that logic must be closely related to natural language, since the most obvious class of expressions carrying the property of truth or falsity are the assertive utterances made by speakers or writers in some natural language. Of course, one can try and make an artificial language whose expressions are bearers of truth values, but one way or another such expressions are all calques, sometimes idealized or streamlined, of natural language expressions.

1.2 The definition of entailment

1.2.1 *The general concept of entailment*

At this point we need to specify more precisely what is meant by ENTAILMENT. We begin by giving a definition of entailment in general:

> ENTAILMENT
> When an L-proposition (or set of L-propositions) P ENTAILS an L-proposition Q (in formal notation P $\models$ Q), then, whenever P is true, Q must of necessity also be true, on account of the specific linguistic meaning of P—that is, for analytical reasons.

For example, the L-proposition underlying the sentence *Jack has been murdered* entails the L-proposition underlying the sentence *Jack is dead* because it is in the meaning of the predicate *have been murdered* that whoever has been murdered must of necessity be dead.

The entailment relation is, however, subject to an essential proviso: both the entailing and the entailed (L-)proposition must be identically KEYED to a chunk of spatio-temporal reality. Definite terms must refer to the same objects and the tenses used must have identical or corresponding temporal values. Thus, in the example given, the proper name *Jack* must refer to the same person and the present tense must refer to the same time slice in both statements. This is the MODULO-KEY CONDITION on the entailment relation. This condition may seem trivial and is, in most cases, silently understood. In fact, however, it is far from trivial. It is defined as follows:

> **THE MODULO-KEY CONDITION**
>
> Whenever a (type-level) L-proposition or set of L-propositions P entails a (type-level) L-proposition Q, the condition holds that all coordinates in the underlying propositions *p* and *q* that link up *p* and *q* with elements in the world take identical or corresponding keying values in the interpretation of any token occurrences of P and Q, respectively.

The Modulo-Key Condition, however, does not allow one to say that if the terms *Jack* and *Dr. Smith* refer to the same person, (the L-proposition underlying) the statement *Jack has been murdered* entails (the L-proposition underlying) the statement *Dr. Smith is dead*, and analogously with the names interchanged. This is so because entailment is a *type-level* relation and *at type-level* it is not given that Jack is the same person as Dr. Smith. To have the entailment it is, therefore, necessary to insert the intermediate sentence *Jack is Dr. Smith*. All the Modulo-Key Condition does is ensure that the term *Jack* is keyed to the same person every time it is used.

The Modulo-Key Condition implies a cognitive claim, since keying is the cognitive function of being intentionally focused on specific objects in the world in a specific state of affairs. This cognitive claim involves at least the existence of a system of coordinates for the mental representation of states of affairs. Whenever the sentences in question are used 'seriously', and not as part of a fictional text presented as such, these coordinates have values that are located in the actual world. For the entailment relation to be applicable, and indeed for the construction of any coherent discourse, the participants in the discourse must share a system of coordinates needed for a well-determined common intentional focusing on the same objects and the same time. The mechanism needed for a proper functioning of such a mental system of coordinates and their values is still largely unknown. We do know, however, that it is an integral part of and a prerequisite for an overall system of discourse construction, both in production and in comprehension—the system that we call *anchoring*. Since most of this system is still opaque, we are forced to conclude that what presented itself as a trivial condition of constancy of keying for entailment relations turns out to open up a vast area of new research, a *terra incognita* for the study of language, meaning, and logic.

In addition to entailment, there is also EQUIVALENCE, normally defined as entailment in both directions: 'P is equivalent with Q' is said to mean that P $\models$ Q and Q $\models$ P. This will do no harm for the moment, but in Chapter 3 it is argued that it is probably not a good way of making explicit what (semantic) equivalence amounts to in natural language and cognition. In natural language and cognition, equivalence is not so much a (meta)relation, yielding truth or falsity when applied to any *n*-tuple of L-propositions, as a cognitive operation taking two or more L-propositions and turning them into one at a certain level of representation. As a *relation*, equivalence makes little cognitive sense, since when two L-propositions are equivalent at some level of cognitive representation, they count as one, not as two. As an *operation*, however, equivalence makes a great deal of cognitive sense, since what counts as two or more at some level of representation can be made to count as one at a different level. In this sense one can say that *Jack sold a car to Jim* is equivalent with *Jim bought a car from Jack* (modulo key). To say that these two sentences are equivalent then amounts to saying that they are turned into one, or are identified, *salva veritate*, at some level, but not necessarily at all levels, of representation.

In the definition of entailment given above we have inserted the condition 'on account of the specific linguistic meaning of P'. This is, in itself, not controversial, but the wording implies that necessarily true L-propositions cannot properly be said to be entailed by any arbitrary L-proposition (the medieval inference rule 'verum per se ex quolibet'), and likewise that necessarily false L-propositions cannot properly be said to entail any arbitrary L-proposition ('ex falso per se ad quodlibet'). These theorems may be said to hold in a strictly mathematical sense, yet they fail to satisfy the definition given, since no specific semantic properties of the entailing L-proposition are involved. We also consider them to be irrelevant for a proper understanding of natural language. The entailments that are relevant are subject to the condition that they derive from the lexically defined meanings of the predicates occurring in the entailing sentence, as it is predicates that produce truth or falsity when applied to objects of the proper kind, due to their satisfaction conditions—that is, the conditions that must be satisfied by any object to 'deserve' the predicate in question. Since more specific conditions imply less specific conditions (for example, the condition of being a rose implies the condition of being a flower), the satisfaction of a more specific predicate by certain objects implies the satisfaction by the same objects of a predicate defined by less specific conditions. This is the basis of the entailment relation we wish to consider. It means that, as long as the objects and the state of affairs involved remain the same, the predicates can do their entailment work. We thus require of the relation of NATURAL ENTAILMENT from P to Q that it be subject to the condition that *the preservation of truth rests on the meaning of the predicates in the entailing sentence P* and on their structural position in *P*. Henceforth, unless otherwise specified, when we speak of entailment, what is intended is natural entailment.

1.2.2 *The specific concept of logical entailment*

A few of Plato's students, in particular Aristotle, discovered that some entailments can be formally computed on the basis of certain specific elements (words) in statements, the so-called LOGICAL CONSTANTS or LOGICAL OPERATORS, known to medieval philosophers as SYNCATEGOREMATA (Moody 1953: 16–17). Statements, or, more precisely, the type-level L-propositions underlying them, allow for a distinction to be made between, on the one hand, logical constants and, on the other, the nonlogical remainder, which are rendered in logical analyses by means of symbols called 'lexical variables'.

Traditionally, the set of logical constants is extremely limited. It consists of the words representing the notions of ALL and its relatives (the universal quantifier), SOME and its relatives (the existential quantifier), NOT (negation), AND (conjunction), OR (disjunction) and, if one wishes, also IF ... THEN (material implication). The quantifiers ALL and SOME do service in PREDICATE CALCULUS, where the lexical variables involved range over predicates. The remaining operators, NOT, AND, and OR (and normally also IF ... THEN), serve in PROPOSITIONAL CALCULUS, where the lexical variables involved range over L-propositions.[2] Since propositional calculus can be incorporated into predicate calculus, the propositional operators can also be put to use in predicate calculus. The propositional operator NOT, in particular, is indispensable not only in propositional calculus but also in any interesting form of predicate calculus.

Further 'fields' of predicate meanings have been discovered, and are perhaps still to be discovered, that allow for the development of a logical system in addition to the predicate and propositional logics we already have. Modal logic, for example, which is as old as predicate logic, has, in addition, the constants NECESSARY and POSSIBLE, and, in modern times, verbal tenses are likewise used as logical constants in tense logics. But the thesis we defend in the present book does not require that we be concerned with logical systems

---

[2] Since Łukasiewicz (1934) it has been known that the logical constants discovered by Aristotle are ALL, SOME, and NOT. Aristotle's syllogistic shows that he had some awareness of the logical force of AND, but he never exploited that. Propositional calculus, based on the logical constants NOT, AND, OR, and IF ... THEN is a product of the Stoic philosophers.

beyond propositional and predicate logic, though there will be occasional references to modal logic.

Those entailments that are formally computable with the help of either predicate calculus or propositional calculus we call LOGICAL ENTAILMENTS. They form a subcategory of the general category of entailments. Semantically necessary truths thus comprise logically necessary truths as a subclass.

Logical entailments are computable on account of the formally defined meanings of the logical constants that occur in sentences. Thus, when we speak of logical entailment, we mean a necessary consequence resulting from a calculus built on the meanings of the logical constants in the entailing sentence:

> LOGICAL ENTAILMENT
> When an L-proposition P LOGICALLY ENTAILS an L-proposition Q (formal-ly P ⊢ Q), then, whenever P is true, Q must of necessity also be true, on account of the meaning(s) of the logical constant(s) in P. Logical entail-ments are by definition formally computable in terms of a logical system.

LOGICAL EQUIVALENCE, moreover, is defined as logical entailment in both direc-tions: 'P is logically equivalent with Q' (or P ≡ Q) means that P ⊢ Q and Q ⊢ P.

Logic is thus a formal calculus for the derivation of entailments. A logic is SOUND when it admits only entailments that are consistent with the entailing L-propositions. We shall see that natural logic adds the condition that the entailing L-proposition must itself have the possibility of truth and that the entailed L-proposition must itself have the possibility of falsity.

All textbooks on logic define the entailment relation without the analyticity condition—that is, without explicitly stipulating that the entailment must be due to the MEANING(s) of the logical constant(s) in the entailing L-proposition. They merely require that when P ⊢ Q, truth of P NECESSARILY requires truth of Q, where necessity is defined negatively as independence of any possible contingent situation. In the actual practice of modern logic, logical entailments are taken to follow from the logical system in the logical language used. And since this logical language consists of logical constants and variables, it is ultimately the constants that define the entailments. But this is not quite the same as saying, as we do, that the entailments are due to the MEANING(s) of the logical constant(s) in the entailing L-proposition. The difference becomes visible when one considers 'nonnatural' or 'constructed' theorems or inference rules, such as the theorem that a necessarily false L-proposition entails any other L-proposition (the old rule 'ex falso per se ad quodlibet' mentioned earlier), or that a necessarily true L-proposition is entailed by any arbitrary

L-proposition ('verum per se ex quolibet'), or the theorem (inference rule), usually called 'addition', which says that, for arbitrary L-propositions P and Q, P ⊢ (P or Q). Such 'entailments' follow from the logical system used, but they are not based on the meanings of the logical constants in the entailing L-propositions and are, therefore, not considered to be entailments in the present context. Although such theorems are mathematically valid, they are considered counterproductive, even 'pathological' (in a nondramatic sense), in the logic of language.

The formal calculus of logical entailments is made possible on account of the fact that the meaning definitions of the logical constants contain as central elements conditions which are defined in terms that allow for formal computation. Therefore, the assumption that sound logical reasoning in natural language is possible implies the assumption that natural language contains expressions that reflect logical constants with meanings admitting of formal computation, which together form a consistent computational system allowing for the derivation of logically necessary consequences. In this perspective, it is an obvious thought that it may be worth our while to see if the logical constants can be legitimately treated as predicates in the logical language of L-propositions. In Section 2.3 it is shown that the logical constants are indeed naturally treated as (abstract) predicates.

Since there are many different possible consistent systems allowing for the formal, computational derivation of logical entailments, each system being defined by the choice and the meanings of the logical constants, the empirical question arises as to exactly which logic underlies logical reasoning in language and, by extension, in thinking. It is often taken for granted, perhaps more by outsiders than by professional logicians, that the bivalent predicate and propositional logic which has been considered standard throughout the twentieth century is the only viable or reasonable logic to operate with. This view, however, is misguided. Standard modern logic may provide a suitable metalanguage for the specification of mathematical truths and entailments, but that does not automatically make it a suitable model for the logic of cognition and of natural language.

There is, of course, an extensive literature aiming at definitions for, and logico-mathematical specifications of, the various quantifiers found in natural language, including and beyond *all* and *some*. Yet this literature somehow seems to miss the point of the present study, which is the logical *system* of cognition and of the object language, the system that safeguards consistency through discourse. Standard logic may provide a suitable descriptive *metalanguage* for the meanings of natural language logical operators (as for well-nigh anything else), but it does not provide a *model* for the logic of language and cognition. The question of what is the, or a, proper *model* for the logic of language has so far received little or no attention. It is this question that is central to the present study.

1.3 The referential independence of logic: no truth-value gaps

Since logical entailments are necessary consequences which derive their necessity from the meanings of the logical constants involved, logic is by definition predicated on the notion of analytical necessity and therefore by definition independent of any contingent state of affairs. The logical machinery must preserve truth through entailment relations regardless of whatever specific state of affairs it is applied to, provided the Modulo-Key Condition is observed. This independence of specific states of affairs we call the *referential independence of logic*. It is essential if logic is to be a calculus of entailments.

The referential independence of logic does not preclude the existence of SPECIFIC LOGICS which look as if they specify entailment relations only for certain states of affairs, or, as is often said nowadays, for certain knowledge states. Such logics can be very useful in practice and, caught under the name of nonmonotonic logics, they abound in the reality of human life. For example, given the fact that prisoners of war are protected by the Geneva Convention, one may say that (the L-proposition underlying) a statement like (1.1a) 'entails' (the L-proposition underlying) the statement (1.1b):

(1.1)   a. All enemy troops have been taken prisoner.
        b. All enemy troops are protected by the Geneva Convention.

But this means no more than that the condition 'All prisoners of war are protected by the Geneva Convention' is silently understood and incorporated into the entailment relation, so that in reality it is not (1.1a) but (1.2) that entails (1.1b):

(1.2)   All enemy troops have been taken prisoner and all prisoners of war are protected by the Geneva Convention.

It stands to reason that specific logics are richer than general unrestricted logics, in the sense that they allow for more conclusions to be drawn. This is part of their usefulness in ordinary life, which again is why practitioners of artificial intelligence set great store by developing all kinds of 'nonmonotonic' logics.

Yet the notion of 'specific logic' is easily misunderstood in that it is believed that such logics are valid only in certain states of affairs and are thus usable within the confines of specific restricted knowledge states. In other words, they presuppose that certain conditions are fulfilled in the states of affairs the logic is to be applied to. That having been said, the feeling is that all is well. In fact, however, such specific logics must be caught under the umbrella of some sound universally applicable logic, or else there is no specific logic at all. In the case of examples (1.1) and (1.2), the 'umbrella' is completed by the addition of a silently understood contingent condition, namely that prisoners of war are protected by the Geneva Convention. In this book, we are not concerned with 'specific' or 'nonmonotonic' logics. What we are concerned with is the more basic, though technologically less challenging, question of the meanings of the logical constants concerned in the overall, universally applicable, 'umbrella' logic.

Consider the well-known example of traditional Aristotelian-Boethian predicate calculus. This logic is sound only for states of affairs where the class of things quantified over is nonnull: it has so-called 'existential import', which makes it nonvalid as a logical system. It is widely believed that this logic is saved from its undue existential import by the mere stipulation that it PRESUPPOSES that the class of things quantified over (the F-class) is nonnull. Once that condition has been stated, so it is thought, the logic is safe. But this cannot be correct. For either Aristotelian-Boethian predicate calculus is to be considered a specific logic, in which case it is in need of a general 'umbrella' logic, or it is meant to be a general logic, in which case it must specify what entailments are valid in any arbitrary state of affairs, no matter whether the class of things quantified over does or does not contain any elements.

Strawson failed to see this when he proposed (1952: 170–6) that (the L-proposition underlying) a statement like (1.3) lacks a truth value (falls into a 'truth-value gap') because there is in fact not a single Londoner alive of that age:

(1.3)   All 150-year-old Londoners are bald.

If Strawson were right, it would follow that (1.3), which otherwise has impeccable papers for serving in Aristotelian-Boethian predicate calculus, falls outside that calculus when used here and now. But as soon as one Londoner were indeed to reach the age of 150 years, (1.3) suddenly would have a truth value and would take part in Aristotelian-Boethian predicate calculus. And then, all of a sudden, it would entail that at least one 150-year-old Londoner is bald—an entailment defined as valid in that logic. It is easily seen that this is in stark conflict with the concept of entailment as used in logic, since it makes entailments dependent on contingencies, on what happens to be or not to be the case, which is precisely what is excluded by the concept of entailment.

Some authors say that (1.3), as used here and now, is truth-valueless but still takes part in a logical calculus. Formally, this amounts to saying that the universal quantifier ALL is a *partial*, not a *total*, function, which refuses as input the otherwise grammatically well-formed expression denoting the F-class when this F-class contains no members. But either this makes the logic dependent on contingent conditions, which is inadmissible, or it surreptitiously uses the term 'truth-valueless' as the name of a truth value and not as a qualification applied to grammatically well-formed but contingently refused inputs. It seems that dependence on contingencies is properly avoided by the introduction of a third truth value in the sense that what is *falsity* in standard bivalent systems is split up into *minimal* and *radical falsity*. This point of view is defended and amply discussed and elaborated in Chapter 10.

A similar predicament arises with sentences that contain a definite term that is either unkeyed (and thus fails to refer), such as *The boy laughed*, said without any context, or is well-keyed but fails to refer to an actually existing entity though the main predicate requires it to do so, such as *The present king of France is bald*. Here again, the predicates *laugh* and *bald* (and the vast majority of predicates in any natural language) can be treated as partial functions refusing unkeyed or not actually existing inputs and thus yielding the 'value' *undefined*. Yet (radical) negation yields truth in *The present king of France is NOT bald* (which makes *The present king of France is bald* radically false), whereas the unkeyed sentence *The boy did NOT laugh* is as devoid of a truth value as its positive counterpart *The boy laughed*. It seems preferable, therefore, to avoid the term and the concept 'undefined' altogether and distinguish, as we do, between the lack of a truth value when a definite term is unkeyed and radical falsity when a definite term is well-keyed but fails to refer to an actually existing object whereas its predicate requires it to do so.

Cases like those exemplified in (1.3) are of great interest to the logic of language. For Frege and Strawson, the truth value of (1.3) is excluded from the calculus as (1.3) is taken to lack a truth value, a position which, as we have seen, is not preferable. In standard modern predicate calculus, (1.3) is considered true. By contrast, as is shown in Chapters 4 and 5, the twelfth-century French philosopher Abelard considered (1.3) false in those circumstances, and the position taken by Aristotle himself implies the same. And to end up with ourselves, we agree with Abelard (and Aristotle) that (1.3) is false, but we assign it a special, marked kind of *radical* falsity, truth-conditionally distinct from unmarked or *minimal* falsity. Opinions galore, all of them derivable from a semantic definition (either of the quantifier ALL or of the main predicate of the sentence). This diversity of opinions makes it all the more mandatory that a decision be reached as regards the real meanings of the logical constants in natural language.

Meanwhile we see that the very fact that an L-proposition about a given state of affairs contains a logical constant makes it fall under the logic that deals with the constant in question. We also see that any L-proposition P about a given state of affairs must have a truth value: it is either true, false, or whatever other value has been introduced, no matter whether the objects referred to are actual or virtual objects. The truth value it has depends on (a) the meaning of P and the expressions in it and (b) the state of affairs that P and its referring expressions are about.

1.4 Logical form and L-propositions

It is commonly, though not universally, accepted that if entailments are to be formally computed it is necessary to reduce the expressions at issue to a 'regimented' form, usually called LOGICAL FORM or SEMANTIC ANALYSIS, which is distinct from the normal or SURFACE FORM in which they occur in actual speech. Since it is likewise commonly accepted that many, if not most, natural language sentences contain one or more logical constants, there is, for every natural language L as a whole, a programme of reduction to the logical language L_L. What we call an L-proposition is the translation of (the propositional part of) a sentence into any given L_L. Since a proper L_L is well-defined, whereas the 'language' of pure mental propositions has so far had to do without any precise definition, we have no choice but to conduct all logical computations in terms of L-propositions.

Given the distinction between surface structure and L-propositional form (semantic analysis), some formal procedure for relating the two must be made available. Until the 1960s, and often still today, the reduction of surface form to logical or L-propositional form and vice versa was mostly done intuitively, by rule of thumb. It was not until the 1960s, when formal semantics and formal linguistics came into being, that this problem was tackled in a systematic, but far from uniform, way. (For some, including the present author, the programme of formulating a mapping relation between surface structure and logical form constitutes the GRAMMAR of L, for others it is part of the SEMANTICS of L.) We will, however, not now enter into the arena of logical form reduction. For now, we simply assume that each sentence of a natural language has a double representation, one at the level of SEMANTIC ANALYSIS (SA) (containing its logical or L-propositional form) and one at the level of SURFACE FORM.

If that is so, there must be a regular mapping system relating the two levels of representation. And it is up to any one individual whether he or she prefers to call that mapping system the grammar of **L** or part of its semantics.

It is customary to say that logical forms or L-propositions are either ATOMIC or COMPLEX. An atomic L-proposition is seen as consisting of a predicate **F** expressing a property and one or more terms used to denote the objects to which the property expressed by **F** is attributed. A complex L-proposition contains at least one propositional operator. We adhere to this distinction, although it should be understood that it is of a purely logical and not of a linguistic or grammatical nature. A sentence like:

(1.4)   Despite the fact that it had been snowing heavily the whole day, she decided to drive to the factory, hoping that she would find the answer there.

is, of course, grammatically complex. Yet it is considered logically atomic, as it contains no propositional operator. It is up to linguistic analysis to show that sentence (1.4) is structured in such a way that indeed a property is assigned to one or more objects. This can only be shown if it is assumed that some objects are of a kind that allows for linguistic expression by means of an embedded sentence or S-structure that functions as a term to a predicate at L-propositional level, so that recursive embeddings of S-structures are allowed. Embedded S-structures must then be considered to refer to abstract objects of some kind (see Section 6.2.3 in Volume I). Seuren (1996) gives an idea of how the *grammatical* analysis of sentences shows up a hierarchical predicate–argument structure. The development of a *semantics* to go with this type of grammatical analysis is part of a comprehensive research programme leading to an integrated theory of language.

So far, we have seen that a logic is a calculus of entailments, and that an entailment of an L-proposition **P**—which may be a set of L-propositions conjoined under AND—specifies on analytical, semantic grounds what L-propositions **Q**, **R**, **S**, . . . (apart from **P** itself) must likewise be true (modulo key) when an assertive token utterance of **P** is true.

1.5 The Bivalence Principle, sentence types, and utterance tokens

It will be clear that a logic must be geared to the system of truth value assignments adopted for the (natural or artificial) language in question. Logic has traditionally followed Aristotle in adopting a *strictly bivalent* system of truth-value assignments, with just two truth values, True and False, in which all L-propositions with a given key always have a truth value. It was not until the 1920s that variations on this theme began being proposed, in particular by the Polish logician Łukasiewicz, but by many others as well (see Rescher 1969, ch. 1). These variations on the theme of multivalence were not, on the whole, supported by linguistic intuitions. On the contrary, they were motivated by a variety of considerations, covering modal logic, future contingency, mathematical intuitionism, undecidable mathematical statements, and logical paradoxes. It was not until after the 1950s that the notion of trivalent logic was mooted in connection with natural language, in particular with presuppositional and vagueness phenomena. Given the great variety in the motivations for multivalued logics, it is understandable that a certain amount of confusion ensued, which in turn led to a situation where investigations into multivalued logics did not achieve a high degree of respectability. In fact, logicians have, on the whole, been anxious to safeguard logic from any incursions of multivalence.

Since we, too, are threatening the bivalent shelter of standard logic, it is important to state as exactly as possible what is meant by the PRINCIPLE OF BIVALENCE. We define the Bivalence Principle as consisting of two independent subprinciples:

PRINCIPLE OF BIVALENCE

(i)   SUBPRINCIPLE OF COMPLETE VALUATION OF L-PROPOSITIONS:
      All well-anchored and well-keyed L-propositions have a truth value.

(ii) SUBPRINCIPLE OF BINARITY:
      There are exactly two truth values, True and False; there are no values between, and no values outside, True and False.

The subprinciple of binarity comprises the (SUBSUB)PRINCIPLE OF THE EXCLUDED MIDDLE (PEM), which says only that there are no values *between* True and False, and says nothing about possible values *beyond* or *outside* simply True and False. The overall principle of bivalence is often confused in the literature with PEM, mainly because Aristotle wrote only about, or rather against, possible truth values *between* true and false, as he wanted to convince his readers that the Sophists, with what he saw as their wishy-washy relativistic notion of truth, were hopelessly wrong because truth and falsity are absolute, nongradable opposites. See, for example, *Metaphysics*, end of book IV, 1010–12, in particular his statement:

There cannot be an intermediate between contradictories, but of one object we must either affirm or deny any one predicate.

To Aristotle, what for him were equivocations and prevarications produced by the Sophists on the notions of truth and falsity were more than he could bear. But he never wrote about, for example, different kinds of falsity, as that question did not weigh upon his mind.

The other subprinciple, that of COMPLETE VALUATION of L-propositions, holds trivially for well-anchored and well-keyed L-propositions as defined above. Any type-level L-proposition that expresses the mental assignment of a property to one or more objects stands by definition in a relation of conformity or nonconformity with regard to reality. When it fully conforms to reality as construed by the human intellect, it is true, and when it does not, it is false. One cannot, mentally or linguistically, assign a property to given objects without some form of truth or falsity arising. Put differently, when a listener successfully interprets a well-anchored and well-keyed statement as produced by a speaker, then the L-proposition underlying that statement bears a relation of corresondence or noncorrespondence to the state of affairs at hand. That relation implies a truth value of some kind, no matter whether the listener or speaker *knows* the exact value. There are, of course, cases where truth is not well-defined, as in sentences with vague predicates such as *grey*, which has vague borders with *white* on the one hand and *black* on the other, or *big*, which is not only vague but also dependent on context-bound evaluation. To cater for such cases one may wish to work with a system of truth values intermediate between True and False, or to set up a grammatical analysis that accounts for the context-bound evaluative factor, as is done in Section 9.3 of Volume I. But even then some truth value will be assigned, so that the subprinciple of complete valuation is not affected.

We are not saying, however, that it is impossible for a *sentence* to lack a truth value. On the contrary, sentences that lack a key lack a truth value. For example, I may, as part of my teaching, write the following sentence on the board, perhaps to explain the grammatical process of auxiliary inversion in English:

(1.5)   Only then did she post the letter.

I may hold forth about this sentence for some time, explaining to the students that it is remarkable for certain linguistic reasons. But it would be absurd for me to ask the students to tell me whether this sentence is true or false, because I have presented it as a type, not as a token utterance expressing a proposition about a given state of affairs with a given person and a given letter. Sentence (1.5), therefore, does indeed lack a truth value when uttered in the teaching situation described, precisely because it is not a well-anchored and well-keyed statement but a mere sentence type.

Of some sentence types, however, it does make sense to ask whether they are true or false regardless of any specific anchor and key. For example, the sentence:

(1.6)   All humans are mortal.

whether written on a blackboard during a grammar lesson or stuck on walls and billboards all over town to admonish people of their mortality, or in whatever other context or situation, does have a truth value. This is so because it contains no definite terms and no deictic tense, and because ALL quantifies over the class of humans, which, one may assume, requires no specific context.[3] This makes it a so-called ETERNAL SENTENCE, following the terminology introduced by the American philosopher Willard Van Orman Quine in his *Word and Object* of 1960. As was shown in Section 3.1.4 of Volume I, Quine opposes eternal sentences to occasion sentences, which need referential focusing on specific objects in a specific state of affairs on account of some definite term or deictic tense occurring in them. Eternal sentences contain only quantified terms, while occasion sentences contain one or more definite referring terms, that is, terms under a definite determiner, such as the definite article *the*, which needs some form of cognitive intentional focusing on one or more specific objects for a proper interpretation. We maintain that it is normal for natural language sentences to be occasion sentences, eternal sentences representing merely a marginal category where the dependency on anchoring and keying has been reduced to zero or near-zero.

The aversion to occasion sentences witnessed in twentieth-century logic was anticipated by Aristotle, who writes (*Prior Analytics* 24a17–22):

A proposition is a positive or negative sentence [lógos] that says something of something. Such a proposition is of three types: universal, particular, or indefinite. A universal proposition is about all or none; a particular proposition is about some, or some not, or not all; an indefinite proposition is about something applying or not applying without any specification as to all or some, as when we say that knowledge of opposites is the same knowledge, or that pleasure is not the same as the good.

---

[3] We leave aside the many cases where universal quantification does require a specific context, as in *Tout Paris était là* (All Paris was present), which, snobbishly, selects only a specific section of Parisian society.

Here we see that Aristotle rules out, perhaps not from his theory of language but certainly from his logic—the main topic of *Prior Analytics*—all propositions that need a specific form of anchoring or keying for the assignment of a truth value—Quine's occasion sentences. Aristotle's entire logic is built on L-propositions corresponding to Quine's eternal sentences. And of these eternal sentences, it is only the universally and existentially quantified ones that play a role in the logic. 'Indefinite', or as we might say, generic, sentences are given a good deal of attention in *On Interpretation*, but they play no part in the logical system. Aristotle would have no truck with occasion sentences, probably, one surmises, because he saw the problems coming, as one cannot deal with the logic, or indeed the semantics, of occasion sentences without taking into account conditions of anchoring and keying, which pose an immediate threat to the simplicity of the system. His refusal, or perhaps his inability, to face this threat was canonized during the first half of the twentieth century and vestiges of that attitude are still found today. This, however, is a luxury we cannot afford when we investigate the logic and the semantics of natural language sentences and words.

On the whole, logicians dislike the complications arising out of the conditions of anchoring and keying. What they want is a logic that operates solely on expressions whose grammatical wellformedness is a sufficient condition for their having a truth value. They want to read the subprinciple of complete valuation of properly anchored and keyed L-propositions as the subprinciple of complete valuation of *sentences* as grammatical objects. But this is totally unrealistic with regard to the logic and semantics of natural language. In natural language, wellformedness of a *sentence* is condition one for an expression to have a truth value (though a great deal of implicit correction is allowed for in practice). Condition two is that it be properly anchored and keyed. Logicians want the latter condition to be either otiose or nonexistent, a wish we must reject as being out of touch with the reality of language. We also say that when an assertive sentence is uttered as a properly anchored and keyed statement, it necessarily has a truth value, because it is impossible mentally to assign a property to one or more objects without there being some form of correspondence or noncorrespondence to what is the case—that is, some form of truth or lack of truth.

The question now is: how many truth values are there in the natural language system? Strawson considered it possible for a properly anchored and keyed statement to have no truth value at all. That must be deemed inadequate, as was shown in Section 1.3. Strawson's proposal invites one to treat his 'lack of truth value' as a truth value after all, though inappropriately named. But if one does that, one needs a logic that takes more than the two values True and False. And this is precisely what we find in natural language, which, in our analysis, operates with the values True, False-1 or 'minimally false', and False-2 or 'radically false' (probably with intermediate values between the three).

So we uphold the subprinciple of complete valuation of properly anchored and keyed L-propositions as being necessary by definition. But we are prepared to tamper with the subprinciple of binarity. We feel free to do so because giving up the subprinciple of binarity enables us to present a more adequate account of the semantics of natural language, and also because in logic this (sub)principle seems to be motivated merely by a desire to keep logic free from the complications arising in connection with anchoring, key-ing, and gradability. We need to consider the possibility not only of two different kinds of falsity and thus of three truth values, but also of fuzzy transitions between truth values. This places the Aristotelian axiom of strict bivalence in a wider metalogical context, in that standard strictly bivalent general logic turns out to be the limiting minimal case of an infinite array of possible, and logically richer, general logics that vary either on an axis of intermediate truth values or on an axis of semantically defined presupposi-tional restrictions to certain contexts.

1.6 Some problems with the assignment of truth values

This leaves us with the question of how to assign truth values to L-proposi-tions. In standard logic it is assumed that truth values are assigned with the help of model theory, which produces a truth value for any well-formed string of terms on the basis of (a) a given well-defined state of affairs and (b) given meaning definitions of the terms and nothing else. In fact, this method of assigning truth values is sometimes considered to be part of logic, rather than merely a preliminary to logic. It is thus understandable that standard logic has a tendency not to take into account the possibility that the machinery that does the assigning of truth values has to be in a particular state in order to be able to deliver a truth value. To the extent that standard logic is at all concerned about the question of how truth values are assigned, it proceeds on the assumption that the following principle holds:

> PRINCIPLE OF COGNITIVE INDEPENDENCE OF TRUTH VALUE ASSIGNMENTS (PCI)
> The cognitive machinery assigning truth values does so independently of any state that the machinery in question happens to be in.

This purified, unworldly view has been of great use to standard mathematics, which is likewise purely formal, never vague and whose dependency on mental contingencies is easily factorized out. But it has also been applied, especially since the 1960s, to the study of linguistic meaning, whereby it was assumed that linguistic meaning, like mathematical meaning, is independent of mental contingencies and nonvague. This assumption has, however, proved unwarranted over the past quarter-century. Not only do most predicate meanings in natural language impose contextual restrictions, called preconditions, which generate presuppositions; they are also often vague and/or they incorporate all kinds of purely cognitive (often evaluative) conditions, besides the conditions to be satisfied by the objects themselves to which the predicate is applied.

We have no choice but to reject PCI as being irreconcilable with natural language. For if sentences normally require anchoring and keying to have a truth value, it follows that the machinery that does the anchoring and the keying—that is, the human mind—must be at some suitable point in the development of a discourse or context and must be intentionally focused on, or keyed to, a particular state of affairs for the truth value assignment to take place successfully.

This is amply borne out by natural language, which violates PCI in a number of ways. For example, most uttered sentences contain DEFINITE TERMS referring to specific objects or sets of objects to which, truly or falsely, a property is assigned. For the reference relation to be successful it is necessary that the means be available to identify the object or objects in question (Clark and Wilkes-Gibbs 1990). In most cases, these means can only be provided if the mind is in a contextually and referentially restricted information state. Reference clearly requires specific anchoring and keying.

The same is found with regard to type-level lexical meanings. There are cases where the satisfaction conditions of predicates depend on (contain an open parameter referring to) what is taken to be normal in any given context. Consider, for example, the predicate *many*. If it is normally so that out of an audience of three hundred taking part in a TV quiz nobody gets the one-million Euro prize, then, when in one session three participants get it, one can say in truth that there were many one-million Euro prize winners in that session. But if only three out of three hundred people voted for me in an election, then, one fears, it is false to say that many people voted for me.

Or consider cases of what is called DYNAMIC FILTERING in Section 9.6.3 of Volume I, found all over the lexicons of natural languages. For example, the conditions for the predicate *flat* to be satisfied differ considerably when it is applied to a tyre, a road, or a mountain. And a definite term like *the office* will have different interpretations according to whether it stands as a subject term to the predicate *be on fire* or, for example, *have a day off*. In the former case the phrase *the office* is interpreted as referring to a building. In the latter case it is interpreted as referring to a group of people.

Or take PREDICATES OF POSSESSION, expressed in words such as *have*, *with*, *without*, or as a genitive or a dative case. As is shown more amply in Section 9.6.3 of Volume I, possession predicates typically require an appeal to world knowledge for decisions about truth or falsity, as is shown by the following two examples:

(1.7)   a. This hotel room has a bathroom.
        b. This student has a supervisor.

Clearly, for (1.7a) to be true, the room in question must have its own individual bathroom, not shared with other rooms. But for (1.7b) to be true no one-to-one relation is required, as one supervisor may serve a number of students. This difference is not linguistic and, therefore, need not be specified in the lexicon, but is caused by the way the world happens to be, as far as hotels or university departments are concerned. The lexical meaning description of possession predicates is thus taken to contain an *open parameter* referring the language user to his or her knowledge base. As is said in Seuren (1998a: 400): 'If the language user does not know "the way it is" with this or that (s)he cannot interpret the utterance in question. For example, an expression like *the room's front wheels* requires either a world picture in which rooms have a known standard relation to front wheels, or otherwise at least a context where this room's relation to front wheels has been explained.'

Cases of what is often called 'viewpoint' are likewise telling (see Section 9.7 in Volume I for more discussion). Consider the case of a fountain and a tree which are located at a distance of, say, twenty yards from each other (cf. Seuren 1998a: 402–3). Now to decide whether sentences like (1.8a) or (1.8b) are true it must be known from what angle the fountain and the tree are being looked at by some 'homunculus' or mental viewer in the mind:

(1.8)   a. There is a tree behind the fountain.
        b. There is a tree to the left of the fountain.

If the mental viewer is standing in the continuation of the line running from the fountain to the tree, (1.8a) is true and (1.8b) is false. But if the homunculus stands at right angles with that line, with the fountain to the right, then (1.8a) is false and (1.8b) is true. Clearly, unless one is describing what is seen on a postcard, the viewpoint is determined by previous discourse.

Viewpoint differences are likewise to be discerned in cases that show an orientation towards or away from a speaker's mental position, as with predicates of the 'come and go'-type:

(1.9)   A few men were waiting to be shown into the office. The door opened and one of them went in. After two minutes another man went in/ came in.

The difference between the two versions is, though clear, hard to express in other than metaphorical terms. With *went in*, the 'camera' (or the homunculus) has, so to speak, remained outside the office. With *came in*, it has 'moved along' with the first man and is now inside the office. Such phenomena are clearly semantic, in that they reflect meaning differences, even though they do not lead to different truth values.

Other lexical restrictions look more like being based on criteria of prototypicality (see Section 8.8 in Volume I). Suppose, for example, that John is a man with no hair on his chest. Then, when one says that his chest is *bald*, that would perhaps not be false in a strict sense but it would certainly be inappropriate, the reason being, probably, that the predicate *bald* prototypically but not truth-conditionally, requires the top of the head when applied to humans. In similar fashion one observes that what we call 'red wine' is called the equivalent of 'black wine' in Modern Greek. We may say in English that a person, when frightened, turns pale, but not, or rather not, that his or her shoulders are 'pale' when not suntanned. Examples like these, of course, come in the thousands.

Lexically fixed prototypicality also has a logical counterpart. For example, when a married man says that he is eating out because *all his wives are ill*, then that may be taken to be true in a strict, logical sense, but not in the ordinary sense which would make one understand that he has a collection of wives. This example probably hinges on an element of prototypicality in the linguistic meaning of the logical word *all*, combined with the fact that quantification in language is to do primarily with plurality.

In view of all this it seems that we are forced to conclude that the Principle of Cognitive Independence lacks empirical backing and seems to have been added merely to avoid complications in the theory of truth. The fact that it is widely considered sacrosanct in circles of logicians is part of what one might call the mythology of logic. Meaning in natural language is a great deal more complex than what we see of it in standard logic. The standard, logically coloured concept of meaning is highly idealized and streamlined, which creates the impression that one may adequately operate with a strictly bivalent system of simple truth and simple falsity. Since, however, natural language is very much more complex and more varied, there is room for the idea that the logical system of language requires a more finely grained set of truth parameters than just True and False. This is one of the questions we explore in this book.

2

Logic: a new beginning

2.1 Entailment, contrariety and contradiction: the natural triangle

We start with the notions in terms of which the machinery of any logic is defined, namely *contrariety, entailment, contradictoriness,* and *subcontrariety.* These are logical relations that may hold between two, or sometimes more, L-propositional types, depending on their logico-semantic properties, which, in their turn, are determined by the logical constants or operators occurring in them. (One remembers that an L-proposition is the type-level linguistic expression of a proposition in the logico-semantic language L_L.) Since these relations are not satisfied by world situations but by combinations of L-propositional types, we should really call them 'metalogical relations', as opposed to the object-language logical relations expressed by the truth-functional operators and quantifiers of L_L. In practice, however, we use the term *logical relations* in all cases where no confusion is to be expected. In general, (meta)logical relations hold (are *valid*) in virtue of the *meanings* of the L-propositional arguments. Within a logical system, they hold in virtue of the meanings of the logical constants in the L-propositional arguments.

(Meta)logical relations should be clearly distinguished from the functors of the object language L_L, also called operators or logical constants, mainly ALL, SOME, NOT, AND, OR, and IF...THEN, which produce truth or falsity depending on token world situations. In standard logic, the functors of negation (NOT) and of material implication (IF P THEN Q) have a direct analog to a (meta)logical relation, as they correspond directly to contradictoriness and entailment, respectively: contradictoriness holds between any L-proposition and its negation; entailment holds when the material implication is true in all admissible situations.

One way of seeing how these (meta)logical relations get off the ground is the following. Let us take as our point of departure the requirement of *consistency* in linguistic interaction. Speakers who commit themselves to the truth of what they assert or who appeal to listeners to fulfil a request or an order must maintain consistency, or else the social fabric will collapse. For that reason it is of the greatest importance, first to language users and secondly to language theorists, to spot inconsistencies or, in logical terms, to spot sets of propositions that cannot simultaneously be true. When such a set consists of just two propositions, we speak of *contrary propositions*. This is, in fact, how Aristotle set up his predicate logic in *On Interpretation*, which revolves around the notions of contrariety and contradictoriness. Aristotle called any two L-propositions which, for semantic reasons, cannot be simultaneously true 'contraries', and any two L-propositions that can, again for semantic reasons, be neither simultaneously true nor simultaneously false 'contradictories'. On the standard (yet oversimplified) assumption that all natural languages have a logical constant of negation—*not* in English—which inverts truth values (modulo key) under the axiom of bivalence, the contradictory of an L-proposition P is its negation $\text{NOT}(P)$, or $\neg P$: the truth of the one entails the falsity of the other, either way.

To give a trivial example, the two sentences in (2.1a) are contraries, since anyone who asserts both is guilty of inconsistency ('$><$' stands for contrariety). This means that when (the L-proposition underlying) *Joe has been murdered* is true, *Joe is not dead* must be false and, therefore, *Joe is dead* must be true (assuming bivalence). In other words, *Joe has been murdered* entails *Joe is dead*, as stated in (2.1b). (One notes that we have silently passed from entailment in a general sense to logical entailment. This is legitimate given the definition of bivalent negation.)

(2.1)   a. Joe has been murdered $><$ Joe is not dead
        b. Joe has been murdered $\models$ Joe is dead

Entailment can thus be defined in terms of contrariety and the contradiction-producing negation operator. It is also possible, of course, to define contrariety in terms of entailment and contradictoriness, but that seems less natural, given the basic requirement of consistency in the use of language. Nor is it how Aristotle proceeded.

Any relation of contrariety between two L-propositions P and $\neg Q$, thus brings along a relation of entailment from P to Q. Figure 2.1 shows the triangular relation arising from the assumed contrariety of P and $\neg Q$, which causes the entailment from P to Q, the contradictory of $\neg Q$.

This triangle is arguably 'natural' in the sense that it may be taken to reflect natural, as opposed to constructed, set-theoretic structures and relations—a supposition that is further elaborated in Chapter 3. It forms the natural basis of the logical system of propositional calculus with the operators AND, OR, and

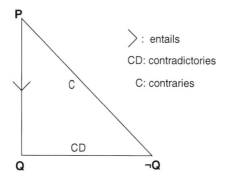

FIGURE 2.1 The natural logical triangle

NOT, and also of Aristotelian-Boethian predicate calculus (ABPC), which is based on the quantifiers ALL and SOME and the propositional operator NOT.

But one can go further, still under the bivalence axiom. Since P and ¬Q in Figure 2.1 are contraries, ¬Q entails the falsity of P, or: ¬Q ⊢ ¬P. This is, of course, nothing but the well-known operation of CONTRAPOSITION: when, for any L-propositions P and Q, P ⊢ Q, then also ¬Q ⊢ ¬P. This is easily shown: suppose Q is false, and therefore ¬Q true, then P cannot be true, for if P were true, Q would also have to be true in virtue of the entailment P ⊢ Q. Since both P and Q have only two options, True and False, it follows that if P ⊢ Q, then in all cases where ¬Q is true, ¬P is also true, that is, ¬Q ⊢ ¬P. This can be added to the triangle of Figure 2.1, leading to the square of Figure 2.2.

Now that the natural triangle has been extended to a square, a new logical relation has emerged, that of SUBCONTRARIETY. By definition, two L-propositions form a pair of subcontraries when they cannot be simultaneously false, though they may be simultaneously true. In this case, Q and ¬P cannot be simultaneously false, because, as the square shows, if Q is false, so is P, and when ¬P is false and thus P is true, Q is true. Clearly, the relation of

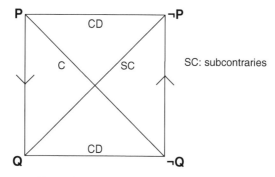

FIGURE 2.2 The natural logical triangle extended with contraposition

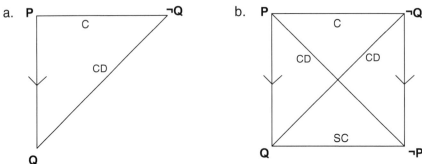

FIGURE 2.3 The logical triangle and square in the Boethian arrangement

contradictoriness is the combination of contrariety and subcontrariety—at least in a bivalent logic with the metalogical relations as defined.

Figure 2.3a shows a different arrangement of the vertices of the natural logical triangle, extended with contraposition to the square of Figure 2.3b. This arrangement has a more familiar look as it reminds one of the famous Square of Opposition in traditional predicate logic, attributed to the Roman-Christian philosopher and statesman Boethius (± 480–524). For that reason, we call this the Boethian arrangement. It is shown, however, in Section 2.2, that the Boethian arrangement is not a very good way of presenting metalogical relations and had better be given up in favour of the arrangement of Figure 2.2.

Apart from this, it will be clear that the square of Figure 2.2, or Figure 2.3b for that matter, cannot be the whole story, since, if it were, both the triangle and the square, in either form, would be dispensable, as they merely reiterate the entailment relation $P \vdash Q$ (or $P \models Q$) in terms of contrariety, contradictoriness and subcontrariety, given the negation as a truth-functional operator inverting binary truth values. The logic would also be pretty poor, consisting only of negation (important though that operator is) and a few new relations that can be defined in terms of each other—hardly sufficient to get a logic off the ground. What makes these new relations important for the machinery of logic is the establishing of logical relations between the *external negations* occurring in L-propositions of the form $\neg P$ on the one hand, and corresponding L-propositions with *internal negation* on the other. What is meant by 'internal negation' is a question to which we turn now.

2.2 Internal negation and duality: the natural square and the Boethian square

Just about the most central operator in any logical system is negation, normally lexicalized as *not* in English. We concentrate first on ordinary external negation over L-propositions. This negation is typically a complement selector. In the simplest case, it selects the complement within a universe **U** of admissible situations.

To make this clear, we fall back again on the notion of valuation space, introduced in Van Fraassen 1971 and briefly discussed in Section 3.3.3 of Volume I. Leaving the formal definition of the notion of 'admissible situation' to Section 2.3.3 below, we define 'valuation space' (VS) as follows:

> Valuation Space
>
> For any L-proposition P expressing the proposition p, the VALUATION SPACE (VS) of P, or /P/, is the set of admissible situations that make P true (modulo key).

Thus, the proposition p (or its L-propositional expression P) is true in all situations that are elements in the set of situations /P/. Given that the standard bivalent negation ¬ selects the complement of /P/ within the universe of all admissible situations **U**, it follows that the proposition expressed by ¬P is true in all situations that form the complement $\overline{/P/}\,(=\textbf{U} -/P/)$ of /P/ in **U**. This simplest case is what is found in standard logic. Since, by definition, an L-proposition P is true just in case the actual situation sit_{act} is an element of /P/ and false otherwise, it follows that ¬P is true just in case sit_{act} is an element of /¬P/—that is, $\overline{/P/}$ —and false otherwise. In the standard, strictly bivalent, system shown diagrammatically in Figure 2.4 no other possibilities than truth and falsity are left open:

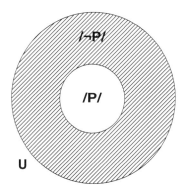

FIGURE 2.4 VS representation of /P/ and /¬P/ in **U**

	P	**¬P**
$\text{sit}_{act} \in /P/$	T	F
$\text{sit}_{act} \in /\neg P/ \ (= \mathbf{U} - /P/)$	F	T

FIGURE 2.5 Truth table of the standard bivalent negation ¬ in terms of VS-modelling

'not true' equals 'false' and 'not false' equals 'true'. Clearly, if P is necessarily false, as, for example, the L-proposition underlying the sentence *He was dead for the rest of his life*, /P/ = Ø; if P is necessarily true, as in *He was alive for the rest of his life*, /P/ = **U**.

Thus defined, negation can be said to 'toggle' between truth and falsity. The property of the negation simply to invert truth values of propositions is expressed in the TRUTH TABLE of the standard negation shown in Figure 2.5 (adapted to a valuation space interpretation), where 'T' stands for True and 'F' for False.

It is possible, however, to vary on this theme. For example, one may define a negation operator that selects the complement of /P/ within a subset of situations in **U** defined on the basis of preceding context or the meaning of the main predicate in P, in which case room is made for more than one negation. In this book we argue that this is, in fact, the situation in natural language, where the main function of the negation NOT is to toggle between the values 'true' and 'minimally false', minimal falsity being caused by those situations that are outside /P/ but within P's subuniverse in **U**. Further comment on this issue is provided in Chapter 3, but a full discussion has to wait till Chapter 10.

But what is meant by internal negation? So as not to complicate matters unduly at this stage, let us say that the internal negation is a negation not over an L-proposition but over a predicate. This is not an adequate definition, since, as is shown in Sections 2.3.5.2 and 2.4.1, internal negation is better defined as a small scope negation over an embedded L-propositional structure, but it will do for the moment. If it is accepted that a predicate, for example *human*, expresses a property possessed by all objects in the world that are indeed human, then the 'negation' of this predicate, *not-human*, functioning as the internal negation of an L-proposition, expresses the lack of that property for all objects that are not human. Call the set of all human objects the EXTENSION of the predicate *human*, or ⟦Human⟧, in the set of all objects **OBJ**. Then the set of objects that are not human is the extension of the predicate *not-human*, or ⟦NOT-Human⟧, in **OBJ**. This makes ⟦NOT-Human⟧ the complement of ⟦Human⟧—that is, **OBJ** minus ⟦Human⟧, or ⟦Human⟧—as long as there are no vague boundaries between what is and what is not human.

The logical interest of internal negation, in the present context, lies in the relation of DUALITY (Löbner 1990):

> **DUALITY**
> Two logical constants X and Y are each other's duals just in case there is logical equivalence between X preceded by the external negation and Y followed by the internal negation and, of course, vice versa.

In standard predicate calculus, for example, the quantifiers ALL and SOME are each other's duals, since in that system an L-proposition corresponding to the form NOT ALL F is G (where F and G are predicates) is equivalent with an L-proposition of the form SOME F IS NOT-G and, analogously, NOT SOME F IS G/NO F is G is equivalent with ALL F IS NOT-G. These equivalences are standardly known as the CONVERSIONS. Henceforth, when dealing with external versus internal negation, we will use the standard symbol '¬' for external negation and the symbol '*' for internal negation. That is, ¬P is the external negation of the L-proposition P and P* is the L-proposition P but with its main lexical predicate negated by the internal negation. Obviously, in a strictly bivalent system, double external negation and double internal negation cancel out: for any L-proposition P, ¬¬P ≡ P and, since for any predicate C, NOT-NOT-C ≡ C, P** ≡ P.

It must be noted, at this point, that the logical properties of two L-propositions P and P* are identical for the simple reason that the choice of lexical predicates is irrelevant for the logic, which is defined by the logical constants only. We call this the MODULO-*-PRINCIPLE. The relevance of the internal negation for predicate logic lies in any logical relation of duality or of a one-way entailment between two logical constants X and Y when one is preceded by the external negation and the other is followed by the internal negation. The Modulo-*-principle provides an extra check for the soundness of a predicate-logic system in that any system that violates the Modulo-*-principle is by definition unsound.

Logicians have observed that a similar relation of duality exists between the propositional operators AND and OR, a form of duality known as DE MORGAN'S LAWS. In standard propositional logic, the operators of negation, conjunction and disjunction are defined in such a way that for the L-propositions P and Q, NOT(P AND Q) is equivalent with NOT(P) OR NOT(Q). Analogously, NOT(P OR Q) is equivalent with NOT(P) AND NOT(Q), or in standard notation: $\neg(P \wedge Q) \equiv \neg P \vee \neg Q$ and $\neg(P \vee Q) \equiv \neg P \wedge \neg Q$.

This is, of course, an intriguing parallel with standard predicate calculus, but if we want to cash in on this parallelism it must first be made clear that here, too, we have to do with internal negation. To do that, the definition of internal negation as predicate negation must be generalized so as to cover the dual quantifiers and the dual propositional operators alike. This is done in Section 2.3, where all logical operators are reinterpreted as (abstract) predicates. The parallelism between the two calculi is then further elaborated in Chapter 4. For the moment, we limit ourselves to the dual quantifiers.

Let us revert to the logical triangle of Figures 2.1 and 2.3a, and the logical squares of Figures 2.2 and 2.3b, respectively, assuming that P and Q are types of L-proposition defined by logical constants that are each other's duals. That is, we assume that:

(2.2) $P \equiv \neg Q^*$ and consequently $\neg P \equiv Q^*$
        $Q \equiv \neg P^*$ and consequently $\neg Q \equiv P^*$

Now the squares of Figures 2.2 and 2.3b are seen to be more than just restatements of the entailment relation and to have real logical power. For now the triangular Figures 2.1 and 2.3a can be expanded to quadrilateral figures that express the duality relation. This is done in Figure 2.6, where (a) corresponds with Figure 2.2 and (b) (in either form) with Figure 2.3b.

It now becomes clear why the arrangement of Figure 2.2 (expanded from the triangle in Figure 2.1) is preferred to the Boethian arrangement of Figure 2.3b (expanded from Figure 2.3a). When the triangles are expanded to squares in such a way that the dual equivalences are expressed, Figure 2.1 results in Figure 2.6a, which we call the NATURAL ISOMORPHIC SQUARE (two parallel lines stand for logical equivalence). But Figure 2.3a turns into Figure 2.6b (in either form), which we call the IMPROVED BOETHIAN SQUARES. The difference is that the natural isomorphic square consists of two triangles that are LOGICALLY ISOMORPHIC in that they display the same logical relations of entailment, (sub)-contrariety and contradiction, the only difference being that the right-hand side triangle has the internal negation added to P, Q, and ¬Q, giving P*, Q*, and ¬Q*, respectively—that is, with a negative instead of a positive predicate. But since the choice of lexical predicates makes no difference to the logic, which is defined by the logical constants alone (the Modulo-*-principle), the two triangles making up the natural square are logically identical. It is their connection through the Conversions that makes a logic spring up.

The interest of their being coupled into the natural square lies in the dual equivalences. By contrast, the two improved Boethian squares in Figure 2.6b

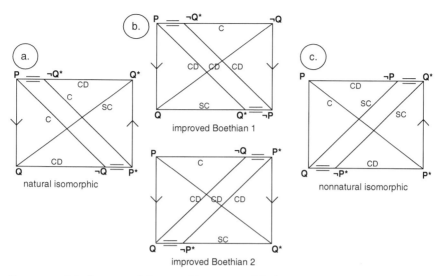

FIGURE 2.6 (a) the natural isomorphic square, (b) the two improved but nonisomorphic Boethian squares, and (c) the nonnatural isomorphic square

lack this regularity. There the triads <P,Q,Q*> and <P,Q,¬Q> of the left-hand side triangles correspond to the nonisomorphic triads <¬Q,¬P,¬Q*> and <P*,Q*,¬P*>, respectively, of the right-hand side triangle. Clearly, the isomorphic representation displays more regularities in the logical system than the nonisomorphic representation.

Figure 2.6c shows a second way of making a square out of two isomorphic triangles with the same logical power.[1] Here we have a triangle <P,¬P,Q>, linked up with the isomorphic triangle <P*,¬P*,Q*>. Now the relations involved are those of entailment, contradiction, and subcontrariety, with contrariety thrown in as a bonus due to the linking up through the Conversions. In Chapter 3, however, it is argued that subcontrariety is not a basic-natural logical relation but a relation that requires a great deal of scholastic training to be grasped, whereas contrariety is just about maximally natural. For that reason, the square of Figure 2.6c is called 'nonnatural isomorphic.' From a strictly logical point of view, the difference is immaterial, but it is not when we are in search of natural logic. Since natural logic is what we are after, we consider Figure 2.6a to be the preferred representation.

---

[1] I am indebted to Dany Jaspers (2005: 34–5) for calling this fact to my attention.

The isomorphy of a representation is important not only because it shows up more regularities in the system than nonisomorphic representations but also because it adds a criterion for the consistency of the logic in question. The criterion can be formulated as follows:

Given the Modulo-*-principle, the (meta)logical relations defined for the operators of predicate calculus (the quantifiers and negation) must be the same no matter whether the main or G-predicate is or is not characterized by internal negation.

In virtue of the Modulo-*-principle, the identity of the logical relations in the two triangles <P,Q,¬Q> and <P*,Q*,¬Q*> in Figure 2.6a, or in <P,¬P,Q> and <P*,¬P*,Q* > in Figure 2.6c, is thus a condition for the soundness of the logic involved. Since the renderings shown in Figures 2.6a and 2.6c actually show the isomorphy, whereas those of Figure 2.6b do not, the former are at least didactically superior to the latter.

The fact that logical systems with *X* and *Y* as duals and an entailment relation from *X* to *Y* are reducible to two logically isomorphic natural triangles, one with and one without the internal negation, connected by the dual equivalences, has so far, as far as I am aware, not been noted in the literature. It is nevertheless of major interest, because traditional Aristotelian-Boethian predicate calculus (ABPC) is built up from precisely the same elements, with the quantifiers ALL and SOME as each other's duals and an entailment from ALL to SOME.

What we call the Boethian arrangement of Figure 2.6b reflects the celebrated Square of Opposition shown in Figure 2.7a and attributed to Boethius

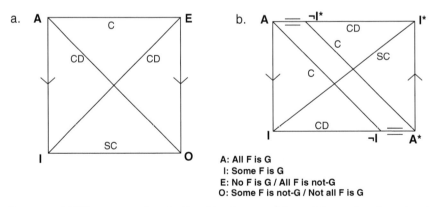

FIGURE 2.7 ABPC represented as the Boethian Square of Opposition and as the natural square consisting of two isomorphic triangles

mentioned earlier. The symbol **A** stands for simple universally quantified sentences of the type ALL F IS G, the symbol **I** stands for simple existentially quantified sentences of the type SOME F IS G. Boethius chose these symbols because they are the first two vowels of the Latin word *affirmo* (I affirm). He added the symbols **E** and **O**, the vowels of the Latin word *nego* (I deny), for the counterparts of **A** and **I** with internal negation—that is, for sentences of the type ALL F IS NOT-G and SOME F IS NOT-G, respectively.

In spite of its august, time-honoured status, we now see that the Boethian Square is a defective way of representing traditional predicate calculus, because it fails to express the function of the internal negation and thus the generalization that the system is representable as two logically isomorphic triangles, $<\mathbf{A},\mathbf{I},\neg\mathbf{I}>$ and $<\mathbf{A}^{*},\mathbf{I}^{*},\neg\mathbf{I}^{*}>$, connected by equivalences (Conversions). We, therefore, dispense with the symbols **E** and **O**, using instead $\mathbf{A}^{*}$ and $\mathbf{I}^{*}$, respectively, in the natural isomorphic square representation of Figure 2.7b.[2] And we replace the arrangement of Figure 2.7a with that of Figure 2.7b.

2.3 Logical operators as predicates

So far we have taken a preliminary look at (meta)logical relations. Now we turn to the internal structure of L-propositions in the object language, in particular to the logical constants, and in doing so we hold on firmly to a linguistic point of view. The logical constants are treated as words or lexical items in a language, with translation equivalents in all natural languages. Being linguistic expressions, they must have a meaning, just like all other linguistic expressions. It is our purpose, in this section, to begin exploring aspects of the linguistic meanings of the logical constants and to show how their specific logical properties follow from their linguistic meaning.

It is argued that the logical operators are best described as *abstract predicates*—that is, predicates in the logical language, L_L, whose L-propositions are taken to be related to the sentences of natural languages through grammar.[3] In formal terms, any function associated with a linguistic construct and

---

[2] Jaspers (2005) calls the **I**-vertex the PIVOT of the triangle, mainly on the grounds that particular existential knowledge is cognitively prior to general knowledge. The concept of pivot is useful in natural logic also because the negation of the pivot establishes the relation of contrariety between the **A**-vertex and the ¬**I**-vertex, thus stressing the triangular character of the relations of contrariety, entailment, and contradictoriness.

[3] Interestingly, the view that quantifiers are, logically speaking, predicates is also found in some nineteenth-century logic textbooks. Thus we find (Sigwart 1895: 160):

with a truth value as output is seen as a predicate. This is obviously so for ordinary unary predicates like *walk*, which deliver a truth value for any given entity as input. And a binary predicate like *love* delivers a truth value for any given pair of entities as input. Likewise, we may consider the quantifier ALL to be a binary predicate, not over pairs of entities but over pairs of sets of entities (which makes it, technically speaking, a higher-order predicate), delivering truth when one set (for example, the set of humans) is included in the other (for example, the set of mortals), and falsity otherwise. Alternative analyses are possible (as in the standard Russell notation), but the predicate format is always useful (and always provides a deeper insight into the matter).

Among the advantages of treating logical operators (constants) as (abstract) predicates are the following—apart from the general consideration that the insight into the nature of logic is greatly enhanced. First, treating logical operators as arguments unifies the format of the semantic definitions of the logical operators with that of common lexical predicates in that both are statable as satisfaction conditions. This allows one to see with greater clarity than before the relation between logic and language. Logic turns out to be a question of lexical semantics: it is the lexical semantic definitions of the logical constants that define the logic associated with them (as long as the definitions make for a consistent system of mathematically definable entailments). It also means that any lexicological standards and principles taken to be valid for predicates in general (such as the possibility of inducing presuppositions) will now equally apply to the logical constants.

Then, assigning predicate status to logical operators facilitates and shows the way towards the development and foundation of alternative logics, thus opening up the possibility of evaluating a variety of logics as possible candidates for the status of the logic of language.

The treatment of logical operators as abstract predicates is also linguistically motivated in that more and more languages are being discovered where what we see as logical operators actually occur as verbs in surface structure (see note 4 for some evidence). In general, as is argued in Seuren (1996), the mechanism of grammar is greatly improved or simplified when *all* elements with lexical meaning are treated as predicates at the level of semantic analysis.

Thus, according to its original meaning. 'All *A*'s are *B*' can only be said in reference to definite particular objects. And here from a logical point of view the 'all' is the predicate (the *A*'s which are *B* are all *A*'s).

That this was not an isolated view is proved by the fact that the linguist Meyer-Lübke held the same view as regards the existential quantifier TWO (Meyer-Lübke 1899: 352; translation mine):

From the point of view of logic there can be no doubt that in the sentence *il arrive deux étrangers* [two foreigners arrive] the subject is *il arrive* while *deux étrangers* is the predicate.

The explicit proposal to treat logical constants formally as predicates is not new. To my knowledge, it was first made, in the context of the theory of grammar, by McCawley (1967, 1972: 516–32), who presented it in his usual visionary way but without much in the way of formal underpinning. Yet, as regards the quantifiers, the formal underpinning was soon provided in the theory of generalized quantifiers (Barwise and Cooper 1981), based on Mostovski (1957). As regards the propositional operators, the basis for their interpretation as predicates is more or less implicit in the standard machinery, which takes the extension of an L-proposition to be its truth value. If all functions to truth values are treated as predicates, the truth functions are automatically predicates, since they are functions from truth values to truth values. We, however, develop a different perspective (see Section 6.2 in Volume I), in which a well-anchored and well-keyed L-proposition is not taken to stand for its truth value but to be cognitively (but without awareness) associated with its *valuation space*—that is, the set of situations in which it is true. It is shown in a moment that in this latter view the propositional operators are even more naturally regarded as (abstract) predicates.

In the surface structures of most natural languages, the logical constants under discussion are, of course, not predicates. They turn up as bound morphemes, particles, determiners, or what not, but never, or very rarely, as surface predicates—that is, as verbs or adjectives.[4] We do not propose to treat the logical constants as verbs or adjectives in surface structure, which would strain even our powers of imagination. What we do propose is to treat them as predicates in L-propositions—that is, in the logical language used for the purpose of semantic analysis, along with the common lexical predicates that may serve as values for the predicate variables.

An interesting question, in this context, is why it should be that the logical constants, if they are 'deep' predicates, tend not to turn up as predicates in

---

[4] In the Finno-Ugric languages, as McCawley observed, the negation operator often turns up as a surface verb, though usually with a defective paradigm (which, in fact, corresponds closely to the defective paradigm of the English modal auxiliary verbs such as *can, may, must, will*). A sentence like *Kevin didn't laugh* comes out as something like 'Kevin notted (to) laugh'. Similar phenomena are found in many other languages. For example, in the Amazonian language Dâw (Andrade Martins 2004: 559), the verbal negation suffix *-ɛ̃h* is derived from the negative verb *mɛ̃h* meaning 'not have'. Brown and Dryer (2008) describe a language, Walman (a Torricelli language of Papua New Guinea), where the conjunctor *and* as a connective linking two or more NPs turns up in surface structure as a verb. Brown and Dryer (2008: 563) are puzzled by this fact, because, in a predicate-logic analysis, there seems to be no way in which the NP-conjoining *and* can be taken to be a verb or a predicate, since a nominal conjunction can be nothing but an argument to a predicate. Their proposal to view this verbal *and* as a serial verb seems plausible for those nominal conjunctions that do not allow for a reduction to clausal conjunction, as in *Vivian and Lesley are a nice couple*. As a clausal connector, *and* is easily seen as a (truth-functional) *n*-ary predicate that takes two or more S-structures as arguments.

surface structure but mostly as adverbials, particles, bound morphemes, determiners, or phonological modifications. This question is part of the larger question of why it should be that humans do not talk to each other in the language of predicate calculus but in surface structures that rather deform the 'deep' predicate-calculus structures of the language L_L of semantic analysis. And this again is part of the even more comprehensive question of why languages should transform SAs into surface structures at all.

It seems that an adequate answer to these questions will at least involve the consideration that all natural language grammars are characterized by the property of MATRIX GREED—the fact that the lexical matrix or nucleus of a sentence structure tends to incorporate all, or almost all, more abstract, functional elements of the auxiliary system and also, as much as possible, nominal, verbal, and adverbial elements of embedded clauses (Seuren 2004: 195–8). The lexical matrix is that part of an SA-structure where the world-related lexical items are concentrated. This makes the lexical matrix the most 'referential' part of the SA-structure—the part specifically housing the relations with objects in the world. It is perhaps not too far-fetched to conjecture that, both from an evolutionary and from a functional point of view, the lexical matrix is somehow the 'core' of the whole sentence, which cannot be missed even in deficient or handicapped forms of human communication. This would provide a basis for a possible answer to the questions just posed.

2.3.1 *Meaning postulates*

Attempts have been made before to break through the traditional barrier between, on the one hand, the logical constants, which are standardly taken to be *sui generis* and, on the other, the propositional or lexical linguistic material, which is standardly treated as providing the values for the lexical variables in a logic. A well-known attempt is Carnap's proposal to treat lexical meanings as logical elements allowing for certain inferences in virtue of so-called MEANING POSTULATES (Carnap 1956: 222–9). For Carnap, the lexical meaning of a predicate like *bachelor* can be said to legitimize on LOGICAL grounds the inference that, for example, if anyone is a bachelor, he is not married. The format used by Carnap for meaning postulates is, exemplified for the item Bachelor:

$$\vdash \forall x(\text{Bachelor}(x) \rightarrow \text{Male}(x) \land \neg\text{Married}(x) \land \ldots \land)$$

or: 'it is a theorem that for all x, if x is a bachelor then x is male, not married, . . .'. When the semantico-logical entailments specified in this meaning postulate are incorporated into the logical system, then the sentence *John is a bachelor* not only semantically but also logically entails that John is male, not married, and so on.

A meaning postulate is thus a stipulated entailment schema or 'inference rule' meant to help define a logical system. It is important to realize that meaning postulates of the type given above must be read as entailment schemata that are part of the logical system, and not as formulae within the system, which would turn them into contingent statements about the world. For example, suppose it happens to be the case that all houses in the village have two bathrooms, then it is true to say 'for all x, if x is a house-in-the-village, then x has two bathrooms'. But this does not provide a licence to describe the lexical meaning of the predicate *house-in-the-village* as implying the condition 'having two bathrooms'. Meaning postulates are not meant to be true about the world but true about the language (which has been incorporated into the logic in so far as it has been fitted out with meaning postulates) and hence, once the language has been fixed, necessarily true in any world. For that reason the entailment sign ⊢ is placed in front of the meaning postulate.

Meaning postulates have had something of a career in formal semantics and in the philosophy of language, where it has been claimed that they can be used to define lexical meanings exhaustively, specifying the severally necessary and jointly sufficient conditions for them to produce truth when applied to their term referents. The dominant view in formal semantics and in the philosophy of language has been to accept the principle 'get your entailments right and you get your meanings right'.

Although this view has a certain appeal, I believe—and have frequently argued in the past—that it is basically flawed. I take sides with Frege in that I take lexical meanings to be defined by satisfaction conditions (Frege's Sätti-gungsbedingungen), which have their roots in cognitive criteria. Natural semantic entailments *follow from* lexical satisfaction conditions but do not define them. In my view, moreover, lexical meaning is more than just truth-conditional satisfaction conditions, in that the satisfaction of lexical semantic conditions, besides leading to truth, often also leads to other sorts of results, often of an ill-understood nature. Some aspects of this question are discussed in Chapters 8 and 9 of Volume I.

The theory of meaning postulates constitutes an attempt at incorporating natural language into, or superimposing it onto, a logical system, which is considered to be given *a priori* and is implicitly taken to be standard modern logic, the only logical system considered viable. What is tried here is the exact opposite. For us, any logical system is part of some (natural or artificial) language. We try to see logical properties as epiphenomena—certainly highly

interesting and important ones but nevertheless epiphenomena—of the semantics of lexical predicates in natural or artificial languages. Instead of
taking the standard logical system as primitive, we regard the logical system,
any logical system, as derived from such lexically given semantic entailments,
in whatever language, as are seen to allow for a formal truth calculus on the
basis of set-theoretic relations defined in, or following from, them. For us,
therefore, the primitive elements are lexical meanings and the semantic
entailments that follow from them. As regards predicate logic, those lexical
meanings that can be specified in the mathematical terms of set theory are
possible candidates for a logical system.

One reason for taking this approach, apart from any possible empirical or
philosophical arguments, is that it enables us to puncture the myth most
formal semanticists and philosophers of language, and also most pragmaticists, implicitly live by, namely that standard modern logic is the only viable
logic and that if that logic turns out not to fit the facts of natural language too
well, the fault lies with natural language, not with the logic. Our approach
creates a space that the theory of meaning postulates denies us, the space
needed to develop sound alternative logics so that we can begin to investigate
which of these logics fits the facts of language best. And this again makes us
put off to a later moment any final answer to the question of the logical
soundness of natural language. For the best part of the twentieth century,
logicians have tried to persuade the world that natural language is vague,
ambiguous, and generally unfit for proper reasoning, with the result that the
new discipline of pragmatics arose, whose practitioners undertake massive
efforts to find functionally motivated excuses for what has been accepted as
being the logical impurity of natural language. We find this premature, since,
in our view, not enough has been done to see if natural language does indeed
suffer from the logical defects imputed to it. And what we have found so far
provides sufficient grounds for assuming that language is not nearly as bad, in
this respect, as it has been made out to be.

It is thus central to our method to regard the traditional logical constants as
the lexical items they are. And since lexical items are, in principle, predicates,
we propose to treat the logical constants as predicates in natural languages.
Not as ordinary 'descriptive' predicates, which are mostly defined in terms of
contingent properties that objects and relations in the world must possess for
truth to come about, but as 'abstract' predicates of L_L, which tend not to
occur as predicates in surface structures and whose satisfaction conditions are
of a mathematical nature.

It follows that we must assume that the human mind is innately equipped
with the machinery required for carrying out such abstract mental

operations, first at a natural, then at a higher, more constructed, level. And since there is no way humans can actually report on the operations in question, it must be assumed that they are wrapped up in, or as part of, a MODULE, beyond any threshold of awareness and taking place in the hidden, 'underground' compartments of the human mind that are screened off from awareness or conscious access. Much of this book is devoted to an exploration of the consequences of this point of view.

2.3.2 *Boolean algebra and the operators of propositional calculus*

But let us revert to the matter at hand. We start with propositional calculus and look at the logical constants AND, OR, and NOT. IF...THEN plays no role in the present context, first because IF P...THEN Q is logically definable as NOT(P) OR Q, and secondly because it is doubtful whether IF...THEN functions as a truth function in natural language (see Kratzer 1979; Evans and Over 2005; see also Section 8.2.4). The three operators AND, OR, and NOT are standardly considered to be TRUTH FUNCTIONS in the sense that they produce a new truth value on the basis of the truth value(s) of their component argument L-proposition(s). The semantic definition of these operators can be presented in different formats. The standard format (introduced in the 1920s, but based on definitions provided by ancient Stoic philosophers; see Łukasiewicz 1934) is that of the TRUTH TABLES. The standard truth tables for these operators are given in Figure 2.8. ('T' stands for truth, 'F' for falsity; the variables P and Q range over L-propositions (modulo key); ∧ is the standard symbol for AND; ∨ stands for OR; ¬ stands for standard bivalent negation.)

Such truth tables may be taken to represent the meanings of the operators concerned in that they specify the conditions under which (token) L-propositions composed by them are true or false. These conditions are exhaustively expressible in terms of the truth values of the component L-propositions, which makes the operators in question truth functions—that is, functions from truth values to truth values.

Usually, ∧ and ∨ are treated as taking two argument propositions. The truth-tables of Figure 2.8 also treat ∧ and ∨ as binary operators. In fact,

P	¬P
T	F
F	T

P ∧ Q	Q: T	F
P: T	T	F
F	F	F

P ∨ Q	Q: T	F
P: T	T	T
F	T	F

FIGURE 2.8 Standard truth tables for ¬, ∧ and ∨

however, there is no limit to the number of argument L-propositions. The general rule is that $P \wedge Q \wedge R \wedge S \wedge \ldots$ is true only if all argument L-propositions are true, and false if at least one of them is false (falsity is 'infectious'). Analogously, $P \vee Q \vee R \vee S \vee \ldots$ is true just in case at least one of the argument L-propositions is true, and false only if all argument L-propositions are false (truth is 'infectious'). The *n*-ary character of these two operators is usually expressed by saying that they are ASSOCIATIVE.

In this truth-functional perspective, which derives from the work of Gottlob Frege (1848–1925), the EXTENSION of an L-propositional token is taken to be its truth value. Just as the extensions (reference objects) of the argument terms of a logically atomic L-proposition P determine the extension (truth value) of P under the lexical predicate of P, in the same way the extensions (in this case the truth values) of the argument L-propositions of a logically complex L-proposition determine its truth value under the logical operator(s) building up the complex L-proposition. Viewed this way, the logical operators of propositional calculus begin to look like predicates.

Alternatively, as a notational variant, these three propositional operators can be defined in terms of the operators of Boolean algebra. George Boole (1815–1864) developed the algebra that carries his name in order to bring logic and mathematics closer together. This algebra turned out to be directly applicable to sets as mathematical objects and thus became the central foundation of set theory.

Boolean algebra has two CONSTANT SYMBOLS, 1 (unity) and 0 (zero), and any number of VARIABLE SYMBOLS or VARIABLES $(x, y, z, \ldots)$ ranging over $1, 0$ and any elements that may be needed for any given interpretation (such as sets in set theory). It has, furthermore, two (associative and commutative) binary operations, ADDITION ($+$) and MULTIPLICATION ($\bullet$) defined as follows ('$=$': mutually substitutable in all contexts; '$\neq$': not mutually substitutable in all contexts):

MULTIPLICATION: (1) $x \bullet x = x$ (3) $x \bullet 0 = 0$
                 (2) $x \bullet 1 = x$

ADDITION: (1) $x + x = x$ (3) $x + 0 = 0$
                 (2) $x + 1 = 1$

It also has a unary operation COMPLEMENT $\bar{x}$, defined as follows:

COMPLEMENT: (1) $\bar{1} = 0$ (4) $\bar{x} \bullet x = 0$
                 (2) $\bar{0} = 1$ (5) $\bar{\bar{x}} = x$
                 (3) $\bar{x} + x = 1$

One may add the (nonassociative, noncommutative) operation SUBTRACTION:

SUBTRACTION: (1) $x - x = 0$ (4) $x - 0 = x$
                 (2) $x - 1 = 0$ (5) $0 - x = 0$
                 (3) $1 - x = \bar{x}$ (6) $x - y = z$ iff $x \cdot z = z$ and $y \cdot z = 0$

Moreover, addition distributes over multiplication and vice versa:

$$x + (y \cdot z) = (x + y) \cdot (x + z) \quad \text{and} \quad x \cdot (y + z) = (x \cdot y) + (x \cdot z)$$

Finally, the following laws hold:
(1) $x + (x \cdot y) = x$ and $x \cdot (x + y) = x$
(2) $x \cdot y = z$ iff $x + z = x$ and $y + z = y$
(3) $x + y = z$ iff $x \cdot z = x$ and $y \cdot z = y$

It is easy to see that Boolean algebra formalizes set theory. Let the variables x, y, z, ... range over sets, while 0 is the null set $\emptyset$ and 1 stands for the domain of objects **OBJ**. Interpret multiplication as set-theoretic intersection ($\cap$), addition as set-theoretic union ($\cup$), and complement as set-theoretic complement($\bar{x}$). Boolean algebra now computes all set-theoretic operations.

Boolean algebra also computes the truth functions of propositional calculus. One way of doing so was developed by Frege. Instead of taking sets as values of the Boolean symbols, Frege took 'truth' as the value of Boolean 1 and 'falsity' as the value of Boolean 0 (which is the origin of the widespread convention, not followed in this book, to use '1' for truth and '0' for falsity). No other symbols are required. NEGATION ($\neg$) is now interpreted as Boolean complement, CONJUNCTION ($\wedge$) as Boolean multiplication and DISJUNCTION ($\vee$) as Boolean addition. Let $\phi(P)$ stand for the truth value, that is the Fregean extension, of any atomic or complex L-proposition P. Figure 2.9 shows how the truth-functional operators of standard propositional calculus are computed as Boolean functions:

All this is generally accepted and part of the standard foundations of propositional logic. It is, however, also widely known, but less widely publicized, that this seductive application of Boolean algebra to the

$\phi(P)$	$\phi(\neg P)$		$\phi(P \wedge Q)$ $\phi(Q)$:	1	0		$\phi(P \vee Q)$ $\phi(Q)$:	1	0
$\bar{x}$			$\bullet$				$+$		
1	0		$\phi(P)$: 1	1	0		$\phi(P)$: 1	1	1
0	1		0	0	0		0	1	0

FIGURE 2.9 Frege's application of Boolean algebra to propositional calculus

truth-functional operators of propositional logic requires an awkward ontology, which must attribute real world existence not only to what are perceived as objects of the kind normally accepted in extensionalist ontologies, but also to Truth and Falsity (see Section 6.1 in Volume I). Standard model theory, in particular, faces the uncomfortable consequence that any 'world' must be defined as containing not only what are normally called objects and sets of (*n*-tuples of) objects, but also the 'abstract' objects Truth and Falsity, a curious intrusion of extreme, and ultimately unsustainable, Platonism in an otherwise strictly nominalist universe.

2.3.3 *Valuation space modelling: a formal definition*

This blemish can be removed by a more direct application of Boolean algebra to the propositional truth functions, without reading Boolean 1 as 'truth' and Boolean 0 as 'falsity', and thus without having to take truth values as extensions of L-propositions. Instead, the machinery of set theory, already seen to be computable by the Boolean operators, can be put to good use by means of the method of valuation space (VS) modelling introduced in informal terms in Sections 3.3 and 2.2.

It is time now to be a little more precise as regards the notion of VS-modelling. VS-analysis takes a logical language L_L whose expressions, L-propositions, are taken to underlie the sentences of a natural language. Given one single set of reference assignments K_i ('key') for all referring and indexical terms in the L-propositions of L_L, VS-analysis assigns to each L-proposition P a valuation space $/P/$, which is the set of admissible situations under K_i, within the totality U of all admissible situations, in which P is true. An ADMISSIBLE SITUATION is defined as a set of truth-value assignments under any given K_i to all L-propositions of L_L. If L_L contains n logically and semantically independent L-propositions, each of which allows for truth (T) or falsity (F) independently of all the others, then, in a standard bivalent system of truth and falsity, there are, under each K_i, 2^n logically and semantically independent valuations—that is, assignments of T or F to each of the L-propositions of the language. Each such set of assignments is called a 'valuation' or 'admissible situation'. Given a particular L-proposition P, its VS $/P/$ is the set of admissible situations (valuations), under any given K_i, in which P is assigned the value T. An L-proposition P is true just in case the actual situation sit_{act} is an element in $/P/$. Clearly, L-propositions formed with the help of one or more truth-functional propositional operators have their truth value assigned depending on the truth values of the component L-proposition(s) and the way the truth function is defined.

For those who are inclined to ask philosophical questions about what is meant by 'situation' here, it is important to realize that one can very well operate theoretically with a formally defined notion of 'situation' while remaining uncommitted as to the precise status of 'situations' in the natural ontology of speakers or, rather, cognizing humans. Although it would be utterly unrealistic to assume that natural speakers have a fully elaborated interpretation of set theory onto a system of valuation spaces at their disposal when interpreting utterances, it is not at all unrealistic to assume that they have an intuitive and not fully elaborated idea, probably beyond the threshold of possible awareness and signalled by physical reactions in the brain, of 'possible truth in an overall set of situations', and hence of notions like (in)compatibility, contradiction, and necessary consequence. Correspondingly, one may assume that notions like mutual exclusion, partial intersection and proper inclusion of sets of situations are likely to be cognitively real. In Chapter 3, a theory is proposed of how naïve, uneducated humans deal with the plural objects we call sets. In this NATURAL SET THEORY, mutual exclusion, mutual partial intersection, and proper inclusion are taken to be the basic-natural set-theoretical notions. If that is so, it easily follows that their logical counterparts, contrariety, contradiction, and necessary consequence (entailment), likewise have some form of psychological reality.

VS-analysis allows for a different interpretation of Boolean algebra onto propositional logic, in that the set-theoretic functions are used as an intermediary. We remember that an L-proposition P, expressing the proposition *p*, has associated with it the set of all admissible situations in which *p* is true—that is, the *valuation space* (VS) of P, or /P/. Since set theory is computable by means of the functions of Boolean algebra, this algebra is applicable to the truth functions of propositional calculus, with valuation spaces as the sets involved and the universe of all admissible situations **U** standing for the universe of all objects **OBJ**. So we use the standard interpretation of Boolean algebra onto set theory, which treats 1 as the universe **OBJ** of all objects and 0 as the null set ∅. Since the Boolean variables are taken to range over sets, set-theoretic COMPLEMENT corresponds to Boolean complement, set-theoretic INTERSECTION to Boolean multiplication, and set-theoretic UNION to Boolean addition. This translates directly onto the truth functions of propositional logic, with VSs as sets and the universe **U** of all admissible situations as **OBJ**, in the following way:

Negation corresponds to set-theoretic complement:

for any L-proposition P: $/\neg P/ = /\bar{P}/$

Conjunction ($\wedge$) corresponds to set-theoretic intersection ($\cap$):

for any L-propositions P and Q: $/P \wedge Q/ = /P/ \cap /Q/.$

Disjunction ($\vee$) corresponds to set-theoretic union ($\cup$):

for any L-propositions P and Q: $/P \vee Q/ = /P/ \cup /Q/.$

On the basis of the principle that when P is true, the actual situation sit_{act} is an element in the valuation space of P, or: $sit_{act} \in /P/$, the truth-functional propositional operators $\neg$, $\wedge$ and $\vee$ are now set-theoretically definable as follows (for the sake of simplicity, the operators $\wedge$ and $\vee$ are treated as binary, rather than as *n*-ary, functions):

(2.3) P is true: $sit_{act} \in /P/$

$\neg P$ is true: $sit_{act} \in /\neg P/$; therefore: $/\neg P/=/\bar{P}/$

$P \wedge Q$ is true: $sit_{act} \in /P/ \cap /Q/$; therefore: $/P \wedge Q/= /P/ \cap /Q/$

$P \vee Q$ is true: $sit_{act} \in /P/ \cup /Q/$; therefore: $/P \vee Q/= /P/ \cup /Q/$

Again, when P is necessarily false, $/P/ = \emptyset$; when P is necessarily true, $/P/ = \mathbf{U}$.

The method of valuation space modelling subdivides the universe $\mathbf{U}$ of all admissible situations for specific L-propositions or classes of L-propositions. Thus, in Figure 2.10a, $\mathbf{U}$ is subdivided for any arbitrary L-proposition P and hence also for its negation $\neg P$, $/P/$, and $/\bar{P}/$ being mutually exclusive and jointly equal to $\mathbf{U}$. Similarly in Figures 2.10b and 2.10c, where $\mathbf{U}$ is subdivided for any arbitrary pair of L-propositions P and Q, which are logically independent in the sense that they can be simultaneously singly true, singly false, both true, and both false. In Figures 2.10b and 2.10c the valuation spaces for $P \wedge Q$ and for $P \vee Q$ are indicated in terms of the logically independent L-propositions P and Q. The corresponding VS for each case is marked by horizontal lines. Figure 2.10 thus shows diagrammatically how the logical truth functions $\neg$, $\wedge$ and $\vee$ are translatable into the set-theoretic functions of complement($\bar{x}$), intersection ($\cap$) and union ($\cup$), respectively.

One notes that, just as the set-theoretic functions apply to any arbitrary set or pair of sets, no matter whether they are null or equal to **OBJ**, the propositional truth functions apply to any arbitrary L-proposition P or pair of L-propositions P and Q, even when they are necessarily true or necessarily false. If P is necessarily true, so that $/P/= \mathbf{U}$, its negation $\neg P$ is necessarily false, so that $/\bar{P}/ = \emptyset$. If either P or Q or both P and Q are necessarily true, then so is $P \vee Q$, since, in that case, $/P/ \cup /Q/= \mathbf{U}$. And if either P or Q or both P and Q are necessarily false, then so is $P \wedge Q$, since, in that case, $/P/ \cap /Q/= \emptyset$.

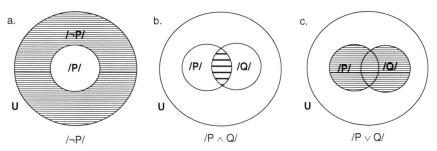

FIGURE 2.10 Valuation spaces in **U** for standard ¬P, P ∧ Q, and P ∨ Q

The standard logical relations of *equivalence* (≡), *entailment* (⊢, ⊨), *contradiction* (#), *contrariety* (><), and *subcontrariety* (>≤) are likewise immediately expressible in the set-theoretic terms of valuation spaces, as is shown in (2.4). One notes that contradictoriness (#) combines the conditions of contrariety (><) and subcontrariety (>≤).

(2.4) For all L-propositions P and Q:

    a. $P \equiv Q$ iff $/P/ = /Q/$

    b. $P \vdash (\vDash) Q$ iff $/P/ \subseteq /Q/$

    c. $P \# Q$ iff $/P/ \cup /Q/ = \mathbf{U}$ and $/P/ \cap /Q/ = \emptyset$ (or: $/P/ = /\bar{Q}/$)

    d. $P >< Q$ iff $/P/ \cap /Q/ = \emptyset$

    e. $P \underset{=}{><} Q$ iff $/P/ \cup /Q/ = \mathbf{U}$

The standard set-theoretic relation of *identity* (=) corresponds to the logical relation of *equivalence* defined in (2.4a). *Inclusion* (⊆) corresponds to *entailment*, as shown in (2.4b). *Contradictoriness* is defined by the set-theoretic relation of *complement*, as in (2.4c). *Contrariety* is defined by the set-theoretic relation of *mutual exclusion*, as in (2.4d). And *subcontrariety* corresponds to a set-theoretic relation that has so far not been honoured with a name in standard set theory but for which we invent the name of FULL UNION (Ů), defined, for sets *A* and *B*, as follows:

(2.5) FULL UNION: A Ů B iff A ∪ B = **OBJ**

It follows from (2.5) that, when A Ů B holds, it will be impossible, for any element *o* in **OBJ**, that *o* ∉ A and *o* ∉ B: *o* has to be an element in either *A* or *B*, or in both. The logical counterpart of full union is subcontrariety, since two L-propositions P and Q are subcontraries just in case it is impossible for both P and Q to be false simultaneously.

The notion of LOGICAL INDEPENDENCE of two L-propositions P and Q is of central importance. VS analysis makes it possible to define this notion in set-theoretic terms. For pairs of sets of objects, *set-theoretic independence* means that an arbitrary object o $\in$ **OBJ** can be an element in either set, or in both sets, or in neither of the two sets involved. For L-propositions P and Q, *logical independence* means that the actual situation sit_{act} can be a member of /P/ but not of /Q/, or of /Q/ but not of /P/, or of both, or of neither. Just as two sets A and B that partially intersect (A $\oslash$ B) and therefore do not severally or jointly equal either **OBJ** or $\emptyset$ are set-theoretically independent, we say that the L-propositions P and Q are logically independent just in case /P/ and /Q/ partially intersect (/P/ $\oslash$ /Q/) and therefore do not severally or jointly equal **U** or $\emptyset$. Relations between sets have now become metalogical relations and vice versa.

It is worth observing, however, that there are also differences, due to the actual needs of the calculi involved. Thus, although 'partially intersect' is a legitimate set-theoretic relation between sets producing truth under certain conditions and 'logically independent' is likewise a legitimate relation between L-propositions producing truth under certain conditions, yet the relation 'logically independent' plays no role in any calculus of entailments—that is, in any logic. Logical (meta)relations are functional only to the extent that they impair the mutual independence of the component L-propositions, so that some form of entailment can be formulated. Similarly, whereas subcontrariety is a well-known relation in propositional logic, its set-theoretic counterpart—here called 'full union'—has not even been given a name in set theory, probably because it can easily be done without.

2.3.4 *Satisfaction conditions of the propositional operators*

Now that it has been shown that the propositional operators can be looked upon as predicates, this perspective can be developed further. Although the same descriptive format is used for ordinary lexical and for logical predicates, it is not implied that there are no differences. As has been said, logical predicates differ from other lexical predicates in that the satisfaction conditions of the former, to the extent that they are part of a logical system, are expressible in terms that allow for a *formal calculus of entailments*. In the case of the standardly known logical constants, it is the purely mathematical terms of set theory that allow for the formal calculus of entailments, but it is not unthinkable that similar semantic properties in other sets of predicates allow for regular logical entailment schemata as well.

It should be borne in mind also that those predicates that fit into some logical system may well have other semantic properties that transcend their strictly logical character and have to do with the often confused or confusing phenomena of reality and experience. Quantifying predicates like FEW or MANY clearly have logical properties. But beyond these they also possess nonlogical semantic properties, such as the implicit appeal to some standard with respect to which it can be said of a set or collection that it has 'many' or 'few' members (see Section 1.6). This shows again that it is both useful and natural to treat logical constants as predicates.

Following this lead we consider ¬, ∧ and ∨ to be predicates. That is, as far as their role in propositional calculus is concerned, we say that ¬ assigns to a (well-anchored and well-keyed) L-proposition P the property that sit_{act} is a member of the COMPLEMENT $\overline{/P/}$ of the associated valuation space, ∧ assigns to the (well-anchored and well-keyed) L-propositions P, Q, R, S, . . . the property that sit_{act} is in the INTERSECTION of the associated valuation spaces—that is, of /P/ ∩ /Q/ ∩ /R/ ∩ /S/ ∩ . . . , and ∨ assigns to the (well-anchored and well-keyed) L-propositions P, Q, R, S, . . . , the property that sit_{act} is in the UNION of the corresponding valuation spaces—that is, of /P/ ∪ /Q/ ∪ /R/ ∪ /S/ ∪ . . . . Using the notation introduced in Section 3.3 of Volume I for the specification of the satisfaction conditions of predicates, we now write (2.6a–c), where '/P/$^{+}$' stands for any set of two or more valuation spaces of corresponding L-propositions:

(2.6)   a. $[\![\neg]\!] = \{P \mid sit_{act} \in \overline{/P/}\}$
(the extension of ¬ is the set of all L-propositions P such that the actual situation sit_{act} is a member of the complement of /P/)

   b. $[\![\wedge]\!] = \{P^{+} \mid sit_{act} \in \bigcap_{/P/^{+}}\}$
(the extension of ∧ is the set of all sets of two or more L-propositions P such that sit_{act} is a member of the intersection of all /P/$^{+}$)

   c. $[\![\vee]\!] = \{P^{+} \mid sit_{act} \in \bigcup_{/P/^{+}}\}$
(the extension of ∨ is the set of all sets of two or more L-propositions P such that sit_{act} is a member of the union of all /P/$^{+}$)

The propositional constants ¬, ∧ and ∨ are presented as predicates over sets of (well-anchored and well-keyed) L-propositions, each such L-proposition having a corresponding valuation space. Technically speaking, the predicates ¬, ∧, and ∨ are thus functions from (sets of) L-propositions to truth values. This makes them a specific kind of predicate: not first-order predicates over individual objects but higher-order predicates over (sets of) L-propositions.

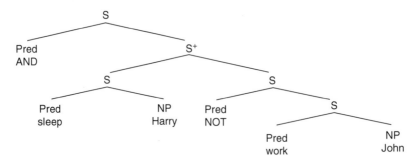

F<small>IGURE</small> 2.11 L-proposition underlying *Harry sleeps and John does not work*

Assuming (simplistically) that ¬, ∧, and ∨ correspond to NOT, AND, and OR, respectively, in English we adopt a modified version of the proposal made in McCawley (1972) to show that these operators also occupy the structural position of predicates in L-propositional structure. We treat the argument of a propositional operator as one term—a single S-term for NOT and a complex S⁺-term for AND and OR—in an L-propositional structure which can be either verb-initial (VSO) or verb-final (SOV) (the verb-initial order is used throughout in the present book). Figure 2.11 shows the L-propositional structure corresponding to the English sentence *Harry sleeps and John does not work* (the operators of assertive speech act and present tense have been omitted). The transformational grammar (see Seuren 1996) then transforms this structure into the appropriate surface structure.

2.3.5 *Satisfaction conditions of the quantifiers*

2.3.5.1 *Russellian quantifiers*   So much for the predicate status of the propositional operators. But how about the quantifiers of predicate calculus? Here one must realize that the notion of quantifier was subjected to considerable refinement during the second half of the twentieth century. In the earlier perspective, quantifiers were functions of a unique kind, introduced by a special rule and provided with a special, not altogether transparent, model-theoretic semantics. Sentences like (2.7a,b) were translated into the language of logic as (2.8a,b), respectively, where '∀' stands for *all* and '∃' for *some.*[5] Let us call the quantifiers as defined in terms of this system R<small>USSELLIAN</small> <small>QUANTIFIERS</small>:

---

[5] The symbol ∃, for the existential quantifier (just like the symbols ∩ and ∪ for set-theoretic intersection and union, respectively, and the symbol ∈ for class membership, being the first letter of

(2.7)   a. All farmers grumble.

      b. Some farmers grumble.

(2.8)   a. $\forall x(\mathsf{Farmer(x)} \rightarrow \mathsf{Grumble(x)})$

       (for all objects x, if x is a farmer, then x grumbles)

      b. $\exists x(\mathsf{Farmer(x)} \wedge \mathsf{Grumble(x)})$

       (for at least one object x, x is a farmer and x grumbles)

This is, on the whole, well known and many readers will still have been brought up in this tradition. What is less well known is the fact that the Russellian quantifiers are open to an interpretation that treats them as *unary higher-order predicates*. To see this, it is important to keep in mind that the extension of a propositional function $\mathsf{F(x)}$, where F is a predicate and x is a variable ranging over the total set of objects **OBJ**, is identical to the extension of the predicate F: $[\![\mathsf{F(x)}]\!] = [\![\mathsf{F}]\!]$—that is, the set of objects in **OBJ** that satisfy the predicate F.

This is easily seen when one realizes that a variable is a symbol that is to be rotated over all objects in its range. Thus, the variable x in the L-propositional function $\mathsf{Horse(x)}$ selects each object in the total set of objects **OBJ** and tests it for satisfaction of the conditions associated with the predicate Horse. Those objects that satisfy the conditions of Horse are marked $+$, those that do not are marked $-$. Now the set of all objects marked $+$ is precisely the set of horses. For that reason, logicians generally follow Frege who stated that, for any (unary) predicate F, $[\![\mathsf{F}]\!]$ equals $[\![\mathsf{F(x)}]\!]$: the variable has no semantic (model-theoretic) effect; all it does is indicate that the predicate in question needs a term in the position of the variable to become an L-proposition.

Moreover, when propositional operators are applied to propositional functions, the result is again a propositional function. Thus, $\mathsf{F(x)} \wedge \mathsf{G(x)}$ is a propositional function and its extension $[\![\mathsf{F(x)} \wedge \mathsf{G(x)}]\!]$ is the intersection of $[\![\mathsf{F(x)}]\!]$ and $[\![\mathsf{G(x)}]\!]$, or $[\![\mathsf{F(x)}]\!] \cap [\![\mathsf{G(x)}]\!]$, or just $[\![\mathsf{F}]\!] \cap [\![\mathsf{G}]\!]$. And $\mathsf{F(x)} \rightarrow \mathsf{G(x)}$ is again a propositional function whose extension $[\![\mathsf{F(x)} \rightarrow \mathsf{G(x)}]\!]$ is the union of the complement of $[\![\mathsf{F(x)}]\!]$ in **OBJ** and $[\![\mathsf{G(x)}]\!]$, or $[\![\overline{\mathsf{F(x)}}]\!] \cup [\![\mathsf{G(x)}]\!]$, or just $[\![\overline{\mathsf{F}}]\!] \cup [\![\mathsf{G}]\!]$.

the Greek *esti* ('is'), was introduced by Giuseppe Peano in the 1890s when he worked at his 'Formulario' project, intended to introduce a unified notational system for the whole of mathematics and logic. The symbol $\forall$, for the universal quantifier, originates with Gerhard Genzen, who introduced it in his 'Untersuchungen ueber das logische Schliessen' (*Mathematische Zeitschr.* 39 (1934) p. 178), as a proper counterpart to $\exists$. An earlier notation for 'for all x', used in Whitehead and Russell (1910–1913) and also in Quine (1952), was '(x)'.

Having said this, we can define the Russellian universal and existential quantifiers as unary higher-order predicates—that is, as unary predicates over sets of objects—in the following way:

(2.9)   For all sets X in **OBJ**:

   a. $[\![\forall]\!] = \{\, X \mid X = \textbf{OBJ}\,\}$

       (the extension of the predicate $\forall$ is the set of all sets that equal **OBJ**)

   b. $[\![\exists]\!] = \{\, X \mid X \neq \varnothing\,\}$

       (the extension of the predicate $\exists$ is the set of all nonnull sets in **OBJ**)

Note that the format used for the specification of the logical predicates $\forall$ and $\exists$ in (2.9a,b), and for the propositional operators in (2.6a–c), is again that used for ordinary lexical predicates as defined in Section 3.3.2 of Volume I. As before, the condition specified after the upright bar is the satisfaction condition of the predicate in question. Technically speaking, therefore, the Russellian quantifiers are treated as functions from sets of objects to truth values.

Consider, for example, (2.8a). An application of the truth table of the material implication shows that when (2.8a) is true, then $[\![\textsf{Farmer(x)} \to \textsf{Grumble(x)}]\!] = \textbf{OBJ}$, since the propositional function $\textsf{Farmer(x)} \to \textsf{Grumble(x)}$ yields truth for any arbitrary object in **OBJ**. (2.8a) is falsified by any object in **OBJ** that does satisfy $\textsf{Farmer(x)}$ but not $\textsf{Grumble(x)}$. But if (2.8a) is true, then any object in **OBJ** either does not satisfy $\textsf{Farmer(x)}$ or it satisfies both $\textsf{Farmer(x)}$ and $\textsf{Grumble(x)}$. Analogously for (2.8b), which is true just in case $[\![\textsf{Farmer(x)} \wedge \textsf{Grumble(x)}]\!] \neq \varnothing$. The predicate status of the Russellian quantifiers is thus saved by the propositional operators of standard logic.

2.3.5.2   *Generalized quantifiers*   During the 1950s, some logicians discovered that the Russellian quantifiers are not satisfactory as logical translations of the natural language quantifying words *all* and *some*. Besides the unnaturalness of the logical translations of quantified natural language sentences—a perennial source of bewilderment for beginning students—the main problem with them is the fact that the method of rendering quantifiers with the help of propositional operators cannot be extended to other quantifiers such as MOST or HALF. This blocks a unified analysis of natural language quantifiers in logical terms, which means an always unwelcome loss of generalization. Since there is an alternative analysis of the quantifiers which restores the generalization, it would seem that that analysis is preferable.

The alternative analysis was presented by Barwise and Cooper (1981), who, falling back on Mostovski (1957), proposed to incorporate the L-propositional function '$\textsf{Farmer(x)}$' into the quantifier in the following way:

(2.10)   a. $\forall$x[Farmer(x)](Grumble(x))
              (for all objects x such that x is a farmer, x grumbles)

         b. $\exists$x[Farmer(x)](Grumble(x))
              (for at least one object x such that x is a farmer, x grumbles)

A semantics can now be provided in set-theoretic terms. As has been shown, L-propositional functions of the form F(x), where F is a predicate and x is a variable ranging over **OBJ**, are interpreted as expressions denoting sets. The set denoted by the incorporated L-propositional function, in this case Farmer(x), is called the RESTRICTOR SET and the set denoted by the remaining propositional function, in this case Grumble(x), is called the MATRIX SET. The corresponding expressions are called the RESTRICTOR TERM and the MATRIX TERM. Now the universal quantifier $\forall$ can be said to require for truth that the restrictor set be a subset of the matrix set, while the existential quantifier $\exists$ can be said to require for truth that the restrictor set and the matrix set share a nonnull intersection. This analysis is known as the theory of GENERALIZED QUANTIFIERS, as it allows for a generalized treatment of all natural language quantifiers.

The analysis provided by Barwise and Cooper can be simplified when one realizes that the quantifiers $\forall$ and $\exists$ express a relation between two sets, the restrictor set and the matrix set. Therefore, the quantifiers are properly regarded as two-place higher-order predicates—that is, as predicates over pairs of sets, rather than over (pairs of) objects, as is the case with first-order predicates. The notation of (2.10a,b) is now no longer desirable and should be replaced by one in which the quantifiers are represented as predicates over two terms, each term denoting a set. This produces the following translations in L_L for the sentences (2.7a,b):[6]

(2.11)   a. $\forall$x(Grumble(x), Farmer(x))
              (the set of farmers is a subset of the set of grumblers)

         b. $\exists$x(Grumble(x), Farmer(x))
              (the set of farmers and the set of grumblers intersect)

---

[6] I deviate from the convention to put the restrictor term first and the matrix term second. My reason for inverting this order is purely linguistic, not logical: it allows for the syntactic rule of OBJECT INCORPORATION (OI), whereby the second (object) term is united with the predicate to form a complex predicate as in, for example, $\forall$x[F(x)](G(x)), or 'for all x that are F: x is G', corresponding to (2.10a). The rule OI has a strong position in universal grammar, whereas SUBJECT INCORPORATION is only weakly supported (Seuren 1996: 300–9). See also note 3 in Chapter 4.

The quantifiers are indexed for the variable they bind. Thus, (2.12a) translates as (2.12b):

(2.12)   a. All farmers groom some horse.
         b. ∀x(∃y(Groom(x,y), Horse(y)), Farmer(x))

In general, sentence types like those given in (2.13a–j) are translated as follows:

(2.13)   a. ALL F is G ∀x(G(x), F(x))   f. SOME F is NOT-G ∃x(¬G(x), F(x))
         b. SOME F is G ∃x(G(x), F(x))   g. ALL NON-F is G ∀x(G(x), ¬F(x))
         c. NOT ALL F is G ¬∀ x(G(x), F(x))   h. SOME NON-F is G ∃x(G(x), ¬F(x))
         d. NO F is G ¬∃ x(G(x), F(x))   i. ALL NON-F is NOT-G ∀x(¬G(x), ¬F(x))
         e. ALL F is NOT-G ∀x(¬G(x), F(x))   j. SOME NON-F is NOT-G ∃x(¬G(x), ¬F(x))

This opens a new window on internal negation, discussed in Section 2.2. It is clear from (2.13a–j) that the negation, ¬, can be used externally, to negate the whole following L-proposition, but also internally, to negate the propositional function in the subject or matrix term: the propositional function ¬G(x) denotes the set of all objects that do not satisfy the predicate G. The language of predicate calculus, and in particular the use of a variable to help denote the extension of a predicate, thus allows for the (internal) negation of any propositional function in any position in an L-propositional structure.

  Normally in predicate calculus, however, only the negated matrix term is used, not the negated restrictor term, although both forms of negation are allowed in the formal language. This is because the negated restrictor term is considered logically less interesting, whereas the negated matrix or subject term plays a major role in predicate logic, owing to the duality of the two quantifiers, as explained in Section 2.2. In general, internal negation is defined as the negation of the matrix term.

  The universal quantifier ∀ can now be defined as assigning the property that the restrictor set is a subset of the matrix set, and the existential quantifier ∃ as assigning the property that the two sets share a nonnull intersection. We do not wish to claim that this is an exhaustive description of the *linguistic* meaning of these two operators, nor even that this description, as far as it goes, is a correct rendering of their purely logical meaning in the logic of language. But it does capture the purely logical meaning of these two quantifiers in standard modern predicate calculus (SMPC). A formal expression of these standard meanings in terms of generalized quantifiers is given in (2.14a,b):

(2.14)   For all sets X and Y:
  a. $[\![\forall]\!] = \{\,<Y,X> \mid X \subseteq Y\,\}$
      (the extension of the predicate $\forall$ is the set of all pairs of sets Y, X, such that X is a subset of Y)
  b. $[\![\exists]\!] = \{\,<Y,X> \mid Y \cap X \neq \emptyset\,\}$
      (the extension of the predicate $\exists$ is the set of all pairs of sets Y, X, such that the intersection of Y and X is nonnull)

Again, the format used for the semantic specification of the logical predicates $\forall$ and $\exists$ in (2.14a,b) is identical to that introduced in Section 3.3.2 of Volume I for nonlogical lexical predicates, with the satisfaction condition specified after the upright bar. Whereas in (2.9a,b) above the Russellian quantifiers were treated as UNARY higher-order predicates, the generalized quantifiers of (2.14a, b) are treated as BINARY higher-order predicates—that is, as functions from PAIRS OF SETS of objects to truth values.

This makes it possible to analyse the quantifier MOST in a way analogous to the standard quantifiers $\forall$ and $\exists$. Sentence (2.15a), translated as the L-proposition (2.15b), contains the binary higher-order quantifier MOST, which is semantically described as in (2.16):

(2.15)   a. Most farmers grumble.
         b. MOST x(Grumble(x), Farmer(x))

(2.16) $[\![\text{MOST}]\!] = \{<Y,X> \mid Y \cap X| > {|X|}/_{2}\}$ (NB: $|X|$: the cardinality of set X)
         (the extension of the predicate MOST is the set of all pairs of sets Y, X, such that the cardinality of the intersection of Y and X is greater than the cardinality of X divided by 2)

A similar analysis for HALF is easily given. This means that there now is a unified category of quantifiers analysed according to one generalized system. Hence the name.

Figure 2.12 shows the L-propositional tree structure for sentence (2.17):

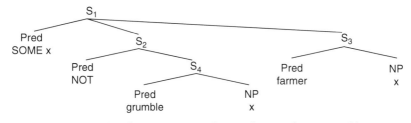

FIGURE 2.12 L-propositional tree structure of *Some farmers do not grumble*

(2.17)   Some farmers do not grumble.

This sentence incorporates the unary propositional operator NOT into the
matrix (subject) term S_2 of the quantifying predicate SOME $(=\exists)$—that is, as
an internal negation. The restrictor term S3 of the predicate SOME, takes
the set of objects that satisfy the predicate *farmer*, i.e. $[\![\mathsf{Farmer(x)}]\!]$, as its
extension. (Syntactically, an L-propositional function $\mathsf{F(x)}$ requires a dominating S-node, so that the tree structure is of the form $_S[\mathsf{F(x)}]$: S is the
dominating node; F is the predicate; x is the (variable) term.) So $[\![S_3]\!]$ gives
the required X-set. But how about the Y-set, represented by S_2? We have seen
that the propositional operator NOT $(= \neg)$ requires the specification of
the VS of its argument-S. We know what is meant by $/\mathsf{F(a)}/$, where a is
a referring term: $/\mathsf{F(a)}/$ is the set of situations that make $\mathsf{F(a)}$ true. But
what is $/\mathsf{F(x)}/$?

By definition, since x is a variable ranging over objects, $/\mathsf{F(x)}/$ is a function
from objects to valuation spaces. That is, for each object $\rho(a)$ (the reference
value of the term a) in **OBJ** the L-propositional function $\mathsf{F(x)}$ produces
precisely one valuation space $/\mathsf{F(a)}/$. The predicate NOT subsequently
produces truth or falsity for the S_2-proposition $\neg\mathsf{F(a)}$ according to whether
sit$_{act}$ is or is not an element in $/\mathsf{F(a)}/$. Thus, a truth value is produced for S_2
for each single substitution of the variable x with an expression referring to
an object in **OBJ**, just as the L-propositional function $\mathsf{Farmer(x)}$ produces
a truth value for S_3 for each single substitution of the variable x with the
name of an object in **OBJ**. Therefore, S_2 gives the Y-set required for (2.17), in
this case the set of all those who do not grumble. The Y-set and the X-set
are now fed into the predicate SOME, so that the proper truth value can be
produced.

All this looks good, much better than the Russellian quantifiers. Other
approaches are possible as well, as shown in Section 4.3, where a modified
system of quantification is presented, the system of *distributive quantifiers*,
which incorporates into the semantics of the quantifiers the parallelism
between the propositional and the quantifying operators.

More importantly, further research into the *discourse-semantic properties* of
the quantifiers reveals that, although the logical form as specified for the
quantifier SOME can be used as input both to the *grammar* of the language in
question and to the *discourse-incrementation procedure*, the same does not
hold for the quantifier ALL. A sentence like *All farmers grumble* can, in its
normal interpretation, only be processed if the discourse already contains
the information that there are farmers, to which the new information that
all farmers grumble is then added. In fact, in the normal interpretation,

a sentence like *All farmers grumble* is equivalent with *All **the** farmers grumble*, which is also how this sentence is rendered in a large number of languages other than English, such as French. Somehow or other, therefore, the universal quantifier ALL must be connected with the definite determiner *the*. There are also interpretations where this is not so, as, for example, with the universal *any* as in *Any doctor will tell you that smoking is bad*. In this case, a formalization with the help of the implication operator IF … THEN seems called for, just as in the Russellian paraphrase of the universal quantifier.

The discourse-sensitive interpretation of ALL complicates matters considerably. It means, for one thing, that universally quantified sentences require an underlying form which differs in important respects from the logical form postulated in our logical system, which does not reckon with discourse factors. As long as it is pure logic that we are concerned with, this complication will be ignored and we will simply keep up the fiction that the universal quantifier runs parallel with its existential counterpart, as is the practice followed in all logical systems in existence. The difficulties and uncertainties surrounding the discourse-sensitive quantifier ALL will be discussed in Chapters 8 and 9 of the present volume.

Meanwhile, we pass on to a discussion of the logical systems of propositional and predicate calculus, looking in greater detail at the logical properties of external and internal negation in relation to the propositional operators and the quantifiers.

2.4 Internal negation, the Conversions and De Morgan's laws

2.4.1 *The internal negation again*

Logic comes off the ground as soon as internal negation is introduced. Although the modern notion of internal negation, that is, negation over a matrix term under a higher operator (small scope negation), was not available to Aristotle, he still observed that there is a special significance to the difference between an external and an internal position of the negation in quantified sentences (L-propositions), and that this significance is lost in nonquantified L-propositions with only definite terms.

Since this is a central element in logic, some precise comment is in order. Consider the nonquantified negative sentence (2.18a), rendered in logical language (L_L) as (2.18b):

(2.18)   a. The flag is not green.
          b. ¬[Green(the x[Flag(x)])]
             (it is not the case that the *x* such that *x* is a flag is green)

The definite determiner the x takes the propositional function Flag(x), denoting the set of all flags, as argument and selects from that set the one particular flag that the discourse happens to be about. Right from Aristotle's day, definite determiners have caused trouble to logicians, the reason being that the function selecting one particular element from a set is not computable by set-theoretic means (it is noncompositional) but depends on knowledge of the discourse and state of affairs at hand. Russell speaks of 'phrases containing *the*' as being 'by far the most interesting and difficult of denoting phrases' (1905: 481).

Definite determiners thus make the interpretation of sentences dependent on cognitive factors, something which twentieth-century logicians have either denied or tried to ignore. In Russell's extremely influential article (1905), which marked the beginning of what Quine called 'the programme of elimination of singular terms', the word *the* is written out of the logic script and is reinterpreted as a lexicalization of a complex quantificational construction. Sentence (2.18a) is analysed there as (2.19a), which, when rewritten in terms of generalized quantifiers, comes out as (2.19b):

(2.19)   a. ∃x[Flag(x) ∧¬[Green(x)] ∧ ∀y[Flag(y) → y = x]]
             (there is an *x* such that *x* is a flag and *x* is not green and such that
             for all *y*, if *y* is a flag, *y* is identical with *x*)
          b. ∃x(¬[Green(x)], [Flag(x) ∧ ∀y(=(y,x), Flag(y))])
             (the set of things that are not green and the set of flags *f* such that
             whatever is a flag is identical with *f* have a nonnull intersection)

This reads as saying that there is a set of flags consisting of just one member and that this set has a nonnull intersection with the set of things that are not green, so that there is exactly one flag and this flag is not green. The sentence should, therefore, be falsified by as little as the existence of a second flag, whether green or not green.

This analysis, though logically sound, is an empirical abomination (for arguments, see Section 10.1.2). It corresponds in no way to the actual use of the definite article and other definite determiners in natural language. Yet it has been the dominant, if not standard, analysis in circles of logicians of language, philosophical logicians, and semanticists throughout the twentieth century. Short shrift is what this analysis deserves. We keep to the analysis presented in (2.18b), accepting as a fact of life that definite determiners are noncompositional and need cognitive input to do their work. (See Seuren et al. (2001) for more comment.)

We recall from Section 1.5 that, in Quine's terminology, sentences containing at least one referring or indexical term are *occasion sentences*, while sentences with only quantified terms are *eternal sentences*. The point here is that in negated occasion sentences without any quantifier it makes no difference whether the external negation (over the whole L-proposition) is interpreted in the normal way as external negation, or is incorporated into the predicate, where it is a complement-taking operator within the total set of objects **OBJ**. That is, sentence (2.18a) can be analysed not only as (2.18b) but also as (2.20):

(2.20)   [NOT-Green](the x[Flag(x)])

with the predicate [NOT-Green], denoting all those things that are not green. In other words, the negated predicate is just another predicate, denoting the complement in **OBJ** of the set denoted by the non-negated predicate. Now there is a logical equivalence between $\neg[G(a)]$ (with G as a predicate and a as a term) on the one hand and [NOT-G](a), where [NOT-G] is the predicate, on the other. The L-proposition $\neg[G(a)]$ is true just in case $sit_{act} \in /\neg[G(a)]/$, and therefore $sit_{act} \in /\overline{G(a)}/$. Since the condition for $sit_{act} \in /\overline{G(a)}/$ is that $\rho(a)$—the reference value of the term a—be an element in $[\![G]\!]$ (the set of objects denoted by the predicate G), the condition for $sit_{act} \in /\overline{G(a)}/$ is that $\rho(a) \in [\overline{G}]$. And since $[\![\overline{G}]\!] = [\![$NOT-G$]\!]$, the condition that $sit_{act} \in /\overline{G(a)}/$ is that $\rho(a) \in [\![$NOT-G$]\!]$, which makes [NOT-G](a) true. Hence $\neg(G(a)) \equiv$ [NOT-G](a) for sentences without any quantifier.

Aristotle already saw this. Calling an affirmative property assignment 'unification' and a negative assignment 'separation', he says (*On the Soul* 430b1–4; see also De Rijk 2002: 253):

Falsehood always involves a unification. For even if you assert that what is in fact pale is not pale you have included 'not-pale' in a unification. But it is equally possible to call all these cases 'separation'.

In his more logically oriented *On Interpretation* (17a32–18a12) he refines the statement that 'falsehood ALWAYS involves a unification'. There he shows that the process of lexical incorporation of the negation into the main lexical predicate is possible *salva veritate* only for occasion sentences whose subject term stands under a definite determiner, such as (2.18a). When the subject term is quantified, the negation can still be lexically incorporated into the lexical main predicate, but now no longer *salva veritate*. In such cases there is a change of truth conditions and hence of meaning.

Take, for example, the following sentences (never mind the plural):

(2.21)   a. Some flags are green.
         b. Some flags are not green.
         c. No (= NOT-SOME) flags are green.

The negation of (2.21a) is not (2.21b) but (2.21c). This becomes clear when one considers the logical analysis of the sentences concerned, given in (2.22a–c), respectively:

(2.22)   a. ∃x(Green(x), Flag(x))
         b. ∃x(¬[Green(x)], Flag(x))
         c. ¬[∃x(Green(x), Flag(x))]

The negation in (2.22c) is the EXTERNAL NEGATION, the negation in (2.22b) is the INTERNAL NEGATION. (2.22b) translates as (2.23), where the negation may be seen as having been unified with the predicate **Green** of the propositional function it stands over (its scope) into one single complex predicate NOT-**Green**:

(2.23)   ∃x([NOT-**Green**](x), Flag(x))

It is widely assumed that, analogously, the external negation of (2.22c) has been unified with the main predicate of the sentence that forms its scope, leading to (2.24), with the complex predicate NOT-SOME, lexically realized as *no* in English:

(2.24)   [NOT-SOME x](Green(x), Flag(x))

Yet although most natural languages have a single lexical item corresponding to English *no* and requiring for truth a null intersection of the two sets involved, closer analysis shows that such quantifiers are probably not instances of lexical unification of NOT with the quantifier SOME but are quantifiers in their own right in a basic-natural system of predicate logic that differs from the standard system (for a full analysis see Section 3.5).

   Occasion sentences with a definite subject term have no equivalent of the internal negation of (2.21b). This is because a definite term, such as the x[Flag(x)], does not consist of a propositional function, although it does contain one. The whole definite term cannot be negated: anything like ¬[the x[Flag(x)]] is uninterpretable (semantically ill-formed). One may object that sentences like (2.25a) or (2.25c), which contain the phrase *not the flag*, are perfectly possible. Here, however, these phrases are not used as terms but as predicates of topicalized sentences corresponding to 'what is green is not the flag (but . . .)'. In the logical analysis of such sentences it is useful to extend the expression the x[Flag(x)] with an identifying copula verb be, as in (2.25d):

(2.25)   a. It is not the flag that is green.
         b. The FLAG is not green (but . . .)
         c. Not the FLAG (but . . .) is green.
         d. ¬[[Be(the x[Flag(x)])](the x[Green(x)])]

In the logical analysis (2.25d) of topicalized sentences like (2.25a–c) the definite subject term is the x[Green(x)] or 'the thing that is green', and the predicate is [be(the x[Flag(x)])] or 'be the flag', unlike its nontopicalized counterpart (2.18b), where the x[Flag(x)] is the logical subject term and Green is the logical predicate. In nontopicalized sentences like (2.18a) there is no way of 'negating' the definite term. Anything like *Not the flag is green* is interpretable only as a topicalized sentence.

Yet, precisely because a definite term CONTAINS a propositional function, some form of 'internal' negation is possible for the propositional function inside the definite term. We have, for example, sentences like (2.26a), analysed as (2.26b), or as (2.26c) with the negation over the propositional function Catholic(x) incorporated into the predicate (again, never mind the plural):

(2.26)   a. The noncatholics are angry.
         b. Angry(the x[¬[Catholic(x)]])
         c. Angry(the x[Noncatholic(x)])

Other than in occasion sentences with a definite subject term, the internal negation typical for quantified sentences does negate a term, namely the matrix term of the quantifying predicate, as in (2.22b). And this is possible (semantically well-formed) because the terms of a quantifying predicate are themselves propositional functions.

2.4.2 *The Conversions and De Morgan's laws*

We can now proceed to a renewed discussion of the internal negation, this time not only in predicate calculus but also in propositional calculus. Let us keep, for the moment, to predicate calculus. As before, we use the following abbreviations, where the asterisk signals the internal negation of the matrix term G(x):

(2.27)   **A** = ∀(G(x), F(x)) (ALL F is G)   **A*** = ∀(¬[G(x)], F(x)) (ALL F is NOT-G)
         I = ∃(G(x), F(x)) (SOME F is G)   **I*** = ∃(¬[G(x)], F(x)) (SOME F is NOT-G)

Since ¬[G(x)] is equivalent with [NOT-G](x), **A*** and **A**, as well as **I*** and **I**, differ only in that **A*** and **I*** have a matrix term with a negative lexical predicate, whereas **A** and **I** have a matrix term with a positive lexical predicate. And since the identity of the lexical predicates is irrelevant to the logical calculus, which is based exclusively on the logical constants (the Modulo-*-principle), the logical properties of **A*** and **A** must be identical, as must those of **I*** and **I**.

Given the definitions of ∀ and ∃ as laid down in (2.14) above for generalized quantifiers and repeated here for convenience:

(2.28)   For all sets X and B:
   a. $[\![\forall]\!] = \{\ <Y,X> \mid X \subseteq Y\}$
   b. $[\![\exists]\!] = \{\ <Y,X> \mid Y \cap X \neq \emptyset\}$

the following theorems, known as the CONVERSIONS, hold for the generalized quantifiers ∀ and ∃ in standard modern predicate calculus:

(2.29)   **Conversions:**
   (a) **A** ≡ ¬ **I*** ∀(G(x),F(x)) ≡¬[∃(¬[G(x)],F(x))]
     (ALL F is G ≡ NO F is NOT-G)
   (b) **I** ≡ ¬**A*** ∃(G(x),F(x)) ≡¬[∀(¬[G(x)],F(x))]
     (SOME F is G ≡ NOT ALL F is NOT-G)

The proofs are simple applications of set theory:

(a) left-to-right:
 If $[\![F]\!] \subseteq [\![G]\!]$, then $[\![F]\!] \cap [\![\overline{G}]\!] = \emptyset$. Hence not $([\![F]\!] \cap [\![\overline{G}]\!] \neq \emptyset)$,
 i.e. ¬[∃(¬[G(x)],F(x))].

 right-to-left:
 If not $([\![F]\!] \cap [\![\overline{G}]\!] \neq \emptyset)$, then $[\![F]\!] \cap [\![\overline{G}]\!] = \emptyset$. Hence $[\![F]\!] \subseteq [\![G]\!]$.
 i.e. ∀(F(x),G(x)).

(b) left-to-right:
 If $[\![F]\!] \cap [\![G]\!] \neq \emptyset$, then not $([\![F]\!] \subseteq [\![\overline{G}]\!])$. Hence $[\![F]\!] \not\subseteq [\![\overline{G}]\!]$,
 i.e. ¬[∀(¬[G(x)],F(x))].

 right-to-left:
 If $[\![F]\!] \not\subseteq [\![\overline{G}]\!]$, then not $[\![F]\!] \cap [\![G]\!] = \emptyset$. Hence $[\![F]\!] \cap [\![G]\!] \neq \emptyset$,
 i.e. ∃ (G(x),F(x)).

As has been said, the relation between the quantifiers ∀ and ∃ established by the Conversions is commonly expressed by saying that they are each other's duals.

The Conversions of predicate logic also hold in propositional logic, where they go under the name of De Morgan's laws, after the nineteenth-century London logician Augustus De Morgan. Analogously to (2.27), we define:

(2.30)   **AND** = $P \wedge Q \wedge R \wedge S \wedge \ldots$ **AND*** = $\neg P \wedge \neg Q \wedge \neg R \wedge \neg S \wedge \ldots$

OR = $P \vee Q \vee R \vee S \vee \ldots$ **OR*** = $\neg P \vee \neg Q \vee \neg R \vee \neg S \vee \ldots$

As before, the asterisk stands for the internal negation, in this case distributed over all members of the set P^+, which is denoted by the syntactic subject (see Section 4.3 for some comment). Again, the logical properties of **AND** and **AND***, as well as those of **OR** and **OR***, are identical, since the identity of the specific argument L-propositions is irrelevant to the calculus.

Given the definitions of $\wedge$ and $\vee$ as given in (2.6b) and (2.6c) and repeated here:

(2.31)   a. $[\![\wedge]\!] = \{P^+ \mid sit_{act} \in_{/P/^+}^{\cap}\}$

(the extension of $\wedge$ is the set of all sets of two or more propositions p, such that sit_{act} is a member of the intersection of all $/P/^+$, each P being an L-proposition expressing p)

b. $[\![\vee]\!] = \{P^+ \mid sit_{act} \in_{/P/^+}^{\cap}\}$

(the extension of $\vee$ is the set of all sets of two or more propositions p, such that sit_{act} is a member of the union of all $/P/^+$, each P being an L-proposition expressing p)

the following theorems hold, which makes **AND** and **OR** each other's duals:

(2.32)   **De Morgan's Laws:**
a.   **AND** $\equiv \neg$**OR***   or: $P \wedge Q \wedge R \wedge S \wedge \ldots \equiv \neg(\neg P \vee \neg Q \vee \neg R \vee \neg S \vee \ldots)$
b.   **OR** $\equiv \neg$**AND***   or: $P \vee Q \vee R \vee S \vee \ldots \equiv \neg(\neg P \wedge \neg Q \wedge \neg R \wedge \neg S \wedge \ldots)$

Again, the proofs are direct copies of theorems in set theory:

(a) left-to-right:
If $sit_{act} \in /P/ \cap /Q/ \cap /R/$, then $sit_{act} \notin \overline{/P/} \cup \overline{/Q/} \cup /R/$, i.e. $\neg[\neg P \vee \neg Q \vee \neg R]$.

right-to-left:
If $sit_{act} \notin \overline{/P/} \cup \overline{/Q/} \cup \overline{/R/}$, then $sit_{act} \in /P/ \cap /Q/ \cap /R/$, i.e. $P \wedge Q \wedge R$.

(b) left-to-right:

   If $sit_{act} \in /P/ \cup /Q/ \cup /R/$, then $sit_{act} \notin /\overline{P}/ \cap /\overline{Q}/ \cap /\overline{R}/$,
   i.e. $\neg[\neg P \wedge \neg Q \wedge \neg R]$.

   right-to-left:

   If $sit_{act} \notin /\overline{P}/ \cap /\overline{Q}/ \cap /\overline{R}/$, then $sit_{act} \in /P/ \cup /Q/ \cup /R/$,
   i.e. $P \vee Q \vee R$.

All this is normal standard logic, though admittedly presented with a slant towards relativizing standard logic and placing it in a wider cognitive and linguistic perspective. The question is: why is this of interest? The following chapters begin to answer that question.

3

Natural set theory and natural logic

3.1 Introductory observations

NATURAL SET THEORY, or NST, is a hypothesis, open to experimental testing. It is a novel hypothesis which, therefore, has not, so far, been subjected to any systematic experimental scrutiny and is based exclusively on what seems to be plausible at an intuitive or pretheoretical level. As a consequence, the present chapter can only be of an exploratory nature. Yet the underlying thought (a) that humans have at their disposal a natural, cognition-based, set theory and a predicate and propositional logic derived from it, (b) that this set theory and this logic are likely to differ in important respects from standard set theory and standard logic, and (c) that these differences may go a long way towards explaining the differences between natural set-theoretic and logical intuitions on the one hand and the corresponding standard systems on the other is, though novel, robust and, it would seem, hard to counter.

NST describes how humans deal cognitively with plural objects. It appears that NST lives by default or prototype and is thus open to correction or overriding as a result of more precise thinking shaped, in particular, by institutional education in more sophisticated societies. NST, like its corresponding logic, is thus open to bootstrapping into higher levels of precision and generality. This implies a gradient cline between two extremes of cognitive achievement, which we name NATURAL SET THEORY and CONSTRUCTED SET THEORY, respectively. However, since too little is known, as yet, to define such a cline in a sufficiently precise format, I follow, for the moment, the easier course of distinguishing different levels of (un)naturalness, in the expectation that these distinctions, when more fully elaborated, will unfold into a system of gradual distinctions. For now, I consider natural set theory to be manifest in two forms: as BASIC-NATURAL SET THEORY (BNST), which stays within the limits imposed by all defaults, and as STRICT-NATURAL SET THEORY (SNST), which overrides one or more defaults. CONSTRUCTED SET THEORY overrides all defaults.

NST instantiates the general hypothesis that there are hidden reserves in the mathematical, or, more generally, the formal powers of human cognition.

Inquisitive and formally creative humans are capable of cranking up the current level of mathematical or, more generally, formal performance to a higher degree of explicitness and formal precision by thinking through the consequences of their formal operations. Prime examples in the context of the Western world are, of course, Aristotle, Euclid, Al Huárizmi—who gave his name to the term *algorithm*—and the many other creators of the modern formal sciences known from history. When such efforts lead to new insights, which are then widely accepted in a given society and integrated into the educational system, we may consider this a measure of the degree of civilization of the society in question.

We thus assume a gradient in the analytical powers of humans ranging from the 'rawest' or most basic level of unsophistication to the most advanced levels of abstract thinking as found in the centres of science. The degree of achievement is taken to depend on the cultural, educational and other conditions that trigger the use and development of available cognitive reserves at the right age interval.

Some extremely interesting and challenging work has been done over the past few decades regarding the arithmetical capacities of infants, schoolchildren, and members of illiterate cultures.[1] Pica et al. (2004) investigated the arithmetical ability of speakers of Mundurukú, an Amazonian language spoken by some 7000, mostly illiterate, Brazilian Indians. The language has no numerals beyond five (the word for 'five' being the equivalent of 'hand', as in many South-East Asian languages), reflecting the fact that the speakers were unable to count beyond five and had great difficulty doing simple arithmetical sums. Yet after some training, they quickly extended their counting and computing abilities both cognitively and lexically, creating expressions like 'two hands', even though their achievements never matched those of humans born into culturally more developed societies.[2]

Butterworth states (1999: 7):

What makes human numerical ability unique is the development and transmission of cultural tools for extending the capability of the Number Module. These tools include aids to counting, such as number words, finger-counting, and tallying; and also the

---

[1] For example, Ginsburg et al. (1984), Dehaene (1997), Butterworth (1999), Pica et al. (2004).

[2] Pierre Pica, p.c. The fact that these speakers created new expressions to name numbers from existing ones strongly suggests, if not proves, that it was not the availability of the lexical items that enabled them to 'think' further along the number line but that it was in the first place their cognitive development that required the new lexical expressions, which were then readily composed and which probably helped them along in a secondary sense, in that the very availability of the expressions enhanced performance.

accumulated inventions of mathematicians down the centuries—from numerals to calculating procedures, from counting-boards to theorems and their proofs.

Though Butterworth is no doubt right as regards the role of culture in the development of human subjects' arithmetical powers, one must fear that he errs on the issue of uniqueness. Far from being unique to the human numerical ability, the power to extend a naturally given ability through cultural development appears to be much more general. Although the exact boundaries of this phenomenon are unknown, it does seem that, along with numeracy and, apparently, also the reading ability, 'significant evolutionary precursors [. . .] may exist for other currently understudied cultural domains of human competence such as geometry, algebra, music and art' (Dehaene 2005: 150–1; see also Dehaene et al. 2006). It thus does not seem too hazardous to surmise that logic and its underlying set theory are also worthy candidates to be considered. This is what is investigated in the present chapter.

The method followed here, however, differs from what is found in the studies mentioned above, which are experimental, performance-driven, and sometimes supported by neurophysiological evidence. Here, a hypothesis is proposed and offered for empirical testing, whereby the data are allowed to be largely intuitive. This method consists in observing how 'ordinary' speakers, whose degree of literacy and cultural sophistication is considered 'normal' in Western society and who distinguish themselves mainly by NOT being academically trained, interpret and use logical expressions—in particular the logical constants—in their daily speech. An attempt is then made to reduce the (well-known) differences with standard modern logic, which is based on highly constructed mathematical set theory, to naturally given restrictions in the human way of cognitively dealing with plural objects.

This difference in method is, to a large extent, motivated by the object of research. In arithmetic or geometry, the technical aspects are relatively simple and straightforward. As regards arithmetic, it doesn't take much theory to define a subject's restricted arithmetical ability when this subject cannot count or carry out arithmetical computations beyond five. Against the background of our superior knowledge of arithmetic, such restrictions are quickly formulated. In fact, we have just done so. It is also easy to understand that early school training will trigger the growth and development of dormant arithmetical powers in the brains and minds of young children who grow up in a culturally developed environment. In fact, a moderately developed arithmetical ability is simply taken for granted in our society, so much so that we are surprised to find out that individuals who grow up in a society without any scholastic tradition are not even able to count beyond the very lowest numbers and, therefore, lack words for higher numbers. We also have a relatively good picture of what it has taken successive Chinese, Indian, Arabic, and Western civilizations to come to the highly sophisticated science of arithmetic that we have today. From the point of view of arithmetical *theory*, therefore, no great obstacles present themselves in the study of basic-natural arithmetic.

As regards logic, however, the situation is different. The very task of formulating restrictions on the logical powers of unsophisticated humans is the opposite of trivial. It requires considerable technical and theoretical effort and insight, and standard logical lore fails to provide the tools for doing so. The foundations and basic notions of logic are far less clear and well understood than those of arithmetic, and the relation with natural cognition and language is still as problematic as ever. It is hardly surprising, therefore, that before one can pass on to any experimental work, one is forced to start with an identification and formulation of the restrictions involved.

The much greater conceptual difficulty of logic compared to arithmetic is borne out by the fact that what looks like the most firmly embedded logical intuitions of the human race appear to support a logic that depends for its application on complete situational knowledge, so that more developed forms of logic were required for use in situations where knowledge is not complete—a development that might explain the well-known discrepancies between natural logical intuitions on the one hand and the concepts and terms of the first, largely Aristotelian, 'official' logic on the other. Such discrepancies do not occur in the case of arithmetic.

One may also look at our hypothesized basic-natural logic in the light of the psychological theory of PROTOTYPES (see also Sections 8.6 and 8.8 in Volume I). In general, prototypes seem to be characterized by the fact that they maximize common features and thus avoid extremes or limiting cases. Thus, it is proposed in Section 3.2.2 below that the first principle of BNST consists in not taking into account the so-called extreme values—that is, the null set (∅), singletons (sets consisting of precisely one element) and the totality of objects (**OBJ**). Perhaps one may, therefore, just as well call BNPC by the name of *prototypical logic*. The problem is, however, that so little is known about the conditions that make for prototypes. Frequency won't do as a criterion, as is shown in Section 8.8 in Volume I. But what will do is simply to a large extent still a mystery, to do with hard-to-define notions such as 'normal' or 'obvious'. Standard modern logic, for its part, can then be seen as the result of the exploration of the extreme cases: when these are taken into account, the basic-natural notions have to be sharpened. When one looks at the question from this angle, it becomes clear why one will have to distinguish degrees of 'naturalness'. This is precisely because the transition from intuitive prototypes to well-defined concepts is gradual.

Anthropological linguists and language typologists, driven as they are by a strong ecologistic motivation, will probably object that it is far from certain that there IS a naturally given, innate 'basis' as part of the genetic endowment of the human race and hence a basic-natural set theory or logic. It is uncertain, they will say, whether all natural languages possess (equivalents of) logical constants, in particular ALL, SOME, NOT, AND, and OR, and, if they do, whether their meanings are the same in all natural languages.[3] All I can say to that is that there *must* be some genetically fixed cognitive substrate for dealing with plurality and for the making of inferences involving plural objects—that is, a predicate logic—or else the entire international machinery of bringing education and other forms of development to underdeveloped parts of the world would be built on quicksand. But, since our knowledge about these matters is as underdeveloped as those parts of the world we treat to our aid programmes, there is little else I can do now but make the famous inductive leap and embrace the simplest and most general hypothesis that, until proven otherwise, the naturally given lexical meanings of the logical operators under scrutiny are universally fixed.[4]

3.2 Some set-theoretic principles of natural cognition

3.2.1 *A résumé of standard set theory*

It is important, at the outset, to emphasize the distinction between set-theoretic functions that map *n*–tuples of sets (a) onto sets and (b) onto truth values. The former are usually just called *set-theoretic functions*; the latter are called *relations*, denoted by *predicates*, since predicates typically

---

[3] Steve Levinson tells me that there are languages which use the same word for 'many' and 'all' and also languages which use the indefinite article or the numeral meaning 'one' for 'some', referring to discussions in Wierzbicka (1996: 74–6, 193–7). What this evidence means remains to be seen. Modern Greek, for example, has the one word *polí* for both 'very' and 'too', making a phrase like *polí megálos* ambiguous between 'very big' and 'too big' (though *megálos* by itself can also mean 'too big', just as English *late* also has the meaning 'too late'). Yet this does not mean at all that Greek speakers cannot or do not distinguish between the concepts 'very' and 'too'. They clearly do and, when pressed, they use *parapolí* for 'too', even though *parapolí* still means 'very much' or 'a whole lot', but it seems to get closer to 'too' than simple *polí*.

[4] The programme thus outlined in effect amounts to an attempt at replacing current Gricean explanations for the disparity between logic and language in terms of generalized conversational implicatures with an explanation based on natural set theory and the cognitive faculty of forming mental propositions. If the objections raised in Section 1.3.3.2 of Volume I against attempted pragmatic explanations along Gricean lines have any validity, this seems a worthwhile exercise.

denote functions from n–tuples of objects (or sets of objects) to truth values. COMPLEMENT, INTERSECTION, UNION, and SUBTRACTION are set-theoretic functions, but INCLUSION, for example, is a relation: for any given sets A and B, the binary relation of INCLUSION, as in A $\subseteq$ B, is either true or false. By contrast, the set functions $\bar{\text{A}}$ (complement), A $\cap$ B (intersection), A $\cup$ B (union), or A–B (subtraction) do not have a truth value. Given the proper number of arbitrary sets (one for complement; more than one for intersection and union; exactly two for subtraction) they denote a new set defined by the Boolean functions complement, intersection, union, and subtraction, respectively. Complement is unique in that it involves the nonarbitrary set **OBJ** (the totality of all objects) as part of its definition. It can be described as a special case of subtraction, with **OBJ**–A as output for any set A. In logic, a further use of the term *complement* is to denote a relation ('be in complement with') yielding truth for two sets A and B just in case A $\cup$ B = **OBJ** and A $\cap$ B = $\emptyset$.

The set-theoretic *relations* have a twofold use in the reduction of logic to set theory. First, they correspond to *(meta)logical relations* expressed in terms of valuation space (VS) analysis. For example, the inclusion relation translates into a possible metalogical statement that, say, the set of situations /P/ is included in the set of situations /Q/—that is, P entails Q (P $\vdash$ ($\models$) Q), which is true or false depending on the meanings of P and Q, including the meanings of any truth-functional propositional operators they may contain. Secondly, some set-theoretic relations correspond to *quantifiers*. For example, ALL F is G translates, in principle, as saying that the set denoted by F is included in the set denoted by G.

By contrast, the set-theoretic *functions* correspond to the propositional logical constants of the object language $\mathbf{L_L}$ as realized in any particular natural language. Just as the set-theoretic functions take sets and deliver sets, the propositional functions take valuation spaces and deliver valuation spaces. For example, the operator AND in an L-proposition of the form P AND Q delivers /P AND Q/—that is, the set of those situations that make P AND Q true, corresponding to /P/ $\cap$ /Q/, the intersection of /P/ and /Q/. Figure 3.1 shows how set-theoretic relations and functions are interpreted onto metalogical relations, object-language quantifiers, and propositional operators.

The counterpart in metalogic of the set-theoretic relation MUTUAL PARTIAL INTERSECTION (henceforth M-PARTIAL INTERSECTION, symbolized as A $\oplus$ B: the two sets A and B partially intersect each other and do not severally or jointly equal either **U** or $\emptyset$, as in Figure 3.3b) is logico-semantic independence, which plays no part in the machinery of logic: when /P/ and /Q/ M-partially

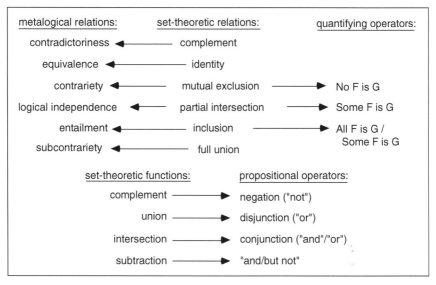

FIGURE 3.1 The reduction of metalogical relations and object-language operators to set-theoretic relations and functions

intersect, the L-propositions P and Q are logically (and semantically) independent in that the actual situation sit_{act} can be in /P/ but not in /Q/, in /Q/ but not in /P/, in both /P/ and /Q/, or in neither /P/ nor /Q/. That is, no entailment relation whatsoever holds between logically independent P and Q.

The relations *complement, identity* and *full union* lack a quantificational counterpart in predicate calculus, perhaps because they lack logical interest or perhaps because the makers of modern logic did not see far enough beyond natural language. Finally, the set-theoretic function *subtraction* appears to lack a single-morpheme propositional counterpart in most languages, but is expressed as *and/but not* in English: the valuation space of an L-proposition of the form P BUT NOT Q is the VS of P minus the VS of Q, or /P/ – /Q/.

Before a start is made with specifying the restrictions we intend to impose on standard set theory so as to slim it down to natural set theory, taken to reflect the way human cognition deals with sets, we will, for the sake of convenience, summarize the standard definitions of the functions and relations of mathematical set theory. The standard Boolean functions of complement, union, intersection and subtraction are defined as follows (**x** ranges over elements in **OBJ**):

(3.1) Standard Boolean functions on sets A and B:
   a. $\overline{A}$ $=_{def}$ the set Z such that for all $x \in Z, x \notin A$ and for all $x \notin Z, x \in A$
   b. $A \cup B$ $=_{def}$ the set Z such that for all and only $x \in Z$, $x \in A$ or $x \in B$
   c. $A \cap B$ $=_{def}$ the set Z such that for all and only $x \in Z$, $x \in A$ and $x \in B$
   d. $A\text{–}B$ $=_{def}$ the set Z such that for all and only $x \in Z$, $x \in A$ and $x \notin B$

The standard relations are defined in (3.2) (x ranges over elements in **OBJ**; FULL UNION has been added for good measure):

(3.2) Standard relations between sets A and B:
   a. COMPLEMENT $\forall x((x \in A \rightarrow x \notin \overline{A}) \wedge (x \notin A \rightarrow x \in \overline{A}))$
   b. IDENTITY $\forall x((x \in A \rightarrow x \in B) \wedge (x \in B \rightarrow x \in A))$
   c. MUTUAL EXCLUSION $\forall x(x \in A \rightarrow x \notin B)$
   d. M-PARTIAL INTERSECTION $\exists x(x \in A \wedge x \in B) \wedge \exists x(x \in A \wedge x \notin B) \wedge$
                            $\exists x(x \notin A \wedge x \in B) \wedge \exists x(x \notin A \wedge x \notin B)$
   e. INCLUSION of A in B $\forall x(x \in A \rightarrow x \in B)$
   f. FULL UNION $\forall x(x \in A \vee x \in B)$

These relations can also be defined in terms of the standard Boolean functions:

(3.3) Standard relations between sets A and B:
   a. COMPLEMENT   iff $A \cup B = \textbf{OBJ}$ and $A \cap B = \emptyset$
   b. IDENTITY   iff $A = B$
   c. MUTUAL EXCLUSION   iff $A \cap B = \emptyset$
   d. M-PARTIAL INTERSEC- iff $A \cap B \neq \emptyset$; $A \cap \overline{B} \neq \emptyset$; $B \cap \overline{A} \neq \emptyset$;
       TION $A \cup B \neq \textbf{OBJ}$;
   e. INCLUSION of A in B iff $A \cup B \neq \emptyset$
   f. FULL UNION: iff $A \cup B = \textbf{OBJ}$

3.2.2 The restrictions imposed by NST

So much for standard set theory and standard logic. The question is now: what restrictions are to be imposed on this system so that the discrepancies between logic and language are correctly predicted? To begin with, let it be assumed that NST entails that the mind, though naturally capable of processing and operating with sets or 'plural objects', does not naturally represent a set as either the null set ($\emptyset$) or the universe of all objects (**OBJ**). It also seems unnatural, for unsophisticated humans, to regard singletons, or sets consisting of just one element, as 'sets', as is borne out by the well-known difficulty of explaining to beginning students of set theory the difference between, say, the individual object a and the set $\{a\}$. As is shown in Section 8.1.2, for natural cognition sets are *per se* plural sets, whose cardinality runs from 2 upward.

This means that, in NST, the null set is not a set at all: the cognitive counterpart of ∅ is the absence of any set, something which is cognitively real and may be called 'null' but cannot play the role of a set. Whereas 'null' still functions cognitively as 'absence of a set', the opposite notion of **OBJ**, as known in standard modern set theory, is typically the product of advanced mathematical and/or philosophical thinking and has no place in natural set theory. It is too nondescript to be cognitively real to formally untrained minds. What does seem to play a role is the notion of RESTRICTED UNIVERSE OF OBJECTS or **OBJ^R**, involving the totality of all objects within a contextually defined universe of discourse. Therefore, all standard set-theoretic definitions involving **OBJ** should, for natural set theory, be redefined as involving the notion of **OBJ^R**, which does count as a natural set. Incidentally, this strategy is chosen also by many mathematically-minded logicians, especially the earlier ones. Thus we read (De Morgan 1847: 37–8):

But the contraries of common language usually embrace, not the whole universe, but some one general idea. Thus, of men, Briton and alien are contraries: every man must be one of the two, no man can be both. Not-Briton and alien are identical names, and so are Not-alien and Briton. The same may be said of integer and fraction among numbers, peer and commoner among subjects of the realm, male and female among animals, and so on. In order to express this, let us say that the whole idea under consideration is *the universe* (meaning merely the whole of which we are considering parts) and let names which have nothing in common, but which between them contain the whole idea under consideration, be called contraries *in, or with respect to, that universe.*

Given these assumptions, we now posit the first principle of natural set theory, PNST–1, which applies to single sets:

PNST–1:   ∅, **OBJ**, AND SINGLETONS ARE NOT NATURAL SETS
Sets are never cognitively represented as having an EXTREME VALUE—that is, as the null set (∅) or as the totality of objects (**OBJ**). Nor are they represented as containing just one element.

Sets that are neither ∅ nor **OBJ** nor a singleton are called 'natural sets'. PNST–1 expresses the fact that NST is a theory of *plural* objects.

In the absence of any experimental data, and hence of any precise scale of naturalness, we posit hypothetically that PNST–1 is both basic-natural and strict-natural in that it strongly resists intellectual construction—perhaps to different degrees for ∅, **OBJ**, and for singletons. Only at a much more advanced level will the cognitive powers of the human race be able to override PNST–1.

A further principle of natural set theory requires the nonidentity, or distinctness, of any two or more natural set representations. When two or more sets are cognitively represented, they are naturally taken to be distinct from each other: any relation of identity is considered to be of a higher level. This gives the second principle of natural set theory, which eliminates the relation of identity:

> PNST–2:   NATURAL SETS ARE DISTINCT
> When sets are distinguished cognitively, they are represented as being extensionally DISTINCT, differing as regards their membership. There is no basic-natural cognitive relation of identity between sets.

Among other things, PNST–2 accounts for the fact that natural intuition reads 'inclusion' as 'proper inclusion' ($\subset$), and not as 'included in or identical with' ($\subseteq$).[5] This principle is, again, taken to be valid at both the basic-natural and the strict-natural level, though it seems to be more easily overridden in the sphere of object-language predicate logic than in the much more abstract metatheory of logic where the metalogical relation of entailment occupies a central place. Thus, whilst it seems relatively easy to gain the insight that ALL F IS G is true when $[\![F]\!] = [\![G]\!]$ (in a logic where ALL F IS G is defined as $[\![F]\!] \subseteq [\![G]\!]$), it seems a great deal harder to convince one that every sentence P entails itself, which amounts to saying that /P/ $\subseteq$ /P/. It takes a considerable amount of advanced analytical thinking—more, apparently, than natural cognition and common natural language can bear—for the latter to be accepted.

In actual fact, PNST–2 is more general. It applies to any kind of object representation, not only of the plural objects we call sets but also of individual objects: basic-natural cognition allows no two objects of any kind to stand in a *relation of identity*, since that would make them one single object. Yet they do allow for a mental *operation of identification*, given distinct levels of representation. This is what underlies the predicate of identity in natural language: what was thought to be distinct becomes one (see Section 5.3.2 in Volume I). Such an operation involves two levels, or stages, of cognitive representation, one at which the two virtual objects or sets are distinct and one at which they have merged into one. If truth is claimed for the latter, two virtual objects or sets have been identified. If truth is claimed for the former, one virtual object or set has been cognitively split up into two.

---

[5] One notes that this is reflected in the lexicon in that the prefix *sub-* requires proper inclusion, not identity: a *subcontinent* is *part of* a continent, a *subsection* is *part of* a section, and so on.

Moreover, as is pointed out in Section 5.3.2 in Volume I, the identity predicate, which identifies as one what were thought to be different objects, is to be distinguished from the value-assigning predicate $\mathbf{Be_v}$, which assigns a value to a parameter, as in *My name is Pieter*, where *my name* denotes the parameter and *Pieter* denotes the value assigned to the parameter. Obviously, $\mathbf{Be_v}$ cannot be missed in a system containing functions. Therefore, $\mathbf{Be_v}$ is admitted, allowing for free substitution of either of its terms in any context. We thus distinguish, wherever it is relevant, between the identity predicate $\mathbf{Be}$ ($=$) and the value-assigning predicate $\mathbf{Be_v}$ written as $=_v$ (or $_v=$ when the value is given first).

We tentatively assume three further principles specifying distinctness conditions, all three less basic than PNST–1 and PNST–2, so that they can be overridden at the strict-natural level. They apply to the set-theoretic functions of UNION, SUBTRACTION, and INTERSECTION and to the set-theoretic relation of INCLUSION:

> **PNST–3:** BASIC-NATURAL UNION REQUIRES TOTAL DISTINCTNESS OF NATURAL SETS
> When two (or more) sets A and B undergo UNION, A and B are natural sets and are, at the level of basic, but not strict, naturalness, TOTALLY DISTINCT, with no element in common, so that $|A \cup B| = |A|+|B|$ ('$|X|$': the cardinality of set X).

Union is thus defined, at the level of basic naturalness, only for any two (or more) totally distinct natural sets. When this condition is not fulfilled, there is, at that basic level, no union. (As is shown in Section 3.4, PNST–3 accounts for the exclusive nature of natural language OR. When PNST–3 is overridden, making it possible for A and B to intersect, exclusive OR is upgraded to inclusive OR.)

PNST–4 is the obverse of PNST–3, in that it requires total (proper) inclusion for the basic-natural function of subtraction:

> **PNST–4:** BASIC-NATURAL SUBTRACTION REQUIRES PROPER INCLUSION OF
>   NATURAL SETS
> When A is subtracted from B, A and B are natural sets and, at the level of basic but not strict naturalness, A is a proper subset of B so that $|B - A| = |B|-|A| \neq 0$.

Again, this restriction is overridden at the strict-natural level. Subtraction is thus taken to be defined, at the level of basic naturalness, for any two natural sets A and B such that, if A is subtracted from B, the remainder is a proper nonnull subset of B. When this condition is not fulfilled, there is, at the basic-natural level, no subtraction. At the strict-natural level, however, one may subtract a set of ginger cats from a set of male cats and find that no male cat remains.

The conditions expressed in the last two subprinciples have been axiomatized in standard arithmetic for the calculus of cardinality. They ensure that, under the principles of basic-natural set theory, Boolean addition and subtraction agree with their arithmetical namesakes as regards the cardinality of the sets involved.

By contrast, the set-theoretic function INTERSECTION, like its Boolean counterpart MULTIPLICATION, does not correspond to any arithmetical function. PNST–5 defines the natural intersection function as excluding both total distinctness and proper inclusion, leaving only M-partial intersection of natural sets:

> **PNST–5:**   BASIC-NATURAL INTERSECTION REQUIRES M-PARTIAL DISTINCTNESS
>   OF NATURAL SETS
> When two (or more) sets *A* and *B* undergo INTERSECTION, *A* and *B* are natural sets and are, at the level of basic, but not strict, naturalness, M-partially distinct, with some, but not all, elements in common.

Basic-natural intersection is thus defined only for sets *A* and *B* (and possibly more) such that (a) $A \cap B \neq \emptyset$ and (b) $A \cap B \neq A \neq B \neq \mathbf{OBJ^R}$. (One remembers that the symbol ⓪, or M-partial intersection, is used for the combination of these two conditions: $X \text{⓪} Y$ just in case $X \cap Y \neq \emptyset \neq X \neq Y \neq \mathbf{OBJ^R}$.) Condition (a) cannot be overridden at any level of set-theoretic or logical sophistication, but condition (b) is overridden at all levels above basic. (This easy overriding allows for the upgrading of SOME excluding ALL to SOME including ALL, as is shown in Section 3.4, and hence for the subaltern entailment schema from ALL **F** IS **G** to SOME **F** IS **G**.)

Thus restricted, the natural intersection function ensures *set-theoretic independence*. That is, if $A \cap B$ has a value under PNST–5, then *A* and *B* are set-theoretically independent and vice versa. It is then ensured that, for any element $o \in \mathbf{OBJ^R}$, it is possible that $o \in A$ and $o \notin B$, or $o \in B$ and $o \notin A$, or $o \in A$ and $o \in B$, or $o \notin A$ and $o \notin B$.

There is a final principle, relating to the recursive application of the set-theoretic functions. Whereas in mathematical set theory one can apply the functions recursively to one's heart's content, this is not so in natural set theory. This applies especially to the function COMPLEMENT, which is taken to be nonrecursive in basic-natural, and only once-recursive in strict-natural set theory:

PNST–6:   Basic-natural complement is nonrecursive and is defined as
the result of basic-natural subtraction

At the level of basic naturalness, COMPLEMENT is restricted to one
application. Further, recursive applications are either strict-natural or
constructed. Moreover, '$\overline{X}$' is defined as $Z - X$, where X and Z are
natural sets and Z functions as a provisional, restricted universe of
objects (**OBJ^R**).

Psychological experiments may disconfirm all or some of this. If they do not,
one should expect them to provide greater clarity and greater precision.

3.3 Consequences for set-theoretic and (meta)logical relations and functions

3.3.1 *Consequences for set-theoretic relations and functions*

Formally, basic NST amounts to an application of Boolean algebra as
defined in Section 2.3.2, whereby the restrictions formulated in (3.4a–f)
hold. In (3.4a–f) a notational distinction is made between the standard
Boolean operators and their basic-natural counterparts, which are provided
with the superscript 'BN' (basic-natural). The BN-operators are defined in
terms of the standard operators.

(3.4)   PRINCIPLES OF BASIC-NATURAL SET THEORY:
   a. **PNST–1:** 0 and 1 are excluded as values of the Boolean variables.
   b. **PNST–2:** the relations $=$ and $\neq$ are eliminated; only the value-
       assigning relation $=_v$ ($_v=$) and its negative counterpart $\neq_v$ ($_v\neq$) are
       admitted.
   c. **PNST–3:** ADDITION $(x +^{BN} y)$ is restricted to x, y such that there is no
       z such that $x \cdot y =_v z$.
   d. **PNST–4:** SUBTRACTION $(x -^{BN} y)$ is restricted to x, y such that $x \cdot y =_v$
       y; $x \cdot y \neq_v x \neq_v \emptyset$.
   e. **PNST–5:** MULTIPLICATION $(x \cdot^{BN} y)$ is restricted to x, y such that $x \cdot y$
       $\neq_v x \neq_v y$; there is a z such that $x \cdot y =_v z$.
   f. **PNST–6:** COMPLEMENT $(\overline{x}^{BN})$ is non-recursive and restricted to an
       independently given element y in the range of the variables such
       that there is a z such that $y -^{BN} x =_v z$.

Thus restricted, Boolean algebra is translatable into basic NST as follows:

(3.5)   a. $\cdot^{BN}$ is interpreted as basic-natural intersection $\cap^{BN}$.
   b. $+^{BN}$ is interpreted as basic-natural union $\cup^{BN}$.

  c. $\overline{X}^{\,BN}$ is interpreted as restricted complement $\overline{X}^{\,R}$.

  d. $-^{BN}$ is interpreted as basic-natural subtraction $-^{BN}$.

This, in its turn, is interpretable onto a logical system when the logical constants are defined in set-theoretic terms. ALL, SOME, and NO are defined in (3.7a–c), where **A** stands for ALL F is G, **I** for SOME F is G ($\equiv$ SOME F is NOT-G), and **N** for NO F is G. For internal or 'subsentential' negation, as in ALL/SOME/NO F is NOT-G, $[\![G]\!]$ is to be replaced with $[\![\overline{G}]\!]^{R}$, the restricted complement of $[\![G]\!]$ in any **OBJ**^{R}. The external negations of sentences with ALL, SOME and NO are defined in (3.7d–f). One notes that (3.7c,e) show that ¬I does not equal **N**, since the conditions of **N** exclude $[\![F]\!] \subset [\![G]\!]$, whereas those of ¬I allow for $[\![F]\!] \subset [\![G]\!]$ (namely, when $sit_{act} \in /\mathbf{A}/$). Basic-natural proper inclusion ($\subset$) is defined, in terms of NST, as in (3.6).

(3.6) A $\subset$ B is true iff there is a natural set C such that B$-^{BN}$ A $=_{v}$ C.

(3.7) a. ALL F is G   true $[\![F]\!] \subset [\![G]\!]$
           (**A**)   iff

       b. SOME F is   true $[\![F]\!] \cap [\![G]\!] \neq_{v} \emptyset \neq_{v} [\![F]\!] \neq_{v} [\![G]\!]$; $[\![F]\!]$, $[\![G]\!]$
           G (**I**)   iff $\neq_{v}$ **OBJ** or: $[\![F]\!] \oslash [\![G]\!]$

       c. NO F is G   true   there is no set H such that H$_{v}$= $[\![F]\!] \cap^{BN} [\![G]\!]$
           (**N**)   iff

       d. ¬**A**   true $sit_{act} \in /\overline{\mathbf{A}}/^{R}$ in **U**^{R}: $sit_{act} \in /\mathbf{I}/$ or $/\mathbf{N}/$
                            iff

       e. ¬**I**   true $sit_{act} \in /\overline{\mathbf{I}}/^{R}$ in **U**^{R}: $sit_{act} \in /\mathbf{A}/$ or $/\mathbf{N}/$
                            iff

       f. ¬**N**   true $sit_{act} \in /\overline{\mathbf{N}}/^{R}$ in **U**^{R}: $sit_{act} \in /\mathbf{A}/$ or $/\mathbf{I}/$.
                            iff

The formal sketch given in (3.4) and (3.5) requires some comment, first as regards the question of psychological plausibility. Most will agree that it would be utterly unrealistic to assume that natural speakers have a fully elaborated interpretation of set theory onto a system of valuation spaces at their disposal when interpreting utterances. Yet it is not at all unrealistic to assume that they have a vague, intuitive idea, probably beyond the threshold of possible awareness, of 'truth in an overall, possibly infinite, set of situations', and hence of notions like necessary consequence, (in)compatibility, and contradiction. It does not seem to matter, for natural cognition, whether a set is finite or, technically speaking, infinite, as the notion 'very large' appears to cover both 'infinite' and 'very large but finite'. One may perhaps even speculate that the formal precision of set-theoretic notions in natural cognition is commensurate with their closeness to the psychological 'ego'.

Infinite and other very large sets would thus become increasingly 'misty' to the mind as they are considered from a greater distance.

Correspondingly, one may assume that notions like mutual exclusion, M-partial intersection and proper inclusion of sets of situations are likely to be psychologically real, these notions being defined without any appeal to the extreme boundaries of the set-theoretic system, namely the null set $\emptyset$ and the totality of all objects **OBJ**. Since mutual exclusion, M-partial intersection and proper inclusion are the key notions in both NST and its application to natural logic, it seems reasonable to assume psychological reality for both NST and natural logic.

From a more formal point of view, we start our comment with *restricted complement* as a function and as a relation between a set A and its complement $\overline{A}^R$. Neither the function nor the relation are current in standard set theory, yet they are of central importance to the study of natural cognition and natural language. The *function*, written as $\overline{A}^R$, is defined in (3.8a): it takes **OBJ^R** as given in any situation and any set A as being properly included in **OBJ^R** ($A \subset$ **OBJ^R**), and it delivers **OBJ^R**–A. The corresponding *relation* RC between a set A and its restricted complement B within **OBJ^R** is defined in (3.8b):

(3.8)   a. $\overline{A}^R =_{\text{def}}$ the set B such that $B_v=$ **OBJ^R** $-^{BN} A$.

b. RESTRICTED COMPLEMENT: RC$(B,A,$**OBJ^R**$)$ iff $B_v=$ **OBJ^R** $-^{BN} A$.

Thus, in Figure 3.2, $\overline{A}^R$ equals **OBJ^R** $-^{BN} A$ (but remember that multiple applications of this function are excluded in virtue of PNST–6). The relation between A and $\overline{A}^R$ (horizontal lines) corresponds to natural contradictoriness (that is, within the restricted complement); that between A and $\overline{A}$ (vertical lines) to the standard metalogical relation of that name.

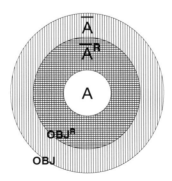

FIGURE 3.2 The relation between the natural set A, its restricted complement $\overline{A}^R$, and its standard complement $\overline{A}$

The set-theoretic relation of *identity* has been eliminated in virtue of PNST–2, as has been said. *Full union* (see Section 2.3.3) is likewise eliminated, at least for basic naturalness: when A and B intersect it is eliminated in virtue of PNST–3; when they do not, full union equals complement. More is said about full union in a moment.

The result is that, when **OBJ** is replaced with **OBJ^R**, there are only four possible basic-natural relations left between any two natural sets A and B: *mutual exclusion, M-partial intersection,* and *proper inclusion* of A in B or of B in A. They are defined, in standard terms, in (3.9a–d) and shown in Figure 3.3a,b,c,d, respectively:

(3.9)   Basic-natural relations between natural sets A and B within **OBJ^R**:

a. MUTUAL EXCLUSION ($A \, OO \, B$)   iff $A \cap B =_v \emptyset$

b. M-PARTIAL INTERSECTION ($A \, \text{\textcircled{O}} \, B$)   iff $A \cap B \neq_v \emptyset$

$A \cap \bar{B}^R \neq_v \emptyset$

$B \cap \bar{A}^R \neq_v \emptyset$

c. INCLUSION of A in B ($A \subset B$)   iff $B - A \neq_v \emptyset$

$A \cap \bar{B}^R =_v \emptyset$

d. INCLUSION of B in A ($B \subset A$)   iff $A - B \neq_v \emptyset$

$B \cap \bar{A}^R =_v \emptyset$

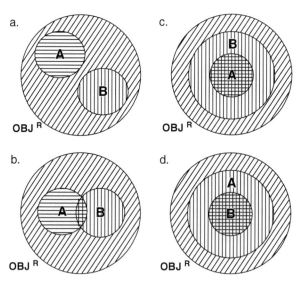

FIGURE 3.3 Mutual exclusion, M-partial intersection, and proper inclusion of A in B and of B in A as the four basic-natural relations between sets A and B

Inclusion has now been reduced to *proper* inclusion, as the difference hinges on the identity of A and B. This is precisely what is needed, since the inclusion relation strikes nonmathematicians as nonnatural for two identical sets. Moreover, *intersection* has been reduced to *M-partial intersection* because when, in standard terms, $A \cap B =_v \emptyset$, there is no intersection, and when $A \cap B =_v A$ or $A \cap B =_v B$, there is (proper) inclusion but not intersection, according to PNST–5 (though, as has been said, this latter condition appears to apply only to basic, not to strict, naturalness).

Mutual exclusion has passed unscathed through the naturalness restrictions. In particular, they still allow for A and $\overline{A}^{\,R}$, as in Figure 3.2, to be called mutually exclusive. What makes Figure 3.2 a special case of mutual exclusion is that the union of A and $\overline{A}^{\,R}$ exhausts **OBJ^R**, or $A \cup \overline{A}^{\,R} =_v$ **OBJ^R**.

The same freedom for the union of the two sets involved to exhaust **OBJ^R** is, however, not granted to A and B when they M-partially intersect, as in Figure 3.4a, or when the one is (properly) included in the other, as in Figure 3.4b. In those cases it may be true in standard terms that $A \cup B =_v$ **OBJ^R**, but it is not true under the restriction imposed by PNST–3, because PNST–3 leaves basic-natural union undefined for cases where A and B are not totally distinct. *Full union*, defined in (2.6) of Chapter 2 and repeated here as (3.10) in a form adapted to NST, is thus equally undefined when A and B are not totally distinct, even when OBJ is replaced with **OBJ^R** ('$\overset{\circ}{\cup}{}^{R}$' stands for full union within any given **OBJ^R**).

(3.10) $A \overset{\circ}{\cup}{}^{R} B$ iff $A \cup^{BN} B =_v$ **OBJ^R**

Whereas it is true, at the level of basic naturalness, that $A \overset{\circ}{\cup}{}^{R} \overline{A}^{\,R}$, as in Figure 3.2, it is false that $A \overset{\circ}{\cup}{}^{R} B$ for the sets A and B represented in Figures 3.4a,b, since A and B are not totally distinct. As for Figure 3.4a, the relation between A and B lacks a name. In standard set theory it lacks one, presumably, because it is mathematically uninteresting. In basic-natural set theory it lacks one because no relation is seen there. Only in strict-natural set theory does it deserve a name ('full union'), because it corresponds to the metalogical relation of subcontrariety, which is relevant in predicate calculus. And, as regards Figure 3.4b, all that is involved is the relation of proper inclusion of A in B. $A \overset{\circ}{\cup}{}^{R} B$ thus delivers truth, in basic-natural set theory, for the natural sets A and B only when $\overline{B}^{\,R} =_v A$ or vice versa—that is, when the one is the restricted complement of the other, as illustrated in Figure 3.2. And since we already have a term for both that relation and that function, the notion of full union appears not to be needed in basic-natural set theory. It begins to be needed as soon as it is realized that the sets A and B in Figure 3.4a are

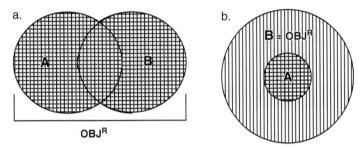

FIGURE 3.4 Basic naturalness has no full union for not totally distinct *A* and *B*

not set-theoretically independent, which makes it desirable, when one de-scribes the system, to reserve a name for the relation that causes this lack of independence.

3.3.2 *Consequences for (meta)logical relations and functions*

The set-theoretic functions and relations can be translated into functions and relations of logic and metalogic. As one reads from Figure 3.1, the set-theoretic *relations* translate into metalogical relations. This is achieved by taking the valuation spaces of L-propositions P and Q, /P/ and /Q/, respectively, as the arguments of the relations and by making the universe of all admissible situations **U** stand for **OBJ**. The set-theoretic relations also translate into the standard operators of quantification in the object-language L_L if $[\![F]\!]$ and $[\![G]\!]$ are the arguments of the relation.

The set-theoretic *functions* are translated into propositional operators (truth functions) in the object-language L_L again by taking /P/ and /Q/ as arguments and by making the universe of all admissible situations **U** stand for **OBJ**. At the same time, a VS-model can be set up for the sentence types ALL F is G, SOME F is G, and NO F is G, showing their metalogical relations, and likewise for the sentence types of conjunction (P AND Q), disjunction (P OR Q), and what we may call 'exjunction' (NEITHER P NOR Q).

Under the conditions imposed by NST, complement is modified into restricted complement ($\overline{A}^R$), as defined in (8a), giving rise to a (presup-position-preserving) *restricted negation*. PNST–6 excludes double negation.[6] Double logically functional negation does occur, but only in culturally

---

[6] Except, of course, when the negation is copied for the functional purpose of reinforcement, as in the Cockney sentence '*E's never been no good to no woman, not never.*

well-developed speech. Treble logically functional negation is rare and confusing.[7] Quadruple logically functional negation is out of the question.

At the level of basic naturalness, disjunction is restricted to nonnull valuation spaces that do not intersect. Conjunction is reduced to M-partial intersection and is defined only over actually intersecting sets of situations (valuation spaces) /P/ and /Q/ such that neither /P/ nor /Q/ equals $\emptyset$ or $\mathbf{U}^{R}$, as in Figure 3.3b. (Subtraction, or /P/ − /Q/, has no counterpart in propositional logic; if it did it would be restricted to valuation spaces /P/ and /Q/ such that /Q/ $\subset$ /P/.)

As regards the relations, one remembers from (2.4) in Section 2.3.3 that the standard metalogical relations of equivalence ($\equiv$), entailment ($\vdash$ or $\models$), contradiction (CD), contrariety (C) and subcontrariety (SC) are expressible as standard set-theoretic relations in terms of valuation spaces:

(3.11) For all L-propositions P and Q:
   a. $\equiv$ (P,Q)   iff /P/ = /Q/
   b. P $\vdash(\models)$Q   iff /P/ $\subseteq$ /Q/
   c. CD(P,Q)   iff /P/ $\cup$ /Q/ $=_v$ **U** and /P/ $\cap$ /Q/ $=_v$ $\emptyset$ (or: /P/ $=_v$ $\bar{\mathbf{Q}}$)
   d. C(P,Q)   iff /P/ $\cap$ /Q/ $=_v$ $\emptyset$
   e. SC(P,Q)   iff /P/ $\cup$ /Q/ $=_v$ **U**

Natural set theory now imposes restrictions on these standard metalogical relations. First, equivalence has to go: it does not exist in natural set theory as a metalogical relation. Yet, as with the identification of objects in general, there is a natural cognitive operation of identification, which takes two sentences that have had different interpretative histories and identifies them at some level of understanding. For example, one may say that *Jack lives in London* is equivalent with *Dr. Smith lives in London* provided the expressions *Jack* and *Dr. Smith* refer to the same person. Likewise, when we say that, in basic-natural set theory, SOME F is G is equivalent with SOME F is NOT-G, what we mean is that they have been identified at some level of theoretical interpretation. Equivalence is, therefore, reinterpreted as identification.

Then, entailment of (3.11b), corresponding to standard inclusion as defined in (3.9c) and redefined in terms of NST in (3.6), is a basic- and strict-natural relation, provided it keeps to natural sets and to proper inclusion. The counterintuitive notion that a necessary falsehood R entails any proposition ('ex falso per se ad quodlibet') has been eliminated, because /R/ $=_v$ $\emptyset$, and $\emptyset$

---

[7] Or, as Larry Horn joked (Horn 1991: 98): 'If Duplex Negatio Negat. [...] But [...] the geometric effect of the three negations is to motivate all too often the more appropriate slogan Triplex Negatio Confundit.'

is not a natural set. Likewise, the equally violently counterintuitive notion that a necessary truth S is entailed by any proposition ('verum per se ex quolibet') has been eliminated, because /S/ $=_v$ U, and U is not a natural set. The concept of naturalness introduced here further restricts the entailment relation in that identity of /P/ and /Q/ is now also excluded, which rules out the counterintuitive notion of self-entailment.

Entailments following from the theorem ('inference rule') of ADDITION have now also been eliminated. Addition, one recalls from Section 1.2.2, is the theorem saying that any L-proposition Q can be extended with ' $\vee$ R' for any arbitrary R. It seems clear that this theorem, though standard, should be qualified as nonnatural, since natural speakers will not agree that, for example, *Joe is dead* entails *Joe is dead or today is Sunday.* NST eliminates this entailment. In standard terms, /Q $\vee$ R/ = /Q/ $\cup$ /R/ and, because /Q/ $\subset$ (/Q/ $\cup$ /R/), one must accept that Q $\vdash$ Q $\vee$ R for any arbitrary Q and R. NST helps out, because in cases where Q and R are logically independent, so that /Q/ and /R/ M-partially intersect, basic-natural union excludes by definition those situations where both Q and R are true. Therefore, the entailment schema or inference rule of addition breaks down for exclusive OR.

A further ground for the elimination of addition as an inference rule lies in the definition of entailment given in Section 1.2.1, which requires not only that truth be preserved but also that this be determined by the specific linguistic meaning of the entailing L-proposition. This latter condition is not satisfied in cases of addition, as there is nothing in the meaning of any arbitrary Q that causes truth to be preserved for Q OR R, R being equally arbitrary. Not so for the inference rule known as SIMPLIFICATION, which says that P AND Q entails both P and Q, since here it is the meaning of AND that causes the entailments. Nothing much thus remains of addition.

All this taken together removes a great deal of counterintuitive excess baggage and, in fact, restricts the entailment relation to semantically motivated entailment, precisely as is wanted. Since logic has no term for the entailment relation as restricted by NST and by the stipulation that entailment is meaning-driven, the term NATURAL ENTAILMENT was suggested in Section 1.2.1. It would seem that this reduction of entailment to natural entailment—that is, to the set-theoretic relation of proper inclusion as restricted under NST and supported by meaning—properly delimits the class of entailments felt to be natural by native speakers, and hence empirically observable or measurable as psychologically valid data.

Contradiction has been slimmed down to a contextually restricted U^R, created by presuppositional restrictions on the admissible situations in any discourse at hand. Contrariety is the only relation that can stand unmodified, apart from the restriction of the VSs at issue to natural sets of admissible situations. Finally, subcontrariety has disappeared from the basic-natural system, as it involves the relation of full union, which has been ruled out. Yet it reappears in the *strict*-natural system of metalogical relations, though not without some considerable cognitive effort.[8]

It is now clear why in Figure 3.5, adapted from Figure 2.6, (a) is preferred to (b). (Figure 2.6b, the improved Boethian square in two guises, is no longer in competition since, in either form, the two component triangles are not isomorphic.) Figure 3.5a consists of two logically isomorphic triangles with the strict- (not basic-) natural relations entailment, contrariety, and contradictoriness, subcontrariety being a 'bonus' due to the duality of the logical constants defining P and Q, as defined in (3.12) (=(2.2) of Section 2.2). (Properly speaking, we should have a special negation sign for the complement within a restricted U^R, but we leave this detail till Chapter 10, where presuppositional logic is discussed. Note also that equivalence (=) is allowed here, owing to the overriding in Aristotelian-Boethian predicate logic of the basic-natural restriction disallowing identity.)

(3.12) $P \equiv \neg Q^*$ and consequently $\neg P \equiv Q^*$
          $Q \equiv \neg P^*$ and consequently $\neg Q \equiv P^*$

By contrast, the two triangles of Figure 3.5b, though likewise isomorphic and made up of three metalogical relations, have the less natural relation of subcontrariety as a constitutive relation for the two triangles and contrariety is the 'bonus' thrown in owing to duality. Thus, where Figure 3.5a has contrariety, Figure 3.5b has subcontrariety and vice versa. This is why Figure 3.5a is considered (strict) natural, as against Figure 3.5b which does not fit into any natural system.

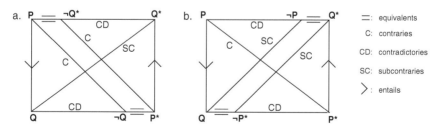

FIGURE 3.5 (a) the natural and (b) the nonnatural isomorphic square

___

[8] Aristotle, with all his logical acumen, failed to identify it as a logical relation (see Section 5.3): it was developed by his commentators. And beginning logic students, who still have to rely on their natural intuitions, tend to find subcontrariety very hard to grasp, as logic teachers know well.

This leaves the following list of basic-natural and strict-natural metalogical relations:

(3.13)   For all L-propositions P and Q such that /P/ and /Q/ are natural sets:
  a. CD(P,Q)   iff /P/ ∪ /Q/ $=_v$ **U**^{R} and /P/ ∩ /Q/ $=_v$ Ø (or:
     /P/$_v$= /Q̄/)
  b. C(P,Q)   iff /P/ ∩ /Q/ $=_v$ Ø
  c. P ⊢ (⊨) Q   iff /P/ ⊂ /Q/ (in virtue of the meanings of P and Q)
  d. Q ⊢ (⊨) P   iff /Q/ ⊂ /P/ (in virtue of the meanings of P and Q)

The missing relation, namely where /P/ ∩ /Q/ $\neq_v$ Ø while both /P/⊄/Q/ and /Q/ ⊄ /P/, and /P/ ≠ /Q/ ≠ **U** ≠ Ø has no corresponding name in logic, for the simple reason that in such a case P and Q are logically independent.

3.4 The basic-natural systems of logic

So far, no great difficulties have been encountered. Problems arise when one looks at the object-logical operators ALL, SOME, NOT, AND, and OR, and the way they interact. As regards the operators of quantification, the only natural relations that can hold between sets *A* and *B*, namely mutual exclusion (with restricted complement as a variant), M-partial intersection, and proper inclusion, as shown in Figure 3.3, look, at first sight, as if they are directly reflected in the quantifiers NO, SOME, and ALL, respectively. Likewise for the propositional truth-functional operators, which look as if they are the direct reflections of the corresponding set-theoretic functions as redefined under NST. Yet when one tries to build a *logical* system—that is a system which maintains consistency—on the basis of these parallels between natural sets on the one hand and logical relations and functions on the other, one finds that there are complications. The main complication consists in the fact that the principles of natural set theory set out above require that SOME F is G be true just in case ⟦F⟧ ⓞ ⟦G⟧, whereas natural intuitions want it to be true not only when ⟦F⟧ ⓞ ⟦G⟧ but also when ⟦G⟧ ⊂ ⟦F⟧—that is, just in case ⟦F⟧ ∩ ⟦G⟧ ⊂ ⟦F⟧, as in *Some children are orphans*.

Before we embark on an analysis of basic-natural predicate logic and its more advanced cousins defined by Aristotle, Boethius, Abelard, and Russell, a clarification is needed regarding the supposedly *monadic* character of these logics. By this is meant the fact that it looks as if these logics allow only for quantification over the subject term, while other quantified terms in sentences (as in *All boys admire some football player*) remain unaccounted for. These logics are thus taken to be less *expressive* than modern predicate logic. It is generally assumed and widely taught that modern logic overcomes this restriction and allows for quantification over any argument term in a sentence. It should be noted, however, that this superior expressivity of modern logic is due not to its logical properties but solely to the *formal language* in which its expressions are couched. Since we use, or anyway can use, the same formal language, with quantifiers, variables and all, for all the different predicate logics concerned, they all have equal expressive power, as they can all express quantification over any argument term in a sentence, embedding one quantifier in the scope of another. Therefore, the fact that we restrict our analyses to the monadic subject–predicate distinction is immaterial. We do this only to keep the exposé within reasonable bounds of size and complexity.

3.4.1 *Basic-natural predicate logic: the necessity of a cognitive base*

Up till now we have assumed that basic-natural predicate calculus (BNPC) is derivable *in toto* from basic-natural set theory (NST), just as standard modern predicate calculus (SMPC) is derivable *in toto* from standard set theory. We shall now see that this assumption is unwarranted. BNPC cannot reasonably be the product of just NST: additional cognitive factors must be invoked. In fact, we shall see, first, that BNPC cannot be constructed solely on a set-theoretic base and requires a wider cognitive base in addition to NST. Then it is shown that SMPC, which finds its apogee in the theory of generalized quantifiers, can only be constructed in terms of set theory, resisting treatment in terms of wider cognitive functions. It is in this sense that SMPC has managed to rid itself from all psychological elements—the ideal that Russell was so keen to achieve. The question is of special relevance as it shows that the reversal of Russell's programme of depsychologization of logic is subject to substantive empirical constraints, which opens up a new and highly interesting area of research in both psychology and logic. Finally, we will see that Aristotelian-Abelardian predicate calculus or AAPC (about which more below), as well as Aristotelian-Boethian predicate calculus or ABPC (best known as the Square of Opposition), are 'mixed' in that they retain some but discard other non-set-theoretic features. The question hinges on the semantic definition of the quantifiers involved.

Obviously, this calls for some explanation. The first stumbling block for a strictly set-theoretic construction of BNPC is the existential quantifier SOME, which, for natural intuition, means 'only some' or 'some but not all'. This means, in set-theoretic terms, that SOME F is G is true just in case $[\![F]\!] \oslash [\![G]\!]$ or $[\![G]\!] \subset [\![F]\!]$. The condition that $[\![F]\!] \oslash [\![G]\!]$ poses no problem with regard to a direct derivation of BNPC from NST in terms of the sets $[\![F]\!]$ and $[\![G]\!]$: a sentence like *Some flags are green* is true when the set of flags partially mutually intersects with the set of green things—as is the case in the actual world. And the relation of M-partial intersection ($\textcircled{0}$) goes well with the notion of natural set theory: it is one of the four basic-natural relations between sets, as shown in Figure 3.3. One would thus expect SOME F is G to be true just in case $[\![F]\!] \textcircled{0} [\![G]\!]$. But what we find in natural language is that SOME F is G is true also when $[\![G]\!] \subset [\![F]\!]$. Consider sentences (3.14a–d), which are obviously true, while $[\![G]\!]$ is properly included in $[\![F]\!]$:

(3.14)   a. Some children are orphans.
        b. Some people are Englishmen.
        c. Some computers are laptops.
        d. Some heavenly bodies are planets.

Moreover, the converses of these sentences raise eyebrows, in that they give rise to the question of whether one should conclude that some orphans are not children, or some Englishmen are not people, and likewise for (3.15c) and (3.15d):

(3.15)   a. Some orphans are children.
        b. Some Englishmen are people.
        c. Some laptops are computers.
        d. Some planets are heavenly bodies.

It is thus clear that, for natural speakers, $I_{BN} \equiv I^*_{BN}$, just as in Hamilton's logic which is discussed below.[9]

The problem is thus that, other than in the remaining three systems, the existential quantifier in BNPC is non-symmetrical, whereas there is no motivated way in which this lack of symmetry can be said to follow from a natural set theory. We may, of course, try to bend NST in such a way that the BNPC existential quantifier follows directly from it, but one has to fear that this will not bear experimental testing: the chances of such a natural set theory being empirically adequate must be deemed minimal. The problem is the more serious because the intuitions that come with the sentences in (3.14) and (3.15) are robust and beyond reasonable doubt. In fact, the problem requires an entire rethinking of quantification theory.

To this end, we distinguish between a COGNITIVE and a SET-THEORETIC approach to quantification. The latter requires just a (basic-)natural set theory. The former requires a cognitive theory of how cognition deals with plural

---

[9] Blanché (1966) uses the type name **Y** for $I_{BN} \equiv I^*_{BN}$. I do not follow him in this respect, as I do not want to make the formalism heavier than it need be.

objects in addition to a (basic-)natural set theory. In a *set-theoretic* analysis, quantifiers are treated as binary higher-order predicates over pairs of sets, in the sense discussed in the previous chapter. A *cognitive* analysis of quantification is formulated in terms of propositions in which a property, expressed as a predicate, is assigned to a plural set (n>1). In this approach, conversion, in the sense of a swap between the matrix and the restrictor predicate (indicated by ! in the discussion below), makes no sense.[10]

In order to make clear what is meant by the cognitive approach, we must dig a little deeper and look at the genesis of logical operators generally. In the cognitive approach, we take it that the logical operators originate as metalinguistic predicates. Thus, the negation operator has as its cognitive origin the metalinguistic qualification 'it is false that' (FALSE). Likewise, at the cognitive level, an assertion stands under the metalinguistic operator 'it is true that' (TRUE), unexpressed (expressed as a zero element) in most languages. Such metalinguistic operators can then, by a process that may be called LOGICAL GRAMMATICALIZATION, be incorporated into the object language, where they appear as object-language operators (or as zero). FALSE thus becomes natural language negation. The advantage is greater flexibility of the object language, in that the negation can then be used (and become part of a semantic calculus) in any embedded L-proposition or L-propositional function.[11]

Pursuing this idea a little further, we can apply it to quantifiers in the following way. Given a nonquantified L-proposition with a definite plural subject term, such as *The flags are green*, we can judge that it is either entirely true, say VERUM IN TOTO (**VIT**), or partially true, say VERUM IN PARTE (**VIP**), or not at all true, say VERUM IN NULLO (**VIN**):

---

[10] Interestingly, Aristotle starts in the cognitive mood, as appears from his term *en mérei* (in part) (and the Latin translation *particularis*) for existential quantification, and, as regards universal quantification, when he says (*Int* 20a9–15; cf. also *Int* 17b-12):

For the word *every* does not make the subject universal but the whole proposition. ... So that the words *every* or *no* add nothing else to the meaning than that, whether affirmatively or negatively, the subject is to be taken as a whole.

Yet his syllogistic, set out in the *Prior Analytics*, is based on the device of letting a predicate (the Middle Term) occur as a subject. In his syllogistic, therefore, Aristotle follows the set-theoretic approach, in which both the restrictor and the matrix term represent sets.

[11] In fact, it makes sense to regard the radical (presupposition-cancelling) negation, discussed in Chapter 10, as having grammaticalized only in part. It has to be constructed, in surface structure, with the finite verb of the main clause and is not allowed in any other, 'noncanonical' position. Moreover, its semantics (echo-effect) shows that it takes a quoted L-proposition as its argument. It would seem that this perspective on the radical negation deserves further reflection.

VIT ['the flags are green']
VIP ['the flags are green']
VIN ['the flags are green']

The 'partial' in VERUM IN PARTE is to be interpreted as saying that some but not all flags are green, in accordance with the basic-natural set-theoretic notion that sees class inclusion as *proper* class inclusion.

Clearly, this creates room for truth values between just true and false, because **VIP** can be specified percentagewise: we can say that it is precisely 70% true that the flags are green, so that, given ten flags, exactly seven flags must be green for truth to be attained. This aspect of the theory is not elaborated here, but it is important to realize that the possibility of an intervalent logic arises *inter alia* when predicates are assigned to plural subject terms.

The three meta-operators **VIT**, **VIP**, and **VIN** can be transferred to the object language, where they can be symbolized as $\forall_{BN}$ (corresponding to the L-propositional type $\mathbf{A}_{BN}$), $\exists_{BN}$ (corresponding to type $\mathbf{I}_{BN}$), and $\mathbf{N}_{BN}$ (corresponding to type $\mathbf{N}_{BN}$), respectively. The truth conditions for the types $\mathbf{A}_{BN}$, $\mathbf{I}_{BN}$ and $\mathbf{N}_{BN}$ are as follows:

(a) $\forall_{BN}$ [the Fs are G] is true iff   all members of $[\![F]\!]$ are G
(b) $\exists_{BN}$ [the Fs are G] is true iff   some but not all members of $[\![F]\!]$ are G
(c) $\mathbf{N}_{BN}$ [the Fs are G] is true iff   no member of $[\![F]\!]$ is G

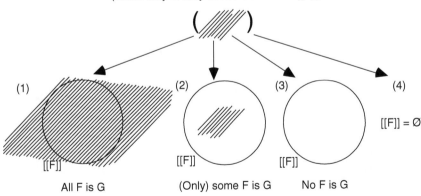

FIGURE 3.6 The four possible situation classes in the cognitive approach

Graphically, the truth conditions can be represented as in Figure 3.6, where the shading indicates the property expressed by the predicate **G**. One notes that these truth conditions are not expressed in terms of two sets but in terms of one set $[\![\mathbf{F}]\!]$, the extension of the plural subject term quantified over. When $[\![\mathbf{F}]\!] = \varnothing$, BNPC does not apply, because the null set does not count as a set in NST. (It is shown below that BNPC remains largely intact when the condition $[\![\mathbf{F}]\!] = \varnothing$ is taken into account.)

The internal negation, symbolized as *, results from placing the argument proposition of **VIT**, **VIP**, or **VIN** under the negation operator:

VIT ['¬[the flags are green]']	$\rightarrow$	$\forall_{\mathrm{BN}}[\neg[\text{the Fs are G}]]$	type: $\mathbf{A}^*_{\mathrm{BN}}$
VIP ['¬[the flags are green]']	$\rightarrow$	$\exists_{\mathrm{BN}}[\neg[\text{the Fs are G}]]$	type: $\mathbf{I}^*_{\mathrm{BN}}$
VIN ['¬[the flags are green]']	$\rightarrow$	$\mathrm{N}_{\mathrm{BN}}[\neg[\text{the Fs are G}]]$	type: $\mathbf{I}^*_{\mathrm{BN}}$

One notes that the argument of **VIT**, **VIP**, and **VIN** is the quoted singular sentence '¬[the flags are green]', which is equivalent with 'the flags are not-green', because 'the flags are green' is a nonquantified, singular sentence, with a definite term as subject. This explains why Aristotle speaks of 'negatives' when what he has in mind is not the external but, in our terms, the internal negation.

Having thus defined the types $\mathbf{A}_{\mathrm{BN}}$, $\mathbf{I}_{\mathrm{BN}}$ and $\mathbf{N}_{\mathrm{BN}}$, and their internally negative counterparts $\mathbf{A}^*_{\mathrm{BN}}$, $\mathbf{I}^*_{\mathrm{BN}}$ and $\mathbf{N}^*_{\mathrm{BN}}$, we can now, with the help of the external negation based on the metalinguistic operator FALSE, define their externally negative versions $\neg\mathbf{A}^*_{\mathrm{BN}}$, $\neg\mathbf{I}^*_{\mathrm{BN}}$, $\neg\mathbf{N}^*_{\mathrm{BN}}$, $\neg\mathbf{A}_{\mathrm{BN}}$, $\neg\mathbf{I}^*_{\mathrm{BN}}$ and $\neg\mathbf{N}^*_{\mathrm{BN}}$. The valuation spaces, in terms of Figure 3.6, for these twelve sentence types are now as follows:

$/\mathbf{A}^*_{\mathrm{BN}}/ = \{1\}$	$/\mathbf{A}^*_{\mathrm{BN}}/ = \{3\}$	$/\neg\mathbf{A}^*_{\mathrm{BN}}/ = \{2,3\}$	$/\neg\mathbf{A}^*_{\mathrm{BN}}/ = \{1,2\}$
$/\mathbf{I}^*_{\mathrm{BN}}/ = \{2\}$	$/\mathbf{I}^*_{\mathrm{BN}}/ = \{2\}$	$/\neg\mathbf{I}^*_{\mathrm{BN}}/ = \{1,3\}$	$/\neg\mathbf{I}^*_{\mathrm{BN}}// = \{1,3\}$
$/\mathbf{N}^*_{\mathrm{BN}}/ = \{3\}$	$/\mathbf{N}^*_{\mathrm{BN}}/ = \{1\}$	$/\neg\mathbf{N}^*_{\mathrm{BN}}/ = \{1,2\}$	$/\neg\mathbf{N}^*_{\mathrm{BN}}/ = \{2,3\}$

Figure 3.7 shows the square representation resulting from the system described, the VS-model (with the four spaces corresponding to Figure 3.6, but with space 4 left idling) and the complete dodecagon of all logical (meta)relations holding in BNPC. This system does not suffer from undue existential import (UEI), although space 4 is inoperative. This is because $\mathbf{A}^*_{\mathrm{BN}}$ entails $\neg\mathbf{I}^*_{\mathrm{BN}}$, and $\neg\mathbf{I}^*_{\mathrm{BN}}$ must be considered true in space 4, regardless of what is done with regard to $\mathbf{A}^*_{\mathrm{BN}}$. But we can, if that is wanted, assign truth values to all twelve types for the situation specified for space 4. When this is done, as in Figure 3.8, it is not possible to assign truth to the types **A** and $\mathbf{A}^*$ in space 4

without cognitive arbitrariness, as type **A** expresses the situation class of space 1 and **A*** the situation class in space 3. There is no good reason why space 4 should be added to these VSs.

One notes that, in BNPC with space 4 operative, **I** and **I*** are still equivalent, but **A** and **N***, and **A*** and **N**, no longer are: there is now a one-way entailment from **A** to **N*** and from **A*** to **N**. Moreover, in this version of BNPC, some relations are missing, so that the dodecagon is no longer complete: it gets a bit undone in the right-hand side area. Yet as a logical system it is sound. And one may marvel at its power and richness. Its only drawback, as we see it, is that it does not allow one to say that *Some flags are green* until all flags have been checked, because *Some flags are green* is false in BNPC when all flags are. This nonlogical but merely functional defect has been repaired in AAPC and ABPC, and of course also in SMPC, but at the expense of considerable logical power, as will become clear in Chapter 4.

We can now take a further step forward on the path from basic- to strict-natural predicate logic and derive Aristotelian-Abelardian predicate calculus (AAPC). This we do by stipulating that AAPC equals BNPC with space 4 operative, as illustrated in Figure 3.8, except that the expression 'part of' is now interpreted in the modern standard sense that if set X is part of set Y, then $X \subseteq Y$, and not $X \subset Y$, as in BNPC. Moreover, we let $\mathbf{A}_{AA}$ be true also when all and only all **F** is **G**—that is, when the extensions of **F** and **G** coincide. In BNPC, ALL **F** IS **G** is interpreted as 'all but not only **F** is **G**'; in AAPC the reading is 'all and possibly only **F** is **G**'. (One already begins to see the need for an analysis in terms of two sets.)

This gives the following valuation spaces for AAPC:

$$/\mathbf{A}_{AA}/ = \{1\} \qquad /\mathbf{A}^{\star}_{AA}/ = \{3\} \qquad /\neg\mathbf{A}_{AA}/ = \{2,3,4\} \qquad /\neg\mathbf{A}^{\star}_{AA}// = \{1,2,4\}$$
$$/\mathbf{I}_{AA}/ = \{1,2\} \qquad /\mathbf{I}^{\star}_{AA}/ = \{2,3\} \qquad /\neg\mathbf{I}_{AA}/ = \{3,4\} \qquad /\neg\mathbf{I}^{\star}_{AA}/ = \{1,4\}$$
$$/\mathbf{N}_{AA}/ = \{3,4\} \qquad /\mathbf{N}^{\star}_{AA}/ = \{1,4\} \qquad /\neg\mathbf{N}_{AA}/ = \{1,2\} \qquad /\neg\mathbf{N}^{\star}_{AA}/ = \{1,2\}$$

We now see that $\neg\mathbf{I}_{AA} \equiv \mathbf{N}_{AA}$ (and, accordingly, $\neg\mathbf{I}_{AA} \equiv \mathbf{N}^{\star}_{AA}\equiv$). This enables us to eliminate the quantifier $\mathbf{N}_{AA}$, and with it the sentence type $\mathbf{N}_{AA}$, from the system, in favour of $\neg\mathbf{I}_{AA}$ and $\neg\mathbf{I}^{\star}_{AA}$. Moreover, the classic subaltern entailments from **A** to **I** and from **A*** to **I*** now hold. The Conversions do not hold, but there is a one-way entailment from $\mathbf{A}_{AA}$ to $\neg\mathbf{I}^{\star}_{AA}$ and from $\mathbf{I}_{AA}$ to $\neg\mathbf{A}^{\star}_{AA}$. This gives rise to the square representation, VS-model, and octagon of Figure 3.9.

Aristotelian-Boethian predicate calculus, or ABPC, best known as the Square of Opposition, is obtained by illegitimately leaving out space 4 from the system. This is illegitimate because leaving out space 4 from AAPC (which was not done by Aristotle, as is widely believed, but by his later

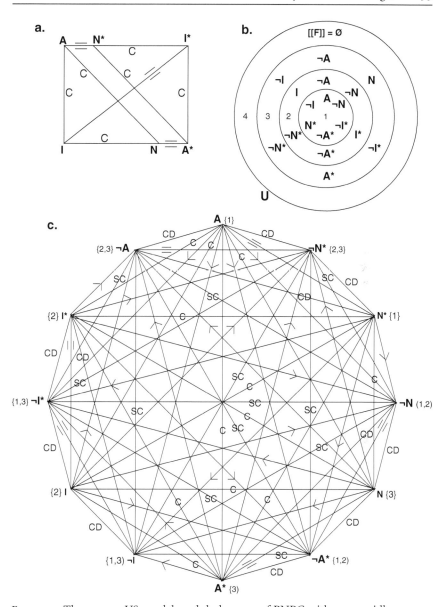

FIGURE 3.7 The square, VS-model, and dodecagon of BNPC with space 4 idle

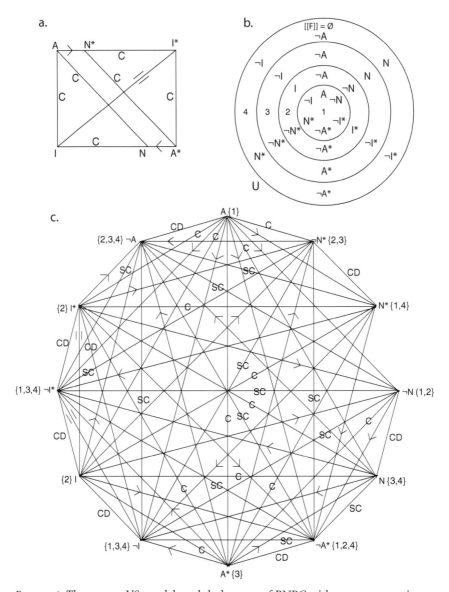

FIGURE 3.8 The square, VS-model, and dodecagon of BNPC with space 4 operative

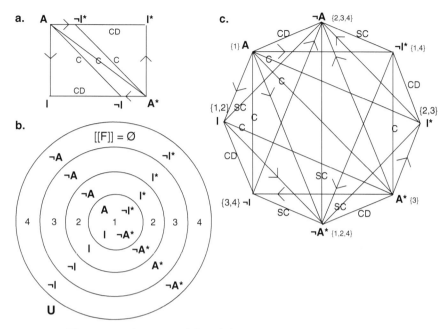

FIGURE 3.9 The square, the VS-model, and the octagon for AAPC

commentators, as is shown in Chapter 5) leads to UEI.[12] Leaving out space 4 yields the classic Square of Opposition, with the VS-model and the octagon of Figure 3.10, as is now easily checked.

We can carry on in the same vein and define SMPC by stipulating that **A** and **A*** are true when $\llbracket F \rrbracket = \varnothing$. The result is shown in Figure 3.11. But such a stipulation is not defensible on cognitive grounds. On cognitive grounds, such a stipulation is arbitrary, because there is no reason in cognition why the situations where all the members of $\llbracket F \rrbracket$ have a certain property should be paired, at the level of linguistic expression, with those where $\llbracket F \rrbracket = \varnothing$. It takes a good deal of formal training to convince oneself that such a pairing does make sense in terms of abstract mathematical set theory. We must, therefore, conclude that SMPC is not constructible in the cognitive mood. Other than BNPC, AAPC, and ABPC, SMPC requires a construction in pure set-theoretical terms.

[12] Even so, ABPC appears to be the optimal strict-natural system of predicate logic. As is shown in Chapter 10, ABPC can remain in full force provided it is extended with a presuppositional component and falsity is split up into presupposition-preserving minimal falsity (F1) and presupposition-cancelling radical falsity (F2).

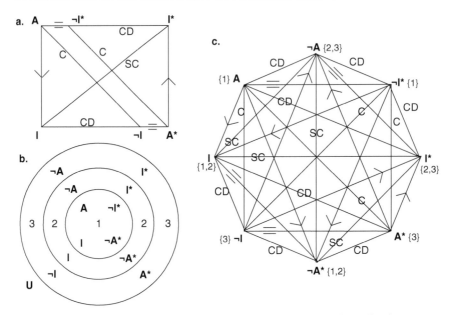

FIGURE 3.10 The square, the VS-model, and the complete octagonal graph of ABPC

One notes that there is no point in maintaining a square notation for SMPC, as **A** and **I**, as well as **A*** and **I***, have now become logically independent and only the (meta)logical relations of contradictoriness and equivalence, in so far as they are involved in the Conversions, have been left. This dramatic decrease in logical power is discussed in Chapter 4.

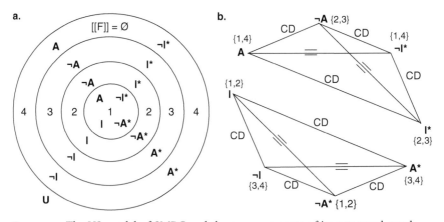

FIGURE 3.11 The VS-model of SMPC and the poor remnants of its octagonal graph

We thus conclude that BNPC can only be constructed in the cognitive mood and that SMPC can only be constructed in the set-theoretical mood. AAPC and ABPC are seen to be 'mixed' in that they contain elements that clearly smack of cognition, but also elements that smack of set theory. In other words, the more 'primitive' the logic, the more it depends on cognitive factors. This makes explicit what precisely is involved in Russell's programme of depsychologization of logic.

Summing up, we may enumerate the following features of the logics concerned:

1. SOME F is G is interpreted as 'only some F is G'
2. ALL F is G is interpreted as 'all but not only F is G'
3. ALL F is G is false when $[\![F]\!] = \varnothing$
4. Space 4 is idle.

These features are distributed as follows over the four predicate logics considered, whereby one notes that ABPC simply results from AAPC if space 4 is made inoperative. SMPC lacks all the features:

BNPC   1, 2, 3, 4
AAPC   3
ABPC   4
SMPC   - -

Does this now mean that the unexpectedly rich, powerful, and sound predicate logic of BNPC carries the day? Not quite yet, because there still are a few empirical problems, one of them consisting in the fact that BNPC fails to account for the strong natural intuition, observed by many authors (notably Jespersen 1917: 86–91), that makes one feel that ¬**A** is equivalent with both **I** and **I***, which means that in the logical system we would like to see an equivalence relation between ¬**A**, **I** and **I***. But BNPC fails to oblige as is easily checked in Figure 3.7b,c. The entailments from **I** and **I*** to ¬**A** hold, but natural intuition requires a stronger relation. In this respect, ABPC fares somewhat better, since, in ABPC, ¬**A** and **I*** are equivalent, though ¬**A** and **I** are mere subcontraries.

The pragmaticists tackle the problem by an appeal to the Gricean maxims, reinforced by Horn's theory of scalarity (Horn 1972, 1989), in virtue of which the negation, when applied to a quantifiable scale, cuts off only the higher part of the scale but leaves the remainder intact. Or, as Jespersen put it (1917: 86), 'in negativing an *A* [ALL F is G; PAMS] it is the *absolute* element of *A* that is negatived'. But this answer, widely subscribed to in pragmatic circles, seems curious for a number of reasons. Thus, while it is accepted that **A** ⊢ **I** (the positive subaltern of the Square), it is at the same time posited that **I** ⊢∼ ¬**A** (where ' ⊢∼ ' stands for Gricean implicature), and while it is accepted that ¬**I** ⊢ **I*** (Square), it is posited that, pragmatically, **I*** ⊢∼ **I**. In nonscalar terms, this would amount to saying that a sentence like *John has been killed* entails *John is dead*, while *John is dead* has the implicature *John has not been killed*. It strikes one as very odd that these logical entailments and these pragmatic implicatures, allegedly derived from conversational principles, should interact in such a way. It seems more sensible to posit different logical systems operating at different levels of cognitive functioning.

Moreover, it is not clear why the psychology of scalarity does not apply to the analogous propositional operators *and* and *or*, which can also be seen to form a quantifiable scale, in that *and* involves as many terms as there are members of the conjunction, while (exclusive) *or* involves just one. Yet **NOT-AND**—that is, NOT(P AND Q AND ... Z)—is not felt to entail P OR Q OR ... OR Z.

We must, therefore, look elsewhere for an explanation. The explanation proposed here for the problem of ¬**A** not being equivalent with **I** and **I*** in BNPC falls back on trivalent presuppositional logic (see Chapter 10) and on the notion of topic–comment structure, also often called 'information structure' (see Chapter 11). Topic–comment structure often comes with negative sentences. If we take it that topic–comment structure is formalizable as an underlying cleft structure and that *all* in a sentence like *Ben didn't eat all of his meal* has comment status, this sentence is then analysed as 'what Ben ate of his meal was not all', which entails presuppositionally that Ben ate some of his meal, excluding the case that he ate nothing. This sentence thus *presupposes*, and hence *entails*, that Ben ate some of his meal and it *asserts* that he did not eat all of it. Similarly for a sentence like *Not all flags are green*, which, if analysed as 'it is not all flags that are green', excludes the case that there are no green flags. In sum, given the sentence form *It is not all flags that are green*, it is presupposed, and hence entailed, that some flags are green and also that some flags are not green (given that **I** ≡ **I***). And because, in BNPC, both **I** and **I*** entail ¬**A**, it follows that ¬**A** both entails and is entailed by **I** and **I***, which makes the three equivalent. This solution requires, however, that ¬**A**-type sentences be given a topic–comment structure with 'not all' as the comment and that BNPC be extended with a presuppositional component.

A further problem arises in connection with the extension of BNPC to a full system of predicate logic catering also for cases where $[\![F]\!] = \emptyset$, as in Figure 3.8. The problem is that, in cases where $[\![F]\!] = \emptyset$, it seems natural to say that **N** is true. Given that this world has no mermaids, it is not hard to agree that *There are no mermaids living in London* must be considered true. But then the corresponding **N*** sentence *There are no mermaids (that are) not living in London* should also be true, because if there are no mermaids, there will be no mermaid among those entities that are living in London nor among those that are not. The disturbing fact is, however, that while *There are no mermaids living in London* is considered true, *There are no mermaids (that are) not living in London* is false for natural intuition and, in fact, felt to be equivalent with *All mermaids live in London*. This latter intuition is accounted for, since, as is shown in Figure 3.7b, both **A** and **N*** are true only in space 1 and false in spaces 2 and 3, which makes them equivalent within the confines of a model where the condition $[\![F]\!] \neq \emptyset$ is left out of account.

But in order to see if BNPC is tenable as a logical system, we must go beyond those confines and take the fourth space into account for cases where $[\![F]\!] = \emptyset$. This has been done in Figure 3.8b, where truth has been assigned to **N** in space 4. But then truth must also be assigned to **N*** on pain of making the semantics of the operator NO inconsistent. It thus follows that if we turn BNPC into a fully fledged logical system that also caters for cases where $[\![F]\!] = \emptyset$, as in Figure 3.8, a gross unnaturalness appears, because truth for **N*** makes **N*** clash with natural intuitions. This is, however, not a problem for the logical system but only for the claim that BNPC reflects natural logical intuitions. Therefore, if this claim is to be upheld, it is essential that space 4 for cases where $[\![F]\!] = \emptyset$ should not be considered to be part of it—owing to PNST–1, which declares $\emptyset$ not to be a set.

Finally, BNPC is still subject to the predicament that it requires complete knowledge of the verification domain before one is entitled to say that existentially quantified sentences are true or false. This is illustrated as follows. Suppose Joe is checking if all the 45 doors in the building are properly locked. He has come to number 15 and so far all has been well. We feel that, as soon as he has found that at least one (or two) doors are properly locked, he ought to be able to say in truth that (at least) some doors are properly locked. But BNPC does not allow him to do so, because *Some doors are properly locked* entails that not all doors are. And Joe cannot vouch for that entailment. In fact, he must wait till he has checked all doors before he can say either that some doors are properly locked or that all are. All he can say after finding that one or more doors are properly locked is that it is not so that no door is properly locked, or: 'not (no door is properly locked)', which entails that at least some and perhaps all doors are properly locked.[13]

This fact is of great epistemological importance. It is already so that **A**- and **N**-statements require full knowledge of the domain before one is entitled to claim their truth. These entitlements are thus restricted to finite and practically surveyable domains. But most domains are infinite or in any case not practically surveyable and yet we profusely help ourselves to positive and negative universal statements about them. Strictly speaking, we cannot vouch for the truth of such statements, yet we venture them, relying on our inductive powers of generalization and thereby taking the risk of falsification. And this is precisely why they are so useful: almost all of what we consider to be our knowledge is inductive knowledge, which has come to be established on the strength of systematic lack of falsification and of the 'sense' they make in terms of larger systems. But this conveys an equal importance to **I**- and **I***-statements as used in traditional and standard modern logic, because these statements have the power of falsification. And for this it is needed that one be entitled to claim their truth *without full knowledge of the domain*, merely on the strength of an observation made. If **I** and **I*** are added to the list of sentence types that require full knowledge of the domain before one can vouch for their truth, this instrument to express a falsification is taken away. In this sense, BNPC is an obstacle to the expansion of inductive knowledge.

This conclusion is to some extent disconcerting. One might propose that natural language *some* is ambiguous between 'some perhaps all' (= NOT NO) and 'some but not all'. But the rules of good methodology make one reluctant to do that. There is, thus, the basic intuition that *some* implies or entails 'not all', but further reflection, manifesting itself at the strict-natural level, makes one see that *some* ought not to be taken that way. If this were cognitive reality, it would put a brake on the extension of inductive knowledge and thus on intellectual development as a whole. Aristotle made the world see that, on reflection, one must concede that **A**-sentences entail the corresponding **I**-sentences, thereby removing the main blemish in any predicate logic constrained by the principles of basic-natural set theory. Needless to say, this

---

[13] Horn (1989: 219) shows that De Morgan was well aware of this epistemological dilemma. Horn quotes Hamilton (1858: 121):

There are three ways in which one extent may be related to another [...]: they are, complete inclusion, partial inclusion with partial exclusion, and complete exclusion. This trichotomy would have ruled the forms of logic, if human knowledge had been more definite. [...] As it is, we know well the grounds on which predication is not a trichotomy, but two separate dichotomies. [...] Must be, may be, cannot be, are the great distinctions of ontology: necessity, contingency, impossibility. This was clearly seen by the logicians. But it was not so clearly seen that this mode of predication tallies, not with the four ordinary forms *A, E, I, O, but with the three forms* A, (OI), E.

Aristotelian upgrading from basic to strict naturalness conquered the world, until it was replaced, a century ago, with the modern, highly constructed, system of predicate logic known as standard modern predicate calculus, which, ironically, banished again the subaltern entailment from **A** to **I** sentences so as to get rid of undue existential import.

In overall perspective, it seems that we have to conclude that SMPC is not fully constructible in the cognitive mood, just as BNPC is not fully constructible in the set-theoretical mood. The question hinges on the semantic definitions of the quantifiers. The existential quantifier SOME must be considered symmetrical for set-theoretic purposes, so that SOME **F** is **G** ≡ SOME **G** is **F** (**I** ≡ **I**!), whereas it must be considered nonsymmetrical for 'cognitive' purposes, so that SOME **F** is **G** ≡ SOME **F** is NOT-**G** (**I** ≡ **I***). The universal quantifier ALL must, for full set-theoretic constructibility, be taken to yield the value *true* in situations without any F, whereas, for full 'cognitive' constructibility, it must be taken to yield the value *false* in such situations. The combination of symmetrical SOME and 'cognitive' ALL, as in AAPC and ABPC, creates the subaltern entailments from **A** to **I** and from **A*** to **I***. They are eliminated by the combination of symmetrical SOME and set-theoretic ALL, as in SMPC.

We have found that all four systems are *definable* in both the cognitive and the set-theoretical mood, but that in *deriving* or *constructing* the various systems from underlying cognitive elements, BNPC is maximally 'cognitive', whereas AAPC and ABPC are more set-theoretically and less 'cognitively' oriented than BNPC. SMPC has shed all 'cognitive' elements. Other than BNPC, AAPC, and ABPC, SMPC requires a construction in pure set-theoretical terms: it is fully depsychologized. The re-introduction of the 'cognitive' element into logic as presented here is motivated by, hitherto unacknowledged, empirical considerations regarding human natural logic, in its various, culture-induced, manifestations.

3.4.2 *Hamilton's predicate logic*

The predicate-calculus system at the level of basic naturalness is strongly reminiscent of, but not identical to, the brand of predicate logic proposed by the Edinburgh philosopher Sir William Hamilton (1788–1856). The main publication in this respect is Hamilton's posthumous (1866).[14] Perhaps

---

[14] Part of Hamilton's claim to fame rests on the drawn-out public polemic between him and the London logician Augustus De Morgan, which was as famous as it was fierce and even made them take each other to the courts of justice. The dispute centred upon Hamilton's predicate logic, which was not to De Morgan's liking. See the Appendix in De Morgan (1847), which contains much of their acrimonious correspondence.

because Hamilton lost his war with De Morgan, and perhaps also because of the unique prestige of modern logic, Hamilton's system of 'quantification of the predicate', as he called it, has largely been forgotten outside circles of historians of logic.[15] Yet, given the undoubted intuitive appeal of at least some of Hamilton's logical notions, the Hamiltonian tradition in logic deserves a closer look. The more so because the Danish linguist Otto Jespersen (1860–1943), who possessed a finely tuned intuition as regards linguistic matters but had no logical knowledge (he had probably never heard of Hamilton), came up with a system of predicate logic that resembles the Hamiltonian system in every respect except for Hamilton's 'quantification of the predicate' (Jespersen (1917: 85–92).

A central feature of Hamilton's logic (see also Cavaliere 2007) is his insistence on quantification of the predicate. This implies that not only the subject but also the predicate in the Aristotelian sentence types should be quantified, despite the grammatical awkwardness of sentences like *All men are some animals.*[16] He even chides Aristotle (Hamilton 1865: 264–5) for 'prohibit[ing] once and again the annexation of the universal predesignation to the predicate' (see note 15), continuing 'Yet this nonsense, (be it spoken with all reverence for the Stagirite,) has imposed the precept on the systems of Logic down to the present day'. In this respect, I do not follow Hamilton and take sides with Aristotle and with standard modern logic, even though one might perhaps attribute to Hamilton the implicit insight that quantification involves two sets, the matrix or predicate set and the restrictor set.

Hamilton does not use anything like quantifiers, but prefixes each set denotation with the operators **t** (total) or **p** (partial), using the symmetrical predicates '$=$' for 'coincides with' and '$||$' for 'excludes'. The following simple composition rule thus generates all expression types (formulæ) of Hamiltonian predicate logic ('$[\alpha / \beta]$' stands for 'either α or β'):

$$\text{Formula} =: [\,\textbf{t} / \textbf{p}\,]X\ [= / \,||\,]\ [\,\textbf{t} / \textbf{p}\,]Y\ \text{(where X and Y are predicates)}$$

---

[15] Hamilton's efforts are part of a tradition of predicate logics with 'quantification of the predicate' that was rejected by Aristotle (*Int* 17b13–16) and occasionally discussed during the late Middle Ages, but which really started in the late eighteenth century and flourished in the nineteenth century (see, for example, Bochenski 1956, Kneale and Kneale 1962: 349, Cavaliere 2007, Lenzen 2008). A major factor in the development of these logics was the wish to enrich and strengthen the classical Aristotelian theory of syllogisms with the help of richer systems of predicate logic.

[16] Some languages, including English, marginally allow for sentences like *Some humans are all Englishmen,* where *all* is a so-called 'floating quantifier', saying that there is a group of humans who are all Englishmen. This, however, does not seem to be what Hamilton intended.

Given that predicates may denote complement sets, there is, for every predicate X, with the extension ⟦X⟧, a negative counterpart NOT-X, with the extension ⟦$\overline{X}$⟧. For the predicates F and G and their negations, there are thus 32 admissible formulæ.

With some effort, such a system can be made good semantic sense of. Despite the grammatical illformedness of quasi-sentences like *All Englishmen are some humans*, there is an intuitive inkling of what they could possibly mean. This inkling can be made formally explicit in a variety of ways. An interpretation that seems to come closest to Hamilton's intentions is the following:

> Read 'tX' as 'the total set of Xs' and 'pX' as 'a nonnull proper subset of Xs' (where X ranges over predicates and ⟦X⟧ $\neq \emptyset \neq$ U). Read '==' as 'coincides with' and '||' as 'excludes'.

A quasi-sentence like *Some computers are all laptops* will then be read, in this interpretation, as pComputer == tLaptop or 'only a nonnull proper subset of computers coincides with the total set of laptops', which is true only if ⟦Computer⟧ ⊃ ⟦Laptop⟧. By contrast, *Some computers are all non-laptops*, translated as pComputer || tLaptop or 'only a nonnull proper subset of computers excludes the total set of laptops', is true if either ⟦Computer⟧ ⊃ ⟦Laptop⟧ or ⟦Computer⟧ ⊙ ⟦Laptop⟧ ('⊙' stands for mutual partial intersection). Then, *Some computers are some laptops* is read as pComputer == pLaptop or 'only a nonnull proper subset of computers coincides with only a nonnull proper subset of laptops', true only if ⟦Computer⟧ ⊙ ⟦Laptop⟧. This is equivalent with *Some computers are some non-laptops*, which reads as pComputer || pLaptop or 'only a nonnull proper subset of computers excludes only a nonnull proper subset of laptops', again true only if ⟦Computer⟧ ⊙ ⟦Laptop⟧.

From a purely logical point of view, this system looks as if it has certain advantages, as the relation of its expressions with set-theoretic constellations is more straightforward than in the logics that quantify only over the subject (restrictor) term. For example, tF == tG is true only if ⟦F⟧ = ⟦G⟧, while tF == pG is true only if ⟦F⟧ ⊂ ⟦G⟧—a distinction that is not expressible in the standard modern rendering of the sentence type ALL F is G, whether in the Peano-Russell notation or in the notation of the generalized quantifiers.

Yet despite its possible advantages for logic as such, Hamilton's logic, whether in his own notation or in any updated version, has an uneasy relation with natural language. Besides the absence of negation, its translations into a natural language such as English result either in artificially regimented, and even ungrammatical, sentences or in sentences that allow for multiple translations into the Hamiltonian system. For example, a sentence type like ALL F is G is true when $\mathbf{tF} = \mathbf{tG}$ or $\mathbf{tF} = \mathbf{pG}$. And SOME F is G is true when $\mathbf{pF} = \mathbf{tG}$, $\mathbf{pF} = \mathbf{pG}$, $\mathbf{pF} \parallel \mathbf{tG}$ or $\mathbf{pF} \parallel \mathbf{pG}$. In other words, Hamilton's insistence on 'quantification of the predicate' may have certain advantages for a system of predicate logic and a concomitant syllogistic, it complicates a translation mapping onto natural language beyond empirical endurance.

This becomes even more apparent when one considers *multiple quantification*, as in *All boys admire some football players*, which are not translatable at all into natural language sentences in terms of quantification of the predicate. One could go as far as 'All boys are some (all) [admirers of some football players]', but then one still has to introduce predicate quantification for 'some football players' and this is something natural language at least has no provisions for. Modern logic, of course, has, in principle, provided adequate logical analyses of multiple-quantification sentences.

If we forget about the quantification of the predicate, we need the three quantifiers ALL, SOME (but not all), and NO, corresponding with the three sentence types $\mathbf{A}_{\text{Ham}}$ for ALL F is G, $\mathbf{I}_{\text{Ham}}$ for SOME but not all F is G (equivalent with $\mathbf{I}^{*}_{\text{Ham}}$ or SOME but not all F is NOT-G), and $\mathbf{N}_{\text{Ham}}$ for NO F is G. The three types $\mathbf{A}_{\text{Ham}}$, $\mathbf{I}_{\text{Ham}}$, and $\mathbf{N}_{\text{Ham}}$ are mutually exclusive and thus form three pairs of contraries. They are defined as follows, in purely set-theoretic terms ($[\![F]\!]$ and $[\![G]\!]$ are natural but not necessarily distinct sets):

$\mathbf{A}_{\text{Ham}}$ (ALL F is G)	true iff	$[\![F]\!] \subseteq [\![G]\!]$
$\mathbf{I}_{\text{Ham}}/ \mathbf{I}^{*}_{\text{Ham}}$ (SOME F is (NOT-)G)	true iff	$[\![F]\!] \supset [\![G]\!]$ or $[\![F]\!] \oslash [\![G]\!]$
$\mathbf{N}_{\text{Ham}}$ (NO F IS G)	true iff	$[\![F]\!] \text{ OO } [\![G]\!]$

If this interpretation of Hamilton's logic is correct, it only differs from BNPC in that the condition for **A**-type sentences is $[\![F]\!] \subseteq [\![G]\!]$ in the former but $[\![F]\!] \subset [\![G]\!]$ in the latter (as Hamilton allows for identity of two sets).

As we have seen, the condition for I-type sentences is irreconcilable with any nonarbitrary natural set-theory hypothesis, due to its cognitively unmotivated putting together of the two conditions $[\![F]\!] \supset [\![G]\!]$ and $[\![F]\!]\oslash[\![G]\!]$. A proper implementation of the set-theoretic restrictions (1) to (6) of Section 3.2.2 yields a logic where I-type sentences are defined as follows ($[\![F]\!]$ and $[\![G]\!]$ are distinct natural sets):

I (SOME F is G)   true iff $[\![F]\!] \oslash [\![G]\!]$

That is, SOME F is G is now read as 'some but not all F is G and some but not all G is F'. In such a logic, other than in the Hamilton system, I is not equivalent with I*, because when $[\![G]\!] \subset [\![F]\!]$, SOME F is G is false (there is no M-partial intersection) but SOME F is NOT-G is true. By contrast, the equivalence of SOME F is G with its converse, SOME G is F (I ≡ I!) holds in such a logic, but not in the Hamiltonian system, again owing to cases where $[\![G]\!] \subset [\![F]\!]$. In such cases, Hamilton makes SOME F is G true but SOME G is F false, while a logic that straightforwardly translates PNST–5 of Section 3.2.2 into SOME makes both false. A logic where both I ≡ I* and I ≡ I! hold is inconsistent.

Examples (3.14) and (3.15) quoted above show that natural intuition supports Hamilton and BNPC and rejects a symmetrical SOME (I ≡ I!). Does this mean that AAPC and ABPC are already somewhat counterintuitive, because in these systems the equivalence I ≡ I! holds, owing to the fact that they count SOME F is G as true when $[\![F]\!] \subseteq [\![G]\!]$? Curiously, and despite cases like (3.14) and (3.15), symmetrical SOME is likewise supported by intuition. When I say that some children are male, you will agree that, therefore, some males are children, and when I say that some males are children, you will agree that, therefore, some children are male, so that the two-way entailment relation makes them seem equivalent. Apparently, the intuitive judgements are influenced by world knowledge. We know that orphans are a proper subclass of the class of children, which makes it possible for us to say naturally that some children are orphans. But we also know that the class of children M-partially intersects with the class of males and also with the class of females, while it properly includes the class of orphans, as in the diagram of Figure 3.12.

It thus seems that, given a constellation like that in Figure 3.12, (3.16a,b,c) are naturally said in truth, but (3.16d) is not:

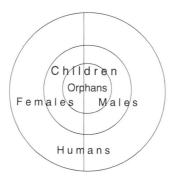

FIGURE 3.12 The set-theoretic relations of children, (human) males, (human) females, and (human) orphans

(3.16)   a. √ Some children are male (female).
         b. √ Some children are orphans.
         c. √ Some males (females) are children (orphans).
         d. ! Some orphans are children.

Yet both AAPC and ABPC, in so far as they can lay claim to naturalness, tell us we should be able to say (3.16d) naturally in truth. Therefore, if we really want to gauge natural intuitions and express them in a logical system, we should hold on to BNPC, which does justice to all the intuitions of (3.16). AAPC and ABPC can thus be said to support natural intuitions less strongly than BNPC, because they allow for (3.16d), which is excluded by intuition.

3.4.3 *Basic-natural propositional logic*

Is there an analog in propositional logic to the basic-natural system of quantification? To a large extent there is, but there are also differences. We recall from Figure 3.1 that, unlike the quantifiers, which express either relations between sets of objects or, in the cognitive mood, distributive assignments of properties to members of a set, the propositional operators are functions mapping n–tuples of VSs on VSs. They become predicates when predicated of the actual situation sit_{act}, as shown in (2.6a–c) in Section 2.3.4 and in (3.17)–(3.18) below.

NEGATION is not immediately problematic (though, when taken in all its aspects, it is perhaps the most complex of all the functions). For now, we adopt the standard definition (2.6a) of Section 2.3.4:

(3.17) $[\![\neg]\!] = \{ P \mid sit_{act} \in /\overline{P}/\}$
         (the extension of $\neg$ is the set of all L-propositions P such that the
         actual situation sit_{act} is a member of the complement of $/P/$)

CONJUNCTION ($\wedge^{BN}$) maps onto the BN-intersection of the VSs of the argument L-propositions, as defined in (3.18a), adapted from (2.6b) in Section 2.3.4 (P^+ stands for any number of semantically compatible L-propositions).

As regards DISJUNCTION (v^{BN}), the situation is more complex. We take the linguistic disjunction operator OR to map onto the BN-union of the VSs of the argument L-propositions, as defined in (3.18b), adapted from (2.6c) in Section 2.3.4:

(3.18)   a. $[\![\wedge^{BN}]\!] = \{ P^+ \mid sit_{act} \in \bigcap_{/P/+} {}^{BN}\}$
         (the extension of $\wedge$ is the set of all sets of two or more L-
         propositions P, such that sit_{act} is a member of the BN-intersection
         of all $/ P/^+$)

b. $[\![\vee^{\mathrm{BN}}]\!] = \{\, \mathbf{P}^{+} \mid sit_{act} \in \overset{\cup}{/\mathbf{P}/+}{}^{\mathrm{BN}}\}$

(the extension of $\vee$ is the set of all sets of two or more L-propositions **P**, such that sit_{act} is a member of the BN-union of all $/\mathbf{P}/^{+}$)

The difference with (2.6b) in Section 2.3.4 is that the argument L-propositions cannot be necessarily true or necessarily false (the VSs would equal **U** and Ø, respectively). Moreover, the conjunction as a whole cannot be necessarily true or necessarily false either. The fulfilment of this latter condition is ensured by the stipulation (PNST–5) that the VSs of the L-propositions involved must M-partially intersect. This ensures, first, that there is at least a chance of all the L-propositions united under conjunction to be true simultaneously. For if the VSs do not intersect, there is no possible situation in which the two L-propositions are both true, which makes them contraries and their conjunction necessarily false. Since AND is the standard discourse-increment function, this condition is, in fact, the same as the condition on any new increment to a discourse domain, discussed in the Sections 7.3.1 and 8.2.1, that it be compatible with all earlier increments, to avoid a reduction of the discourse domain's VS to zero.

Secondly, M-partial intersection ensures that, given the L-propositions **P** and **Q**, /**P**/ does not include /**Q**/ or vice versa, which would make the conjunction necessarily true. The basic-natural semantics of AND thus selects the M-partial intersection in the basic-natural intersection relation in Figure 3.3b, which is, therefore, defined only for L-propositions that neither include nor exclude each other in virtue of their meaning.

L-propositions made up with AND are classified as type **AND** (conjunction); those with OR as type **OR** (disjunction); those made up with NEITHER . . . NOR as type **NOR** (exjunction). **AND** thus says that the actual situation sit_{act} is an element in the intersection of /**P**/ and /**Q**/ of Figure 3.13.

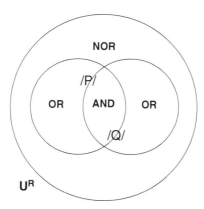

FIGURE 3.13 VSs for logically independent **P** and **Q** and their logical compositions

As regards the sentence type **OR** ($\vee^{BN}$), the situation is more complex. We take the linguistic disjunction operator OR to map onto the BN-union of the VSs of the argument L-propositions, as defined in (3.18b) above. Under the restrictions imposed on union by the criteria of basic naturalness, the component VSs must not only be natural sets (neither $\emptyset$ nor **OBJ**), but, according to PNST–3, they must also be totally distinct—that is, without any intersection. However, natural language OR cannot be restricted to contrary argument L-propositions: in a disjunction of the form P OR Q, P and Q must be allowed to be logically independent, so that their VSs, /P/ and /Q/, actually intersect, as in Figure 3.13. A sentence like (3.19), for example, is perfectly normal even though it is *possible* for both disjuncts to be true at the same time:

(3.19)   He either eavesdropped or he went through your papers.

To satisfy PNST–3, it is, therefore, necessary to reformulate P OR Q for the purpose of linguistic interpretation at the level of basic naturalness in such a way as to ensure that the two or more arguments of the union function are totally distinct.

This can be done by considering P OR Q to be tacitly understood as:

(3.20)   P OR (NOT-P AND Q); formally: $P \vee (\neg P \wedge Q)$

Sentence (3.19) is then interpreted as 'He either eavesdropped or he did not eavesdrop and/but went through your papers'. Now the two disjuncts have totally distinct VSs, which, therefore, allow for the basic-natural union operation, even in cases such as (3.19) where the VSs of the disjuncts M-partially intersect on account of their being semantically independent.

The tacit understanding as formulated in (3.20) has the advantage of accounting for the unnaturalness of a disjunction where one disjunct entails the other as in:

(3.21)   !The man is dead or he has been killed.

If this is tacitly understood as 'either the man is dead or the man is not dead and he has been killed', then the second disjunct is necessarily false owing to the contrariety of 'the man is not dead' and 'he has been killed'.

The tacit reading of (3.20) also accounts for the otherwise problematic anaphora (donkey anaphora) in sentences like (3.22), again discussed in Section 8.2.2:

(3.22)   There is no letterbox in this street or **it** is well hidden.

According to the book, the anaphoric *it* in the second disjunct should not be possible as it appears to lack an antecedent. Yet when read according to

(3.20)—as 'there is no letterbox in this street or there is one and it is well hidden'—there is no problem in this regard, because the second disjunct provides the antecedent, albeit a tacit one.

The disadvantage of (3.20), however, is that it still fails to guarantee that the two or more arguments of the OR-function are mutually exclusive for semantic—that is, analytical—reasons, since the truth of the one disjunct P is still sufficient for the truth of the whole disjunction $P \vee (\neg P \wedge Q)$. As a result, type-**AND** L-propositions still entail type-**OR** L-propositions, which must be avoided in basic-natural propositional logic. One might, therefore, think of a more drastic reformulation which makes OR truly exclusive with regard to its two or more disjuncts. This can be done if one regards P OR Q to be tacitly understood as (3.23), which is not equivalent with standard $P \vee Q$:

(3.23)   (P AND NOT-Q) OR (NOT-P AND Q); formally: $(P \wedge \neg Q) \vee (\neg P \wedge Q)$

This, however, has the disadvantage of going against the book, as it seems to fail to account for (3.22): a reading like 'there is no letterbox in this street and *it* is not well hidden, or there is one and it is well hidden' appears to leave the first occurrence of *it* without a proper antecedent. This obstacle, however, is removed when the negation in *it is not well hidden* is treated as the metalinguistic radical presupposition-cancelling NOT discussed and defined in Chapter 10. On that reading, the problematic *it* refers to an intensional object and thus needs the radical NOT to achieve truth. The disjunction operator OR now selects the union of /P/ and /Q/ in Figure 3.9, minus their intersection.

This appears to account for the intuition that natural language OR is exclusive, excluding cases where both P and Q are true. At the same time, as is shown in Section 9.2.4, it accounts for a number of clashes between intuitive judgements regarding conditionals (sentences of the form if P then Q) and their standard logical analysis in terms of material implication.

But how does this work out for the logic? In the reading (3.23), /**AND**/ and /**OR**/ are mutually exclusive and together form standard /**OR**/. The only space not covered in U^R is the restricted complement of standard /**OR**/—that is, /$\overline{OR}$/^{R}—normally denoted by the linguistic operator *neither a . . . nor b*, also realized as *not . . . (either) a or b* and here called **NOR** (exjunction).[17] One notes that **NOR** cannot be the negation of the exclusive **OR** of this system, since the

---

[17] In Seuren (1974) it is argued that an L-propositional structure of type **AND*** (AND [¬P, ¬Q]) is grammatically transformed into **NOR** (NEITHER P NOR Q) by the rule of NEGATIVE RAISING. Likewise, ALL F is NOT G is taken to be transformed into NO F is G. This conforms to the basic-natural propositional and predicate logic as proposed here and shown in Figure 3.10.

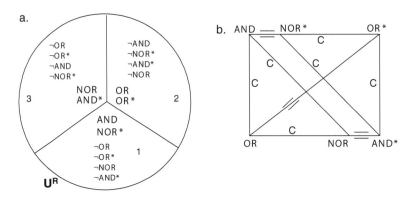

FIGURE 3.14 Basic-natural analog for propositional logic with NOR ≠ ¬OR

complement of /**OR**/, /$\overline{\text{OR}}$/$^\text{R}$, comprises /**AND**/, and *neither* P *nor* Q clearly means NOT-P AND NOT-Q, excluding P AND Q. Therefore, just as English *no* does not correspond to basic-natural NOT-SOME but constitutes a separate quantifier in BNPC, English *nor* does not correspond to basic natural NOT-OR but constitutes a separate sentence-type, which may be called EXJUNCTION, in the NST-constrained system of propositional logic. Consequently, **NOR** is equivalent, in this system, with **AND*** (within **U**$^\text{R}$), as shown in Figure 3.14. (One remembers from Section 2.4.2 that the internal negation for the propositional operators AND and OR distributes over the component L-propositions. Thus, **AND*** stands for ¬P ∧ ¬Q ∧ ... and **OR*** stands for ¬P ∨ ¬Q ∨ ....)

NOR*, ¬**NOR**, and ¬**NOR*** may be taken to be undefined at the level of basic naturalness, due to PNST–6 (the mind baulks at repeated applications of the complement function). As before, however, they are still taken into account in Figure 3.14, because we need to know the ultimate logical consequences of the system.

Empirical evidence for this analysis is derived, for example, from the fact that a sentence like (3.24a) is naturally and immediately interpreted as (3.24b), whereas (3.25a) is not at all naturally and immediately interpreted as (3.25b), even though, from a standard logical point of view, both (3.24) and (3.25) merely instantiate De Morgan's laws. This is a fact on which neither the Gricean maxims, nor indeed the whole of pragmatics, have anything to say:

(3.24) a. He doesn't like planes or trains.
　　　 b. He doesn't like planes and he doesn't like trains.

(3.25) a. He doesn't like planes and trains.
　　　 b. He doesn't like planes or he doesn't like trains.

Given the analysis presented above, one now sees why this should be so. Consider *not... planes or trains* in (3.24a) to be an instance of basic-natural **NOR**: 'He neither likes planes nor does he like trains'. Figure 3.14 shows that, in this reading, **NOR** is equivalent to **AND***, both sharing the same VS. By contrast, *not ... planes and trains* in (3.25a) realizes ¬**AND**, the restricted negation of AND: 'It is not so that he likes planes and he likes trains'. The VS of ¬**AND** comprises the combined VSs of **NOR** (≡ **AND***) and **OR** (≡ **OR***). Since in basic-natural propositional logic, ¬**AND** is not equivalent with **OR***, the transition from (3.25a) to (3.25b) is a matter of strict-natural or standard modern logic and thus requires a more complex computation at a higher level of achievement.

There is, however, again the problem of consistency through discourse. As has been widely observed, **OR** is typically used in situations where the speaker is uncertain as to which of the disjuncts provides the correct answer to the question he or she is entertaining but where the speaker has concluded that either disjunct will do as a good enough answer. This conclusion is naturally expressed by the auxiliary of epistemic necessity *must*. A speaker may say (3.26b), in response to the question (3.26a):

(3.26)   a. How did the journalist know?
         b. The journalist must have spoken to Ann or to Jeremy.

If it were then found out that the journalist had spoken to both Ann and Jeremy, it would be incorrect to say that the person who uttered (3.26b) had been wrong, even if that speaker had failed to think of the possibility that the journalist had spoken to both Ann and Jeremy.

Therefore, in parallel with the basic-natural system of quantification, consistency through discourse requires an entailment from **AND** to **OR**. This time it was the Stoic philosophers who, roughly a century after Aristotle, discovered this fact and upgraded the natural propositional logic of language and cognition to full consistency through discourse by introducing the

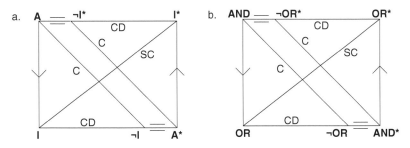

FIGURE 3.15 The strict-natural Squares for predicate and propositional logic

entailment from **AND** to **OR**, thereby creating the inclusive OR of standard propositional calculus.

The introduction of the parallel entailment schemata **A** ⊢ **I** and **AND** ⊢ **OR** has thus brought about a complete parallelism of the two strict-natural systems of predicate and propositional logic. The former results in strict-natural predicate calculus, which is identical with the traditional Square of Opposition and is shown in Figure 3.15a. The latter results in strict-natural propositional calculus, which is isomorphic with standard propositional calculus and is shown in Figure 3.15b.

3.5 Neither *nand* nor *nall*: NST predicts their absence

3.5.1 *The problem and the solution proposed by pragmaticists*

We have reached a point where a question can be discussed which has recently attracted some attention. After it had been observed by Thomas Aquinas (see Horn 1989: 253; Jaspers 2005: 1), it was again observed more recently (Zwicky 1973; Horn 1972, 1989: 252–67; Levinson 2000: 69–71) that while a large majority of languages have what is taken to be a single-morpheme expression for NOT-SOME (such as English *no*), a single-morpheme expression, say *nall*, for the complex negative predicate NOT-ALL or its presumed equivalent SOME-NOT has not so far been attested. Analogously, while many languages have a lexeme for NOT (P OR Q) or equivalently NOT-P AND NOT-Q (English *neither... nor*), a lexeme corresponding to *nand*, for NOT (P AND Q), or equivalently NOT-P OR NOT-Q, is thought to be either nonexistent or at most extremely rare.

One must, however, be careful. Is it indeed so that *nand* and *nall* represent systematic gaps in the lexicons of the world's languages? It does not look as if Horn or others who have presented this problem have made a systematic inquiry in this respect, although there are reasons for doubting the universality of these lexical gaps. The Tamil specialist Eric Pederson, for example, has informed me that Tamil does have a single lexeme meaning 'not and' or 'either one of the two or none'. And Aimable-André Dufatanye, who is a native speaker of Kenya-Rwanda and a near-native speaker of Kirundi (both African languages of the Bantu group), tells me that in his language(s) there are fully lexicalized lexemes for 'not-all'. Thus, he gave me the forms (subject to the nominal classification system in the language) *sibose* ('not all people'), *sihose* ('not everywhere'), *siyose* ('not the whole house'), *sizose* ('not all houses'), as opposed to *ntanzu* ('no house'), *nta muntu* ('no person'), and so on. It is, therefore, far from certain that the lexical gaps in question are universal. Whether they occur in a significant majority of languages and, if so, whether they are systematic in the languages in which they occur, is yet to be established.

If there is indeed a systematic absence of equivalents of *nall and *nand in the languages of the world, such a gap appears to be matched by similar gaps in other lexical fields. Thus, it is said, whereas one finds lexicalized equivalents of epistemic NOT-POSSIBLE, lexicalizations of epistemic NOT-NECESSARY are found nowhere (lexicalized agentive NOT-NECESSARY, such as English *unnecessary* is widely attested). Likewise, NOT-CAUSE is never lexicalized, while NOT-ALLOW is frequently found in lexicalizations such as *disallow, forbid*, or *prohibit*. Typically, predicates like NECESSARY or CAUSE show semantic characteristics that may lead one to think that they can or should be classified along with ALL and AND: they all belong to an 'all-yes' section of the lexicon, while POSSIBLE and ALLOW typically belong to the group of 'perhaps-yes-perhaps-no' predicates, which also comprises the existential quantifier and the propositional connective **OR**. The question is: are these similarities reducible to a single principle and if so, what is it? This question is interesting as it forces one to probe natural set theory in both the logic and the lexicalization processes of natural language.

Horn, Levinson, and others seek an answer in the pragmatics of language use. Restricting themselves to *nand and *nall, they argue, in essence, as follows. Since OR is normally exclusive for pragmatic reasons and pragmatically equivalent to OR-NOT, excluding the case that both argument propositions are true, there appears to be no need left for an item like *nand which excludes the simultaneous truth of both argument propositions and may be taken to imply pragmatically that at least one of the argument propositions is true. Then, given the pragmatic equivalence of *or* and *nand, the item without the incorporated negation—that is, *or*—would be preferred on grounds of simplicity in the lexicon, so that *nand is ruled out. Similarly, since SOME, SOME-NOT, and NOT-ALL are pragmatically equivalent, conveying the intended meaning 'some but not all', it is assumed that there is no need left for a lexicalized form like *nall meaning 'not-all', which is somehow, either logically or pragmatically, equivalent to SOME-NOT and hence to SOME. Since the pragmatically equivalent but cognitively and semantically simpler operators *or* and *some* are already available, there is no need for surface lexicalizations like *nand or *nall (Levinson 2000: 70). Therefore, the lexicalized expressions *all, some*, and *no* will do for the quantifiers, and *and, or*, and *neither . . . nor* for the propositional operators.

This reasoning can be summarized as follows:

(a) The English quantifier word *no* and its equivalents in other languages are lexicalizations of underlying NOT-SOME. Analogously, *neither . . . nor* stands for NOT-OR.

(b) Lexicalizations take place at a Gricean-pragmatic level of processing.

(c) At that level, SOME-NOT is equivalent with SOME, both implying NOT-ALL, and OR-NOT [i.e. NOT-P OR NOT-Q] is equivalent with (exclusive) OR, both implying NOT-AND.

(d) Since SOME-NOT is also, if not logically in any case pragmatically, equivalent with NOT-ALL, and OR-NOT with NOT-AND, it follows that NOT-ALL and NOT-AND are, at the Gricean-pragmatic level of processing, equivalent with SOME and OR, respectively.

(e) Given the lesser semantic complexity of SOME vis-à-vis SOME-NOT and NOT-ALL, and given the lesser semantic complexity of OR vis-à-vis OR-NOT and NOT-AND, it is SOME and OR that are the preferred candidates for lexicalization.

For the authors who propose this explanation such a system is not a logical system but represents the way listeners construct a quantified mental model of a state of affairs described, on the presumption that the speaker has full and adequate knowledge of that state of affairs and has the intention to be as informative and helpful as possible—that is, that speakers will commit themselves to the maximum of what they know. The main criterion of such a system is not truth but information value on the presumption of full cooperativity and complete knowledge. It is not meant for the computation of solid entailments grounded in strictly semantic properties, but for practical inferences. To say that two expressions are pragmatically equivalent then amounts to saying that they have the same information value on the presumption specified.

3.5.2 *Preliminary objections*

The question is, however, whether one may justifiably posit that linguistic lexicalizations depend on 'information value on the presumption of full cooperativity and complete knowledge'. It would seem that such a position is unwarranted, since the use of language is not restricted to authoritative and maximally cooperative reporting on states of affairs fully known to the speaker. For one thing, as has been said, reporting often consists in informing the listener of what has been found out so far. When inspecting a population of children, a reporter may say that so far no, or so far some, or so far all, children have proved to be undernourished, without any commitment as to what is still to be found out. This point was made by Hoeksema, who first asks (Hoeksema 1999: 4) 'If *nall* is not needed, due to the presence of *some*, then why is *not all* used at all? ' and then observes (Hoeksema 1999: 5):

In contexts where the speaker has only partial knowledge, there is not even pragmatic equivalence. If I say that some of my students are gay, one should not infer immediately that not all my students are gay. Perhaps I am unaware of the sexual preferences of the remainder. But if **I** and **O** are often not even pragmatically equivalent, because the conditions for the Gricean implicatures are not met, then why should **O** be superfluous?

Since any cognitive theory of linguistic interpretation depends primarily on pre-existing linguistic meanings, rather than on a presumption of full co-operativity and complete knowledge, it would seem that the pragmatics answer is not satisfactory on its own terms.

Moreover, as is argued in Chapter 4 of Volume I, speech is not primarily meant to be a form of reporting or information transfer but consists, in principle, in taking a socially binding position with respect to a given proposition. Speaking consists primarily in vouching for truth, or in making a suggestion or a request, issuing an order, asking a question, uttering a wish, and so on, all with respect to the proposition expressed. The issue, therefore, is not what factual information is provided by the speaker but what the speaker commits himself or herself to.

3.5.3 *The main objection and a stronger solution*

But there is a more decisive argument, related to point (a) in the Horn-Levinson analysis and, one fears, destroying it. Throughout their analysis, Horn and Levinson take it for granted that the surface quantifier *no* stands for, or is a lexicalization of, NOT-SOME and that *neither . . . nor* lexicalizes NOT-OR. But that is far from obvious. As has been shown, BNPC is tenable only if it is assumed that *no* does not stand for NOT-SOME but is a quantifier—the quantifier NO—in its own right. And analogously for *neither . . . nor* and NOT-OR. One may, of course, posit a pragmatic equivalence of NO with NOT-SOME (cutting out the ALL option), and of NOR with NOT-OR (cutting out the AND option), but it is not clear what pragmatic principle would be strong enough to underwrite such an equivalence. Of course, the equivalence holds in standard predicate and propositional logic, which may explain why one is so easily led into accepting that it also holds at a basic-natural cognitive level, but it is not to be found at that level, owing to the fact that, at that level, SOME entails both NOT-ALL and NOT-NO but is not equivalent with either of them. And analogously for OR, which entails both NOT-AND and NOT-NOR but is not equivalent with either of them.

We have no problem with the principle that, by and large, lexicalizations take place at a basic-natural level, be it pragmatic or cognitive in a more formal sense—though, as is shown below, lexicalizations involving double negation also occur, no doubt created at a more advanced level of cultural development. But the point is that, at the basic-natural level, *no* is not a lexicalization of NOT-SOME—to stay with predicate logic. If anything, *no* incorporates *any*, not SOME, but we don't really know what *any* amounts to.[18] In many languages, including English, (the equivalent of) *no*, which lexicalizes the natural set-theoretic relation of mutual exclusion, clearly does contain an incorporated negation, but not in combination with a quantifier of the same logical system. Latin *nullus*, for example, is a combination of the negation word *ne* and *unulus*, the diminutive of *unus* (one), like the Dutch expression *niet eentje* ('not a little one'). Greek *oudeis* (nobody) is literally 'not one' and so on. Such lexicalizations all deny the presence of even the smallest common element in the two sets involved, $[\![F]\!]$ and $[\![G]\!]$. It is merely accidental that this coincides with the negation of existentially quantified L-propositions—that is, with $\neg I$—in both traditional and standard modern predicate calculus. English *no* and its equivalents in many other languages thus appear not to lexicalize the meaning NOT-SOME but, rather, the absence of even the smallest common element in the two sets at issue—both linguistically and psychologically a plausible form of lexicalization, which, moreover, lends itself to being incorporated into a variety of sound predicate-logic systems. An analogous analysis applies to propositional logic.[19]

Horn (1989) recognizes that his pragmatic system reflects the Hamilton/ Jespersen predicate logic, but fails to mention that in that logic NO does not stand for NOT-SOME, and analogously for NOR, which does not stand for NOT-OR, NO and NOR being operators in their own right. Yet if the negation is considered to be a complement selector, there is no way one can combine the thesis that SOME excludes ALL with the thesis that NO equals NOT-SOME. And if the negation is not taken to be a complement selector, it is incumbent on the pragmaticist authors in question to provide a proper definition of negation, since in that case it is unclear what negation is or does.

There are thus, at the level of naturalness at which lexicalizations are deemed to take place, no single-morpheme expressions for NOT-SOME and NOT-OR. This, in effect, takes the bottom out of the question of why lexicalizations for NOT-ALL and NOT-AND are systematically absent, as it arose in the first

---

[18] English *fuck all* stands for ALL-NOT, which is equivalent to NO in BNPC as Figure 3.7 shows.

[19] In Seuren (2002) it is observed that both in traditional predicate logic and in propositional logic no key role is reserved for vertices named $\neg A$ or $\neg AND$, which is presented as an explanation for the systematic absence of lexicalizations like **nand* or **nall*. The present analysis shows that this conclusion was premature. See Jaspers (2005) for ample comment.

place because NOT-SOME and NOT-OR were thought to lack counterparts for ALL and AND, respectively. In fact, however, given the lack of single-morpheme lexicalizations for NOT-SOME and NOT-OR, NST predicts the absence of such lexicalizations for NOT-ALL and NOT-AND, which in turn, if that absence proves real, is valuable confirmation for the correctness of our reconstruction of basic-natural logic.

The real question is not why *no* and *neither . . . nor* have no corresponding counterparts **nall* and **nand* but, rather, why NOT does not merge with either SOME or ALL (or with either OR or AND), though it does occasionally merge with NO, which, with its double negation, is a mild infringement of point (b) in the Horn-Levinson analysis (lexicalizations of NOT-NOR do not seem to occur).

The answer may well be found in the consideration that mergers of the form NOT-SOME or NOT-ALL would unite incompatibles. As has been said, NOT-SOME would cover both ALL and NO, which will never form a natural cognitive unit. The same goes for NOT-ALL, which would cover both SOME and NO, again a very unlikely candidate for lexicalization. Only NOT-NO, which covers both SOME and ALL, would seem to form an acceptable natural cognitive unit encompassing the semantic field 'some, perhaps all'. And indeed, lexicalizations of NOT-NO, usually in the stylistic form of an idiomatized understatement (litotes), are, though not frequent, not too hard to come by. As mentioned by Horn, Latin has a number of instances (see also Jespersen 1917: 90): *nonnemo* 'not-nobody → several persons', *nonnulli* 'not-none → several', *nonnihil* 'not-nothing → a considerable amount', *nonnumquam* 'not never → quite often', *nonnusquam* 'not nowhere → in several places'. Dutch has *niet-niks* 'not-nothing → quite something'. Semi-lexicalizations for 'not-without → with a notable amount of' are frequently found. A careful search will no doubt yield a significant number of examples of this nature in various languages.

3.5.4 *Parallel lexical gaps in epistemic-modal and causal logic?*

A word must be said here about the presumed analogous gaps in the lexicalizations of epistemic modal logic and the logic of causality. As regards epistemic modal logic, observations have been made to the effect that there is an epistemic-modal lexicalization *impossible* but not *unnecessary*, though *unnecessary* is, of course, a current predicate in nonepistemic contexts. Likewise, it has been observed that NOT-ALLOW is frequently lexicalized in forms such as *disallow, forbid, keep from, prohibit*, whereas NOT-CAUSE does not seem to be lexicalized ever.

Given these observations, one may object that the solution proposed for predicate calculus lexicalizations, which is based on the fact that in basic-natural logic *no* does not stand for NOT-SOME but is a quantifier in its own right, contrarily opposed to SOME and ALL, does not apply in epistemic modal or in causal logic, because it can hardly be denied that *impossible* is a lexicalization of NOT-POSSIBLE, or that *disallow* stands for NOT-ALLOW.

To this objection I reply that although *impossible* is, of course, a lexicalization of NOT-POSSIBLE, the predicate POSSIBLE in question does not belong to epistemic modal logic. *Impossible* has incorporated the predicate POSSIBLE in a variety of its senses, but not in the modal-epistemic sense of 'it may be true that . . .'. The Oxford English Dictionary (OED) gives the following two main senses for *possible*, the second of which clearly comprises epistemic possibility:

1. That may be (i.e. is capable of being); that may or can exist, be done, or happen (in general, or in given or assumed conditions or circumstances); that is in one's power, that one can do, exert, use, etc.
2. That may be (i.e. is not known not to be); that is perhaps true or a fact, that perhaps exists.) (Expressing contingency, or an idea in the speaker's mind, not power or capability of existing, as in 1; hence sometimes nearly = credible, thinkable.)

But for *impossible* the OED merely gives the negation of *possible* 1, not of *possible* 2:

1. Not possible; that cannot be done or effected; that cannot exist or come into being; that cannot be, in existing or specified circumstances.

That is, the OED describes *impossible* as occurring only as the negative counterpart of *possible* in the main sense 1, not in the main sense given under 2. There is, in other words, no negated counterpart of sense 2 of *possible*. *Impossible* is naturally used in phrases like *an impossible task, an impossible construction, an impossible person*, even *an impossible truth*, and also in, for example, *It is impossible to clear up that mess* or *It is impossible for the man to climb the stairs*, but never with a *that*-clause in the sense of 'it cannot be true that . . .'. A sentence like *It is impossible that he is right* strikes one as deviant.[20]

---

[20] I hesitate about the litotes *not impossible*, as in *It is not impossible that he is right*, which sounds a great deal better than *It is impossible that he is right*. Also, as was pointed out by Isidora Stojanovic, people often react to a piece of new information by saying *That's impossible*, meaning 'That can't be true'. It seems obvious that much still remains to be sorted out in this area.

Moreover, whereas the adverbial clausal modifier *possibly* normally occurs in an epistemic sense, as in (3.27a), its negative counterpart *impossibly* cannot occur in that sense, as one sees from the ungrammatical (3.27b). The proper negation of (3.27a) is (3.27c), with epistemic *can't* as the proper negation of epistemic *may* but idiomatically combined, probably for reasons of functional emphasis, with an otherwise superfluous *possibly*:

(3.27) a. The man had possibly eaten too much.
         b. *The man had impossibly eaten too much.
         c. The man can't possibly have eaten too much.

It seems, therefore, that there is no lexicalization of NOT-POSSIBLE in a postulated basic-natural epistemic modal logic ('POSSIBLE' stands, of course, for the 'exclusive' possibility operator, which excludes NECESSARY). Worse, there does not seem to be a basic-natural epistemic modal logic, because if there was one, one would expect to find a lexical analog of basic-natural *no*, something like *no way*, meaning 'neither POSSIBLE nor NECESSARY', but no convincing analog exists, now that *impossible* has been discarded. Logically sound modal thinking is probably a product of at least some degree of civilization and the concomitant cognitive development and would thus not form a logical system at a basic-natural level, but only at a strict-natural level, at which NECESSARY(**P**) entails POSSIBLE(**P**) and does not exclude it, as it would do at a basic-natural level. In such a logic, NOT-POSSIBLE will do, without further lexicalization.

As regards the logic of causality, one observes that the predicate *disallow*, unlike *forbid*, *keep from*, or *prohibit*, is the only predicate that is transparently derived from a negation plus *allow*. But *disallow*, together with *forbid*, denotes an injunction not to DO something, not a causal blocking that keeps an event from HAPPENING. *Disallow* and *forbid* belong to the semantic paradigm of permission, not to that of causality. Interestingly, *keep from* and *prohibit* may be used in a strictly causal sense, but they are not demonstrably composed of a negation plus a predicate of causal possibility. This is interesting because we see a parallel here between causal *allow* and epistemic *possible*.

In other words, if there are analogies between the lexicalizations in predicate and propositional logic on the one hand and those in epistemic modal logic and the logic of causality on the other, they follow the pattern predicted by the analysis presented here, and not the pattern based on the assumption that the negative existential quantifier *no* is to be analysed as NOT-SOME.

4

Logical power, Abelard, and empirical success rates

4.1 Aristotelian predicate calculus rescued from undue existential import

As one can see from Figure 3.15 in the preceding chapter, standard propositional calculus and traditional Aristotelian-Boethian predicate calculus (ABPC) run completely parallel and thus have the same logical power. As long as $[\![F]\!] \neq \emptyset$, there is a complete parallelism between, on the one hand, the universal quantifier and conjunction and, on the other, between the existential quantifier and disjunction. This analogy has not passed unnoticed in logical circles. It has often been observed that the universal and existential quantifiers correspond to the conjunction and disjunction operators, respectively: if $\forall x(G(x),F(x))$ is true, then, for all $a_1, a_2, a_3, \ldots a_n \in [\![F]\!]$, $G(a_1) \wedge G(a_2) \wedge G(a_3) \wedge \ldots \wedge G(a_n)$ is likewise true. Analogously, if $\exists x(G(x),F(x))$ is true, then $G(a_1) \vee G(a_2) \vee G(a_3) \vee \ldots \vee G(a_n)$ is also true. In relation to this, the Conversions of predicate calculus are analogous to De Morgan's laws in propositional calculus. Except when $[\![F]\!] = \emptyset$, because then there simply is no conjunction or disjunction. It is for this reason that this analogy has never been elaborated in the existing formalizations of the quantifiers.[1] In Sections 4.2.4 and 4.3, however, it is shown that this analogy can, within the context of a strictly extensional logic, be saved to a considerable extent, even for cases where $[\![F]\!] = \emptyset$. But then the Conversions of predicate logic must be sacrificed: they must be weakened to e-way entailments.

The entailment schemata of propositional calculus thus correspond to those of ABPC, but not to those of its twentieth-century successor STANDARD MODERN PREDICATE CALCULUS (SMPC). This in itself would not be of much

---

[1] Yet the analogy between the universal quantifier and the propositional operator $\wedge$ on the one hand, and between the existential quantifier and $\vee$ on the other, was expressed in the symbol 'Λ' for the universal quantifier and the symbol 'V' for the existential quantifier in the so-called 'Californian' notation, which was much used during the 1960s and 1970s but eventually had to yield to what is now the standard notation.

concern, were it not that ABPC, just like propositional calculus, has maximal logical power, whereas SMPC, as is shown in Section 4.2.3, sees its logical power dramatically reduced when compared with ABPC. The loss of logical power in SMPC is due to the fact that SMPC has given up the subaltern entailment schema **A** ⊢ **I** (*All F is G* entails *Some F is G*), which is considered valid in ABPC, just as **AND** ⊢ **OR**, the analog in propositional calculus, is valid in propositional calculus. Logicians, who like the idea that SMPC is the ultimate *ne plus ultra* of predicate calculus, have never been very vocal as regards this dramatic loss of logical power, but there is no denying that it is there. Moreover, as is shown in Chapter 6, the logical power of ABPC turns out to be highly functional for the transmission of quantified information. Therefore, if ABPC can be saved for natural language, our respect for this logic will be considerably enhanced (many philosophers of language who dare not doubt the inviolability of SMPC still look back to ABPC with nostalgia).

The situation as it is creates a dilemma in that SMPC is logically sound but has bought its health at great cost, whereas avoiding that cost seems to mean a faulty logic. It is time now to spell out the question in greater detail.

The reason why ABPC was replaced with SMPC in the wake of scholars like Frege and Russell about a century ago lies in the fact that ABPC, as it stands, suffers from what is known as UNDUE EXISTENTIAL IMPORT (UEI). By this is meant the fact that ABPC only functions when $[\![F]\!]$, the extension of the predicate F in the standard sentential schema used for predicate logic, is nonnull—that is, when, in the world as it is, $[\![F]\!]$ contains at least one actually existing object properly characterized by the predicate F. This is unbearable to a logician, because logic is meant to be based on meanings only, not on contingencies in the world. When ABPC is applied to a situation where $[\![F]\!] = \varnothing$, then, given that it is based on a strictly extensional ontology of actually existing objects only, just as SMPC does, an inconsistency arises under universal quantification. Consider the sentences (4.1a) and (4.1b), whose universally quantified subject terms contain a predicate expression $[\![F]\!]$ with a null extension, either because of the contingent conditions of the world, as with the predicate *be a dodo* (the dodo became extinct around the year 1700), or because of a semantic inconsistency, as with the predicate *be living dead*. The question is whether sentences like (4.1a) or (4.1b) are true or false in the actual world:

(4.1) a. All dodoes are in good health.
       b. All living dead are in good health.

If they are true, it follows in ABPC (by the subaltern entailment schema) that their existential counterparts should also be true:

(4.2)   a. Some dodoes are in good health.
        b. Some living dead are in good health.

The sentences of (4.2), however, entail, by the entailment schema of EXISTENTIAL IMPORT, that there is at least one actually existing dodo and at least one actually existing entity that is dead while being alive, neither of which is the case.

In ABPC, SMPC and other varieties of predicate logic, existential import is semantically induced by the existential quantifier (SOME), which requires that there be a nonnull intersection of $[\![F]\!]$ and $[\![G]\!]$. In a strictly extensional ontology, this means the actual existence of at least one element in the intersection. Since this condition is not fulfilled in (4.1a,b), these sentences cannot be true. But if they are false, then their negations (4.3a) and (4.3b), respectively, should be true:

(4.3)   a. Not all dodoes are in good health.
        b. Not all living dead are in good health.

Now, however, the problem appears again, because, owing to the duality relation between the universal and the existential quantifiers (the Conversions), (4.3a,b) are equivalent to (4.4a,b), respectively:

(4.4)   a. Some dodoes are not in good health.
        b. Some living dead are not in good health.

And here, existential import rears its head again, as (4.4a,b) entail again that there is at least one actually existing dodo and at least one actually existing entity that is dead while being alive, respectively—*quod non*. Therefore, (4.1a,b) cannot be false either. And since ABPC does not allow for any value but true or false and does not allow for the absence of a truth value, ABPC appears to be in trouble.

More technically minded readers may wish to see a more formal definition of undue existential import. All right then, here are two possible definitions:

> A system of predicate logic suffers from UNDUE EXISTENTIAL IMPORT when every admissible expression in the system entails a proposition of the type **I** or **I***—that is, entails the existence of at least one entity of the **F**-class quantified over.
> Alternatively, a system of predicate logic suffers from UNDUE EXISTENTIAL IMPORT when there is a proposition or proposition type **T** such that both **T** and ¬**T** entail a nonnecessary (contingent) proposition of the type **I** or **I***, which makes **I** or **I***, as the case may be, a necessary truth.

Figure 4.5c shows that this is indeed the case in ABPC. To solve this problem, something must be done. The solution embodied in Russellian SMPC consists in cutting out the subaltern entailment schema **A** ⊢ **I** and declaring (4.1a,b) true in the actual world, in accordance with standard set theory which says that the null set ∅ is included in all sets. This solution has the advantage of mirroring mathematical set theory and thus of agreeing with those forms of mathematics that lend themselves to application to physical matter. For that reason, Russellian logic has had a great career during the twentieth century and has acquired unique prestige. Yet it has landed the study of language in another dilemma, this time not of a logical but of an empirical nature, because SMPC grossly offends natural linguistic intuitions—much more than traditional ABPC. Parsons' description of the mathematical logicians' typical, not altogether forthcoming, reaction is true to life (Parsons 2006: 3):

The common defense of this is usually that this is a logical notation devised for purposes of logic, and it does not claim to capture every nuance of the natural language forms that the symbols resemble. So perhaps '$\forall x(S\, x \to P\, x)$' does fail to do complete justice to ordinary usage of 'Every S is P', but this is not a problem with the logic. If you think that 'Every S is P' requires for its truth that there be Ss, then you can have that result simply and easily: just represent the recalcitrant uses of 'Every S is P' in symbolic notation by adding an extra conjunct to the symbolization, like this: $\forall x (Sx \to Px)$ & $\exists x Sx$. This defense leaves logic intact and also meets the objection, which is not a logical objection, but merely a reservation about the representation of natural language.

This, however, is mere palliative therapy. It amounts to saying that all one should do to appease speakers' logical conscience is define ALL **F** is **G** not just as $[\![F]\!] \subseteq [\![G]\!]$ but as $[\![F]\!] \subseteq [\![G]\!]$ and $[\![F]\!] \neq \emptyset$, adding the clause 'and $[\![F]\!] \neq \emptyset$', and all is well. But all is not well, because if one does that, De Morgan's laws make NOT ALL **F** is **G** come out as meaning 'either $[\![F]\!] \nsubseteq [\![G]\!]$ or $[\![F]\!] = \emptyset$', which again violates natural intuitions: SOME **F** is NOT-**G** clearly implies intuitively that NOT ALL **F** is **G** (in fact, both SMPC and ABPC take the two to be equivalent). But SOME **F** is NOT-**G** stipulates the existence of at least one **F** and thus rules out the possibility that $[\![F]\!] = \emptyset$, which disqualifies the disjunct 'or $[\![F]\!] = \emptyset$'. The addition of the clause 'and $[\![F]\!] \neq \emptyset$' to the definition of the universal quantifier thus merely makes the clash of intuitions rear its head elsewhere. Therefore, whichever way one takes it, SMPC does not sit at all well with the facts of language. (See Section 5.2.4 for further comment.)

In overall perspective, the following steps are taken. First, in accordance with the arguments set out in Chapter 2 of Volume I, we give up the restriction to a strictly extensional ontology and let in the full realm of intensional entities. This is necessary because a proposition is by definition contextually anchored and thus automatically creates the intensional objects needed for reference when there are no corresponding actually existing objects, according to the reference hierarchy described in Section 3.5.2 of Volume I. This makes it intrinsically impossible for ⟦F⟧ to be null, since the very fact that an object, or a class of objects, has been conceived implies the virtual, or intensional, being of that object or class of objects and thus makes it possible for that object to be referred to or for that class of objects to be quantified over. Views of this nature were often aired during the nineteenth century, but they never caught on, due not only to the unclarity, during that period, regarding the nature of intensional objects but also to a lack of formal expertise. When accepted, this view, in effect, removes the obstacle to the subaltern entailment schema from **A**-type to **I**-type L-propositions and allows for the reinstatement of the subalterns. This means that SMPC can be discarded for the purposes of language and cognition—though not for the purposes of the nonmentalistic worlds of physical matter and mathematics, to which partially defined mind-created intensional objects as described in Chapter 2 of Volume I are alien.

We thus take it that natural language operates with universal and existential quantifiers that lack existential import but merely induce an entailment of being, which can be actual existence or virtual being, depending on whether the position of the term quantified over with regard to the matrix predicate is or is not extensional. An extensional term position induces the entailment of existence; an intensional term position does not. The difference is taken to be presuppositional: each predicate does or does not *presuppositionally* require the actual existence of the referent of any of its terms. In order to uphold both logical consistency and empirical adequacy, the Aristotelian principle of strict bivalence is relativized so as to allow for two kinds of falsity, RADICAL FALSITY for presupposition failure and MINIMAL FALSITY for failure to satisfy the nonpresuppositional, or update, conditions of the matrix predicate. This makes ALL/SOME MERMAIDS are IMAGINARY true in the actual world, because the matrix predicate *imaginary* is intensional with respect to its subject term. But given that the predicate *have a bank account* is extensional with regard to its subject term, ALL/SOME MERMAIDS have A BANK ACCOUNT is false in the actual world—in fact, radically false since the falsity rests on presupposition failure. (It can achieve truth only when it occurs as an instance of implicit intensionalization, as explained in Chapter 5 of Volume I.) Thus, other than in SMPC, ALL F is G and SOME F is G are radically false when the ⟦F⟧-class is extensionally null and the matrix predicate G requires actual existence for the subject-term referent,

but they may be true when the matrix predicate does not pose that requirement. As far as the language system is concerned, existential import is thus
properly regulated by the lexicon, not by the machinery or the axioms of logic.

This allows language to profit from the maximal logical power of ABPC
within the confines of those situations where all presuppositions are fulfilled
and thus within the confines of the default conditions of linguistic interaction. Chapter 10 contains a detailed description of this logic, which allows for
intensional entities.

Thus protected, ABPC can be saved for language and cognition, though
perhaps not for general mathematics and the physical sciences. The question
is whether the protective measures are justified and how they actually work.
The arguments for intensional objects were given in Chapter 2 of Volume I, so
that we consider that question settled. The presuppositional machinery and
the concomitant logic are defined in Chapter 10. The history and precise
analysis of ABPC is sketched in Chapter 5, while its surprising functionality is
demonstrated in Chapter 6. What remains to be done is show the logical
power of ABPC and of propositional calculus (which, unlike predicate calculus, has not been superseded by a modern variant). This is what is undertaken
in the following section.

4.2 The notion of logical power

It seems intuitively reasonable to assume that a logical system Φ is less
powerful to the extent that there are more logically independent pairs of
basic expression types in the logical language defined for Φ. We call *basic
expression types* the expression types in terms of which the logical system Φ
has been defined (without vacuous repetitions of negations). We speak of
logical independence of a pair of basic expression types just in case no
(nonnegative) logical relation holds between its members. The term *pair* is
used here not in the sense of 'ordered pair' but merely to refer to a set
consisting of exactly two members, so that, for any entities *a* and *b*, <a,b>
and <b,a> are the same pair.

On this basis we may introduce the notion of LOGICAL POWER of a logical
system Φ, based on the number and proportion of logically independent pairs
of basic expression types in Φ: the more logically independent pairs of basic
expression types, the weaker the system. The sum total of the pairs of basic
expressions in Φ that are not logically independent then constitutes the logical
power of Φ. Other, more refined, metrics are possible, but all we want to
achieve at this moment is to provide some formal support for what is already
clear intuitively.

Propositional calculus is defined in terms of the following eight basic types, as specified in Section 2.4.2 (P and Q range over L-propositions):

AND stands for $P \land Q \land \ldots$ **¬AND** stands for $\neg(P \land Q \land \ldots)$
OR stands for $P \lor Q \lor \ldots$ **¬OR** stands for $\neg(P \lor Q \lor \ldots)$
AND* stands for $\neg P \land \neg Q \land \ldots$ **¬AND*** stands for $\neg(\neg P \land \neg Q \land \ldots)$
OR* stands for $\neg P \lor \neg Q \lor \ldots$ **¬OR*** stands for $\neg (\neg P \lor \neg Q \lor \ldots)$

Analogously for the varieties of predicate calculus we are considering, which are all defined in terms of the following twelve basic types (F and G range over predicates):

A stands for ALL F is G   **¬A** stands for ¬(ALL F is G)
I stands for SOME F is G   **¬I** stands for ¬(SOME F is G)
N stands for NO F is G   **¬N** stands for ¬(NO F is G)
A* stands for ALL F is NOT-G   **¬A*** stands for ¬(ALL F is NOT-G)
I* stands for SOME F is NOT-G   **¬I*** stands for ¬(SOME F is NOT-G)
N* stands for NO F is NOT-G   **¬N*** stands for ¬(NO F is NOT-G)

(In AAPC, ABPC, and SMPC, $N \equiv \neg I$, which reduces the number basic types to eight.)

The logical power of the systems under consideration can be visualized in a simple way by arranging their basic types in a polygon with the corresponding basic types as vertices and connecting lines between any two vertices symbolizing the logical relations defined for the system. For an octagonal arrangement, there are at most 28 such relations, so that the maximal score for the systems considered is 28. Anything less means a loss of logical power.

One remembers from Chapter 3 that BNPC has twelve basic expressions, requiring a dodecagonal representation as in Figure 3.7c or 3.8c in Section 3.4.1. And since the dodecagon that represents BNPC is complete (fully filled in) (see Figure 3.7c), one must conclude that BNPC is the most powerful system of predicate logic in existence, more powerful even than ABPC and vastly more powerful than SMPC, the mathematics-based standard modern system.

It may seem more paradoxical to some than to others, but it does appear as if the most primitive natural system of predicate logic is at the same time the most powerful, and that the power of predicate-logic systems decreases the more closely their operators reflect the Boolean functions set in mathematical space. For the time being it is hard to interpret this fact in the context of philosophical questions relating to the position of mankind in the physical world. But it does seem certain that it will prove to be of at least some significance in future discussions of this nature.

4.2.1 *The logical power of propositional calculus*

But before we proceed to computing the values for the systems concerned, let us revert to the Square notation, which is where we left off in Chapter 2. First we consider propositional calculus, in particular the entailment schema **AND** ⊢ **OR**, which gives rise to a natural logical triangle as shown in Figure 2.1, with **AND**, **OR**, and ¬**OR** for P, Q, and ¬Q, respectively. Given the equivalences resulting from De Morgan's laws, a second, isomorphic triangle with the internal negation can be added, whose vertices are **AND***, **OR***, and ¬**OR***. The two triangles link up by the De Morgan equivalences at the AND and ¬OR* vertices and again at the ¬**OR** and **AND*** vertices.

The logical properties of the two triangles are identical, as they should be, since whether or not the argument L-propositions are negated is irrelevant for the logic of **AND** and **OR**: all that counts is the logical properties of the truth-functional operators themselves. The subcontrariety between OR and OR* is an additional bonus: since ¬**OR** and ¬**OR*** are contraries and thus cannot both be true at the same time, their contradictories **OR** and **OR*** cannot both be false at the same time and thus form a pair of subcontraries. Figure 4.1 shows the result (repeated from Figure 3.15b).

Yet although Figure 4.1 may *contain* the whole story, it does not *show* it. A minimalist graph consisting of just the equivalences and the contrariety of **AND** and ¬**OR** likewise contains the whole story, but to *show* it, more is needed. A more revealing way of displaying the calculus is by means of a hexagon, as in Figure 4.2, which specifies more logical relations than the square notation. The two natural triangles, printed in heavy lines, have remained unchanged, but more logical relations have been added, such as the entailment from ¬**OR** to **OR***. Yet, compared with Figure 4.1, Figure 4.2 does not add new information, since those logical relations that are shown in Figure 4.2 and not in

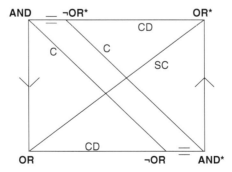

FIGURE 4.1 Propositional calculus represented as a natural square formed by two logically isomorphic natural triangles

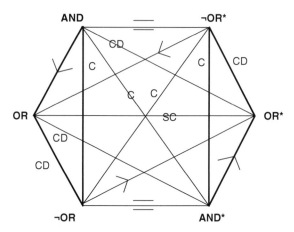

FIGURE 4.2 Hexagonal graph for propositional calculus

Figure 4.1 can easily be deduced from the latter. All Figure 4.2 does is make explicit some logical relations that are not shown in Figure 4.1. But if that is what we want, we should present a model that shows *all* logical relations between *all* possible vertices.

A complete representation requires an octagonal model, as in Figure 4.3, where the natural triangles are again printed in heavy lines. To facilitate the checking of the logical relations specified in the octagon, the VS of each vertex is indicated, according to the VS-model of Figure 4.4 and listed in (4.5) below. This octagon, with its dense network of metalogical relations, may look forbidding, yet it should be remembered that it simply follows from the combination of the subaltern entailment (**AND** ⊢ **OR**) with standard bivalent negation and the De Morgan equivalences.

In the octagon of Figure 4.3 all edges between vertices represent some logical relation, giving a complete octagonal graph. No edge between two vertices would mean that the corresponding L-propositional types are logically independent: their VSs have a nonnull intersection but neither includes the other and their union does not equal **U**. The absence of logically independent pairs makes the graph COMPLETE in the standard terminology of graph theory. This puts the logical power of this system at the maximum of 28, according to the rough metric introduced earlier.

Figure 4.4 shows propositional calculus in terms of a valuation space (VS) model. It subdivides **U** in terms of the eight L-propositional types **AND, OR, AND*, OR***, and their negations. Space 1 is reserved for cases where all component L-propositions are true, space 2 for those where one or more are true and one or more are false, and space 3 for cases where all are false. For example,

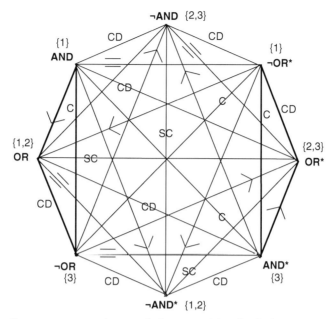

FIGURE 4.3 Octagon as a complete graph for propositional calculus

given the two logically independent sentences *The earth is round* and *Venus is a planet*, **U** is subdivided for the eight sentences *The earth is round AND Venus is a planet, The earth is round OR Venus is a planet, The earth is NOT round AND Venus is NOT a planet, The earth is NOT round OR Venus is NOT a planet*, and their

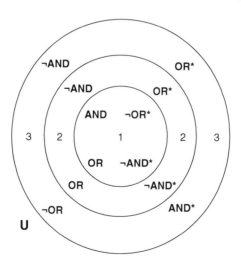

FIGURE 4.4 VS-representation of standard propositional calculus

external negations. When the two (or more) component L-propositions are not logically independent because, say, there is a contrary pair among them, then /**AND**/ = Ø since their conjunction is never true. When the component L-propositions exhaust **U**, then /**OR**/ = **U**, because their disjunction is always true. (The reader may try to work out for himself or herself what the VS-model will look like when the component L-propositions of **AND** and **OR** are equivalent: $P \land P$, $P \lor P$, $\neg(P \land P)$, $\neg(P \lor P)$, etc.)

The simple diagram of Figure 4.4, again, represents the whole of standard propositional calculus. The VSs of the various L-propositional types are specified as follows (the numbers stand for the spaces as they are numbered in Figure 4.4):

(4.5) /**AND**/   =   {1}   /**¬AND**/   =   {2,3}
      /**OR**/   =   {1,2}   /**¬OR**/   =   {3}
      /**AND***/   =   {3}   /**¬AND***/   =   {1,2}
      /**OR***/   =   {2,3}   /**¬OR***/   =   {1}

Since {1} ⊂ {1,2}, the entailment **AND** ⊢ **OR** holds. Likewise for the entailment **AND*** ⊢ **OR***, since {3} ⊂ {2,3}. Moreover, **AND** and **¬OR*** are equivalent since their VSs coincide. Likewise for **OR** and **¬AND***. Then, **AND** and **AND*** are contraries because their VSs do not intersect. And **OR** and **OR*** are subcontraries because the union of their VSs taken equals **U**: {1,2} ∪ {2,3} = {1,2,3} = **U**. It is thus easily seen that the VS representation of Figure 4.4, when written as an octagon, returns Figure 4.3.

4.2.2 *The logical power of Aristotelian-Boethian predicate calculus*

Let us now do for ABPC what we did for propositional calculus, disregarding, for the moment, the blemish of undue existential import. In the light of what has been done for propositional logic, this exercise is simple, because ABPC is defined by the same logical relations, including the equivalences, due to the duality of the universal and existential quantifiers. One only has to replace **AND** with **A** and **OR** with **I**. The result is Figure 4.5 (repeated from Figure 3.10), with the VS specification (4.6). Note that space 1 is reserved for cases where $[\![F]\!] \subseteq [\![G]\!]$ and $[\![F]\!] \neq Ø$; space 2 for cases where either $[\![F]\!]$ Ⓞ $[\![G]\!]$ (M-partial intersection: $[\![F]\!] \cap [\![G]\!] \neq Ø \neq [\![F]\!] \neq [\![G]\!]$) or $[\![G]\!] \subset [\![F]\!]$ (so that $[\![F]\!] \neq Ø$); space 3 for cases where $[\![F]\!]$ OO $[\![G]\!]$ ($[\![F]\!]$ and $[\![G]\!]$ are mutually exclusive) and $[\![F]\!] \neq Ø$. As with propositional calculus, the system has maximal logical power, in the terms in which this notion has been defined, given the subaltern entailment schema from **A** to **I**, given standard bivalent negation and given the Conversions due to duality.

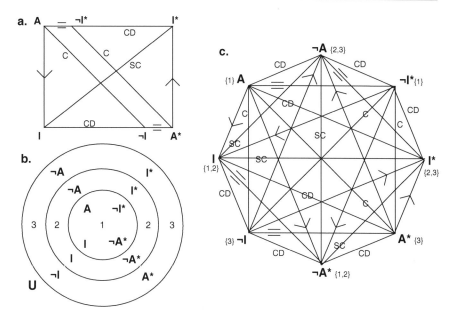

FIGURE 4.5 The Square, the VS-model, and the complete octagonal graph of ABPC

$$(4.6) \quad \begin{array}{llll}
/\mathbf{A}/ & = & \{1\} & /\neg\mathbf{A}/ & = & \{2,3\} \\
/\mathbf{I}/ & = & \{1,2\} & /\neg\mathbf{I}/ & = & \{3\} \\
/\mathbf{A}^*/ & = & \{3\} & /\neg\mathbf{A}^*/ & = & \{1,2\} \\
/\mathbf{I}^*/ & = & \{2,3\} & /\neg\mathbf{I}^*/ & = & \{1\}
\end{array}$$

The VS-modelling of ABPC given in Figure 4.5b shows again the fault of undue existential import: since there is no space where both **I**-type and **I***-type L-propositions are false, there is no space for those situations where $\llbracket\mathbf{F}\rrbracket = \varnothing$. Therefore, a fourth space is required containing those situations where $\llbracket\mathbf{F}\rrbracket = \varnothing$. The logical power of ABPC is again 28, as for propositional calculus.

4.2.3 *The logical power of standard modern predicate calculus*

We now do the same for SMPC, as before under a strictly extensional ontology. In SMPC, the generalized universal and existential quantifiers are defined as in (2.14) of Section 2.3.5.2, repeated here as (4.7):

(4.7)   For all sets X and Y:
       a. $\llbracket\forall\rrbracket = \{ <Y,X> \mid X \subseteq Y \}$
            (the extension of the predicate $\forall$ is the set of all pairs of sets Y, X, such that X is a subset of Y)

b. $[\![\exists]\!] = \{ <Y,X> \mid Y \cap X \neq \emptyset \}$
  (the extension of the predicate $\exists$ is the set of all pairs of sets Y, X,
  such that the intersection of Y and X is nonnull)

ALL F is G is considered true just in case $[\![F]\!] \subseteq [\![G]\!]$, and SOME F is G is
considered true just in case $[\![F]\!] \cap [\![G]\!] \neq \emptyset$. When $[\![F]\!] = \emptyset$, ALL F is G is
automatically true because, in set theory, $\emptyset$ is a subset of any set (for all sets X
and Y, $X \subseteq Y$ iff $X \cdot Y = X$ and $X + Y = Y$—a condition always fulfilled when
$X = \emptyset$).

Figure 4.6 (repeated from Figure 3.11) does for SMPC what Figure 4.5
does for ABPC. In Figure 4.6a, space 1 represents cases where $[\![F]\!] \subseteq [\![G]\!]$
and $[\![F]\!] \neq \emptyset$; space 2 cases where either $[\![F]\!] \oslash [\![G]\!]$ or $[\![G]\!] \subset [\![F]\!]$ and
$[\![F]\!] \neq \emptyset$; space 3 cases where $[\![F]\!]$ OO $[\![G]\!]$ and $[\![F]\!] \neq \emptyset$; and space 4 cases
where $[\![F]\!] = \emptyset$—the class of situations absent in ABPC. In space 4, **A**-type
and **A***-type L-propositions both count as true and **I**-type and **I***-type
L-propositions as false.

Figure 4.6a parallels Figures 4.5b and 4.4, but whereas Figure 4.4 is in no need
of a fourth space, Figure 4.6a must have one, since, without it, it fails to cater for
situations where $[\![F]\!]$ lacks the required supply of extensional objects. Standard
propositional calculus does not need a counterpart to extensionally null predicates: a set may be null, but a proposition has nothing to reciprocate with.

Under a strictly extensional ontology, the system of Figure 4.6 is logically
sound: there is no undue existential import and the system is fully consistent—even if it clashes with natural intuitions. But look what has happened to
its logical power, which now amounts to a mere 12. The extra space 4, with
truth for **A**-type sentences, destroys most of the beautiful, rich logic of Figure
4.5. The logically complete and maximally powerful octagonal graph of Figure

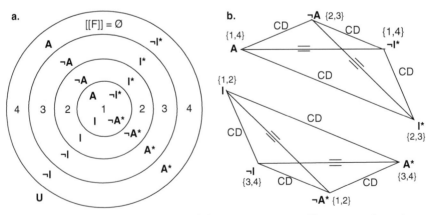

FIGURE 4.6 The VS-model of SMPC and the poor remnants of its octagonal graph

4.5c has been largely dismantled and the traditional Square has vanished altogether. In effect, the octagon has disappeared and given way to two isomorphic trapezoids, shown in Figure 4.6b, whose isomorphism reflects the elementary fact that the internal negation may be added without consequences for the semantics of the vertices (note that $\mathbf{A}^{**} \equiv \mathbf{A}$ and $\mathbf{I}^{**} \equiv \mathbf{I}$). The entire logical power of the trapezoids derives from the equivalence $\neg\mathbf{I} \equiv \mathbf{A}^*$ (or $\neg\mathbf{I}^* \equiv \mathbf{A}$)—that is, from the Conversions. Almost all connections between vertices have been lost, which means that the vertex pairs in question represent the vacuous relation of logical independence.

The striking news about SMPC is, of course, its heavy loss in logical power when compared with ABPC, whose 28 logical relations have dwindled to a paltry twelve: two quadruples $<\mathbf{A}, \mathbf{I}^*, \neg\mathbf{I}^*, \neg\mathbf{A}>$ and $<\mathbf{A}^*, \mathbf{I}, \neg\mathbf{I}, \neg\mathbf{A}^*>$, which are logically isomorphic owing to the Modulo*-Principle. This loss of logical power is solely due to the stipulation made in SMPC that $\mathbf{A}$- and $\mathbf{A}^*$-sentences are true in space 4, where $[\![\mathbf{F}]\!] = \varnothing$. But alas, ABPC is logically faulty, as it fails to cover situations where $\mathbf{G}$ requires nonnull membership of $[\![\mathbf{F}]\!]$ yet $[\![\mathbf{F}]\!]$ fails to oblige.

To make things worse, SMPC also clashes badly with natural intuitions about truth and falsity. In fact, for natural language SMPC is an unmitigated disaster. Consider, for example, sentence (4.8), said by a mechanic to justify an exorbitant bill for the servicing of a car with a diesel engine, which, as one knows, has no spark plugs:

(4.8)   All spark plugs have been changed.

For SMPC this sentence is true, but any judge presiding over the case brought by the car owner against the mechanic will consider the latter a liar.

Or take the sentences (4.9a,b), which, in the SMPC book, should both be counted as true in any situation, common enough in the actual world, where there are children but no real baby dinosaurs:

(4.9)   a. Some children played with all baby dinosaurs.
         b. Some children didn't play with any baby dinosaur.

In fact, given the absence of baby dinosaurs, SMPC makes both sentences equivalent to the statement that there was at least one child. Yet ordinary people will consider (4.9a) false in a situation with at least one child and no baby dinosaurs. And (4.9b) may have to count as true in such a situation, but only in a trivial and uninformative way.

Pragmatic principles make both sentences equally inappropriate in the actual world, where everyone knows that there are no living baby dinosaurs. To utter such sentences will thus violate a number of Gricean maxims. Yet these maxims fail to explain why (4.9a) is felt to be false while (4.9b) is considered true by unsuspecting speakers. More examples of this nature are easily thought up. In practically all cases the conclusion is that ABPC fits natural intuitions much better than SMPC, even though the latter reigns supreme in the world of modern logic and the former is still far from full empirical adequacy.

4.2.4 *The logical power of Aristotelian-Abelardian predicate calculus*

Does this mean that SMPC is the best deal possible, within the constraints of a strictly extensional ontology? Far from it. There is at least one alternative way to repair ABPC in such a way that the loss of logical power sustained by SMPC is significantly reduced while natural linguistic intuition is served more adequately. This remedy was proposed by the medieval philosopher Peter Abelard (1079–1142) and it is most probably the logic that Aristotle himself envisaged but failed to elaborate. (Chapter 5 is devoted to a detailed historical and text-critical analysis of this question.) We call this system ARISTOTELIAN-ABELARDIAN PREDICATE CALCULUS or AAPC.[2]

The gist of the Abelardian solution lies in keeping the subalterns but giving up the Conversions for one-way entailments from **A** to ¬**I*** and, analogously, from **A*** to ¬**I**, but not vice versa. This step results in the system shown in Figure 4.7 (repeated from Figure 3.9). Figure 4.7b does have the required fourth space for cases where $[\![F]\!] = \emptyset$ but where, significantly, **A**-type L-propositions where $[\![F]\!] = \emptyset$ are not considered true, as in SMPC, but false, which agrees much better with natural intuitions. This is the only difference between SMPC and AAPC, as is easily checked by comparing the VS-models of Figures 4.6a and 4.7b: in Figure 4.7b, **A** and **A*** are false in space 4, while in Figure 4.6a **A** and **A*** are true. It is amazing to see how such a small difference can provoke such a large difference in logical power.

Undue existential import has been eliminated in AAPC because **A** is false when $[\![F]\!] = \emptyset$ and, in cases where **A** is false, nothing follows with regard to any other L-propositional type: as shown in Figure 4.7c, the ¬**A**-vertex entails no other vertex and occurs only at the receiving end of some other vertices. As a reward for the weakening of the Conversions, the octagon has lost less logical power than the depleted system of SMPC: the metric adopted puts its logical power at 24, so that it scores better than SMPC, which achieves a mere

---

[2] In Seuren (2002) a solution is proposed for undue existential import that is identical to Abelard's. I named it *Revised Aristotelian predicate calculus* or RAPC. At the time, I was not aware of the fact that Abelard had proposed an identical solution nine hundred years earlier. To give Abelard his due, I have renamed the system in question *Aristotelian-Abelardian predicate calculus*.

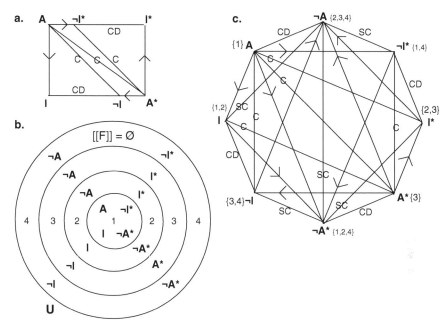

FIGURE 4.7 The square, the VS-model, and the octagon for AAPC

12, but less well than ABPC, which comes to 28. Moreover, intuitions are better respected. AAPC has thus freed itself from all the restrictions of natural set theory, whether basic or strict, but has been able to reduce the price for this freedom considerably by adopting a definition of the universal quantifier ∀ that differs from the definition adopted in SMPC.

It thus appears that, from a strictly logical point of view, ABPC represents a retrograde development with regard to AAPC, which preceded it in time (if one grants Aristotle the honour of being the originator of AAPC). Not only did ABPC introduce the logical defect of undue existential import, it also failed to eliminate the principles of natural set theory. Yet this logical blunder, if that is what one wishes to call it, was offset by a great advance as regards the functionality of predicate logic in real life situations. As is shown in Chapter 6, ABPC has the advantage of cutting out the informational redundancy of SMPC and it has greater logical power.

It is, therefore, questionable whether SMPC does indeed deserve the exalted status of inviolate doctrine it enjoys. For nonmentalistic, purely extensional applications, for which SMPC is fully valid, AAPC is likewise fully valid, but it appears to be a better, because more powerful, logic. Nowhere do the founding fathers of modern logic or their followers provide reasons for keeping the

Conversions and giving up the subalterns rather than the opposite. In fact, they appear to have opted for the most immediately obvious, but not necessarily the most useful, application of Boolean algebra to predicate calculus. This, however, is a question that falls outside the scope of the present work. What we can show—and do show in the following section—is that it is not too hard to provide a simple and logically interesting mathematical characterization of the AAPC quantifiers.

Yet no matter how interesting, perhaps even revolutionary, the Abelardian solution to the problem of undue existential import may be, it does insufficient justice to the requirements of cognitive realism (Section 1.3.1 in Volume I), as it fails to take into account the fact that natural language quantifies with equal ease over extensional as it does over intensional objects, as well as the fact that certain predicates yield truth when applied to intensional objects, as is shown in Chapters 2 and 5 of Volume I. For that reason AAPC cannot be considered a viable candidate for the post of logic of language, even though it is a highly interesting and intriguing pointer.

Therefore, if it proves possible to resolve or circumvent the problem of undue existential import, ABPC, also known as the Square of Opposition, will turn out, after all, to be the most preferable predicate-logic system for natural language and cognition, *pace* our mathematical friends.

4.3 Distributive quantifiers

To make AAPC work, the definition of the universal quantifier must be changed. One way of doing this is by adding the condition $X \neq \emptyset$ to the condition specified for the generalized universal quantifier in (2.14a) of Section 2.3.5.2, so that $\forall$ is semantically defined as follows:

(4.10)   For all sets X and Y:
$$\llbracket \forall \rrbracket = \{ \ <Y,X> \mid X \subseteq Y \text{ and } X \neq \emptyset \ \}$$
(the extension of the predicate $\forall$ is the set of all pairs of sets Y, X, such that X is a subset of Y and X is nonnull)

This does the job, at least for purely extensional purposes, but not in a very illuminating way. It merely patches up the standard definition for the purpose of natural language, thereby destroying the Conversions and, in effect, turning SMPC into AAPC.

A more principled way is by means of what we call the DISTRIBUTIVE QUANTIFIERS. This solution can not only be made to encompass intensional as well as extensional entities, it also shows up the parallelism between, on the one hand, universal quantification and conjunction and, on the other, existential quantification and disjunction. As was said in Section 4.1, the universal quantifier yields truth just in case the conjunction $G(a_1) \wedge G(a_2) \wedge \ldots \wedge G(a_n)$ is true, where a_1, a_2, $\ldots$, a_n denote the elements in the extension $[\![F]\!]$ of F. Analogously, the existential quantifier yields truth just in case the disjunction $G(a_1) \vee G(a_2) \vee \ldots \vee G(a_n)$ is true, where, again, a_1, a_2, $\ldots$, a_n denote the elements in $[\![F]\!]$. The reason why this correspondence is not at all popular in modern standard logic lies in the fact that the correspondence is lost when $[\![F]\!] = \emptyset$, because then there is no conjunction and no disjunction. In the present perspective, however, this is not a weakness but, rather, an aspect that can be turned to the advantage of AAPC.

Just like the Russellian quantifiers (see (2.9) in Section 2.3.5.1), the distributive quantifiers are defined as unary higher-order predicates over sets. Other than the Russellian quantifiers, however, and more like the generalized quantifiers, the distributive quantifiers are defined with respect to a designated predicate (Γ) and require that the members of $[\![F]\!]$ satisfy the condition of the quantifier with respect to the extension of the matrix predicate G. Given the predicates F and G, the condition for $\forall_F$ is, in simple terms, that for all $x \in [\![F]\!]$, $G(x)$ is true, whereas $\exists_F$ requires merely that for at least one $x \in [\![F]\!]$, $G(x)$ is true.

The quantifiers are thus, in fact, predicates over restrictor-predicate extensions with respect to a matrix predicate G. When it is said that *All flags are green*, or *Some flags are green*, then these sentences are interpreted as statements about the set of flags. Provided $[\![Flag]\!] \neq \emptyset$, the statement is that, for $\forall_{Flag}$, truth is achieved only if $Green(a_1) \wedge Green(a_2) \wedge \ldots \wedge Green(a_n)$ is true, and, for $\exists_{Flag}$, only if $Green(a_1) \vee Green(a_2) \vee \ldots \vee Green(a_n)$ is true, where a_1, a_2, $\ldots$, a_n denote the elements in $[\![Flag]\!]$.

On the basis of this we say that, for $\forall_F$, the set of objects $[\![F]\!]$ must satisfy the predicate G under conjunction and that, for $\forall_F$, the set of objects $[\![F]\!]$ must satisfy the predicate G under disjunction, for truth to come about. The notion of a set of objects satisfying a predicate under a propositional operator is defined as follows:

> The set of objects $[\![F]\!]$ SATISFIES THE PREDICATE G UNDER CONJUNCTION just in case either $F(a) \wedge G(a)$ is true, where a is the only element in the extension of F ($= [\![F]\!]$), or there is a true conjunction $[F(a_1) \wedge G(a_1)] \wedge \ldots \wedge [F(a_n) \wedge G(a_n)]$, where a_1, $\ldots$, a_n form the extension of F.

> The set of objects $[\![F]\!]$ SATISFIES THE PREDICATE G UNDER DISJUNCTION just in case either $F(a) \wedge G(a)$ is true, where a is the only element in the extension of F ($= [\![F]\!]$), or there is a true disjunction $[F(a_1) \wedge G(a_1)] \vee \ldots \vee [F(a_n) \wedge G(a_n)]$, where a_1, $\ldots$, a_n form the extension of F.

This enables us to define the distributive universal and the existential quantifier with respect to the restrictor predicate F as follows:

(4.11) For all predicates F and G:
a. $[\![\forall_F]\!] = \{ [\![F]\!] \mid [\![F]\!]$ satisfies the predicate G under conjunction $\}$
b. $[\![\exists_F]\!] = \{ [\![F]\!] \mid [\![F]\!]$ satisfies the predicate G under disjunction $\}$

Now, when $[\![F]\!] = \emptyset$, falsity results for both the universal and the existential quantifier. This is so because, in the absence of any $x \in [\![F]\!]$, $F(x) \wedge G(x)$ is false for any element x in **U**, which makes both ALL F is G and SOME F is G false. It is easily seen that this predicate logic represents the AAPC variant of the cognitive approach to predicate logic described in Section 3.4.1.

To facilitate understanding, a toy VS-model can be set up illustrating how these definitions work. Such a model must be kept extremely small, because the number of valuations increases exponentially with the number of elements and/or predicates. Consider a toy model $\mathbf{M}_{toy}$ with two semantically independent predicates F and G and three elements a, b, and c. The total number of valuations (situations) for $\mathbf{M}_{toy}$ is $(2^3)^2 = 64$, as shown in Figure 4.8. (With four elements and two predicates, the total number of valuations or situations would be $(2^4)^2 = 256$.)

Figure 4.8 shows $\mathbf{M}_{toy}$ written out as a system of separate valuations, each of which marks each basic proposition and each conjunction of the form $F(x) \wedge G(x)$ *plus* (true) or *minus* (false), thereby giving a breakdown of **U**.

Val:	1	2	3	4	5	6	7	8	9	10	11	12	13	14	15	16
Fa	+	-	+	-	+	-	+	-	+	-	+	-	+	-	+	-
Fb	+	+	-	-	+	+	-	-	+	+	-	-	+	+	-	-
Fc	+	+	+	+	-	-	-	-	+	+	+	+	-	-	-	-
Ga	+	+	+	+	+	+	+	+	-	-	-	-	-	-	-	-
Gb	+	+	+	+	+	+	+	+	+	+	+	+	+	+	+	+
Gc	+	+	+	+	+	+	+	+	+	+	+	+	+	+	+	+
Fa ∧ Ga	+	-	+	-	+	-	+	-	-	-	-	-	+	-	-	-
Fb ∧ Gb	+	+	-	-	+	+	-	-	+	+	-	-	+	+	-	-
Fc ∧ Gc	+	+	+	+	-	-	-	-	+	+	+	+	-	-	-	-

Val:	17	18	19	20	21	22	23	24	25	26	27	28	29	30	31	32
Fa	+	-	+	-	+	-	+	-	+	-	+	-	+	-	+	-
Fb	+	+	-	-	+	+	-	-	+	+	-	-	+	+	-	-
Fc	+	+	+	+	-	-	-	-	+	+	+	+	-	-	-	-
Ga	+	+	+	+	+	+	+	+	-	-	-	-	-	-	-	-
Gb	-	-	-	-	-	-	-	-	-	-	-	-	-	-	-	-
Gc	+	+	+	+	+	+	+	+	+	+	+	+	+	+	+	+
Fa ∧ Ga	+	-	+	-	+	-	+	-	-	-	-	-	-	-	-	-
Fb ∧ Gb	-	-	-	-	-	-	-	-	-	-	-	-	-	-	-	-
Fc ∧ Gc	+	+	+	+	-	-	-	-	+	+	+	+	-	-	-	-

Val:	33	34	35	36	37	38	39	40	41	42	43	44	45	46	47	48
Fa	+	-	+	-	+	-	+	-	+	-	+	-	+	-	+	-
Fb	+	+	-	-	+	+	-	-	+	+	-	-	+	+	-	-
Fc	+	+	+	+	-	-	-	-	+	+	+	+	-	-	-	-
Ga	+	+	+	+	+	+	+	+	-	-	-	-	-	-	-	-
Gb	+	+	+	+	+	+	+	+	+	+	+	+	+	+	+	+
Gc	-	-	-	-	-	-	-	-	-	-	-	-	-	-	-	-
Fa ∧ Ga	+	-	+	-	+	-	+	-	-	-	-	-	-	-	-	-
Fb ∧ Gb	+	+	-	-	+	+	-	-	+	+	-	-	+	+	-	-
Fc ∧ Gc	-	-	-	-	-	-	-	-	-	-	-	-	-	-	-	-

Val:	49	50	51	52	53	54	55	56	57	58	59	60	61	62	63	64
Fa	+	-	+	-	+	-	+	-	+	-	+	-	+	-	+	-
Fb	+	+	-	-	+	+	-	-	+	+	-	-	+	+	-	-
Fc	+	+	+	+	-	-	-	-	+	+	+	+	-	-	-	-
Ga	+	+	+	+	+	+	+	+	-	-	-	-	-	-	-	-
Gb	-	-	-	-	-	-	-	-	-	-	-	-	-	-	-	-
Gc	-	-	-	-	-	-	-	-	-	-	-	-	-	-	-	-
Fa ∧ Ga	+	-	+	-	+	-	+	-	-	-	-	-	-	-	-	-
Fb ∧ Gb	-	-	-	-	-	-	-	-	-	-	-	-	-	-	-	-
Fc ∧ Gc	-	-	-	-	-	-	-	-	-	-	-	-	-	-	-	-

FIGURE 4.8 $\mathbf{M}_{toy}$ for two predicates F and G and three objects called a, b, and c

A set of objects $[\![F]\!]$ satisfying the predicate **G** under conjunction is found in precisely the following set $V_{\forall_F}$ of situations (valuations):

$$V_{\forall_F} = \{1, 2, 3, 4, 5, 6, 7, 10, 12, 14, 19, 20, 23, 28, 37, 38, 39, 46, 55\}.$$

And the set of valuations $V_{\exists_F}$ such that for each valuation in $V_{\exists_F}[\![F]\!]$ satisfies the predicate **G** under disjunction is:

$$\begin{aligned} V_{\exists_F} = \{&1, 2, 3, 4, 5, 6, 7, 9, 10, 11, 12, 13, 14, 17, 18, 19, 20, 21, 23, 25, \\ &26, 27, 28, 33, 34, 35, 37, 38, 39, 41, 42, 45, 46, 49, 51, 53, 55\} \end{aligned}.$$

Since $V_{\forall_F} \subset V_{\exists_F}$, it follows that **A**-type L-propositions entail their **I**-type counterparts.

If one reads Flag for **F** and Green for **G**, then ALL Flags are Green is true in all and only the valuations (situations) of $V_{\forall_F}$ because for all and only these situations is it possible to enumerate the elements in $[\![Flag]\!]$ and ascertain that they are also marked plus for the predicate Green. Notably, in those situations where there is no flag—that is, in $\{8,16,24,32,40,48,56,64\}$—ALL Flags are Green is false because there is no true conjunction of the required sort. SOME Flag(s) is(are) Green is false when there are no flags or there are flags but none of them is green—that is, in the complement of $V_{\exists_F}$, namely $\{8,15,16,22,24,29,30,31,32,36,40,43,44,47,48,50,52,54,56,57,58,59,60,61,62,63,64\}$.

The missing fourth space for situations where $[\![F]\!]=\varnothing$ can thus be incorporated into the VS-model of the system in Figure 4.7b, but, other than in SMPC, universally quantified L-propositions are valued 'false' in such situations, just like existentially quantified L-propositions. This amounts to AAPC, Abelard's amendment of Aristotle's predicate logic.

The definitions of (4.11a,b) also shed some light on the fact that in order to maintain the parallelism between propositional and predicate logic it is necessary to distribute the internal negation over all arguments of the non-unary propositional operators. One remembers from (2.30) in Section 2.4.2 that **AND*** and **OR*** distribute their internal negation over all their arguments: **AND**$^* = \neg P \wedge \neg Q \wedge \neg R \wedge \ldots \wedge \neg Z$ and **OR**$^* = \neg P \vee \neg Q \vee \neg R \vee \ldots \vee \neg Z$. Under the definitions of (4.11a,b), **A*** and **I*** distribute their internal negation over all the instances of the matrix predicate: if the matrix predicate is $\neg G$, then the condition is, for **A***, that $sit_{act} \in /(F(a_1) \wedge \neg G(a_1)) \wedge \ldots \wedge (F(a_n) \wedge \neg G(a_n))/$ and, for **I***, that $sit_{act} \in /(F(a_1) \wedge \neg G(a_1)) \vee \ldots \vee (F(a_n) \wedge \neg G(a_n))/$, for all a_i in $[\![F]\!]$. If the propositional operators $\wedge$ and $\vee$ can be redefined in such a way that they extend over propositional functions under a quantifier, the generalizing principle may be seen to stem from the quantifiers. This aspect, however, is not elaborated here.

Given the fact that the quantifiers are now restrictor-bound predicates over matrix-predicate extensions, their L-propositional syntax had better be changed as well. Sentences like (4.12a,b) are now better rendered syntactically as the L-propositions (4.13a,b), where the restrictor predicate is attached to the quantifier. The syntax of the quantifier now corresponds to (2.10a,b) of Section 2.3.5.2:[3]

(4.12)   a. All farmers grumble.
   b. Some farmers grumble.

(4.13)   a. ∀x[Farmer(x)](Grumble(x))
    (for all objects x such that x is a farmer, x grumbles)
   b. ∃x[Farmer(x)](Grumble(x))
    (for at least one object x such that x is a farmer, x grumbles)

The corresponding L-propositional tree structure is now different from that assumed for generalized quantifiers. On this analysis, a sentence like *Some farmers do not grumble* is assigned the L-propositional tree structure of Figure 4.9. This configuration makes it possible to use the same variable x for both the predicate *farmer* and the predicate *grumble*. In practice, this means that the whole structure S_1 is true just in case the disjunction ¬Grumble(a_1) ∨ ¬Grumble(a_2) ∨ ... ¬Grumble(a_n) is true, where a_1, a_2, ..., a_n range over [[Farmer(x)]], or, in the terminology defined above, the set of farmers satisfies the predicate not-Grumble under disjunction.

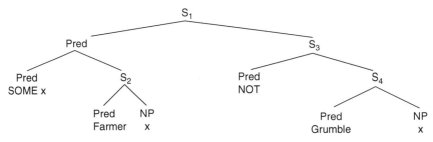

FIGURE 4.9 L-propositional tree structure of *Some farmers do not grumble*

---

[3] Compared with (2.11a,b) in Chapter 2, Figure 4.9 shows the result of the transformational syntactic rule of OBJECT INCORPORATION or OI—a rule frequently found in the syntax of natural languages. Examples are English expressions like *take care of* or *pay attention to*, where the object terms *care* and *attention* have been incorporated into the predicate, as is seen from the passives *She has been taken care of* or *She has been paid attention to*. Full lexicalizations where an object term has been incorporated are, for example, English *bearhunting, seafaring, globetrotting, golddigging, brew* ('make beer'), *price* ('put a price on'), *pencil* ('use a pencil to write'). Such formations are frequent in many other languages as well. See also note 6 in Chapter 2.

As long as $[\![F]\!] \neq \varnothing$, the distributive quantifiers ∀ and ∃ convert in the normal way, just like their counterparts in traditional and standard modern predicate logic. But unlike modern predicate logic, in cases where $[\![F]\!] = \varnothing$, falsity results for both the universal and the existential quantifier, with or without internal negation.

Of course, we want to know what happens to nonstandard quantifiers like MOST or HALF when these are defined as distributive quantifiers. Let us look again at (2.15a,b) of Chapter 2, repeated here in the form adapted as necessary:

(4.14)   a. Most farmers grumble.
         b. MOST $x_{[Farmer(x)]}$[Grumble(x)]

The tree structure corresponding to the L-proposition (4.14b) is shown in Figure 4.10.

The semantic definition of the predicate MOST is given in (4.15):

(4.15)   For all predicates F and G:
         $[\![MOST_F]\!] = \{[\![F]\!] \mid$ there is a subset $Y \subseteq [\![F]\!]$ such that $|Y| > |[\![F]\!]|/2$
         and Y satisfies G under conjunction}
             NB: |X|: the cardinality of the set X)

         (the extension of the predicate MOST is the set of all sets $[\![F]\!]$ such that
         there is a subset Y of $[\![F]\!]$ whose cardinality is greater than the
         cardinality of $[\![F]\!]$ divided by 2 and Y satisfies G under conjunction)

Thus, if most farmers grumble, there is at least one subset Y of the set of farmers such that Y consists of more than half the number of farmers, and all members of Y grumble. Clearly, when there are no actually existing farmers, Y equals Ø and, therefore, cannot contain more than half the number of farmers. There is then, moreover, no actual situation in which a farmer grumbles. Therefore, when $[\![F]\!] = \varnothing$, sentence (4.14a) is false. The interested reader is invited to formulate an analogous definition for the quantifier HALF.

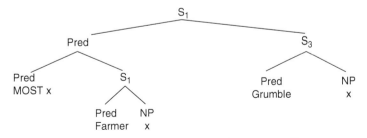

FIGURE 4.10 L-propositional tree structure of *Most farmers grumble*

4.4 Predicate logics and intuitions: a scale of empirical success

Let us now take provisional stock and see how the various systems score, at this stage of the analysis, given their satisfaction conditions for SOME, NO, and ALL. First we list seven natural logical intuitions. Then we list the satisfaction conditions for SOME, NO, and ALL in four systems of predicate logic. Finally, we list the empirical success scores of the four systems considered with regard to the intuitions listed. (The Hamiltonian system has been left out because it is identical to BNPC but for the condition that ALL F is G is true in BNPC just in case $[\![F]\!] \subset [\![G]\!]$ whereas in the Hamiltonian system it is true just in case $[\![F]\!] \subseteq [\![G]\!]$.) The empirical success scores of the various systems are shown in terms of the following seven natural logical intuitions ('⊢': 'is felt to entail'; '≡': 'is felt to be equivalent'):

Natural logical intuitions:

1. SOME F is G ⊢ NOT-ALL F is G $I \vdash \neg A$
2. SOME F is G ≡ SOME F is NOT-G $I \equiv I^*$
3. SOME F is G ≡ SOME G is F $I \equiv I!$
4. ALL F is G ⊢ SOME G is F $A \vdash I!$
5. ALL F is G ⊢ SOME G is NOT-F $A \vdash I!^*$
6. NO F is NOT-G ≡ ALL F is G $N^* \equiv A$
7. NOT-ALL F is G ≡ SOME F is G ≡ SOME F is NOT-G $\neg A \equiv I \equiv I^*$

Satisfaction conditions for SOME, NO, and ALL in four systems:

SOME: satisfaction condition:
  BNPC $[\![F]\!] \cap [\![G]\!] \subset [\![F]\!]$ ($[\![F]\!]$, $[\![G]\!]$ are distinct natural sets)
  AAPC $[\![F]\!] \cap [\![G]\!] \neq \emptyset$
  ABPC $[\![F]\!] \cap [\![G]\!] \neq \emptyset$
  SMPC $[\![F]\!] \cap [\![G]\!] \neq \emptyset$

NO: satisfaction condition:
  BNPC $[\![F]\!] \, OO \, [\![G]\!]$ ($[\![F]\!]$, $[\![G]\!]$ are distinct natural sets)
  AAPC $[\![F]\!] \cap [\![G]\!] = \emptyset$
  ABPC $[\![F]\!] \cap [\![G]\!] = \emptyset$
  SMPC $[\![F]\!] \cap [\![G]\!] = \emptyset$

ALL: satisfaction condition:
  BNPC $[\![F]\!] \subset [\![G]\!]$ ($[\![F]\!]$, $[\![G]\!]$ are distinct natural sets)
  AAPC $[\![F]\!] \subseteq [\![G]\!]$ and $[\![F]\!] \neq \emptyset$

ABPC $\llbracket F \rrbracket \subseteq \llbracket G \rrbracket$ (applicable only if $\llbracket F \rrbracket \neq \varnothing$)
SMPC $\llbracket F \rrbracket \subseteq \llbracket G \rrbracket$

Empirical success scores for four systems of predicate logic:

BNPC   1, 2, 4, 5, 6
AAPC   3, 4,
ABPC   3, 4, 6
SMPC   3, 6

The first thing that strikes one is that none of the logical systems under discussion is able to account for intuition 7, which says that NOT-ALL F is G is felt to be equivalent with both SOME F is G and SOME F is NOT-G. Apparently, intuition 7 is a special case. In Section 3.4.1 it has been made clear that intuition 7 is accounted for in BNPC when NOT-ALL F is G is assigned a topic–comment structure and BNPC has been extended with a presuppositional component, which, incidentally, makes the logic trivalent. Extending AAPC with a presuppositional component establishes the equivalence of NOT-ALL F is G and SOME F is NOT-G, lacking in nonpresuppositional AAPC. The equivalence felt to exist between NOT-ALL F is G and SOME F is G is, of course, not attainable in either AAPC or ABPC, since these two systems have the subaltern entailment from **A** to **I**.

BNPC scores best, though it lacks an account for intuition 3 which makes the quantifier SOME symmetrical (**I** $\equiv$ **I**!). This question has been commented on in Sections 3.4.1 and 3.4.2, where it is argued that intuition 3 is deceptive in that it appears to depend on world knowledge regarding the actual extensions of the predicates at issue.

AAPC and ABPC (the Square) successfully account for intuitions 3 and 4 because in both systems SOME is symmetrical. Moreover, ALL F is G cannot be true unless SOME G is F is also true, under the definitions for SOME and ALL in these systems. One notes that the combination of intuitions 3 and 4 makes for the intuition that the subaltern entailment (**A** $\vdash$ **I**) holds. ABPC, in addition, accounts for intuition 6, because in ABPC the Conversions hold, so that $\neg\textbf{I}^{*}\equiv$ **A**. In AAPC, as has been shown, all that can be said is that **A** $\vdash$ '$\neg$ **I*** but not vice versa. Finally, SMPC satisfies the intuitions 3 and 6. It satisfies intuition 3 because in SMPC **I** $\equiv$ **I**! and it satisfies intuition 6 because in SMPC the Conversions hold.

It thus results that BNPC (along with the Hamiltonian system) is the most intuitively satisfying system of predicate logic in existence. It is also internally consistent and logically faultless. In particular, it does not suffer from undue existential import. All it suffers from, as has been explained in Section 3.4.1, is its inability to warrant the truth of quantified statements under the operators ALL, SOME, or NO as long as no full situational knowledge has been achieved—a defect that will hardly have been felt for most of the period in which natural language came into being and was the vehicle of linguistic interaction in illiterate, tribal communities. Presumably, BNPC's failure to be knowledge-independent began to be important only a mere five thousand years ago when literate civilizations began to spring up all over the world, in South and Central America, China, Mongolia, Northern India, Mesopotamia, and Egypt.

5

Aristotle, the commentators, and Abelard

5.1 A recapitulation of ABPC

As was shown in the previous chapter, ABPC, for many centuries the one and only predicate logic in existence, is an exact parallel to standard propositional logic created by the Stoics. Every student of logic will remember the traditional Square of Opposition, presented in Figure 5.1a and expressed in terms of the Boethian symbols **A**, **I**, **E**, and **O** (see also Section 2.2).

The entailments from **A** to **I** and from **E** to **O** are known by the traditional names of positive and negative subalterns, respectively. **A** and **E**, moreover, are known as the universal positive and the universal negative, respectively, and **I** and **O** as the particular positive and the particular negative, respectively.

The relations expressed in the square representation must be extended by stipulating that **I**-type L-propositions 'convert', in the original Aristotelian sense of 'conversion' (antistrophḗ), defined in the *Prior Analytics* and discussed briefly in Section 3.4.1. 'Antistrophḗ' or conversion is the process whereby the F- and G-predicates are interchanged. In ABPC, it can be applied to **I**-sentences *salva veritate*: SOME F is G is equivalent to SOME G is F (**I** ≡ **I**!). Since **O**-sentences are **I**-sentences with a negated G-predicate, SOME F is NOT-G is equivalent with SOME NOT-G is F. Moreover, as **E**-sentences are, in fact, negated **I**-sentences, the converse of NOT[SOME F is G] is NOT[SOME G is F]. Then, F and G are interchangeable in **A**-sentences provided both F and G are made negative (contraposition): ALL F IS G is equivalent with ALL NOT-G IS NOT-F. Moreover, ALL F IS G entails, but is not equivalent with, SOME G IS F and hence SOME F IS G (the subaltern entailment).

As has been mentioned several times in the preceding chapters, we consider the Boethian notation in the form of the classic square unsatisfactory, even though it was in use for many centuries, mainly because it fails to express

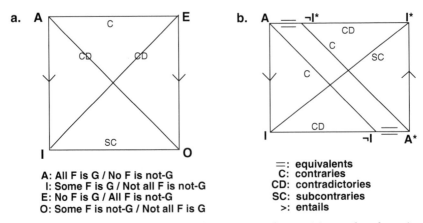

FIGURE 5.1 ABPC represented as the Boethian Square of Opposition and as the strict natural square consisting of two isomorphic triangles

the roles of external and internal negation and because it fails to express the Modulo*-Principle. For these reasons, we decided, in Section 2.2, to replace the symbols **E** and **O** with **A*** and **I***, respectively, so as better to be able to express the fact that **E**-sentences are in fact **A**-sentences (that is, universals) and that **O**-sentences are in fact **I**-sentences (particulars), in both cases with an internal negation on the G-predicate, represented by the asterisk. We also adopted the sign ¬ for standard (external) negation so as to express the fact that contradictoriness is systematically caused by negation.

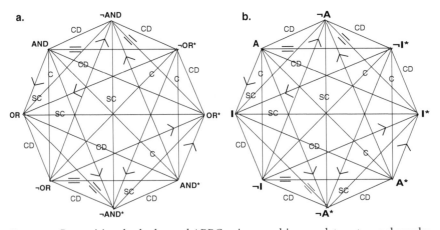

FIGURE 5.2 Propositional calculus and ABPC as isomorphic complete octagonal graphs

It has been shown, in the preceding chapters, that, apart from the notation used for the vertices, ABPC is better represented not as a square with two crossing diagonals but as a combination of two triangles connected at two of their vertices by equivalence relations, as in Figure 5.1b, just as was done for propositional calculus in Figure 4.1. In Chapter 4, however, it was shown that the optimal representation for both propositional and predicate calculus is maximalist: it takes the form of an octagonal graph, as in Figure 5.2, repeated from Figures 4.3 and 4.5.

Section 4.1 has made it sufficiently clear that, under a strictly extensional ontology, ABPC suffers from UNDUE EXISTENTIAL IMPORT (UEI). What interests us here is the historical development of ABPC and of its unknown variant Aristotelian-Abelardian predicate calculus or AAPC.

5.2 The not quite Aristotelian roots of ABPC

5.2.1 *Aristotle's own predicate logic*

What did Aristotle's own predicate logic, found mainly in his *On Interpretation* (*Int*), look like?[1] Specialists say, no doubt correctly, that Aristotle did not complete his system of predicate logic and elaborated only some aspects. And, as everyone does who is working at a new formal system, he also dwelled on aspects of the system that were not, in the end, incorporated into it.

Thus he spends some time on a sentence type called 'adióristos' in the first chapter of *On Interpretation*. This term means literally 'indefinite', but it is perhaps best rendered as 'generic'. It is described formally by saying that it lacks any specific quantifier (ALL or SOME) and semantically, somewhat cryptically, as 'about a universal class but not universal in character' (*Int* 14b7). His example is *Man is white*, where 'man' denotes a universal class but the sentence does not imply that all men are white. In fact, Aristotle allows for both *Man is white* and *Man is not white* to be true simultaneously despite the fact that, grammatically speaking, the latter is the negation of the former and should therefore be its logical contradictory (*Int* 17b31–32). He fails, however, to specify the quantificational truth conditions that would make this possible. It is easy to see that this sentence type, as long as it remains as ill-defined as it is, can hardly play a role in any sound predicate

---

[1] The most detailed and authoritative study on Aristotle's *On Interpretation* (*Perì Hermēneías*) is Weidemann (1994), where one finds a translation that is better than most, along with a discussion of the chronology and authorship of the work, a complete survey of the manuscript tradition, the tradition of interpretation in Antiquity, the Arab world and the Middle Ages, and the translation tradition. What it does not have is an analysis of the actual logic involved.

logic. Such lapses are understandable, given the high degree of difficulty of predicate calculus and given the fact that Aristotle had to create logic out of nothing, without any existing terminology and without any formalization techniques to build on. Many things that were still opaque to him are clearer to us now.

In the matter of existential import, however, Aristotle appears to have seen the problem more sharply than most later logicians and many modern historians of logic, who tend to gloss over it too lightly or even fail to see it. When one reads Aristotle's text literally, one sees that he hedges precisely on the point where existential import becomes relevant. He rejects the classic Conversions and thus saves his logic from the blemish of undue existential import, as will be clear in a moment. That Aristotle may well have seen the danger of undue existential import looming at the horizon is seldom taken into consideration, presumably, one is inclined to think, because his commentators, followers, and critics did not, on the whole, discern it as clearly as they could have. It was not until the late nineteenth century that the logical problem of existential import began to receive full attention. Until that time, awareness of this problem seems to have been desultory and incomplete. Since we have no inclination to underestimate Aristotle, who is undoubtedly one of the greatest intellectual giants in Western history, we will have a closer look at the issue.

What we see, when we read the text of *On Interpretation* closely, is that Aristotle stops short of stating the Conversions—that is, the equivalence of NO F is G and ALL F is NOT-G and of SOME F is G and NOT ALL F is NOT-G. The Kneales noticed this (Kneale and Kneale 1962: 57):

Aristotle [. . .] allowed that *Every man is not white* could be said to entail *No man is white*, but rejected the converse entailment.

Yet these authors failed to see the relevance of this rejection. Further down in their book, when discussing Abelard's rejection of the Conversions and his appeal to Aristotle who, like Abelard, considered NOT EVERY human is white and not SOME human is NOT-white, to be the contradictory of EVERY human is white, their comment is (Kneale and Kneale 1962: 210):

It is true, of course, that Aristotle wrote Greek words corresponding to *Non omnis homo est albus* [Not every human is white], but it seems clear that he did not intend to convey by these words anything different from the doctrine later attributed to him by Boethius.

This not only contradicts what they wrote on p. 57, but it is also, one must fear, just wrong. Why should Aristotle not be taken at his actual words?

If that is done, what results is a sound, though incomplete, system of predicate logic.

The actual passages in Aristotle are *Int* 17b16–26 (translations mine):

I use the term 'contradictorily opposed' for positive and negative statements, the one attributing a property universally and the other not universally to the same objects, such as *Every human is white* versus *Not every human is white*, or *No human is white* versus *Some human is white*. The term 'contrarily opposed' is used for the pair universal positive and universal negative, such as *Every human is white* versus *No human is white*, or *Every human is just* versus *No human is just*. It is impossible for these latter two to be simultaneously true, but their contradictories can sometimes be simultaneously true of the same class, as in *Not every human is white* versus *Some human is white*.

and *Int* 20a16–23:

Since the contrary of *All animals are just* is the statement meaning *No animal is just*, it is clear that these two will never be true at the same time nor be predicated of the same thing. But their contradictories, that is *Not all animals are just* and *Some animal is just*, will sometimes be simultaneously true. Then we have the following entailments: *All men are not-just* entails *No man is just*, and *Some man is just* entails the former's contradictory *Not all men are not-just*. For in that case there must be at least one just man.[2]

These passages are crucial. For if, as Aristotle actually does here, the Conversions are given up for one-way entailments ($\mathbf{A}^* \vdash \neg\mathbf{I}$, and therefore also $\mathbf{A} \vdash \neg\mathbf{I}^*$, because if $\mathbf{A}^* \vdash \neg\mathbf{I}$ then also $\mathbf{A}^{**} \vdash \neg\mathbf{I}^*$, and $\mathbf{A}^{**} \equiv \mathbf{A}$) but not vice versa, the logic is sound: it then no longer suffers from its central logical defect, undue existential import. This fact is too important for it to pass unnoticed and it seems less than fair to Aristotle to ascribe this crucial avoidance of a basic logical error to mere good luck on his part.

Yet it is true that Aristotle fails to be explicit on several points where one would have liked him to be a little less sparing of his words. For example, he gives no evidence of an explicit awareness of the subaltern entailments. Yet they follow directly from what he does present explicitly. He does say clearly and repeatedly that the truth of ALL F is G requires the falsity of its contrary NO F is G. He also says explicitly and repeatedly that the contradictory of NO F is G is its nonnegative counterpart SOME F is G. Given this, it is hard to imagine

---

[2] This last sentence is problematic owing to the extreme density of Aristotle's style at this point. The literal translation of the Greek *Anángkē gàr eînaí tina* is 'For there must be some'. Most existing translations leave the opacity of this sentence unclarified. I have followed Weidemann's translation (Weidemann 1994: 20): 'denn notwendigerweise ist denn ja irgendeiner gerecht', which makes perfect sense: if there is one just man, then it cannot be the case that all men are unjust.

that he failed to see that, therefore, the truth of ALL F is G requires the truth of SOME F is G—that is, the positive subaltern entailment. And analogously for NO F is G, which, by contraposition, entails NOT ALL F is G—that is, the negative subaltern entailment for the negation of ALL F is G (though not necessarily for its supposed equivalent SOME F is NOT-G). Moreover, he implies the validity of the subaltern entailments at *Prior Analytics* (25a8–14):

> The positive sentence does convert [in the Aristotelian sense; PAMS], though not as a universal but as a particular, for example, if every pleasure is a good, then some good must be a pleasure. Of particular sentences the positive does convert (since if some pleasure is good, then some good will also be a pleasure), but the negative particular does not convert, because if some animal is not human, it does not follow that some human is not an animal.

This says that an **A**-sentence entails the converse (antistrophḗ) of the corresponding **I**-sentence and that an **I**-sentence and its converse are equivalent. It follows immediately, of course, that an **A**-sentence entails the corresponding **I**-sentence. Any impartial reader will agree that, therefore, Aristotle does have the subaltern entailments. He should, in any case, be given the benefit of the doubt in this respect.[3]

In similar manner we notice that Aristotle fails to posit the relation of subcontrariety explicitly. He certainly has no term for it. While his term for contraries was *enantíai* and for contradictories he used the terms *antíphasis* and *antiphatikôs antikeímenos* ('contradictorily opposed'), as at *Int* 17b16–17, or sometimes simply *antikeímenos* ('opposed'), as at *Int* 17b24 (see also De Rijk 2002: 103), there is no term for subcontraries. The first known occurrence of the concept of subcontrariety is in the logical treatise *Perí Hermēneías*, written in the second century CE and reliably attributed to the Latin author Apuleius (best known for his *Metamorphoses* or *The Golden Ass*). In this treatise, the Latin term *subpares* ('nearly equal') is used for subcontraries, *incongruae* for contraries and *alterutrae* for contradictories (Sullivan 1967: 65; Londey and Johanson 1987: 56, 88–89, 111). (Apuleius has no term for the subalterns (Londey and Johanson 1987: 109) and is a little reticent on the subject of the Conversions (Sullivan 1967: 71), though he does use the term *æquipollens* for them.)

The first known occurrence of the Greek term *hypenantíai*, which underlies Latin *subcontrariae*, is in the fifth-century Greek commentary on Aristotle's *On Interpretation* by Ammonius, who writes: 'The particulars are called *sub-contraries* (*hypenantíai*), because they are placed below the contraries [in the

---

[3] See also Kneale and Kneale (1962: 58), where these authors express essentially the same conclusion.

Square; PAMS] and follow from them.' (Busse 1897: 92). (One may surmise that diagrams were commonly used in classroom teaching, or else it is hard to understand how Ammonius could use the expression 'below the contraries'; see also Section 5.2.3.)

At *Int* 17b25 and 20a17–18 (quoted above) Aristotle says that the contradictories of contraries may be simultaneously true. But he does not, or not explicitly, draw the further consequence that the falsity of the one excludes the falsity of the other: they cannot be simultaneously false. Had he done so, he would have established the relation of subcontrariety between **I**-type and ¬**A**-type sentences. We shall be generous and assume that Aristotle did know about subcontrariety, even though he did not give it a name. Aristotle may not have seen all the details, but to deny him the insight that if two sentences cannot be simultaneously true, their contradictories cannot be simultaneously false, would seem to do him an injustice. In this we are supported by the Kneales, who take it that Aristotle was, in fact, aware of the relation of subcontrariety even though he had no term for it (Kneale and Kneale 1962: 56):

The two particular statements [i.e. **I** and **I***; PAMS] have been said by later logicians to be *subaltern* to the universal statements under which they occur in the figure and *subcontrary* to each other. Although he does not use these expressions, Aristotle is interested in the relations so described, and assumes that sub-contraries cannot both be false though they may both be true. This is shown by his description of them as contradictories of contraries.

Yet while one appreciates the Kneales's generosity vis-à-vis Aristotle as regards subcontrariety, one must note their apparent confusion on the subject of the Conversions. For in Aristotle's system of predicate logic (AAPC), the pair $< \textbf{I},\textbf{I}^* >$ is not part of the relation of subcontrariety, whereas the pair $< \textbf{I},\neg\textbf{A} >$ is, as are the pairs $< \textbf{I}^*,\neg\textbf{A}^* >$, $< \neg\textbf{A},\neg\textbf{I}^* >$, and $< \neg\textbf{I},\neg\textbf{A}^* >$, as one can read from Figures 5.3 and 5.6a. Aristotle merely accepted the one-way entailments from **A** to ¬**I*** and from **A*** to ¬**I** and therefore from **I*** to ¬**A** and from **I** to ¬**A***, which makes **A** and **I***, and **A*** and **I**, contraries, but not ¬**I** and ¬**I***, so that **I** and **I*** cannot be subcontraries.

What appears to be the authentic Aristotelian system as it can be culled from his texts is based on the two independent stipulations (i) and (ii), from which further theorems follow ('$\times$' stands for contrariety; '$\asymp$' for subcontrariety):

(i)   **A** $\times$¬**I** (*contraries*)   (ii) **A*** $\vdash$ ¬**I** (*entailment*)

From this follow the theorems: From this follow the theorems:

¬**A** $\asymp$ **I** *subcontraries*)   **A*** $\times$ **I** *(contraries)*
A $\vdash$ **I** *(positive subaltern)*   ¬**A*** $\asymp$ ¬**I** *(subcontraries)*
¬**I** $\vdash$ ¬**A** *(contraposition)*   **I** $\vdash$ ¬**A*** *(contraposition)*
A* $\times$ ¬**I*** *(Modulo*-Principle)*   **A** $\times$ **I*** *(Modulo*-Principle)*
¬**A*** $\asymp$ **I*** *(subcontraries)*   ¬**A** $\asymp$ ¬**I*** *(subcontraries)*
A* $\vdash$ **I*** *(negative subaltern)*   **A** $\vdash$ ¬**I*** *(Modulo*-Principle)*
¬**I*** $\vdash$ ¬**A*** *(contraposition)*   **I*** $\vdash$ ¬**A** *(contraposition)*

This system, incomplete as it is, is presented in Figure 5.3, which differs from Kneale and Kneale (1962: 55) and Parsons (2006: 4), but is in agreement with Thompson (1953: 259). The relation of contradictoriness of any pair < **T**, ¬**T**> (**T** stands for any of the sentence types defined) has been added because it is implicit in Aristotle's definition of sentential negation. This system is, though not fully elaborated, logically sound, other than ABPC, which is not.

As has been shown, Aristotle rejected the Conversions, cutting them down to the one-way entailments specified above. That this is sufficient to avoid undue existential import is not apparent from the incomplete Figure 5.3, but it is from Figure 5.7a, where all the missing logical relations have been filled in. There one sees that the types ¬**A**, ¬**I**, ¬**A***, and ¬**I*** do not entail any **I**-type or **I***-type sentence, which absolves the system of the charge of undue existential import. In Figure 5.2b, however, which represents ABPC, one sees that all

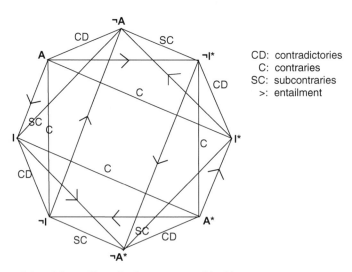

FIGURE 5.3 Aristotle's predicate logic as presented in his texts

sentence types as represented by the vertices entail an **I**-type or an **I***-type sentence, which restricts the system to situations where $[\![F]\!] \neq \varnothing$.

5.2.2 *The ancient commentators*

There is a remarkable contrast between, on the one hand, the very long history of predicate logic and, on the other, the amount of persistent misunderstanding and misattribution.[4] There is no doubt that the Master laid the foundations for predicate logic, and in better-informed circles (e.g. Kneale and Kneale 1962; De Rijk 2002) it is also known that his own system of predicate logic differs in certain important respects from traditional ABPC as developed by his commentators, especially the Latin author Apuleius ($\pm$125–180 CE), the Greek Ammonius ($\pm$440–520 CE), and his younger Roman contemporary Boethius ($\pm$480–524 CE)—that is, five to eight centuries after Aristotle.

One should realize that formal predicate logic, as presented in Aristotle's texts, was not at all a popular subject in ancient times. There was a rich tradition of writing commentaries on Aristotle's works, in the context of higher-education teaching of Aristotelian philosophy, but the interest was almost entirely focused on questions of the compatibility or incompatibility of Platonic and Aristotelian doctrines and, after the third century CE, also the more mystically oriented philosophy introduced by Plotinus known as Neo-Platonism. There was a secondary focus on Aristotle's theory of the syllogism, but clearly no focus at all on predicate calculus (for documentation, see Sorabji 1990, 2004).

Until the advent of the Middle Ages, formal predicate logic was but a sideshow of a sideshow. Compared with the large number of known ancient commentators on Aristotelian philosophy in its each and every aspect (see Sorabji 2004), the number of commentaries written on Aristotelian predicate logic is extremely small.[5] Apuleius, Ammonius, and Boethius are, to my

---

[4] The same goes for propositional calculus, where it took Łukasiewicz (1934) to show that this calculus did not originate with Aristotle, as had been widely thought till then, but with the Stoics. Significantly, Łukasiewicz wrote (Borkowski 1970: 198): 'The history of logic must be written anew, and by an historian who has fully mastered mathematical logic.' Admittedly, the situation has changed to some extent during the seventy-odd years that have passed since, but not enough to make Łukasiewicz's words irrelevant. It is still so that historians of logic can do with some additional formal training. Just as technical translators need knowledge not only of the languages concerned but also of the subject matter of the text, historians of a technical subject need not only historical, linguistic, and textual knowledge but also the expertise required for a proper grasp of the subject at hand. Unfortunately, this latter requirement is too often not met.

[5] With the exception of the three authors mentioned, all the ancient authors known to have written commentaries on Aristotelian logic restricted themselves either to basic semantic notions (such as the

knowledge, the only three who commented on the machinery of Aristotelian predicate logic and whose works have survived. And for them, too, formal predicate logic was but a minor sideline.

Apuleius was a North-African intellectual with a wide range of interests, including the writing of literature, as has been said above. Ammonius was a professor of philosophy in Alexandria. As regards his interest in logic, we may quote Ebbesen (1990*b*: 445):

[T]hough Ammonius taught lots of logic classes in his time, he never managed to become really interested in the discipline. Like most of his contemporaries, he considered acquaintance with the *Organon* as only a stepping-stone on the way to real philosophy.

Boethius was a Christian-Roman aristocrat who not only became prominent in political life but was also a writer and intellectual of note. Despite his short life (he fell into disgrace with the king, Theodoric the Great, and was executed at the age of 44), he left an impressive œuvre, of which his work on Aristotelian predicate logic was only a small part. Since the formal-logical interest of all three authors was merely marginal, one may confidently surmise that their insight into the nature and the technical details of predicate logic was limited, to say the least.

Yet it was the ancient commentators, in particular Ammonius and Boethius, who shaped predicate logic into a form that was passed on to the Middle Ages and reigned supreme till the beginning of the twentieth century.

5.2.3 *The Square representation*

The classic Square of Opposition was only partially Boethius' own invention—if at all. The historical roots of the tradition to represent Aristotelian predicate calculus in the form of a rectangular figure are not entirely clear. Aristotle himself appears to imply some sort of geometrical figure for expository purposes, but according to Londey and Johanson (1987), the actual square notation goes back to the treatise *Perì Hermēneías* mentioned in Section 5.2.1 and reliably attributed to the Latin author Apuleius (±125–180 CE). The text of Apuleius' treatise (which is written in Latin despite its Greek

---

relation between thought, word, and thing) or to the theory of the syllogism. This goes, for example, for Alexander of Aphrodisias (±205 CE) and also for the Neo-Platonist Porphyry (±234–±305 CE) mentioned by Ebbesen (1990*a*). The immensely influential ancient authority on medical science, Galen of Pergamon (±129–199 CE), is thought to have written a commentary on Aristotelian predicate logic. Unfortunately, however, the relevant parts of this commentary have not, as far as is known, survived the wear of time. Sorabji (2004), a source book of Aristotelian commentaries on logic and metaphysics, has nothing at all on predicate logic.

title) makes it clear that Apuleius saw that a rectangular arrangement would capture Aristotelian predicate logic as set out in his *On Interpretation* and modified through a few centuries of teaching practice.

Apuleius describes in detail what the 'quadrata formula' (Sullivan 1967: 64) should look like. It is made up of the four vertices **A** ('omnis voluptas bonum est' or 'every pleasure is a good'), **A***** ('omnis voluptas bonum non est' or 'every pleasure is not a good'), **I** ('quaedam voluptas bonum est' or 'some pleasure is a good') and **I***** ('quaedam voluptas bonum non est' or 'some pleasure is not a good')—though, of course, Apuleius did not use these symbols. The positive and negative universals (**A** and **A***) are to be placed 'in superiore linea' and the positive and negative particulars (**I** and **I***) 'in inferiore linea' (Sullivan 1967: 110). This terminology strongly suggests a teaching practice where it was customary to actually draw the diagram.

One may assume that something like a square representation, whether or not actually drawn, was used in whatever teaching in predicate logic took place during subsequent centuries. It was left to the Roman Boethius, who probably fell back on his slightly older contemporary the Greek Ammonius, to complete Aristotle's logic and cast it into the mould of the classic Square of Opposition, which subsequently became part of the stock-in-trade of predicate logic.

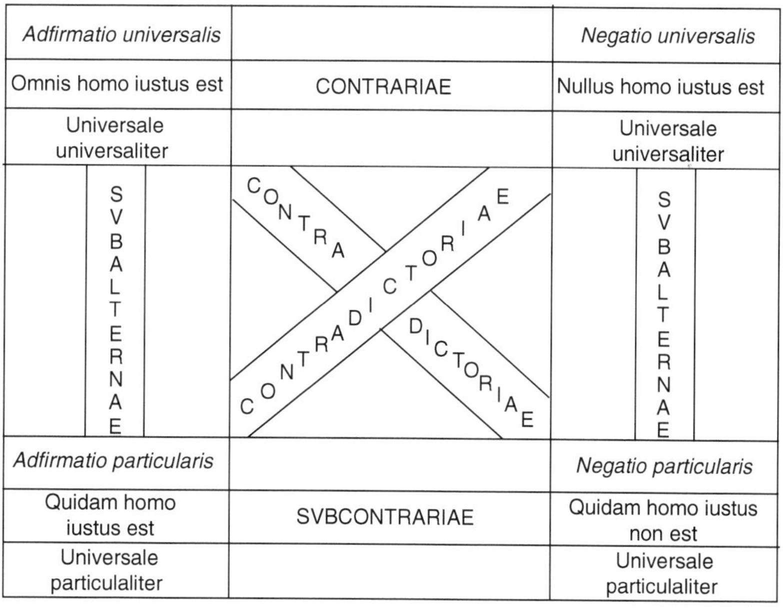

Adfirmatio universalis		Negatio universalis
Omnis homo iustus est	CONTRARIAE	Nullus homo iustus est
Universale universaliter		Universale universaliter
SVBALTERNAE	CONTRADICTORIAE	SVBALTERNAE
Adfirmatio particularis		Negatio particularis
Quidam homo iustus est	SVBCONTRARIAE	Quidam homo iustus non est
Universale particulaliter		Universale particulaliter

FIGURE 5.4 Boethius' own diagram of the Square of Opposition

Source: Meiser 1880: 152

For Boethius' text in this regard I consulted Meiser (1880). There one finds that Boethius did actually draw the Square diagram, prefacing it by the words (Meiser 1880: 152):

Superioris autem disputationis integrum descriptionis subdidimus exemplar, quatenus quod animo cogitationique conceptum est oculis expositum memoriae tenacius infigatur.

[We have provided an integral descriptive diagram of the above discussion, since what is understood by the mind and by thought is more enduringly fixed in memory when shown to the eye.]

Then follows the diagram, of which Figure 5.4 is an exact replica.

5.2.4 *An aside on Horn's and Parsons' proposal as regards the **O**-corner*

An aside must be inserted here regarding a view found in Horn (1989, 1997) and followed up in Parsons (2006, 2008). The view reduces to two claims. The first, which one finds discussed in one or two late medieval texts but which was abandoned by the end of the Middle Ages and revived in the 1950s by a few American historians of logic, in particular Moody (1953), amounts to saying that it is not the universals (**A** and **A***/¬**I**) that generate existential entailment but the positives (**A** and **I**), as opposed to the negatives (**A*** and **I***/¬**A**), which do not. The view is summarized by the formula that it is not 'quantity' but 'quality' that is responsible for existential import: the *affirmative* categorical types are taken to have existential import but the corresponding *negatives* (that is, with internal negation) can be true when $[\![F]\!] = \emptyset$. In more direct parlance, it is said that the **I*** and **A***-corners should be allowed to 'leak'. We shall see that this claim is correct in so far as the logic based on the quantifiers thus defined does not suffer from undue existential import (UEI). The second claim is that this has in fact been the way the **O**-corner has been interpreted throughout the logical tradition. We will see that the second is incorrect and fails to do justice to historical truth.

If, like Horn, one belongs to the pragmatics camp, such a view appears, at first sight, to make good sense. For if the Square can be saved from UEI and thus be shown to be logically sound after all, the gap between pragmatics and logic is narrowed considerably, since the Square stays much closer to natural intuitions than SMPC does. But clearly, for that remedy to work, the Square must not have to be re-interpreted in a way that makes the clash with the same natural intuitions worse than it was before. Unfortunately, it is to be feared that this condition is not fulfilled. On the new interpretation, the clash with natural intuitions is even worse than it was with respect to SMPC.

Logically speaking, one might be tempted to think that letting the **I*** and **A***-corners 'leak' has a great deal going for it because it looks as if the classic Square is preserved in full glory when **A*** and **I*** no longer require that the F-class should be nonnull, as becomes clear when one sets up a VS-model and an octagonal representation along these lines, as in Figure 5.5 below. In virtue of considering space 4 a truth-maker for **A*** and **I*** but not for **A** and **I**, the resulting octagon turns out identical to that of the Square (Figure 5.2b). This may well give rise to the idea that the Square can be saved in full if the truth assignments are made in this way. But, as is shown below, this advantage is bought at the price of having to admit an ambiguity in the semantic definition of the existential quantifier.

Horn (1989: 23–30) is at pains to convince his readers of the historical legitimacy of the view that 'existential import is determined by the *quality* of the proposition; affirmative (**A** and **I**) propositions entail existence, while negative ones (**E** and **O**) do not' (Horn 1989: 24). He assigns an impressive pedigree to this view, tracing it back to Aristotle in so far as Aristotle denies the truth of a singular, nonquantified sentence like *Socrates' son is ill* when Socrates has no son. Just as *Socrates' son is not ill* is true when Socrates has no son, *Not all Socrates' children are ill* should likewise be considered true, and thus *All Socrates' children are ill* should be considered false, when the good man has no children. Yet, although this parallel is sometimes drawn (e.g. Thompson 1953: 257), it is false, since Aristotle clearly distinguishes between 'singular sentences' ('occasion sentences' in Quine's terminology) and quantified sentences or categoricals (Quine's 'eternal sentences'). Moreover, neither Aristotle nor any other ancient author has been found prepared to maintain that *Some of Socrates' children are not ill* is true when Socrates is childless.

Moody (1953) proposes a more modest pedigree. Trying to defend the logical soundness of the Square, he claims (1953: 50–3), followed by Klima (1988: 18–19), that the medievals generally held that only the affirmatives in the Square have existential import while the negatives do not. Buckner, however, clearly showed in his conference paper (2007) that this is at best tendentious and at worst just wrong, since this interpretation of the intended meaning of **I***-type propositions is overwhelmingly belied by the medieval philosophical literature. It appears to be closer to the truth to say that during the fourteenth century and only then this view was discussed but far from generally accepted.

In Moody's defence it must be said that he recognizes the fact that, even though withholding existential import from the **O**-corner saves the Square from UEI, it clashes with natural intuitions (Moody 1953: 51–2):

The particular negative must, as negation of the universal affirmative, be analyzed as a disjunction of the negations of the two parts of the universal affirmative. Consequently the formula of the particular negative *is not properly represented by the word formula* 'Some *F* is not a *G*', but only by the formula, 'Not every *F* is a *G*', which is satisfied either because nothing is an *F*, or because something is an *F* which is not a *G*. (italics mine)

The same observation is made by Thompson, who agrees with Moody's analysis (Thompson 1953: 253):

Even if we agree with the new defenders of Aristotle that the decision which leads to the modern analysis is repugnant to ordinary speech, we can still argue that this is more desirable than a decision repugnant to logical analysis itself.

Our perspective, however, is the opposite of Thompson's: we are primarily interested in *natural* human logic, and an **O**-corner as envisaged by Moody and Thompson is, therefore, of no interest to us, even if it were tenable from an abstract, and inevitably artificial, logical point of view.

Horn, who closely follows Moody, agrees (Horn 1989: 27):

... an **O**-type ... statement corresponds more exactly to the nonentailing *Not every F is a G* than to the entailing *Some F is not a G*. The former is automatically true but the latter false in a state of *F*-lessness.

Yet he fails to draw the conclusion that, therefore, this interpretation of the Square is artificial and unhelpful for an understanding of the natural logic of human language and cognition.

In Horn (1997) one finds a shift towards what Thompson, in the quote given above, calls 'logical analysis itself' and away from natural usage. Here, Horn defends the view that only affirmative propositions in the Square of Opposition have existential import, while the negatives do not, so that *Some F is not a G* should be taken to be automatically true 'in a state of *F*-lessness'. This view, which is, again, called 'traditional' (Horn 1997: 157), is attributed to Aristotle's commentators Apuleius and Boethius, to the twelfth-century French philosopher Abelard, and to a few modern authors, in particular Carroll (1896), Strawson (1952), and Kneale and Kneale (1962).

These references, however, do not stand up to scrutiny. As has been shown in Section 5.2.2, the commentators certainly did not subscribe to the analysis proposed by Horn and Parsons. Abelard did not even have an **O**-corner, as is shown in Section 5.3, because, like Aristotle, he distinguished **I***, which does have existential import, from **¬A**, which does not. The eccentric but well-informed Oxford mathematician-logician-writer-photographer Charles Dodgson, better known under his *nom de plume* Lewis Carroll, wrote a logic textbook for children (Carroll 1896). This author clearly assigns existential import to **I***, as is shown by his reduction of *Some apples are not ripe* to:

Some | existing Things | are | not-ripe apples (Carroll 1896: 77).

Horn's statement (Horn 1997: 157) that Carroll defended the position that the **O**-corner lacks existential import is thus clearly erroneous.

The same applies to his reference to Strawson's logic textbook. There we read, for example (Strawson 1952: 166):

It is already agreed that the **I** and **O** forms are to be regarded as having existential import.

And as regards the Kneales's famous book on the history of logic, we read (Kneale and Kneale 1962: 58):

. . . the assertion of the existence of a man who is white, or not-white, as the case may be, already involves an assertion of the existence of a man.

Parsons (2006), which, mainly through its publication on the internet,[6] has had a considerable influence, repeats Horn's claim to an ancient pedigree. Apparently, Parsons considers this historical claim important, as it occurs in the opening paragraph of his article (Parsons 2006: 1):

For most of this history [of the Square; PAMS], logicians assumed that negative particular propositions ('Some *S* is not *P*') are vacuously true if their subjects are empty.

Yet no evidence is provided for this statement, which, to the best of my knowledge, does not hold water. What one does find in the thirteenth and fourteenth centuries is a debate on whether *Every man is an animal* is true with no men existing.[7] In this case, the example itself is important because *animal* is an essential, not an accidental, property of *man*. The debate ran mainly along party-philosophical lines. The nominalists (Ockham, Buridan) argued that, with no men existing, *Every man is an animal* is false. They concluded that, therefore, *Some man is not an animal* is true, not realizing that this conclusion is false, because when ¬**A** is considered false with no **F** existing, there is an entailment from **I*** to ¬**A** but not vice versa, as is shown in Figures 4.7c and 5.7a. But the realists (Scotus, Aquinas) ruled this out on grounds of philosophical *a priori*: if it is part of the essence of man to be an animal, then falsity for *Every man is an animal* is ruled out as a matter of

---

[6] Parsons (1997) is a larger version of Parsons (2006), published in the normal, old-fashioned way.
[7] I owe this information to Edward Buckner (email correspondence).

principle. Since the Church backed the realists (Ockham was excommunicated in 1328), their view prevailed and the nominalist view, which erroneously implied that the **O**-corner has no existential import, was marginalized. But one should note that this debate was not triggered by the question of UEI, which, apparently, did not figure at all prominently in the minds of the philosophers involved, but by the great metaphysical debate on universals. It might well have been superfluous if both parties had taken the trouble to have a closer look at the Aristotelian-Abelardian version of predicate logic.

Moody states (1953: 51):

Since existential import was considered to belong only to affirmative sentences, it is sufficient, for the falsity of an affirmative and hence for the truth of the contradictory negative, that one of the terms stands for nothing.

This statement, however, is not backed up with any crucial quotation. The closest he comes is a quote from Buridan's *Sophismata*, Ch. 2, Concl. 14 (Moody 1953: 51):

Omnis particularis negativa vera, ex eo est vera ex quo universalis affirmativa sibi contradictoria est falsa.
[Every true particular negative is true on the grounds that the universal affirmative which is its contradictory is false.]

But Buridan does not go so far as to state that particular negatives are vacuously true when the subject class is empty. Moody's statement that 'existential import was considered to belong only to affirmative sentences' is, therefore, based on his *interpretation*, not on *textual evidence*. One may wonder why the medieval authors did not put into words what Moody takes them to imply. Did they baulk at the idea of having to call a sentence like *Some unicorns are not animals* true despite the absence of unicorns in this world or is this simply not what they implied?

Abelard, as shown in Section 5.3, solved the predicament, in the early twelfth century, by giving up the Conversions and letting the **O**-corner keep its existential import. In this he was followed by Walter Burleigh in his *De Puritate Artis Logicae*, written around 1328 in reply to Ockham's *Summa Logicae*, which was written around 1323. For Burleigh, as is shown in Section 9.4.2, an **A**-type sentence like *Every man who has a son loves him* and its corresponding **I***-type *Some man who has a son does not love him* are not contradictories but only contraries.

In any case, Moody's skewed interpretation of medieval logic is now widely taken to reflect historical reality, especially in North America. Many or most American authors now take it for granted that it was 'the general medieval view that affirmative sentences are false if their subjects are empty, whereas negative sentences are true if their subjects are empty' (King 2005: 266). Yet never is one presented with an actual reference to that effect: it very much looks as if Moody has been believed on the strength of his authority, not on the strength of actual evidence.

Nor, it seems, on the strength of actual insight. When providing the truth conditions for the four Aristotelian sentence types, King, in his otherwise excellent article, unwittingly assigns the same conditions to ¬**I** as he does to **I***, which suggests a less than full grasp of the issue. Yet the issue seems to weigh on his mind, or else it is hard to see why he should start his enumeration of truth conditions for the four types with an **I***-sentence whose subject term is empty (King 2005: 266):

Truth conditions for assertoric present-tense categorical sentences are straightforward. For instance, the particular negative sentence 'Some vampires are-not friendly' is true just in case what 'friendly' personally supposits for, namely people who are friendly, does not include anything—note the negative copula—for which 'vampire' personally supposits. Universal affirmatives ('Every S is P') are true when everything their subjects supposit for their predicates also supposit for; particular affirmatives ('Some S is P') when their predicates supposit for at least one thing their subjects supposit for; universal negatives ('No S is P') when the predicate does not supposit for anything the subject supposits for.

Parsons (2008: 5) does come up with something that looks like evidence, quoting a passage from Ockham, who lived in the fourteenth century. This passage, however, occurs in a wider context which I quote here more fully, both in Latin and in my English translation (Ockham, *Summa Logicae* II.3). The text opens Chapter II.3 of Ockham's *Summa Logicae*, entitled 'What is required for the truth of propositions that are both indefinite and particular' (I have italicized the parts that are quoted by Parsons):[8]

Viso quid sufficit ad veritatem propositionis singularis, videndum est quid requiritur ad veritatem propositionis indefinitae et particularis.

Et est primo sciendum quod si non vocetur propositio indefinita nec particularis nisi quando terminus subiectus supponit personaliter, tunc semper indefinita et particularis convertuntur, sicut istae convertuntur 'Homo currit', 'Aliquis homo currit'; 'Animal est homo', 'Aliquod animal est homo'; 'Animal non est homo', 'Aliquod animal non est homo'. Et *ad veritatem talium sufficit quod subiectum et praedicatum supponant pro aliquo eodem, si sit propositio affirmativa* et non addatur signum universale a parte praedicati;

---

[8] The quote is taken from: http://individual.utoronto.ca/pking/resources/Ockham/Summa_logicae. txt

quod dico propter tales 'Aliquod animal est omnis homo', 'Aliquis angelus est omnis angelus'. Sed *si talis sit negativa*, requiritur quod subiectum et praedicatum non supponant pro omni eodem, immo *requiritur quod subiectum pro nullo supponat, uel quod supponat pro aliquo pro quo praedicatum non supponit*. Et hoc quia ad veritatem talium sufficit veritas cuiuscumque singularis. Sicut ad veritatem istius 'Aliquod animal est homo' sufficit veritas istius 'Hoc animal est homo' vel 'Illud animal est homo'; similiter ad veritatem istius 'Animal non est homo' sufficit veritas istius 'Hoc animal non est homo', quocumque demonstrato. [. . .] *Et ideo si nullus homo nec aliquod animal sit nisi asinus, haec consequentia non valet 'Homo non est asinus, igitur aliquod animal non est asinus'*. Similiter non sequitur 'Homo albus non est animal, igitur homo non est animal' nisi ista propositio sit vera 'Homo albus non est homo'. Tamen affirmative bene sequitur [. . .] quia semper, sive homo sit animal sive non, bene sequitur 'Homo currit, igitur animal currit', similiter bene sequitur 'Homo albus est animal, igitur homo est animal', sive homo sit albus sive non. Sic igitur patet quomodo indefinita vel particularis est vera si subiectum supponat pro aliquo pro quo non supponit praedicatum. Hoc tamen non semper requiritur, sed quandoque sufficit quod subiectum indefinitae vel particularis negativae pro nullo supponat. Sicut si nullus homo sit albus, haec est vera 'Homo albus non est homo', et tamen subiectum pro nullo supponit quia nec pro substantia nec pro accidente.

[Now that we have seen what suffices for the truth of singular propositions, let us see what is required for the truth of propositions that are both indefinite and particular.

First we note that, if the label 'indefinite' or 'particular' is assigned to a proposition only when the subject term has individual reference, then indefinites and particulars are always interchangeable, as in 'A man runs' and 'Some man runs'; 'An animal is a man', 'Some animal is a man'; 'An animal is not a man', 'Some animal is not a man'. And *it is sufficient for the truth of such propositions that the subject term and the predicate refer to some same thing, if the proposition is affirmative* and no universal sign is added to the predicate; I am saying this because of examples like 'Some animal is every man', 'Some angel is every angel'. But *if such a proposition is negative*, it is required <for its truth> that the subject and the predicate do not refer to all identicals—that is, *it is required either that the subject refers to nothing or that it refers to something to which the predicate does not refer*. And this is because it suffices for the truth of such propositions that at least one, no matter which, singular proposition is true. Just as it suffices for the truth of 'Some animal is a man' that 'This animal is a man' or 'That animal is a man' is true, in like manner it suffices for the truth of 'An animal is not a man' that there be some, no matter which, animal that can be actually pointed at, of which 'This animal is not a man' be true. [. . .] *And therefore, if there are no men and no animals except a donkey, the following argument is not valid: 'A man is not a donkey; therefore, some animal is not a donkey'*. In the same way, the following is not valid 'A white man is not an animal; therefore, a man is not an animal', unless it is also true that 'A white man is a man'. Yet these arguments are valid in the affirmative form [. . .] because, whether a man is an animal or not, the argument 'A man runs; therefore, an animal runs' is always valid. Or, to take another example, 'A white man is an animal; therefore, a man is an animal' is a valid argument, whether a man is white or not. Thus it is clear why an indefinite or particular proposition is true in case the subject refers to something to which the predicate does not. But this is not always required, for sometimes it suffices for the truth of a negative indefinite or particular proposition that the subject refers to nothing. For example, when there are no white men, 'A white man is not a man' is true even though the subject refers to nothing because it refers neither to a substance nor to an accident.]

I apologize for this very long quote, but it is necessary because it places the quote given by Parsons in an entirely different light. In this passage, Ockham appears to be making an attempt at incorporating a logic of indefinites into that of the Square, as one sees from the opening sentence, where he does not speak simply of particulars but of propositions that are both indefinite—that is, 'generic', without a quantifier—and particular. Ockham systematically distinguishes indefinites (generics) from particulars in that he uses the bare noun (adorned with the indefinite article in the translation) in indefinites but the noun preceded by *aliquod* or *aliquis* ('some') in particulars. In other words, Parsons misquotes Ockham when he translates 'ad veritatem talium sufficit' as 'it is sufficient for the truth of [a particular] proposition' because *talium* (such) does not simply stand for particular propositions but for propositions that are both indefinite and particular.

We remember from Section 5.2.1 that Aristotle spends some time over indefinites (adióristoi) in the first chapter of *On Interpretation*, without coming anywhere near a logic for them. Apparently, Ockham is now at pains to achieve what Aristotle had failed to do. It is clear from the text that Ockham withholds existential import from internally negative indefinites, as he considers *A man is not a donkey* true in cases where there are no men but there is a donkey, which in itself is quite reasonable (*A unicorn is not a donkey* is reasonably called true in the actual world). In fact, all his examples where internal negation yields truth when the subject class is empty are examples of indefinites, not of particulars.

But it is also clear that he is pushing for an identification of indefinites and particulars: 'indefinites and particulars are always interchangeable'. And the last-but-one sentence of the quote reads: 'But this is not always required, for sometimes it suffices for the truth of a negative indefinite *or particular* proposition that the subject refers to nothing.' Apparently, Ockham has some qualms about this, because he continues: 'For example, when there are no white men, "A white man is not a man" is true *even though the subject refers to nothing*', giving again an example of an indefinite, and not a particular, negative. The overall impression is that he is unhappy with the unnaturalness of this truth assignment to internally negative particulars, more so than to internally negative indefinites.

In any case, the passage shows that Ockham is experimenting here, in very much the same way as so many other logicians (such as Hamilton, Moody, Thompson, or Parsons) have done, with remedies for the Square.[9] But this is a far cry from saying that it was traditionally or generally accepted in medieval philosophy that the **O**-corner lacks existential import, or that existential import is restricted to the affirmatives while the negatives are without it. Parsons' generalizing statement that this is how 'late medieval logicians understood' the Square (2008: 5) is, therefore, unsupported by sufficient evidence, or, to put it bluntly, just a myth.

As hardly anything of note was presented on this issue between the Middle Ages and the nineteenth century, I will now turn to that century and we will see that there is hardly a trace of the thesis that the **O**-corner lacks existential import. Fowler (1892), for example, implicitly assumes existential import for the **O**-corner without mentioning the problem of the null **F**-class or the distinction between extensional and intensional being (Fowler 1892: 36, 79). Schiller (1912), though apparently unaware of the LOGICAL problem of existential import in connection with the Square, is acutely aware of the ONTOLOGICAL distinction between extensional and intensional being (Schiller 1912: 107–8). He also assumes existential import for the **O**-corner without further comment (Schiller 1912: 154–5).

The German logician Sigwart mentions the logical problems caused by existential import (Sigwart 1895: 172):

The negation of 'all *A*'s are *B*' means 'the *A*'s which are *B* are not all *A*'s'; and the way in which we understand the negation must depend upon whether the judgement was intended as empirically or as unconditionally universal. [...] Aristotle taught [...] that universal affirmative [= **A**] and particular negative [= **I***] judgements, and universal negative [= **A***] and particular affirmative [= **I**] judgements are contradictorily opposed. This doctrine leads to false conclusions unless attention is paid to the difference between empirically valid and [unconditionally] valid [universal] judgements.[10]

---

⁹ King (2005: 243) writes 'Ockham's *Summa Logicae* (*The Logic Handbook*), written *ca.* 1323, is a manifesto masquerading as a textbook', implying that the book was meant to promote Ockham's grand nominalist philosophical conception. Be that as it may, it is clear that the *Summa Logicae* does not represent standard views that were taught in the Arts faculties of medieval universities.

¹⁰ The text, which is itself a translation from the German original, reads 'empirically valid and universally valid judgements', which makes no sense; I have restored the text according to the only possible intended meaning.

He thus seeks a solution in a distinction between empirically universal and unconditionally universal 'judgements', the former with, the latter without, existential import (Sigwart 1895: 163):

If a judgement concerning 'all' is unconditionally universal, then it is clear that no direct statement is made about the actual existence of the subjects, though this is most certainly presupposed by empirical judgements if they refer to actual things at all.

The distinction is then reduced to one of necessity versus possibility—a solution that smacks of medieval metaphysics and would not satisfy nowadays. Interestingly, Sigwart noted (Sigwart 1895: 173) that Aristotle avoided the equivalence of ¬**A** and **I***, quoting exactly the passage from *Int* 17b16 given in Section 5.2.1, and thereby belying his statement, made one page earlier, that 'Aristotle taught ... that universal affirmative and particular negative judgements ... are contradictorily opposed'. In this respect, therefore, Sigwart and the Kneales are of a kind. Be that as it may, Sigwart's text would make no sense if the **I***-form were to lack existential import.

The not so traditional nineteenth-century logician De Morgan (followed in this respect by Carroll 1896: 70) uses his notion of restricted universe of discourse (see Section 3.2.2) to circumvent the problem of existential import, though he does not discuss the issue explicitly. This allows him to accept the traditional Square, which he does, complete with existential import for the whole Square and hence also for the **I***-form (De Morgan 1847: 6).

In Volume II of his *Collected Works*, entitled *Elements of Logic*, Peirce writes (Peirce 1974: 223, paragr. 2.376):

... the distinction between affirmative and negative propositions is purely relative to the particular predicate. No doubt many logicians have assumed that negative propositions are distinguished from ordinary affirmative propositions in not implying the reality of the subject. But what, then, does 'Some patriarch does not die' mean? Besides, all admit that propositions *per se primo modo* do not imply the existence of the subject, although they be affirmative. At any rate, the resulting syllogistic, if consistent, is very objectionable.

Again, one sees that this philosopher rejects the Horn–Parsons analysis, because it clashes not only with ordinary usage but also with syllogistic reasoning.

This, more or less random, selection of texts rather bodes ill for Parsons' (and Horn's) contention that 'For most of this history, logicians assumed that negative particular propositions ("Some *S* is not *P*") are vacuously true if their subjects are empty'.

But, history aside, does it make semantic or logical sense to deny the **O**-corner existential import? At first sight one might think it does, because if the **A**-corner has existential import, one would expect it to follow that ¬**A**, and thus its alleged equivalent **I***, do not. Yet a little reflection will show that this makes the semantics of the natural-language existential and universal quantifiers SOME and ALL inconsistent in a strictly extensional system. According to Horn and Parsons, existential import is induced by the universal and existential quantifiers only when they combine with a nonnegative predicate G but not when they combine with a negative predicate not-G. This would make their satisfaction conditions dependent on the lexical choice of the main predicate. But in extensional predicate logic the main predicate is represented by a lexical variable—in this case, G or not-G—and should, therefore, have no bearing on the logical properties of the operators that define the logic. The Horn–Parsons position has the extraordinary implication that, for example, *Some men are bachelors* has existential import, but *Some men are not married* hasn't, or that *All John's views are erroneous* has existential import, but *All John's views are not right* hasn't!

Logically speaking, Parsons' proposal amounts to a VS-model and an octagon as shown in Figure 5.5. Here one sees that, in a state of F-lessness, **A** and **I** are taken to be false but **A*** and **I*** true. This has the surprising effect that the corresponding octagon remains identical with that holding for traditional ABPC, as is easily checked when one compares Figure 5.5b with Figure 5.2b. It may well have been this fact that has motivated Parsons and

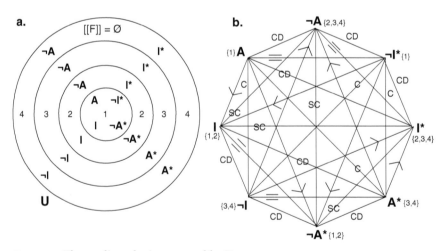

FIGURE 5.5 The predicate logic proposed by Parsons

those he follows to propose the view that the Square can be saved by assuming that the affirmatives have existential import while the negatives do not. Yet there is a big problem, in that this interpretation of ABPC makes it impossible to provide consistent definitions for the two quantifiers ∀ and ∃, or, in traditional terms, for the words ALL and SOME.

This is easily shown. If, as Parsons does, one takes **A**, or ALL **F** is **G**, to be true just in case $[\![F]\!] \neq \emptyset$ and $[\![F]\!] \cap [\![\overline{G}]\!] = \emptyset$, then **A***, or ALL **F** is NOT-**G**, must be taken to be true just in case $[\![F]\!] \neq \emptyset$ and $[\![F]\!] \cap [\![G]\!] = \emptyset$, which gives both **A** and **A*** existential import. Likewise, if **I**, or SOME **F** is **G**, is taken to be true just in case $[\![F]\!] \cap [\![G]\!] \neq \emptyset$, then **I***, or SOME **F** is NOT-**G**, must be taken to be true just in case $[\![F]\!] \cap [\![\overline{G}]\!] \neq \emptyset$ which gives both **I** and **I*** existential import. The reason for this is that ∀ (ALL) and ∃ (SOME) are binary higher-order predicates expressing relations between two sets X and Y, no matter which. Therefore, it makes no difference whether X or Y is characterized by positive or by negative satisfaction conditions. Yet Parsons defines **A** as requiring that $[\![F]\!] \neq \emptyset$ and $[\![F]\!] \cap [\![\overline{G}]\!] = \emptyset$, as above, but **A*** as requiring that $[\![F]\!] = \emptyset$ or $[\![F]\!] \cap [\![G]\!] = \emptyset$, which precludes one single definition for ∀ (ALL). Likewise, Parsons defines **I** as requiring that $[\![F]\!] \cap [\![G]\!] = \emptyset$, as above, but **I*** as requiring that $[\![F]\!] = \emptyset$ or $[\![F]\!] \cap [\![\overline{G}]\!] \neq \emptyset$, which again precludes one single definition for ∃ (SOME). In other words, ALL and SOME have become ambiguous between those cases where the G-predicate is positive and those where it is negative. In the latter case it (arbitrarily) loses its natural existential import. Parsons and company thus buy the logic of the Square of Opposition but have to live with ambiguous quantifiers.

This forces Parsons to give up the classic notion of quantifier and thus to reject both the traditional Aristotelian syntactic template (NOT) ALL/SOME **F** is (NOT-)**G** and the modern notation, whether in the Russellian or in the generalized-quantifier format. And this is exactly what he does. Parsons (2006, 2008) falls back on the device of 'quantification of the predicate' discussed in Section 3.4.2 in connection with Hamilton's predicate logic. (This device was also known to Ockham, as one sees from the long quote given above from Ockham's *Summa Logicae*.) Like Moody and Thompson, however, he dismisses naturalness as a criterion (Parsons 2008: 5):

What is important is that the logical notation be coherent and useful. If it does not perfectly match the usage of ordinary language, that is not on its own important for a system of logic. Indeed, if you are sure that ordinary language universal affirmatives should be false when their subject term is empty, then you may represent that fact by translating them into modern logical notation adding a conjunct. Instead of symbolizing 'Every A is B' by '∀x(Ax → Bx)', symbolize it as '∃xAx & (Ax → Bx)'.

Yet he does not mention the disastrous consequences this has for the naturalness of the logic when this proposal is combined with the requirement that the Conversions stay intact. Horn and like-minded pragmaticists should realize that this does not help them at all.

In this context, Parsons devises an entirely new logical language which is severely at odds with natural language, both syntactically and semantically, and where SOME and ALL are defined not as words but syncategorematically, and in terms not just of what may be the case 'in the model' but also of 'truth under an assignment σ. Following Klima (1988), Parsons then introduces an artificial 'zero element' which, arbitrarily, makes ALL F is G and SOME F is G false but ALL F is NOT-G and SOME F is NOT-G true. I will not here comment on the logical merits of this proposal, since it is irrelevant for the natural logic of language and cognition. All I wish to note here is that proposals to the effect that only the Aristotelian affirmatives have existential import while the negatives do not are doomed to take leave from the world of natural intuitions and to disappear into abstract logical space.

5.2.5 *Logic and mysticism: what made logic popular?*

But let us revert to our original topic. As we know, Boethius determined the form of predicate logic until the twentieth century. It is usually said that this is in virtue of the fact that he was a Christian and that he wrote in Latin, Greek being almost universally unknown till the thirteenth century. In fact, most of the standard Latin terminology is due to him (though many specialists believe that in presenting his version of Aristotelian predicate logic he heavily depended on Ammonius). This, however, is only part of the story. It seems safe to surmise that the primary cause of Boethius' enormous influence on the history of logic lies in the general human penchant to look for mystic messages in formal systems.

In this respect, the medieval literati had a field day. The seeds of mysticism that had been sown during late Antiquity now had the chance to come to full fruition, no longer suppressed by a pagan imperial power that had, on the whole, connived at the spread of mystical currents, including Christianity with its Eastern roots, among the slaves and the labourers but had stifled such tendencies among the military, the educated, and the ruling classes. No sooner had Christianity been given full rein than the hidden reserves of esoteric mysticism and occultism exploded, despite the frantic efforts of the official Church to contain the explosion. The subsequent rise of Islam only added fuel to the flames.

During the Middle Ages, one witnesses not only a genuine professional interest in logic, both syllogistic and predicate calculus (as shaped by Boethius), but also a dramatic increase in mystic, kabbalistic and other occult exercises, all of a well-defined formal nature, connected with letters of the alphabet, geometrical figures, esoteric symbols, heavenly bodies, and numbers. One thinks, for example, of the mysticism woven around the Fibonacci numbers and the golden ratio, also known as the golden section or the divine proportion—a mysticism that has been of all times but was particularly strong during the Middle Ages.

Syllogistic and predicate logic, with their nice geometrical designs, likewise offered a wonderful opportunity for mystics and kabbalists to look for hidden messages sent down from the clouds of eternity. A good example is the Catalan Ramon Llull (±1232–1316), who developed a system based on a nonagon (reminiscent of Aristotle's nine categories) listing the attributes of God: goodness, greatness, eternity, power, wisdom, will, virtue, truth, and glory. From these he meant to derive deductively all important eternal truths, especially the Christian dogmas. The nonagon was realized in four different 'figures', the first of which was designed to generate the Aristotelian syllogisms. The other three had different functions, all of a 'cosmic' nature (Eco 1995: 56–64; Wikipedia s.v. *Ramon Llull*).

Tellingly, the Arabic word for logic is *manṭiq*, from the Greek word *mantikē* (prophecy, fortune-telling). For a long time, logic and kabbalistic mysticism were closely linked—a fact which, paradoxically, strongly contributed to the increased popularity and prestige of logic. Once the political shackles of the Roman Empire had been shed and Christianity had gained the ascendancy, esoteric formal symbolisms began to cast their spell not only on the common folk, as in late Antiquity, but also on the educated classes and the lay rulers. And most of these were fascinated more by the mystical depths attributed to the formal systems than by their purely intellectual content (to the extent that there was any).

In modern times, we have, by and large, managed to banish occultism from mathematics, logic, and science and to a large extent also from the prevailing social norm system, if not quite from actual practice.[11] But the irony is that

---

[11] One should realize that even reputable academics have, at times, indulged in kabbalistic and similar occult exercises. Mark Alford writes the following about Isaac Newton (Alford 1995):

In fact, Newton was deeply opposed to the mechanistic conception of the world. A secretive alchemist and heretical theologian, he performed countless experiments with crucibles and furnaces in his Cambridge chambers, analyzing the results in unmistakably alchemical terms. His written work on the subject ran to more than a million words, far more than he ever produced on calculus or mechanics. Obsessively religious, he spent years correlating biblical

the 'scientific attitude', which began to be manifest during the late Middle Ages and has dominated Western culture ever since, may well owe its growth and its enormous influence in large part to the very craving for hidden truths and for contact with the supernatural that it so successfully managed to get rid of.

5.3 Abelard's remedy

Petrus Abaelardus, known in the English world as Abelard (1079–1142), was the opposite of a mysticist but he was destroyed, one may say, by one who was, St. Bernard of Clairvaux. Abelard is, of course, best known on account of his passionate but deeply unhappy relationship with Héloïse, tragically scarred by his violent castration at the behest of Héloïse's 'uncle' (more likely her natural father), canon Fulbert of Notre Dame in Paris. Although Abelard and Héloïse found themselves forced by the powers that were to lead separate monastic lives, leaving their son Astralabius in the care of Abelard's sister, they remained devoted to each other for the rest of their unhappy days. All this is well known. Less known is the fact that this brilliant, flamboyant, and amazingly independent thinker, teacher, writer, and composer of religious hymns and (now lost) popular love songs was excommunicated twice by the Holy Church and died a broken man, having been the victim of a persistent and extremely vicious defamation campaign led by envious countrymen, especially the obscurantist St. Bernard of Clairvaux. The Church then ensured his lasting vilification through its centres of education. He was the first to apply the term *theology* to the rational investigation of the nature of God—an activity considered blasphemous by Bernard and by the Pope (as well as by the Islam religious authorities of the period). In this context, he wrote extensively

prophecy with historical events. He became deeply convinced that Christian doctrine had been deliberately corrupted by the false notion of the trinity, and developed a vicious contempt for conventional (trinitarian) Christianity and for Roman Catholicism in particular. Newton's religious and alchemical interests were not tidily separated from his scientific ones. He believed that God mediated the gravitational force, and opposed any attempt to give a mechanistic explanation of chemistry or gravity, since that would diminish the role of God.

The Dutch mathematician Luitzen E. J. Brouwer (1881–1966), founder of Intuitionism in mathematics, had strong mystical tendencies. In 1905, Brouwer published a pamphlet entitled 'Leven, Kunst en Mystiek' ('Life, Art and Mysticism' see Brouwer 1966), a text drenched in romanticism, in which he attempted to integrate mathematics and mysticism (see also Van Dalen 1999). Wittgenstein's 'mathematical' work was likewise not without a fair shot of mysticism, and his *Tractatus Logico-Philosophicus* has been much more influential among speculative thinkers and in the artistic literature than among more sober-minded philosophers. One wonders if it would have had the same appeal if it had lacked its quasi-formal style and structure.

Another example is Ferdinand de Saussure, one of the founding fathers of modern linguistics, who, for the last twenty years of his life, indulged in 'occult speculations about hidden messages in Greek and Latin poetry, based on occurrences or repetitions of syllables and sounds' (Seuren 1998a: 146; see also Starobinski 1979). Many more such examples could be mentioned.

on the mystery of the Trinity. A century after his death, under the influence of Thomas Aquinas, the Church reversed its position on the legitimacy of theology and in particular the study of the Trinity, but Abelard was never duly acknowledged, let alone rehabilitated.[12]

Apart from all this, however, Abelard was also a consummate logician, who was probably the first, after Aristotle, to be aware of the problem of undue existential import in ABPC. He proposed a solution which is not only as sound as it is simple but also reflects Aristotle's original intention: dissolve the Conversions into one-way entailments from **A** to ¬**I**[*] and from **A**[*] to ¬**I**. Yet, perhaps because the Church was keen to erase Abelard's heritage from history, this solution never came to the surface. It has played virtually no role in the tradition of logic, where, to the extent that its existence was acknowledged, it was not understood and hence misrepresented.[13]

One sometimes finds, as, for example, in Horn (1997) and Parsons (2006) discussed in Section 5.2.4, Abelard discredited with the view that **I**[*]-sentences have no existential import, which would mean that the existential quantifier is taken to induce existential import when followed by a positive, but not when followed by a negative matrix predicate. If Abelard had indeed held this view, he would be subject to the same criticism as has been voiced in Section 5.2.4 with regard to Horn's and Parsons' description of ABPC. For Abelard, however, what is at issue is not whether **I**[*]-sentences have existential import (which he was sure they have) but whether ¬**A**-sentences have it. One should realize that in SMPC ¬**A**-sentences do have existential import, while in ABPC there is a clash of truth values when ¬**A**-sentences are subjected to this question. It is the denial of existential import to ¬**A**-sentences, and the attribution of existential import to **I**[*]-sentences, that makes Aristotle's and, after him, Abelard's logic worthwhile and saves it from inconsistency. It has, apparently, been hard for logicians to see that the Conversions are far from unassailable.

Kneale and Kneale (1962) also mention Abelard's solution and, apparently, likewise fail to see his point. They do, however, acknowledge Abelard's importance for the history of logic, as appears from the following passage (Kneale and Kneale 1962: 204; translation between square brackets mine):

---

[12] One may consult McLeod 1971, Gilson 1978, or Clanchy 1997 for authoritative and highly readable accounts of this dramatic episode in human history.

[13] In Seuren (2002) a solution is proposed for undue existential import that is identical to Abelard's. I named it *Revised Aristotelian predicate calculus* or RAPC. At the time, I was not aware of the fact that Abelard had proposed an identical solution nine hundred years earlier. To give Abelard his due, I have renamed the system in question *Aristotelian-Abelardian predicate calculus*.

Abelard's mind was the keenest (though not in all respects the most admirable)[14] that had been devoted to the subject for more than a thousand years, and he approached his task with the belief that it was still possible to make discoveries: 'Non enim tanta fuit antiquorum scriptorum perfectio ut non et nostro doctrina indigeat studio, nec tantum in nobis mortalibus scientia potest crescere ut non ultra possit augmentum recipere' (De Rijk 1956: 535). [For the perfection of the ancient writers was not such that their doctrine could not profit from our investigations, nor is it possible for science to grow to such an extent in us mortals that it can no longer be improved.]

What Abelard proposed was that, for cases where $[\![F]\!] = \emptyset$, **A**- and **A***-sentences, as well as **I**- and **I***-sentences, should be considered false, while their negations should be considered true (Kneale and Kneale 1962: 210–11):

while he [=Abelard] admits that *Nullus homo est albus* [No human is white] can be regarded as the contradictory of *Quidam homo est albus* [Some human is white] because *nullus* is merely an abbreviation of *non ullus*, he now refuses to allow that *Quidam homo non est albus* [Some human is not white] is the contradictory of *Omnis homo est albus* [All humans are white], as Boethius had maintained, and says that Aristotle dealt with the question more subtly when he offered *Non omnis homo est albus* [Not all humans are white] as the contradictory. It is true, of course, that Aristotle wrote Greek words corresponding to *Non omnis homo est albus*, but it seems clear that he did not intend to convey by these words anything different from the doctrine later attributed to him by Boethius. Abelard, on the other hand, thinks that *Non omnis homo est albus* is something distinct in meaning from the particular negative proposition *Quidam homo non est albus*, and therefore outside the usual scheme of four categorical forms. His reason for introducing this complication is that he assumes existential import for *Omnis homo est albus*, though apparently not for *Nullus homo est albus*. The assumption seems curious after his explicit statement that the word *est* occurring as pure *copula* involves no assertion of existence; but there can be no doubt of his doctrine on this point, since he insists that even the seeming tautology *Omnis homo est homo* would be false if there were no men: 'Cum autem *Quidam homo non est homo* semper falsa sit atque *Omnis homo est homo* homine non existente, patet simul easdem falsas esse: unde nec recte dividentes dici poterunt' (De Rijk 1956: 176) [But since *Some human is not human* is always false and *All humans are humans* is false when no humans exist, it follows that these two can be false at the same time, so that it must be incorrect to call them contradictory opposites]. We must therefore suppose that in his view it is the word *omnis* which introduces existential import.[15]

---

[14] One wonders about the relevance, or indeed the stringency, of the Kneales's moral reservations. This remark about Abelard's allegedly not so admirable 'mind' is best taken as a late reflection of the biographical and other historical facts mentioned at the outset of the present section. The Kneales ought to have known better.

[15] On Abelard's doctrine of the existential value of the copula verb *esse*, see Rosier-Catach (2003 *a*). Since Rosier-Catach's meticulous analysis shows that Kneale and Kneale appear to be right on this

This is a curiously interesting passage, since it shows not only that Kneale and Kneale, with all their barely hidden irony, failed to see Abelard's point—a failure they share with the entire logical tradition—but also, more important-ly, that Abelard's analysis is perfectly coherent and, as was shown in the preceding section, in accordance with what can be gathered from Aristotle's own text, despite Kneale and Kneale's assurance to the contrary. Since Abe-lard's proposal is in full agreement with Aristotle's text, it is legitimate to speak of ARISTOTELIAN-ABELARDIAN PREDICATE CALCULUS, or AAPC. But let us turn to Abelard's own texts so as to unravel what he himself actually proposed.

In his *Dialectica*, his main work on logic (full edition De Rijk 1956), Abelard is at pains to distinguish as clearly as possible between the external ('pre-posed') negation, which always creates contradiction, and the internal ('inter-posed') negation, which creates contrariety under the universal quantifier. We read, for example (De Rijk 1956: 177; translation mine):

The preposed negation thus has a different logical power from the interposed negation. A sentence that says *Every human is not white* is not equivalent with *Not every human is white*, and *Some human is not white* says something different from *Not any human is white*.[16]

In this context Abelard argues, in accordance with the Stoics, that the only real guarantee for pure contradiction is the preposing of the negation and not the insertion of an internal negation combined with a change from universal to existential quantifier or vice versa (De Rijk 1956: 176; translation mine):

Similarly for categorical propositions, where the only real truth-value-inverting (dividens) contradiction of any arbitrary positive proposition appears to be the one

complex issue, we subscribe to their conclusion that, for Abelard, 'it is the word *omnis* [and not the suppletive copula verb *esse*; PAMS] which introduces existential import'. One will note that, according to the analysis presented in the present book, existential import is not induced by any quantifier either but by the extensionality of argument-term positions under any given predicate (see Section 10.7 and Section 3.5.1 in Volume I).

16 It is not clear to what extent Abelard was aware of the distinction between sentences and their underlying L-propositions (logical form), though valuable details for a reconstruction are presented in Rosier-Catach (1999, 2003*b*, 2003*c*). Had he used a modern European language, he would have noticed that in sentences with a definite, non-quantified subject term the external (sentential) negation is not 'preposed' but woven into the surface sentence (in many languages in construction with the finite verb form). But he used Latin, where the logically external negation can always be literally preposed, that is, placed at the beginning of the surface sentence, although most of the times it does not actually occupy that position. His insistence on the syntactic distinction between preposed (external) and interposed (internal) negation suggests that he was thinking in terms of a logical language with both propositional and predicate variables, combining Aristotelian and Stoic logical analyses.

that has the negation preposed to it so that all its entailments are lost (*totam eius sententiam destruit*). For example, the contradictory of *Every human is human* is *Not every human is human,* and not *Some human is not human,* since there are situations where the first and the third are simultaneously false. For when not a single human exists, both of these two propositions are false: *Every human is human* and *Some human is not human.* [...] The proposition *Some human is not human* [...] is always false. For what it says is totally impossible: it cannot be the case and nature can offer no instance of it. [...] In no situation can the same thing be both human and not human at the same time. For it is a well-nigh eternal law that what is not included under negation is excluded under it. [...] But since *Some human is not human* is always false and *All humans are humans* is false when no humans exist, it follows that these two can be false at the same time, so that it must be incorrect to call them contradictory opposites.

The quintessence of Abelard's proposal is that the Conversions should be given up in favour of the one-way entailments from **I*** to ¬**A** and from **I** to ¬**A*** (or, equivalently, from **A** to ¬**I*** and from **A*** to ¬**I**), resulting in a system where the subalterns are preserved as entailments from universal to existential quantification (and thus not from ¬**I*** to **I** or from ¬**I** to **I***) and where **A**-type and **A***-type sentences are false in cases where ⟦**F**⟧=∅. The method of VS-modelling enables us to complete the system without effort and to show immediately and precisely what the logical consequences are of this move.

AAPC as shown in Figure 5.6b differs from SMPC of Figure 5.6a only in that space 4 (the outer ring), which represents the situations where ⟦**F**⟧=∅, makes **A**-type and **A***-type sentences false instead of true. In fact, all four

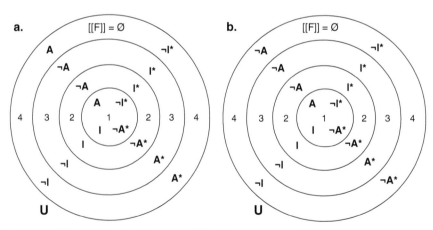

F<small>IGURE</small> 5.6 VS representation of (a) SMPC and (b) AAPC

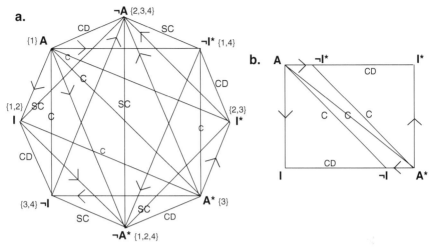

FIGURE 5.7 The octagonal (a) and the square (b) representation for AAPC.

Aristotelian sentence types are made false in AAPC by the situations in space 4. (One remembers from Section 4.2.4 that space 1 covers the situations where $[\![F]\!] \subseteq [\![G]\!]$, space 2 covers those where $[\![F]\!]$ ⓪ $[\![G]\!]$ or $[\![G]\!] \subset [\![F]\!]$, and space 3 those where $[\![F]\!]$ OO $[\![G]\!]$.)

Given the logical relations as defined in (4) of Section 2.3.3, one reads from Figure 5.6b that the Conversions have been replaced with one-way entailments from **A** to ¬**I*** (or from **I*** to ¬**A**) and from **A*** to ¬**I** (or from **I** to ¬**A***), since /**A**/⊂ /¬**I***/ and /**A***/⊂ /¬**I**/, but not vice versa.[17] Then, the subaltern entailments from **A** and **A*** have been preserved, since /**A**/ ⊂ / **I**/ and /**A***/ ⊂ /**I***/.[18] The subcontrariety between **I** and **I*** has been lost, but **I** and ¬**A** are still subcontraries, since /**I**/ ∪ /¬**A**/=**U** (and, of course, analogously for **I*** and ¬**A***).[19] In addition, the number of contrary pairs has increased.

---

[17] /**A**/= {1} and /¬**I***/= {1,4}; therefore /**A**/ ⊂ /¬**I***/; therefore **A** ⊢ ¬**I*** but not vice versa. Then, /**A***/ = {3} and /¬**I**/= {3,4}; therefore /**A***/⊂/¬**I**/; therefore **A** * ⊢¬**I** but not vice versa.

[18] /**A**/= {1} and /**I**/= {1,2}; therefore /**A**/ ⊂ /**I**/; therefore **A** ⊢ **I** but not vice versa. Then, /**A***/= {3} and /**I***/= {2,3}; therefore /**A***/⊂/**I***/; therefore **A*** ⊢ **I*** but not vice versa.

[19] /**I**/= {1,2} and /¬**A**/= {2,3,4}; so /**I**/∪/¬**A**/= **U**; so **I** and ¬**A** are subcontraries. Then, /**I***/= {2,3} and /¬**A***/= {1,2,4}; so /**I***/∪/¬**A***/= **U**; so **I*** and ¬**A*** are subcontraries. Note that **I** and **I*** are not subcontraries: {1,2} ∪ {2,3} ≠ **U**. This means that **I** and **I*** are logically independent in this system: they can be both true, both false, singly true, and singly false.

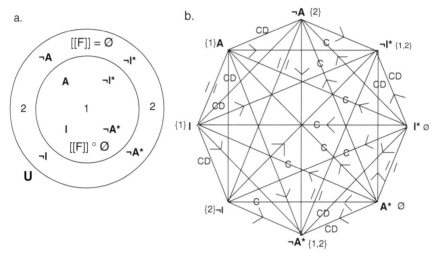

FIGURE 5.8 VS-model and octagon for ALL F IS F and so on

The corresponding octagonal graph is shown in Figure 5.7a, where the valuation spaces of Figure 5.6b are given for each vertex. A comparison with the graph-theoretically complete octagonal graph for ABPC of Figure 5.2b above shows that AAPC is less powerful than ABPC but a great deal more powerful than SMPC, whose poverty is shown in Figure 4.6b.

Abelard devotes some space to sentences where the F- and G-predicates are identical, as in his example EVERY human is human, SOME human is NOT-human, and so on. In such sentences, AAPC remains intact, as it should, but acquires a number of extra entailment relations, many of which are counter-intuitive. Since the extensions of the F- and G-predicates coincide, the spaces 1 and 2 of Figure 5.6b collapse into one space. Space 3 disappears, as there can be no difference between two identical predicate extensions, and space 4 remains intact, leaving just two spaces, one for $[\![F]\!] \neq \emptyset$ and one for $[\![F]\!] = \emptyset$, as shown in Figure 5.8a, which returns the octagon of Figure 5.7b. In Figure 5.8a, $\mathbf{A}^*$ and $\mathbf{I}^*$ are not represented, since in AAPC sentences of the form ALL F is NOT-F and SOME F is NOT-F are necessarily false, as noticed by Abelard. (It is an interesting exercise to read Abelard's text quoted above with the Figures 5.7 and 5.8 at hand.)

The octagonal graph of Figure 5.8b is graph-theoretically complete, in that there is at least one, sometimes two, logical relations between every two vertices, but the important point is that all logical relations of AAPC, as shown in Figures 5.5b and 5.6a, are preserved and in some cases reinforced. Figure 5.8b just has a much richer supply of logical relations than ordinary AAPC, though the relations it has in excess of those of ordinary AAPC are largely counterintuitive, owing to the fact that in AAPC with two identical predicates sentences of the types **A*** and **I*** are necessarily false and thus have a null VS. That being so they mathematically entail any arbitrary sentence—a form of entailment that counts as nonnatural and counterintuitive, as is argued in Chapter 3. At the same time, they are contrary with regard to any arbitrary sentence, since they will never be true together with any sentence, including themselves. The combination of entailment and contrariety is, of course, highly counterintuitive. But then, predicate calculus with two identical predicates is something of a logician's prank and is not part of ordinary language or cognition. One remembers that one of the principles of natural set theory proposed in Chapter 3 specifically rules out the identity of sets that have been introduced as sets in their own right and hence the identity of predicate extensions that have been given different names.

What results from all this is that giving up the Conversions for one-way entailments and declaring **A**-type and **A***-type sentences false for situations where $[\![F]\!] = \emptyset$ results in a better logical and linguistic deal than keeping the Conversions and declaring **A**-type and **A***-type sentences true in such situations, as SMPC does.

Why Abelard's solution has never been incorporated into the logical tradition is hard to say. In the absence of a specialized study on the Abelard tradition, one can only guess at the reasons for this historical anomaly.[20] In the context of the present work, Abelard's contribution is highly significant, as it brings us one step closer to the isolation of the situations where $[\![F]\!] = \emptyset$ by declaring all four Aristotelian sentence types false in those situations.

Yet, even with Abelard's solution, we are still far removed from an adequate treatment of the logic of quantification in natural language. Somehow, space 4 must be 'put on hold' and treated as being *hors concours*, but this cannot be done with the means at our disposal at this point in the exposition. It is done in Chapter 10, where the principle of strict bivalence is sacrificed in the

---

[20] One can think of a few possible reasons, given his superior intellect, combined with his gift for debating and ridicule, his insistence on rational as opposed to mystic thinking, his frequent clashes with official theology, and his defiant attitude with regard to the stifling moral prescriptions imposed and enforced by the Church, which twice condemned him for heresy.

context of the theory of presupposition and contextual anchoring. What can be shown, however, within the confines of strict bivalence and a strictly extensional ontology, is that the setting apart of the situations where $[\![\mathbf{F}]\!] = \varnothing$ as a separate, marked class is functional with regard to linguistic interaction. This is done in the following chapter.

6

The functionality of the Square and of BNPC

6.1 How to isolate the cases with a null F-class: the purpose of space 4

The previous chapters have shown that when no account is taken of situations where $[\![F]\!] = \varnothing$ (space 4 in most of the VS-models considered), SMPC is isomorphic with propositional calculus and identical with both AAPC and ABPC. *Prima facie*, therefore, it would be very helpful if situations where $[\![F]\!] = \varnothing$ could be dispensed with in predicate logic, since that would leave only BNPC to cope with as a possible alternative. In fact, one of the final conclusions of this book, reached in Chapter 10, is that the logic of language has indeed proved capable of doing away with situations where $[\![F]\!] = \varnothing$, which are, in the end, reserved for cases of presupposition failure. Language and logic have thus, in a way, 'screened off' presupposition failure from the default, presupposition-preserving systems of both propositional and predicate logic—and with good reason.

In the present chapter we will see that this 'default turn' taken by natural language and cognition is, perhaps unexpectedly, highly functional. The avoidance not only of the null set but also of the total set of all objects **OBJ**, as required in our natural-set-theory hypothesis (Section 3.2), automatically reduces SMPC not only to ABPC but, with the BNPC quantifiers as defined in Section 3.4.1, also to BNPC.

We are not proposing, of course, to dispense with situations where $[\![F]\!] = \varnothing$ just like that. Quantifiers express relations between sets and the null set plays its part not only in the set-theoretic game but also in real-life situations. Actual situations where $[\![F]\!] = \varnothing$ abound in any world. A sentence like:

(6.1) All dodoes are in good health.

is both perfectly grammatical and perfectly interpretable. It may even be a normal sentence in some fictional story, or in some story about the island

Mauritius as it was before the year 1700, when there were still dodoes alive. It must, therefore, be considered to be a rightful member of the class of **A**-sentences even if the **F**-class, the class of dodoes, happens not to be instantiated in the actual world as it is now. No logic can afford to leave such sentences out of account: **U** is the set of ALL possible situations, not just of those that happen to have a nonnull **F**-class. Nor can the predicate variable **F** be restricted to those predicates that happen to have a nonnull extension. Space 4, therefore, reserved for situations where $[\![F]\!] = \emptyset$, cannot be eliminated from the system.

It can, however, be isolated and 'put on hold'. For one thing, space 4 is special in that it is only needed for the purpose of catering for situations where $[\![F]\!] = \emptyset$. This is shown as follows. For a situation *sit* to belong to space 1 or 2, it is necessary that $[\![F]\!] \neq \emptyset$ and $[\![G]\!] \neq \emptyset$, since both spaces make **I**-sentences true, which require a nonnull intersection of $[\![F]\!]$ and $[\![G]\!]$. For *sit* to belong to space 3, which houses the situations where SOME **F** is NOT-**G** is true, $[\![F]\!]$ and $[\![\overline{G}]\!]$ must be nonnull, but $[\![G]\!]$ is free: either $[\![G]\!] = \emptyset$ or $[\![G]\!] \neq \emptyset$, since all that is required is a nonnull intersection of $[\![F]\!]$ and the complement of $[\![G]\!]$. Only in space 4 is it allowed, and necessary, that $[\![F]\!] = \emptyset$, while $[\![G]\!]$ may or may not be null.

This insight is not revolutionary. It is widely known that SMPC is the result of adding situations where $[\![F]\!] = \emptyset$ to the set of situations in which ABPC is valid. Yet it is useful to look at this fact a little more closely. Let us speak of FACT 1:

> FACT 1
> If the set of situations where $[\![F]\!] = \emptyset$ is disregarded, SMPC is transformed into traditional Aristotelian-Boethian predicate calculus (ABPC or the Square) and becomes logically isomorphic with standard propositional calculus. This provides a wealth of logical relations that are absent in SMPC.

FACT 1 is important because there is more. It is not hard to see that, if the set of situations where $[\![F]\!] = \emptyset$ can somehow be put on hold, it is only the VS-extension of **A**-type or **A***-type sentences that is affected. The reason is simple: space 4 in the VS-model of SMPC (Figure 3.11), which is reserved for the situations where $[\![F]\!] = \emptyset$, only makes sentences of type **A** and **A*** true; the **I**-type or **I***-type sentences still remain restricted to spaces 1, 2, and 3. This gives us FACT 2, which is likewise not revolutionary, yet much less present in the minds of the professionals than FACT 1, despite its relevance in the context of the logic of language:

> FACT 2
> The reduction of SMPC to ABPC only affects **A**-type or **A***-type sentences and has no effect on the VS-extension of **I**-type or **I***-type

sentences. Under a strictly extensional ontology, the difference between the two calculi must therefore lie in the semantics of the universal quantifier $\forall$.

6.2 Extreme values are uninformative in standard modern predicate calculus

Now we come to a point which has so far not played any role at all in the literature even though it appears to be of great importance for an adequate insight into the way logic is incarnated in human language and cognition. Let us define the notion of *extreme value* for a set variable as follows:

> When we say that, for a predicate X, its extension $[\![X]\!]$ has an EXTREME VALUE, we mean to say that either $[\![X]\!] = \emptyset$ or $[\![X]\!] = \mathbf{OBJ}$.

The point we wish to make is that when $[\![F]\!]$ or $[\![G]\!]$ or both have an extreme value, then the set-theoretic relation between the two sets involved is fully determined. Hence, the truth value, in SMPC, of quantified L-propositions in the language of predicate calculus ($\mathbf{L_{PredC}}$) involving the predicates F and G, with or without the external or internal negation, follows automatically: their truth or falsity is determined by Boolean computation alone, no further inspection of the world being needed. But when the situation is such that neither $[\![F]\!]$ nor $[\![G]\!]$ has an extreme value, the truth value of an L-proposition describing that situation depends on the contingent set-theoretic relation between $[\![F]\!]$ and $[\![G]\!]$. The class of situations characterized by the condition that neither $[\![F]\!]$ nor $[\![G]\!]$ has an extreme value we call the CLASS OF CONTINGENT (OR MUNDANE) SITUATIONS. The sentences that describe a contingent situation we call CONTINGENT (OR MUNDANE) SENTENCES.

Some comment is in order. What is said is that in all cases where $[\![F]\!] = \emptyset$ or $[\![G]\!] = \emptyset$ or $[\![F]\!] = \mathbf{OBJ}$ or $[\![G]\!] = \mathbf{OBJ}$, the truth value of any L-proposition in $\mathbf{L_{PredC}}$, involving the predicates F and G is fully determined by Boolean computation. This is so because:

(a) The extreme values $\emptyset$ and $\mathbf{OBJ}$ are instances of Boolean 0 and 1, respectively.
(b) The quantifiers in SMPC are exclusively defined in terms of the set-theoretical functions $\cap$, $\cup$, and Complement.
(c) The set-theoretical functions $\cap$, $\cup$, and Complement correspond to the Boolean functions of multiplication, addition, and complement, respectively.

(d) These Boolean functions are defined in terms of the constants $1, 0$ and at most one variable symbol (see Section 2.3.2).

As regards (d), one should note that, as soon as more than one variable symbol is involved whose value is not Boolean 1 or 0, the values of the Boolean functions are no longer determined *a priori* but depend on any values the variable symbols may have in any application of Boolean algebra to some domain.

From (a)–(d) it follows that, in all cases where $[\![F]\!]$ or $[\![G]\!]$ or both have an extreme value, the truth value of any quantified L-proposition in $\mathbf{L_{PredC}}$ involving the predicates F and G is computable from these values, while this is not so when both $[\![F]\!]$ and $[\![G]\!]$ are natural sets in the sense of Chapter 3 and thus avoid extreme values. The inverse does not hold. For example, when $\forall x$ (Gx,Fx) is true (in SMPC), both $[\![F]\!]$ and $[\![G]\!]$ may be null or nonnull or equal to **OBJ**, though not in every combination. The existential quantifier is more restrictive: when $\exists x[Gx,Fx]$ is true, neither $[\![F]\!]$ nor $[\![G]\!]$ may be null, though either may be equal to **OBJ** (provided **OBJ** $\neq \emptyset$). We thus formulate FACT 3:

> **FACT 3**
> When $[\![F]\!] = \emptyset$ or $[\![G]\!] = \emptyset$ or $[\![F]\!] = $ **OBJ** or $[\![G]\!] = $ **OBJ**, the truth value of any L-proposition in $\mathbf{L_{PredC}}$ involving the predicates F and G is fully determined by Boolean computation.

The reason this is relevant is that the use of an L-proposition of $\mathbf{L_{PredC}}$ in natural language is now seen to be informative only for situations belonging to the class of contingent situations, that is, for situations where $[\![F]\!] \neq \emptyset \neq$ **OBJ** and $[\![G]\!] \neq \emptyset \neq$ **OBJ**. In the other cases, where the truth value simply follows from an extreme value, it is more informative to specify the status of $[\![F]\!]$ and $[\![G]\!]$, which gives the set-theoretic relation between them as an automatic consequence. The relevance of FACT 3, therefore, lies not so much in the logic itself as in more pragmatic considerations regarding the functionality of human language.

6.3 The functionality of excluding extreme values

The next step in the argument is easy to guess: it is shown that logic itself ferrets out redundancy. In doing so, it provides the instruments for an optimal application to the practical needs of language users—a point of view not so far developed in pragmatics or semantics. The argument is that, if the evolution of human language has favoured informativeness in sentences and if it turns out that those sentence types that are by definition informative happen to fit into a logical system whose application is restricted but which is (much) more powerful than SMPC (or even AAPC), then one will not be surprised to find that language has made the more powerful but restricted logical system its own and has sought remedies for the parts that had to be cut off.

In other words, human language will then be seen to favour the more powerful predicate logic that comes with the contingent class of situations where $[\![F]\!] \neq \emptyset \neq$ **OBJ** and $[\![G]\!] \neq \emptyset \neq$ **OBJ**, and to have done so without compromising the soundness of the system. How this *tour de force* has been achieved is described in global terms in Section 4.1, and in more precise terms in Chapter 10. For the moment we ask the reader to bear with us while we unravel the standard system of SMPC.

The clearest way of showing what is at issue is to present a graphic breakdown. Consider Figure 6.1, which presents a matrix for the various possible situations that make L-propositions in $\mathbf{L_{PredC}}$ with the predicates **F** and **G** true, without the restriction that neither $[\![F]\!]$ nor $[\![G]\!]$ may be null or equal to **OBJ**. The status of $[\![F]\!]$ and $[\![G]\!]$ is specified for each of the ten columns: they are either null or nonnull or equal or not equal to **OBJ**, which is itself again nonnull or null.

In Figure 6.1, the following notational conventions are used.

(a) '$[\![X]\!]$' is replaced with '**X**' for any predicate **X**.
(b) '$O_\emptyset$' stands for NULL **OBJ** (therefore $O_\emptyset = \overline{O}_\emptyset$).
(c) 'O_+' stands for NONNULL **OBJ** (therefore $\overline{O}_+ = \emptyset$).
(d) '**X** $\neq$ ev' ('ev': extreme value) stands for '$[\![X]\!] \neq \emptyset \neq$ **OBJ**' for any predicate **X** (in terms of Chapter 3 we say: **X** is a natural set).
(e) '**X** ⓪ **Y**' stands for **X** ∩ **Y** $\neq \emptyset$; **X** $\neq$ **Y** $\neq$ ev; **X** $\not\subset$ **Y**; **Y** $\not\subset$ **X** (mutual-partial intersection of two natural sets).

Each possible combination of $[\![F]\!]$ and $[\![G]\!]$ status with each of the eight set-theoretic relations that are possible between $[\![F]\!]$ and $[\![G]\!]$ has a slot in the matrix. There are 80 such slots for the combined $[\![F]\!]$ and $[\![G]\!]$ status and the set-theoretic relations specified. The marking '–' for a slot means that the values specified for the column entail that the set-theoretic relation specified for the row cannot hold. Such slots, therefore, represent impossible situations. The marking '+' means that the values specified for the column entail that the set-theoretic relation specified for the row must hold. The marking '?' means that the values specified for the column are insufficient to determine whether the set-theoretic relation specified for the row does or does not hold.

Take, for example, slot 3, the top slot in column iii: when $[\![F]\!] = O_+$ and $[\![G]\!] \neq$ ev—that is, $[\![F]\!]$ equals a nonnull total set of objects **OBJ** and $[\![G]\!]$ is a

		i	ii	iii	iv	v	vi	vii	viii	ix	x
		$F \neq ev$ $G \neq ev$	$F = \emptyset$ $G \neq ev$	$F = O+$ $G \neq ev$	$F \neq ev$ $G = \emptyset$	$F = \emptyset$ $G = \emptyset$	$F = O+$ $G = \emptyset$	$F \neq ev$ $G = O+$	$F = \emptyset$ $G = O+$	$F = O+$ $G = O+$	$F = O\emptyset$ $G = O\emptyset$
1	$F \subset G$	1 ?	2 +	3 −	4 −	5 −	6 −	7 +	8 +	9 −	10 −
2	$G \subset F$	11 ?	12 −	13 +	14 +	15 −	16 +	17 −	18 −	19 −	20 −
3	$F = G$	21 ?	22 −	23 −	24 −	25 +	26 −	27 −	28 −	29 +	30 +
4	$F \circledcirc G$	31 ?	32 −	33 −	34 −	35 −	36 −	37 −	38 −	39 −	40 −
5	$F \cap G = \emptyset$	41 ?	42 +	43 −	44 +	45 +	46 +	47 −	48 +	49 −	50 +
6	$\overline{F} \subset G$	51 ?	52 −	53 +	54 −	55 −	56 −	57 +	58 −	59 +	60 −
7	$\overline{F} = G$	61 ?	62 −	63 −	64 −	65 −	66 +	67 −	68 +	69 −	70 +
8	$F \subset \overline{G}$	71 ?	72 +	73 −	74 +	75 +	76 −	77 −	78 −	79 −	80 −

FIGURE 6.1 Situation table for $\mathbf{L_{PredC}}$

natural set of objects and thus a proper part of **OBJ**—the relation of proper inclusion of $[\![F]\!]$ in $[\![G]\!]$ ($F \subset G$) cannot possibly hold, so that slot 3 must be marked '−' and thus represents an impossible situation. Or take slot 7, the top slot in column vii. Here it is specified that $[\![F]\!]$ is a natural set ('$F \neq ev$') and $[\![G]\!]$ equals nonnull **OBJ** ('$G = O_+$'). That being so it simply follows that $[\![F]\!]$ is properly included in $[\![G]\!]$. One notes that the condition of row 4 ($[\![F]\!]$ and $[\![G]\!]$ are both natural sets and intersect partially) is compatible only with the condition of column i and incompatible with those of all other columns.

What does Figure 6.1 tell us? First, it is clear that column i represents the class of contingent situations as defined above, since it is only in column i that both $[\![F]\!]$ and $[\![G]\!]$ avoid the extreme values $\emptyset$ and **OBJ**. This illustrates the fact that when either $[\![F]\!]$ or $[\![G]\!]$ has an extreme value, the truth value of a set-relational statement is predicted on *a priori* grounds. This is perhaps undramatic, but it does no harm to see it visually illustrated.

The next point has a little more drama to it. The reduction of the predicate-logical constants to set theory allows us to set up valuation spaces for the various L-proposition types of $\mathbf{L_{PredC}}$. The procedure specified in (6.2) allows us to list the slots that yield truth for any L-proposition of SMPC and thus compose a VS-model:

(6.2) Check for each slot *n* whether **formula** is true given **R** and **C**, where:
formula stands for any predicate-logic L-proposition,
R for the set-theoretic relation specified for the row and
C for the status of $[\![F]\!]$ and $[\![G]\!]$ specified for the column.
When **formula** is true, add the slot number *n* to the list.

For example, given the predicate-logical L-proposition ALL F is G or **A**, formally written $\forall x[Gx,Fx]$, we list, for row 1, the following slots: 1, 2, 7, and 8. Row 2 yields no slot, since $\forall x[Gx,Fx]$ cannot be true when $[\![G]\!] \subset [\![F]\!]$. Row 3 yields the slots 21, 25, 29, and 30, because $\forall x[Gx,Fx]$ is always true when $[\![F]\!] = [\![G]\!]$. Row 4 again yields no slot because $\forall x[Gx,Fx]$ is false when $[\![F]\!]$ ⓪ $[\![G]\!]$ and all other slots in row 4 represent impossible situations. It is a bit tedious to do this for all eight L-proposition types of SMPC and for all rows and columns, but the result is given in (6.5).

One should note that the procedure defined in (6.2) automatically selects only those matrix slots that are marked '+'. This is because the slots marked '–' represent impossible situations, given their combined values in **R** and **C**. These slots, therefore, cannot play a part in a valuation-space model listing all possible situations. It is useful to have the universe **U** of all possible situations at hand:

(6.3) The universe **U** of all possible situations (all slots marked '?' or '+'):
{ **1**,2,7,8,**11**,13,14,16,**21**,25,29,30,**31**,**41**,42,44,45,46,48,50,**51**,53,57,59,**61**,66, 68,70,**71**,72,74,75}

Some situations have been printed in boldface and larger font. This has been done to make them stand out as the members of the class of contingent situations, listed separately in (6.4). These, one remembers, are the situations where, given the status of $[\![F]\!]$ and $[\![G]\!]$, their set-theoretic relation does not follow automatically.

(6.4) {**1**,**11**,**21**,**31**,**41**,**51**,**61**,**71**}

In all other situations the set-theoretic relation stated for $[\![F]\!]$ and $[\![G]\!]$ in a row follows from their status specified for them in their column. Take, for example, situation (slot) 2: given the column condition $[\![F]\!] = \emptyset$, $[\![G]\!] \neq$ ev, it is necessarily so that $[\![F]\!] \subset [\![F]\!]$. Or take situation 44 with the column condition $[\![F]\!] \neq$ ev and $[\![G]\!] = \emptyset$. Here it is necessarily so that $[\![F]\!] \cap [\![G]\!] = \emptyset$. Analogously for all situations whose numbers are not printed in bold.

Here, then, is the valuation-space table for all eight basic expressions in SMPC:

(6.5) a. /∀x[Gx,Fx]/ (/**A**/) = {1,2,7,8,**21**,25,29,30,42,45,48,50,57,59,68,70,72,75}
       b. /¬∀x[Gx,Fx]/ (/¬**A**/) = {**11**,13,14,16,**31**,**41**,44,46,**51**,53,**61**,66, **71**, 74}
       c. /∀x[¬Gx,Fx]/ (/**A***/) = {2,8,25,30,42,45,46,48,50,66,68,70, **71**,72,74,75}
       d. /¬∀x[¬Gx,Fx]/ (/¬**A***/) = {**1**,**7**,**11**,13,14,16,**21**,29,**31**,**41**,44,**51**,53,57,59,**61**}
       e. /∃x[Gx,Fx]/ ≡ / ∃x(Fx,Gx)/ (/**I**/) = {**1**,**7**,**11**,13,14,16,**21**,29,**31**,**41**,44,**51**,
          53,57,59,**61**}
       f. /¬∃x[Gx,Fx]/ ≡ /¬∃ x(Fx,Gx)/ (/¬**I**/) = {2,8,25,30,42,45,46,48,50,66,68,70,
          71,72,74,75}
       g. /∃x[¬Gx,Fx]/ (/**I***/) = {**11**,13,14,16,**31**,**41**,44,46,**51**,53,**61**,66,**71**,74}
       h. /¬∃x[¬Gx,Fx]/ (/¬**I***/) = {1,2,7,8,**21**,25,29,30,42,45,48,50,57,59,
          68,70,72,75}

Note that Figure 6.1, the procedure (6.2), the universe **U** of all possible
situations (6.3), the class of contingent situations (6.4) and the valuation-
space table (6.5) are all based on SMPC, where the subalterns do not hold but
the Conversions do.

All this illustrates the point, made above in connection with FACT 3, that
quantified sentences (which describe set-theoretic relations between two sets)
are maximally informative when describing contingent situations—that is,
those listed in (6.4) and in column i of Figure 6.2. This is so because when
they describe a noncontingent situation, it is superfluous to express the
relation that holds between the sets involved, since it is implicit in the values
specified for them. In such cases, therefore, it is more economical merely to
specify these values—something which is usually implicit in the current
context or situation.

We are now coming closer to the conclusion we have been after for the
past few pages. Suppose it were possible to construct a partial logic just for
the class of contingent situations specified in (6.4) and therefore involving
only natural sets, then the resulting predicate logic would be identical
to ABPC, described by a complete octagonal graph as in Figures
4.5c or 5.2b. This is easily shown by simply singling out the bold numbers
from (6.5):

(6.6) a. /∀x[Gx,Fx]/ (/**A**/)   = {1, 21}
       b. /¬∀x[Gx,Fx]/ (/¬**A**/)   = {11, 31, 41, 51, 61, 71}
       c. /∀x[¬Gx,Fx]/ (/**A***/)   = {71}
       d. /¬∀x[¬Gx,Fx]/ (/¬**A***/)   = {1, 11, 21, 31, 41, 51, 61}
       e. /∃x[Gx,Fx]/ (/**I**/)   = {1, 11, 21, 31, 41, 51, 61}

    f. /¬∃x[Gx,Fx]/ (/¬I/)   =   {71}
    g. /∃x[¬Gx,Fx]/ (/I*/)   =   {11, 31, 41, 51, 61, 71}
    h. /¬∃x[¬Gx,Fx]/ (/¬I*/)   =   {1, 21}

Now **A** ⊢ **I**, since {1, 21} ⊆ {1, 11, 21, 31, 41, 51, 61} and likewise **A*** ⊢ **I***, since {71} ⊆ {11, 31, 41, 51, 61, 71}, two entailments that do not hold for (6.5). Moreover, the Conversions hold since /**A**/ = /¬**I***/, /**A***/ = /¬**I**/, /**I***/ = /¬**A**/ and /**I**/ = /¬**A***/. It thus seems that a concentration on column i of Figure 6.2 brings along a very significant enrichment of the logical power of the system involved.

This was to be expected, since it is well known that ABPC is valid when $[\![F]\!] \neq \emptyset$ and $[\![G]\!] \neq \emptyset$, conditions that are satisfied by column i. But the validity of ABPC can be extended well beyond column i, provided, of course, the logic can be kept sound despite the cancelling of certain classes of situations. In fact, in order to save ABPC all that has to be got rid of is columns ii, v, viii, and x, where $[\![F]\!] = \emptyset$. The universe of situations **U** of SMPC is then reduced to **U**^{R}, which comprises only the following 20 situation types:

(6.7) **U**^{R} = {1,7,11,13,14,16,21,29,31,41,44,46,51,53,57,59,**61**,66,**71**,74}

The valuation spaces thus restricted then look as follows:

(6.8)   a. /**A**/   =   {1,7,**21**,29,57,59}
        b. /¬**A**/   =   {11,13,14,16,**31**,41,44,46,**51**,53,**61**,66,**71**,74}
        c. /**A***/   =   {46,66,**71**,74}
        d. /¬**A***/   =   {1,7,**11**,13,14,16,**21**,29,**31**,41,44,**51**,53,57,59,**61**}
        e. /**I**/   =   {1,7,**11**,13,14,16,**21**,29,**31**,41,44,**51**,53,57,59,**61**}
        f. /¬**I**/   =   {46,66,**71**,74}
        g. /**I***/   =   {11,13,14,16,**31**,41,44,46,**51**,53,**61**,66,**71**,74}
        h. /¬**I***/   =   {1,7,**21**,29,57,59}

Now ABPC still holds: **A** ⊢ **I**, since {1,7,**21**,29,57,59} ⊆ {1,7,**11**,13,14,16,**21**,29, **31**,41,44,**51**,53,57,59,**61**} and **A*** ⊢ **I***, since {46,66,**71**,74} ⊆ {11,13,14,16,**31**, 41,44,46,**51**,53,**61**,66,**71**,74}. The Conversions also still hold, since, again, /**A**/ = /¬**I***/, /**A***/ = /¬**I**/, /**I***/ = /¬**A**/ and /**I**/ = /¬**A***/.

Incidentally, AAPC equals SMPC but for the fact that 2, 8, 25, 30, 42, 45, 48, 50, 68, 70, 72, and 75 are moved from (6.5a) to (6.5b) and from (6.5c) to (6.5d), because **A** and **A*** are judged false in AAPC but true in SMPC when $[\![F]\!] = \emptyset$.

This yields AAPC. AAPC also holds for the mundane situations plus those where $\llbracket F \rrbracket \neq \emptyset$, but it stops being valid when the situations where $\llbracket F \rrbracket = \emptyset$ are taken into account. Within these constraints, however, AAPC is not maximally powerful: ABPC, which operates within the same constraints, is more powerful. But AAPC has the advantage of lacking UEI.

We thus see in clear detail what we had suspected all along: if the elimination of the class of situations where $\llbracket F \rrbracket = \emptyset$ is feasible, that will be sufficient to boost the predicate logic from the impoverished SMPC to the maximally powerful ABPC. What has also been shown is that the elimination of situations with a null F-class does not affect the valuation spaces of **I**-type and **I***-type sentences: their valuation spaces in (6.8) are identical to those in (6.5). It is therefore only the **A**-type and **A***-type sentences and, of course, the complements of the **I**-type and **I***-type sentences, that are affected by the shrinking from **U** to **U**$^{\mathbf{R}}$. This illustrates what was stated above in FACT 2.

6.4 The functionality of BNPC

What we have not investigated so far is what happens to SMPC when all situation classes (slots) that are incompatible with the restrictions valid for BNPC are removed from Figure 6.1 on account of these slots not being operative in the cognitive machinery at basic-natural level. In order to carry out such an investigation, we must specify the semantics of the quantifiers $\forall$, $\exists$ and N (NO for sentence type **N**) in BNPC. This is done in the following manner. In BNPC, the quantifier $\forall$ is defined as requiring that $\llbracket F \rrbracket \subseteq \llbracket G \rrbracket$ ($\llbracket F \rrbracket$ is a subset of $\llbracket G \rrbracket$) and $\llbracket F \rrbracket$, $\llbracket G \rrbracket \neq$ ev. The quantifier $\exists$ is defined as requiring that $\llbracket F \rrbracket \oplus \llbracket G \rrbracket$ ($\llbracket F \rrbracket$ and $\llbracket G \rrbracket$ M-partially intersect) or $\llbracket G \rrbracket \subset \llbracket F \rrbracket$ (that is, just in case $\llbracket F \rrbracket \cap \llbracket G \rrbracket \neq \llbracket F \rrbracket$). The quantifier N is defined as requiring that $\llbracket F \rrbracket \oplus \llbracket G \rrbracket$ (that is, $\llbracket F \rrbracket \cap \llbracket G \rrbracket = \emptyset$, while $\llbracket F \rrbracket$, $\llbracket G \rrbracket \neq$ ev). This eliminates columns ii–x as well as row 3, reserved for the nonnatural identity relation of the natural sets $\llbracket F \rrbracket$ and $\llbracket G \rrbracket$. (External and internal negation are standard, but for Restriction 6 of Section 3.2.2.)

All that remains of Figure 6.1 when cut down in the manner indicated is column 1, listing the mundane situation classes, minus slot 21. The valuation spaces specified for the eight basic sentence types in SMPC were given in (6.5) above. The reduction of (6.5) by the elimination of columns ii–x and of row 3 in Figure 6.2 gives (6.9a–h). The new BNPC-quantifier N as defined above, giving rise to the basic sentence types **N**, **N***, **¬N** and **¬N***, makes for (6.9i–l):

(6.9)   a. /**A**/   =   {**1**}
        b. /¬**A**/   =   {**11, 31, 41, 51, 61, 71**}
        c. /**A***/   =   {**41, 61, 71**}
        d. /¬**A***/   =   {**1, 11, 31, 51**}
        e. /**I**/   =   {**11, 31, 51**}
        f. /¬**I**/   =   {**1, 41, 61, 71**}
        g. /**I***/   =   {**11, 31, 51**}
        h. /¬**I***/   =   {**1, 41, 61, 71**}
        i. /**N**/   =   {**41, 61, 71**}
        j. /¬**N**/   =   {**1, 11, 31, 51**}
        k. /**N***/   =   {**1**}
        l. /¬**N***/   =   {**11, 31, 41, 51, 61, 71**}

The following logical relations are now seen to hold, precisely as specified in Figure 3.7 of Chapter 3:

(6.10) $\mathbf{A} \equiv \mathbf{N}^*$ $\neg\mathbf{A} \equiv \neg\mathbf{N}^*$
        $\mathbf{A}^* \equiv \mathbf{N}$ $\neg\mathbf{A}^* \equiv \neg\mathbf{N}$
        $\mathbf{I} \equiv \mathbf{I}^*$ $\neg\mathbf{I} \equiv \neg\mathbf{I}^*$
        $\mathbf{A} \vdash \neg\mathbf{A}^*$ $\mathbf{N}^* \vdash \neg\mathbf{A}^*$
        $\mathbf{A} \vdash \neg\mathbf{I} / \neg\mathbf{I}^*$ $\mathbf{N}^* \vdash \neg\mathbf{I} / \neg\mathbf{I}^*$
        $\mathbf{A} \vdash \neg\mathbf{N}$ $\mathbf{N}^* \vdash \neg\mathbf{N}$
        $\mathbf{A}^* \vdash \neg\mathbf{A} / \neg\mathbf{N}^*$ $\mathbf{N} \vdash \neg\mathbf{A} / \neg\mathbf{N}^*$
        $\mathbf{A}^* \vdash \neg\mathbf{I} / \neg\mathbf{I}^*$ $\mathbf{N} \vdash \neg\mathbf{I} / \neg\mathbf{I}^*$
        $\mathbf{I} \vdash \neg\mathbf{A} / \neg\mathbf{N}^*$ $\mathbf{I}^* \vdash \neg\mathbf{A} / \neg\mathbf{N}^*$
        $\mathbf{I} \vdash \neg\mathbf{A}^* / \neg\mathbf{N}$ $\mathbf{I}^* \vdash \neg\mathbf{A}^* / \neg\mathbf{N}$

We may also keep the BNPC-definitions of the three quantifiers ∀, ∃ and N but disregard the basic-natural restrictions of Section 3.2.2, thereby reading BNPC as an unrestricted logic. When we do that, BNPC is extended to cover all situation classes of Figure 6.2. The VSs thus specified are listed in (6.11):

(6.11) The VSs of the basic sentence types of BNPC as an unrestricted logic
        a. /**A**/ =   {**1**}
        b. /¬**A**/ = {2,7,8,**11**,13,14,16,**21**,25,29,30,**31,41**,42,44,45,46,48,50,
                    51,53,57,59,**61**,66,68,70,**71**,72,74,75}
        c. /**A***/ = {**41,61,71**}

d. /¬**A***/ = {1,2,7,8,**11**,13,14,16,**21**,25,29,30,**31**,42,44,45,46,48,
       50,**51**,53,57,59,66,68,70,72,74,75}

e. /**I**/   = {**11,31,51**}

f. /¬**I**/ = {1,2,7,8,13,14,16,**21**,25,29,30,**41**,42,44,45,46,48,
       50,53,57,59,**61**,66,68,70,**71**,72,74,75}

g. /**I***/ = {**11,31,51**}

h. /¬**I***/ = {1,2,7,8,13,14,16,**21**,25,29,30,**41**,42,44,45,46, 48,50,
       53,57,59, **61**,66,68,70,**71**,72,74,75}

i. /**N**/   = {**41,61,71**}

j. /¬**N**/ = {1,2,7,8,**11**,13,14,16,**21**,25,29,30,**31**,42,44,45,46,48,50,
       51,53,57,59,66,68,70,72,74,75}

k. /**N***/ = {**1**}

l. /¬**N***/ = {2,7,8,**11**,13,14,16,**21**,25,29,30,**31,41**,42,44,45,46,48,50,
       51,53,57,59,**61**,66,68,70,**71**,72,74,75}

Here one sees that even when extended to cover all situations, the six nonnegated basic sentence types of BNPC, **A**, **A***, **I**, **I***, **N**, and **N***, are still restricted to the mundane situations represented in column i. This remarkable property is not shared by ABPC, as is shown by (6.8) above.

It thus appears that BNPC, though invariably dismissed as unimportant by professional logicians, is not only a superbly powerful logic but is also highly functional in that it automatically focuses its nonnegated basic expressions on the mundane situations. Yet it has the fatal drawback of not allowing for existential statements in the absence of complete knowledge of the domain. BNPC also has a second, less serious drawback, to do with expressive power. As a result of the incorporation of PNST–2 ('natural sets are distinct') into the semantics of the BNPC quantifiers, BNPC is unable to produce a true quantified sentence when $[\![F]\!] = [\![G]\!]$: the slots 21, 25, 29 and 30, filling the row characterized by the relation $[\![F]\!] = [\![G]\!]$, do not occur in the VS of any of the six nonnegated basic sentence types of BNPC.[1] The same does not hold for the slots in row 7, defined by the relation $[\![\overline{F}]\!] = [\![G]\!]$ (or, equivalently, $[\![F]\!] = [\![\overline{G}]\!]$): slot 61 figures in both /**A***/ and /**N**/ of (6.11), which, as one can see, are identical. This is because in row 7 the sets $[\![F]\!]$ and $[\![G]\!]$ are both natural sets and distinct from each other. Hamilton and Jespersen can thus rest in peace: their logic has finally found the recognition it deserves, even though it has its limitations.

---

[1] This lack of expressive power does not occur in Hamilton's notation as presented in Hamilton (1866). As is shown in Section 3.4.2, Hamilton writes tF = tG when $[\![F]\!] = [\![G]\!]$.

6.5 Conclusion

It is time to summarize our conclusions. The first conclusion is that our analysis of predicate calculus has shown that if there is a way to restrict predicate calculus to those situations where $[\![F]\!] \neq \emptyset$, predicate calculus will have the same maximal logical power as propositional calculus, as both will then conform to the logical entailment system described by the complete octagonal graphs of Figure 4.5c.

The second conclusion concerns a fact that has so far either been unknown or been allowed to lie unexploited. We have been able to single out a core class of contingent situations characterized by the condition that both $[\![F]\!]$ and $[\![G]\!]$ avoid extreme values, that is, the condition that $[\![F]\!] \neq \emptyset \neq$ **OBJ** and $[\![G]\!] \neq \emptyset \neq$ **OBJ**. This class is significant (a) because the quantifying L-propositions of $\mathbf{L_{PredC}}$ are maximally informative when they describe such situations (in all other cases the truth or falsity of an $\mathbf{L_{Predc}}$ L proposition follows from the status of $[\![F]\!]$ or $[\![G]\!]$) and (b) because a predicate logic restricted to this class of contingent situations is maximally powerful (given its eight basic expressions), while the general system of SMPC has only weak logical power. Therefore, functionality will be boosted if a system of predicate logic can be developed that sustains the restriction to the class of contingent situations, so that quantifying sentences describing these situations can benefit from a maximally powerful logic. In addition, we have found that such a system will apply not only to the situations of the contingent class but also to those other noncontingent situations where the F-class is nonnull. The loss to the general SMPC system will thus remain limited, while the gain will be maximal.

Finally, we have seen that BNPC is not only an extremely powerful predicate calculus but is also an extremely functional one, in that, when all restrictions are lifted, its nonnegated basic expressions automatically restrict their valuation spaces to the mundane situations of column i.

The question we are facing now is the following: how will the predicate logic of language cater for the situations that are missing in the restricted $\mathbf{U^R}$? This question is answered in the following chapters.

7

The context-sensitivity of speech and language

7.1 What is context-sensitivity?

The context-sensitivity of natural language has been a spanner in the works of all formal theories of language and its logic. Formal logicians, starting with Aristotle, have tended to flee into the safety of eternal sentences, either leaving occasion sentences out of their account or trying to reduce them to eternal sentences. In linguistic theory, context-sensitivity has cropped up only recently and during that short period it has mostly been treated at an informal (pragmatic) rather than at a formal level. In this and the following chapters we try to gain an overall view of all aspects involved in what we consider context-sensitivity to be, and in doing so we attempt to push up the level of formality, and hence of clarity and precision, of the analysis and description of the phenomena concerned.

In succinct terms, context-sensitivity is the fact that, as a matter of principle, natural language utterances need an appeal to both encyclopedic and contextual knowledge for their proper interpretation. Apart from (ad hoc or conventionalized) nonlinguistic cues, such as gestures, that normally come with spoken utterances, sentences (types) underlying utterances (tokens) contain systematic lexical and grammatical devices that refer the listener in specific ways to available encyclopedic and contextual knowledge. And speakers must build into their sentences the appropriate context-related devices needed for a proper interpretation.

Context-sensitivity, in other words, is the fact that listeners must integrate their *comprehension* of the utterance as an expression of an underlying type-level L-proposition or semantic analysis (SA) into the proper overall *interpretation* in the token situation. We use the term *comprehension* for the identification of the type-level, schematic, linguistically encoded message, so that it can be repeated, written down, or transcribed, or said to be ambiguous or uninterpretable. *Interpretation*, by contrast, is taken to be the full reconstruction of the *hic et nunc* intent—that is, speech act-cum-proposition—conceived and expressed by the speaker, or, if one wishes, the application of the schematically organized linguistic expression to a unique situation complete with the multitude of facets and angles from which it can be considered.

In order to be properly interpreted, utterances need context, in the sense of cognitive backing shared between speaker and listener. In fact, this dependency on shared knowledge is so deeply ingrained in the semantic system of human language that one is entitled to say that, across the board and as a matter of principle, utterance interpretation needs a shared-knowledge base for it to work properly. The few utterance types that appear to be interpretable without shared knowledge may be considered cases whose context-sensitivity, and thus their dependency on shared knowledge, has been reduced to zero, but their occurrence is far rarer than logicians and some philosophers of language would have us believe. This is the well-known SHARED-KNOWLEDGE THESIS, defended in particular by Clark (1992) as an indispensable prerequisite for the proper interpretation of utterances.

For the shared-knowledge thesis to work, the schematic and incomplete information carried by the incoming utterance has to be integrated somehow with what speaker and listener possess in the way of accessible knowledge (memory). This integration requires, *inter alia*, a mechanism which we call ANCHORING, described in Chapter 3 of Volume I and appealed to repeatedly in subsequent chapters. Anchoring is the process of linking up utterances with a specific memory called DISCOURSE DOMAIN (**D**), which accumulates the information contributed by successive utterances into a cognitively coherent complex. The information carried by a single utterance consists, in principle, in the INTENT associated with the utterance in question, as defined in Sections 3.1.1 and 4.3 of Volume I—that is, the total package of the committal or speech-act force and the propositional content. This intent is stored in, or, in the technical jargon, incremented to, the **D** at hand. Once a well-anchored interpretation is achieved, the result is again fed and integrated into cognition in specific ways. The fact that, as a matter of principle, utterances require anchoring is constitutive for natural human language. Natural language production and comprehension are, by constitution, incremental.

Context-sensitivity is nature's way of ensuring that the time and energy-consuming effort of producing physical utterances is minimized. This is achieved by maximizing the dependency on what speaker and listener assume to be knowledge shared between them: what is already known need not be said, provided the speech material that is made physically available contains the necessary cues as to what elements in the common knowledge are called upon. Sometimes it is elements in speaker–hearer's general encyclopedic or world knowledge, sometimes it is the knowledge of features in the speech situation, and in all but the rare instances of eternal sentences it is knowledge of what has been built up between speaker and listener in the way of a specific discourse domain: anchoring to an available **D** is an essential prerequisite for successful interpretation, the result of which is then, in its turn, incremented to the **D** at hand and subsequently to cognition as a whole.

Sentence-types are tailored to the anchoring requirements of the utterances realizing them. They contain elements, call them 'anchor hooks' if you like, that make their utterance tokens fit for interpretation only when the anchor hooks are properly attached to the available **D**. This, of course, also poses conditions on any **D** for the acceptance and integration of newly uttered sentences: sentence-types are made, semantically, and also grammatically, in such a way that they fit only into certain classes of **D** and not into others. Sentence types pose conditions on **D**s for proper anchoring and thus for proper interpretation.

As far as is known today, there are at least four specific devices ensuring that the anchoring conditions of sentences are satisfied: external anaphora, presupposition, topic–comment structure, and open parameters in lexical meanings, also called free variables. The latter are discussed in Section 7.4 (having been the topic of discussion in Sections 1.3.3.2, 8.2.1, 9.6.3, and, especially, 9.7 of Volume I). The former three form the contents of Chapters 9, 10, and 11, respectively. But before we take a closer look at these devices, we turn our attention to the notion of discourse domain.

7.2 Discourse domains

It is probably premature to try to give a formal definition of the notion 'discourse domain' at the present primitive state of our knowledge about them. The best we can do is build up the notion gradually, starting from what seems to be required intuitively. With this proviso, we can say that *a discourse domain **D** is a form of memory storing both the speech-act quality and the fully interpreted L-propositional content of the utterances produced by the participants in a linguistic exchange, possibly a monologue, in their order of production.*

A discourse domain is thus assumed to store token-level, fully contextually integrated interpretations, not just type-level meanings. This assumption seems to be justified by the consideration that there would be little point in having a memory for unfinished products, while great advantages accrue from having a memory for products that have just functioned in a specific context. It is thus, so to speak, at the gate of a discourse domain that open access is required to all available conscious knowledge of speaker and hearer, who can thus channel any appeal to the shared-knowledge base required for proper interpretation. Having said this, one must admit to the humbling fact that the mechanisms for linking up discourse domains with the whole of conscious knowledge have so far remained almost totally undisclosed.

Discourse domains must, to some degree at least, be specific for the use of natural language utterances, since they show properties and mechanisms that are not found in other forms of memory. Yet they also have properties and mechanisms in common with other forms of memory, in particular with general episodic memory. For example, a discourse domain shares with general episodic memory the property that its degree of detail corresponds, on the whole, with the recency of the token event: the older the event or utterance, the more global and the less detail-specific the storage—apart from token occurrences that stand out for some reason, often because of some emotionally salient association. Yet discourse domains are also subject to laws and principles that are not found in general episodic memory. It is these that we focus on in the present context, taking for granted that memory, with all its different compartments, its intricate storing and retrieval systems, its distortions over time, and its subconscious caves, is still largely a mystery.

It is important, right at the outset, to clear up a misunderstanding which is as widespread as it is confusing. It is often thought, especially among philosophers, that assertions are defined by the speaker's intention to say only what is true or at least what the speaker believes to be true and by the listener's presumption that that is what the speaker does. Take, for example, Dummett's view, discussed earlier in Section 4.2 of Volume I, according to which assertions differ from other speech acts in that they do not establish a socially binding commitment on the part of the speaker but are merely meant to make the listener believe, on the presumption of the speaker's honesty, that their propositional content is true (Dummett 1973: 301–2):

A command has definite consequences: disobedience to a command given by a person in authority confers on that person a right to punish, or at least reproach, the person commanded. . . . An assertion has no such definite consequences. [. . .] Assertions take place against the background of a custom of uttering them with the intention of saying something true.

Another example, likewise discussed in Section 4.2 of Volume I, is found in Fodor (1983: 132):

Strictly speaking, I suppose, a convention must be something one can adhere to if one chooses; so perhaps the principle at issue is not 'Say only what is true' but rather 'Say only what you believe.' General adherence to the latter injunction will license inferences from utterances to how the world is, given the assumption (which is, anyhow, in all sorts of ways epistemologically indispensable) that much of what people believe is true.

Though plausible enough as a description of what often happens in verbal interaction, an appeal to the principle of 'saying only what you believe to be true' and to the fact that 'much of what people believe is true' utterly misses the essential function of assertions—not to mention other kinds of speech act. As has been emphasized repeatedly, the essential function of an assertion is to enable the speaker to enter a commitment as to the truth of the proposition expressed. It is this function that determines the incrementation of assertions to discourse domains. Incrementations of either assertions or other kinds of speech act have nothing to do with belief and only a little with actual truth. They merely register what has been said and under what social commitments, no matter whether anyone believes the propositional content stored to be true or false—as long as there is something to be taken to be true or false. It follows from the speech-act analysis presented in Chapter 4 of Volume I that the primary operator over any **D** is not belief but some form of commitment, appeal, or allowance. All compartments or subdomains of a **D** are linked up to an overarching **D** which either commits the speaker to its truth, or constitutes the speaker's overall appeal to the listener, or sets rules of behaviour.[1] Let us call this overarching domain the COMMITMENT DOMAIN (even though it is a partial misnomer), as distinct from any of its subdomains.[2]

---

[1] Appellations (name-callings) may seem to form a special case. They hardly ever extend over a whole discourse domain, though marvellous extended invectives are known in world literature.

[2] The notion of commitment domain was first introduced in Hamblin (1970), who speaks of *commitment background.*

7.2.1 The commitment domain and further subdomains

7.2.1.1 The notion of subdomain   The internal structure of a discourse domain has thus far been explored only to a very limited extent. For one thing, as has been said, the fact that the speech-act quality of utterances must be recorded has so far been largely neglected in both the more formally oriented and the more impressionistic literature. Nor is there an even remotely complete account, formal or informal, of the fact that the contributions made by different speakers must be stored in different subdomains, labelled for each speaker. How these different speaker domains are interrelated is, though perhaps intuitively clear in individual cases when one sets oneself to think about them, a question that still lacks a precise general answer. Some limited amount of work has been done, in the context of model-theoretic semantics, on intensional subdomains (treated as sets of possible worlds) and their relation to the commitment domain, but close to nothing is known about the interrelations between various intensional subdomains, nor is anything known about the nonintensional subdomains created by negation, disjunction, implication, and conjunction. And the reason for this remarkable state of affairs is to be sought in the fact that, since the 1960s, logic-inspired model-theoretic semantics, which held total sway over theoretical semantic studies, has been more interested in keeping up the paradigm as defined by its originators than in discovering the facts of language. Semantics, in other words, has been allowed to swerve far too much over to formalism, which has disturbed the delicate balance that is to be observed between formalism and ecologism (see Section 1.3 in Volume I).

There being thus not much to go by, it seems sensible to make a fresh start and develop an uncluttered view of what the notion of subdomain can sensibly be taken to involve. In defining, or describing, what is meant by subdomain, we disregard for the moment the distinction between nonintensional or extensional subdomains on the one hand and intensional subdomains on the other (the former having been left largely uninvestigated in the formal-semantic literature). One remembers from Section 6.1 in Volume I that the difference resides in the fact that free substitution of co-referring terms *salva veritate* is blocked in intensional subdomains while it is not in their extensional counterparts.

To define the notion of subdomain, we start with defining embedded sentential terms (S-terms) in L-propositional structure (see also Section 6.2.3 in Volume I):[3]

---

[3] For an elaborated grammatical theory of S-term embedding, see Seuren (1996).

An EMBEDDED S-TERM is an argument term to an L-propositional predicate (which may be a logical operator, possibly ending up in surface structure as an adverbial or morphological element) structurally defined as an S-structure which can function both as a full L-proposition with a truth value and as an L-propositional function whose variable is bound by a higher quantifier (see Section 2.3.5.1).

S-structures embedded under quantifiers are thus not embedded S-terms as defined here, because these S-structures are *per se* propositional functions containing at least one bound variable and can thus never function as a full L-proposition. Analogously for relative clauses, which again obligatorily contain a variable linking them up with the antecedent.

The most straightforward cases of embedded Ss are, of course, direct-object complement clauses under verbs like *know, believe, hope, see,* etc., no matter whether these clauses occur as fully tensed finite clauses under a complementizer (*that, if*) or whether they are reduced to an infinitival or a participial. But subordinate clauses under a conjunction (*because, while,* etc.) are likewise embedded Ss, since they can be analysed as sentential (phrasal) argument terms to the conjunction, which is then analysed as a predicate. A sentence like *She left because she felt unwell* is then analysed, at SA-level, as 'Because $(_{S_1}$[she left], $_{S_2}$[she felt unwell]}', where S_2 is the direct-object clause and S_1 the subject matrix-S. The grammar makes the predicate *because* incorporate the object clause $_{S_2}$[she felt unwell], giving the complex predicate $_{PRED}[_{PRED}$[Because]$_S$ [she felt unwell]], which is then, as a whole, lowered into the subject matrix-S to a peripheral position—that is, either to the far left or to the far right. These syntactic details are of lesser interest in the present context (see Seuren 1996 for a fully elaborate theory). What counts here is the general notion of embedded S-term.

The incrementation of an embedded L-propositional S-term either creates or augments a SUBDOMAIN.

A SUBDOMAIN within the overall commitment domain **D** is a subunit of incrementation in which, subject to the kind of subdomain, either an entire intent or just the L-propositional content is stored by incrementation.

7.2.1.2 Extensional and intensional subdomains   Some subdomain-creating predicates (operators) are such that an increment in their subdomain has direct and unambiguous consequences for the commitment domain, or, more precisely, for the immediately superordinate domain. Negation, for example, is taken to increment the L-propositions in its scope in a separate subdomain. But any L-proposition forming the scope of negation is immediately marked as being banned from the immediately superordinate domain, on pain of inconsistency. Similarly for the disjunction operator OR: its two or more component L-propositions are lodged in separate (mutually exclusive; see Sections 3.3.2 and 8.2.3) subdomains, with the condition attached that one of them is to be incremented to the immediately superordinate domain, though it is as yet uncertain which. IF also creates its own subdomain, with the condition attached that as soon as the antecedent L-proposition is incremented to the immediately superordinate domain, so must the consequent L-proposition be. And the conjunction operator AND may be seen as creating a subdomain storing the component L-propositions in their order of occurrence and requiring that the corresponding increments are immediately added to the superordinate domain at hand.

In similar fashion, increments to the subdomain created by the object S-term of the predicate *cause* and its cognates are immediately incremented to the superordinate domain (see Section 6.2.3.1 in Volume I). When I say, for example:

(7.1)   The storm made the roof collapse.

the information that the roof collapsed is immediately understood as having been added to my commitment domain as I spoke, if it had not been added earlier (when 'the storm' is comment and 'what made the roof collapse' is topic).

Many other subdomain-creating predicates, however, are not so simple. It is well-known that FACTIVE PREDICATES induce the presupposition that their factive S-term has been incremented to the superordinate domain before the utterance sporting the factive predicate as its main predicate can be incremented. As a rule, factive predicates create or continue INTENSIONAL SUBDOMAINS, in which SSV is disallowed, as is seen from the sentences (2a,b), repeated from Section 6.2.3.1 in Volume I, which are semantically independent in that they may both be true, or both false, or singly true, or singly false, even though the terms *morning star* and *evening star* denote the same actual object:

(7.2)   a. John realizes that the morning star is uninhabited.
      b. John realizes that the evening star is uninhabited.

Not all factive S-terms, however, are intensional in this standard sense. Consider the factive subject clause in (7.3a). Replacement of the term *Jackson* by the term *the butler* does not affect the truth value of the utterances in question as long as Jackson and the butler are the same person, even if this fact is unknown to speaker and/or listener. If (7.3a) is true, so is (7.3b), and if (7.3a) is false, so is (7.3b):

(7.3)   a. That Jackson's fingerprints are on the glass proves that he is the murderer.
      b. That the butler's fingerprints are on the glass proves that he is the murderer.

In general, an intensional subdomain that blocks SSV stands under an operator (predicate) requiring reference to someone's THOUGHTS for truth to arise. This was Frege's position and, as was pointed out in Section 6.1 in Volume I, it seems to be correct in principle, the principle being that the terms occurring in thoughts mentally denote cognitive representational packages or 'addresses' representing actually existing or merely thought-up entities. Addresses thus may or may not be instantiated by actual entities and they may have to be identified or disidentified for truth to arise. How intensional and nonintensional (extensional) subdomains are incremented is the subject of discussion in Sections 8.1.3 and 8.2.

The intensional subdomains most commonly dealt with are created (or continued), on the one hand, by the so-called PREDICATES OF PROPOSITIONAL ATTITUDE, such as *believe, hope, expect, wish*, and many others, all of which contain an appeal to the subject's world of thought and, on the other, by the MODAL PREDICATES, although, as is argued in the following section, the intensional status of modal subdomains is highly questionable.

In general, domains under a propositional attitude predicate are not restricted by the consistency criterion, since one may well truthfully attribute to a human being inconsistent beliefs, hopes, wishes, and so on.[4] Nor is SSV freely allowed in these subdomains, since thoughts have wings of their own and may fly off to virtual realms whose relation to the world construed as being actual may become as tenuous as in Alice's Wonderland, or more.

---

[4] For example (with thanks to Barbara Partee), a person may very well believe in evolution theory and at the same time believe that of necessity every human individual must have had two human parents.

7.2.1.3 The epistemic modal subdomains   By contrast, domains under an epistemic modal predicate are fully subject to the consistency criterion. Whether they are also intensional in the sense of blocking free SSV is a moot point. Epistemic modals are complex and hard to understand. In the formal-semantics literature they take pride of place, next to predicates of propositional attitude, as prototypical creators (or continuators) of intensional contexts. Yet a closer analysis reveals that it is at least not obvious that they block free SSV in their embedded S-terms. They are thus not, or at least not clearly, intensional in the intended sense. We will now have a somewhat closer look at the epistemic modal predicates. Yet, since a full treatment of natural language modals would require a monograph in its own right if not more, we must content ourselves here with a summary discussion.

Let it be observed first that natural language modal predicates are either EPISTEMIC or AGENTIVE, but never metaphysical. Metaphysical modalities are philosophical constructs which vary with the ontology adopted. Natural languages are, on the whole, unaffected by such philosophical lucubrations. What one finds in the lexicons of natural languages is, to begin with, a basic distinction between epistemic and agentive modalities. Within these two main divisions, modalities occur in many guises which, however, seem to gravitate around the two poles of NECESSITY and POSSIBILITY. In this respect they resemble the quantifiers, which also occur in many different guises but gravitate around a universal and an existential pole. It has often been pointed out that universal quantification corresponds with necessity in modal logic, while existential quantifiers are on a par with operators of possibility.

What epistemic possibility operators express is partly to do with the compatibility of the proposition expressed in the argument S-term with speaker's knowledge at the time of speaking. In other words, it is implied that, as far as speaker's knowledge goes, nothing excludes the actuality of the virtual situation referred to by the argument S-term. Analogously, part of what epistemic necessity operators say is that, as far as speaker's knowledge goes, the actuality of the virtual situation referred to by the argument S-term is a necessary consequence, on grounds of deduction, induction, or knowledge of causal laws. Thus, when I say (7.4a), I imply that it is compatible with my knowledge at the time of speaking that the fire was caused by witchcraft. And when I say (7.4b), I imply that it follows from what I know at the time of speaking that the fire was caused by witchcraft.

(7.4)   a. The fire may have been caused by witchcraft.
   b. The fire must have been caused by witchcraft.
   c. The fire cannot have been caused by witchcraft.

Yet epistemic modal statements are not simply statements about compatibility with, or necessary consequence of, speaker's knowledge at the time of speaking. If that were so, such statements would be true or false depending merely on the relation of compatibility or necessary consequence invoked for the modalized proposition with regard to what the speaker's knowledge amounts to at the time of speaking. But that is not what epistemic modal statements are. One cannot say, for example, that (7.4a) is false and hence (7.4c) is true, merely because the speaker's knowledge state, whatever it amounts to, leaves no room for the possibility that the fire was caused by witchcraft. (7.4a) may also be false, and (7.4c) true, because the speaker's knowledge state, in so far as it pertains to the cause of the fire, is factually incorrect. There are thus two conditions that must be fulfilled for (7.4a) to be true, one of compatibility with the speaker's knowledge base and one of factual correctness of that knowledge base. So perhaps (7.4a) should be read as saying what is said in (7.5a), and (7.4b) as (7.5b):

(7.5)   a. My relevant knowledge state **K** is correct and it is compatible with **K** that the fire was caused by witchcraft.
   b. My relevant knowledge state **K** is correct and it follows from **K** that the fire was caused by witchcraft.

Interestingly, it is not evident that this blocks SSV in the embedded S-terms. Consider (7.6a,b), with the corresponding paraphrases (7.7a,b):

(7.6)   a. The morning star may be inhabited.
   b. The morning star must be inhabited.

(7.7)   a. My relevant knowledge state **K** is correct and it is compatible with **K** that the morning star is inhabited.
   b. My relevant knowledge state **K** is correct and it follows from **K** that the morning star is inhabited.

Is the term *morning star*, in (7.7a,b), freely interchangeable *salva veritate* with the coreferential term *evening star*? This is a difficult question.

Let us consider first the case that (7.7a) or (7.7b) is true. Then, on the present analysis, speaker's knowledge state **K**, in so far as it pertains to the possible inhabitation of the morning star, is correct. But does this mean that the speaker also knows that the terms *morning star* and *evening star* refer to the same object? If so, SSV is ensured and the operator *may* does not create an intensional subdomain. But perhaps the speaker does not know that the morning star and the evening star are the same planet and perhaps his evidence shows that the evening star cannot be inhabited, though the morning star just may be, given the conditions under which the planet has been observed. In that case, SSV is effectively blocked, which would make at least the operator *may* intensional. But then again, an interlocutor might say that if (7.6a) is true, then so must (7.8a) be, because *morning star* and *evening star* are just different names for the same object. And the speaker who produced (7.6a) will then have no choice but to agree. And analogously for (7.6b) and (7.8b):

(7.8)   a. The evening star may be inhabited.
        b. The evening star must be inhabited.

The issue seems to turn on the meaning of the word *relevant*: what does one take the '*relevant* knowledge state **K**' to amount to? It doesn't look as if this question can be resolved here and now. We will, therefore, allow it to rest until new insights arise. It may be added that the question of free SSV, even though it triggered essential developments in semantics during the twentieth century, is less important for an adequate understanding of natural language than it is for an adequate philosophical notion of what 'truth' amounts to.

By contrast, if (7.7a) or (7.7b) is false, SSV appears to be freely applicable. For in that case either **K**, in so far as it is relevant, is incorrect, in which case substitution of the one term for the other does not affect the truth value, or **K**, in so far as it is relevant, is correct but there is no compatibility or necessary consequence, in which case SSV again fails to affect the truth value.

In actual fact, the widespread belief that epistemic modal subdomains are intensional in the sense of disallowing SSV simply is a consequence of the wildly unrealistic philosophical construct which reduces the extension of S-terms embedded under modal predicates to sets of possible worlds. Since the set of possible worlds in which the morning star is inhabited is different from the set of possible worlds in which the evening star is inhabited, SSV must, according to this analysis, be blocked. But this analysis is typically generated by philosophical and formal *a prioris*. It lacks any psychological plausibility, let alone any empirical support.[5]

---

[5] The tangle was confounded by W. V. O. Quine (1953: 143–4), who, in an effort to show that SSV is blocked in modal contexts, confused the value-assigning predicate be_v with the predicate *be* of identification (see Section 5.3.2 in Volume I). Quine wrongly regards a sentence like (i) as an identity statement and not as a statement assigning a value to the parameter 'the number of planets', which is what it is. Following up on this mistake, he shows that a replacement of the term

As regards *agentive* modals, in particular those of permission and obligation, SSV seems to be fully warranted. As a matter of intuitive observation, (7.9a) and (7.9b) are seen fully to allow for the substitution of *Mount Everest* for *Chomolungma* and vice versa (one remembers from Section 3.1.1 of Volume I that the two are different names for the same mountain). No-one can say that the addressee has not fulfilled the obligation imposed by (7.9b) because (s)he has climbed Mount Everest and not Chomolungma; and analogously for (7.9a):

(7.9)　a. You may now climb Mount Everest.
　　　　b. You must now climb Chomolungma.

The agentive modal *may* may be seen as saying that the set of rules and norms of behaviour actually in force is compatible with the event mentioned in the embedded S-term to be realized. Analogously, agentive *must* may be seen as saying that the existing set of rules and norms of behaviour requires the realization of the event mentioned in the embedded S-term.[6] Clearly, the realization of an event is insensitive to the terms used to refer to the entities mentioned, which means that SSV is freely allowed.

Apart from this factual, truth-conditional use, however, agentive modals are also open to performative use. (7.9a,b), for example, can be read not only as statements of fact about the existing set of rules of behaviour, but also, in a performative sense, as speech acts whereby the speaker uses his or her authority to bring about a change in the existing set of rules of behaviour by either allowing or ordering the addressee to carry out a specific act.[7]

---

nine in (ii) with *the number of planets* leads to the obvious falsity (iii), which is why he holds that the modal necessity operator does not allow for free SSV and is, therefore, intensional:

(i)　　The number of planets is nine.
(ii)　　Nine is necessarily greater than seven.
(iii)　The number of planets is necessarily greater than seven.

Needless to say, this argument, influential though it may have been, comes to nothing.

[6] The L-propositional form of epistemic and agentive modal statements is taken to be identical. In many languages, including most languages of Europe, the modal predicate forms part of the Auxiliary System and takes an embedded subject-S-term. The modal predicate is lowered into the subject-S-term, where it may end up as a finite verb form (as in English), or as a morphological element (as, for example, in Turkish). See Seuren (1996: 79–84, 111–16, 159–60, 221–2) for extensive discussions and analyses in different languages.

[7] Dutch and Low-German allow for an agentive prepositional phrase with agentive modals, under the preposition *van* (*von*). Sentences like (i) are normal standard Dutch:

(i) Hij moet van zijn leraar de sommen afmaken.
　　he must of his teacher the sums finish
　　His teacher has told him to finish his sums.

Dutch *van* was, until a few centuries ago, the standard preposition for passive agent phrases (standard modern Dutch has *door*); German *von* still has that function. This suggests that, at least for these languages, the agentive modals may represent underlying passive predicates approximately of the form 'it has been made possible/necessary (by A) for B to do C'. We will, however, not pursue this issue here.

7.2.2 *The Principle of Maximal Unity*

There is a principle at work in the overall construction of domains which ensures the maximal unity of the entire commitment domain including its subdomains. Let us speak of the PRINCIPLE OF MAXIMAL UNITY or PMU. PMU is akin to the OSTA Principle discussed in Section 3.4.2 of Volume I, which optimizes sense, truth, and actuality, both principles being of a strictly functional nature. PMU ensures that increments are, by default, managed in such a way that only minimal changes are brought about in the existing **D**. The principle can be overridden, but such overridings of the default process always involve a *post hoc* correction and hence a metalinguistic statement.

As far as can be seen at present, PMU manifests itself mainly in four ways, which we call transdominial referential transparency, upward presupposition projection, subdomain unification, and minimal **D**-change, respectively.

7.2.2.1 *Transdominial denotational transparency* By transdominial denotational transparency is meant the phenomenon that addresses occurring in any domain or subdomain are retrievable from any other domain or subdomain. (The term *denote* is used for the connection made between a definite noun phrase in an uttered sentence and the corresponding *discourse address*. The term *refer* is reserved for the connection made between a definite noun phrase (or the corresponding address) and the actual or virtual object represented by the address in question. Reference is thus mediated by a discourse address.)

The denotation function, which thus takes a definite noun phrase and delivers it at a discourse address, is free to roam through the speaker/listener's entire **D**, as indeed through the speaker/listener's entire knowledge base, to establish denotation, and hence reference. An apparent exception, as is explained in Sections 7.3.3, 8.2.2, and 10.8 seems to be the use of sentential negation, which may seem to ban the incrementation of the negated proposition to the domain or subdomain that is operative at the time the negation is used and thus to make impossible any denotation of an address thus created (see Section 10.8 for further comment).

Disregarding negation for the time being, we see, for example, that, given an address for the Eiffel Tower in the commitment domain at hand, this address is immediately retrievable for the purposes of any subdomain. Consider sentence (7.10):

(7.10)   Ann fears that the Eiffel Tower has been hit.

It is not necessary for the subdomain under *fear* to be construed as requiring the existential introduction of an address for *the Eiffel Tower* into the subdomain itself before (7.10) can be processed, as in (7.11), even though such an interpretation is not excluded:

(7.11)   Ann fears that there is a thing called 'Eiffel Tower' and that it has been hit.

The normal reading of (7.10) is such that the Eiffel Tower is taken to be a really existing object, which can be given an address in the commitment domain. Yet the actual existence of the Eiffel Tower is not entailed by (7.10), as can be seen from (7.12), whose first conjunct, *Ann is under the illusion that there is a thing called 'Eiffel Tower'*, entails that there is no such thing as the Eiffel Tower. If the second conjunct, *she fears that it has been hit*, entailed that the Eiffel Tower exists, the conjunction as a whole would be incoherent or inconsistent, but it is not: (7.12) is a fully coherent piece of discourse:

(7.12)   Ann is under the illusion that there is a thing called 'Eiffel Tower' and she fears that it has been hit.

Transdominial referential transparency likewise holds between subdomains. Consider the following sequence of sentences:

(7.13)   Roy is thought to have a sister. One hopes that *she* is more honest than him.

In (7.13), *she* stands for the intensional object 'Roy's reputed sister', who may not exist at all. This object is represented in the intensional subdomain of what people think. Yet it recurs in the intensional subdomain of what people hope. This is made possible by the principle of transdominial referential transparency.

When an inconsistency arises between any domains or subdomains where mutual consistency is required, this inconsistency is not due to transdominial reference but to a conflict between actual and virtual being (see Section 10.8). Thus, sentence (7.14) does allow for transdominial reference, but suffers from inconsistency between the subdomains of knowledge and hope:

(7.14)   !! I know Roy has no sister, but I hope that *she* is more honest than him.

The formal system, or, if one wishes, the logic of transdominial consistency has so far not been given any attention in the literature. No attempt is made here to develop such a logic. Further research will have to bring greater clarity.

7.2.2.2 Upward presupposition projection Transdominial denotational transparency by itself is, however, insufficient to explain the fact that (7.10) is *normally* interpreted as implying the actual existence of the Eiffel Tower. All it does is make it possible for (7.10) to be interpreted in such a way that the term *the Eiffel Tower* refers to an actually existing object, represented in the commitment domain. But that does not explain the *preference* for such an interpretation. To account for that, we have to assume that sentence (7.10), *by default*, induces the invited inference that the Eiffel Tower has actual existence.

Unlike entailments, which cannot be overridden or neutralized, invited inferences can, as is shown in (7.11) and (7.12). Thus, while (7.15) entails that the Eiffel Tower actually exists, owing to the fact that the predicate *hit* is extensional with regard to its object term (Section 3.5 in Volume I), (7.10) merely invites the inference that it actually exists:

(7.15)   The Eiffel Tower has been hit.

This weakening of entailment to invited inference is based on a default mechanism which we call 'upward presupposition projection' (following the introduction of the term *presupposition projection* in Langendoen and Savin (1971) in the context of the projection of presuppositions from subdomains into higher domains). Presuppositions have a tendency to percolate upwards and they do so under a variety of conditions and in different guises.

The notion of upward presupposition projection, or just presupposition projection, is defined as follows:

> (Upward) presupposition projection:
> (Upward) presupposition projection is the incrementation of presuppositions generated within an embedded S-term S_n, or of presuppositions or invited inferences that originated as presuppositions and were projected into S_n, to the higher domain of the embedding L-proposition, either as full presuppositions or as invited inferences.

The projection problem consists in defining the conditions under which presuppositions or invited inferences of embedded S-terms do in fact project—that is, are incremented to the immediately higher domain and any higher domain over it prior to the incrementation of the whole sentence—and in what form. This problem dominated the presuppositional literature during the 1970s, at the expense, one must say, of more basic research into the question of what presuppositions are and how they are generated.

Mostly, when presuppositions project upwards, they are weakened to invited inferences, as is demonstrated in the following sentences:

(7.16)   a. Maggie hopes that her boyfriend has come back.
        b. Maggie's boyfriend has come back.
        c. Maggie's boyfriend has been away.
        d. Maggie has a boyfriend.

Sentence (7.16b) expresses the L-propositional object term of (7.16a), (7.16c) is a presupposition of (7.16b), and (7.16d) of (7.16c). The question is: are (7.16d) and (7.16c) also presuppositions of (7.16a)? That is, does (7.16a) also, like (7.16b), presuppose that Maggie has a boyfriend and that her boyfriend has been away? The answer is that the presuppositions (7.16d) and (7.16c) do make it to the superordinate domain of (7.16a), but only in the weakened form of an invited inference. Full presuppositions form a subclass of entailments, but (7.16a) does not entail that Maggie has a boyfriend and that the young man has been away. It only invites that inference and that invited inference can be overridden, as is shown by (7.17), which entails that Maggie does not have a boyfriend, so that he cannot have been away:

(7.17)   Maggie has deluded herself into believing that she has a boyfriend and she hopes that he (her boyfriend) has come back.

Here, the presupposition (7.16d), carried by (7.16c), is restricted to the subdomain under the predicate *believe*.

In the terminology that was introduced in Karttunen (1973: 178) and which was much *en vogue* during the 1970s, predicates like *hope* or *believe* are FILTERS in that they let presuppositions through in the weakened form of default invited inferences which are open to cancellation. By contrast, predicates introducing or continuing a subdomain that need not be consistent, either internally or with respect to the superordinate **D**, in particular all metalinguistic predicates, including predicates of verbal reporting like *say, ask,* or *mention,* are PLUGS, in that they block the upward projection of presuppositions. A final category of predicates, in Karttunen's taxonomy, is formed by the so-called HOLES, which let presuppositions through as full presuppositions, no matter when and where. Factive predicates are clear holes, in that they induce the presupposition that their factive embedded S-term is true, which requires in turn the truth of the presuppositions entailed by the embedded S-term in question.

The empirical question of the precise conditions for presupposition projection is discussed in detail in Section 10.5, where the hole-filter-plug terminology is given up and where it is argued that PMU is indeed the main guiding principle, given the lexical meanings of the predicates concerned. Here we only wish to point out that presuppositions of embedded clauses are under pressure to project upwards, so that they have a maximally restrictive effect on the overall total **D** in question and thus make it maximally informative. How and when this tendency is thwarted is a matter for discussion in Section 10.5. The conclusion there is that the reasons for the thwarting of this tendency are, on the whole, grounded in PMU, though there is a remainder of cases where PMU appears to be restricted by linguistic form.

A case in point is *natural language negation*. It has been, and still is, a moot question whether natural language negation (*not* in English) is a hole, a filter, or a plug. According to standard propositional logic, it must be a plug, since the standard logical negation blocks any entailment of its argument proposition, except necessary truths, which follow from any proposition. According to accepted lore in pragmatics, it must be a filter turning presuppositions of the embedded proposition into invited inferences, which can be overridden on pragmatic grounds. For those authors who support this view, in particular Horn (1985, 1989), pragmatics should also be able to account for metalinguistic uses of negation, where the negation signals the speaker's dissatisfaction with the choice of words in a previous utterance.

In Seuren (1980, 1985, 1988, 2000) the position is defended that normal unmarked, *minimal negation* is a hole, letting the presuppositions of its argument-S through in full force. But next to minimal negation, a strongly marked metalinguistic *radical negation* is posited, which cancels all presuppositions and requires special accent to do so. This position is based on the fact that the possible occurrence of both the minimal and the radical negation is universally constrained by certain grammatical and lexical environments, which are unrelated to any pragmatic factors (for a detailed discussion see Section 10.4).

Moreover, the radical negation clearly has a metalinguistic character, but, as argued in Seuren (1988), distinct from other metalinguistic uses of negation. *Prima facie* at least, these facts appear to support the assumption of a true ambiguity between minimal and radical NOT, the latter being obligatorily metalinguistic and each being excluded in certain linguistic contexts and uniquely possible in others. Yet, if we have to do with an ambiguity of the negation operator, it is not an idiosyncratic ambiguity such as are found all over the lexicon. On the contrary, since the semantic behaviour of negation is most probably subject to systematic grammatical and lexical restrictions that apply across the languages of the world, any ambiguity of the negation operator should be the result of yet unknown universal semantico-grammatical principles. Moreover, as indicated in note 12 of Chapter 3, the metalinguistic character of the radical negation may well be a not fully grammaticalized remnant of an original truly metalinguistic operator 'Not true (the utterance *u*)'.

7.2.2.3 *Subdomain unification: transdominial consistency*   A further manifestation of PMU consists in subdomain unification. By this is meant the fact that (sub)domains maximally pool their resources under the condition of semantic consistency and according to available world or situational knowledge. Consider the following sentences:

(7.18)   a. Paul may be at home and he may be having his breakfast.
          b. Paul may be at home and he may be in hospital.

The first conjunct of (7.18a), *Paul may be at home*, introduces a subdomain of possibility. The second conjunct, *he may be having his breakfast*, continues that same subdomain, since, by default, one's home is where one has one's breakfast. Typically, in cases of domain unification or continuation, subsequent additions restrict earlier additions. Thus, in the possibility subdomain of (7.18a), having one's breakfast restricts the being at home, in that one can do a variety of things when one is at home: cook, read, watch TV, entertain guests, or indeed have one's breakfast.

By contrast, the second conjunct of (7.18b), *he may be in hospital*, does not continue the subdomain of possibility introduced by the first conjunct. Here we have two subdomains of possibility, one in which Paul is at home and one in which he is in hospital. The reason is, obviously, that being in hospital is, in all but highly exceptional cases, incompatible with being at home. Moreover, being in hospital does not restrict being at home, as being in hospital is not something one normally does at home. Consequently, (7.18b) results in two distinct possibility subdomains, one for Paul's being at home and one for his being in hospital.

In cases of domain-splitting, as in (7.18b), one often finds the connective *or* instead of the perhaps more regular *and*. This is no doubt due to the fact that (7.18b) forces a choice between two subordinate domains, only one of which can be true. This is remarkable because normally OR leaves a choice not between two parallel operators over subdomains but between two parallel domains, as in:

(7.19)   Paul is at home or he is in hospital.

The use of *or* in cases like (7.18b) is semantically anomalous since the juxtaposition of two possibilities calls for *and*:

(7.20)   Possible[Paul is at home] and Possible[Paul is in hospital]

If, as some say it is, this use of OR is natural for speakers of natural languages, an adequate semantic analysis should show that this use of OR is a regular consequence of the semantics of OR. This, however, is more than we can achieve here.

A further consequence of domain splitting is the blocking of CONJUNCTION REDUCTION. Whilst (7.18a) can be reduced to (7.21a), (7.18b) cannot, *salva veritate*, be reduced to (7.21b):

(7.21)   a. Paul may be at home and be having his breakfast.
          b. !! Paul may be at home and in hospital.

This means that the syntactic process of CONJUNCTION REDUCTION applied to subdomains must be taken to be conditional upon domain unification. This may be taken as an argument against the thesis that grammatical processes are modular—that is, operating on mere formal input and algorithmically delivering a mere formal output, without any external interference (see Section 7.2.2 in Volume I). It follows that if both the modularity thesis for grammars and the syntactic rule of CONJUNCTION REDUCTION are to be upheld, the input structures to a grammar must, where relevant, carry a formal mark indicating whether the second domain is or is not unified with the first: domain split/unification must then be encoded in the syntax. We must, unfortunately, leave this question unresolved here.

Inverting the order of the conjuncts in (7.18a), as in (7.22a), leads to a different interpretation. But in (7.18b), where domain unification is blocked, the difference is at most stylistic:

(7.22)   a. Paul may be having his breakfast and/or he may be at home.
          b. Paul may be in hospital and/or he may be at home.

Normal world knowledge makes (7.22a) anomalous. Normally, or by default, the second conjunct restricts the first and not vice versa. Since, in (7.22a), the first conjunct restricts the second, an anomalous interpretation imposes itself. As a result, (7.22a) forces a scenario in which Paul's having his breakfast does not take place at home but elsewhere, in a hotel, for example. Such an interpretation blocks domain unification and hence conjunction reduction.

*7.2.2.4 Minimal **D**-change*   If we extend the PRINCIPLE OF MAXIMAL UNITY through time, we get the PRINCIPLE OF MINIMAL CHANGE, which implies that listeners appeal to all their cognitive resources in order to keep their current discourse domain from being unnecessarily crowded. On the one hand, this is an application of the general cognitive principle in virtue of which the mind strives for maximal efficiency. It seems an inborn feature of the mind to keep natural ontologies minimal and subject to functional classification. Babies quickly learn to identify different occurrences of the same person or object as being precisely that. They also quickly acquire the ability to identify different individual objects or persons as belonging to one type or class—Leibniz's 'identity of indiscernibles'. This activity of creating maximal order in the mind with a minimum of expenditure and effort is naturally extended to the construction of discourse domains. On the other hand, however, it is also a matter of the listener's 'aligning' his or her current discourse domain with that of the speaker, on the overall assumption that speakers likewise minimize their models of the situation under discussion—that is, their discourse domains (Pickering and Garrod 2004).

One manifestation of this principle was discussed in Section 7.2.2.3, where the case was discussed, in connection with example (7.18), of two modal subdomains being automatically united by default into one domain when world knowledge supports such unification. More examples are provided by the phenomena of transdominial referential transparency and of presupposition projection discussed in Sections 7.2.2.1 and 7.2.2.2, respectively.

A further illustration of this principle is the practice of especially journalists and reporters to enrich anaphoric reference with new information by replacing a simple pronoun with a full lexical NP, as in (7.23):

(7.23)   Yesterday evening a Swiss banker was arrested at Heathrow Airport. The fifty-year-old bachelor declared that he had come to Britain to kidnap the queen.

Here the NP *the fifty-year-old bachelor* adds new information about the banker who is said to have been arrested at Heathrow Airport, not about a hitherto unmentioned individual introduced into the discourse domain by means of the device of *post hoc* suppletion (accommodation). In other words, *post hoc* suppletion is activated only as a last resort, as when I start a story in something like the following way:

(7.24)   The fifty-year-old bachelor was at the end of his tether. No matter whom he approached in the street, they all shied away as if he were a leper.

Now there is nothing for the NP *the fifty-year-old bachelor* to link up with, so that the listener or reader is left with no other option than to apply *post hoc* suppletion of the presupposition carried by (7.24), namely that there apparently was a fifty-year-old bachelor approaching people in the street. But no such measure is needed for (7.23), because world knowledge easily allows for an identification of the Swiss banker and the fifty-year-old bachelor mentioned in the news item. The principle of Minimal **D**-change now says that because such an identification is *possible*, it is *mandatory*, unless blocked by specific information provided in the discourse or in the situation at hand. The principle of minimal **D**-change thus amounts to a restriction imposed on any new incrementation process to minimize the number of subdomains and the number of addresses for individual objects or sets of objects.

7.3 Conditions for text coherence

The main principle underlying discourse incrementation processes is the closest possible approximation of the nature and the location of what is meant to be the TARGET SITUATION, which is the situation the speaker aims at describing. Or, in less ponderous terms, discourse incrementation is the search for the target situation. This search must safeguard consistency, since inconsistency of a discourse leaves no possible situation in which it can be true. It must be informative in the sense that every new increment helps to home in on the target situation, restricting the number of possible situations in which **D** can be true (unless a new increment recapitulates what has been achieved so far). And it must keep subdomains apart whenever that is necessary. These three conditions are discussed, in that order, in the following subsections.

7.3.1 *Consistency*

Any **D** must be internally consistent for the simple reason that an inconsistent set of statements cannot be true for any situation at all. Speakers and listeners have a profound awareness of this condition, as any discourse comes to a halt when an inconsistency is detected.

Although it does not matter much whether a **D** in course is actually true or not, it does matter whether it *can* be true. There is a CONSTRAINT OF POSSIBLE TRUTH with regard to the propositional content of any commitment domain. A commitment domain must, as a whole, be consistent, so that there is something to the truth of which the speaker is committed, or whose truth the speaker wants to be realized through the listener, who is requested, allowed, or obliged to bring it about. (One remembers from the opening sentences of Chapter 1 that it is because of the importance of textual consistency that so much attention is paid to logic in the present book.)

A commitment domain is like a novel: no matter how strange or outlandish the story, complete with the linguistic utterances of each character, it must be at least consistent or else the novel will fail to interest readers and it might even simply break down. The moment an inconsistency is detected by a hearer in a commitment domain, it gives rise to puzzlement and possibly even to incomprehensibility. Inconsistency makes it impossible for a commitment domain to be true and thus makes it unfit for any truth commitment or for any appeal to the listener to make it true, or for any rule-setting to be followed properly. Even so, however, inconsistencies may occur in certain kinds of subdomain. Obviously, a subdomain under the operator INCONSISTENT is expected to contain inconsistent information. Or the inconsistency may be attributed to a given speaker, who will then be understood as making inconsistent utterances. But the overall commitment domain, the overarching tale, appeal, or rule-setting must be consistent, or rather, must not contain any detected inconsistencies.

Interestingly, the consistency condition of commitment domains may be seen as resulting from the principle of natural set theory PNST–5, presented in Section 3.2.2 and stating that, at a basic-natural cognitive level, the intersection of two sets A and B must be M(utual)-PARTIAL intersection (A ⦾ B, or: $A \cap B \neq_v \emptyset \neq_v A \neq_v B$). Given that this intersection function translates into basic-natural propositional logic as the functor AND, it follows that the conjunction of two L-propositions P, Q must leave a nonnull valuation space, so that there is at least one possible situation in which P AND Q is true (modulo key). Since AND is also the prototypical incrementation function of utterances, PNST–5 formally ensures logico-semantic consistency of commitment domains as well as of any subdomain that requires consistency.

In actual fact, the condition of consistency should be carried further and extended to the speech-act force of utterances. Just as propositional content is subject to *truth conditions*, the speech-act character of utterances, as specified in Section 4.3 of Volume I, is subject to *liability conditions*, which have to do more with interpersonal relations than with truth. (There may even be a legal aspect to speech-act commitments or appeals, as interpersonal relations very much involve giving and taking, as well as pleasing and offending.) It follows that the notion of consistency applies not only to propositional content but also, at a higher level, to speech-act commitments, appeals, or rule-settings, which have their own consistency criteria.

Something was said about this latter aspect in Section 4.2 of Volume I, with regard to a few examples from the literature showing a clash between speaker's overtly expressed commitments or appeals on the one hand and his or her loyalty to the commitment or appeal on the other. The examples discussed were Austin's quote from Euripides' *Hippolytus*: 'my tongue took an oath, but my mind remained unsworn', Hamblin's 'I am obliged to order you to do D, and I hereby do so; but my private advice to you is not to', as well as the famous Moore paradox 'the cat is on the mat, but I don't believe it'. And the conclusion was that the existing literature is largely unclear with regard to speech-act consistency. In general, the speech-act force of utterances has been neglected in linguistic, semantic, philosophical, and pragmatic studies, where all attention has been focused on propositional content. To remedy that situation and bring greater clarity to the issues concerned is, however, a research programme of such magnitude that we cannot possibly hope to do much about it within the confines of the present study.

7.3.2 *Informativity*

A new increment to any **D** must be *informative* in the sense that it narrows down the set **U** of possible situations in the direction of the target situation, or else it must recapitulate what has been achieved so far and draw an inference that has not so far been made explicit, as is typically the case in sentences starting with *therefore*. In general, we speak of the PRINCIPLE OF INFORMATIVITY or PI. The underlying rationale of PI seems to be a basic need in linguistic interaction to home in on the target situation, which is to be described up to the degree of precision needed for the purpose at hand. Given our system of valuation-space modelling, this requirement can be cast into a formal mould.

Formally speaking (and without taking into account the class of inference-drawing increments), the principle of informativity (PI) is defined as follows:

> PRINCIPLE OF INFORMATIVITY (**PI**)
> Each successive increment in a discourse domain **D** must constitute a further restriction of /**D**/, provided the restricted /**D**/ $\neq \emptyset$.

Noncompliance with PI results in either an erratic or an incomprehensible discourse (the latter in particular when /**D**/ is reduced to $\emptyset$).

Consider, in an abstract formal sense, the universe of all possible situations **U** to be the disjunction (in the standard sense) of all possible propositions, and hence the union of the VSs of all infinitely many possible L-propositions: /P_1/ $\cup$ /P_2/ $\cup$ /P_3/ $\cup$ ... .As a general principle we say that before any discourse has started /**D**/ = **U**. Although this makes the initial /**D**/ (= **U**) a nondescript entity, and hence unfit for natural cognition, it helps to see how a discourse can start with the implicit question, anticipated by the speaker: 'Exactly what proposition do you, speaker, want to increment for the purpose of the present interaction?' Any first L-proposition **P** presented for incrementation can be regarded as an answer to that question. **P** then restricts the initial /**D**/ (= **U**) to /**P**/, in the sense that the target situation is an element in the new, more restricted, /**D**/.

   We will speak of any given (old) **D** as **Do**, and of the resulting new **D** as **Dn**. It is not required that, for an increment of **P**, /**P**/ be included in /**Do**/, which would make **P** entail **Do**. But it is not forbidden either. When /**Do**/ contains /Dan is human/ and /**P**/ is /Dan is a student/, or, presuppositionally, when /**Do**/ contains /Dan was married before/ and /**P**/ is /Dan is divorced/, then **P** entails **Do** and the discourse is still coherent and informative. In most cases, however, **P** and **Do** will be semantically independent with regard to each other, so that /**Dn**/ will consist of the nonnull intersection of /**P**/ with /**Do**/. This process of incrementing **P** to **Do** is shown graphically in Figure 7.1. Anticipating the analysis of presuppositional phenomena in Chapter 10, we posit that, for normal or default negation, /NOT(**P**)/ is the complement of /**P**/ within /**Do**/, since an incrementation of NOT(**P**) is an answer to the (implicit or explicit) question 'P?' within the interpretative limits of **Do**. In Figure 7.1, /**Do**/ is marked by horizontal lines, and /**Dn**/ by vertical lines. Since by definition /**Dn**/ is included in /**Do**/, /**Dn**/ is, in fact, marked by both horizontal and vertical lines. This makes the standard incrementation procedure an instance of AND-conjunction.

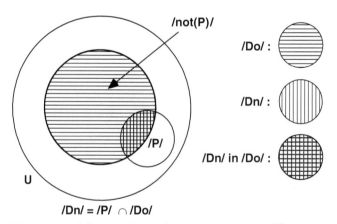

FIGURE 7.1 /**Do**/ narrowed down to /**Dn**/ after incrementation of **P**

7.3.3 *Subdomain hierarchies: subsidiary subdomains*

Although there is, as yet, no fully elaborated logic encoding the conditions of transdominial consistency, it may be observed that there are *hierarchies* of subdomain-creating predicates (see Seuren 1985: 417–22). Consider the following sentences:

(7.25)   a.   Dan knows that Philip has a sister who is a divorcee.
       b.   Dan believes that Philip's divorced sister has a daughter.
       c.   Dan hopes that Philip's sister's daughter is still a child.

When these sentences are ordered serially, with normal anaphoric provisions and conjunctive concatenation, the following coherent text comes about:

(7.26)   Dan knows that Philip has a sister who is a divorcee. He believes that she has a daughter and he hopes that this daughter is still a child.

From a presuppositional point of view, these sentences may be taken to have the following structure (where Y_X stands for 'Y presupposing X', X, Y, . . . ranging over L-propositions):

(7.27)   a.   Dan knows that P.
       b.   Dan believes that Q_P.
       c.   Dan hopes that R_Q.

The point is that the text of (7.26) becomes incoherent when the main predicates are exchanged, as, for example, in:

(7.28)   ! Dan hopes that Philip has a sister who is a divorcee. He believes that she has a daughter and he knows that this daughter is still a child.

The first sentence in (7.28) is not incoherent. But the second sentence strikes one as both an incoherent continuation of the first and incoherent in itself. (7.28) can be improved by the insertion of conditionals, as in:

(7.29)   Dan hopes that Philip has a sister who is a divorcee. He believes that, *if Philip has a divorced sister,* she has a daughter and he knows that, *if she has a daughter,* this daughter is still a child.

This sentence is, though a little odd for pragmatic reasons, fully coherent in itself. To remove the pragmatic oddity one must invent a proper context, no matter how far-fetched. For example, one may assume that Dan has been told about Philip's sister and her daughter from a marriage that has been dissolved. He doesn't know if this is true, but he hopes that it is at least true that Philip has a divorced sister, because he wants to marry into Philip's family, which is quite rich. Since this sister has always been mentioned in connection with a daughter, Dan believes that, if Philip has a sister, this sister has a daughter. Dan knows that Philip's parents are in their mid-forties, which makes it practically impossible for them to have a grown-up granddaughter. Therefore, Dan knows that, if Philip's sister has a daughter, this daughter must still be a child. Perhaps a starting point for a suspense thriller!

Subdomain hierarchies do not infringe upon the principle of transdominial denotational transparency discussed in Section 7.2.2.1, as one might be inclined to think. This is because that principle is about interpretational *accessibility* of addresses in the commitment domain or any subdomains, whereas subdomain hierarchies are about *coherence*. Although a sequence of sentences like (7.28) may be deemed incoherent on account of its transgressing the boundaries set by subdomain hierarchies, there is no problem as regards the denotations of the various definite noun phrases: *she* in the second sentence clearly denotes the sister-address set up in the first sentence, even though a subdomain of belief does not fit well into a subdomain of hope.

An attempt at setting up a few subdomain hierarchies was made in Seuren (1985: 417–22). One such scale, intended to apply to descending epistemic strength, is shown in Figure 7.2. Such scales imply that the discourse may proceed from the column marked 0 to any column marked by a higher number, while predicates in the same column are not subject to a sequentiality constraint.

The predicates of column 1 are all factive predicates, which means that the truth of the object *that*-clause is presupposed. This makes it possible, though perhaps only marginally so, to formulate a coherent sequence of conjuncts as exemplified in (7.30):

(7.30)   Molly regrets that her brother is in jail but (it is true that) the man is dangerous.

This is not a counterexample to the epistemic-strength scale of Figure 7.2, because factive predicates induce a presupposition of truth for their *that*-clauses, so that whatever is said in the *that*-clause is retrievable from the higher truth domain.

0 →	1 →	2 →	3
true	know	believe	hope
	realize	think	wish
	regret	…	want
	…		try
			…

Figure 7.2 Intensional scale for epistemic strength

0	→	1	→	2	→	3
true		must		probable		may
		necessary		likely		possible
		…		…		…

FIGURE 7.3 Intensional scale for epistemic inference

A further intensional scale may be set up for predicates of epistemic modality, discussed in Section 7.2.1.3. Such a scale is presented in Figure 7.3 and more such scales can be constructed.

A theory of subdomain hierarchies is important not only for a proper understanding of how subdomains are interrelated, and thus for an adequate insight into the criteria for textual coherence and consistency, but also for another, equally important and more specific, reason, to do with presupposition projection (see Section 10.5). Suppose the sentence (7.25c) occurs in a context where it is given that Philip has no sister. Now the presuppositions 'Philip has a sister' and 'Philip's sister has a daughter' of the embedded clause *that Philip's sister's daughter is still a child* cannot be projected into the commitment domain **D** and must remain restricted to a subdomain. The question is: which subdomain? It cannot be the subdomain of what Dan hopes, because then the interpretation would be 'Dan hopes that Philip has a sister and that this sister has a daughter and that this daughter is still a child', which is not the way (7.25c) is interpreted. On the contrary, Dan may well hope that Philip does not have a sister and that, if Philip does have a sister, that this sister does not have a daughter. But, if these hopes are dashed by the way things are, he may hope that at least this daughter is still a child. The question is, therefore, if these presuppositions are prevented from rising into a higher subdomain and also from staying within the subdomain of what Dan hopes, where do they go? The answer must be that they go into the sub-domain of what Dan *believes* to be the case, even if Dan's beliefs have not been the topic of discussion in the current **D**.

When a subdomain requires a different subdomain for the storage of nonprojected presuppositions, we call it a SUBSIDIARY SUBDOMAIN. Subsidiary subdomains have to refer to a RECIPIENT SUBDOMAIN for the storage of non-projected presuppositions of embedded clauses. In all cases, whether the presuppositions of embedded clauses are projected or not, they are ENTAILED in the associated recipient subdomain. Thus, in all cases where it is true to say that Sandra hopes that her son has returned, it follows by way of semantic entailment that Sandra believes that she has a son and that this son has been away. They are actually *projected* as default inferences as long as the current discourse domain is compatible with Sandra having a son and this son having been away.

Subdomains created by the predicate hope are thus subsidiary subdomains and they have to fall back on a recipient subdomain of what the subject-term referent of hope believes, to cater for nonprojected presuppositions.

To the best of my knowledge, this particular phenomenon has not so far been discussed in the literature. If this is so, it is surprising because the phenomenon is of considerable importance for a proper understanding of the processes of utterance interpretation. It seems, incidentally, that the class of predicates that create subsidiary subdomains is identical with the class of emotive factive predicates that do not allow for substitition *salva veritate* of topic–comment modulation—a phenomenon hitherto unknown and discussed in Sections 3.2 and 6.2.3.2 of Volume I. We revert to this important topic in Section 10.5.2 and in Chapter 11.

Right now, we leave these and related questions open and merely point out that these aspects of discourse incrementation have been neglected in the literature, despite their obvious relevance.

7.4 Open parameters in lexical meaning

In the present section, we take some time to look at the lexical aspects of context-sensitivity, keeping in mind what was said at the outset of the present chapter, namely that sentences underlying utterances contain systematic lexical and grammatical devices that refer the listener in specific ways to available encyclopedic and contextual knowledge.

It is often thought or implicitly assumed that predicate meanings, as codified in their satisfaction conditions, are lexically fixed in such a way that they automatically produce truth or falsity when applied to appropriate reference objects. This assumption, however, though not unreasonable in itself, is unwarranted because it fails to take into account the important fact that in many, perhaps most, cases, the satisfaction conditions imply an appeal to nonlinguistic world or situational knowledge, not codified in the language system acquired during childhood. The truth and falsity of assertive utterances are thus not just the product of linguistic compositional computation, but are co-determined by nonlinguistic knowledge, either of a general encyclopedic or of a context-bound, situational nature. Formal semanticists should be worried by this, since such appeals to general or situational knowledge prove that they have been wrong in insisting that the truth conditions of sentences are compositionally derivable from the satisfaction conditions of the predicates occurring in them and the structural positions they occupy. Let us consider a few examples, some of which have been discussed earlier, especially in Sections 9.6 and 9.7 of Volume I, though in a slightly different context.

Gradable adjectives provide a prime example. These are adjectives that allow for grade modifiers such as *rather, very,* or *a little.* They also allow for comparatives and superlatives.[8] Typical examples are *expensive, old, large, wide, smart, popular, rich, safe, fast,* and many others, as opposed to, for example, *closed, empty, rectangular, frontal, dead, postprandial,* which are, in principle, nongradable. The applicability of gradable adjectives (when used absolutely, that is, not in a construction that implies a form of comparison) depends on, usually socially recognized, standards, such as standards of cost, age, size, monetary value, etc., for the objects denoted by their subject terms. The description of such standards is not part of the description of the language concerned but of (socially shared) knowledge. Thus, when I say:[9]

(7.31)   He is an old man.

the truth of what I say depends on socially acknowledged norms for calling a man *old.* How the norm is selected is still largely unknown. It is unclear, for example, what norm is to be applied in a case like *Apes are intelligent.* Are they meant to be intelligent with regard to humans, or compared to other animals? There is a large amount of literature dealing with gradable adjectives, and many issues have so far remained unresolved. But it is clear, across the board, that no solution will be found unless cognitive factors are fully integrated into the semantics of gradable adjectives. The point here is that the criteria for truth or falsehood are not given in the linguistic description of the meanings of these adjectives but in (socially shared) knowledge. Such adjectives thus need an open parameter (sometimes also called 'free variable') in their

---

[8] Interestingly, some adjectives are nongradable in literal use but become gradable when used metaphorically. For example, the adjective *self-contained* is nongradable when applied to an apartment but gradable when applied to a person's character. Likewise for *square, round, full, angular, pedestrian, human, savage,* and many other adjectives, which are nongradable when used literally (especially in a technical context), but gradable when used nonliterally or less strictly.

[9] One recalls from Section 9.3 in Volume I the proposal that a sentence like (7.31) is to be analysed as 'He mans oldly' (or 'He olds his being a man'), in analogy with *He is a good teacher* and *He teaches well.*

semantic description referring the speaker/hearer to the relevant elements in general knowledge.[10]

Further examples of cognitive dependency are *possession predicates*, like English *have, lack, with, without*, and whatever lexical specification is needed for genitives, datives, and possessive pronouns. These clearly require general encyclopedic knowledge, and often also contextual knowledge, for their proper interpretation and thus for the assignment of truth values. Consider the following examples (repeated from (7.17a,b) in Section 9.6.3 of Volume I, where they are discussed in a different context):

(7.32)   a. This hotel room has a bathroom.
         b. This student has a supervisor.

For (7.32a) to be true it is necessary that there be one unique bathroom directly connected with the room in question, whose use is reserved for the occupants of that room. When the room has a note stuck to the door saying that its bathroom is at the end of the corridor to the right, while the same bathroom serves all the other rooms in the corridor, (7.32a) is false—not just misleading but false, as any judge presiding over a court case brought by a disgruntled hotel guest will agree. But for (7.32b) to be true no such unique-ness relation is required, as one supervisor may, and usually does, have many students to look after. The predicate *have* does not determine the precise nature of the relation between the referents of the subject and object terms. What is needed for full interpretation is, for (7.32a), knowledge of the world of hotels and, for (7.32b), knowledge of the world of universities or similar institutions of higher education. The same goes for the parallel sentences:

(7.33)   a. This is a hotel room with a bathroom.
         b. This is a student with a supervisor.

Possession predicates, therefore, must be specified in the lexicon as involv-ing an appeal to what is normally the case, or has been specified to be the case, regarding their term referents. Linguistically, they merely express a *known relation of appurtenance* between the kind of object referred to in subject position and the kind of object referred to in object position (see Janssen 1976). The semantic description (satisfaction condition) of *have* and other

---

[10] Typically, in the case of gradable adjectives, the boundary between truth and falsehood forms what is often called a 'grey area', in which gradable statements are neither clearly true nor clearly false, letting in a 'fuzzy' logic with transitional truth values. Gradability thus goes hand in hand with fuzzy truth values.

possessive predicates is thus taken to contain a parameter for 'what is known', making the interpretation of this predicate in each token occurrence truth-conditionally dependent on situational or world knowledge.

Possessive pronouns appear to allow for a larger range of 'known relations of appurtenance' than, for example, *have*. Sentence (7.34) may be uttered by a gardener who has no proprietary rights to 'his' flower beds other than his duty to tend them:

(7.34)   Please don't mess up my flower beds.

To say 'I have flower beds' would be inappropriate in the circumstances.

Many such examples can be given. Consider the predicate *flat* said of a road, a tyre, a mountain, a face, or the world. There is an overall element 'spread out, preferably horizontally, without too much in the way of protrusions or elevations', but that in itself is insufficient to determine what 'being flat' amounts to in these cases. The full meaning comes across only if it is known what roads, tyres, mountains, faces, and the world are normally thought to be like. Dictionaries, even the best ones, limit themselves to giving examples, hoping that the user will get the hint.

Another example is the predicate *fond of*, as in the following sentences (copied from Section 9.6.3 in Volume I):

(7.35)   a. John is fond of his dog.
         b. John is fond of cherries.
         c. John is fond of mice.

Clearly, there are different, incompatible, kinds of fondness, depending on how socially shared world knowledge tells us to practise it. Sentence (7.35c) is ambiguous in this respect, as John's fondness may be of the kind expressed in (7.35a) or of the kind expressed in (7.35b). The common element in the status assigned to the object-term referents is something like 'being the object of one's affection or of one's pleasure', but such a condition is insufficient to determine full interpretation. It is no doubt for that reason that a sentence like (7.36) strikes one as somehow infelicitous:

(7.36)   John is fond of his dog and of cherries.

Cognitive dependency is an essential aspect in the description of predicate meanings. The fact that many predicate meanings contain a parameter referring to an available nonlinguistic, language-independent knowledge base means that neither utterance-token interpretation nor sentence-type meaning are compositional in the accepted sense of being derivable by (model-theoretic) computation from the linguistic elements alone. As regards utterance-token interpretation, this is already widely accepted, owing to the deconstructivist forces at work in pragmatics. The noncompositionality of sentence-type meaning, defined at the level of language description, is now likewise beginning to be accepted by theorists of natural language. This type-level noncompositionality, however, does not force the conclusion that the specification of the satisfaction conditions of predicates is not truth-conditional, only that standards embodied in socially accepted knowledge and information provided by context may become part of the truth conditions of sentences in which the predicate occurs.

As was said in Section 9.6 of Volume I, the term *polysemy* is often used for phenomena such as those presented above. At the same time, however, it is widely recognized that this is, in fact, little more than a label used to give the problem a name. The problem itself lies in the psychology of concepts. One may assume that there are socially shared concepts like 'possession', 'flatness', 'fondness', but it is not known in what terms such concepts are to be defined. In a general sense, Fodor (1975, 1998) is probably right in insisting that lexical meanings are direct reflexes of concepts that have their abode in cognition but outside language. Yet both the nonlinguistic concepts and the corresponding lexical meanings must be defined one way or another. And the question is whether this can be done in terms of the famous necessary and sufficient conditions. If so, then, according to Fodor, the language in which such conditions are to be formulated cannot be any form of natural human language but must be a 'language of thought', which is categorially different from any natural language and whose terms and combinatorial properties will have to be established as a result of psychological theorizing. We are still very much in the dark as regards such questions. It is clear, in any case, that phenomena like those shown in (7.31)–(7.35) pose a serious threat to any attempt at setting up a model-theoretic theory of lexical meaning, such as Dowty (1979). The neglect of the cognitive factor quickly becomes fatal in lexical semantics.

As is explained in Section 9.7 of Volume I, context-bound or situational knowledge plays a role in the interpretation of predicates that involve a VIEWPOINT or PERSPECTIVE, such as the pair *come* and *go*, or predicates like *to the right/left of, in front of, behind*. Consider, for example, the sentences:

(7.37)   a. John looked around. The box was to his left.
         b. I looked around. The box was to John's left.

In (7.37a), the viewpoint is taken by John, and the box must be to his left as *he* sees it. In (7.37b), this is not necessary: the box must be to John's left as *I* (speaker) see it, while for John it may be anywhere around him. That predicates like *left*, *right*, *in front of*, *behind*, and so on, and also pairs of the type *come* and *go*, are sensitive to viewpoint is no doubt due to the fact that they involve ego-related localizations. (One thinks of the quasi-problem of why mirrors invert left and right but not up and down.)

Moreover, FUNCTION is known to be a determining factor in lexical meanings, in particular in the domain of artefacts. What makes a coat a coat is not its size, shape, material, or what not, but its intended function—a criterion to be satisfied not by the object itself but by the use to which it can be put according to whatever, possibly very creative, cognitive criteria.

A further source of cognitive dependency lies in a semantic component of *evaluation*. As was already pointed out by the Greek Sophists, the truth of a sentence like *There is a pleasant breeze* depends primarily on what humans perceive as 'pleasant', under varying conditions, and only in a secondary sense on the physical properties of the object so predicated. This point has great philosophical importance, as philosophers argue about the question of whether predicates like *good* and *just* (the central concepts in ethics), and *beautiful* (central in aesthetics), are to be defined in terms of world properties alone, or in terms that co-involve personal evaluation. As is shown in Section 3.4 of Volume I, this question applies likewise to the predicate *true*.

One further source of vagueness lies in the fact that satisfaction conditions of predicates often centre around *prototypical* 'ideals' (Rosch 1975). Some objects are closer to the intended prototype than others. A sparrow, for example, is closer to the prototype of 'bird' than an ostrich or a penguin. The notion of prototypicality plays a role in lexical semantics, in that preconditions (the class of satisfaction conditions that give rise to presuppositions) often select prototypical circumstances. The preconditions of the German predicate *kahl* (bald, bare), for example, include the condition that the subject-term referent is *prototypically* a human being or his/her head, *prototypically* covered with hair on the top of the head. The prototypicality appears from the fact that subjects, when asked what they think of first on hearing the word *kahl*, almost invariably answer that they think of a human head. Yet the subject-term referent may also, nonprototypically, be another kind of object, normally covered with other growth, such as feathers or leaves, or with decorative artifacts.

The update condition (giving rise to standard entailments) is simply that the growth or decoration which is normally there, is not there. This allows for phrases like *der kahle Kopf* (the bald head), *der kahle Mann* (the bald man), *der kahle Baum* (the bare tree), *der kahle Vogel* (the bald bird), *die kahle Landschaft* (the bare landscape), *die kahle Wand* (the bare wall). One notes, incidentally, that English has two predicates to cover this semantic field: *bald* and *bare*. Yet, when asked what the English equivalent is of German *kahl*, most people will reply *bald*, not *bare*. This is because of the prototype of *kahl*, which centres on hair on the human head, so that the more marginal cases slide out of focus. Prototypicality is thus an autonomous cognitive parameter that plays a role in the satisfaction conditions of many predicates.

This is as far as we can go in the present context. But even this cursory discussion shows that lexicographers are not all that wrong when they view theoretical semantics with a fair amount of scepticism.

8

Discourse incrementation

8.1 The incrementation procedure

So far, we have spoken only informally about what we call addresses—that is, cognitive representations of either actually existing or somehow thought-up entities or sets of entities. We shall now try to be a little more precise.

Addresses have their place in the general knowledge base of any individual human being (and also of many nonhuman animals). A large proportion of these addresses is intentionally related to really existing entities, but some are lodged in some subdomain of the general knowledge base capable of representing virtual entities. For example, you and I have an address for Sherlock Holmes, but we both know that Sherlock Holmes never existed but was thought up by the great nineteenth-century writer of detective stories Arthur Conan Doyle. The address for Sherlock Holmes is, therefore, lodged in a separate general-knowledge subdomain labelled 'In the stories by Arthur Conan Doyle'. And that subdomain is itself related to an actually existing set of books and stories, whose existence is partially grounded in actual books, consisting of actual paper (or in electronic form), and partially also in what we have called *social reality* in Section 2.1.2 of Volume I.

The general knowledge base may thus be seen as containing at least two kinds of unit: (a) ENTITY ADDRESSES known to represent actually existing entities or sets of entities and (b) DOMAIN ADDRESSES each again encapsulating entity and/or domain addresses, and so on. Entity addresses that are thus encapsulated in a domain address are, for the most part, intensional addresses. An intensional address is an entity representation, but the corresponding entity does not necessarily have to have actual existence. It may be a virtual entity in the sense explained in Chapters 2 and 5 of Volume I. It often happens that the title-holder of the knowledge base in question is uncertain as to the ontological status of an entity. In such cases, the address is lodged in a subdomain of uncertainty or doubt. If this were not so, hypotheses and theories would not be possible.

If this is acceptable in principle, we may posit that each commitment domain **D** is itself a, possibly ephemeral, intensional subdomain in the domain of general knowledge, indexed for the linguistic exchange at hand. We further posit that, at each mention of an entity by the speaker, the listener activates the corresponding address in his or her general knowledge base.

It follows that even in cases where reference is made in direct speech to an actually existing entity, that reference is intrinsically intensional, as it is processed through the intensional commitment domain at hand. It is for that reason that we spoke of the *intensionalization of extensions* in the last sentence of Chapter 2 in Volume I. All semantics is intensional. Necessarily, the commitment domain **D** is itself a mental construct, just like the mental constructs that are considered intensional (and hence block substitutivity). The commitments laid down in the commitment domain often apply to imagined situations whose relation to what is considered the real world is codified by the governing predicate. Thus, when I say that John thinks that the moon is made of green cheese, I have made myself responsible for the truth of the statement that John thinks that the moon is made of green cheese, not for the truth of the statement that the moon is made of green cheese. This latter putative fact is stored in a subdomain indexed for what John thinks. There are thus intensional subdomains for what the speaker, or a person mentioned in the discourse, hopes, realizes, has forgotten, and so on, or for what he or she considers possible, probable, fortunate, and so on.

The speaker may, of course, wish to introduce a new entity into the discourse, knowing or anticipating that the listener does not yet have a corresponding entity address in his or her general knowledge base. The proper thing for the speaker to do, in such cases, is to use an existentially quantified statement. In practice, however, speakers, and certainly fiction writers, are not so accommodating and throw the listener (reader) so to speak *in medias res* by using a definite description for the entity referred to, leaving it to the listener (reader) to infer that an address for such an entity has to be set up. This is what we have called *post hoc suppletion* or *accommodation*, exemplified in example (7.24) of Section 7.2.2.4.

8.1.1 *Singular entity addresses and address closure*

It is useful to have a formal notation for the processes mentioned, not only because formal notations add to the clarity of the theory but also because they often reveal complications that had hitherto remained unobserved. In this section, some elementary symbolism is introduced for the representation of the process of incrementation to a given discourse domain **D**, leaving out the more complex cases involving plurality and quantification, and also incrementation to subdomains of **D**. These more complex procedures, along with a more complex notation, are proposed in the following two sections.

Let us assume that a speaker wishes to introduce a new address by uttering the deceptively simple sentence *There was a cat*. The example is, of course, a little stilted, and it hardly represents a normal speech event, but that is how formalisms have to be built up. We use the following notation for the new address just introduced:

(8.1)   **d–1** [**a** | Cat(a)]

(8.1) is to be read as follows. '**d–1**' is the address label facilitating address retrieval (the number 1 is arbitrary). The part between the square brackets reads as 'There is an **a** such that **a** is a cat', or 'There is an **a** such that **a** ∈ ⟦Cat⟧'. Tense is disregarded for the time being; tense domains are not discussed here. The symbol '**a**' thus acts as a unary (Russellian) existential quantifier requiring that ⟦Cat⟧ be nonnull. If the sentence had been *There was a cat that ran away* or *Some cat ran away*, the address would be as in (8.2):

(8.2)   **d–1** [**a** | Cat(a), Run away(a)]

requiring for truth that the intersection of ⟦Cat⟧ and ⟦Run away⟧ M-partially intersect (or, for BNPC, that ⟦Run away⟧ may be properly included in ⟦Cat⟧; see Section 3.4.1). If spoken in direct discourse, (8.1) and (8.2) have a truth value which depends on the state of affairs (situation) referred to on the one hand and the satisfaction condition defined for the existential quantifier **a** and for the predicates Cat and Run away on the other.

Now let the sentence *There was a cat* be followed by *The cat ran away*. The definite description *the cat* needs an existing address to 'land at', or denote. The question is: what happens to the address **d–1** when the information carried by the sentence *The cat ran away* is incremented to it? One might think that the information 'the cat ran away' is simply added to the address (8.1), as in (8.2), which is read as 'There was a cat that ran away', with both occurrences of the variable **a** bound by the quantifier **a**. But this cannot be correct, even though it (or its counterpart in predicate logic) is widely assumed to be correct by logicians and formal semanticists.

A quick way to see why this is so is the following. Compare the following two sentences (see also (8.25a,b) below):

(8.3)   a. John has a girlfriend and this girlfriend is Australian.[1]
        b. John has a girlfriend who is Australian/an Australian girlfriend.

---

[1] (8.3a) may be rephrased as *John has one girlfriend,—who is Australian*, with a nonrestrictive relative clause. Nonrestrictive relative clauses have the force of a subsequent conjunct, as appears from the fact that they may be followed by a polar tag with speech-act force, as in: *John has one girlfriend,—who is Australian, isn't she?*

These two sentences differ radically in what they say. Sentence (8.3a) implies that John has a girlfriend, who is Australian. (8.3b), by contrast, is compatible with a sequel like *and many others who are not*. (8.3a) is a conjunction of two sentences; (8.3b) is not. It is clear that *this girlfriend* in (8.3a) cannot represent a variable bound by the existential quantifier, represented by the indefinite article *a*, if only because one can say *I believe that John has a girlfriend and I hope that this girlfriend is Australian*, where binding of *this girlfriend* under one single quantifier is impossible. The principle of generality dictates that the same must then apply to *this girlfriend* in (8.3a).

Nothing changes for (8.3a) when the definite description *this girlfriend* is replaced with the anaphoric pronoun *she* which, again, cannot represent a variable bound by the indefinite article (quantifier) *a*. But what does it represent? We say that it represents an instance of PRIMARY ANAPHORA—that is, anaphora where the antecedent is not itself a referring expression but an address that has been set up existentially just before and is 'visited' by a subsequent anaphoric expression for the first time.

The problem for (8.3a), with *she* for *this girlfriend*, is—and this is the basic problem of primary anaphora, further discussed in Chapter 9—how to account for the status of the anaphoric pronoun *she* as a referring pronoun not bound by the existential quantifier represented by *a*, but somehow recovering its antecedent from the preceding existentially quantified sentence. In anticipation of the treatment of this problem in Chapter 9, we now introduce the technique of ADDRESS CLOSURE, which ensures that a pronominal reference used in primary anaphora is not bound by the preceding quantifier but is represented as a definite term in **D**.

First look at (8.4), where address closure has taken place. We say that an address that has not been closed is an OPEN ADDRESS. Thus, **d–1** in (8.1) is an open address, where **a** is an existential quantifier. An open address is closed the moment a definite term retrieves its denotation from a preceding existentially quantified sentence and thus becomes a referring term. Address closure is represented as '*//*'. The incrementation of *The cat ran away*, uttered right after *There was a cat*, thus looks like (8.4):

(8.4)   **d–1 [a | Cat(a) // Ran away(the a(Cat(a)))]**

Address closure is needed to establish reference. It changes **a** from being a quantifier—that is, a function from sets to truth values—to being a reference function selecting an object (the referent) from a set of objects. Reference is a function that takes a set and delivers a specific element in that set. The reference function has been a source of discomfort to modern semantics because it cannot be defined within the confines of standard compositional model theory: there is no way of selecting one specific individual from a plural set by mathematical means alone. For it to work, an external input from cognition is needed, in particular from knowledge of and about the context and situation of the utterance and the (restricted) universe of objects **OBJ**^{R} that the speech is about. This is a further indication that compositionality is not a hard-and-fast principle of the interpretation of natural language utterances.

The effect of closure is thus that **a** no longer functions as an existential quantifier, as in (8.1) or (8.2), but as a definite determiner over the propositional function Cat(a), or, in other words, as a function from the predicate extension ⟦Cat⟧ to a particular object in ⟦Cat⟧, its reference or ρ-value. Before address closure, **a** is an existential quantifier, but, after address closure, **a** has become a definite determiner and the whole address **d–1** has become a cognitive representation of an entity.

As in the case of (8.3a), it is natural to replace the phrase *the cat* with the anaphoric pronoun *it*, which is then an instance of primary anaphora. The incrementation of *There was a cat. **It** ran away* will then be something like:

$$\text{d-1} \; [\, \mathbf{a} \mid \text{Cat(a)} \; // \; \text{Run away (1)} \,]$$

The symbol '1', acting as the subject term to the predicate *Run away* and corresponding with the address label **d–1**, is not a bound variable but a resumptive pronominal expression resuming 'the *a* such that *a* was a cat'.[2] The address **d–1** can thus be read as 'The *a* such that *a* was a cat,—it ran away', where '**a** | Cat(a)' represents the referential part of the address and where the propositional content is located in the part that follows address closure.

It is by means of the device of address closure that the difference between (8.3a) and (8.3b) is accounted for. (8.3a) is assigned a discourse representation with address closure: 'There is an *a* such that *a* is a girlfriend of John's, and this *a* is Australian' or 'John has a girlfriend,—who is Australian'. But (8.3b) is assigned one without address closure, read as 'There is an *a* such that *a* is a girlfriend of John's and such that *a* is Australian' or 'John has a girlfriend who is Australian'. It is, if you wish, the difference between a nonrestrictive and a restrictive relative clause.

Now we extend the mechanism so as to show how addresses are generated from the semantic analyses (SAs) of sentences—that is, from L-propositions. Consider again the sentence *There was a cat*, as in (8.5a), with its (matrix-S)

---

[2] One might think of using the notation 'Run away(a)' for the part after closure. This, however, would make it impossible to make cross-references, as in (8.8c,d) below.

SA (8.5b), represented as an L-propositional (SA) tree structure in (8.5c), and resulting in the **D**-address (8.5d):

(8.5)   a. There was a cat.

b. $AN_x[Obj(x), Cat(x)]$

c.

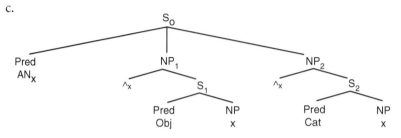

d. **d–1** [**a** | Cat(a)]

In (8.5b,c), AN is the existential quantifier, also known as ∃, but AN is reserved for a single entity, as opposed to SOME, which is reserved for the plural existential. AN is treated as a binary higher-order predicate over pairs of sets, with, in this case, the subject term $Obj(x)$ (see Section 5.6 in Volume I) and the object term $Cat(x)$. The index x in AN_x binds the variables x in $Obj(x)$ and $Cat(x)$. The operator AN requires for truth that there be at least one element common to the sets denoted by the two terms.

There is a problem here regarding actual and virtual being. Following the argument developed in Section 5.6 of Volume I, (8.5a) should not entail the *actual existence* of a cat, since the predicate $Obj(x)$ is intensional, which would allow it to intensionalize the set of cats in virtue of Virtual Object Attraction discussed in Section 5.4 of Volume I. That (8.5a) is felt to entail actual existence might be attributed to the fact that a sentence like (8.5a) is normally used under an operator of place, as in *There were cats in the cellar*, where the operator *in the cellar* ensures an extensional interpretation. Since, in natural speech, the verification domain is normally restricted to a given situation known and accepted by speaker and listener to be actual and not just virtual, the default interpretation of (8.5a) would then implicitly impose that situation as a local restrictor turning the sentence into an extensional statement. Yet intuitively, (8.5a) does entail actual existence. For example, when asked *Are there unicorns?* I can reply in truth *No, only in stories*. We revert to this question below.

The SA-structure (8.5c) is the tree-structure counterpart of (8.5b). NP₁ is the subject term, NP₂ the object term, and the caret symbol '∧' is a set-denoting operator: 'the set of things x such that . . .'. The grammatical process transforming (8.5c) into (8.5a) is not at issue here. (Roughly, NP_2 is incorporated into $_{PRED}$[AN], forming the complex predicate $_{PRED}$[AN -^x [Cat(x)]], which is then lowered into the position of the subject term x of **Obj**, which is lexicalized as **Be there**. For details see Seuren (1996: 300–9).)

The present concern is the incrementation procedure **IP** turning (8.5c) into the **D**-address (8.5d). **IP** scans the highest SA-predicate first. In the case at hand, the highest predicate is AN, which is an instruction to create a new singular address (a first-order address over individuals). An ADDRESS LABEL **d–1** is set up (the number 1 is arbitrary), identifying the address for later reference. The contents of the address is given between square brackets. Here **a** is the ADDRESS HEAD, representing AN and binding the variables. It stands for the Russellian first-order existential quantifier—a function from sets of individuals to truth values, typed $((e,t),t)$.[3]

For (existential) quantifiers, the object term NP_2, denoting the restrictor set, is incremented first for at least two reasons. The first reason is that this procedure guarantees the proper scope order, as is demonstrated in (8.10) below. The second reason is that it is by the restrictor set that the address is identified and selected for closure as a result of a following definite NP (such as *the cat*).

This gives the new address **d–1** [**a** | Cat(a)]. Normally, the subject term is then added, but not in the case of **Obj(x)**, it being axiomatically understood that there are (actual or virtual) things. Therefore, only NP_2 is incremented after the upright bar indicating the scope of **a**. (One notes the analogy of **d–1** with the Russellian formula $\exists x[Cat(x)]$.) The address **d–1** has a truth value and is read as 'there is/was a cat'. Existentially quantified addresses are open addresses.

Now we turn for a moment to the question of existential import. In standard logic, the existential quantifier posits *actual existence* of the common element. But that will not do for language, given sentences like (8.6a) which do not entail that the cat in question actually existed:

---

[3] Typing of terms and predicates is a commonly used device in formal semantics, introduced by the Polish logician Ajdukiewicz during the 1930s. It is based on the typing of entities as *e* (entity) and truth values as *t* (the symbols are due to Montague). It enables one to follow a compositional function calculus from entities to truth values, as done in categorial grammar, where the finally resulting value must be typed *t*. A set of entities, denoted by what is known as a first-order predicate, is typed (e,t), that is, a function from individual entities to truth values. A Russellian quantifier is a unary second-order predicate, typed as $((e,t),t)$, that is, a function from sets of individual entities to truth values. The existential quantifier, for example, takes a set of individuals and assigns it the value TRUE just in case the set is nonnull and otherwise the value FALSE.

(8.6)　a. A cat was worshipped there.
　　　　b. AN$_x$[Be worshipped(x), #Cat(x)]
　　　　c. **d–2** [**a** | #Cat(a), Be worshipped(a)]

(8.7)　a. A child laughed.
　　　　b. AN$_x$ [Laugh(x), Child(x)]
　　　　c. **d–3** [**a** | Child(a), Laugh(a)]

For the semantics of language it is stipulated that when the matrix term of the existential quantifier is an intensional predicate denoting a cognitive process and capable of yielding truth for both actual and thought-up entities (Frege's 'thought predicates'), while the restrictor term is extensional, yielding truth only for actually existing objects, the extensional term is *intensionalized*, so that it applies to thought-up entities as well. This is the rule of VIRTUAL OBJECT ATTRACTION (VOA) presented in Section 5.4 of Volume I. Since in (8.7b) both terms are extensional by nature, as only really existing individuals can truthfully be said to laugh or to be a child, (8.7a) is rendered as (8.7b). But in (8.6a) **Be worshipped** is an intensional predicate as it may yield truth also for fictitious objects. Therefore, **Cat(x)** is intensionalized to #Cat(x), where '#' indicates that the set denoted by #Cat(x) may also contain virtual or thought-up cats as a result of VOA. This allows true existential quantification over virtual objects.

Obj(x) in (8.5) is taken to be intensional by nature denoting the axiomatically given nonnull set of actual and virtual objects that 'are there'. But since **Obj(x)** is not a thought predicate, it does not intensionalize the other term under AN but is itself automatically extensionalized when the other term is extensional, since an extensional predicate **F(x)** denotes a purely extensional set ⟦F(x)⟧, which makes the intersection of ⟦F(x)⟧ and ⟦Obj(x)⟧ again purely extensional. This ensures an entailment of actual existence for extensional terms, but also the absence of such an entailment for intensional terms, as in *There was an imaginary cat* or *There are nonexistent unicorns*.

Now back to address closure. As we have seen, an open address is closed when denoted in a subsequent clause by a definite term. Address closure, symbolized by a double oblique stroke, changes the address head from being a function to truth values to being a reference function selecting an object (the referent) from a set of objects. Reference functions over individuals are typed ((e,t),e) (taking a set and delivering an individual), and are thus type-reducing. It has been said a few times already that this function is not compositional, not even given a model.

Now let D contain the open address **d–1** as in (8.5d) above and also an open address **d–2** [**a** | Mouse(a)]. Then a sentence like (8.8a), with the SA (8.8b), results in the two parallel increments (8.8c) and (8.8d):

(8.8) a. The cat caught the mouse.

b.

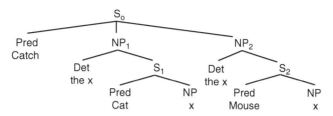

c. **d–1** [**a** | Cat(a) // Catch(1,2)]
d. **d–2** [**a** | Mouse(a) // Catch(1,2)]

NP_1 in (8.8b) reads 'the x such that x is a cat', and analogously for NP_2. In (8.8c) and (8.8d), the head **a** has been retyped from $((e,t),t)$ to $((e,t),e)$; the propositional function preceding closure—Cat(a) or Mouse(a)—denotes the input set typed (e,t). Catch(1, 2) is the proposition saying that the individual selected by the reference function **a** in **d–1**—the cat—caught the individual selected in **d–2**—the mouse. The incrementation procedure **IP** first scans the predicate of S_0. Catch being a binary lexical verb (and not a quantifier), **IP** is put to work on the definite NP_1 first, to be followed by the definite NP_2.

The DENOTATION PROCEDURE **d** for definite NPs is as follows:

For any NP_i under a definite-NP operator, say, **the**:
(a) **the** takes the predicate of the S under NP_i and selects the matching address **d–n**. There must, in principle, be only one such address in **D** (but see Section 9.5.1 on primary anaphora and the reference-assignment procedure).
(b) **d–n** is closed (if still open), and the SA-tree is added to the closed address, with the number *n* of **d–n** for the NP_i-constituent.

Thus, **d**(NP_1) in (8.8b) selects **d–1** [**a** | Cat(a)], and NP_1 is replaced with **1**; **d–1** is closed and the SA-tree, with **1** in place, is added to the now closed **d–1**:

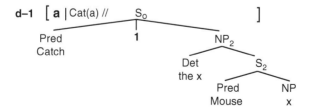

The procedure is repeated for NP_2 in **d–1**, yielding the two parallel increments:

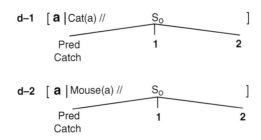

For practical reasons trees are written as bracketed strings, giving (8.8c) and (8.8d), respectively.

A sentence like (8.9a), with SA (8.9b) is incremented as follows, with **D** containing **d–1** [**a** | Cat(a)]:

(8.9)   a. The cat caught a mouse.
        b.

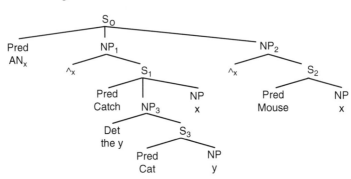

        c. **d–2** [**a** | Mouse(a), Catch(1,a)]
        d. **d–1** [**a** | Cat(a) // [**b** | Mouse(b), Catch(1,b)]]

The new **d–2**, created in virtue of $_{PRED}$[AN], is fitted out with S_2 and S_1, in that order (with **a** for **x**):

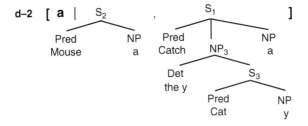

d–1 in (8.9d) contains a subordinate open address. An open address can be stored under another address **d–n** provided it contains either the variable bound by **d–n** (for open addresses) or the definite term **n** (for addresses after closure).

Double existential quantification is treated analogously. (8.10a), with SA (8.10b), yields the open address (8.10c):

(8.10) a. A cat caught a mouse.

  b.

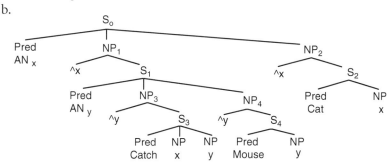

  c. **d–1** [**a** | Cat(a), [**b** | Mouse(b), Catch(a,b)]]

IP causes **d–1** to be set up in such a way that the cat-address takes scope over the mouse-address: 'there is a cat *a* such that there is a mouse *b* such that *a* caught *b*'. Since, however, it is possible to refer subsequently to the mouse caught by the cat, as when one says *The mouse escaped*, an independent open address for the mouse in question is also required. To that end, an address of the form (8.11) is set up in virtue of a process of inferential bridging:

(8.11) **d–2** [**a** | Mouse(a), [**b** | Cat(b), Catch(b,a)]]

Here the mouse-address takes scope over the cat-address, but the difference is irrelevant, as scope differences do not matter for two successive existential quantifiers. The discourse may now continue with definite terms like *the cat that caught a mouse*, closing **d–1**, or *the mouse that was caught by a cat*, closing **d–2**.

The difference is not irrelevant, however, in more complex cases, such as:

(8.12) John claims that he owns a Ferrari, but I have never seen it.

Here, *it* stands for 'the Ferrari John claims he owns' and thus needs an address for that Ferrari to land at and close if necessary. It would appear that such an address, if still open, must look like

  d–3 [**a** | Ferrari(a), Claim(John, Own(John,a))]

This, however, requires for truth an *actual* specific Ferrari, claimed by John to be owned by him. But the Ferrari in question may well be, and probably is, a *virtual* Ferrari because John may well be bluffing about his racing monster. So there we are: the Ferrari claimed by John to be his property may well be a virtual vehicle but to refer to it it looks as if we need an open address that asserts its actual existence.

The only solution available, given the machinery as developed so far, is to apply the intensionalization operator #, as in (8.7) above, and establish an address like (8.13) for 'There is a Ferrari John claims he owns':

(8.13)   **d–3** [**a** | #Ferrari(a), Claim(John, Own(John,a))]

This correctly speaks of a *specific* Ferrari, namely the one John claims he owns, but, owing to the fact that the existential quantifier no longer entails actual existence by itself, this specific Ferrari need not actually exist. The assignment of the intensionalization operator # to the predicate $[\![$Ferrari(a)$]\!]$ is driven by the fact that the open address originates in the intensional context created by the predicate Claim, in whose scope the open address for the Ferrari was set up. The still open address **d–3** can now be selected by the phrase *the Ferrari John claims he owns* to land at and close.

8.1.2 *Plurality and quantification*

8.1.2.1 *Plurality and existential quantification*   Now we turn to plurality. The semantics of plurality is among the most difficult topics in the study of natural language and, perhaps for that reason, among the least studied, despite plurality being a basic category in the grammars of languages. There is a certain amount of daring and incisive literature on plurality, especially from the point of view of quantification, in the tradition of formal model-theoretic semantics, but even though this literature has clearly advanced the frontiers of our knowledge, the new ground it has conquered is far from fully explored. What I can offer in this respect is, therefore, tentative, fragmentary, and suggestive, even more so than in most other parts of this book.

One thing is clear. Since in most natural languages plurality starts with cardinality 2, plurality, in these languages, requires the notion of PLURAL POWER SET ($\mathscr{P}_{pl}$), which differs from what is standardly called the 'power set' operator, symbolized as $\mathscr{P}$. The *standard power set* of a set X, $\mathscr{P}(X)$, is the set of all subsets of X, including the null set $\varnothing$ and all sets consisting of just one element, the so-called singletons. The *plural power set* of a set X differs in that, for any set X, $\mathscr{P}_{pl}(X)$ is $\mathscr{P}(X)$ minus $\varnothing$ and all singletons.[4] We might also say that $\mathscr{P}_{pl}(X)$ is the set of all *natural subsets* of X plus X itself, following the definition of natural set given in Chapter 3.[5] The very fact that plurality as a linguistic category requires the notion of plural power set as just defined, as opposed to the standard notion of power set, demonstrates, if not the validity, certainly the reasonableness of the natural set theory hypothesis put forward in Chapter 3.

To express this distinction formally, we can usefully employ the type-raising distributive operator '::', defined over predicates, for the language of SAs and discourse addresses. Let $[\![P(x)]\!]$ denote, as before, the extension of the predicate $P(x)$—the set of individuals x such that x satisfies P—then $[\![::P(\bar{x})]\!]$ is defined as follows ($\bar{x}$ ranges over sets of individuals):

$$[\![::P(\bar{x})]\!] =_{\text{Def}} \mathscr{P}_{pl}\Big([\![P(x)]\!]\Big)$$

The extension of $::P(\bar{x})$ is thus the set of sets of at least two individuals x such that each x satisfies P. The expression $::\text{Happy(the children)}$ reads as 'the set of children in question is an element in $\mathscr{P}_{pl}([\![\text{Happy(x)}]\!])$, the plural power set of Happy'. In other words, the sentence *The children are happy* is true just in case the set of children in question is a natural subset of the total set of those individuals that are happy. This requires that more than one child is happy, because singletons are excluded from plural power sets. When P is transitive and both of its terms are definite and plural, $::$ distributes indiscriminately over the subject and the object term referents.

An open plural address is normally of the form (8.14c), representing (8.14a) with SA (8.14b):

(8.14) a. There were (some) cats.

  b.

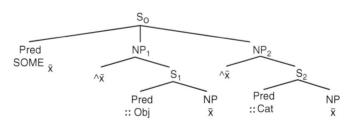

  c. **d**–4 $[\bar{\mathbf{a}} \mid ::\text{Cat}(\bar{a})]$

[4] For languages, such as classical Arabic and Ancient Greek, with a morphological category 'dual', in addition to 'singular' and 'plural', special provisions must be made for sentences quantifying over two elements. It is not clear, at this stage of the enquiry, whether an underlying numeral *two* will suffice for the purpose.

[5] Standardly, if X has cardinality n, $\mathscr{P}(X)$ has cardinality 2^n. For plural power sets, as one will easily figure out for oneself, if X has cardinality n, $\mathscr{P}_{pl}(X)$ has cardinality $2^n-(n+1)$.

Assuming ABPC to be the logic in charge (but SMPC will do as well in this case), the plural existential quantifier SOME yields truth just in case there is a nonnull intersection of at least one plural set of individuals of the two term extensions concerned, which now are sets of sets of individuals. SOME is again an instruction to set up a new address of the right type. In (8.14c), **a̅** represents plural SOME and binds the variable. (**8.14c**) thus requires that there be at least one set of at least two actually existing cats.

The distributive operator :: makes it possible to account for a sentence like (8.15a), rendered by the SA (8.15b) and the corresponding open address (8.15c):[6]

(8.15)   a. There were cats (that were) running away.
         b.

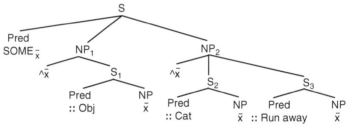

c. **d–5** [**a̅** | :: Cat(ā), :: Run away(ā)]

When the predicate is second order by nature and thus typed ((e,t),t), such as the predicates *disperse, congregate, disband,* or numeral predicates such as *three,* or nominal predicates such as *team* or *platoon,* (army unit consisting of men), the distributive operator :: is not needed. Thus, a sentence like *There is a platoon* results in the singular address (8.16a), with the second-order predicate **Platoon** over the plural variable **a̅**. The two forms can be combined, as in (8.16b,c) representing, respectively, *Some cats dispersed* and *There were three cats*:

(8.16)   a. **d–6** [**a̅** | Platoon(ā)]
         b. **d–7** [**a̅** | :: Cat(ā), Disperse(ā)]
         c. **d–8** [**a̅** | :: Cat(ā), 3(ā)]

---

[6] Sentence (8.15a) is meant to be taken in the purely existential way, and not as *Some of the cats were running away,* which is perhaps better treated in a format analogous to that of *All (of) the cats were running away,* as in (8.30) below. Perhaps all quantifiers should be open to a double treatment, one in which they do and one in which they do not involve a definite restrictor term.

Mathematically, an address can be of any order, yet, apart from exceptional cases, language stops at second-order predicates requiring third-order addresses for their plurals, as in (8.17), which reads *There are platoons.* Any higher-order nouns are treated as second-order.

(8.17)   **d–9** [$\bar{\bar{\mathbf{a}}}$| :: Platoon($\bar{\mathrm{a}}$)]

Plurals are difficult, and only some of the problems can be dealt with here. One such problem is the distinction between distributive and collective readings. In the collective reading, *The men carried the bags* reads as saying that the men as a group carried the bags as a group (while, say, the women carried the pots), leaving it open whether there were subgroups of men carrying subgroups of bags. The distributive reading says that each of the men carried one or more bags and each of the bags was carried by one or more men. The linguistic expression thus underdetermines the actual state of affairs.

Collective readings are incremented analogously to singular increments. Thus, given an open plural cat-address, such as **d–4** in (8.14c), the addition *They ran away* is incremented either as in (8.18a), where the cats are said to have run away as a group, or as (8.18b), where the cats are said to have run away individually. Closure has turned $\bar{\mathbf{a}}$ into a second-order determiner or reference function $(((e,t),t),(e,t))$, selecting a set from a set of sets:

(8.18)   a. **d–10** [$\bar{\mathbf{a}}$ | :: Cat($\bar{\mathrm{a}}$) // Run away(10)]
          b. **d–10** [$\bar{\mathbf{a}}$ | :: Cat($\bar{\mathrm{a}}$) // :: Run away(10)]

To compute the truth value of Run away(10) in (8.18a), it is necessary to type-raise the predicate Run away from (e,t) to $((e,t),t)$, so that it can process an input of type (e,t), that is, a set of objects. The type-raising is triggered by the fact that the address head is $\bar{\mathbf{a}}$ not $\mathbf{a}$. Type-raising of a predicate P implies that, despite the transition from individuals to groups, the satisfaction conditions of P remain unchanged.

This condition cannot be fulfilled by all predicates. Most nominal predicates, such as *cat, dog, tree, house,* being reserved for individual predication, disallow type-raising, because a group of cats cannot itself again be a cat, and likewise for the predicates *dog, tree, house* and whatever object-naming predicates one has in mind. These predicates must be marked in the lexicon as blocking type-raising, as opposed to, for example, *run away* or *be happy* or *carry,* because a group can run away as well as an individual can, and likewise for being happy and carry.

(8.18a) is thus read intuitively as 'the set of cats referred to by [$\bar{\mathbf{a}}$ | :: Cat($\bar{\mathrm{a}}$)] is a set of at least two individuals running away as a group'. The distributive reading of *They ran away,* incremented as in (8.18b), lets the cats in question run away individually.

Typical collective readings are found in sentences like:

(8.19)   a. The mice have been at the cheese.
          b. The Americans were the first to land on the moon.

In their common reading, these do not imply that all the mice have been at the cheese, or that all Americans were the first to land on the moon, as they are about the mice, or the Americans, as a group. (Embarrassingly, these sentences are true even if there was one single mouse at the cheese or one single American on the moon—a fact that our formalism is as yet unable to account for.)

Now consider the at least three-way ambiguous (8.20a) with the SAs (8.20b) (in two versions) and (8.20c):

(8.20)   a. The men carried a bag.
          b.

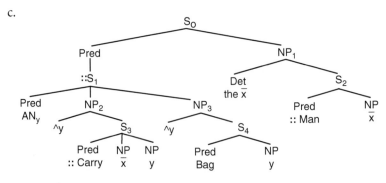

d. d–11 [**b**| Bag(b), $(::)$Carry(12,b)]
e. d–12 [**ā**| $::$Man(ā) // [**b** Bag(b), $(::)$Carry(12,b)]]
f. d–12 [**ā**| $::$Man(ā) // $::\lambda\bar{x}$ [**b** | Bag(b), $::$Carry($\bar{x}$,b)](12)]

The SA (8.20b) has two guises, one with and one without the distributive operator :: over the predicate **Carry**. With ::, (8.20b) says that there was a bag that the men carried individually, so that the same bag was carried as many times as there were men. Without ::, we have the group reading, saying that the men combined forces to carry one single bag. **IP** produces **d–11** in (8.20d) as the result of (8.20b), with or without the distributive operator :: over **Carry**. In either reading there is just one single bag. Supposing **D** already contains the open address

$$\text{d–12}[\bar{\mathbf{a}} \mid :: \text{Man}(\bar{a})]$$

('there were men'), this address is now closed, analogously to **d–1** in (8.11d), resulting in (8.20e), again with or without the distributive operator :: over **Carry**.

(8.20c), however, does not speak of one single bag but says that the set of men in question is one of those sets of individuals such that each individual had a bag to carry, so that there were at most as many bags as there were individuals, and perhaps less, if two or more of the men carried a single bag. This latter reading is incremented as (8.20f): the set of men referred to by **d–12** was such that for each man there was a bag carried by him (alone or with one or more others).

The main predicate of (8.20c) is the propositional function (=predicate) S_1. S_1 is a tree-structure version of what is known in logic as a LAMBDA PREDICATE. The lambda operator λ creates predicates, enabling one to incorporate quantificational and other operators into a predicate. In this case, the lambda predicate denotes the set of those sets of at least two individuals who have a bag to carry, individually or collectively. A variable is needed to ensure that this lambda predicate is a propositional function rather than an open address with a truth value. This variable is of a different register from those used so far in the address notation. For that reason we revert to the end of the alphabet and use $\mathbf{x}$, here type-raised to $\bar{\mathbf{x}}$ because the carriers are groups of at least two individuals. The lambda predicate is incorporated as such into the address notation.

With this lambda predicate, the sentence says that the set of men in question is one of those sets of at least two individuals who have a bag to carry, individually or collectively. The collective or group reading need not be represented, as it is already given in (8.20b) without :: over **Carry**, which may be seen as an instance of lambda reduction. Therefore, (8.20c) only gives the distributive reading, which is not captured by (8.20b). This reading requires two occurrences of the distributive operator ::, one for the predicate :: $\lambda\bar{x}$ [**b** |

Bag(b), ::Carry(x̄,b)] and one for the embedded predicate ::Carry(x̄,b). It is needed for the former so as to get as many bags as there are carriers; it is needed for the latter to ensure that the bags can be distributed over individual carriers. (The first occurrence of:: in (8.20f), just before λ, ensures that (8.20f) is not merely a lambda-extracted version of (8.20d) with ::).

How does **IP** work for (8.20) in its various versions? Let **D** contain an open address **d–12** [ā | ::Man(ā)]. Then for (8.20b) **IP** creates a new open address **d–13** [**b** | Bag(b), (::)Carry(12,b)], saying that there is/was a bag which the men of **d–12** carried collectively (without ::) or individually (with ::). **d–12** is now closed, analogously to **d–1** in (8.11d), representing the two readings of (8.20b). This gives (8.20d) in its two versions.

As regards (8.20c), its group reading selects the open address **d–12** [ā| ::Man(ā)], closes it and adds the lambda predicate without the two occurrences of ::. Lambda reduction reduces the result to **d–12** in (8.20e). The distributive reading of (8.20c) again selects the open address **d–12** [ā | ::Man (ā)], but places the distributive operator :: both before the main (lambda-) predicate and before the embedded predicate Carry, as explained above.

This reading requires the setting up, by inferential bridging, of an open *plural* bag-address creating room for subsequent reference to the bags distributed over the men carrying them. The formal elaboration of this form of inferential bridging requires an open plural address saying something like 'There is a plural set of bags such that each bag belonging to it was carried by one (or more) of the men referred to by **d–12** of (8.20e)'. This address can then be closed to allow reference to 'the bags that the men carried' in the context of interpretation (8.20c) of the sentence *The men carried a bag*—that is, given (8.20f). The technical and notational elaboration of such an address is something I happily leave to others. For the moment we will let such technicalities rest.

We now turn to the quantifiers MANY and FEW in sentences of the type (8.22a)—that is, without any implication that the cats were numerous within a given group, as in *Many of the cats were asleep*. Sentences that contain existential quantification of the sort 'some of the X' or 'few/many of the X' are perhaps better treated in a format analogous to that of (8.30) (see note 6). That there is a clear semantic difference is shown by examples like (8.21a,b). (It is worth noting that this difference has not been accounted for in any semantic theory in existence.)

(8.21)   a. Six elephants were travelling with the circus.
       b. Six of the elephants were travelling with the circus.

In the strictly existential sense, the quantifiers MANY and FEW are treated as variants of the neutral existential quantifier SOME, regarded as a binary second-order predicate over sets. Thus, a sentence like (8.22a), with the SA (8.22b), comes out as (8.22c) (leaving aside, of course, the question of what gradable MANY and FEW imply in any given context):

(8.22)   a. Many cats were asleep.
         b.

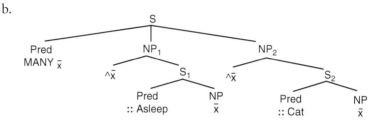

c. **d** 14 [MANY **ā** | :: Cat(ā), Asleep(ā)]

Like SOME, the quantifying predicates MANY and FEW are higher-order by nature, requiring terms denoting sets of sets. (8.22b) says, in effect, there is a nonnull intersection between the set of plural cat sets and the set of plural object sets of beings that were asleep, while the intersection of the set of cats and the set of beings that are asleep has a high cardinality.

Formally, we define the semantics of the quantifiers MANY and FEW in the following way (cf. (2.14b) in Section 2.3.5.2):

(8.23)   For all sets X and Y:
         a. $[\![\text{MANY}]\!] = \{ <Y,X> \mid \mathscr{P}_{pl}(Y) \cap \mathscr{P}_{pl}(X) \neq \varnothing, |Y \cap X| \text{ is high} \}$
            (the extension of the predicate MANY is the set of all pairs of sets Y, X, such that the intersection of $\mathscr{P}_{pl}(Y)$ and $\mathscr{P}_{pl}(X)$ is nonnull and the cardinality of the intersection of Y and X is high)
         b. $[\![\text{FEW}]\!] = \{ <Y,X> \mid \mathscr{P}_{pl}(Y) \cap \mathscr{P}_{pl}(X) \neq \varnothing, |Y \cap X| \text{ is low} \}$
            (the extension of the predicate FEW is the set of all pairs of sets Y, X, such that the intersection of $\mathscr{P}_{pl}(Y)$ and $\mathscr{P}_{pl}(X)$ is nonnull and the cardinality of the intersection of Y and X is low)

One notes that this definition makes a sentence like *Few cats were asleep* false when there was only one sleeping cat, because in such a case $\mathscr{P}_{pl}([\![\text{Asleep}]\!]) \cap \mathscr{P}_{pl}([\![\text{Cat}]\!]) = \varnothing$, singletons being excluded from plural power sets. If one finds that unsatisfactory, one may reduce the satisfaction conditions for MANY and FEW to simply '$|Y \cap X|$ is high' and '$|Y \cap X|$ is low', respectively, leaving out the condition $\mathscr{P}_{pl}(Y) \cap \mathscr{P}_{pl}(X) \neq \varnothing$. It then follows automatically that $Y \cap X \neq \varnothing$.

One is reminded of what is said in Section 3.2 of Volume I regarding example (3.12), repeated here as (8.24a), and in Section 9.3 of Volume I regarding example (9.5), repeated here as (8.24b):

(8.24) a. Coffee does not grow in Africa.
       b. John does not get up at five in the morning.
       c. John did not catch many fish.

The point is that the negation applies specifically to the predicate of the highest S-term under the negation operator, as it denies the assignment of the property expressed by that predicate to its argument term(s). The more deeply embedded S-terms thus remain unaffected. The same is found in (8.24c). Just as, in a normal interpretation, (8.24a) does not deny that coffee grows or that there is coffee but that it is in Africa that coffee grows, and just as (8.24b) does not deny that John gets up but that it is at five in the morning that he does, in the same way (8.24c) does not deny that John caught fish but, rather, that the fish he caught were plentiful. This confirms the analysis presented in (8.22b), where MANY is the highest predicate.

For operators like MANY or FEW, the closure operation is important for empirical reasons, as appears, for example, from (8.25a,b), whose obvious semantic difference is unaccounted for in most semantic theories:

(8.25) a. Nob had few students who failed.
       b. Nob had few students, and they failed.

The difference corresponds with the closure operation. Let **D** already contain an address **d–15** [**a** | 'Nob'(a)], standing for 'There is an **a** called "Nob"'. Both (8.25a) and (8.25b) set up a new address **d–17** for the students Nob had. For (8.25a) **d–16** is left open, but for (8.25b) **d–16** is closed:

(8.26) a. **d–16** [FEW $\bar{\mathbf{a}}$ | $::$ Student(ā), $::$ Have(15,ā), $::$ Fail(ā)]
       b. **d–16** [FEW $\bar{\mathbf{a}}$ | $::$ Student(ā), $::$ Have(15,ā) // $::$ Fail(16)]

Now consider (8.27), which has both a group and a distributive reading. The existential predicates FEW and MANY say that the intersecting set required by the existential quantifier is small or large, respectively:

(8.27)   a. Few cats caught many mice.

b.

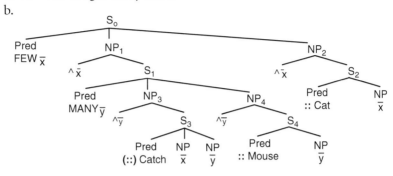

c. **d-17** [FEW **ā** | :: Cat(ā), [MANY **b̄**| :: Mouse(b̄), (::)Catch(ā,b̄)]]

The group reading says 'a small group of cats caught a large group of mice'. In this reading subsequent definite reference can be made to the large group of mice, as in *These mice had escaped from a laboratory*, which requires the inferentially added address:

(8.28)   **d-18** [MANY **ā** | :: Mouse(ā), [FEW **b̄**| :: Cat(b̄), Catch(b̄,ā)]]

But in the distributive reading, with :: Catch(b̄,ā), subsequent definite reference is not possible, which means that inferential bridging of the kind at issue must be blocked. The passive of (8.27a):

(8.29)   Many mice were caught by few cats.

is equivalent to (8.27a) only in the group reading. In the distributive reading scope differences destroy the equivalence.

8.1.2.2 *Discourse-sensitive universal quantification*   We now pass on to the universal quantifier ALL. Here we must refer to what was said at the end of Section 2.3.5.2 regarding the discourse-sensitivity of the universal quantifier ALL in its normal interpretation. A great deal was said in the chapters on logic about the logical properties of this quantifier and its existential counterpart without taking into account any complications that might arise in the context of discourse semantics. It is now time, however, to be serious about the context-sensitive aspects of the universal quantifier.

Since the only way of introducing entity representations into a **D** is by means of existential quantification, it follows that universal quantification cannot open a discourse and needs previous existential quantification to fall back on. In other words, universally quantified sentences (type **A**) are *per se* occasion sentences, not eternal sentences. If standard modern predicate calculus (SMPC) treats **A**-type sentences as eternal sentences, it can only do so by assuming a nonnull universe **OBJ** of extensional objects (an implicit assumption seldom present, nowadays, in the minds of logicians) and by letting the variables range over **OBJ**.[7] In principle, therefore, SMPC pushes the context-sensitivity of the universal quantifier to the very limit of the universe of objects as a whole. This fact is recognized by a number of formal semanticists, who have proposed various strategies for restricting the domain of universal quantification (e.g. Stanley and Szabó 2000; Peters and Westerståhl 2007). I will not discuss these proposals here, as they fit into a very different theoretical frame, which I reject for general reasons. The point here is that presupposition, and in particular the accommodation mechanism, must be taken to play a central part in any such strategy. For the rest, the problem seems reducible to the general problem of fixing definite reference.

In any case, some restriction on the domain of the universal quantifier is required if justice is to be done to natural language. A sentence like *All farmers grumble*, is only interpretable if **D** already contains an (open or closed) address for a set of at least two farmers. And likewise for variants of *all*, such as *every* or *each*. This is, it would seem, the origin of the existential import assigned to ALL in Aristotelian-Abelardian and Aristotelian-Boethian predicate calculus.

This perspective requires a rethinking of universal quantification as a whole—an enterprise which is not feasible within the constraints of the present text. What can be presented here is, therefore, again, tentative and provisional. I propose to treat the quantifier ALL from now on as a binary higher-order predicate expressing a relation between a *definite* restrictor set and a set of elements satisfying the matrix predicate. The truth condition does not change. An **A**-type sentence is still true just in case the (definite) restrictor set is an element in the plural power set of the matrix set: ALL **F** is **G** is true just in case $[\![F]\!] \in \mathscr{P}_{pl}([\![G]\!])$.[8]

---

[7] It is possible to hide the discourse-dependency of the universal quantifier in a conditional (see Section 8.2.4), as when one says *If there is a set of farmers, then all farmers grumble*, which seems to be a sentence type involving the use of *any* as in *Any doctor will tell you that smoking is bad*. But here again, the set of farmers has to be introduced first, albeit under the conjunction *if*. And, of course, saying *If there is a set of farmers, then all farmers grumble* is not the same as saying *All farmers grumble*.

[8] One notes that the condition $[\![F]\!] \in \mathscr{P}_{pl}([\![G]\!])$ is equivalent with the condition $[\![F]\!] \subset [\![G]\!]$, with $[\![F]\!]$ and $[\![G]\!]$ as natural sets, just as $[\![F]\!] \in \mathscr{P}([\![G]\!])$ is equivalent with $[\![F]\!] \subseteq [\![G]\!]$. The advantage of the formulation $[\![F]\!] \in \mathscr{P}_{pl}([\![G]\!])$ is that it provides a unified solution to the type problem caused by standard analyses for sentences like *All the farmers dispersed*. The analysis $\forall x(\text{Farmer}(x) \rightarrow \text{Disperse}(x))$ or, in terms of generalized quantification, $\forall x(\text{Disperse}(x), \text{Farmer}(x))$ will not do because $\text{Disperse}(x)$ contains a type error. Interestingly, the standard analysis may be taken to explain why the tenseless 'eternal' sentence *All farmers disperse* is infelicitous, but it fails to account for the felicitousness of an occasion sentence like *All the farmers dispersed*. The analysis given here provides

The definite restrictor set is thus commanded, in SA-structure, by the definite determiner *the*, as shown in (8.30b). This analysis establishes a link between ALL and the definite determiner *the*, which, in fact, optionally occurs with *all* in ordinary English sentences such as *All the farmers grumble*, or *All of the farmers grumble*, or, in the 'floating quantifier' version, *The farmers all grumble*, where *all* occupies the place of an adverbial expression. In French and Italian, the definite article is even obligatory: *Tous **les** paysans grognent* or *Tutti **i** contadini brontolano.*

For sentence (8.30a), this gives the SA presented in (8.30b) and the resulting incrementation shown in (8.30d), based on a previously existing (open) address (8.30c):

(8.30)   a. All (the) farmers grumble.

   b.

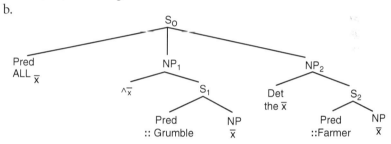

   c. **d–19** [$\bar{\mathbf{a}}$ | ∷ Farmer(ā)]
   d. **d–19** [$\bar{\mathbf{a}}$ | ∷ Farmer(ā) // ALL[∷ Grumble(19)]]

In this version of ALL, (8.30b) is read as 'the individual grumbling of each farmer was total as regards the set of farmers'. The quantifier ALL thus functions as an adverbial modifier of the L-proposition **Grumble(the farmers)**.[9]

For (8.30a) to be incremented, **D** must already contain **d–19** [$\bar{\mathbf{a}}$ | ∷ Farmer (ā)] ('there are farmers'), thus ensuring that the class of farmers is nonnull. The address **d–19**, if still open, is closed, following the primary definite reference to this particular set of farmers. [∷ Grumble(x̄)] denotes the set

the answer. Even so, 'occasion' ALL is not suitable for just any higher-order predicate. A sentence like *All farmers are numerous* is incoherent even though *numerous* is an intrinsically higher-order predicate. The reason seems to be that the natural language semantics of ALL requires that no member of the restrictor set (the set of farmers, in this case) be left out—a condition that makes sense for predicates like *disperse* or *sit in a circle* but not for a predicate like *numerous*.

[9] This might help explain the hitherto unexplained fact that *all* is allowed to 'float', occupying an adverbial modifier position, as in *The farmers all grumble*, whereas such 'floating' is impossible, or anyway much less current, for existential quantifiers. Note that 'floating' quantifiers typically occupy adverbial positions in the sentence, not only in English but in all languages I have so far checked.

of sets of at least two individually grumbling individuals. ALL (::Grumble(19)) says that the grumbling of the farmers in question applies to the full set of farmers at issue. This makes, strictly speaking, ALL(::Grumble(19)) equivalent with ::Grumble(19), though it emphasizes that the predicate ::Grumble applies to all the farmers without exception. The difference between ALL and plural **the** is thus taken to be that while they both select the set of farmers defined by the address head of **d-19** after closure, and let the sentence say that this set of farmers is an element in the set of sets defined by the type-raised predicate ::Grumble, ALL specifically requires, redundantly, one would say, that no member of the set of farmers be left out.

We are now in a position to say that, whereas the existential quantifier is an instruction to set up a new open address, the universal quantifier is an instruction licensing the closure, if necessary, of any still open address for any representative of the restrictor set and the addition of the predication of the matrix set.

Thus, suppose **D** contains an address **d-20** [**a** | Farmer(a), See(I,a)] saying 'I see/saw a farmer', the universal quantifier as used in (8.30a) licenses the closure of **d-20** and the addition of the predication Grumble(20), resulting in:

(8.31)   **d–20** [**a** | Farmer(a), See(I,a) // Grumble(20)]]

It seems that EVERY distinguishes itself from 'occasion' ALL mainly in that EVERY excludes group readings. The specifics of EACH are not touched upon here. Nor will I attempt to disentangle the complexities of universal or existential ANY, which has so far eluded all researchers.[10]

8.1.3 *Subordinate subdomains*

As has been said, a **D** may contain subdomains. These are either *instructional* or *alternative* or *subordinate*. INSTRUCTIONAL SUBDOMAINS are set up in virtue of some increment instruction, as with the universal quantifier discussed in the previous section, or the negation, discussed in Section 8.2.2. ALTERNATIVE

---

[10] What has remained unexplained in the account given above is the possibility of the negative polarity item *any* occurring in restrictive relative clauses attached to the restrictor term of sentences quantified with *all* and *every*, but not, at least according to many speakers, with *each*:

(i) Every student who had done any work passed.
(ii) All students who had done any work passed.
(iii) *Each student who had done any work passed.

Nor do I have an explanation for the fact that *each* and *all* are allowed to 'float', as in *The students each (all) went home*, while this possibility does not exist for *every*: *The student every went home*.

SUBDOMAINS are created by OR (disjunction) and IF (implication), to be discussed in Sections 8.2.3 and 8.2.4, respectively. SUBORDINATE SUBDOMAINS are the topic of the present section. They are a special kind of address. Like ordinary addresses, they can be open or closed. They also have **D**-properties, in that they may contain their own addresses, increments and instructions. They are represented both as a special kind of address, labelled **D–n**, and as an indexed domain.

Let us consider an example, by way of succinct explanation. A sentence like (8.32a) is incremented as (8.32b), where the variable D ranges over virtual facts (see Section 6.2.3.1 in Volume I). (8.32b$_1$) reads 'there is a possible fact D'. **Possible** carries an instruction to set up a subdomain specifying the virtual fact in question. This subdomain is represented in (8.32b$_2$) read as 'There is a planet called "Minerva" and it is inhabited':

(8.32)　a. There may be a planet Minerva and it may be inhabited.
　　　　b$_1$. **D–1 [D | Possible(D)]**
　　　　b$_2$. ⌞　**D–1: d–1 [a | Planet(a), 'Minerva'(a) // Inhabited(1)]**

'D–1' in (8.32b$_1$) is the label of the subdomain introduced as a result of the predicate **Possible**. The sign '⌞' specifies the contents of the new **D–1**.

It in (8.32a) refers opaquely, as it finds its antecedent within **D–1**. Transparent reference, with open **d–21** given in the superordinate **D**, is shown in (8.33). In (8.33c) **d–21** is closed and the predication **D–1[Inhabited(21)]** is added, saying that **21** is represented as being inhabited in the possibility subdomain **D–1**:

(8.33)　a. There is a planet Minerva and it may be inhabited.
　　　　b. **D–1 [D | Possible(D)]**
　　　　　⌞　**D–1: Inhabited(21)**
　　　　c. **d–21 [a | 'Minerva'(a), Planet(a) // D–1[Inhabited(21)]]**

A few general principles hold for subdomains. First, addresses from the commitment domain 'percolate downward' into subdomains as shown in (8.33), where **d–21** in **D–1** is taken from **D**. This downward percolation is stopped only if the subdomain in question explicitly blocks the address in question. Then, presuppositions of clauses incremented in subdomains 'percolate upward' into higher domains, including **D**, unless blocked either by their explicit negation or by lack of cognitive backing. This process is called PROJECTION. Both processes follow from the Principle of Maximal Unity, in particular its subprinciple of Minimal **D**-change, discussed in Section 7.2.2.4, both of which serve the functional purpose of ensuring maximal unity and coherence in the overall **D**-structure.

Anaphora may delve into subdomains under intensional predicates. In (8.34a), for example, the brother Marion believes she has is anaphorically referred to by *he* under the intensional predicate *be the talk of the town*. In (8.34b), the movie Geert says he has made (but may well not exist at all) is referred to by the anaphoric pronoun *it* in the second conjunct standing under the intensional predicate *be all over the news*:

(8.34)   a. Marion believes that she has a brother, and he is the talk of the town.
        b. Geert says he has made an anti-Islam movie and it's already all over the news.

The machinery of the incremental construction of discourse domains and subdomains is the main explanatory factor for the lack of substitutivity *salva veritate* in intensional contexts, which has been the dominant driving force in theoretical semantics during the twentieth century.

8.2 Instructions

The incrementation procedure **IP** is also able to follow INSTRUCTIONS constraining the further development of any given **D**. All standard operators of propositional logic are, from a discourse-semantic point of view, instructions. The logic of the propositional operators is seen as an emergent property of basic-natural set theory combined with the discourse-semantic incrementation instructions. In the following subsections it is shown how this 'emergence' can be traced in detail. This way, our combined theory of basic-natural set theory and discourse-semantic incrementation is meant to provide an alternative to the currently dominant pragmatic accounts.

8.2.1 *Conjunction*

The sentential functor AND is, in principle, nothing but an instruction to increment the conjuncts in the order given. It is the basic discourse-incrementation functor. In many cases, **IP** is iconic in that it follows the temporal, causal, or motivational order of the events or situations described, as appears from the difference between (8.35a) and (8.35b):

(8.35)   a. She went to Spain and married. (A Spaniard?)
        b. She married and went to Spain. (Alone or with her husband?)

This is not always so, as will become clear in a moment. When the incrementation is iconic, we speak of an ORDERED INTERPRETATION.

Whether the difference between (8.35a) and (8.35b) is truth-conditional or not is hard to say.[11] If I hear (8.35a) and am then told that, in fact, she married first and then went to Spain, I think I would feel cheated and I might be prepared to say that what I was told was false. Standard logic is unable to account for this, but it is consistent with a dynamic logic as proposed in Groenendijk and Stokhof (1991).

But this is by no means always so. In sentence (8.36), the order of the conjuncts is definitely relevant but not, it seems, truth-conditionally so:

(8.36)   It's raining and we're out of booze.[12]

Here the ordered interpretation is motivated by the speaker's wish to paint a picture of utter misery. It wouldn't be so bad if it were raining and speaker and company still had a sufficient supply of spiritual refreshments, but being out of booze while it's raining is, one gathers, the ultimate agony for speaker and company.

As is said in Section 7.2.2.3, the second conjunct normally restricts the first and not vice versa, precisely because, as is said in Section 7.3, the normal function of every new increment consists in homing in on the target situation, restricting the number of possible situations in which **D** can be true. This is, however, not an absolute rule, because sometimes the new increment recapitulates what has been said or draws a conclusion, as in (8.37), where (in terms of valuation spaces) the fact of John's being in his office is restricted by the fact that his light is on. Yet in (8.37) *John's light is on* precedes *he is in his office*, which is made possible by *therefore*, which draws a conclusion:

(8.37)   John's light is on and, therefore, he is in his office.

The standard function of every new increment to restrict the set of possible situations in which **D** is true is naturally expressed in terms of VS-modelling (see also Figure 7.1 in Section 7.3.2). Take the two logically and semantically independent sentences (where *she* is keyed to the same person):

---

[11] According to Cohen (1971) the difference is truth-conditional, but according to Gazdar (1979: 69–71) it is a Gricean implicature, defeasible by, for example, the addition of *in reverse order* to a sentence like (8.35a). Gazdar's argument, however, fails to convince, because the sentence with that addition is not the sentence without it: the one may have an entailment which the other lacks.

[12] See Blakemore and Carston (2005) for related and highly interesting cases of *and*-conjunction such as, for example, *Paul can't spell and he is a linguist*.

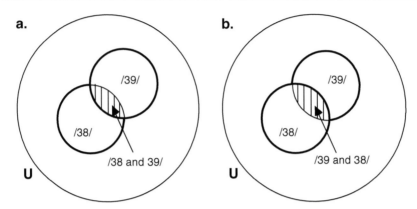

FIGURE 8.1 The order of incrementation reflected in 'superimposition'

(8.38)   She went to Spain.
(8.39)   She married.

Their valuation spaces are rendered in Figure 8.1 as /38/ and /39/, respectively. The VSs /38/ and /39/ have an M-partial intersection precisely because (8.38) and (8.39) are logico-semantically independent, so that it is possible for both to be true, both to be false or for the one to be true and the other to be false. If **D** consists of the combined increments of (8.38) and (8.39), /**D**/ is the intersection of /8.38/ and /8.39/, as shown in Figure 8.1, no matter whether one takes Figure 8.1a or Figure 8.1b. The *order* of incrementation is reflected in the suggestion of superimposition. Figure 8.1a shows the result of incrementing (8.38) first, followed by (8.39), as in (8.35a). Figure 8.1b represents the inverse order, corresponding to (8.35b). In Figure 8.1a her marrying took place against the background of her already being in Spain. In Figure 8.1b her going to Spain took place in the context of her already being married. A three-dimensional representation would perhaps do a better job, but the reader no doubt gets the idea.

Yet, as linguists know, the word *and*, or its equivalents in the languages of the world, is used in several distinct ways that give the impression of multiple ambiguity. In English one finds full speech-act conjunction, as in, for example, *Go home and nobody will know what has happened*. This form of conjunction has received relatively little attention in the linguistic literature on conjunction. L-propositional conjunction, as in *John lives in Paris and Harry lives in London*, is the form studied by logicians, who also look at the conjunction of L-propositional functions, typically under quantifiers, as in

Some politicians only do politics and forget about policy—a conjunction type that linguists tend to stay away from.[13]

It won't do to speak of multiply ambiguous *and* unless one is forced to. The ideal solution would be to reduce all existing varieties of conjunction to speech-act or propositional conjunction, but the literature is far from unanimous on the success of that enterprise.

The reduction of natural language *and* to full L-propositional conjunction is complicated by the fact that the conjunctor AND does not conjoin full L-propositions in surface structure but induces the grammatical process of CONJUNCTION REDUCTION (CR). The grammars of all languages allow for a variety of ways to shorten full L-propositional conjunction in the corresponding surface structures, which then require a reconstruction of the full L-propositional form by way of a syntactic parsing procedure.[14] In this regard, some notable success has been booked in linguistics, except for so-called PHRASAL CONJUNCTION, as in (8.40), which is, of course, not reducible to 'John is a nice couple and Rose is a nice couple':

(8.40)   John and Rose are a nice couple.

Phrasal conjunction clearly requires a separate analysis, which may result in the conclusion that here, too, one has to do with L-propositional conjunction, albeit in an encapsulated form. But no well-motivated answer to this question has so far come to light.[15]

CR is already visible in (8.35a,b), where the common subject of both L-propositional conjuncts is eclipsed in the second conjunct. More drastic cases of CR are shown in (8.41) (the commonly used labels for the type of CR have been added:

(8.41)   a. (Both) Bert and Alex bought a new car.   (Left CR)
          b. Bert bought a car for Mary and a horse for Sue. (Right CR)
          c. Bert bought a car and Alex b̶o̶u̶g̶h̶t̶ a horse.   (Gapping)
          d. Bert likes and Alex hates the play.   (Right-Node Raising)

What we now see is that some of these reduced forms are and some are not open to an ordered interpretation. To begin with, the form of CR known as

---

[13] But see Seuren (1996: 325–6) for the scope-sensitivity of AND with regard to quantifiers and the ensuing restrictions on the syntactic processes of CONJUNCTION REDUCTION.

[14] For more detailed discussions, see, for example, Van Oirsouw (1987), Seuren (1996: 323–38).

[15] Nor do I have an account of the idiosyncratic use of *and* in texts like:

(i) Moving now to sports—*and* in London, Arsenal have qualified for the Europe cup.

As far as I am aware, this use of *and* is restricted to BBC radio English.

'Left CR' appears not to be sensitive to the order of incrementation. Consider the following examples (where *his widow* is to be read as 'the woman Bert was married to before he died' and not as, for example, 'the widowed woman he was dating'):

(8.42)   a. Bert and his widow each died in a car crash.
          b. His widow and Bert each died in a car crash.
          c. The same car was rented by Bert and by his widow.
          d. The same car was rented by Bert's widow and by him.

Clearly, Bert's widow can't be said to have died in a car crash unless Bert died first, when his wife was not yet a widow. Yet (8.42b) is not anomalous, which suggests that Left CR is indifferent to ordered interpretation.

The situation is more complex for cases of Right CR, as in (8.42c,d) or (8.43) and (8.44). (8.43a) and (8.44a) seem all right but the corresponding b-sentences do not, presumably because an ordered interpretation forces itself on the sentences involved. Yet both (8.42c) and (8.42d) also seem both all right, despite the fact that they involve Right CR. I know of no literature about such questions, but *prima facie* it would seem that perhaps the crucial factor is whether or not the underlying L-propositions have a common main verb, in which case there is no order-sensitivity, or different main verbs, in which case the interpretation is order-sensitive.

(8.43)   a. Alex killed Bert and married his widow.
          b. !Alex married Bert's widow and killed him.

(8.44)   a. Alex emptied the bottle and threw it away.
          b. !Alex threw the bottle away and emptied it.

Gapping again makes for conjunctive sentences that are not sensitive to an ordered interpretation, as one can see from (8.45a,b). Although, normally speaking, one has to die before one can be buried, sentence (8.45b) does not strike one as anomalous:

(8.45)   a. Bert filmed the woman's death and Alex filmed her burial.
          b. Alex filmed the woman's burial and Bert filmed her death.

Right-Node Raising again requires an ordered interpretation, since (8.46a) tells a different story from (8.46b). Here, the difference comes again close to being truth-conditional, especially when the word *again* is placed in final position. (8.46c) is anomalous as *again* lacks an antecedent:

(8.46)   a. Bert closed and Alex opened the door (again).
        b. Alex opened and Bert closed the door (again).
        c. !Alex opened again and Bert closed the door.

It thus seems that Left CR and Gapping result in sentences that are not sensitive to an ordered interpretation, whereas Right CR may and Right-Node Raising does result in sentences that are. As far as can be seen, the difference resides in the fact that the L-propositional forms underlying cases of Left CR and Gapping have the same main lexical predicate in both conjuncts, whereas those underlying cases of Right CR and Right-Node Raising may have different main lexical predicates. This, together with an 'event' interpretation of the L-propositions concerned (at least for temporal ordering), may be the necessary and sufficient conditions for successively ordered interpretation, but there may well still be further factors involved. The matter must remain undecided for the moment.

8.2.2 *Negation*

Negation looks simple but that appearance is deceptive. It has all the complexities one should expect of natural language phenomena. Like AND, it primarily takes propositions and propositional functions in its scope, but, unlike AND, it cannot stand over a speech-act operator. It may restrict itself to predicates, as in *nonconformist, non-Catholic*, but such cases can, in principle, be treated as negation over a propositional function because that is what first-order predicates are, propositional functions that take one or more individuals and deliver a truth value—that is, of type (e,t). The same applies to the internal negation of predicate calculus, as in *Some fishermen do not swim*. Here again, the negation is construed as applying to a propositional function, in this case the function $\neg :: \text{Swim}(\bar{x})$.

Lexically incorporated negation, discussed in Section 8.6.4 of Volume I, presents many problems, as already noted by Aristotle. The words *polite* and *impolite* denote not contradictory but only contrary properties. Neither *immoral* nor *amoral* is the contradictory of *moral*, though both are contrary with it. This, however, is a matter of lexical semantics, not relevant in the present context.

What is relevant is the phenomenon of metalinguistic usage, as in:

(8.47)   a. Not Liz, you twit, but Queen Elizabeth has just been on TV.
        b. The man isn't intelligent, he's a whopping genius.
        c. In this house, we don't eat grub, we eat food.
        d. I did NOT only see Act One, Two, and Three, I only saw Act One.

Cases like these are discussed in Horn (1985, 1989) and, in their wake, in a flurry of publications during and after the 1990s. The main trend, in this literature, is to treat these cases as instances of a 'pragmatic' transfer from the standard 'descriptive' negation to a metalinguistic, more or less 'metaphorical', negation, but how exactly this metamorphosis takes place, has never been made clear in a proper falsifiable way.

In Seuren (1988, 2000) I argue that if such pragmatic accounts predict anything, it is this: when someone suggests that, say, some politician is a crook by quoting the famous ironical line *And Brutus is an honourable man* from Shakespeare's *Julius Caesar*, a second person, who strongly believes that the politician in question is entirely blameless, should, if the pragmatic account is correct, be able to rebut this suggestion by saying *And Brutus is* NOT *an honourable man*, which, of course, does not work. All such a person can do is say something like *To hell with your Brutus!* It is also argued there that, while cases like (8.47a,b,c) are instances of lexical-choice correction, cases like (8.47d), though likewise of a 'metalinguistic' nature, belong to a separate category, namely the category of presupposition denials. This latter point is taken up in Section 10.4, and we will not touch on it here. Cases of lexical-choice correction are discussed below.

Leaving aside, for the moment, distracting phenomena such as those mentioned above, we start with ordinary sentential negation. For **IP**, sentential negation, as in NOT-**S**, is an instruction banning the incrementation of S from **D**. The banning order is symbolized in **D**-representations as '*'. Ordinary (default) negation is presupposition-preserving, which means that the non-negated proposition must be normally incrementable, or, if you like, must 'have the right papers', for the **D** at hand. **IP** takes the subject-S (the scope) of NOT in the SA-tree and processes it first without negation (if it hadn't been processed already, for it to be negated subsequently by a second speaker). Subsequently, NOT places an asterisk before the increment.

Double negation bans the banning, and thus establishes incrementation in a roundabout way, based on inferential bridging. Treble negation, as is easily seen, makes one dizzy and confused, in accordance with the principle of natural set theory **PNST–6**, discussed in Section 3.2.2, which says that the function COMPLEMENT is nonrecursive in basic-natural, and only once-recursive in strict-natural set theory. Quadruple negation is, though formally well defined, entirely unrealistic as a cognitive process—unless, of course, the later negations are not logically functional but serve only to lend emphasis to the first, original, negation, as in the New York Black-English sentence (8.48a), taken from Labov (1972: 130), or the London Cockney (8.48b), taken from the 1960s BBC TV play *Cathy Come Home* (see also note 23 in Chapter 8 of Volume I):

(8.48)   a. It ain't no cat can't get in no coop.

   b. 'E's an odd fella. 'E ain't never been no good to no woman, not never.

Grammatically, both (8.48a) and (8.48b) have four negations (if we disregard the rhetorical addition *not never* in (8.48b)) but only the first is logically functional; the other three result from the well-known grammatical process of NEGATION COPYING, found in a vast number of languages in some form or other, and putting a copy of the 'original' negation on some or all subsequent existential operators (see Seuren 1996: 269). (8.48a), where the copying of the negation even penetrates into a relative clause, is equivalent to standard English *There isn't any cat that can get into any coop.* (8.48b) reads as the standard English *He is an odd fellow. He hasn't ever been any good to any woman*, which, somehow, makes less of an impression than (8.48b).

Following the argument in Chapter 2, we treat negation as an abstract predicate in SA-structure, like the other propositional operators and the quantifiers. Its subject-S is what is normally called its scope. Thus, (8.49a) has the SA (8.49b). (8.49c) is the incremental result on the basis of the pre-existing and therefore pre-recorded open address **d–2** [**a** |Mouse(a),[**b** | Cat (b), Catch(b,a)]] ('A cat caught a mouse') given above in (8.11).

(8.49)   a. The mouse did not escape.

   b.

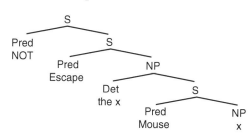

   c. **d–2** [**a** | Mouse(a), [**b** | Cat(b), Catch(b,a)] // *Escape(2)]

Sentential negation, as exemplified in *John has no car*, thus amounts to an instruction for the **D** at hand to refuse the existential introduction of an address for a car of John's and the addition, after closure, of the predication [**b** | Car(b), Have(22,b)] to any, possibly open, address **d–22** [**a** | 'John'(a)] for someone called 'John'. Thus, given the, possibly open, address **d–22** [**a** |

'John'(a)], its extension to (8.50a) is banned, just as the introduction of an address of the form (8.50b):

(8.50)   a. **d–22** [**a** | 'John'(a) // *[**b** | Car(b), Have(22,b)]]
        b. *d–23 [**a** | Car(a), Have(22,a)]

Negated open addresses cannot be closed, as there is nothing to close. This explains the incoherence of, for example, (8.51a), where *it* calls upon an address that has just been banned:

(8.51)   a. !John has no car. It is in the garage.
        b. John has no car. So it can't be in the garage.
        c. John has no car. His car (?It) is a figment of your mind.

In (8.51b), we detect an echo effect, in that it fits naturally into a context in which someone has just said that, or has put up the question of whether John's car is in the garage. The second sentence of (8.51b) is thus to be read as 'the car just said (suggested) to be John's car cannot be in the garage (because John has no car)'. Analogously for (8.51c), which seems to fall back, again, on an assertion (or question) uttered earlier by someone asserting that (or questioning whether) John has a car. The second sentence declares that object to be a figment of the previous speaker's mind. Why it should be that, in cases of this nature, the full NP (*his car*) goes down much better than the anaphoric pronoun *it*, is, admittedly, a question to which I have no answer. (Incidentally, such examples show again the necessity of accepting that speakers naturally make reference to nonexistent or virtual objects; see Section 10.8 for more detailed discussion of anaphoric reference to objects said not to exist.)

A sentence like (8.52a) is thus incremented as (8.52b):

(8.52)   a. No mouse was caught.
        b. *d–24 [**a** | Mouse(a), Be caught(a)]

But (8.52a) is not equivalent with (8.53a,b) (in the sense in which ALL takes scope over NOT), though (8.53a,b) is equivalent with (8.54a,b):

(8.53)   a. All the mice were not caught.
        b. **d–25** [**ā** | ::Mouse(ā) // ALL*(::Be caught(25))]

(8.54)   a. None of the mice were caught.
        b. **d–26** [**ā** | ::Mouse(ā) // *SOME(Be caught(26))]

Now back to (8.47a–c), repeated here for convenience:

(8.47)   a. Not Liz, you twit, but Queen Elizabeth has just been on TV.
         b. The man isn't intelligent, he's a whopping genius.
         c. In this house, we don't eat grub, we eat food.

These are cases of lexical-choice correction and, therefore, of a metalinguistic use of the negation. No grammar and no proper semantics has
been set up, as yet, for cases of this nature, probably because the dominant
attitude has been, over the past twenty years, to relegate such phenomena
to pragmatics.

It cannot be our purpose here to present a full formal account of such
sentences, as that would require a separate monograph. What we can do is
point out that sentences of this type have a common structure representable
as something like (8.55a), where the quotation marks signal the metalinguistic
nature of the sentences at issue. A more formal (SA) rendering of (8.55a)
would be (8.55b), where the caret quotes secure reference to the phonological
(or, if appropriate, the phonetic) form of the words in the range of the
variables **a** and **b** and where **Be$_v$** is the value-assigning predicate discussed
in Section 3.2:

(8.55)   a. The proper expression for **x** in '—**x**—' is not 'a' but 'b'.
         b. NOT [Be$_v$ ^a^ (the proper expression for x in ^—**x**—^)];
            Be$_v$ ^b^ (the proper expression for x in ^—**x**—^)

(8.47a) is then read as 'The proper expression for who has just been on TV is
not ^Liz^ but ^Queen Elizabeth^'. (8.47b) is read as 'The proper expression
for what this man is is not ^intelligent^ but ^a whopping genius^', while
(8.47c) reads as 'The proper expression for what we eat in this house is not
^grub^ but ^food^'.

In the analysis given in (8.55b), this type of sentence is a metalinguistic variety
of the cleft construction, expressing a topic–comment-modulated proposition.
This is confirmed by the fact that the isolation of **x** from '—**x**—' is subject to
the normal isolation—that is, extraction or insertion—constraints that have
found to be valid in grammars, as appears from, for example, (8.56a), where
Liz's cannot be isolated from the position occupied by *Queen Elizabeth's*
because the position involved is a modifier genitive position and modifiers
cannot be isolated from S-structures (we can say *John whose wife died* but
not *John's who wife died*). Not so in (8.56b), where the position involved is
that of a full NP, not of a modifier, or in (8.56c,d), where no isolation has taken
place:

(8.56) a. *It isn't Liz's, you twit, that he praised hat but Queen Elizabeth's.
    b. √ It isn't Liz, you twit, that he praised the hat of but Queen Elizabeth.
    c. √ He praised not Liz's, you twit, but Queen Elizabeth's hat.
    d. √ He praised the hat not of Liz, you twit, but of Queen Elizabeth.

Similar observations can be made regarding (8.47b) and (8.47c):

(8.57) a. *It isn't an intelligent man's that he is son but a whopping genius's.
    b. √ It isn't an intelligent man that he's the son of but a whopping genius.
    c. √ He is not an intelligent man's but a whopping genius's son.
    d. √ He is the son not of an intelligent man but of a whopping genius.

(8.58) a. *In this place, it isn't grub we have standards but food.
    b. √ In this place, it isn't grub we have standards for but food.
    c. √ In this place, we don't have grub but food standards.
    d. √ In this place, we have standards not for grub but for food.

How exactly the grammar turns a (8.55b)-type structure into a corresponding surface structure, or what parameters are required in a semantic theory for a proper formal interpretation of cases like (8.47a–c) are, as has been said, questions that have so far received no attention at all in the linguistic literature. Given this unsatisfactory state of affairs, it would be futile even to try to present an incrementation procedure for such cases.

8.2.3 *Disjunction*

The disjunctive operator OR is far from analogous to its conjunctive counterpart AND. While AND can be used to conjoin speech acts, as in the sentence *Go home and nobody will know what has happened* quoted above, it is not at all clear that OR can be used in an analogous way. One might think of an example like (8.59a), but it is unclear how it should be read in the systematic terms of speech act operators and propositions. We revert to this issue below, when discussing the tacit expansion of disjunctions to the form specified in (8.66).

(8.59) a. Don't try, or you'll get caught.
    b. Do you want coffee or do you want tea?

(8.59b) is likewise not without problems. One may presume that it reads as something like 'I am asking which: what you want is coffee or what you want is tea'. If that is correct, OR is used in combination with the specific-question operator WHICH asking for a choice to be made among given alternatives. Little is known about how such a combination works, owing to the primitive state of research on the grammar of speech acts. One notes, incidentally, that (8.59b) is unambiguous as regards the scope of OR, unlike (8.60), which is ambiguous (unless intonation is taken into account):

(8.60)   Do you want coffee or tea?[16]

Like NOT, OR can be used to correct lexical choices, as in:

(8.61)   He was a sad, or rather pathetic, man.

AND can only be used this way when followed by NOT, as in (8.62a), and in such cases it can be left out. One notes that the use of *but* instead of *and*, as in (8.62b), takes away the metalinguistic reading, leaving only the object-language reading:

(8.62)   a. He was a sad, (and) not a pathetic, man.
         b. He was a sad, but not a pathetic, man.

Like AND, OR has a form of phrasal coupling, as in the example *John and Rose are a nice couple* quoted above as an instance of phrasal conjunction. The disjunctive version would be something like:

(8.63)   Aberdeen or Inverness is an impossible choice.

Yet phrasal disjunction, as in (8.63), has a metalinguistic flavour which phrasal conjunction lacks. (8.63) reads as '"Aberdeen or Inverness" is an impossible choice'.

   One remembers from Section 7.2.2.3 the curious reduction of (8.64a) to (8.64b):

(8.64)   a. Paul may be at home and he may be in hospital.
         b. Paul may be at home !and/ √or in hospital.

On the whole, the relation between natural language AND and OR is far from clear. It is certainly not exhausted by the purely logical account of these two operators.

---

[16] There is an anecdote about Bertrand Russell, said to have replied 'Yes' to a stewardess asking him (8.60). According to the anecdote, Russell wanted to teach the poor lady that *or* is inclusive, not exclusive, but, if that is so, he would have had to ignore the stewardess's intonation, which, in all likelihood, had a rising tone on *coffee* and a falling tone on *tea*.

The most common use of OR, however, is its use as a propositional connector, as in (8.65a), which can be reduced by grammatical reduction processes to (8.65b):

(8.65)   a. This house has no basement or this house has no garden.
          b. This house has no basement or no garden.

A variant of full propositional OR is OR connecting propositional functions, as in:

(8.66)   Most of our students are Portuguese or Brazilian.

As regards full propositional OR, we hark back to Section 3.4.3. There it is proposed that, at a basic-natural level, OR is best accounted for by assuming that sentences of the type P OR Q (limiting ourselves to binary disjunction) should be analysed, at some underlying level, as (8.67), repeated from (3.23) in Section 3.4.3:

(8.67)   (P AND NOT-Q) OR (NOT-P AND Q); formally: $(P \land \neg Q) \lor (\neg P \land Q)$

The reason for this assumption is, as one remembers, that it is only in this way that the basic-natural requirement that the arguments of the OR-function are mutually exclusive can be met, even though P and Q are themselves logically and semantically independent, meaning that /P/ Ⓞ /Q/. In order to ensure that the two disjuncts are mutually exclusive even though P and Q are logically and semantically independent, we expand P to P AND NOT-Q and Q to NOT-P AND Q. The tacit exclusion (negation) of the second disjunct in the first and vice versa rests on the TRUE ALTERNATIVES CONDITION for Ds, requiring that the alternative increments under disjunction be truly distinct. This explains the much-debated 'exclusive' character of OR as resulting from principles of coherent discourse construction.

When we say that P OR Q is to be 'tacitly' read as (8.67), what we mean is not that the underlying SA, which is the input to the grammar module, should be of the form (8.67). This would go against all principles of sound grammatical theorizing. What is meant is that the expansion from P OR Q to (8.67) should be specified (a) as part of the (basic-natural) lexical semantics of OR and (b) as part of the **IP**-instruction associated with OR. This way the expansion to (8.67) is kept out of the syntax, as it should be.

We posit that the **IP** for normal propositional OR is an instruction, in the sense defined above, of the following form, which ensures that the 'tacit' reading is materialized in the **IP**-result, not in the grammar. Each subdomain now corresponds automatically to a valuation space that excludes the others:

INSTRUCTION FOR L-PROPOSITIONAL OR

For a propositional disjunction DIS of the form P_1 OR P_2 OR...P_n, expand the disjunct P_1 of DIS to P_1 AND NOT-P_2...NOT-P_n and analogously for all P_m ($1 < m \leq n$). Then set up as many separate subdomains as there are expanded disjuncts, whereby each subdomain must be properly anchored to the given **D**.

It must be stressed that the instruction to expand disjunctions to the format of (8.67) is taken to hold only at a basic-natural level. At stricter natural levels, the instruction must be taken to start with the second sentence: 'Set up as many separate subdomains as there are expanded disjuncts.' Yet the basic-natural interpretation stays with us all the time, even when we operate at a stricter level of naturalness, or else the type of donkey anaphora shown in (8.68) would not be a problem for formal semanticists.

The subdomains set up as a result of the OR-instruction naturally give rise to the explicit or (mostly) implicit question of which of the subdomains should be elected to continue the **D** at hand. This is not only one of the sources of topic–comment modulation, it also drives the further development of **D** in that the participants in the discourse feel urged to look for arguments that will decide in favour of one of the alternatives.

The **IP** for OR accounts for the possibility of 'donkey' anaphora, as in (8.68), where the anaphoric pronoun *it* appears to lack an antecedent:

(8.68)   Either Socrates does not own a donkey or he feeds *it*.

Given the condition in the OR-instruction saying that the two expanded disjuncts must be well-anchored to the current **D**, one sees that both 'Socrates does not own a donkey and (therefore) he does NOT feed it' (with presupposition-cancelling radical NOT) and 'Socrates owns a donkey and he feeds it' are proper increments to one and the same given **D**.

There is a problem with OR as a connector of propositional functions, as in (8.66) above. Sentence (8.66) appears to lack the 'exclusive' character generally adhering to OR, as it seems readily and naturally to allow for truth when some of the students in question are both Portuguese and Brazilian, having dual nationality. The sentence may then be taken to want to say that most of the students speak some variety of Portuguese. And indeed, donkey anaphora seems to lose its facilitation in existentially quantified sentences like (8.69a). This would then be explained by the assumption that (8.69a) is not subject to the expansion procedure specified above. But this does not apply to (8.69b), the propositional-function equivalent of (8.66) with MOST, where donkey anaphora appears fully acceptable.

(8.69)   a. ??Some farmers do not own a donkey or they feed *it*.
          b. √Most (of the) farmers do not own a donkey or they feed *it*.

We must leave this problem open and hope that future research will produce an answer.

The expansion of **P** OR **Q** to (8.67) has a wider application than to just propositional OR. It applies, in an analogous but far from fully understood way, also to the quasi-speech-act OR of (8.59a) and (8.59b). The first disjunct of (8.59a) is, perhaps, expandable to 'I urge you not to try and I predict that you will not get caught', but it is unclear what is to be done with the second conjunct *or you'll get caught*, which is not readily expandable to 'I urge you to try and I predict that you'll get caught'. As regards (8.59b), if the reading proposed above holds, it expands to 'I am asking which: what you want is coffee and not tea, or what you want is tea and not coffee'. Likewise for phrasal disjunction, as in (8.63), which expands naturally to 'Aberdeen and not Inverness or Inverness and not Aberdeen is an impossible choice'. Where the expansion does not seem to apply in any way at all is in cases of metalinguistic lexical-choice correction, as in (8.61) above.

Yet another of the many problems connected with OR (and IF) that there is no space to explore more fully is the following. Given the expansion of disjunctions according to the format of (8.67), the logic of OR need not account for its exclusive character: OR itself can remain inclusive, as logic prefers it to be. But do we also follow the logicians in claiming that the subdomains set up as a result of the OR-instruction are fully extensional? That is, do these subdomains freely allow for substitution *salva veritate* (SSV) of co-referential terms? The question is of no direct relevance to the **IP**, but it is directly relevant to the semantics of discourse domains. Consider the following sentence:

(8.70)   Either the morning star is the evening star, or there are ten planets.

According to standard propositional calculus, SSV is guaranteed in these cases. If, for example, the term *evening star* is replaced with *morning star*, as in (8.71), the result may be a little quaint but in the actual world, where the two names refer to the same entity—the planet Venus—the truth value does not change:

(8.71)   Either the morning star is the morning star, or there are ten planets.

It is clear that (8.70) and (8.71) express quite different speaker commitments, just as Frege's original *The morning star is the evening star* expresses a quite different speaker commitment from *The morning star is the morning star*. But this is due to the different truth conditions. The actual identity of the morning star and the evening star ensures that, despite the different truth *conditions*, the truth *value* stays unchanged.[17]

As regards **D**-structures, it seems to be generally so that subdomains created in virtue of an instruction associated with a propositional operator are always extensional in the sense defined. This holds for conjunction, negation, disjunction, and also, as will become clear in a moment, for conditionals and it seems to be due to the fact that the increments stored in these subdomains must be well-anchored—that is, ready for direct attachment to the current **D** (they must have 'the right papers' for the current **D**). Being a subdomain set up under such an instruction is thus a sufficient condition for the subdomain to be extensional, but it is not a necessary condition. For there are extensional subdomains that are not the result of such an instruction but are embedded under a lexical predicate, such as the subdomain embedded in the object position of the verb **Cause**, as in (8.72a), or the factive subdomain embedded in subject position under verbs like **Prove** or **Suggest**, as in (8.72b):

(8.72) a. The arrival of the police caused the butler to flee.
   b. That the butler had fled suggested that he was guilty.

Suppose the butler in question is identical with the person referred to by the phrase *the man with the white gloves*, any truth value of (8.72a) or (8.72b) remains unchanged when *the man with the white gloves* is substituted for *the butler*.

Semantically, it is clear why this should be so. Just as Frege said (see Section 7.2.1.2), a subdomain is intensional when it reflects the thought-contents of a thought-predicate, usually in object position. Since **Cause** is not a thought-predicate, it is listed in the lexicon as extensional with regard not only to its subject but also to its (possibly sentential) object term, while **Suggest** is lexically marked as extensional with regard to its subject term, whether sentential or nominal, but intensional with regard to its object term because **Suggest** is a thought-predicate and its object term contains the contents of what is suggested.

---

[17] I have wavered on this issue in the past but, on reflection, I think I must come down in favour of the standard position and retract what I argued for in Seuren 1985: 396.

It would seem that this difference must be formally marked in **D**-structures, as it has not so far been shown to follow from any structural or otherwise formally recognizable feature in **D**-structures. The simplest way of doing so is to borrow the marking used for the lexicon (in our notation, the asterisk; see Section 5.3 in Volume I). But it would be preferable if the intensional nature of any given subdomain were seen to follow from independent factors formally rendered in **D**-structure representations.

8.2.4 *Conditionals*

Let us now have a look at conditionals—that is, sentences of the type **if P then Q**. Ever since the Stoic philosophers set up their propositional logic during the third century BCE, natural language ɪꜰ has been widely regarded, especially by philosophers and logicians, as representing the truth-functional operator of material implication—a view that immediately gave rise to public controversy, as appears from a little epigram written by the Alexandrian librarian and poet Callimachus in the third century BCE, saying 'Even the crows on the rooftops caw about the nature of conditionals' (Kneale and Kneale 1962: 128). The question is: were the Stoics, and with them the logical tradition till the present day, right or wrong in considering ɪꜰ a truth-functional propositional operator? The answer to that question is not simple. Perhaps one should say that to a considerable extent they were right, but to some extent they were not. Such an answer, of course, calls for some comment.

Most semanticists assume that the natural language subordinating conjunction *if* represents the well-known truth-functional operator '→' of propositional logic, also known as 'material implication', which yields falsity only when the antecedent clause (or *if*-clause, also called by the ancient Greek name *prótasis*) is true and the consequent clause (also known as *apódosis*) is false, and truth in all other cases. Yet the same semanticists accept, or admit, that this assumption is tenable only with a heavy supply of pragmatic support. It seems incontrovertible that the equation of natural language *if* with material implication falls far short of accounting for the way *if* is naturally used by speakers, which gives rise to the question of whether the deficit is to be made up for by pragmatics or by a different kind of logic, for example basic-natural logic, combined with the mechanics of discourse incrementation. The latter is preferable on methodological grounds, as it makes for greater precision.[18] It is also the view defended here.

---

[18] Johnson-Laird (1986) agrees that context plays an important role in the interpretation of conditionals, but he takes a dim view of the powers of logic to account for their vagaries. He writes (1986: 73):

In searching for a logical, or in any case formal, basis we are helped a great deal by what we have found regarding the semantics of OR. In standard logic, of course, $P{\rightarrow}Q$ is equivalent with $\neg P \lor Q$, and it is interesting to see to what extent this parallelism can be sustained—an issue to which we return below. Meanwhile we can say that the parallelism fails in some respects. For example, it fails with regard to the number of propositional terms taken by IF: whereas OR can take any number of arguments IF is restricted to two. There is a parallel in that speech-act conditionals are as unclear as regards their analysis as are speech-act disjunctions. A sentence like (8.73), though perfectly normal from the point of view of English usage, has not so far received a proper analysis:

(8.73)   Shoot me, if you dare.

NP-conditionals, as a parallel to NP-disjunctions and NP-conjunctions, are questionable. (8.74a) is quaint, though better with *also*; (8.74b) is a great deal better:

(8.74)   a. ?If Aberdeen then (also) Inverness is an impossible condition.
          b. If not Aberdeen then Inverness is an impossible dilemma.

Finally, conditionals seem to be subject to different conditions of contextual fit from disjunctions. For example, if someone asks 'Why does Philip pay so much income tax?', (8.75a) may be an appropriate answer but (8.75b) can hardly be:

(8.75)   a. Either he doesn't know the law or he is a bachelor.
          b. If he knows the law, he is a bachelor.

There are, therefore, considerable differences between conditionals and disjunctions, despite the fact that they are logically interchangeable.

How do people interpret conditionals? They set up a mental model based on the meaning of the antecedent, and on their beliefs and knowledge of the context. They then determine the nature and the degree of the relation between antecedent and consequent. This process may lead to a recursive revision in the antecedent model. Finally, if need be, they set up a scenario relating the model of the consequent to the antecedent model. The relation may be merely that the consequent state of affairs is relevant to a protagonist in the antecedent model, or it may be a logical, temporal, causal or deontic relation between the two models.

What are the logical properties of conditionals? They are many and various. Conditionals are not creatures of a constant hue. Like chameleons, as I once put it, they take on the colour suggested by their surroundings. Their logical properties depend on the relation between antecedent and consequent, and that in turn depends on beliefs.

Although I can agree with Johnson-Laird in certain respects, I do find him more than a little failing in his duty to be precise. In particular, to say that the logic of conditionals is like a chameleon, taking its properties from 'the relation between antecedent and consequent' is a little too vague to my taste. Greater precision is possible and should, therefore, be striven for.

But let us now look at the similarities. The schema IF P then Q does not oblige the listener to add either P or Q to D. What it says is that there are two possibilities: either P is to be incremented, but then also Q, or else NOT-P is incremented. The question is: what happens when NOT-P is incremented? Strict-natural and constructed standard logic say that no commitment is entered with regard to Q in case NOT-P is incremented: Q may be true (incremented) or false (not incremented). But this is not what basic-natural logic says. Basic-natural propositional logic follows the principle of natural set theory PNST–3, formulated in Section 3.2.2, and repeated here:

When two (or more) sets A and B undergo union, A and B are natural sets and are, at the level of basic, but not strict, naturalness, totally distinct, with no element in common, so that $|A \cup B| = |A| + |B|$.

In standard logic, as one knows, IF P then Q is equivalent with IF P then (P AND Q), just as NOT-P OR Q is equivalent with NOT-P OR (P AND Q). Intuitively, this makes sense in that, according to the instruction for conditionals given below, IF P then Q tells the listener that the incrementation of P licenses the incrementation of Q, *salva veritate*. The normal choice between incrementing or not incrementing P is thus enriched with the information that the former option carries Q as an extra bonus—a central element in inductive thinking.

Basic-natural logic saves the equivalence of IF P then (P AND Q) and NOT-P OR (P AND Q), but now under the conditions that hold for basic-natural OR, making it 'exclusive'. That is, NOT-P OR (P AND) Q is rephrased as (8.76), according to the expansion scheme of (8.67). This is so because if the two possibilities mentioned in $(P \wedge Q) \vee \neg P$ are to be mutually exclusive for the antecedent clause ¬P and the consequent clause Q, the possibility of both being true must be excluded. Thus, exactly as in the case of disjunction discussed in Section 3.4.2, conditionals must be expanded according to the schema formulated in (8.67) above, that is as (8.76), thereby eliminating the possibility of NOT-P and Q being true simultaneously. Exclusive OR and bi-implicational IF are thus of a piece:

(8.76)   (P AND Q) OR (NOT-P AND NOT-Q); formally: $(P \wedge Q) \vee (\neg P \wedge \neg Q)$

This, in effect, makes IF P then Q equivalent with standard logical $P \leftrightarrow Q$, just as basic-natural intuition wishes it to be.

Given this, let us now formulate what we see as the incrementation instruction for the conditional IF-operator at a basic-natural level of operation. It seems that the following will do:[19]

INSTRUCTION FOR 'IF **P** then **q**'

For a conditional COND of the form IF **P** then **Q**, expand COND to IF **P** then **Q** AND IF **Q** then **P**. Then set up two subdomains, one for **P** AND **Q** and one for NOT-**P** AND NOT-**Q**. In case **P** is incremented to **D**, there is a licence, *ceteris paribus*, for **Q** to be incremented subsequently, and in case ~**P** is incremented to **D**, there is a licence, *ceteris paribus*, for ~**Q** to be incremented subsequently, both *salva veritate*, whereby each subdomain must be properly anchored to the given **D**.

At a strict-natural level of operation the expansion is limited to IF **P** then **P** AND **Q**, which is equivalent with standard logical **P** → **Q** and amounts to saying that once **P** is incremented there is a licence, *ceteris paribus*, for **Q** to be incremented as well, without further ado.

It is thus clear that at both the basic-natural and the strict-natural level donkey anaphora is warranted, as in a sentence like:

(8.77)   If Nancy has a husband, *he* is Norwegian.

This so because once 'Nancy has a husband' has been incremented, the new husband-address provides an anchor for the pronoun *he*.

The incrementation instruction for conditionals implies that it is uncertain whether **P** can or must be incremented to **D**. It thus gives rise to the explicit or (mostly) implicit question of whether **P** can be incremented. As such, conditionals are, like disjunctions, a major source for topic–comment modulation discussed in Chapter 11. And, again as with disjunctions, participants in the linguistic interaction taking place will feel urged to look for arguments that will decide whether or not **P** can be incremented to **D**.

It also implies that both **P** and NOT-**P** must be properly anchored to, or, as has been said, must have the 'right papers' for, the **D** of the moment, while the 'right papers' for **Q** (or, as the case may be, NOT-**Q**) are predicated on the **D** of the moment enriched with **P** (or, as the case may be, NOT-**P**). This is important for a correct assessment of the conditions for presupposition projection in conditionals, as is explained in Section 10.5.

---

[19] In anticipation of Chapter 10, the negation operator is considered to be the presupposition-preserving minimal negation ~ and not standard bivalent¬.

As long as **P** has not been incremented, the *if*-clause is held in abeyance, in a separate nonintensional subdomain. In this respect, the antecedent **P** may be regarded as a *yes/no*-question. Instead of saying *If you are ready, come with me*, one may also say *Are you ready? (If so/ Then) come with me*. In many languages, in fact, conditionals have a grammatical form that equals, or is strongly reminiscent of, *yes/no*-questions.[20]

Yet what we call *if*-clauses may also be expressed in a number of different grammaticalized expression modes. Thus, one sometimes finds *and*-conjunctions for the expression of conditionals ('You are right and we must sell the business'). In the West-European languages this form is mostly reserved for cases where the antecedent clause is an imperative, as in *Do that and I'll lock you up*. In Turkish, this form is appropriately used, next to the canonical form of a conditional clause with the suffix *-se/-sa*, to emphasize that the antecedent cannot possibly be true, as in *Sen yapmadın da kim yaptı?* (You didn't do it and who did?) (Lewis 1984: 268). Prepositional (postpositional) phrases under a pre(post)position meaning 'in the event of', in construction with a nominalized clause, are also found ('In the event of your being right, we must sell the business'). This latter mode of expression for conditionals is found in a fair number of languages, including some Papuan languages (Wegener 2008: 267) and Turkish (with the postposition *takdirde*; Lewis 1984: 186). Sometimes, the antecedent is in the imperative, as in Turkish: *Uzatma, bırakır giderim* (Don't carry on, I'll stop and go) (Lewis 1984: 268). And this list surely does not exhaust the possibilities available to the human race for the expression of conditional propositions.

Clearly, a conditional sentence leads to incoherence, or at least to vacuity, when the current discourse **D** already contains the information that the antecedent clause is false. All one can do, in such a case, is use a counterfactual

---

[20] Comrie (1986: 87) mentions examples (i) and (ii), in German and English, respectively, where the antecedent has the grammatical form of a question. Dutch has the same phenomenon, as shown in (iii):

(i) Hätte er das getan, wäre ich glücklich gewesen.
(ii) Had he done that, I would have been happy.
(iii) Had hij dat gedaan, was ik gelukkig geweest.

Harris (1986: 276–7) points at the frequently found parallel between conditional clauses and embedded or indirect questions: 'We must now look briefly at one quite separate use of si/*si*/se in Romance, namely as the complementizer required when the embedded sentence was originally a polar question.' The same phenomenon is found in English, which uses *if* for both conditional antecedents and embedded polar questions.

Turkish regularly uses questions, next to other constructions, to express conditionals: *O geldi mi, ben burada durmam* (Did he come? I won't stop here) (Lewis 1984: 267).

construction of the type *If you were clever, you wouldn't buy shares,* counter-factuals being analysed as IF P then Q, with the presupposition that P is false.

But apart from these discourse-related aspects of conditionals, there is a great deal of explanatory profit to be gained from expanding, in the sense of (8.76), IF P then Q to IF P then Q AND IF Q then P—that is, from reading the material implication as the material bi-implication. It is widely known among formal semanticists (though much less outside these circles) that the standard logical material implication leads to strongly counterintuitive results, often called 'paradoxes' when applied to natural language condi-tionals.[21] The following analysis shows that most of the 'paradoxes' resulting from the application of the material implication to the semantics of natural language conditionals simply vanish as soon as natural language *if* is read as *if and only if.*

Just for the sake of clarity, let us set up a truth table for the propositions P, Q, and R and four relevant compositions in the following way:

TABLE 8.1. Truth table for P, Q, and R and four compositions

valuations:		1	2	3	4	5	6	7	8	
P		T	F	T	F	T	F	T	F	VS: $\{1,3,5,7\}$
Q		T	T	F	F	T	T	F	F	VS: $\{1,2,5,6\}$
R		T	T	T	T	F	F	F	F	VS: $\{1,2,3,4\}$
a.	$(\neg P \wedge \neg Q) \vee (P \wedge Q)$ or: $P \leftrightarrow Q$	T	F	F	T	T	F	F	T	VS: $\{1,4,5,8\}$
b.	$(\neg R \wedge \neg P) \vee (R \wedge P)$ or: $R \leftrightarrow P$	T	F	T	F	F	T	F	T	VS: $\{1,3,6,8\}$
c.	$(\neg R \wedge \neg Q) \vee (R \wedge Q)$ or: $R \leftrightarrow Q$	T	T	F	F	F	F	T	T	VS: $\{1,2,7,8\}$
d.	$(\neg(P \wedge R) \wedge \neg Q) \vee ((P \wedge R) \wedge Q)$ or: $(P \wedge R) \leftrightarrow Q$	T	F	F	T	F	F	T	T	VS: $\{1,4,7,8\}$

The translation of Table 8.1 into a standard VS-model for the logically and semantically independent L-propositions P, Q, and R is shown in Figure 8.2. For the three sentences P, Q, and R, there are eight valuations such that all possible combinations of truth (T) and falsity (F) are represented. Given the truth values for P, Q, and R in each column (valuation), the truth values of their logical compositions follow automatically. I have selected four specific compositions for reasons that will become clear in a moment.

Composition *a*: $(\neg P \wedge \neg Q) \vee (P \wedge Q)$ or: $P \leftrightarrow Q$

representing NOT-P OR Q (or: IF P, then Q, or: IF Q, then P) as construed on the principles of basic-natural logic, is true in the valuations 1, 4, 5, and 8,

---

[21] An incisive study in this regard is Veltman (1985), to which we refer below.

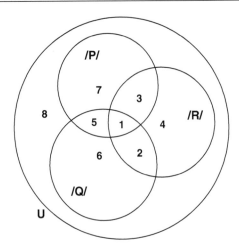

<small>FIGURE 8.2</small> The valuation spaces of Table 8.1 in a VS-model

giving the valuation space {1,4,5,8}: P and Q are either jointly true or jointly false.

Composition b: $(\neg R \wedge \neg P) \vee (R \wedge P)$ or: $R \leftrightarrow P$

representing basic-natural NOT-R OR P (or: IF R, then P, or: IF P, then R), is true in the valuations 1, 3, 6, and 8, giving the valuation space {1,3,6,8}: R and P are either jointly true or jointly false.

Composition c: $(\neg R \wedge \neg Q) \vee (R \wedge Q)$ or: $R \leftrightarrow Q$

representing basic-natural NOT-R OR Q (or: IF R, then Q, or: IF Q, then R), is true in the valuations 1, 2, 7, and 8, giving the valuation space {1,2,7,8}: R and Q are either jointly true or jointly false.

Composition d: $(\neg(P \wedge R) \wedge \neg Q) \vee ((P \wedge R) \wedge Q)$ or: $(P \wedge R) \leftrightarrow Q$

representing basic-natural IF P and R then Q (or: IF Q then P and R), is true in the valuations 1, 4, 7, and 8, giving the valuation space {1,4,7,8}: either P, Q, and R are jointly true or P and R are jointly false or Q is false.

It is now easy to read off what entails what. Thus, $a \wedge b \vdash c$ (implication is a transitive relation), because {1,4,5,8} ∩ {1,3,6,8} = {1,8} and {1,8} ⊆ {1,2,7,8}. But $a \nvdash d$, because {1,4,5,8} ⊄ {1,4,7,8}, which means that the embarrassing standard-logic entailment from IF P then Q to IF P and R then Q (antecedent strengthening) no longer holds. We will come back to this in a moment, when we discuss example (8.84).

This analysis provides a number of solutions to old problems. As has been noted by many authors, treating the IF-operator as truth-functional material implication leads to serious clashes with intuition, often referred to by the embellishing term 'paradoxes'. These come in two classes. Some are solved with the help of basic-natural logic, so that implication is read as bi-implication, but others withstand such a solution. For the latter, a remedy is to be sought in the discourse-semantic aspects of conditionals. We first consider a few cases that are solved in terms of the basic-natural logical analysis of conditionals as bi-implication.

First and obviously, this analysis accounts directly for the intuition that IF P then Q is naturally, but not in an analytically compelling way, understood as implying the converse IF Q then P, or, equivalently, as IF NOT-P then NOT-Q, turning the antecedent clause from a merely sufficient into a sufficient and necessary condition (the reading $P \leftrightarrow Q$ (composition *a*) for IF P then Q is throughout symmetrical for P and Q, and thus also allows for the expression IF Q then P). This intuition does not reflect analytical necessity, but it clearly has the weaker status of an invited or default inference, which can be overridden by a modicum of careful thought. This phenomenon is an obvious target both for pragmatics and for our basic-logic hypothesis. It has given rise to a rather large body of, mostly pragmaticist, literature over the past thirty or so years, so much so that it has acquired a special name: since Geis and Zwicky (1971), this phenomenon has been known as CONDITIONAL PERFECTION, or, in the words of Horn (2000), the move from IF to IFF.[22] It has been shown above that, like exclusive OR, the much discussed phenomenon of conditional perfection follows from the principles of basic-natural set theory.

A further 'paradox', likewise solved by an appeal to the basic-natural logical analysis of implication as bi-implication, is the following. Consider the following pair of sentences:

(8.78)   a. If Amsterdam is in Belgium, the present pope is German.
         b. If Amsterdam is in Belgium, I am the pope.

Elementary world knowledge tells us that the antecedent clause of (8.78a) is false but the consequent clause true. This would make the whole of (8.78a) true, but I am confident that any systematic testing of speakers' judgements will reveal that this is not what speakers feel (8.78a) to be. The truth of (8.78b), where both the antecedent and the consequent (at least if uttered by someone other than the pope) are false, is easier to accept. (8.78b) can be

---

[22] For a survey of the literature in this respect, see Van Der Auwera (1998) and also Declerck and Reed (2001). See also Johnson-Laird (1986: 59–60) for an illuminating discussion.

used to lend strong emphasis to the speaker's assertion that *Amsterdam is in Belgium* is false, because if you accept one obvious falsity, you may as well accept any.

This discrepancy is explained by the natural tendency to interpret conditionals as biconditionals ('conditional perfection'). For if (8.78a) were intuitively felt to be true, given world knowledge, then (8.79a,b) would also have to be felt to be true because basic-natural logic allows both for obversion (contraposition) of a conditional, as in (8.79a), and for the negation of both clauses, as in (8.79b), as is easily read off from Table 8.1. Both obversion and negating both clauses leave the truth conditions of IF P then Q unchanged because all positions of P and Q in composition *a* are symmetrical and adding a negation throughout to each elementary sentence likewise changes nothing.

(8.79)   a. If the present pope is German, Amsterdam is in Belgium.
          b. If Amsterdam is not in Belgium, the present pope is not German.

But both (8.79a) and (8.79b) are clearly false, and felt to be false, in the present world. Therefore, the alleged truth of (8.78a) clashes with the intuition that conditionals are 'really' biconditionals, since both the negating and the exchanging of the antecedent and consequent clauses lead to clear-cut falsity. But when the same test is applied to (8.78b), we see that the strengthening to a biconditional makes no difference for its truth value as felt intuitively: both (8.80a) and (8.80b) remain true, also for natural intuition:

(8.80)   a. If I am the pope, Amsterdam is in Belgium.
          b. If Amsterdam is not in Belgium, I am not the pope.

A further, well-known, 'paradox' of this nature is exemplified in (8.81). In the standard analysis, where IF P then Q is considered false only when P is true and Q false, and true in all other cases, a sentence of the form NOT(IF P then Q) amounts to the assertion that P is true and Q false, because when NOT(IF P then Q) is true, P is true and Q is false. But this is highly counterintuitive. It would turn a demonstration of the truth of (8.81) into a proof for the nonexistence of God:

(8.81)   It is not so that if God does not exist, there are no moral rules.

Sentence (8.81) sounds quite reasonable, and is, in fact, a central tenet in humanist moral philosophy. Yet if we apply a standard-logic truth-table test to (8.81), the result is clearly incompatible with the way it is naturally understood. Let 'P' stand for 'God exists' and 'Q' for 'there are moral rules', then the logical structure of (8.81) is as shown in (8.82), which shows that truth is obtained for this formula by assigning falsity (F) to **P** and truth (T) to **Q**.

(8.82)

$$\neg\,(\neg\,P\ \rightarrow\ \neg\,Q)$$

$$\begin{array}{ccc} \underline{F} & & \underline{T} \\ T & \rightarrow & F \\ \multicolumn{3}{c}{\underline{F}} \\ T \end{array}$$

According to the standard truth table for the material implication, the only way for ¬**P** → ¬**Q** to be false is for ¬**P** to be true and for ¬**Q** to be false, and hence for **P** to be false and **Q** to be true, as in (8.82). Only then can the falsity of ¬**P** → ¬**Q** be turned into truth by the wide-scope negation. All other truth-value assignments to **P** and **Q** will lead to falsity for the whole formula.

On this, standard, interpretation, (8.81), in fact, expresses the assertion that God does not exist and that there are moral rules. But this is not the way (8.81) is understood by normal speakers. No (normal) humanist philosopher will accept that the truth of (8.81) amounts to saying that God does not exist but moral rules do. What (8.81) says is, rather, that the nonexistence of God does not license the claim that there are no moral rules.

Again, an appeal to a basic-natural-logic interpretation helps out. When translated in terms of exclusive OR, (8.81) reads as follows:

(8.83)   It is not so that either God exists and there are moral rules,
           or God does not exist and there are no moral rules.

In formal notation, this amounts to: $\neg((P \wedge Q) \vee (\neg P \wedge \neg Q))$. Now it is no longer so that the only way for (8.83) to be true is for **P** to be false and for **Q** to be true, as in (8.82). To see this, just take composition *a* of Table 8.1, representing IF **P**, then **Q**, and invert the truth values. This gives the valuation space {2,3,6,7}, the complement of {1,4,5,8}. In the valuations 2, 3, 6, and 7, it is not so that **P** is always false and **Q** is always true, as is the case for $\neg(\neg P \vee Q)$. On the contrary, in the valuations 2, 3, 6, and 7, **P** and **Q** never have the same truth value: if the one is true, the other is false and vice versa. Therefore, all that is needed for the truth of (8.83), and thus for the basic-natural truth of (8.81), is that **P** and **Q** have different truth values. The 'paradox' of (8.81) thus evaporates under the analysis in terms of basic-natural logic.

A further interesting example, provided by Veltman (1985: 194), is the following:

(8.84)   a. If you add sugar to your coffee, it tastes good.
          b. Ergo: if you add sugar and petrol to your coffee, it tastes good.

In standard logic, a true conditional remains true when the antecedent is strengthened with further conditions ('antecedent strengthening'), because the antecedent merely states a sufficient condition for the truth of the consequent, not a necessary one. Antecedent strengthening seems to follow from ordinary reasoning, yet it leads to strongly counterintuitive results. One is inclined to reason that if it is true that adding sugar to my coffee makes it taste good, then, if I add both sugar and petrol, I do add sugar, which should thus still make my coffee taste good. But it doesn't make my coffee taste good at all.

One immediate answer is that, apparently, IF is not truth-functional but merely provides a licence to add the consequent clause 'ceteris paribus'—that is, without any relevant additional changes in the situation. This is why the Instruction for IF P then Q, as formulated above on page 273, is predicated on the *ceteris paribus* condition.

Apart from this, however, basic-natural logic helps out. Let P be *You add sugar to your coffee*, Q *The coffee tastes good* and R *You add petrol to your coffee*. The basic-natural analysis of (8.84a) is then $(\neg P \wedge \neg Q) \vee (P \wedge Q)$, or composition *a* of Table 8.1, with the valuation space $\{1,4,5,8\}$. The basic-natural analysis of (8.84b) is $(\neg(P \wedge R) \wedge \neg Q) \vee ((P \wedge R) \wedge Q)$, or composition *d* of Table 8.1, with the valuation space $\{1,4,7,8\}$. Clearly, since $\{1,4,5,8\} \not\subseteq \{1,4,7,8\}$, (8.84a) does not entail (8.84b). Therefore, the annoying problem of antecedent strengthening does not arise in basic-natural logic.

The basic-natural analysis is even better than that. Add to (8.84a) the statement:

(8.84)   c. If you add petrol to your coffee, it does not taste good.

Antecedent strengthening now gives:

(8.84)   d. If you add petrol and sugar to your coffee, it does not taste good.

Yet at the same time antecedent strengthening based on (8.84a) gives (8.84b), so that one must conclude that if one adds both petrol and sugar to one's coffee it does and does not taste good at the same time—as long as one adheres to the standard analysis of IF and thus to antecedent strengthening.

The standard analysis of conditionals fails to give an answer: (8.84a) entails (8.84b) and (8.84c) entails (8.84d), but nothing follows when (8.84b) and (8.84d) are asserted simultaneously, even though our intuition warns us that (8.84b) and (8.84d) are incompatible. In the basic-natural analysis, however, (8.84b) and (8.84d) turn out to be contradictories. This is quickly shown in terms of VS-analysis:

(8.84a) /If P then Q/ $= \{1,4,5,8\}$ (see Table 8.1, comp. a)
(8.84b) /If P and R, then Q/ $= \{1,4,7,8\}$ (see Table 8.1, comp. d)
(8.84c) /If R then not-Q/ $= \{3,4,5,6\}$ (check in Table 8.1)
(8.84d) /If P and R, then not-Q/ $= \{2,3,5,6\}$ (check in Table 8.1)

There are no entailment relations between (8.84a) and (8.84b) or between (8.84c) and (8.84d)—that is, there is no antecedent strengthening—but (8.84b) and (8.84d) are both mutually exclusive (contraries) and in full union (subcontraries), hence contradictories. This is obviously in much better agreement with natural intuitions than what results from the standard analysis.

So far, we have solved a number of 'paradoxes' by means of the bi-implicational analysis corresponding with basic-natural logic. There are, however, other 'paradoxes' that resist such a solution. Veltman (1985: 194–5) provides the following example:

(8.85) If Jones wins the election, Smith will retire to private life.
        If Smith dies before the election, Jones will win it.
        Ergo: If Smith dies before the election, he will retire to private life.

In standard terms, the logic of this argument is sound, since the relation of material implication is transitive: if $P \rightarrow Q$ and $Q \rightarrow R$, then $P \rightarrow R$. But, other than in the preceding cases, if the material implication is replaced with the biconditional, the argument remains logically sound: if $P \leftrightarrow Q$ and $Q \leftrightarrow R$, then $P \leftrightarrow R$. Yet the argument is, in fact, absurd. Why should this be so?

Here we need stronger measures than just basic-natural logic. As was said at the very outset of Section 8.2, the logic is an EMERGENT PROPERTY of the discourse-semantic incrementation instructions.[23] In fact, IF becomes a logical operator only when discourse factors are left out of account. This implies that the incrementation instructions are richer than the logic emerging from them. It is this extra, nonlogical but purely discourse-semantic resource afforded by the incrementation instructions that we must fall back on now.

The discourse-semantic account of conditionals proposed here implies that incrementation of *Jones wins the election* will only license the incrementation of *Smith will retire to private life* if the **D** at hand is not changed in any significant way by subsequent incrementations, and analogously for the second premiss of the argument *If Smith dies before the election, Jones will win it*. The argument as a whole is valid only if the combined incrementations

---

[23] Cf. Johnson-Laird (1986: 55): 'A corollary of this theory is that the logical properties of conditionals derive from their interpretation and not from any formal rules associated with them.'

of *Jones wins the election* and *Smith dies before the election* still licenses the incrementation of *Smith will retire to private life*. And this is, of course, not so.

This, by the way, is also the conclusion reached in Veltman (1985). Veltman argues that the logic of conditionals, to the extent that it can be a natural logic, is predicated upon a given 'data base'. In our terms, this means that the logic of conditionals must be restricted by a *Modulo D* or *ceteris paribus* condition. It would seem that such a condition hardly lends itself to full formalization, though attempts are made in artificial intelligence to solve the formalization problem by means of nonmonotonic logics.

Further 'paradoxes' resisting a solution in purely logical terms arise in the context of what is known as CONTRAPOSITION. In standard logic the theorem holds that whenever $P \rightarrow Q$ is true, so is $\neg Q \rightarrow \neg P$ and vice versa. In other words, $P \rightarrow Q \equiv \neg Q \rightarrow \neg P$. The same theorem holds in basic-natural logic, because the full expansions of $P \rightarrow Q$ and of $\neg Q \rightarrow \neg P$ are identical: namely $(\neg P \wedge \neg Q) \vee (P \wedge Q)$. Yet, as is observed by McCawley (1981: 50), there is a clear difference between (8.86a) and (8.86b):

(8.86)   a. If you don't have somebody to take my place, I won't leave.
         b. If I leave, you have somebody to take my place.

The first puts a condition on my leaving, while the second expresses a conclusion that can be drawn *post hoc* in the event that I leave. McCawley does not say so, but the difference seems to be connected with the fact, discussed in Section 8.2.1, that, as a matter of default, discourse incrementation follows the temporal, causal, or motivational order of the events or situations described. Given the IF-instruction, this means that the antecedent P is literally an 'antecedent': the *if*-clause is incremented *before* the consequent clause. Sentence (8.86a) respects this principle, since the lack of a replacement is the reason for my not leaving. (8.86b) does too, but in a different way. What (8.86b) says is that in case I leave one may conclude that a replacement has been available. Here my leaving precedes the drawing of the conclusion.[24]

---

[24] Comrie (1986: 83–4) implicitly confirms the principle that, normally, the *if*-clause is incremented before the consequent clause:

Greenberg (1963: 84–5) states the following Universal of Word Order 14 concerning the linear order of the two clauses:

> In conditional statements, the conditional clause [=protasis, BC] precedes the conclusion [=apodosis, BC] as the normal order in all languages.

Work leading up to the present paper has uncovered no counterexamples to this generalization. Although many languages allow both orders, protasis–apodosis and apodosis–protasis, many grammars note explicitly that the usual order is for the protasis to precede, and presumably the same will hold for many languages where the grammars are silent on this point. In some languages the protasis must precede the apodosis, in particular in languages with a rigid rule requiring the finite verb of the main clause to stand sentence-finally (e.g. Turkish). Since the positioning of

In conclusion, we may say that some headway has been made towards the realization of the programme of reducing the deviations from the standard logical analysis of conditionals observed in ordinary language usage to the differences between standard and basic-natural logic and to the design properties of discourse domains, including the instruction for conditionals. To the extent that this programme is successful, an appeal to mostly not very well defined pragmatic principles becomes unnecessary.

protases in such languages can be viewed as just a special case of the general rule whereby subordinate clauses must precede main clauses, this does not necessarily say anything specific about conditional constructions. However, this same restriction to protasis-apodosis order is also found in some languages which do not have a strict subordinate–main clause order restriction, suggesting that there is indeed something special about conditional clauses in this respect, i.e. the preponderance of the protasis–apodosis order in languages with free clause order is not 'just statistical', but does reflect something significant about language.

Primary and donkey anaphora

9.1 Introduction

Apart from the continuous appeal to shared knowledge, there are in principle four main devices in natural language serving the purpose of linking up utterances with the current discourse in such a way that coherence is safeguarded: *anaphora, presupposition, topic–comment modulation,* and *open parameters* in lexical meanings. The latter have been discussed in Section 7.4 and we will not deal with them again. The remaining three devices are relevant in this and the following two chapters because they show up the inadequacy of the Russellian-Quinean-Montagovian paradigm of natural language semantics, with standard modern predicate calculus (SMPC) at its centre. Even though the standard paradigm is meant to account for just the truth-conditional properties of natural language sentences, leaving out the clutter due to the exigencies of communicative usage, it breaks down on a particular form of external anaphora, commonly called *donkey anaphora,* discussed in the present chapter. It also breaks down on presupposition, as is shown in Chapter 10. And one draws a total blank, not only in semantics but also in the theory of grammar, when one looks for any account at all of topic–comment modulation as distinct from predicate–argument structure. Topic–comment modulation, already amply commented upon in Section 3.2 of Volume I, is taken up again in Chapter 11, where its role in the cementing of discourse coherence is further elaborated and situated in a more general cognitive and linguistic context.

The last three chapters of this book are thus a three-pronged attack on the standard paradigm. But the standard paradigm has to cope with other threats as well, less to do with the context-sensitivity of natural language and the criteria for textual coherence. The main threat, apart from the three discussed in Chapters 9, 10, and 11, is the problem of propositional attitudes, discussed earlier in Sections 2.1.1 and 6.1 of Volume I. The inability of the standard paradigm to account for this problem has proved to be due to the very basic tenets of this paradigm, in particular its strictly extensional house ontology, which is incapable of dealing with intensional phenomena. Here, too, the assumption of a cognitive discourse domain, storing all information of any discourse at hand regarding actual or virtual entities and facts, provides the theoretical space required for an adequate solution.

This critique of the standard paradigm does not come out of the blue. Over the past twenty or thirty years there has been a growing awareness of its insufficiency, the emphasis being variably on one or more of the issues mentioned above. One may say that a movement has been gaining ground that no longer supports the rarified, logic-inspired view of natural language and its semantics but aims at developing a more ecological perspective, hard though that proves to be.

During the 1980s, a spate of publications saw the light, all trying to develop a context-sensitive semantics for natural language sentences by means of the introduction of a cognitive intermediary station—called *data base, discourse domain, discourse representation, mental space*, whatever—housing mental representations of anything spoken about, whether actually existing or only virtual. In these theories, reference is no longer seen as some sort of extrasensory, ectoplasmic link, established by some Kripkean flight of metaphysics between definite terms occurring in utterances on the one hand and world objects on the other. Instead, the somewhat more reasonable view is taken according to which definite expressions establish reference via mental representations of entities of whatever kind, our 'addresses', set up earlier in the discourse by means of existential quantification. What mechanism accounts for the intentional relation between the addresses and the objects focused on is still largely a mystery, but at least it is a general mystery—the mystery of what is known as intentionality—affecting all existing theories of the mind.

One important consequence of this new perspective is that definite terms in sentences are now seen as being directed to discourse addresses before any possible relation to really existing world entities can be established. In practical terms this means that the Russell-Quine programme of elimination of singular terms has been given up: referring expressions have been reinstated, after almost a century of exile. The king of France has again become the king of France, even though he does not exist. The referential problem created by his nonexistence is taken to be solvable, in principle, by the introduction of the intermediary station of a discourse domain.

Seuren (1972, 1975), Isard (1975), and Stalnaker (1978) were early harbingers, setting out the perspective of a store accumulating the information carried by successive utterances in a discourse and thus being added to by every new utterance. The first more formally precise approach was DISCOURSE REPRESENTATION THEORY (DRT), introduced in Kamp (1981) and further elaborated in Kamp and Reyle (1993). The roots of this theory lie in the donkey-anaphora problem, discussed in Section 9.2.2, which is correctly diagnosed as potentially fatal for the established paradigm of possible-world formal semantics. In this theory, the mechanism of reference is mediated by a cognitive system of mental representations, whose relation to any actual world is a matter of independent concern. The discourse representations envisaged by Kamp and Reyle not only contain entity representations but also store any propositional information about the intended referents provided by prior linguistic input. This halfway station of mental representations creates the extra room needed for a semantic account of donkey anaphora. DRT is not a logical theory but a formal theory of utterance incrementation, even though the format in which newly incremented information is represented looks very much like the well-known structure of SMPC expressions. The actual corresponding logic has been investigated by Groenendijk and Stokhof in a number of joint publications, notably their 1991 paper on 'Dynamic Predicate Logic'. The main difficulty with DRT is that its focus is too much on the donkey-anaphora problem, leaving entirely out of account the notion of presupposition, let alone that of topic–comment modulation, indispensable though these are for any adequate theory of discourse incrementation. Nor does it offer a principled solution to the problem of reference to nonexisting entities: there is no theory of virtual or intensional entities. In general, one may say that DRT is a typical example of a theory that has been fully formalized before the object of the theory has been looked at from all angles so that one's familiarity with the object gives one an adequate idea of what is to be formalized. Such premature formalization may impress the world for some time, but it is detrimental to the advancement of lasting knowledge.

Practitioners of DRT have not been insensitive to the criticism that their theory fails to account for presuppositions. Van der Sandt (1992) made an attempt at incorporating presupposition theory into the anaphora-based framework of DRT by equating presupposition with anaphora. This made it look as if the presupposition deficiency of DRT could be remedied in one swoop by declaring anaphora and presupposition one—a point of view readily taken over by DRT-practitioners who were all too eager to dispose of presuppositions, which they had all along regarded with diffidence and suspicion and which they were only too glad to get rid of. In fact, in the short section on presupposition in the article on DRT in the *Stanford Encyclopedia of Philosophy* (Geurts and Beaver 2007), the authors take it for granted that, indeed, presupposition and anaphora are of a piece. Since this misunderstanding has meanwhile gained some currency, a separate section (Section 10.8) has been added to Chapter 10, dedicated to its refutation. There it is shown that this *prima facie* absurd view is sustainable only if the notions of presupposition and of anaphora are kept fuzzy and essential facts are ignored.

The SITUATIONAL SEMANTICS of Barwise and Perry (1983) is another representative of this class of theories. This theory sprouts mainly from the authors' dissatisfaction with two aspects of the standard paradigm, namely its inability to cope with propositional attitudes (see Sections 2.1.1 and 6.1 in Volume I) and the lack of a proper demarcation of the contextually and situationally restricted universe of discourse in terms of which utterance interpretation takes place. No attention is paid to the donkey-anaphora problem, nor is there an account of reference to nonexisting entities. Presuppositions likewise stay out of the picture, even though their function in the delimitation of restricted universes of discourse should have been obvious. The question of topic–comment modulation remains untouched.

In Fauconnier (1985) a system of 'mental spaces', complete with 'subspaces', is proposed in order to account for what is called 'transdominial denotational transparency' in Section 7.2.2.1. This highly readable but entirely informal little book concentrates on examples like *The girl with brown eyes has blue eyes* (see also Section 5.3 in Volume I). Contrary to what one might expect, this sentence is not internally inconsistent. Suppose there is a picture containing the portraits of a number of girls, one of whom is portrayed as having brown eyes, even though in reality she has blue eyes. In such a situation, the sentence is true. The expression *the girl with brown eyes* then refers to the girl as portrayed in the picture, which is mentally represented as a special subspace. The predication *has blue eyes* takes the listener back to the real world, mentally represented as the overall commitment domain. But the same sentence may also be taken as saying that the girl who in reality has brown eyes has blue eyes in the picture. Which of the two readings applies, depends on the context in which the sentence is uttered. This essay is illuminating in many ways but its scope is too restricted, and its elaboration too informal, for it to qualify as a theory of context-sensitive utterance interpretation.

All three theories or approaches mentioned thus lack the generality that is required for a proper theory of context-sensitive utterance interpretation. I myself started out on this road as early as 1972, with my lengthy paper (1972) in *Leuvense Bijdragen*, which contains a fairly elaborate section on discourse incrementation and presupposition as a condition on incrementability. I believe this was the first publication, even preceding Isard (1975), where the notion of discourse incrementation was mooted (apart from Stout 1896, mentioned and quoted extensively in Section 3.2 in Volume I). Yet it was never acknowledged, then or later, though many protagonists of the new contextually oriented semantics were Dutch and thus had no difficulty reading it. This was followed by Seuren (1975), which was again written in Dutch, again contained lengthy sections on discourse semantics and was again left unacknowledged by the Dutch establishment, though not by the establishments in neighbouring countries. In 1979, I presented a paper at the Mannheim *Institut für deutsche Sprache* on the three-valued logic which I take to be required for presupposition theory, published as Seuren (1980). Hans Kamp, whose seminal article appeared in 1981, had been invited to reply to this paper. Then came my 1985 book *Discourse Semantics*, where a fairly elaborate theory of discourse incrementation is presented, complete with the notion of address closure discussed in Section 8.1.1. In that book, the basis of the theory of discourse semantics is widened to include not only its original starting point of presupposition theory but also donkey anaphora and topic–comment modulation, as well as the question of propositional attitudes. The present book may be seen in part as a sequel to my *Discourse Semantics* of 1985, in that it attempts to lay as broad a basis as possible for the new theory.

9.2 Reference by anaphora

Let us start with the problem of donkey anaphora, which, however, needs some introduction. The word *anaphora* is Greek and it means literally 'pick-up' or 'uptake'. What we mean by anaphora in linguistics is, roughly, the phenomenon that certain nominal expressions exercise their referential power via another expression or element in the discourse domain, called the *antecedent*, which is either a directly referring nominal expression or a quantifier or, in cases of what we call 'primary anaphora', the open address established by a previous existentially quantified sentence. Anaphoric expressions are usually third person personal or possessive pronouns, but they may also be full lexical noun phrases, such as the English phrases *the former*, *the latter*, or the so-called 'epithet' pronouns, about which more in a moment, or the indirectly referring noun phrases serving as 'enriched' pronouns illustrated in the Swiss banker example (7.23) of Section 7.2.2.4. Many languages, such as the languages of Europe, have number and gender distinctions for their anaphoric pronouns—whereby gender corresponds variably to either grammatical or natural gender—to facilitate anaphoric uptake, but not all languages do. Creole languages, for example, tend to do without gender distinctions and Malay even does without number distinctions.

There is a vast, but not entirely conclusive, literature that attempts to establish rules and principles for the uptake function of anaphoric expressions, called *anaphora resolution*. The commonly accepted view is that a primary distinction must be made between sentence-internal and sentence-external anaphora, depending on whether the antecedent is to be located within the same sentence or outside it. This view is largely, but not entirely, correct. It is true that sentence-internal anaphora is subject to structural conditions in a way that external anaphora is not—a difference that is reflected in the fact that it is mostly grammarians who write on internal anaphora resolution, whereas the literature on external anaphora is largely psycholinguistic and/or pragmatic.[1] But the two cannot be separated too strictly, as the following will make clear.

Let us, for a moment, look at sentence-internal anaphora, which is subject to sentence-internal structurally definable restrictions. First consider clause-internal anaphora, as in (9.1a–d). One notes that in (9.1a,b) the possessive pronoun *his* is ambiguous between a reading in which the office belongs to John (the internal reading) and one in which it belongs to some other person who is not mentioned (the external reading). But in (9.1c,d), the anaphoric pronoun *he* must refer to an external person and cannot take the noun phrase *John* as its antecedent:

(9.1)   a. In his office John reads detective stories.
         b. John reads detective stories in his office.
         c. In John's office he reads detective stories.
         d. He reads detective stories in John's office.

The least one can deduce from this is that there are structural restrictions on the choice of antecedents for anaphoric uptake. That these are not trivial transpires when one looks at clause-external but still sentence-internal anaphora, as in (9.2a–d). Here, both the internal and the external reading are possible for (9.2a,b,c) but not for (9.2d), which only allows for the external reading:

(9.2)   a. While his office was being cleaned, John stood on the balcony.
         b. John stood on the balcony while his office was being cleaned.
         c. While John's office was being cleaned, he stood on the balcony.
         d. He stood on the balcony while John's office was being cleaned.

---

[1] For detailed discussions of sentence-internal anaphora, see Reinhart (1983), Seuren (1985: 346–86; 1986*b*) and Weijters (1989).

The odd one out is the c-variant in (9.1) and (9.2): (9.1c) only allows for the external reading, but (9.2c), like (9.2a,b), allows for both the internal and the external reading.

The matter becomes even more intriguing when EPITHET PRONOUNS are taken into account (see also the examples in (4.41) of Chapter 4 in Volume I). These are, grammatically speaking, not really pronouns but full lexical noun phrases, though with an anaphoric function. They are always unstressed and usually express an evaluation of some kind. Examples are the following (the epithet pronouns are in italics):

(9.3)   a. Where is John? I just saw *the great genius* leaving the building.
        b. As John entered the room, *the maniac* saw it was empty.

Now consider again (9.1a–d), but with the epithet pronoun *the fool* instead of the neutral *his* or *he*:

(9.4)   a. In the fool's office John reads detective stories.
        b. John reads detective stories in the fool's office.
        c. In John's office the fool reads detective stories.
        d. The fool reads detective stories in John's office.

One sees that the internal reading has disappeared altogether: all four sentences only allow for the external reading. However, the same does not hold for the epithet analogs of (9.2):

(9.5)   a. While the fool's office was being cleaned, John stood on the balcony.
        b. John stood on the balcony while the fool's office was being cleaned.
        c. While John's office was being cleaned, the fool stood on the balcony.
        d. The fool stood on the balcony while John's office was being cleaned.

Here, as in (9.2), the internal reading is allowed for (9.5a,b,c) but not for (9.5d).

The epithet-substitution test is a useful but neglected diagnostic in anaphora theory. It shows, for example, that there must be some hidden difference between the status of *his* in (9.1a,b) as opposed to (9.2a,b). This difference is expressed formally in some languages, like Latin or Swedish, which both distinguish between a reflexive and a nonreflexive third person possessive pronoun. In Latin, the reflexive possessive pronoun is the adjectivally declined *suus*, while the nonreflexive variant is expressed in the singular by the genitive *eius* (of him/her/it) of the third person personal pronoun *is* (this, he) and in the plural by *eorum* (of them). Analogously, Swedish distinguishes between the adjectival *sin* and the personal pronoun genitive *hans*, the former being the reflexive, the latter the nonreflexive *his*. In both

Latin and Swedish, the translations of (9.1a,b) differentiate between the internal reading, which has *suus* or *sin*, and the external reading, which has *eius* or *hans*, respectively. By contrast, (9.2a,b) are ungrammatical in Latin and Swedish with *suus* or *sin*, but grammatical (and ambiguous) with *eius* or *hans*, respectively.

A similar phenomenon crops up in *that*-clauses and dependent questions:

(9.6) a. John told me that *he* was unable to attend the meeting.
       b. John told me that *the great hero* was unable to attend the meeting.
       c. John asked whether it was all right for *him* to leave.
       d. John asked whether it was all right for *the poor sod* to leave.

Again one sees that insertion of an epithet pronoun blocks the internal reading.

Pronouns occurring in a position where they are bound by a quantifier never allow for substitution *salva resolutione* by an epithet pronoun:

(9.7) a. Somebody must have been thinking that *he* would win.
       b. Somebody must have been thinking that *the brute* would win.
       c. In those days, every husband expected his wife to obey *him*.
       d. In those days, every husband expected his wife to obey *the brute*.

Clearly, the expression *the brute* in (9.7b) and (9.7d) blocks the bound-variable reading of *him* in (9.7a) and (9.7c), respectively, thus leaving the external anaphoric reading as the only possible one.

Sentence-external anaphora is, on the whole, less subject to structural restrictions than to considerations of distance and pragmatic plausibility. It is also the form of anaphora that plays a major role in the machinery that links up utterances with the discourse and the situation at hand. Inevitably, therefore, sentence-external anaphora is more relevant, for the present purpose, than sentence-internal anaphora. Yet sentence-internal anaphora cannot be ignored, because there is an issue in the literature as to the status of certain pronouns that cannot be rendered in SMPC, the so-called *donkey pronouns*. According to some, these should be treated as sentence-internal pronouns, but it is argued here that they represent a particular form of sentence-external anaphora called *primary anaphora*.

In order to discuss these issues properly, we need to be able to fall back on at least a summary survey of the restrictions valid for sentence-internal anaphora. For that reason, we posit the following tentative and incomplete list of anaphor categories and their resolution conditions:

I *Clause-internal anaphora.*
   a. Reflexive anaphora: takes subject (sometimes indirect object) as antecedent; not always formally marked.
   b. C-command anaphora: anaphor must be C-commanded by antecedent.[2]
   c. Non-C-command anaphora: antecedent must precede anaphor.

II *Clause-external but sentence-internal anaphora.*
   a. Indirect reflexive anaphora: occurs only in complement clauses and anaphor takes subject, direct or indirect object of commanding clause as antecedent; rarely formally marked.
   b. Nonreflexive anaphora: occurs in clauses of any rank and anaphor takes any NP in any other clause as antecedent, but if antecedent is in a lower clause, it must precede the anaphor.[3]

III *Bound-variable anaphora.* The anaphor stands for a bound variable in the semantic analysis (SA) of the sentence in question and is, therefore, subject to the structural conditions of variable binding in L_L, not in surface structure.

IV *Sentence-external anaphora.* The antecedent is any overt or implicitly understood NP in preceding text or in the situation given. Anaphora resolution is subject to gradable criteria of closeness, pragmatic probability, and syntactic function, besides, of course, to restrictions imposed by gender and number, if any.[4,5]

---

[2] *C-command* (Reinhart 1983) is a tree-structural notion defined as follows:

A node **A** C-commands a node **B** just in case the first node up from **A** dominates **B** and **A** does not dominate **B** and **B** does not dominate **A**.

There is C-command anaphora in (i) but not in (ii); (iii) is probably a case of formally unmarked reflexive anaphora ('*' stands for 'epithet substitution not permitted'):

 (i) She told John about his (*the bugger's) parents.
 (ii) She told John's daughter about his (the bugger's) parents.
 (iii) His (*the bugger's) mother told John to stop laughing.

[3] Hence the difference between (9.2a,b,c) on the one hand and (9.2d) on the other. In (9.2a,b,c), *John* can be the antecedent of *his*, but in (9.2d) it cannot, because *John* occurs in a lower clause but does not precede *his.*

[4] It is pointed out in Tasmowski-de Rijck and Verluyten (1982) that external anaphora to objects given in the situation but not mentioned in previous text is subject to gender restrictions that follow the grammatical gender of the noun that would have been used had the object actually been named, as is shown by the following examples, both meaning 'you will never get it through the door':

 (i) Tu ne *le* feras jamais passer par la porte. (said of a desk, French: *le bureau*)
 (ii) Tu ne *la* feras jamais passer par la porte. (said of a table, French: *la table*)

[5] An extremely interesting category of external primary anaphora was discovered by Moxey and Sanford (1986/7) (see also Sanford et al. 2007). They found that a large majority of test subjects, who

We stipulate, furthermore, that epithet anaphora is possible, *salva resolutione*, only for the categories Ic, IIb, and IV. These can be grouped together as *unbound anaphora*; the remaining categories can be grouped as *bound anaphora*. Whereas bound anaphora is subject to a variety of structurally defined forms of binding, the main, and perhaps even necessary, condition on unbound anaphora is antecedent precedence. Cases of a sentence-external 'antecedent' following later in the text are extremely rare, as opposed to bound anaphora, where this phenomenon is sometimes called by the name of *cataphora*.

Having said this, we now pass on to primary anaphora, which has been our target all along: all that has been said about anaphora so far was only said because we needed to get at primary anaphora, a central but hitherto unsolved problem in the semantics and the logic of natural language.

9.3 Primary anaphora: bound variable or external anaphor?

Primary anaphora is a particular form of sentence-external anaphora, namely that form of anaphora where the antecedent is not a referring expression or a universal quantifier but an existentially introduced address. A primary anaphor usually occurs right after the existential introduction of its antecedent, which, again, is not a linguistic element in preceding text but the newly introduced address. Primary anaphora has caused a great deal of confusion owing to the wish of certain prominent investigators to treat primary anaphors as bound-variable pronouns. It is argued here that this is misguided. Primary anaphora is a category in its own right.

A typical example of primary anaphora is given in sentence (9.8), where the pronoun serving as primary anaphor has been printed in italics:

(9.8)   Socrates owns a donkey and he feeds *it*.

I have deliberately used a 'donkey' example, to make it clear that cases of primary anaphora are of a piece with the well-known cases of donkey

---

were given the task of completing sentences like (i) interpreted the pronoun *they* as referring to the members who were **not** at the meeting—a form of anaphora for which they invented the term *complement anaphora*:

(i) Few students were at the meeting. *They* ...

The subjects would, for example, complete the sentence as *They had gone out with their girl-friends*. The only way to explain this seems to be the assumption of a discourse address established for the students who were **not** at the meeting, the complement of the set delimited by FEW. If anything, this shows the necessity to fall back on cognition-driven discourse incrementation processes for the explanation of reference fixing.

anaphora. But I might as well have adopted the example *There was a cat; it ran away* discussed in Section 8.1.1 in connection with the procedure of address closure, which, as we shall see, is essential in the present context.

Why is primary anaphora important? It is important in its own right because it is a central instrument for maintaining coherence in discourse, but it is also important because it constitutes a problem for the logical analysis of natural language sentences that has hitherto not found a final solution. It turns out that established logic lacks the means to account for primary anaphora and that this failure is entirely due to its decision to keep occasion sentences away from the analysis. In other words, standard modern logic trips over primary anaphora and it does so precisely because it fails to make room for context-sensitivity.

9.4 Donkey sentences

The problem of donkey anaphora is extremely well known and has been so since the publication of Peter Geach's 1962 book *Reference and Generality.* Owing to this book, the problem has acquired its curious name 'donkey-sentences problem', since the relevant examples in Geach (1962) all involve mention of donkeys. We shall see in a moment that Geach was less than frank about his sources, but before that, let us see what the problem actually amounts to.

9.4.1 *The problem*

In terms of modern logic, the problem is that the status of *it* in a sentence like (9.8) is unclear. In (first-order) SMPC, a term in a proposition that has a truth value must either be an expression referring to an actually existing entity or set of entities, or be a variable bound by a quantifier and ranging over such entities. In fact, SMPC went further and adopted Quine's 'programme of elimination of singular terms', trying to avoid the problem of reference to nonexisting entities by reducing all definite descriptions to quantified terms. A systematic application of this programme should, in Quine's eyes, provide answers to all the many problems connected with reference. In his *Word and Object* (1960: 181–6), Quine supported and generalized Russell's analysis of definite terms, proposing that the regimented 'canonical' form of sentences, which displays just their logical properties without the clutter accrued from the impure conditions of usage, should contain no referring expressions at all. All statements about the world could then be expressed with the help of the two standard quantifiers and propositional functions containing the variables bound by them. In principle, this leaves SMPC sentences with only one kind of argument term: variables that are bound by a quantifier. Hence Quine's slogan: 'To be is to be the value of a variable' (Quine 1953: 13, 15). The problem is that the so-called donkey anaphors do not fit into this theory.

Consider *it* in sentence (9.8). If this *it* is a referring expression and, therefore, (9.8) has the logical form 'P ∧ Q', there are two problems. First, in case P is false, the *it* in Q fails to refer, so that Q remains without a truth value, which is against the rules. Secondly, suppose Socrates has two donkeys, one of which he feeds while the other he does not, then (9.8) is true, but so is (9.9a), analysed as (9.9b):

(9.9)   a. Socrates owns a donkey and he does not feed *it*.
        b. P ∧ ¬Q

And this is intolerable, as propositional logic tells us that P ∧ Q and P ∧ ¬Q are contraries. It thus looks as if the *it* of sentence (9.8), or, for that matter, of sentence (9.9a), cannot be a referring term and must, therefore, be a bound variable.

This is, in fact, what is proposed in Geach (1972: 115–27). There, Geach analyses (9.8) and (9.9a) as (9.10a) and (9.10b), respectively (using the Russellian and not the generalized quantifiers):

(9.10)   a. ∃x[Donkey(x) ∧ Own(Socrates,x) ∧ Feed(Socrates,x)]
         b. ∃x[Donkey(x) ∧ Own(Socrates,x) ∧ ¬Feed(Socrates,x)]

Yet, as was pointed out in Seuren (1977, 2001: 316–18), Geach failed to consider sentences like (9.11a,b), with each conjunct under an independent higher operator:

(9.11)   a. Socrates must own a donkey and he may feed *it*.
         b. I believe that Socrates owns a donkey and I hope that he feeds *it*.

No binding of *it* under a quantifier, as in (9.10a,b), is possible here. For either the quantifier must have large, overall scope for *a donkey*, turning (9.11a,b) into sentences about a specific donkey that Socrates must own and may feed, or that I believe Socrates owns and I hope he feeds. But this is not what these sentences mean. Or else, to ensure proper binding, the second operator (*may, hope*) must be placed in the scope of the first (*must, believe*), in something like the following way:

(9.12)   a. MUST[∃x[Donkey(x) ∧ Own(Socrates,x) ∧ MAY[Feed
(Socrates,x)]]]
    b. Believe(I,∃x[Donkey(x) ∧ Own(Socrates,x) ∧ Hope(I,
Feed(Socrates,x))])

Or, in the language of decent citizens:

(9.13)   a. It is necessary that Socrates owns a donkey and that he may feed it.
    b. I believe that Socrates owns a donkey and that I hope that he
feeds it.

It is obvious that (9.13a,b) do not mean what (9.11a,b) do. In fact, what
(9.13a,b) mean is a little quaint, to say the least. What one would like to see
is an analysis of, indeed, the form P ∧ Q, but with a stranded variable in Q for
the pronoun *it*. But stranded variables are anathema in modern predicate
logic. It thus appears that Geach's analysis comes to nothing and, worse, that
the *it* in question constitutes an embarrassment for SMPC.

The cases with intervening operators, such as (9.11a,b), have already been
taken care of in Section 8.1.1, where the sentence, here repeated as (9.14), is
discussed:

(9.14)   John claims that he owns a Ferrari, but I have never seen *it*.

The mechanism set out in Section 8.1.1 sets up an open intensional address for
the specific but not necessarily actually existing Ferrari John claims he owns.
Owing to the fact that the existential quantifier has been robbed of existential
import, this address does not entail that it is an actually existing Ferrari that is
at issue. After all, the Ferrari may well be, and probably is, nothing more than
a virtual object. This address can then be fallen back on for closure and
definite reference. The donkey pronouns *it* in (9.11a,b) or (9.14), and all
other donkey pronouns, are, in my theory, to be analysed as external definite
anaphoric pronouns that take an earlier established address as their antecedent. According to the Principle of Maximal Unity of discourse domains
(Section 7.2.2), there are no domain restrictions on pronominal anaphora:
all (sub)domains are anaphorically accessible from all (sub)domains.

A second reason why Geach's attempt at solving this problem does not
work, besides the intervening operators as in (9.11), is provided by the epithet-
substitution test. In the following sentences, the anaphora resolution remains
unchanged, which shows that the anaphoric expressions cannot stand for
bound variables but must be cases of external anaphora and thus belong to
category IV:

(9.15)   a. Socrates owns a donkey and he feeds *the animal.*
         b. Socrates must own a donkey, and he may feed *the animal.*
         c. I believe that Socrates owns a donkey, and I hope that he feeds *the animal.*

But this is not all. In formal semantics, the problem of donkey sentences started out with sentence types different from the simple conjunctions of (9.8) or (9.9a). The standard types of donkey sentence are exemplified in (9.16a,b,c):

(9.16)   a. Either Socrates does not own a donkey or he feeds *it.*
         b. If Socrates owns a donkey, he feeds *it.*
         c. Every farmer who owns a donkey feeds *it.*

Here, the same problem crops up. In standard model-theoretic semantics, based on SMPC and standard propositional logic, these sentences must be considered true in worlds not containing any donkey at all. As regards (9.16a), *Socrates does not own a donkey* is true in such a world, which should make (9.16a) true were it not for the fact that the pronoun *it* in the second disjunct *he feeds it* cannot be subjected to the Russell treatment for definite descriptions because it isn't a definite description but a pronoun. It must, therefore, represent a bound variable.

Likewise for (9.16b). In a world without any donkeys, *Socrates owns a donkey* is false, which should make (9.16b) true in such a world. But again, the pronoun *it* in the consequent clause resists Russell's treatment, so that it must represent a bound variable. Similarly again for (9.16c). In a world without donkeys there can be no donkey-owners, which should make (9.16c) true in such a world. Again, however, a logical translation of (9.16c) requires that the pronoun *it* be taken to represent a bound variable. However, as is shown in (9.17a–c), the normal and most straightforward translation method of natural language sentences into SMPC leads to trouble because *it* refuses to be bound (the 'asinus' symbol @ stands for the term that causes the binding trouble):

(9.17)   a. $\neg\exists x[\text{Donkey}(x) \wedge \text{Own}(\text{Socrates},x)] \vee \text{Feed}(\text{Socrates}, @)$
         b. $\exists x[\text{Donkey}(x) \wedge \text{Own}(\text{Socrates},x)] \rightarrow \text{Feed}(\text{Socrates}, @)$
         c. $\forall y[\text{Farmer}(y) \wedge \exists x[\text{Donkey}(x) \wedge \text{Own}(y,x)] \rightarrow \text{Feed}(y, @)]$

The problem is, obviously, that the variable x, which one would like to see in the position of the asinus @ in (9.17a–c), is not allowed to occur there because it falls outside the scope of any of the quantifiers involved.

And, again, the analyses given in (9.17a–c) fail to satisfy the epithet-substitution test, which shows that the *it*-pronouns in question cannot be bound-variable pronouns but must be instances of either clause-external but sentence-internal anaphora (category IIb), or sentence-external, in particular primary, anaphora (category IV):

(9.18)   a. Either Socrates does not own a donkey or he feeds *the animal*.
          b. If Socrates owns a donkey, he feeds *the animal*.
          c. Every farmer who owns a donkey feeds *the animal*.

Quine (1960) shows no awareness of the donkey-anaphora problem. He does, however, deal with a similar problem posed by sentences of the type (1960: 138):

(9.19)   If any member contributes, *he* gets a poppy.

If the word *any* is taken to represent the existential quantifier, the pronoun *he* is left stranded, or, as Quine says (1960: 139), 'left high and dry':

(9.20) $\exists x[Member(x) \land Contribute(x)] \rightarrow \exists y[Poppy(y) \land Get(@,y)]$

Quine then proposes not to use the existential quantifier and get the universal quantifier to do all the work, stipulating that 'by a simple and irreducible trait of English usage', *every* always takes the smallest and *any* the largest possible scope. (9.19) would then translate into SMPC as (21):

(9.21) $\forall x[[Member(x) \land Contribute(x)] \rightarrow \exists y[Poppy(y) \land Get(x,y)]]$

This proposal was used later in an attempt to solve the problem of the stranded variables in cases like (9.17a–c). The idea was to translate (9.16a–c) with the help of the universal quantifier only:

(9.22)   a. $\forall x[Donkey(x) \rightarrow [\neg Own(Socrates,x) \lor Feed(Socrates,x)]]$
          b. $\forall x[Donkey(x) \rightarrow [Own(Socrates,x) \rightarrow Feed(Socrates,x)]]$
          c. $\forall x \forall y[[Donkey(x) \land Farmer(y) \land Own(y,x)] \rightarrow Feed(y,x)]$

This does indeed eliminate the scope problem raised by (9.17a–c). Yet the medicine has proved worse than the ailment. First, one wonders why natural language chooses to use, clearly without any problem for natural interpretation processes, surface-structure representatives of the existential quantifier (*a donkey, no donkey*), allowing unbound variables to dangle, instead of the perfectly available surface-structure representatives of the universal quantifier, if that is the quantifier used in the underlying logico-semantic structure. In other words, one wonders what could justify the sudden change in the translation or mapping relation between the logico-semantic and the grammatical form of the sentences involved. A Quinean appeal to 'simple and irreducible traits of English usage' obviously won't do.

Secondly, Quine failed to mention that in a sentence like *If **some** member contributes, **he** gets a poppy* the same scope problem occurs for *it* as in *If **any** member contributes, **he** gets a poppy*. One wonders if he would have shrunk from putting forward the daring proposal to treat the word *some* as a representative of the universal quantifier.

Thirdly, the epithet-substitution test shows that *he* in (9.19) cannot represent a bound variable. And finally, and most seriously, Quine's universal quantifier ploy falls again foul of possible intervening operators, as is shown by the following sentences:

(9.23)　a. Either Socrates no longer owns a donkey or he still feeds *it*.
　　　　 b. If it's bad that Socrates owns a donkey, it's good that he feeds *it*.
　　　　 c. Every farmer who is thought to own a donkey is expected to feed *it*.

The only way of binding *it* under the spurious universal quantifier is to place the quantifier over the whole structure, as in (9.24a,b,c), respectively.

(9.24)　a. $\forall x[\text{Donkey}(x) \rightarrow [\text{NO LONGER}[\text{Own}(\text{Socrates},x)] \lor \text{STILL} [\text{Feed}(\text{Socrates},x)]]]$
　　　　 b. $\forall x[\text{Donkey}(x) \rightarrow [\text{BAD}[\text{Own}(\text{Socrates},x)] \rightarrow \text{GOOD}[\text{Feed} (\text{Socrates},x)]]]$
　　　　 c. $\forall x \forall y[[\text{Donkey}(x) \land \text{Farmer}(y) \land \text{Thought}[\text{Own}(y,x)]] \rightarrow \text{Expected}[\text{Feed}(y,x)]]$

Yet (9.24a,b,c) are incompatible with what the sentences in question mean. (9.24a) is true, in SMPC, when there are no donkeys at all, and also, if there are donkeys, when Socrates still feeds them all even if he has never owned any of them. But (9.23a) cannot be considered true in such a case.

Likewise for (9.24b), which fails because it is gratuitously true (in SMPC) if there are no donkeys, whereas (9.23b) cannot be true in such a case. (Since both operators *it's bad* and *it's good* are factive, (9.23b) presupposes that Socrates owns and feeds a donkey, and presupposition failure cannot lead to truth.) Moreover, (9.23b) is not a statement about all donkeys, but rather says that if it's bad that Socrates is a donkey-owner, it's good that he feeds the donkey he owns.

Likewise again for (9.24c), which is true in all cases where there is no specific donkey thought to be owned by any specific farmer. In that case, no donkey and no farmer will satisfy $\text{Thought}[\text{Own}(x,y)]$, which makes (9.24c) gratuitously true. But (9.23c) can be false in such a case, namely when there is at least one farmer thought to be a donkey-owner (though no-one has an idea about which donkey he owns) but not expected to feed the animal he is thought to own. For (9.23c) is not about all donkeys but about farmers who are thought to be donkey-owners.

And again, the epithet-substitution test shows that the *it*s in (9.23a,b,c) cannot be bound-variable pronouns but must be external anaphors. One is, therefore, forced to conclude that SMPC is unable to account for them in a way that bears normal scientific generalization and avoids ad hoc solutions. The same conclusion holds for sentences of the types illustrated in (9.8), (9.11), (9.16), (9.19) and (9.23).

The upshot is, therefore, that there is a hard core of sentences, those containing donkey anaphora, which resist translation into SMPC. With or without Russell's analysis of definite descriptions, or Quine's programme of elimination of singular terms, SMPC is intrinsically unable to account for donkey anaphora. The donkey sentences contain definite expressions, pronouns, or pronominal epithets, which are neither directly referring expressions nor bound variables but indirectly referring expressions whose antecedent is hidden in a preceding existentially quantified sentence—the category of primary anaphora, which is not catered for in SMPC. One must conclude that, for such sentence types, SMPC is, by the terms of its own charter, unable to provide an empirically adequate and methodologically sound logico-semantic analysis.

9.4.2 *The history of the problem*

Something like the donkey-anaphora problem was already known in the late Middle Ages. As has been said, the currency of the term 'donkey sentences' in modern formal semantics originates with the 1962 book *Reference and Generality* by the British philosopher Peter Geach, whose discussion of certain sentences, all about donkeys, awakened the interest of modern logicians. But Geach did not mention—apart from token references on page 116 to 'another sort of medieval example' and on page 118 to 'medieval logicians'—that he took his cue from the British nominalist philosopher Walter Burleigh (±1275–after 1344), who introduced donkey sentences in the context of supposition theory, the medieval equivalent of reference theory.[6] In Burleigh (1988: 92), written around 1328, one finds examples like:

---

[6] I owe this information to Joachim Ballweg of the *Institut für deutsche Sprache* in Mannheim.

(9.25)   Omnis homo habens asinum videt illum.
        Every man owning a donkey sees it.

Burleigh's problem has nothing to do with the empirical inadequacy of SMPC as an analytical-descriptive language for natural language meanings. That problem would have been an anachronism in his day, even though the truth conditions for quantified sentences were the subject of widespread debate. His problem was of a different nature. Although SMPC was not yet about, it was known, in Burleigh's day, that there are what we now call bound-variable pronouns, as in:

(9.26)   All boys feared that the dogs would bite *them*.

Burleigh investigates the question of anaphora resolution for bound-variable pronouns and puts forward the principle that these may never take as antecedent a constituent of the clause containing the quantifying expression. In this context, he presents (9.25) as an apparent counterexample, since the pronoun *illum* takes as antecedent *asinum*, which stands under the same verb (*videt*) and is thus in the same clause. His answer is that one should not look at the surface structure but at the underlying logical structure, where *asinum*, the antecedent of *illum*, is not a constituent of the same clause but of the subordinate relative clause *qui habet asinum* (who owns a donkey), which saves his principle. Presumably, Burleigh did not realize that in his analysis *illum* is not a bound-variable pronoun but an instance of external anaphora, in fact, a special case of primary anaphora.

Geach (1962) discusses the same problem and in the same context: how to account for the antecedent relation when the antecedent occurs in a relative clause under a quantified term. His treatment of (9.25) and similar cases in his (1962) is, on the whole, rather circumstantial and not always entirely perspicuous, due, it seems, to his double perspective of medieval and modern theories of reference and quantification. But it does transpire that he disagrees with Burleigh, though without ever mentioning him. Other than Burleigh, and in accordance with the twentieth-century trend to disenfranchise definite terms, he insists on treating *illum* as representing a bound variable. He must, therefore, look for some way of binding *illum* in the way of standard modern quantification theory or SMPC.

It would stand to reason, he says (1962: 117), to treat *man who owns a donkey* in the sentences (9.27a,b), which he considers to be contradictories, as a complex predicate 'replaceable by the single word "donkey-owner"'. But if we do that, (9.27a,b) 'become unintelligible [...] because "it" is deprived of an antecedent':

(9.27)   a. Any man who owns a donkey feeds it.
      b. Some man who owns a donkey does not feed it.

A solution could conceivably be found in rewording these sentences as (9.28a,b) (1962: 117):

(9.28)   a. Any man who owns a donkey, owns a donkey and feeds it.
      b. Some man who owns a donkey owns a donkey and does not feed it.

Yet, he says, (9.27) and (9.28) are not equivalent: whereas (9.27a) and (9.27b) are contradictories, in accordance with the logic of both the classic Square of Opposition and SMPC, (9.28a) and (9.28b) are not (1962: 118):[7]

[F]or both [(9.28a) and (9.28b)] would be true if each donkey-owner had two donkeys and beat only one of them. Medieval logicians would apparently have accepted the alleged equivalences; for they argued that a pair such as [(9.27a)] and [(9.27b)] could both be true [...] and were therefore not contradictories. But plainly [(9.27a)] and [(9.27b)], as they would normally be understood, are in fact contradictories; in the case supposed, [(9.27b)] would be true and [(9.27a)] false.

The 'medieval logicians' Geach argues against are in fact none other than the never-mentioned Walter Burleigh, who adds the following comment to his discussion of (9.25), thereby denying that (9.27a) and (9.27b) are contradictories (1988: 92–3; translation mine):

It follows that the following are compatible: 'Every man owning a donkey sees it' and 'Some man owning a donkey does not see it'. For assuming that every man owns two donkeys, one of which he sees and one of which he does not see, then it is not only true to say 'Every man owning a donkey sees it', but also to say 'Some man owning a donkey does not see it'. In the same way, suppose that every man who has a son also has two sons, and that he loves the one but hates the other, then both the following are true: 'Every man who has a son loves him' and 'Some man who has a son does not love him'.

Burleigh and Geach are thus seen to disagree on account of the truth conditions of sentences like (9.27a,b). For Burleigh, these two sentences are compatible and not contradictories. For Geach, however, they are contradictories.

---

[7] Geach has his farmers *beat* their donkeys. As this would offend the feelings of many readers with more developed notions of animal rights, I use *feed*, rather than *beat*, in my examples.

Geach's solution is to analyse a relative clause under a quantified term as an implication under universal and a conjunction under existential quantification:

(9.29)   a. Any man, if he owns a donkey, feeds it.
          b. Some man owns a donkey and he does not feed it.

This, he says, 'is quite unforced and does give us a pair of contradictories, as it ought' (Geach 1962: 118). He does not say what precise SMPC renderings he has in mind for (9.29a,b), but we can give him the benefit of the doubt and translate them as (9.30a,b), respectively:

(9.30)   a. $\forall x[Man(x) \rightarrow \forall y[[Donkey(y) \wedge Own(x,y)] \rightarrow Feed(x,y)]]$
          b. $\exists x \exists y[Man(x) \wedge Donkey(y) \wedge Own(x,y) \wedge \neg Feed(x,y)]$

Whether this is indeed 'quite unforced' is a matter of taste, but it is true that all variables are properly bound and that (9.30a,b) are indeed contradictories in the terms of SMPC. Yet, as before, the analysis founders on intervening independent operators, as in:

(9.31)   a. Any man, if he wants to own a donkey, must promise to feed it.
          b. Some man wants to own a donkey and he does not promise to feed it.

It is thus clear that Geach's analysis fails on all counts.

As regards the truth value of sentences like (9.27a,b) or (9.16c) in cases where someone (some farmer) owns two donkeys, one of which he feeds while he lets the other starve, for all predicate logics discussed, whether (9.27a) and (9.27b) are taken to be contradictories, as in SMPC and ABPC, or contraries, as in BNPC and AAPC, when (9.27b) is true, (9.27a) is false. This means that a single man who owns a donkey he does not feed is a counterexample to (9.27a), which is exactly what intuition tells us should be the case.[8]

It also means that it is no longer sufficient for the verification of universal statements, such as (9.27a), to check for each individual member *m* of the class of donkey-owners quantified over whether the statement '*m* owns a donkey and (s)he feeds it' is true. The OSTA principle, discussed in Section

---

[8] Isidora Stojanovic pointed out that a sentence like *Every time Mary goes out with a Frenchman, he pays for her drinks* does not seem to be falsified by some occasion where Mary goes out with two Frenchmen, only one of whom pays for her drinks, although then there is a Frenchman she goes out with who does not pay for her drinks. I consider this a valid objection and all I can say is that, depending on contextual or situational factors, the phrase *a Frenchman*, or, as in (9.27a), *a donkey*, is apparently interpreted as 'one or more Frenchmen' or 'one or more donkeys', respectively. The sentences in question would then read as 'Any man who owns one or more donkeys feeds them' and

3.4.2 of Volume I, will automatically assign truth to such a statement as soon as *m* owns one donkey (s)he feeds, thereby opening the possibility that donkeys owned but not fed by *m* are left out of account so that many possible counterexamples are missed out on. What is needed for the verification of, say, (9.27a) is the *absence* of any true statement of the form ' *m* owns a donkey and (s)he does not feed it'. This may well have consequences for the philosophy of knowledge or for theories of scientific methodology, but I can hopefully be forgiven for not elaborating this aspect any further.

9.5 The reference-fixing algorithm

It has become clear from what has been said so far that donkey anaphors cannot be treated adequately in terms of variable binding. The solution proposed by Geach has been shown to be unworkable. Donkey anaphors must be treated as definite unquantified pronouns that take as their antecedents not a definite or indefinite noun phrase in a preceding clause or sentence but an open discourse address set up in the current **D** as a result of a preceding existential quantification. In other words, donkey anaphora is primary anaphora. This statement is important because it shows that discourse structures are now seen to take on part of the burden of explanation of hitherto problematic facts. For that reason it is important to have as clear an idea of what primary anaphora amounts to as can be achieved in the light of what has so far been found.

One way of doing that is the following. In the context of the principle of optimization of sense, truth and actuality, the OSTA principle discussed in Section 3.4.2 of Volume I, it was observed that, in cases of possible referential ambiguity, pronouns and definite descriptions automatically key on to the reference object that makes for truth. An example, given in (3.31) of Section 3.4.2 of Volume I, is the case of two professors of English in the same department, one a Dutch and the other a British national. That being so, the pronoun *he* in the sequence of sentences *There is a professor of English in this department. He is British* automatically selects the British national as reference object because that is the reference object that makes for truth. The first sentence is true of two individuals in the situation at hand; the second sentence provides the information needed for a proper referential keying of its own subject term *he*, which is an instance of primary anaphora.

'Every time Mary goes out with one or more Frenchmen, they pay for her drinks', respectively. What the appropriate conditions are for such a reading will then be a matter of further investigation. See also Neale (1990: 222–63) for an interesting but inconclusive discussion of much the same cluster of problems within the terms of Russell's Theory of Descriptions.

Given the situation as described, the second sentence *He is British* cannot be false because there is no way the pronoun *he* can be made to refer to the professor who is a Dutch national. In general, in cases of referential ambiguity such as these, reference fixing takes place the moment enough information is provided to identify the correct reference object. This procedure can be caught in terms of a simple algorithm, which is presented in Figure 9.1.

Figure 9.1 shows the algorithm for the fixing of definite singular reference after address closure. The general principle is that reference is fixed for a definite term as soon as the predications stored for an address in **D** determine a unique object a in the verification domain **OBJ**^{R}. Once reference has been fixed for a definite term t—that is, once $\rho(t)$ has a as a unique value—that value remains unchanged for the remainder of the discourse, provided no second object is added to or discovered in **OBJ**^{R} also satisfying the conditions satisfied by a so as to qualify as $\rho(t)$.

If the predications stored before address closure fail to determine a unique object a because more objects satisfy the criteria, as when I speak of John's son when John has more than one son, then the predications *after* closure are called upon to secure reference. If that fails to yield the desired result, no reference object is fixed so that no proposition comes about and, strictly speaking, no truth value results, though the future possibility of truth remains open.

But if no reference value can be fixed because no object satisfies the predications provided, as when I speak of John's son when John has no son, then, as is argued in Section 9.3, the normal consequence is that radical falsity ensues. In such a case truth is possible only when the main predicate is intensional with respect to the term position occupied by t, as when John has no son and I say that John's son is imaginary.

Thus, when **OBJ**^{R} contains exactly one donkey owned by Socrates, the sentence *Socrates owns a donkey* is true of one donkey and, therefore, $|\ [\![Own(S,x)]\!] \cap [\![Donkey(x)]\!]\ | = 1$ (the vertical bars around a set denotation stand for the cardinality of the set in question). This condition suffices for the reference fixing of the primary anaphoric pronoun *it* in the subsequent sentence *He feeds it*. Consequently, if that is the way it is in **OBJ**^{R}, this latter sentence is true just in case that one donkey owned by Socrates is indeed fed by him, and false otherwise.

But now suppose Socrates owns two donkeys, one of which he feeds while the other he does not. Now the sentence *Socrates owns a donkey* is true of two donkeys and the subsequent sentence *He feeds it* is in danger of failing to pick a referent for *it*. For this eventuality, the algorithm calls in the after-closure predication Feed(Socrates,x) to help fix reference. This measure is success-ful if **OBJ**^{R} contains exactly one donkey owned by Socrates and fed by him, as we have stipulated it does. In such a situation, remarkably, the sentence *He feeds it* CANNOT BE FALSE, because its very truth is a necessary condition for the fixing of reference. When no reference can be fixed (for example because Socrates does not feed either of his two donkeys), there is either no truth value or the third value of radical falsity—depending on the theory one embraces— but there is certainty that it cannot be true.

If Socrates owns three donkeys but he feeds only two of them while the third is left starving, the sentence *He feeds it* simply fails to pick a referent for *it* and the sentence must remain without a truth value (or be radically false) until reference is fixed in a possible later sentence, which then again cannot be false because its truth is a necessary condition for the reference fixing of *it*. If **OBJ^R** contains three donkeys, all owned by Socrates but only two being fed by him, as before, while of the two donkeys fed by Socrates only one is brown, the sentence *It is brown* fixes reference and is automatically true. Clearly, this same story can, in theory, be repeated indefinitely, though in practice appeals to after-closure predications for the fixing of reference will be relatively rare and restricted to one after-closure appeal.

The definite-singular-reference-fixing algorithm is a partial, but only a partial, formalization of the OSTA Principle. In the cases where a sentence containing a primary anaphor cannot be false because the very reference fixing for the anaphor makes the sentence true, the algorithm guarantees the optimization of truth: it would be absurd to say that sentence (2) in Figure 9.1 is false because the speaker wants *it* to refer to the donkey not fed by Socrates. Yet it must be borne in mind that many other factors play a role in reference fixing that are not taken into account in the algorithm.

REFERENCE FIXED FOR *it*:	TRUE IFF:
(1) Socrates owns a donkey	
(NO REFERENCE FIXING)	$[\![\mathrm{Own(S,x)}]\!] \cap [\![\mathrm{Don(x)}]\!] \neq \varnothing$
(2) He feeds *it*	
$\big| [\![\mathrm{Own(S,x)}]\!] \cap [\![\mathrm{Don(x)}]\!] \big| = 1$	$\rightarrow \alpha \in [\![\mathrm{Feed(S,x)}]\!]$
$\big| [\![\mathrm{Own(S,x)}]\!] \cap [\![\mathrm{Don(x)}]\!] \cap [\![\mathrm{Feed(S,x)}]\!] \big| = 1$	$\rightarrow \alpha \in [\![\mathrm{Feed(S,x)}]\!]$ (cannot be false)
(3) *It* is brown	
$\big| [\![\mathrm{Own(S,x)}]\!] \cap [\![\mathrm{Don(x)}]\!] \big| = 1$	$\rightarrow \alpha \in [\![\mathrm{Brown(x)}]\!]$
$\big| [\![\mathrm{Own(S,x)}]\!] \cap [\![\mathrm{Don(x)}]\!] \cap [\![\mathrm{Feed(S,x)}]\!] \big| = 1$	$\rightarrow \alpha \in [\![\mathrm{Brown(x)}]\!]$
$\big| [\![\mathrm{Own(S,x)}]\!] \cap [\![\mathrm{Don(x)}]\!] \cap [\![\mathrm{Feed(S,x)}]\!] \cap [\![\mathrm{Brown(x)}]\!] \big| = 1$	$\rightarrow \alpha \in [\![\mathrm{Brown(x)}]\!]$ (cannot be false)
...and so on	
NB: α is the one member of set X when $\big| \mathrm{X} \big| = 1$.	

FIGURE 9.1 The definite-singular-reference-fixing algorithm and truth conditions

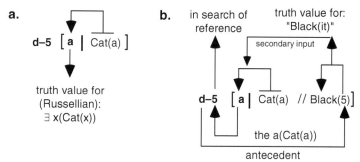

FIGURE 9.2 Function structure of an open and a closed address

As a matter of interest, Figure 9.2 schematically shows the function structure of (a) the open address for *There is a cat* (= (8.1) in Section 8.1.1) and (b) the closed address for *There is a cat. It is black* (corresponding to (8.4) in Section 8.1.1). In Figure 9.2a, which it is useful to compare with Figure 7.10 in Chapter 7 of Volume I, the predicate Cat(a) (where a is a bound variable) is fed into the existential quantifier **a** yielding truth just in case $[\![\text{Cat(a)}]\!] \neq \emptyset$. In Figure 9.2b, the predicate Cat(a) is again fed into **a**, but **a** is no longer an existential quantifier but has become a definite determiner as a result of address closure. The definite determiner **a** searches the verification domain **OBJ**^{R} for a proper reference value (ρ-value) for the address **d–5**, which has now become an object representation in **D**. At the same time, **d–5** is the antecedent of the pronoun '5' serving as the subject term for the predicate Black. 'Black(5)' is now a proposition with a truth value, provided the reference search in **OBJ**^{R} has been successful. If the search results in indeterminacy because there is more than one cat, the proposition Black(5) is called upon as a secondary input to the reference function **a**, which will then no longer search for just a cat but for a *black* cat.

9.6 The solution

We can now proceed to a discussion of the donkey-anaphora problem proper. It would seem that the solution to this problem is to be sought in reducing all forms of donkey anaphora to primary anaphora, so that the mechanism of address closure can be applied to all donkey anaphors. We deal with the three kinds of donkey anaphora as exemplified in (9.16a,b,c) in that order.

9.6.1 *Donkey anaphora under disjunction*

Let us start with donkey anaphora under disjunction, as exemplified in (9.16a), repeated here as (9.32):

(9.32)   Either Socrates does not own a donkey or he feeds *it*.

Here the solution was already formulated in Section 3.4.2, where it was argued, on grounds of basic-natural set theory, that a surface-structure disjunction of the form 'P OR Q' should be tacitly understood as (P AND NOT-Q) OR (NOT-P AND Q), making the disjuncts mutually exclusive. As explained in Section 8.2.3, this 'tacit' reading is given concrete form in the result of the incrementation procedure (**IP**) for OR. This turns (9.32) into (9.33):

(9.33)   Either Socrates does not own a donkey and does not feed *it*, or he owns a donkey and feeds *it*.

The second *it* has now found its antecedent and turns out to be an instance of primary anaphora. Yet, as was pointed out in Section 3.4.2, the first *it*, which does not occur in the surface form (9.32), is problematic since its would-be antecedent is barred from the discourse by the negation, so that anaphora should be excluded. The only way to bestow a coherent interpretation on the first disjunct of (9.33) is to interpret *not* as the radical, presupposition-cancelling negation. The first disjunct of (9.33) improves when the word *therefore* is inserted after the first *and*, indicating that what follows is a metalinguistic comment, and the negation is given heavy accent, indicating that it is the radical, rather than the minimal, negation that is being used. Donkey anaphora under disjunction is thus seen to be a case of primary anaphora requiring address closure.

One notes that intervening operators do not nullify this analysis. Sentence (9.34a), repeated from (9.23a), survives the expansion of the type '(P AND NOT-Q) OR (NOT-P AND Q)' without a hitch, as one sees in (9.34b), where both occurrences of *it* are instances of primary anaphora (we take it, as is argued in Section 10.4, that minimal NOT over *still* gives *no longer*, and minimal NOT over *no longer* gives *still*):

(9.34)   a. Either Socrates no longer owns a donkey or he still feeds it.
          b. Either Socrates no longer owns a donkey and he no longer feeds it, or he still owns a donkey and he still feeds it.

The solution to the donkey-anaphora problem in disjunctions is thus to be sought not in the logico-semantic analysis of disjunctive sentences—their semantic analyses or SAs—but in the instruction for their incrementation.

9.6.2 *Donkey anaphora in conditionals*

Donkey anaphora in conditionals was exemplified in (9.16b) above, repeated here as (9.35):

(9.35)   If Socrates owns a donkey, he feeds *it*.

Here again, the reduction to primary anaphora in terms of discourse incrementation is unproblematic. As is argued in Section 8.2.4, conditional *if* activates the
instruction that in case the *if*-clause is incremented to the current **D**, the
subsequent incrementation of the main clause is licensed. That is, if *Socrates
owns a donkey* is incremented, *he feeds it* may also be incremented, giving rise to
the sequence *Socrates owns a donkey (and) he feeds it*—again a case of primary
anaphora, this time embedded in the subdomain reserved for conditional *if*-
clauses. Intervening operators present no problem. As in (9.14) above, the
pronoun *it* in (9.36) is a case of address closure across (sub)domains:

(9.36)   If Socrates claims that he owns a donkey, I want to see *it*.

9.6.3 *Donkey anaphora under universal quantification*

Finally, we come to donkey anaphora under universal quantification, as it
occurs in the example sentence (9.16c), repeated here as (9.37):

(9.37)   Every farmer who owns a donkey feeds *it*.

According to the instruction associated with ALL specified in Section 8.1.2.2
(and assuming an isomorphy between ALL and EVERY), EVERY licenses the closure,
if necessary, of any still open address for a representative of the restrictor set—that
is the closure of any address containing the information stored in (9.38a): 'there is
a farmer such that he owns a donkey'. The address in (9.38a) induces, in virtue of
inferential bridging as shown in (8.10) and (8.11) of Section 8.1.1, the setting up of
an address **d–m** for the donkey owned by the farmer in question. This second
address **d–m** reads: 'there is a donkey such that some farmer owns it'.

(9.38)   a. **d–n** [**a**| Farmer(a), [**b** | Donkey(b), Own(a,b)]
          b. **d–m** [**a** | Donkey(a), [**b** | Farmer(b), Own(b,a)]

The quantifier EVERY in (9.37) now licenses the closure of **d–n** plus the
addition of the information that the farmer in question feeds the donkey he
owns, and similarly for every address for a donkey-owning farmer to be found
or yet to be set up in **D** in conformity with the verification domain (situation)
at hand. That is, (9.38a) is expanded to (9.39), which is read as 'the farmer
feeds the donkey he owns':

(9.39)   **d–n** [**a** | Farmer(a), [**b** | Donkey(b), Own(a,b)] // Feed(**n,m**)]

And likewise for any other address for a donkey-owning farmer. At the same
time, as we have seen, the instruction for the universal quantifier blocks the
addition of ¬Feed(**n,m**) to any address **d–n**, thus blocking any possible counterexamples due to the OSTA principle and the reference-fixing algorithm.

The SA-structure postulated for sentence (9.37) is something like (9.40), where the asinus symbol @ represents the problematic donkey pronoun.

(9.40)

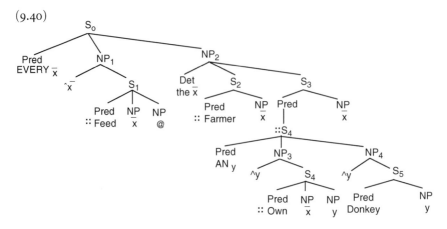

It is clear that @ lacks a proper variable binding so that it remains marooned and should lead to uninterpretability. This is so not only in the technical notation adopted here but also in any other notational or notional variety of predicate logic. Therefore, the fact that sentence (9.37) is fully and effortlessly interpretable cannot be explained by an appeal to the logico-semantic analysis of sentences. It seems, however, that it can be explained in terms of the incrementation procedures associated with sentences of this type. The problematic @ is referentially resolved through the operation of address closure and thus through primary anaphora as occurring when the instruction associated with the universal quantifier is applied to specific cases.

It is important to realize, in this connection, that we are forging ahead into largely uncharted territory. That being so, one must be ready to admit that not all questions can be answered right away and that it is as yet early days for a complete formalization of the machinery envisaged. In fact, one must reckon with the possibility that the aim of complete formalization will be unrealistic for quite some time to come and perhaps forever, given the complexity of the system and the manifold ways in which it links up with and is integrated into the whole of the human mind. We are still finding our feet.

Yet there are plenty of signs that we are not totally off course. The machinery that has been set up or envisaged is beginning to yield explanations, or at least possible explanations, for facts that have been troublesome for a long time because they would simply not adjust to the theories developed so far. Thus, we now see that the donkey-anaphora problem seems to find its solution in terms of the machinery of discourse incrementation and not in terms of logical analysis.

10

Presupposition and presuppositional logic

10.1 Presupposition as an anchoring device

It is now time to pass on to presupposition, the second main device for the maintenance of coherence in discourse. Though central to the theory of language, the phenomenon of presupposition did not become the subject of systematic study till the second half of the twentieth century. When it did, it quickly became one of the wedges that helped to prise open the hitherto intractable mysteries of context-sensitivity in language.

Essentially, presuppositions are discourse restrictors for the sentences carrying them. A presupposition P carried by a sentence Q restricts the universe of discourse to what can be true or false on the assumption that P is true. Normally, in the flow of a natural discourse, subsequent increments narrow down the universe U of all admissible situations to an ever more restricted U^R to which new increments can again be added. A presupposition P, being part of the semantics of its carrier sentence Q, automatically shortens that process in that it makes its carrier sentence fit for use only in the restricted class of discourses where P has been or can be incremented. When we say that a sentence must have 'the right papers' for a given discourse D, part of what is meant is that D must (be able to) contain, or *satisfy*, P.

The situations that belong to the complement of U^R in U are, so to speak, put on hold for the time being. If necessary, they can be fallen back on, as happens, for example, when the discourse must be repaired owing to the need to remove an incorrect or undesirable previous increment from the current discourse. But on the whole, the situations that fall outside the U^R at any stage in a discourse play no role in the communicative process.

All the indications are that presuppositions are generated by the *language system*, not by whatever factors happen to play a role in any contingent speech situation. This appears in particular, but not exclusively, from the fact that a sentence carrying a presupposition evokes a context where that presupposition is fulfilled without that context being actually provided. This phenomenon goes by the name of *accommodation* (Lewis 1979) or *post hoc suppletion* (Seuren 1988). Thus, when I say *John is divorced*, it is not necessary for me to say first that he was married before, because that information is accommodated, or supplied *post hoc*, by the semantics of the predicate *be divorced*. Since the actual physical realization of speech takes a great deal of time and energy compared with the mere cognitive processing involved, presupposition is seen to be a powerful device for the saving of time and energy.

The latter point is of great functional importance. One grand way in which the language system enables speakers to economize on the effort of speaking and hit directly on the *hic et nunc* target of linguistic interaction is the device of presupposition. We leave implicit a great deal that could be said explicitly, not only, as is well known, because of shared knowledge (Clark 1992, 1996), but also because the lexical meanings of the predicates we use are more often than not reserved for special classes of situations, so that the mere use of such a predicate carries the information that what is said is meant to be restricted to the class of situations associated with the predicate at hand. This latter device is encoded in the form of *preconditions* in the satisfaction conditions of predicates, discussed earlier in Sections 3.1.5 and 9.4 of Volume I. It is these preconditions that generate the presuppositions.

From a strictly logical point of view, presuppositions are entailments. When I say that a sentence like *John is divorced* presupposes that he was married before, I also say that *John is divorced* entails that he was married before, because it is implicit in the meaning of the predicate *be divorced* that one must have been married before one can get divorced. But the strictly logical point of view is insufficient to account for what presupposition really is. The essence and *raison d'être* of presupposition lies in its function of context abridger and guardian of contextual coherence.

10.1.1 *Some early history*

As is our custom, we first take a brief look at the history of the topic at hand. The first to see that presuppositions pose a threat to Aristotle's celebrated Principle of the Excluded Third (PET) was his somewhat older contemporary Eubulides of Miletus (±405–±330 BCE; see Kneale and Kneale 1962: 113–17), who taught philosophy at Megara, not far from Athens (the Megarian school of philosophy was one of the main sources of the great Stoic tradition in ancient philosophy). Eubulides is mainly known for his four paradoxes, the Liar, the Sorites, the Electra, and the Horned Man, and for the bitter personal animosity between him and Aristotle.

Strangely, the significance of his paradoxes was never properly understood in the history of logic. Probably as a result of the enormous influence exerted by Aristotle, Eubulides has consistently been depicted as a fool who made flippant jokes without any real depth. Yet the Liar paradox was a much discussed 'insoluble' during the Middle Ages. It was rediscovered about a century ago, when Russell and subsequent mathematical logicians saw how profoundly significant the Liar paradox is for logic and semantics (the currently standard Russellian answer to it—the prohibition to mix object language and metalanguage—is still open to serious doubt; see Seuren 1987). But the historians of logic had meanwhile lost the connection with modern mathematical logic, so that the sudden revival of the Liar paradox failed to alert them to the relevance of Eubulides' work. The Kneales are an exception. In their standard 1962 work on the history of logic, they begin to suspect that something is afoot in this respect, even though they fail to see exactly what. They write (1962: 114–15) that Eubulides 'must surely have been trying to illustrate some theses of Megarian philosophy' and that 'the Megarian study of the paradoxes was a serious affair and not mere perversity'. In our day, most professional logicians do not even realize that their cherished Liar paradox originated with Eubulides of Miletus.

Nowadays, in the context of modern semantics, we are in a position to see that the four Eubulidean paradoxes constitute a highly significant head-on attack on Aristotelian truth theory and logic, in particular the thesis of truth as correspondence and the Principle of the Excluded Third. They also summarize the core of well-nigh the entire research programme of twentieth-century semantics, including the problems of vague predicates (Sorites), intensional contexts (Electra), and presuppositions (Horned Man). It is a surprising and highly significant fact that a contemporary of Aristotle already spotted the main weaknesses of the Aristotelian paradigm (see Seuren 2005 for a detailed discussion).

What interests us here is Eubulides' paradox of the Horned Man. It runs as follows (Kneale and Kneale 1962: 114):

> What you have not lost you still have. But you have not lost your horns. So you still have your horns.

This paradox rests on presupposition. Read **B** for *You have lost your horns* and **A** for *You had horns*. Now **B** presupposes **A** (**B** >> **A**), because the predicate *have lost* has the precondition that what has been lost was once possessed. Eubulides implicitly assumed (like, much later, Strawson) that presuppositional entailments are categorically preserved under negation: **B** ⊢ **A** and NOT

(B) ⊢ **A.** Under PET, this would make **A** a logically necessary truth, which is absurd for a contingent sentence like *You had horns*.[1] To avoid this, PET would have to be dropped, very much against Aristotle's wish. Although Aristotle himself was unable to show Eubulides wrong—his grumpy reaction was to say that Eubulides' paradoxes were just silly (átopa)—there is a flaw in the paradox. It lies in the incorrectly assumed entailment in the first premiss 'What you have not lost you still have'. For it is possible that a person has not lost something precisely because he never had it.

To the best of present knowledge, there was no explicit awareness of presuppositional phenomena until Frege, or perhaps more accurately, until well into the twentieth century. We now know that the solution to Eubulides' Paradox of the Horns lies in an adequate analysis of presuppositions, but there are no signs that Eubulides himself was aware of that fact. All the same, the proper answer to Eubulides' Paradox of the Horns is still in conflict with the classic Aristotelian Principle of the Excluded Third, as is shown below.

The issue is not raised in any of the Ancient literature on logic or the philosophy of language. Nor did the medievals, otherwise so resourceful and so creative, have much to say about presuppositions. Occasionally, however, they came close. In an anonymous text, *Ars Meliduna*, probably written between 1154 and 1180 (Nuchelmans 1973: 165), Aristotle's celebrated Principle of the Excluded Third is called into question. One of the grounds for doubt in this respect consists in the fact that utterances may be neither true nor false but 'nugatory'. In De Rijk's edition of the *Ars Meliduna* we read (De Rijk 1967: 363):

...enuntiables such as that 'Socrates is white because it is him' or that 'he loves his son' appear to become nugatory when Socrates is no longer white or no longer has a son. [...] We must, therefore, posit that such enuntiables may become nugatory [...] even if that goes against Aristotle ....

No further attempt, however, is made in this treatise to investigate the concepts of truth and falsity within given contextual conditions.

Another near miss was the medieval doctrine of *exponibles*—expressions that require special explication in terms of separate propositions. A proposition containing such an expression is an *exponible proposition*. Examples are given in an anonymous *Tractatus Exponibilium* (incorrectly attributed to

---

[1] It is a safe bet that Eubulides meant to tease the prudish Aristotle by confronting him with the absurd and somewhat disconcerting consequence that his logic made it a necessary truth for every man to be a cuckold. See Seuren (2005), where it becomes apparent that Aristotle was not amused.

Peter of Spain by Mullally 1945):[2] 'exclusives' (*only*), 'exceptives' (*except*), 'reduplicatives' (*insofar as*), time-aspectual verbs (*begin, stop*), comparatives, superlatives, etc. Though some of these, in particular the exclusives, had been known at least since Abelard in the early twelfth century (Mullally 1945: lxxv), exponibles did not become a topic until about 1340.[3]

Some space is devoted to the exclusives (*only*-sentences) in the logical treatise *Syncategoreumata* (edition De Rijk 1992), probably authored by Peter of Spain (±1212–1277). In the fourteenth century we have, besides the *Tractatus Exponibilium* mentioned above, William of Ockham (±1285–±1349) writing on exponibles in his *Summa Logicæ* and Walter Burleigh (±1275–±1357) doing the same in his *De Consequentiis* (Green-Pedersen 1980) and in separate tracts on exclusives and exceptives (De Rijk 1985, 1986). All these authors divide an exponible proposition into two exponent propositions, the *propositio praeiacens* ('proposition that comes first') and the *propositio superveniens* ('proposition that comes after'). Thus we read Walter Burleigh on exclusive propositions (De Rijk 1985: 49–50):

> ... the proposition *only man walks* is exposed in the following way: 'man walks and nothing but man walks'. The one exponent, i.e. 'nothing but man walks', it has in virtue of the exclusive expression; but the other, 'man walks', it has in virtue of its prejacent. For this is the prejacent: 'man walks'.

The two exponents are conjoined by *and* to give the meaning of the whole exponible proposition. Therefore, in Peter of Spain's words: 'every true

---

[2] According to De Rijk (1972: xcix) it begins to crop up at the end of manuscripts of Peter of Spain's *Summulae Logicales* starting from about 1350.

[3] An observation by Horn (1985: 123; 1996: 300, and elsewhere) has caused some confusion in this respect. Horn notes that the term *praesupponere* occurs in the *Tractatus Exponibilium* mentioned above (Mullally 1945: 112), which he, following Mullally, incorrectly attributes to Peter of Spain (it was written about a century later by an unknown author; see De Rijk 1972: xcix). Horn takes over Mullally's translation 'presuppose'. But this cannot be correct. The term is used in the context of a sentence-type called 'reduplicatives', such as: *insofar as man is rational, he is capable of weeping*. My best translation of the passage in question is:

The first rule is that a reduplicative word ['insofar as'; PAMS] anticipates (praesupponit) that some predicate inheres in some entity and says (denotat) that the clause to which it is immediately attached expresses the cause of that inherence.

That is, the expression *insofar as* anticipates that some predicate (in this case 'capable of weeping') inheres in some entity ('man'), and means in addition that 'insofar as man is rational' expresses the cause of man's being capable of weeping. Since there can be no question of 'man is capable of weeping' being presupposed by the sentence mentioned, one must conclude that *praesupponere* is used here in a different sense from what *presuppose* means today, just as *supponere*—the medieval Latin term for 'referring'—does not mean what *suppose* means today. As a matter of fact, *praesupponere* does not occur anywhere else in the whole of the philosophical literature written in Latin.

exclusive proposition leaves its prejacent true' (De Rijk 1992: 110–11), or: presuppositions are entailed by their carrier sentences.

Although the exclusives were the most discussed among the exponibles, nothing suggests an awareness of their specific, discourse-related, presuppositional character. Burleigh applies, in principle, standard propositional logic to exposed exclusives. Since *only man walks* is equivalent with *man walks and nothing but man walks*, its negation, *not only man walks*, is true if at least one of the conjuncts is false. He writes (Green-Pedersen 1980: 119):

Note that the opposite of an exclusive proposition has two grounds for truth: because no man walks, or because something other than man walks.

He thus denies the entailment from *not only man walks* to *man walks*, despite the natural intuition that it does hold. Had he followed intuition and thus done justice to language, he would have found that, in this respect, language is in conflict with standard logic, and he might have embarked on an analysis of presuppositions. Unfortunately, however, this did not happen.

Subsequent centuries do not even come close to presuppositions. Till Frege (1892), there is no development at all on the presuppositional front. Strawson (1950, 1952, 1954) follows up on Frege, but specifically with regard to existential presuppositions and only in a strictly logical perspective. Like Eubulides and Frege, Strawson assumed full entailment of presupposition under negation for all cases and concluded that PET had to go. In Strawson's view, nonfulfilment of a presupposition leads to both the carrier sentence and its negation lacking a truth value altogether.

Frege (1892) had come to the same conclusion, though from a different angle. In a sentence like (10.1) the subject term lacks a referent in the actual world, though the existence of such a referent is presupposed in virtue of the existential precondition on the subject term of the verb *run*:

(10.1)   The unicorn ran for its life.

This makes it impossible to test the truth of (10.1): given that there is no actually existing unicorn, there is no way to check whether it (whatever this *it* may stand for) actually ran. Therefore, Frege, like Strawson more than half a century later, concluded that (10.1) lacks a truth value.

This posed a profound problem for standard logic in that the applicability of standard logic to, say, English would have to be made dependent on contingent conditions of existence—a restriction no logician will accept. In the effort to solve this problem two traditions developed, the *Russell tradition* and the *Frege-Strawson tradition*.

10.1.2 *The Russell tradition*

In his famous 1905 article 'On denoting', Russell proposed a new analysis for sentences with definite terms, like (10.2a). Putting the new theory of quantification to use, he analysed (10.2a) as (10.2b), or 'there is an individual x such that x is now king of France and x is bald, and for all individuals y, if y is now king of France, y is identical with x' (for a more philosophical critique, see Section 2.1.1 in Volume I):

(10.2) a. The present king of France is bald.
        b. $\exists x[\text{KoF}(x) \wedge \text{Bald}(x) \wedge \forall y[\text{KoF}(y) \rightarrow x = y]]$

In order to save bivalence, Russell thus replaced the time-honoured subject–predicate analysis with an analysis in which the definite description *the present king of France* no longer forms a constituent of the logically analysed sentence, but is dissolved into quantifiers and propositional functions.

The linguistic negation of (10.2a) is (10.3a). Accordingly, one would expect its logical analysis to be (10.3b)—that is, (10.2b) preceded by the negation operator. However, Russell observed, speakers often prefer, for reasons best known to themselves, to interpret (10.3a) as (10.3c), with internal negation over $\text{Bald}(x)$:

(10.3) a. The present king of France is not bald.
        b. $\neg\exists x[\text{KoF}(x) \wedge \text{Bald}(x) \wedge \forall y[\text{KoF}(y) \rightarrow x = y]]$
        c. $\exists x[\text{KoF}(x) \wedge \neg\text{Bald}(x) \wedge \forall y[\text{KoF}(y) \rightarrow x = y]]$

This makes sentences like (10.3a) ambiguous.

This analysis, known as Russell's THEORY OF DESCRIPTIONS, was quickly accepted by logicians and philosophers of language, as it saved strict bivalence—a principle most were afraid to tamper with and hence dear to their hearts. At the same time, however, it drove logicians and linguists apart, first because it defies any notion of sentence structure as conceived of by the linguists of the day, but then also on account of the strident unnaturalness of taking (10.2b) as the logico-semantic analysis of (10.2a).

Russell tried to save natural intuitions of truth and falsity as much as possible by dispensing with the—otherwise very natural and intuitive—notion of 'aboutness'. It is with that purpose in mind that he presented his famous theory of descriptions, which is, in fact, a programme aimed at the elimination of all definite referring terms, like *the present king of France*, from the expressions of logic, including those that purport to render the meaning of natural language sentences.

Besides all kinds of linguistic, semantic, and pragmatic objections, his theory of descriptions fails to account for the natural intuition that a sentence like (10.4a) is simply true. In Russell's analysis, (10.4a) should be read as 'there is a god Apollo who was worshipped in the island of Delos and who is identical with nothing else', rendered formally as (10.4b):

(10.4)   a. The god Apollo was worshipped in the island of Delos.
         b. ∃x[God Apollo(x) ∧ Be worshipped in Delos(x) ∧ ∀y[God Apollo(y) → x = y]]

Nobody conversant with ancient mythology will deny that (10.4a) is true, as opposed to (10.5), which is historically and factually false:

(10.5)   The god Poseidon was worshipped in the island of Delos.

Yet, Russell's analysis makes them both false, since neither Apollo nor Poseidon ever enjoyed actual existence. For Russell, as for almost the entire body of standard twentieth-century logic, the existential quantifier 'there is' has existential import: it induces an entailment of actual, tangible, existence for individual objects. Sentence (10.4a), therefore, should entail the actual, tangible, existence of the god Apollo. And since Apollo never tangibly existed, (10.4a) turns out false in Russell's analysis.

The conclusion must be, therefore, that Russell's attempt at saving natural intuitions was a failure. It may perhaps be thought to account for the natural intuition that (10.6) is false, since no-one will doubt that it is not true that there is a god Apollo who lives in Kathmandu and is unique of his kind, but it fails, as a matter of principle, to account for the truth of (10.4a):[4]

(10.6)   The god Apollo lives in Kathmandu.

Russell was not totally unaware of this difficulty, but one has the impression that he tended to be dismissive with regard to the facts of natural language. One reads (Russell 1905: 491):

---

[4] In his (1905: 485), Russell quips about the king of France's alleged baldness:

By the law of the excluded middle, either 'A is B' or 'A is not B' must be true. Hence either 'the present King of France is bald' or 'the present King of France is not bald' must be true. Yet if we enumerated the things that are bald, and then the things that are not bald, we should not find the present King of France in either list. Hegelians, who love a synthesis, will probably conclude that he wears a wig.

We may paraphrase this for the case at hand, saying that if one searches among the inhabitants of Kathmandu one will not find Apollo there; yet if one looks among those who live elsewhere one will not find him either. A Hegelian synthesis that makes him be of no fixed abode will not be of much use either, because Apollo will be equally absent from the vagrants of this world.

All propositions in which Apollo occurs are to be interpreted by the above rules. If 'Apollo' has a primary occurrence [has large scope; PAMS], the proposition containing the occurrence is false; if the occurrence is secondary [has small scope; PAMS], the proposition may be true.

But the theory of descriptions fails to show how *Apollo* in sentence (10.4a) can possibly be assigned small scope in such a way that it turns out true. Nor is it likely that any form of linguistic or semantic analysis will achieve such a feat, as (10.4a) is in no way ambiguous. I fully agree with Zalta (1988: 11):

[O]ne might offer Russell's infamous theory of descriptions as the means of analyzing away the propositions in question. Unfortunately, this theory not only fails to do justice to the apparent logical form of the propositions in question, but more importantly, when applied generally, it fails to preserve the intuitive truth value of a wide range of other propositions. For example, it turns the historical fact that Ponce de León searched for the fountain of youth into a falsehood. Results such as this suggest that the theory of descriptions is, at best, not general and, at worst, false.

The solution lies, of course, in the fact that a predicate like *be worshipped* is nonextensional (intensional) with regard to its subject term, while a predicate like *search for* is nonextensional with regard to its object term. But if one wants to account for the facts at hand by an appeal to the occasional nonextensionality of predicates with regard to their terms, the semantic definition of the existential quantifier must be changed so as no longer to imply actual existence but rather 'being' in a wider sense than mere existence. This, in turn, requires, besides an extension of the logical machinery, a thorough revision of the concomitant ontology, not found in the relevant logical literature.[5]

Further objections may be raised as regards what is known as the 'uniqueness clause' in (10.2b): $\forall y[KoF(y) \rightarrow x = y]$, meant to say that only one king of France exists. Russell added the 'uniqueness clause' in order to account for the uniqueness expressed by the definite determiner *the*. In fact, however, the

---

[5] Richard Montague's model-theoretic possible-worlds semantics comes closest, but it fails irreparably on account of its inability to account for substitutivity *salva veritate* in intensional contexts. Dowty et al. write: (1981: 175):

We must acknowledge that the problem of propositional attitude sentences is a fundamental one for possible world semantics, and for all we know, could eventually turn out to be a reason for rejecting or drastically modifying the whole possible world framework.

Meanwhile, a quarter century has passed, but no solution has appeared at the horizon. I take it, therefore, that Montague's programme of 'extensionalisation of intensions' has foundered on the cliffs of the human mind.

definite article implies no claim to uniqueness of existence, only to discourse-bound uniqueness of identifying reference. Saying *John and Harry met in the pub after work* in no way implies that the world contains just one pub. Since the world is full of pubs, its Russellian translation would make it false. Yet it may well be true, provided John and Harry met in a particular pub whose identity has been fixed by shared speaker–hearer's knowledge and is thus taken for granted. Russell is his usual off-handed self when he writes (1905: 481):

> Now *the*, when it is strictly used, involves uniqueness; we do, it is true, speak of '*the* son of So-and-so' even when So-and-so has several sons, but it would be more correct to say '*a* son of So-and-so'.

But this superior, if not arrogant, attitude with regard to the facts of natural language blinded him to the basic truth that definite reference in language is unrelated to uniqueness of existence and fully related to uniqueness of identification.

Then, this analysis is limited to definite descriptions and is unable to account for other kinds of presupposition. Factive and categorial presuppositions, and those derived from words like *all*, *still*, or *only*, fall outside its coverage.

To account for other than existential presuppositions some have proposed to change Russell's analysis into (10.7) or 'there is a king of France, and *he* is bald'.

(10.7) $\exists x[KoF(x)] \wedge Bald(he)$

He is now no longer a bound variable but an instance of primary anaphora outside the scope of the existential quantifier. With a logical mechanism for such anaphora (as in Kamp 1981 or Groenendijk and Stokhof 1991), this analysis can be generalized to all categories of presupposition. A sentence B_A (that is, B presupposing A) is now analysed as A AND B_A, and NOT(B_A), though normally analysed as A AND NOT(B_A) with the negation restricted to the second conjunct, can also, forced by discourse conditions and marked by special accent (see below), be analysed as NOT$(A$ AND $B_A)$, with the negation over the whole conjunction. This analysis, which saves PET, is known as the CONJUNCTION ANALYSIS for presupposition.

Anaphora is needed anyway, since Russell's analysis fails for cases like (10.8), where quantifier binding is impossible for *it*, which is in the scope of *I hope*, while *I hope* is outside the scope of *I know*:

(10.8)   I know that there is a dog and I hope that it is white.

The conjunction analysis, however, still cannot account for the fact that (10.9a) is coherent (though perhaps a little ponderous) but (10.9b) is not:

(10.9)   a. There is a dog and it is white, and there is a dog and it is not white.
          b. !There is a dog and it is white and it is not white.

(10.9a) speaks of two dogs, due to the repetition of *there is a dog*, but (10.9b) speaks of only one. Yet the conjunction analysis cannot make that difference, since the repetition of *there is a dog* makes no logical or semantic difference for it.

Attempts have been made to incorporate this difference into the logic (e.g. Kamp 1981; Heim 1982; Groenendijk and Stokhof 1991) by attaching a memory store to the model theory which keeps track of the elements that have so far been introduced existentially. Though this is no doubt a move in the right direction, it still falls short of what is needed, logically, philosophically, and linguistically. And even when these needs are satisfied, the conjunction analysis still postulates existence for term referents whose existence is denied:

(10.10)   Santa Claus does not exist.

(One notes that the negation *not* in (10.10) in no way needs to be marked by special accent nor be forced to take large scope by discourse factors.)

10.1.3 *The Frege-Strawson tradition*

Some time before the advent of Russellian logic, the German mathematician Gottlob Frege (1848–1925) was already deeply engrossed in questions of meaning and reference. One may rightly say that the modern history of presupposition theory started with a footnote in Frege (1884: 87–8), which runs as follows:

The expression 'the largest real fraction', for example, has no content because the definite article has a claim to the possibility of pointing at a unique object. [...] If one were to determine, by means of this concept, an object that falls under it, two things would no doubt have to be shown first:

1. that there is an object falling under this concept;
2. that there is no more than one object falling under it.

Since the first of these assertions is already false, the expression 'the largest real fraction' makes no sense.

This is clearly reminiscent of the *Ars Meliduna* mentioned earlier, but the difference is that this time the observation was followed up. Even so, however, it still took some time for presupposition theory to flourish.

The follow-up started in Frege's famous 1892 article 'Ueber Sinn und Bedeutung' (On sense and reference). There he discusses, among other things, what truth values are with regard to sentences and how truth values are assigned to them. For Frege, the use of a definite term normally presupposes (setzt voraus) the actual existence of its reference object. When we say *The moon is smaller than the earth* we presuppose that there is an actual moon and an actual earth, and we say of the former that it is smaller than the latter (Frege 1892: 31). Only if this presupposition is fulfilled can the sentence have a truth value. If not, the sentence may still have a sense or meaning, as in fictional contexts, but it lacks a truth value.

Frege takes the medieval distinction between the extension and the intension of predicates as his point of departure and extends this distinction to cover argument terms and sentences as well (see Section 6.1 in Volume I). He considers a sentence to be composed of a predicate and its argument terms, and he follows Aristotle in saying that when the referents of the argument terms possess the property expressed by the predicate, the sentence is true; otherwise it is false.

For Frege, the *extension* of a (definite) argument term is an individual reference object, while its *intension* (or sense) is the way by which a speaker-hearer cognitively arrives at the reference object—the search or reference procedure. The extension of a predicate is a set of individual objects, while its intension is the corresponding concept. And, surprisingly, the extension of a sentence (Satz) is its truth value, while its intension is defined as the underlying thought. We read (Frege 1892: 32–3; translation mine):

Let us assume, for the time being, that the sentence has a reference! If we replace one of its words with another word that has the same extension (=reference object; PAMS) but a different sense, such replacement will have no bearing on the extension of the sentence. But we see that the thought does change; for the thought underlying a sentence like *The morning star receives its light from the sun* is different from the thought underlying *The evening star receives its light from the sun*. Someone who does not know that the morning star is identical with the evening star, might take the one thought to be true and the other to be false. Therefore, the thought cannot be the extension of the sentence. Rather, we take the thought to be its sense. But then, how about its extension? Is it anyway appropriate to ask that question? Maybe the sentence as a whole only has a sense and no extension? One may anyhow expect such sentences to occur, just as there are sentence parts with a sense but without an extension. Sentences with nominal expressions that lack a reference will be of that nature. The sentence *Odysseus was put ashore at Ithaca while sound asleep* obviously has a sense. But since it is doubtful that the name *Odysseus* occurring in this sentence has an extension, it is equally doubtful that the whole sentence has one. Yet one thing is certain: if one seriously takes this sentence to be true or false, one also assigns an extension to the name *Odysseus*, and not just a sense. For it is to the extension of this name that the predicate is assigned or denied. [...]

Why do we want every name to have not only a sense but also a reference? Why is the thought alone insufficient? Because, and in so far as, we care about its truth value. This is not always the case. For example, when we listen to an epic poem, it is, besides the euphony of the language, only the sense of the sentences and the images and feelings aroused by them that will captivate us. But as soon as we ask about the truth of the story, we leave the precinct of aesthetic pleasure and enter upon the territory of scientific investigation. As long as we take the poem as no more than a work of art, the question of whether a name like *Odysseus* has an extension may remain a matter of total indifference to us. It is, therefore, the effort to achieve truth that invariably drives us forward from the sense to the reference.

Obviously, this is a suggestive, not a conclusive, argument. Yet the overall coherence and force of this suggestive picture, together with its Aristotelian basis and the lack of an equally powerful alternative, gained it the hearts and minds of logicians and philosophers of language during the century to come. The Fregean point of view that a predicate is a function from entities to truth values (type e,t) became the basis of twentieth-century Categorial Grammar.

It follows, in this perspective, that when a nominal expression fails to refer to an actually existing object, the predicate function lacks an input and therefore cannot produce an output: the sentence in question will thus lack a truth value. For the sake of clarity, the Fregean system of extensions and intensions for terms, predicates and sentences is schematically rendered in Figure 10.1.

Frege never directly opposed Russell's theory of descriptions, which dates from 1905, though he must have had grave reservations about it. The first to

type of expression	categorial type	extension (Bedeutung)	intension (Sinn)
term	e	entity	search procedure
predicate	e → t	set of entities	concept
sentence	t	truth value	thought

FIGURE 10.1 Frege's system of extensions and intensions for terms, predicates, and sentences

oppose Russell directly was Peter Geach in a curious little article of 1950, in which Geach deals with presuppositions (the term is used only in passing), referring to the footnote in Frege (1884) quoted above. The article is a critique of Russell's theory of descriptions, first on account of its failure to recognize presuppositions in ordinary language, then on account of Russell and White-head's defective definition of the iota operator in *Principia Mathematica*. About the former, Geach writes (Geach 1950: 84–5):

On Russell's view 'the King of France is bald' is a false assertion. This view seems to me to commit the fallacy of 'many questions'. To see how this is so, let us take a typical example of the fallacy: the demand for 'a plain answer – yes or no!' to the question 'have you been happier since your wife died?' Three questions are here involved:

1. Have you ever had a wife?
2. Is she dead?
3. Have you been happier since then?

The act of asking question 2 presupposes an affirmative answer to question 1; if the true answer to 1 is negative, question 2 *does not arise*. The act of asking question 3 presupposes an affirmative answer to question 2; if question 2 does not arise, or if the answer to it is negative, question 3 *does not arise*. When a question does not arise, the only proper way of answering it is to say so and explain the reason; the 'plain' affirmative or negative answer, though grammatically possible, is *out of place*. (I do not call it 'meaningless' because the word is a mere catchword nowadays.) This does not go against the laws of contradiction and excluded middle; what these laws tell us is that *if* the question arose 'yes' and 'no' would be exclusive alternatives.

Similarly, the question 'Is the present King of France bald?' involves two other questions:

4. Is anybody at the moment a King of France?
5. Are there at the moment different people each of whom is a King of France?

And it does not arise unless the answer to 4 is affirmative and the answer to 5 is negative.

What Geach describes here is, of course, a gapped bivalent logic, which does violate the Principle of the Excluded Third (not the Law of the Excluded Middle, since what is at issue is not a truth value *between* 'true' and 'false', but, rather, the *absence* of a truth value). But the interesting thing about this article is that the existential presupposition is brought in line with other kinds of presupposition, a step that was repeated soon afterwards in the linguistic literature.

Geach's article appeared at roughly the same time as Strawson (1950), which was further elaborated in Strawson (1952, 1954, 1964). Strawson reinstated the traditional subject–predicate analysis, which had been destroyed by Russell's theory of descriptions. He discussed only existential presuppositions, probably because he considered the other presupposition categories less relevant to philosophy, or perhaps because he just was not aware of them. His main thesis revolves around negation. Strawson considered negation to be presupposition-preserving, which means that both B_A and NOT(B_A) entail **A**. In order to escape from the unwanted consequence that this would make **A** a necessary truth, Strawson gave up PET and introduced, besides 'true' and 'false', the possibility of lacking a truth value, realized in cases of presupposition failure.

He remained unclear, however, as to what 'truthvalueless' should be taken to mean. If taken literally, it is the absence of a truth value for sentences with presupposition failure. This, however, is problematic not only because it is possible to make such sentences true by the use of emphatic *not*, as in (10.12a–c) below, but also because the whole machinery of logic is based on the notion that its L-propositions express token propositions that are bearers of truth values.

It seems sensible, therefore, to treat Strawson's 'truthvalueless' as a truth value after all, but one that is 'infectious' in that it produces a lack of truth value whenever it figures in the input to any of the truth-functional propositional functions. The resulting propositional calculus is known as GAPPED BIVALENT PROPOSITIONAL CALCULUS, shown in Figure 10.2, where the negation operator is symbolized as '~' rather than '¬', since the negation is no longer the standard bivalent operator of standard logic. The alleged absence of a truth value is symbolized as '*'.

One sees that, in so far as the values T and F are assigned, Gapped Bivalent Propositional Calculus preserves standard propositional logic, while * is 'infectious' and makes any truth function inert (cf. Dummett 1973: 432).

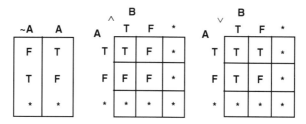

FIGURE 10.2 Strawson's Gapped Bivalent Propositional Calculus

Strawson's definition of presupposition is strictly logical. For him, 'B presupposes A' (B >> A) simply means that both B and ~B entail A. When A is false, both B and ~B 'lack a truth value.' This, purely logical, definition of presupposition is given in (10.11):

(10.11)   B >> A $=_{Def}$ B ⊢ A and ~B ⊢ A

This Frege-Strawson paradigm was attacked by Wilson (1975) and Boër and Lycan (1976), who side with Russell and his theory of descriptions. Their argument is that natural language negation is not invariably presupposition-preserving, as Frege and Strawson have it, but can very well be used to cancel presuppositions. This is correct, at least for many cases but not across the board (see Section 10.2). Wilson (1975) provides an effusion of examples illustrating this point, but fails to look for counterexamples. Thus, (10.12a–c) are well-formed and coherent, though they require some sort of emphatic, discourse-correcting accent, normally both on NOT and on the finite verb of the correcting sentence, as in (10.12a–c), or only on the latter when the correcting sentence takes the form of a *because*-clause, as in (10.13a–c):

(10.12)   a. The present king of France is NOT bald. There IS no king of France!
          b. Jill has NOT forgotten that Jack is her student. Jack ISN'T her student!
          c. Jack is NOT divorced. He never MARRIED!

(10.13)   a. The present king of France isn't bald because there IS no king of France!
          b. Jill hasn't forgotten that Jack is her student because Jack ISN'T her student!
          c. Jack isn't divorced because he never MARRIED!

Wilson, as well as Boër and Lycan, consider classical bivalent logic adequate for natural language: presuppositional entailments differ from classical entailments only 'pragmatically'. Their argument, however, is specious, no matter how forceful it may appear. It fails on several counts. First, these authors appear a little too gullible when accepting Russell's theory of descriptions without further ado and despite the weighty arguments against it. Then, their appeal to a 'pragmatic' explanation of presupposition-cancelling (radical) negation would be more convincing if such an explanation were available. Sadly, however, all one is presented with in Wilson (1975), as in whatever else has been written on a possible pragmatic account of radical negation, is a collection of suggestive, rhetorical, and sometimes just mistaken disquisitions, but no systematic observation of data and no *modus explanandi*. Had

Wilson (and Boër and Lycan) looked more carefully, they would have found, for example, that the presupposition-cancelling 'echo' negation NOT is not always possible, or that, by contrast, it is sometimes the only negation possible. Since that is clearly so, the conclusion must be that their 'pragmatic' way out is basically flawed. The matter is important enough to deserve a closer look. This is done in Section 10.4, but first we must provide some clarity on the nature and structural basis of presuppositions and on the operational criteria for recognizing them.

10.2 The origin and classification of presuppositions

The question of the origin of presuppositions has never been answered satisfactorily. It has been customary to speak of 'presupposition inducers', which, supposedly, could be listed but not, or hardly, explained or at least reduced to some stable parameters in linguistic descriptions. These presupposition inducers could be lexical predicates, as in the case of the predicate *be divorced*, or adverbials, as with *only*, or *still*, which induces the presupposition that the propositional content was true before the reference time and entails in the standard way that it is true at the time of reference. The quantifier *all* and the definite determiner *the* were likewise—mistakenly—taken to induce an existential presupposition with regard to the class quantified over or the intended reference object, respectively. Ever since this question arose, I have found this answer unsatisfactory, no matter how widely accepted it may have been, mainly because it is merely taxonomic and ad hoc, but also because it fails to integrate presuppositions into the machinery of semantics—quite apart from the factual errors it is based on.

Instead, I have always attempted to reduce presuppositions to the lexical meanings of the predicates occurring in a sentence, whereby the principle holds that every lexical item is a predicate at the level of semantic analysis (SA), including not only adjectives and verbs but also those elements that make their appearance in surface structure as prepositions, conjunctions, adverbs, quantifiers, negation, and other logical connectives. The main or matrix predicate is, on the whole, the predicate figuring as the main finite verb in surface structure, but it may also be an infinitival or participial, when, for example, an auxiliary predicate is realized in surface structure as the finite verb attracting finite-verb morphology (as with the perfect-tense auxiliary *have* in English). It is a matter of considerable delicacy to decide what presuppositions should be assigned to what predicates.

Presupposition inducers such as the adverbs *only* or *still* and many other items that do not have verbal status in surface structure are thus considered to be underlying predicates at the SA-level of representation. This, of course, requires a machinery to transform SAs into well-formed surface structures. The viability of this account of the origin of presuppositions thus depends in part on whether or not there is a chance that a syntactic theory reducing all presupposition inducers to 'deep' or underlying predicates in SAs will carry the day. The programme of developing such a syntactic theory is known as *Generative Semantics*, or, more properly, as *Semantic Syntax* (Seuren 1996). The requirement of a sound theory of syntax is thus seen to be far from trivial.

This approach has the double advantage of unifying presupposition theory and placing it in a functional context. It also provides for a uniform format for the specification of presuppositions, which are taken to be induced by certain given preconditions of lexical predicates. This can be shown as follows. A normal way of specifying lexical meanings is by means of a specification of the extension of any given lexical predicate F, defined by the conditions to be fulfilled by any object or *n*-tuple of objects to qualify for F. These conditions are called the *satisfaction conditions* of F. For example, one may think of specifying the satisfaction conditions of the predicate Feed as follows:

$$\|\text{Feed}\| = \{<\text{x,y}> \mid \text{x causes y to eat by bringing food to y's mouth or body}\}$$

to be read as 'the extension of Feed equals the set of all pairs of objects x, y, such that x causes y to eat by bringing food to y's mouth or body'. This may be satisfactory up to a point, but it fails to express the fact that only existing objects can feed and that only living objects can be fed. These conditions can be incorporated into the meaning description of Feed by splitting up the satisfaction conditions into, on the one hand, PRECONDI-TIONS and, on the other, UPDATE CONDITIONS. For the predicate Feed we do this in the following manner:

$$[\![\text{Feed}]\!] = \{<\text{x,y}> : \text{x and y actually exist; y is an animate being} \mid \text{x causes}$$
$$\text{y to eat by bringing food to y's mouth or body}\}$$

to be read as 'the extension of Feed equals the set of all pairs of objects x, y, such that (a) x and y actually exist and y is an animate being, and (b) x causes y to eat by bringing food to y's mouth'. Conditions listed under (a) are preconditions; conditions listed under (b) are update conditions.

Similarly for, for example, Be divorced:

⟦Be divorced⟧ = {x : x actually exists; x has been married till time *t* | x's marriage has been dissolved by legal procedure since time *t*}

or: 'the extension of **Be divorced** equals the set of all objects **x** such that (a) **x** actually exists and **x** has been married till the time *t* of the process of getting divorced, and (b) **x**'s marriage has been dissolved by legal procedure since time *t*'. (Clearly, the predicate **Be married** again has its preconditions, and so on.)[6]

Predicates that carry a precondition of actual existence with respect to a term **a** are called *extensional* with respect to **a**. Since most predicates are extensional with respect to their terms, we consider that to be the default case, which can be left without special notation. Some predicates, however, are not extensional with respect to some term. For example, the predicate *think about* is extensional with respect to its subject term, but not with respect to its object term, because one can think about anything at all, including nonexisting entities, such as mermaids, unicorns, or dodoes. When a predicate **F** is nonextensional (intensional) with regard to a term **a**, we asterisk that term position in the semantic specification. Thus, in the specification of the predicate **Think about** we asterisk the object-term position:

⟦Think about⟧ = {<x,y*> : x is endowed with cognitive powers | . . .}

This notation makes it clear that **Think about** is extensional with respect to its subject term but not with respect to its object term.

When predicates are used in sentences, their preconditions become presuppositions of the sentences in which they are used. This is how a sentence like *Jack is feeding the dog* acquires its presuppositions that both Jack and the dog actually exist and that at least the dog is an animate being. This is also how a sentence like *Jack is divorced* evokes a context in which it has been established that he was married until the moment the divorce became effective.

Often predicates are 'misused' in the sense that they do not fit into the current discourse. For example, when I say *The trees whispered in the wind*, in a context about a picnic in the woods, then, clearly, the verb *whisper* is out of

---

[6] Isidora Stojanovic correctly pointed out that the precondition of existence and that of having been married before, though presented as being on a par, intuitively seem to have a different status. I do not expand on this difference in the present text, but it seems to be reducible to the fact that the contextual role of existential presuppositions differs considerably from that of categorial presuppositions induced by specific lexical items such as *be divorced*. Denials of existence tend to have a much more profound effect on discourse construction than denials of specific lexically bound properties. Moreover, existential preconditions do not lend themselves to metaphoric use, as categorial preconditions do.

place, because it carries the precondition that the one who does the whispering must be a living being capable of speech. Since trees do not satisfy that condition, the wrong context is evoked and (radical) falsity should ensue. The current term for such a 'misuse' is CATEGORY MISTAKE. Some category mistakes, however, are evocative in a way that turns out to be inspiring or amusing or perhaps even moving, in that the object failing the precondition in question is regarded, for the purpose of the current discourse, as satisfying that precondition. The fact that the wrong context is evoked is exploited precisely for the purpose of evocation and association. When this is the case, one speaks of METAPHOR. In the sentence at hand, for example, the trees in question are regarded, for the purpose of the current discourse, as living beings capable of speech, which evokes a magical world of comparisons and associations.

A presupposition is thus a semantically defined property of a sentence making that sentence fit for use in certain contexts and unfit for use in others. This property is partly based on the fact that if a sentence Q presupposes a sentence P ($Q \gg P$), then Q entails P ($Q \vdash P$): whenever Q is true, P is necessarily also true—given the same situational reference points—in virtue of the meanings of Q and P. Presuppositions are thus a subclass of entailments, which, for the purpose of the present discussion, we call P-ENTAILMENTS. Entailments that are not presuppositional are called CLASSICAL or C-ENTAILMENTS. (10.14) illustrates a C-entailment ($\vdash_c$); (10.15a–d) illustrate P-entailments or presuppositions ($\gg$):

(10.14)   Jack has been murdered. $\vdash_c$ Jack is dead.

(10.15)   a. Jack lives in Manchester. $\gg$ Jack exists.
    b. Jill has forgotten that Jack is her student. $\gg$ Jack is Jill's student.
    c. Jack is divorced. $\gg$ Jack was married before.
    d. Only Jack left. $\gg$ Jack left.

(10.15a) is an instance of *existential presupposition*: to be murdered one must be an actually existing entity. (10.15b) exemplifies *factive presuppositions* (Kiparsky and Kiparsky 1971): the factive predicate *have forgotten* requires the truth of the *that*-clause.[7] (10.15c) is a case of *categorial presupposition*, derived from the lexical meaning of the main predicate *be divorced*. (10.15d) belongs to a *remainder category*, the presupposition in question being due to the particle *only*. For such cases, the generalization that presuppositions are

---

[7] Some predicates are WEAK FACTIVES, in that the truth requirement of the factive complement clause is not absolute but can be overruled, albeit with some difficulty. Examples of weak factive predicates are *regret, surprise, anger*, as in:

induced by lexical preconditions can be upheld only in terms of a well-founded theory that reduces surface particles like *only* to a predicate in the semantic analysis of any sentence in which it occurs.

10.3 Operational criteria for the detection of presuppositions

There are various differences between P-entailments and C-entailments. The first intuitively striking difference is that when $Q \gg P$, P is somehow 'prior' to Q. On further analysis it appears that this intuition arises from the fact that P restricts the domain within which Q is interpretable. Then, presuppositions present themselves specifically, dependent as they are on lexical meaning descriptions, whereas C-entailments are 'unguided' in that they are infinite in number and need not be semantically connected, as in the case of inconsistent sentences (like *All living animals are dead*), which, technically speaking, entail any arbitrary sentence. C-entailments thus lack the function of restricting the interpretation domain. This makes presupposition relevant for the cognitive aspects of linguistic information transfer.

But let us look now more specifically at the question of how one recognizes a presupposition. Since presuppositions are part of the language system, and not of the pragmatics of use, they are detectable ('observable') irrespective of actual token use. Like C-entailments, P-entailments can be read off isolated sentences, regardless of special context. This makes it possible, as has been observed, for P-entailments to evoke a context all by themselves—something C-entailments cannot do. (10.15a), for example, requires it to be contextually given that there actually exists someone called 'Jack' and thus evokes such a context, while it asserts that he lives in Manchester. (10.15b) evokes a context where Jack is Jill's student, while asserting that Jill has forgotten that. (10.15c) requires a context where Jack was married, and asserts that the marriage has been dissolved. And (10.15d) requires a context where Jack left, while asserting that no one else did. This, together with the criteria for detecting entailments to be discussed presently, provides a set of operational criteria to recognize presuppositions.

First, as has been said, if $Q \gg P$ then $Q \vdash P$. But on what grounds does one conclude that one sentence entails another (apart from the fact that in standard logic every sentence entails itself)? The usual heuristic criterion for

---

(i) Harold was under the illusion that his son had failed and this (namely that his son had failed) angered him.

Weak factive predicates invariably involve an emotive factor. See Gazdar (1979: 119–22) for some discussion.

an entailment $Q \vdash P$ is the incoherence of the juxtaposition of NOT(P) with Q. On the whole, this works well as a criterion for entailment in the general sense. For example, (10.16a) does not entail, and therefore does not presuppose, (10.16b), since (10.16c) is still coherent.

(10.16)   a. Lady Fortune neighs.
           b. Lady Fortune is a horse.
           c. Lady Fortune is not a horse, yet she neighs.

But this criterion overkills when the entailing sentence is qualified by an epistemic possibility operator, like English *may*, as in (10.17a), which does not entail (10.17b) even though (10.17c) is incoherent. Epistemic possibility requires compatibility of what is said to be possible with what is given in discourse or knowledge (see Section 7.2.1.3). Therefore, if $Q \vdash P$, then with NOT$[P]$ in the knowledge base, Possibly$[Q]$ results in inconsistency, even though Possibly$[Q]$ does not entail P. This means that the criterion for entailment must be refined. A viable refinement, without loss of generality, consists in testing the (in)coherence of the juxtaposition of Possibly [NOT$[P]$] with Q, as in (10.17d). Since (10.17d) is coherent, (10.17a) does not entail, and therefore does not presuppose, (10.17b) ('!' marks incoherence):

(10.17)   a. Jack may have been murdered.
           b. Jack is dead.
           c. !Jack is not dead, yet he may have been murdered.
           d. Jack may not be dead, yet he may have been murdered (and thus be dead).

By contrast, (10.18a) entails (10.18b), because one cannot coherently say (10.18c):

(10.18)   a. Jack has been murdered.
           b. Jack is dead.
           c. !Jack may not be dead, yet he has been murdered.

Further criteria are needed, however, to distinguish P-entailments from C-entailments. First there is the PROJECTION CRITERION: if $Q \gg P$ and Q stands under an entailment-cancelling operator like Possibly or NOT or Believe, P survives not as a P-entailment but as a more or less strongly INVITED INFERENCE (>) which can be overridden. Generally, O$[Q_P] > P$, where 'Q_P' stands for 'Q presupposing P' and 'O' for an entailment-cancelling operator. In standard terminology: the presupposition P of Q is PROJECTED through the operator O as an invited inference. To work out the conditions under which and the form in which presuppositions of embedded clauses are projected through higher operators constitutes the PROJECTION PROBLEM OF PRESUPPOSITION, discussed in Section 10.5.

Projection typically comes with P-entailments, as in (10.19a), not with C-entailments, as in (10.19b):

(10.19)   a. Jill believes that Jack is divorced > Jack was married before
          b. Jill believes that Jack has been murdered ⊅ Jack is dead

The projection criterion is mostly used with NEGATION as the entailment-cancelling operator. Strawson (1950, 1952) held, incorrectly, that presupposition is always preserved as entailment under negation. In his view, a sentence like (10.20a) still presupposes, and thus entails, that there exists a king of France, who therefore, if (10.20a) is true, must lack wisdom. However, according to the entailment criterion specified above, Strawson was wrong, because one can coherently say (10.20b):

(10.20)   a. The present king of France is not wise.
          b. The present king of France may not exist, but he is, in any case, not wise.

Although presuppositions are, in fact, normally weakened to invited inferences under negation, there are cases where they are not but remain presuppositions in the full sense of the term. More is said on this issue in Section 10.4 below. For the moment it suffices to say that, apart from such special cases, presuppositions are normally weakened to invited inferences under negation, as they are under other entailment-cancelling operators.

In Strawson's day, it was still customary to take what is in fact the default function of negation in presupposition-carrying sentences for a categorical function. As a result, Strawson's 'negation test' became the standard test for presupposition. We now know that this test is unreliable, for reasons set out in Section 10.4. If we still want to use it, it has to be heavily qualified.

We fare better with the DISCOURSE CRITERION: a discourse bit *P and/but Q$_P$* (with allowance for anaphoric processes) is felt to be consistent with the context given, orderly, and informative—that is, SEQUENTIAL. The condition of sequentiality is used to characterize stretches of acceptable text that have their presuppositions spelled out ('^{S}' signals sequentiality):

(10.21)   a. ^{S} There exists someone called 'Jack', and he lives in Manchester.
          b. ^{S} Jack is Jill's student, but she has forgotten that he is.

    c. ^S Jack was married, but he is divorced.

    d. ^S Jack left, and he is the only one who did.

C-entailments and inductive inferences lack the property of sequentiality. When they precede their carrier sentence the result may still be acceptable, yet there is a qualitative difference, as shown in (10.22a,b), where a colon after the first conjunct is more natural ('^C' marks nonsequential but coherent discourse):

(10.22)   a. ^CJack is dead: he has been murdered.

       b. ^CJack earns money: he has a job now.

The discourse criterion still applies through projection: P AND/BUT O[Q$_P$] is again sequential (the entailment-cancelling operators are printed in bold face):

(10.23)   a. ^S Jack really exists, and Jill **believes** that he lives in Manchester.

       b. ^S Jack is Jill's student, but she has **probably** forgotten that he is.

       c. ^S Jack was married in the past and he has **not** got divorced.

       d. ^S Jack left, and he is **not** the only one who did.

These tests reliably set off P-entailments from C-entailments. They thus form an operational test for the detection of presuppositions.

10.4 Some data that were overlooked

It appears that neither the Russell tradition (including the analysis proposed in Wilson 1975 and Boër and Lycan 1976) nor the Frege-Strawson tradition can carry the day. The former holds that natural-language negation *always* cancels all entailments (except those that are necessarily true in virtue of the meaning of the entailing sentence or sentences); the latter holds that negation *always* leaves presuppositional entailments intact and it seeks a way out of the predicament of having to call all presuppositions necessary truths by allowing an infringement of PET. The problem with both traditions is that they have both overlooked the fact that natural language negation does not *categorically* either cancel or preserve presuppositional entailments. Close inspection of the facts shows that, although *most of the time* natural language negation allows for the cancelling of presuppositions (provided it is invested with emphatic accent), it *sometimes precludes* and *sometimes requires* presupposition cancelling. Moreover, the criteria for optional or obligatory preservation or cancelling of presuppositions are of a systematic linguistic nature, which excludes, as a matter of principle, any kind of pragmatic account.

Let us have a closer look. Although no claim of completeness can be made, and further cases will probably come to light as research proceeds, we can say that in the following classes of cases negation is *per se* presupposition-preserving:

A. MORPHOLOGICALLY INCORPORATED NEGATIONS
Negative prefixes like *un-*, *in-*, *dis-*, *a-*, cannot fulfil the cancelling role of NOT. Thus, (10.24a) is felt to be inconsistent, whereas (10.24b) easily allows for the cancelling interpretation (initial '!' indicates inconsistency):

(10.24)   a. !Tim is UNrealistic about the risk. He doesn't know there to be one!
          b. Tim is NOT realistic about the risk. He doesn't know there to be one!

B. NEGATIONS IN NONCANONICAL POSITIONS
By 'canonical position' is meant the position of ordinary, unmarked sentence negation. For English, this is the position in construction with the finite verb form, with or without *do*-support. Remarkably, negations in any other position than the canonical one are necessarily presupposition-preserving, even when they are logically speaking the highest operator and thus function as sentence negation:[8]

(10.25)   a. !NOT only Harry laughed. He didn't laugh at all!
          b. It is not true that only Harry laughed. He didn't laugh at all!

(10.26)   a. !NOT all doors were locked. There wére no doors!
          b. All doors were NOT locked. There wére no doors!

Native intuition clearly says that the first sentence of (10.25a), with or without the emphatic accent on *not*, entails that Harry laughed, just as the same sentence without the initial *not*. As a whole, therefore, (10.25a) is incoherent, with or without the emphatic accent on *not*. This, in fact, is one of the clearest and most convincing cases showing that sentential negation in natural language is sometimes obligatorily presupposition-preserving. All one can do to make the negation cover the presupposition as well is to say something like (10.25b).

---

[8] The only exception, as was pointed out to me by Larry Horn (p.c.), is the English construction with *not even*, as in *Not even John was disappointed*. This semantically and grammatically complicated construction is discussed in Section 11.4.

As regards (10.26), both (10.26a) and (10.26b) are to be understood with the negation as the highest operator, followed by the universal quantifier. (10.26a) poses no problem for SMPC: since the first sentence of (10.26a) entails the existence of doors, owing to the equivalence in SMPC of ¬**A** and **I***, it is incompatible with the second sentence. But (10.26b), which should have the same analysis, does pose a problem for SMPC, precisely because its two sentences are compatible to the native speaker.

(10.26b) is of particular relevance because it conflicts with standard modern predicate logic and, therefore, with the conjunction analysis discussed above. For SMPC, NOT[ALL DOORS were LOCKED] is equivalent with SOME DOORS were NOT LOCKED and should, therefore, entail the existence of doors. This would make the conjunction *There were no doors and not[all doors were locked]* inconsistent. In fact, however, it is not, provided the negation is placed in the canonical position and is provided with heavy emphatic accent, as in (10.26b).

C. Negations in nonassertive clauses or in the scope of higher operators
Negations in nonassertive main sentences and in many subordinate clauses or infinitivals cannot cancel presuppositions:

(10.27)   a. !Tim seems NOT to be back. He hasn't been away at all.
           b. √Tim does NOT seem to be back: he hasn't been away at all.

(10.28)   a. !Tim may NOT be divorced. He never got married in the first place.
           b. √Tim can't be divorced: he never got married in the first place.

(10.29)   !Do NOT go back to your wife. You haven't even left her.

D. Negations with certain quantifiers
As was demonstrated in (10.26b), the negation with the quantifier ALL can be used to cancel presuppositions, provided it is placed in the canonical position. Not so, however, it seems, with, for example, *each* (*of the*), or *both* (*of the*):

(10.30)   !Each of the children was NOT given a sweet. There wére no children!

(10.31)   !Both of his children are NOT spoiled. He hás no children!

E. Nonextraposed factive subject clauses
When a factive *that*-clause in semantic subject position is preposed (or, if one prefers, nonextraposed) in surface structure, the negation over the factive

main verb is, though in the canonical position, unable to cancel the factive presupposition, as shown in (10.32a), though it may affect other presuppositions, as is made clear by (10.32c). Only if the factive subject clause is extraposed, as in (10.32b), can the (canonically placed) negation cancel the factive presupposition:

(10.32)   a. !That Tom is clever does NOT irritate Joanna. He ISN'T clever!
          b. It does NOT irritate Joanna that Tom is clever. He ISN'T clever!
          c. That Tom is clever does NOT irritate the king of France. There IS no king of France.

One notes, moreover, that when the factive clause is pronominalized by means of *that*, the factive presupposition still remains intact under negation, as is shown in (10.33a). But when the negation is reinforced with epistemic possibility and comes out as *cannot*, the factive presupposition can be cancelled, as in (10.33b):

(10.33)   a. !That does NOT irritate Joanna. He ISN'T clever! (cf. (10.32a))
          b. That CANNOT (possibly) irritate Joanna. He ISN'T clever!

These observations were not made in either Wilson (1975) or Boër and Lycan (1976). Had they been made, they would have undermined their analysis.

F. CLEFT AND PSEUDOCLEFT CONSTRUCTIONS

As is well known, cleft and pseudocleft constructions have a specific existential presupposition associated with the clefted WH-constituent: if in the noncleft version of the sentence this constituent requires a really existing object for the sentence to be true, so does the clefted constituent, whether in cleft or in pseudocleft constructions. This presupposition is uncancellable by negation:

(10.34)   !What he said was NOT 'Damn!'. He said nothing at all!

Here the existential presupposition applies to the WH-constituent *what he said*, since for something to be said it must, albeit for a brief moment, actually exist. But other presuppositions not directly associated with the clefted constituent are fully cancellable:

(10.35)   Who wrote the letter was NOT Mr. Davis. Mr. Davis doesn't exist!

Here it is presupposed that someone wrote the letter, since in order to write a letter one must actually exist. But Mr. Davis's existence is not presupposed, because in the semantic analysis of the cleft sentence *be Mr. Davis* is the value-assigning predicate *be$_v$*.

G. CONTRASTIVE ACCENTS

Contrastive accents form an exact parallel to the (pseudo)cleft constructions. In sentences with contrastive accent the accented constituent serves as a predicate establishing the identity of the entity mentioned in the nonaccented part. This latter entity is presupposed to exist in all cases where it is in the corresponding sentence without contrastive accent. This presupposition cannot be cancelled under negation:

(10.36)   !The WAITER did NOT start the argument. Nobody did!

Again, however, other presuppositions, such as those associated with the accented part functioning as an underlying predicate, are freely cancellable:

(10.37)   The WAITER did NOT start the argument. There wás no waiter!

H. NEGATIONS WITH NEGATIVE POLARITY ITEMS

As is well known, every language has a, usually large, number of so-called 'negative polarity items' (NPIs). These are words, constructions, or expressions which, mostly for unknown reasons, require a negation or, for some NPIs at least, a negative word, when used in simple declarative sentences. (Their behaviour in other clause-types differs in ways that have as yet never been exhaustively studied.) Some, but not all, NPIs allow for emphatic auxiliaries (*do*-support when there is no auxiliary) as a form of negativity. In the examples below the NPIs are italicized. (10.38a) is a standard case. In (10.38b,c) one has NPIs with negative words (*hardly, difficult*). (10.38d) is a case of emphatic *do*-support:

(10.38)   a. She *could*n't *possibly* have known that.
           b. She could hardly breathe *any more*.
           c. It was difficult (*easy) for him to go on *any longer*.
           d. It DOES *matter* that Jones is an alcoholic.

The negation required in simple assertive clauses with NPIs (if there is no other negative word and no auxiliary emphasis) is *per se* presupposition-preserving, for all presuppositions in the sentence. Thus, the examples of (10.39) are all felt to be inconsistent, if not outright ungrammatical:

(10.39)   a. !It does NOT *matter* that Jones is an alcoholic. He ISN'T! (factive)
   b. !Jones does NOT live in Paris *any more*. He doesn't exist!
      (existential)
   c. !He did NOT *at all* acknowledge my presence. I wasn't there!
      (factive)

NPIs have a counterpart in so-called 'positive polarity items' (PPI). When a PPI stands directly under negation, the sentence loses its default property of inviting presuppositional inferences and acquires what is known as an 'echo-effect' to an even stronger degree than in presupposition-cancelling sentences without a PPI: it sounds as if the same sentence but without the negation has been uttered (or strongly suggested) in immediately preceding discourse, preferably by a different speaker. Take, for example, the PPI *still*, which induces the presupposition that what is said in the rest of the sentence, if in the present tense, was true at least till the moment of utterance, and the sentence as a whole asserts that that situation continues to obtain. Contrast this with the NPI *any more*, which induces the same presupposition but lets the sentence, with the obligatory negation, assert that that situation has ceased to obtain. Thus, given a sentence with the PPI *still*, its natural negation will not be that sentence with the default-cancelling and 'echoing' NOT but rather that sentence with *still* replaced by *not... any more*, as in the following pair:[9]

(10.40)   a. Harold *still* lives in Paris.
   b. Harold *doesn't* live in Paris *any more*.

The test is now that the presuppositions of (10.40a) have not become invited inferences but are cancelled altogether when simple *not* is inserted, whereas those of (10.40b) are not cancellable, just as in (10.39b):

(10.41)   a. Harold does NOT still live in Paris: he has never set foot in France.
   b. !Harold doesn't live in Paris *any more*: he has never set foot in France.

Examples of English PPIs are (see also Seuren 1985: 233): *rather, far from, hardly, terrific, daunting, ravenous, staunch, as fit as a fiddle, at most, at least, perhaps, already, certainly, surely, awful, even, each, both, most, some, several,*

---

[9] For the reader's reassurance, I have often tested this out with my students. The reader, if in a teaching position, might do the same. He or she will then find out that, when the students are asked to give the negation of a sentence like (10.40a), their answer will be (10.40b).

few, not. Note that the negation word *not* is itself a PPI: a succession of two or more occurrences of *not* has the effect of cancelling all presuppositions and creating an echo. But if there is no stark succession of two *not*s, as in (10.42) below, they can both be presupposition-preserving.

Thus, generally, when a PPI stands in the immediate scope of NOT it cancels the presuppositions of the sentence, not leaving even an invited inference. It then also produces an echo-effect. However, Baker (1970) observed that, interestingly, this is not so when there is double negation (other than stark succession of *not*s), as in (10.42), with the PPI *rather*:

(10.42)   There is nobody here who wouldn't *rather* be in Montpelier.

This sentence carries no echo-effect and contains no radical negation, despite the occurrence of *rather*. Baker's observations are tantalizing, but still unexplained.

A further unexplained complication is that some, but not all, PPIs can stand under an unaccented *not* when an explicit or implicit comparison is made:

(10.43)   a. You are not *still* building (as we are).
         b. She hadn't *already* finished (as you had).

Such sentences have a (slight) echo-effect, but preserve presuppositions in so far as these are not induced by *still* or *already*.

PPIs are generally excluded in the scope of implicitly negative operators (or, if one prefers, operators with underlying negation), such as the comparative *than*, as shown in (10.44a). In (10.44b), the PPI *some* is outside the scope of *than* (as opposed to *any* in the same position); this sentence is interpreted as 'there are some of her colleagues who she is richer than' ('*': ungrammatical):

(10.44)   a. *She is richer than you *already/still* are.
         b. She is richer than some of her colleagues.

If the comparative particle *than* is analysed as containing an underlying negation (see Seuren 1973), this agrees with the observation made in **A** above that morphologically incorporated negations are necessarily presupposition-preserving and cannot take PPIs in their immediate scope.

Just as it is, for the most part, unknown what causes the phenomena mentioned under **A–H**, it is not known what system or mechanism is responsible for the emergence of polarity items, whether positive or negative, and their behaviour. Nor is much known about the question of what factors lie behind the fact that often the negation word cancels presuppositions as entailments but leaves them as invited inferences, while in certain classes of cases it preserves some or all of the presuppositions in the sentence at hand, and in other classes of cases it eliminates even the invited inference of the presuppositions—the projection problem. It would seem that a theory of topic–comment modulation might lay bare the grounds of the necessary preservation of presuppositions in the categories **E** (non-extraposed factive clauses), **F** ((pseudo)clefts) and **G** (contrastive accents). Sentences that fall under these categories have a grammatically fixed topic–comment structure built into them in such a way that the presupposition adheres to the topic, and presupposition-cancelling can probably be shown to be incompatible with topic-hood. Yet on the whole, our theoretical insights still fall short of an explanation of the facts concerned.

Even so, however, the answer cannot be merely that the negation operator in language is just the simple bivalent truth-functional operator known from standard logic, somehow modified by pragmatic factors. Pragmatic types of analysis are in principle unable to cope with the clear-cut difference between the cases where presuppositions are necessarily preserved and those where they are necessarily cancelled. The minimal conclusion to be drawn is that there are at least three systematically differing ways of using the negation: (i) with the presuppositions necessarily preserved, (ii) with the presuppositions reduced to invited inferences, and (iii) with even the invited inferences removed. The question is now: what theory has the best chance of coming to grips with the facts observed above? A Gricean pragmatic theory may be considered for certain peripheral parts of the question, but it does not seem the first choice for the central problems, given the known failure, so far, of such theories in those areas. The observed facts are anyway too linguistically structural to be a natural object for pragmatics, whose typical hunting ground is the nonlinguistic interactional aspects of communication by means of utterance tokens.

If presupposition is not a pragmatic phenomenon, is it a logical phenomenon? Again, the answer appears to have to be negative. If, as we have posited, presuppositions originate in the preconditions of predicates, and if the *raison d'être* of these preconditions is to restrict the use of predicates to certain classes of situations, then presupposition is primarily a semantic property of sentences, whose function it is to restrict the use of sentences to certain classes of contexts (discourses). Presupposition is thus a discourse-semantic phenomenon with, as one might expect, consequences for the logic of language. These consequences, however, are epiphenomenal on the true nature of presuppositions; they do not define presuppositions. This enables us to modify the Strawsonian definition of presupposition given in (10.11) above in the following way (again, one notes that the symbol used for negation is '~', not the standard bivalent '¬'; the symbol '≃' stands for the radical, presupposition-cancelling negation):

(10.45)   If $B \gg A$ then $B \vdash A$ and $\sim\!B \vdash A$ and $(\sim\!A$ or $\underset{\sim}{\sim} A) \vdash \underset{\sim}{\sim} B$.[10]

What this means for propositional logic is explained in Sections 10.6 and 10.7.

10.5 Presupposition projection

10.5.1 *What is presupposition projection?*

As was said in Section 7.2.2.2, presupposition projection is the phenomenon that presuppositions of embedded clauses (E-PRESUPPOSITIONS) tend to percolate upward into higher domains, either as fully entailed presuppositions, or as default inferences. In the former case they *require*, in the latter case they *prefer*, a higher **D** admitting them. If the requirement is not met, the sentence in question is unfit for the **D** at hand and is rejected. If the preference is not met, the sentence in question is still acceptable in **D** but the E-presupposition stays within its own subdomain (or, as is explained below, is relegated to a more general recipient subdomain).

The driving force behind this phenomenon is the *Principle of Maximal Unity of discourse domains*, discussed in Section 7.2.2. This principle makes listeners keep their **D**s as compact as possible. Since maximization of compactness is a general feature of human interpretative processes (Ockham's razor is one manifestation of it, and so is the principle of induction), presupposition projection is a direct consequence of the way the mind deals with its environment in a general sense. For that reason, presupposition projection is maximal: it will make concessions only when forced to.

A powerful means of upward percolation of E-presuppositions is provided by the process of accommodation or post hoc suppletion discussed in Section 10.1. It takes little effort to see that in cases where presuppositions have not

---

[10] The inverse does not hold. It is possible for both B and $\sim\!B$ to entail A, without A being a presupposition of B (or $\sim\!B$). For example, both B and $\sim\!B$ entail any necessary truth T, but T is most probably not a presupposition of B (or $\sim\!B$). Or consider the fact that if B and/or $\sim\!B$ entail A, they also entail $A \lor C$ (the entailment schema of addition; see Section 3.3.2), where C is any arbitrary sentence, but $A \lor C$ is highly unlikely to be a presupposition of A. Moreover, as is shown in Section 10.6, conjunctions of the form $B \land B_A$ cannot be taken to presuppose A, even though (minimal or radical) falsity of A leads to the radical falsity of $B \land B_A$.

been spelled out explicitly, their post hoc suppletion will take them as far as possible into the higher domains. That process is stopped only when the introduction into a higher domain leads to inconsistency either with the domain itself or with independently available situational or world knowledge. In other words, E-presuppositions will percolate upward as long as they are *compatible* with any higher domain they are about to invade. It is for that reason that presupposition projection is, normally speaking, a *default* process, which can be overruled by contrary information. It is stopped by inconsistency and enforced when the presupposition in question is entailed in the domain in question. In between there is a gliding scale of possibilities, which is analysed in some detail in the present section.

For sentences that are looked at in isolation, regardless of any specific context they may occur in, the question of whether an E-presupposition makes it upward or not, and if so in what form, depends on the predicate or the instruction that has created the subdomain, given the principles of **D**-construction. Following Karttunen (1973: 178), the literature has made a distinction between (a) HOLES: predicates which cannot stop presuppositions and let them through as full entailing presuppositions because they entail and often presuppose their argument clauses, (b) FILTERS: predicates which let presuppositions through but in the weakened form of default inferences, and (c) PLUGS: predicates which categorically stop presuppositions from creeping upward.

During the 1970s and 1980s, presupposition theory was entirely dominated by the question of what formalism would account for presupposition projection, whereby no account was taken of the fact that the entire projection mechanism is driven by, and becomes transparent in the light of, the Principle of Maximal Unity that governs discourse incrementation processes. Instead, one looked for a strictly formal calculus, very much in the tradition of formal semantics that was en vogue during that period. The total disregard for the ecology of the phenomena at issue led to a situation where the debate became sterile and fruitless, as a result of which it inevitably petered out. Now that a more realist course is taken in discourse semantics and some greater clarity exists regarding **D**-structures and incrementation processes, the question can be looked at in a new and more explanatory light.

10.5.2 *Projection from lexical subdomains*

Let us look at sentence (10.46), containing the main verb **Hope**, which creates (or continues) an intensional subdomain.

(10.46)   Joan hoped that her son's new girlfriend would have better manners than the previous one.

Taken in isolation (10.46) carries the following default inferences: (a) Joan had a son, (b) Joan's son had a girlfriend, (c) Joan's son had a previous girlfriend, and (d) her son's previous girlfriend's manners could be improved. In a context containing the information (a), (b), (c), and (d), (10.46) is perfectly sequential—that is, consistent with the context given, orderly, and informative. Yet none of these inferences are entailed, as they can all be cancelled. Let us start with (d). (10.46) is still fully sequential if preceding context says that Joan's son's previous girlfriend had perfectly good manners but Joan herself thought less well of the manners of this girl. The default inference (c) is equally vulnerable, because the preceding context may contain the information that Joan's son's actual girlfriend was his first one, in which case the default inference (c) is cancelled and prevented from projecting, but the text remains fully sequential. Likewise for the default inference (b), because preceding text may have told the listener/reader that Joan had been misinformed and that, in fact, her son never had a girlfriend at all, which still leaves (10.46) fully sequential. Similarly again for the default inference (a), which can likewise be eliminated by preceding context. **D** may contain the information that Joan lives in a world of her own making. Poor Joan never had any children but in her own fantasy she had a son, who once had an ill-mannered girlfriend. In such a context, (10.46) may well describe Joan's latest delusion. In sum, the more default inferences are scrapped, the more Joan seems to be out of touch with reality. The conclusion is that the verb **Hope** is a so-called 'filter', letting through its E-presuppositions as default inferences as long as they are not stopped by contrary information stored in higher domains or in available knowledge.

One would expect presuppositions that do not make it into a higher domain to stay put as presuppositions of the domain in which they have been generated. While this is true for many subdomain-creating predicates, it is not true for all. As was pointed out in Section 7.3.3, there appears to be a class of predicates that do not let their subdomains take in nonprojected presuppositions but, instead, send them to a subdomain created by a predicate that is higher in the subdomain hierarchy. *Hope* is one such predicate. In a context where the default inference (d) of (10.46) is blocked, (10.46) is not interpreted as saying something like (10.47a), but rather as saying something like (10.47b). The blocking of the default inference (c) requires a specification of a subdomain for Joan's belief about her son's previous girlfriend or girlfriends:

(10.47)   a. Joan hoped that her son's previous girlfriend's manners could be improved and that her son's new girlfriend would have better manners.

        b. Joan believed that her son's previous girlfriend's manners could be improved and she hoped that her son's new girlfriend would have better manners.

Those subdomains that need an appeal to a different subdomain for the storage of nonprojected presuppositions are called *subsidiary subdomains*, while the receiving subdomain is named *recipient subdomain* (Section 7.3.3). As far as can be seen, given the present state of the enquiry, it looks as if subsidiary subdomains are created or continued either exclusively or typically by *emotive* complement-taking predicates.

These include predicates like *hope* or *fear*, but also the weak factive predicates like *regret*, or *surprise*. In the case of strong or weak factives, projection does not primarily affect the E-presuppositions of the weak factive complement clause but the clause itself in its entirety or any of its semantic, including presuppositional, entailments. Weak factives differ from ordinary strong factives in that a negation of their presupposed *that*-clauses in **D** or in available knowledge strongly resists, but in the end does yield to, the incrementation of the sentences in the superordinate **D** (see note 7). In Sections 3.2 and 6.2.3.2 of Volume I it was observed that weak factives do not allow for substitition *salva veritate* of topic–comment modulation and the following examples were given, repeated here as (10.48a,b):

(10.48)   a. It surprised/angered Ann that JOHN (and not Kevin) had sold the car.

        b. It surprised/angered Ann that John had sold THE CAR (and not the speedboat).

It requires little effort to see that (10.48a) differs truth-conditionally from (10.48b)—a fact that has so far remained undiscussed in the semantics or pragmatics literature.

Weak factive predicates are thus almost 'holes', but not quite. Contextual overruling seems possible, since sentences like (10.49a,b) are still sequential— that is, consistent and informative—albeit perhaps with some difficulty:

(10.49)   a. Kevin had been falsely told that John had left the country and it surprised/angered him that John had done that.

        b. Someone had whispered into Ann's ear that John had sold the car, although John had done nothing of the sort, and it surprised/ angered her that JOHN had done that.

What we now see is that nonprojection of the presupposed complement clause or any of its presuppositional or other semantic entailments on account of contextual blocking requires a subdomain for Ann's *belief*, not for her *surprise* or *anger*, to store the nonprojected subordinate clause or its entailments. Suppose someone had whispered into Ann's ear that John had sold the car, whereas John had done nothing of the sort, the proper interpretation of (10.48a) is not (10.50a) but (10.50b):

(10.50)   a. It surprised/angered Ann that John had sold the car and that it had been JOHN to do so.
          b. Ann had been made to believe that John had sold the car and it surprised/angered her that it had been JOHN to do so.

We thus have subsidiary subdomains, created by complement-taking emotive predicates and needing a recipient subdomain for the storage of nonprojected presuppositions. A subclass of the complement-taking emotive predicates creating subsidiary subdomains is the class of weak factives, which are still admissible when the current **D** contains the information that the factive *that*-clause is false, in which case they relegate the presupposed factive *that*-clause to the recipient subdomain of what the repository of the emotion in question believes to be true. It also seems that, in general, the emotive predicates creating subsidiary subdomains disallow the substitution *salva veritate* of topic–comment modulation in their complement clauses.

Now consider the causative predicates. In sentence (10.51), the embedded infinitival *her seek shelter in the basement of her house* carries the E-presuppositions that (a) she had a house and (b) the house had a basement. These E-presuppositions must be projected upward on pain of the discourse becoming inconsistent and thus incoherent. This is so because, given the metaphysical fact that what has been physically caused has actual being, predicates like *make* or *cause* require full incrementation of the entire content of the object clause in the superordinate **D**. As a result, they are not intensional with regard to their sentential object term:

(10.51)   The bombing made her seek shelter in the basement of her house.

Sentence (10.52) is different, in that here the main predicate *realize* is a strong factive—that is, it presupposes the truth of its object clause with all its E-presuppositions and other entailments, even though it is intensional with regard to its object clause and thus does not allow for *substitution salva veritate* in it. Therefore, when used in the commitment domain, (10.52) requires the incrementation of its object clause before it can itself be incremented, and, with its object clause, also the presuppositions thereof.

(10.52)   She realized that she would never get her husband to give up smoking.

In Karttunen's terms, the predicate *realize* is, therefore, also a 'hole', but not for the same reason that makes causative predicates 'holes'.

Now to the epistemic modal predicates *may* and *must*. Epistemic *may*, discussed earlier in Section 7.2.1.3, strongly projects its E-presuppositions into any **D** that is compatible with them. It has the peculiar property that, on the one hand, it does not entail its argument clause or that clause's E-presuppositions, while, on the other hand, the whole modal sentence is refused in a **D** (with the concomitant knowledge base) where that argument clause or any of its E-presuppositions have been declared false, as is shown by (10.53b) below. Incrementation in an incompatible **D** of a sentence with a main predicate of epistemic possibility results in a strong intuition of inconsistency. Yet such a sentence does not entail its argument clause. When the current **D** is not explicit on the truth or falsity of the complement clause and/or its presuppositions and thus leaves open the possibility that they are true, the E-presuppositions are projected into a subdomain of epistemic possibility. We shall see in a moment that the truth-functional disjunctive operator OR shares with MAY the property of being blocked by negative information on either of its disjuncts in **D** while not entailing them, merely requiring compatibility. Just as MAY, OR strongly projects its E-presuppositions in any compatible **D**, but does not entail them. What is entailed is that the disjuncts, together with their projected E-presuppositions, are *possible*.

The following sentences illustrate the projection properties of epistemic MAY:

(10.53)   a. Andy may have left his car in the garage.
           b. !!Andy doesn't have a car but he may have left it in the garage.
           c. Andy may have a car and he may have left it in the garage.
           d. Andy may not have a car but he may (also) have left it in the garage.

In (10.53a), the embedded infinitival 'Andy have left his car in the garage' presupposes that Andy has a car. This E-presupposition, though not entailed under MAY, is not only blocked from projecting if it is negated in the higher **D** but such blocking makes the whole modal sentence unacceptable, as is shown by (10.53b), which is strongly felt to be inconsistent. The reason for this is that, as argued in Section 7.2.1.3, epistemic MAY requires truth of the relevant present knowledge state **K**, besides the requirement that the embedded infinitival clause is consistent with **K**. This makes it inconsistent to say first that Andy has no car and then that he left his car in the garage. But it does allow for a knowledge state that is not explicit on whether Andy has a car, because Andy having left his car in the garage is consistent with such a knowledge state.

Sentence (10.53b) is thus felt to be inconsistent. (10.53c) shows that the E-presuppositions of MAY project into a subdomain of possibility unless blocked by negative information in **D**. And (10.53d) shows that 'Andy has a car' is not entailed by (10.53a).

Like MAY, epistemic MUST requires a knowledge state that contains or still admits the incrementation of 'Andy has a car'. But unlike MAY, epistemic MUST entails its embedded clause, because it requires for truth that the relevant knowledge state **K** of the speaker is correct and that the deduction schema followed for the MUST-statement is valid. These two conditions suffice for the entailment of the embedded clause complete with its presuppositions. The difference between epistemic MAY and MUST shows up in (10.54a–d). (10.54a) and (10.54b) run parallel with (10.53a) and (10.53b), respectively. (10.54c) is incoherent on account of the fact that it violates the domain hierarchy for epistemic inference shown in Figure 7.3 in Section 7.3.3. The incoherence of (10.54d) shows that (10.54a) entails 'Andy has a car' (according to the operational criterion developed in Section 10.3):

(10.54)   a. Andy must have left his car in the garage.
           b. !!Andy doesn't have a car but he must have left it in the garage.
           c. !Andy may have a car and he must have left it in the garage.
           d. !Andy may not have a car but he must have left it in the garage.

10.5.3 *Projection from instructional subdomains*

• *Conjunction*[11]

The conjunction predicate AND (sometimes realized as BUT) immediately and obligatorily secures the incrementation of both conjuncts to the current **D**, in the order in which they are presented. That is, the first conjunct is

---

[11] A large part of the recent literature on the projection properties of the propositional connectives is, though formally very elaborate, in fact irrelevant, as it fails to take into account the ecological embedding of language in cognition and society. To take just one example, Schlenker (2007) criticizes the dynamic approach proposed in Heim (1990) and in principle endorsed in the present book on the grounds that (Schlenker 2007: 327–8):

incremented first while all its non-incremented presuppositions are supplied post hoc (accommodated). Then the second conjunct is incremented, while all its non-incremented presuppositions are supplied post hoc in the **D** as it is after the full processing of the previous conjunct. And so on for any following conjuncts.

This means that conjunctions project their E-presuppositions conjunct by conjunct, each conjunct being a separate incrementation unit. This is important in the light of the often heard objection that if AND is taken to project its E-presuppositions the way other 'holes' do, primary-anaphora cases like (10.55) lead to the paradox that conjunction sentences both classically and presuppositionally entail what is asserted in the first and presupposed in the second conjunct:

(10.55)   John has a car and [his car/it] is in the garage.

This objection loses its force when it is stipulated that AND does not inherit any presuppositions of its argument conjuncts but treats them as independent but successive incrementation units. Such a stipulation is, of course, not arbitrary but follows from the fact that AND is the primary conjoiner of successive increments.

In many cases, as the discussion in Section 8.2.1 makes clear, the order of incrementation has an extra *iconic force* in that it reflects the temporal, causal, or motivational order of the events described. In such cases we speak of *ordered interpretation*. The precise conditions of ordered interpretation of AND-conjunctions are not clear, though it appears that, at least for temporal ordering, the conjuncts must have an event, and not a situational, interpretation. It, moreover, looks as if nonidentity of the main predicates in the conjuncts involved plays a major role, in that it appears to be a necessary but not sufficient condition for an ordered interpretation that the two main predicates involved must not be identical (see examples (8.41) to (8.46) in Section 8.2.1). Be that as it may, as far as the 'dynamic' projection is concerned

---

Heim's dynamic semantics is just *too* powerful: it can provide a semantics for a variety of operators and connectives which are never found in natural language. To make the point concrete, it suffices to observe that in Heim's framework one could easily define a deviant conjunction *and** with the same classical content as *and* but a different projection behavior [...] with the order of the conjuncts reversed.

It should be obvious that Schlenker's *and** is unnatural for reasons that have nothing to do with the formalities of presupposition projection and everything with the fact that the order of incrementation corresponds with the order of presentation of successive utterances (with post hoc suppletion as a functional artifice making it possible to economize on the effort of speaking). One thus sees how research can get out of touch with reality as a result of an all too narrow formalist approach.

of the presuppositions of the successive conjuncts of AND, it is safe to assume that across the board the treatment is as sketched above, no matter whether or not the conjunction is open to an ordered interpretation: the conjuncts are anyway incremented in the order of occurrence and their presuppositions are, if necessary, obligatorily projected along with them, but always after the incrementation of the preceding conjunct.

• *Negation*

In the light of what has been said in Section 10.4, we can be brief about the projection properties of the minimal and radical negation operators. The minimal negation entails and thus obligatorily projects the E-presuppositions of its argument L-proposition. When any such E-presupposition is incompatible with **D**, the negative sentence is inadmissible in **D**. In such cases, the speaker/listener must fall back on the radical negation, which takes its argument L-proposition as a linguistic object (hence the echo-effect induced by radical NOT) and declares it inadmissible in **D** on account of presupposition failure.

• *Disjunction*

The disjunctive operator OR, as has been said, is in many ways like epistemic MAY. It does not entail its disjuncts and projects their E-presuppositions as default inferences so as to ensure maximal unity in the overall discourse domain. But it requires a superordinate **D** that is compatible with the disjuncts as well as with their negations, since there is no point in presenting the disjuncts as possible increments if **D** has already banned them. When the superordinate **D** is compatible with but silent about the E-presuppositions of a disjunct, the E-presuppositions in question are *projected* into **D** as relatively strong default inferences and they are *entailed* in a subdomain of epistemic possibility: P (AND NOT-Q) OR (NOT-P AND Q) entails that both P (AND NOT-Q) and (NOT-P AND Q) are epistemically possible.

The OR-expansion defined in (8.67) of Section 8.2.3 incorporates AND but this makes no difference for the projection mechanism. All one has is two or more alternative incrementation packages.

• *Implication*

In Section 8.2.4 we surmised that the conditional structure IF P then Q is, at a basic-natural level, expanded to the biconditional IF P then Q AND IF Q then P and at a strict-natural level to IF P then P AND Q, which is logically equivalent with the standard material implication. Two alternative subdomains are set up, one for P AND Q and one for NOT-P AND NOT-Q at a basic-natural, and for just NOT-P at a strict-natural level. The difference with OR is that, for implication, the relation between the overt antecedent and the overt consequent clause is the dynamic relation that exists between successive conjuncts. The disjunctive operator OR has no such relation between the overt disjuncts.

The projection properties of natural language implication follow from this description. The antecedent clause requires a **D** that is compatible with it and hence with its E-presuppositions, so that the whole conditional sentence is inadmissible in a **D** that contains information contrary to what is said or presupposed in the antecedent clause. The consequent clause requires compatibility with **D** as it is after the incrementation of the antecedent clause. Primary anaphora is thus allowed in conditionals, as shown in (10.56a). In (10.56b), the antecedent clause presupposes that Nancy has a husband. If **D** contains information that is incompatible with the news that Nancy has a husband, the whole of (10.56b) is inadmissible in **D**. (10.56b) thus entails that it is possible that Nancy has a husband and it projects the invited inference that she has one, in accordance with the Principle of Maximal Unity proposed in Section 7.2.2. The consequent clause of (10.56b) has the factive, and thus entailed, E-presupposition that Nancy's Norwegian husband is faithful. This E-presupposition is obligatorily projected not in the **D** as it was before **IP** started work on (10.56b) but in the **D** as it will be after the antecedent is incremented, ensuring that a text like 'Nancy has a husband. He is Norwegian. He is faithful. She knows that he is.' is fully sequential—that is, consistent with the context given, orderly, and informative.

(10.56)   a. If Nancy has a husband, he is Norwegian.
            b. If Nancy's husband is Norwegian, she knows that he is faithful.

All the, partly far-fetched, examples adduced in Gazdar (1979: 83–7) and later literature regarding the projection properties of conditionals are accounted for by the incrementation mechanism proposed here and the ecological context in which it is placed.

10.5.4 *Summary of the projection mechanism*

All the properties illustrated in Sections 10.5.1 to 10.5.3 are epiphenomenal on (a) the structure of **D**s and the processes involved in incrementation, and (b) the meanings of, or the instructions associated with, the predicates in question. An overall survey of the entailment and projection properties of S-embedding predicates is given in Figure 10.3, where the boxes contain

Entailment scale / Projection scale	Entailed	Not entailed			
	Requires compatible D Refused in contrary D		Not refused in contrary D	Indifferent to contrary D	Requires contrary D
strong ▲	1 Causatives Factives Epistemic MUST Minimal not	2 Epistemic MAY OR (2x) Antecedent IF of conditionals	3 Weak (emotive) factives Belief verbs Emotives (hope, complain) antifactives counter-factuals	4	5
Projected / **weak** ▼					
Not projected				Verbs of saying	Radical NOT

FIGURE 10.3 Projection chart for E-presuppositions

predicates creating or continuing recipient subdomains in the sense defined above.

Figure 10.3 shows the relation between entailment and projection. All entailing predicates project obligatorily, in a descending order of strength: causatives more strongly than factives, factives more strongly than epistemic MUST, and epistemic MUST, it seems, more strongly than minimal NOT. Non-entailing predicates also project, except verbs of saying and radical NOT. Verbs of saying do not project because of the very fact that they report on what someone has said or will say, which may be in a **D** that has no relation to the current **D**. As a result, they are indifferent to any possible contrary **D**. Radical NOT goes further in this respect. For a sentence under radical NOT to be properly anchored, a **D** is required that is incompatible with one or more E-presuppositions. For example, for (10.57) to be properly anchored, it is necessary that **D** contain, or be made to contain, the information that the E-presupposition of the L-proposition embedded under NOT saying that John has a dog is false:

(10.57)   John's dog has NOT been put in quarantine. He hás no dog!

The predicates that do not induce the entailment of their E-presuppositions yet may project their E-presuppositions under certain conditions are more interesting. Of these, some require a **D** that is compatible with their E-presuppositions, while others allow for a **D** that is not. The former class comprises epistemic MAY, OR and the conditional IF in antecedent clauses. These pose the heaviest restrictions on **D** in that they cannot be anchored, let alone project their E-presuppositions, in a **D** that contains information that leads one to conclude that one or more of their E-presuppositions are false. When **D** does not contain the positive information that an E-presupposition *P* of any of these predicates has been stored in it (though it may be), these predicates induce the entailment that *P* is *possible* in **D**, with the result that *P* ends up in the recipient subdomain of epistemic possibility. Thus, sentence (10.58a) is incoherent because, owing to the satisfaction conditions of MAY (see Section 7.2.1.3), **D** must be at least compatible with the information that John has a dog for *John's dog may be in quarantine* to be incrementable. Likewise for OR and IF of the antecedent of conditionals, as is demonstrated in (10.58b) and (10.58c), respectively.

(10.58) a. !!John has no dog but his dog may be in quarantine.
       b. !!John has no dog but his dog is either in quarantine or in the park.
       c. !!John has no dog but if his dog is in quarantine it will be well fed.

That the second sentences in (10.58a–c) do not *entail* that John has a dog appears from the coherence of (10.59a–c) (see Section 10.3):

(10.59) a. John may have no dog but he may have one and then it may be in quarantine.
       b. John may have no dog but he may have one and then it is either in quarantine or in the park.
       c. John may have no dog but he may have one and then if it is in quarantine it will be well fed.

By contrast, the predicates listed in column 3 of Figure 10.3 do allow for anchoring in a **D** that is inconsistent with their E-presuppositions. Consider the following sentences:

(10.60) a. John has no dog but he thinks he has one and that it is in quarantine.
       b. John has no dog but he thinks he has one and he regrets that it is in quarantine.

    c. John has no dog but he thinks he has one and he hopes that it is in quarantine.

    d. John has no dog but he thinks he has one and he is under the illusion that it is in quarantine.

    e. John has no dog but, if he had one and it was in quarantine, he would miss it.

Sentence (10.60a) is a classical example of projection blocking: since **D** is inconsistent with the E-presupposition that John has a dog, this E-presupposition is not projected but stays with John's belief-domain. (10.60b,c,d) are examples of projection blocking whereby the blocked E-presupposition is confined to the recipient subdomain of John's beliefs. (10.60d) instantiates the ANTIFACTIVE main verb *be under the illusion*. Antifactives are predicates inducing a presupposition not of the *truth* but of the *falsity* of their embedded clauses. Examples are *be under the illusion that, lie that, falsely suggest that,* or German *wähnen* (used by Frege in his 1892 article). They form a neglected category, yet it is a real one. In so far as antifactives involve a sincere but false belief, as with *be under the illusion that*, their E-presuppositions are relegated to a recipient subdomain of belief.

    (10.60e) is a counterfactual construction. Counterfactual IF carries the precondition that the clause *C* in its scope has been coded in **D** as being false. Thus, the sentence *If John's dog were in quarantine, John would miss it* presupposes that John's dog is not in quarantine, while the counterfactual IF-clause has the E-presupposition that John has a dog. Now in cases where **D** says or entails that John has no dog, it also entails that John's dog cannot be in quarantine, thus providing a proper anchoring base for (10.60e). The E-presupposition that John has a dog is now prevented from projecting and must stay within the subdomain created by counterfactual IF.

10.6 The presuppositional logic of the propositional operators

Although, as has been stressed repeatedly, presupposition is not a logical but a discourse-semantic phenomenon, it does allow for a logic to be distilled from it. This logic is trivalent in that it has, besides truth, two kinds of falsity and two negations. MINIMAL FALSITY (F1) ensues when an update condition of the main predicate (which generates a classical and not a presuppositional entailment) is not satisfied; it is repaired to truth by the default MINIMAL NEGATION ($\sim$). RADICAL FALSITY (F2) ensues when a precondition of the main predicate (generating a presuppositional entailment) is not satisfied; this kind of falsity is repaired to truth by the marked RADICAL NEGATION ($\simeq$). This presupposition-related distinction between two kinds of falsity was made, but not further elaborated, in Dummett (1973: 425–6) and further elaborated in Seuren (1980, 1985, 1988, 2000).

We repeat the discourse-semantic definition of presupposition in terms of a logical condition given in (10.45) above:

(10.45)   If B >> A then B ⊢ A and ~B ⊢ A and (~A or ≃A) ⊢ ~B.

Together with the semantics of radical NOT for presupposition failure, the principle that F2 has priority over F1 and F1 over T for ∧, and that T has priority over F1 and F1 over F2 for ∨, makes for the following truth tables for the propositional operators concerned in strict-natural or standard propositional logic:

A	~A	≃A
T	F1	F1
F1	T	F1
F2	F2	T

∧ conjunction (B across top, A down side):

∧	B: T	B: F1	B: F2
A: T	1 T	2 F1	4 F2
A: F1	2 F1	3 F1	5 F2
A: F2	4 F2	5 F2	6 F2

∨ disjunction (B across top, A down side):

∨	B: T	B: F1	B: F2
A: T	1 T	2 T	4 T
A: F1	2 T	3 F1	5 F1
A: F2	4 T	5 F1	6 F2

FIGURE 10.4 Three-valued Presuppositional Propositional Calculus (PPropC₃)

The minimal negation operator (~) makes minimal falsity true and leaves radical falsity unaffected, whereas the radical negation operator (≃) makes radical falsity true and leaves minimal falsity unaffected, both making truth minimally false. The ~ operator yields truth when all preconditions of the main predicate are satisfied but at least one update condition is not. The ≃ operator says that at least one precondition of the main predicate is not satisfied. The standard bivalent negation ¬, though probably not occurring in natural language, remains operative in that it yields truth when either a precondition or an update condition is not satisfied. Thus, for any sentence A, ¬A ≡ ~A ∨ ≃A.

Conjunction (∧) is defined by the condition that radical falsity (F2) is infectious in the sense that when at least one conjunct is radically false, so is the conjunction. Then when neither conjunct is radically false, minimal falsity (F1) is infectious in that, when at least one conjunct is minimally false, so is the conjunction. A conjunction is true only when both disjuncts are true. Conversely, disjunction (∨) is defined by the condition that truth (T) is infectious in the sense that when at least one disjunct is true, so is the disjunction. Then when neither disjunct is true, minimal falsity (F1) is infectious in that, when at least one disjunct is minimally false, so is the disjunction. A disjunction is radically false only when both disjuncts are radically false. This yields the truth tables of Figure 10.4.

It is important to note that, if the condition that falsity of A leads to the radical falsity of B were a *defining* condition of B >> A, then a conjunction of the form A ∧ B$_A$ would presuppose A, because the falsity of A makes the whole conjunction radically false. Yet we do not want to say that A ∧ B$_A$ >> A, because then A ∧ B$_A$ would both assert and presuppose A. Thus, even though it follows from the *logic* of conjunction that conjunctions of the form A ∧ B$_A$ are radically false when A is (minimally or radically) false, this does not mean that B *presupposes* A. The reason is that presupposition is not a *logical* but a *discourse-semantic* notion, and the latter takes precedence over the former. The conjunctive sentence operator AND may have a logic as an emerging property, but it is *defined* as a discourse-incrementer: 'A and B' carries the instruction, and thus means, 'increment A first and then B', as specified in Section 8.2.1. And since presupposition is defined as a condition on preceding discourse, A ∧ B$_A$ can only have a presupposition C if C is required in the discourse that precedes A ∧ B$_A$ as a whole.

In Figure 10.4, the slots for conjunction and disjunction have been given numbers 1–6. This has been done to render it possible to state the various valuation spaces and hence the entailment relations holding in the system. There are nine valuations (3^2 for two L-propositions and three truth values), but only six VSs are needed, since the operators ∧ and ∨ are symmetrical. The numbers in the slots of Figure 10.4 correspond to the following combinations of T, F$_1$, and F$_2$:

VS:	1		2		3	4		5		6
A	T	F$_1$	T	F$_1$	F$_2$	T	F$_2$	F$_1$		F$_2$
B	T	T	F$_1$	F$_1$	T	F$_2$	F$_1$	F$_2$		F$_2$

We use the following notation:

AND:	A ∧ B	~AND:	~(A ∧ B)
OR:	A ∨ B	~OR:	~(A ∨ B)
AND*:	~A ∧ ~B	~AND*:	~(~A ∧ ~B)
OR*:	~A ∨ ~B	~OR*:	~(~A ∨ ~B)
≃AND:	≃(A ∧ B)	AND≚:	≃ A ∧ ≃B
≃OR:	≃(A ∨ B)	OR≚:	≃ A ∨ ≃B
≃AND*:	≃(~A ∧ ~B)	....	
≃OR*:	≃(~A ∨ ~B)	....	

This gives the VS-model of Figure 10.5. The circle around space 3 in Figure 10.5 has been printed bold because the valuation spaces 1, 2, and 3 form

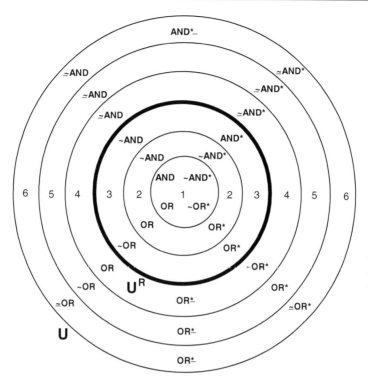

FIGURE 10.5 Valuation-space representation of strict natural PPropC$_3$

the presuppositionally restricted universe $\mathbf{U^R}$ of situations causing no pre-supposition failure and thus no radical falsity. Figure 10.6 gives the polygonal representation of PPropC$_3$, but without the radical negation (the superscript '$\mathbf{R}$' over the metalogical relations restricts the validity of the relation to the spaces 1, 2, and 3). Within $\mathbf{U^R}$ standard propositional logic is valid (with standard $\neg$ for the presuppositional minimal negation $\sim$). When all spaces are taken into account, one sees that $\sim(A \wedge B) \vdash \sim A \vee \sim B$ but not vice versa, while $\sim A \wedge \sim B \vdash \sim(A \vee B)$ but not vice versa. Also, $\sim A \vee \sim B$ entails none of the other admissible conjunctions or disjunctions or their minimal or radical negations. With minimal negation, De Morgan's laws thus do not hold but have been reduced to one-way entailments.

A polygonal representation of the entire system may result in an aestheti-cally pleasing picture of a polygon with 18 vertices, each standing for a basic expression with and without minimal or radical external and/or internal negation, but it would seem that such a labour of love should rather be left to the true devotees who are interested in the logical system as such, regardless of what is required for the use it is put to in natural linguistic interaction.

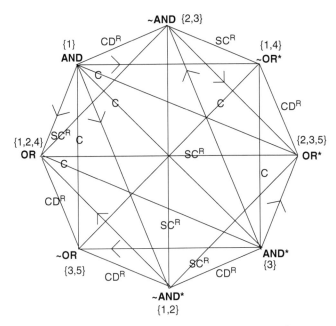

FIGURE 10.6 Octagonal representation of strict-natural (= standard) PPropC$_3$ without radical negation

Meanwhile, the reader will quickly ascertain that the following expression types of PPropC$_3$ correspond with the valuation spaces specified:

/AND/ = {1}	/~AND/ = {2,3}	/$\underset{\sim}{}$AND/ = {4,5,6}	/AND*/ = {6}
/OR/ = {1,2,4}	/~OR} = {3,5}	/$\underset{\sim}{}$OR} = {6}	/OR*/ = {4,5,6}
/AND*/ = {3}	/~AND*/ = {1,2}	/$\underset{\sim}{}$AND*/ = {4,5,6}	....
/OR*/ = {2,3,5}	/~OR*} = {1,4}	/$\underset{\sim}{}$OR*} = {6}	....

One also finds that the following duality relations hold between **AND** and **OR**:

$$\underset{\sim}{}OR \equiv AND^* \equiv \sim OR^* \quad \underset{\sim}{}AND \equiv OR^* \equiv \underset{\sim}{}AND^*$$

That is, **AND** and **OR** are duals only under the radical negation. Moreover, De Morgan's laws do hold for the radical negation $\underset{\sim}{}$ and also for the standard negation ¬ but not for the minimal negation ~, as is easily shown. This means that PPropC$_3$ is isomorphic with standard bivalent propositional calculus for the negation operators $\underset{\sim}{}$ and ¬, but not for the minimal negation ~. Figure 10.6 shows immediately that, for the minimal negation, **AND** ⊢ ~**OR*** but not

OR (∨)

∨	B: T	F1	F2
A: T	[1] F1	[2] T	[4] T
F1	[2] T	[3] F1	[5] F1
F2	[4] T	[5] F1	[6] F2

NOR (•)

•	B: T	F1	F2
A: T	[1] F1	[2] F1	[4] F2
F1	[2] F1	[3] T	[5] F2
F2	[4] F2	[5] F2	[6] F2

FIGURE 10.7 Truth tables for OR (∨) and NOR (•) in basic-natural $PPropC_3$

vice versa, and **~AND*** ⊢ **OR** but not vice versa. Moreover, **~AND** ⊢ **OR*** and **AND*** ⊢ **~OR**, but not vice versa.

As is shown in Weijters (1985), $PPropC_3$ can be expanded to $PPropC_n$ with $n–1$ negations and n truth values, for $n > 1$. Standard propositional calculus is thus seen to be just the extreme minimal instance of $PPropC_n$, while $PPropC_3$ represents the three-valued variant. In Seuren et al. (2001) it is shown that the Kleene calculus (Kleene 1938, 1952) is likewise the three-valued variant of a system with, in principle, an unlimited number of truth values between, not beyond, any given pair of successive truth values. The Kleene set of many-valued propositional logics can be combined with the presuppositional set of many-valued logics, resulting in a system of propositional logic with an unlimited number of definite truth values and an equally unlimited number of values that are intermediate between any pair of successive definite truth values. This rather extends the number of possible propositional logics natural language could choose from when it started on its evolutionary path.

Basic-natural $PPropC_3$ differs in certain respects from its strict-natural or standard counterpart. The operators ~, ≈ and ∧ are not affected, but the operator ∨ is. Moreover, as one recalls from Section 3.4.2, there is the further operator NEITHER NOR, symbolized here as '•', and occurring in the sentence type **NOR**, which is defined as ~A ∧ ~B. The three-valued truth tables for basic-natural $PPropC_3$ are as given in Figure 10.7.

Basic-natural (exclusive) OR differs from strict-natural or standard OR in that it produces truth only when one of the constituent L-propositions is true. Given this, it is still so that T has priority over F1 and F1 over F2. Basic-natural NOR is defined on the basis of the assumption that the negations involved are minimal negations. On this assumption, NOR produces truth only when both (all) constituent L-propositions have the value F1—that is, in space 3. Given this, the principle holds that F2 has priority over F1 and F1 over T (as for the conjunctive operator ∧). The corresponding VS-model is shown in Figure 10.8.

Here we see that **NOR** is equivalent with **AND***, both sharing the VS {3}. Moreover, **OR*** entails **~AND** but not vice versa, since {2} ⊂ {2,3}. This is of

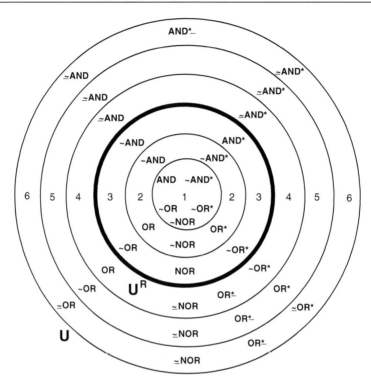

FIGURE 10.8 Valuation-space representation of basic-natural PPropC$_3$

special interest in the light of examples (3.24) and (3.25) of Section 3.4.2, repeated here as (10.61) and (10.62):

(10.61)   a. He doesn't like planes or trains.
          b. He doesn't like planes and he doesn't like trains.

(10.62)   a. He doesn't like planes and trains.
          b. He doesn't like planes or he doesn't like trains.

The point is that (10.61a) is naturally reduced to (10.61b), while a reduction of (10.62a) to (10.62b) is highly unnatural and requires a good deal of reflection. In Section 3.4.2 it was shown that in *bivalent* basic-natural propositional logic (10.61a) is equivalent with (10.61b), whereas (10.62a) is not equivalent with (10.62b). Here we see that the same holds in *trivalent* basic-natural propositional logic, so that the explanation given in Section 3.4.2 for this difference can be maintained.

But is natural language negation really ambiguous between a minimal and a radical negation as defined above? Horn (1985) does not think it is. Horn first posits that a distinction must be made, in natural language, between a 'descriptive' and a 'metalinguistic' negation, the former being negation as used in the normal flow of speech and meant to deny the truth of the proposition in its scope, while the latter is used to deny the appropriateness of specific words or expressions, the phonology or the pronunciation, or indeed of the whole sentence. Examples of metalinguistic negation, in Horn's sense, are:

(10.63) a. No Johnny, aunt Bessie isn't SPLITTING tomorrow, she is LEAVING.
  b. He doesn't hate SOME of his pupils. He hates them ALL.
  c. He is not in his 'læb'r´ 'tori but in his l´ 'bor´t´ri.
  d. It is NOT sad that she died so young. She is still very much alive.

While it is certainly correct and very necessary to distinguish between a descriptive and a metalinguistic use of negation and to classify the radical negation as being metalinguistic on account of the echo-effect it provokes, it is highly doubtful whether the radical negation, as exemplified in (10.63d) (as well as in (10.12), (10.13) and many other examples above), is sufficiently accounted for by placing it in one 'natural class' along with cases of lexical selection or phonological realization such as (10.63a–c). The reason for this doubt lies in the fact that, as has been pointed out, the negation that cancels presuppositions cannot occur in any other position in the sentence than what has been called the canonical position, which, for English, is the position in construction with the finite verb form (see category **B** in Section 10.4: negation in noncanonical positions necessarily preserves presuppositions). The point is that the metalinguistic negation as exemplified in (10.63a–c) does not have to be in the canonical position, witness, for example, sentences like the following:

(10.64) a. Not several but all guests left after the row.
  b. Not Lizzy, please, but Her Majesty the Queen is wearing a
     funny hat.   (cf. Horn 1985: 133)

In (10.64a,b) the negation precedes the surface subject, and is, therefore, not in the canonical position. One notes, moreover, that the quantifier *several*, which is, as we have seen, a PPI, does not function as a PPI here, apparently because the word used is not *several* but its quoted counterpart '*several*'. If it had been a PPI here, the negation would have had to occupy the canonical position, and would have been presupposition-cancelling. This difference is real, and considerably weakens Horn's thesis that all cases of utterance correction form one natural class, which must, therefore, be accounted for uniformly. Note, for example, the difference between (10.65a), which is an acceptable case of presupposition-cancelling, and (10.65b,c), which are not, because of their being inconsistent:

(10.65)   a. He did NOT only lose a thousand pounds. He lost nothing at all!
          b. !Not/NOT only did he lose a thousand pounds. He lost nothing at all!
          c. !He not/NOT only lost a thousand pounds. He lost nothing at all!

A theory like Horn's will have to explain why (10.65b,c) do not work, while (10.64a,b) do.

This is not just a grammatical problem (though, if it were, it would be serious enough), it is also a semantic problem. For, contrary to what this theory predicts, the negation over 'ordinary' cases of metalinguistic negation, correcting lexical choice or phonological realization, does not cancel presuppositions. Take, for example, (10.63a,b) above, and try replacing the second sentence—that is, the correction—by a presupposition denial. The result is unacceptable:

(10.66)   a. !No Johnny, aunt Bessie isn't SPLITTING tomorrow. There is no aunt Bessie!
          b. !He doesn't hate SOME of his pupils. He doesn't exist!

It seems unlikely, therefore, that presupposition denials belong in one single class with the other cases of metalinguistic negation. A further distinction appears to be called for, setting presupposition denials apart from other cases of metalinguistic negation.

Then, there is the problem why English, and with it all known languages, does not systematically distinguish between the two functions reserved for negation—a problem raised by Gazdar (1979: 65–6):

But no language, to the best of my knowledge, has two or more different types of negation such that the appropriate translation of *John doesn't regret having failed* could be automatically 'disambiguated' by the choice of one rather than the other.

This is a problem that plagues all theories of ambiguous *not*. One might counter this argument by saying that such 'universal' ambiguities do occur. No language is known, for example, to distinguish formally between the two senses of:

(10.67)   There's a fly in the middle of the picture.

Such ambiguities are likely to come with the language machine the human race is natively endowed with. Even so, however, it must be admitted that a theory that manages to subsume all different varieties of negation under one, formally precise umbrella definition, covering the logical differences as well as the differences of a more pragmatic nature, is preferable to a theory that makes negation (multiply) ambiguous without any unifying formula. No such umbrella definition, however, has been found to date.

10.7 The presuppositional logic of quantification

10.7.1 *The presuppositional version of the Square and of SMPC*

We define the universal quantifier in trivalent presuppositional predicate calculus (PPredC$_3$) as in (10.68) (one recalls that the colon is followed by the preconditions and the upright stroke by the update conditions of the predicate defined):

(10.68) $[\![\forall]\!] = \{< [\![G]\!], [\![F]\!] > : [\![F]\!]$ satisfies the preconditions of $G \mid [\![F]\!] \subseteq [\![G]\!]\}$

(The universal quantifier $\forall$ denotes the set of all pairs of predicate extensions $[\![G]\!]$ and $[\![F]\!]$ such that (precondition) all elements of $[\![F]\!]$ satisfy the preconditions of the predicate G, and (update condition) $[\![F]\!]$ is included in $[\![G]\!]$.)

The quantifier $\forall$ thus inherits the preconditions of the matrix predicate G, which are to be satisfied by the members of the set denoted by the restrictor predicate F. As a result of the presuppositionalization of the universal quantifier the distinction we were forced to maintain between strict-natural **ABPC** and constructed SMPC has now vanished. When $\forall$ in SMPC is presuppositionalized as in (10.68), it turns out to be identical with ABPC, whose undue existential import has now been subsumed under, and solved by, the general precondition that the elements in $[\![F]\!]$ should satisfy the preconditions of the matrix predicate G. For, if $[\![F]\!] = \emptyset$, then the truth value of type-**A** sentences will depend on whether the G-predicate is or is not extensional with respect to the restrictor term. If G is extensional with respect to the restrictor term and thus requires that $[\![F]\!] \neq \emptyset$ (in a purely extensional version of the logic concerned), then ALL F is G will be radically false when $[\![F]\!] = \emptyset$. And likewise for all other possible preconditions of G. This is the force of the Cartesian argument *Cogito ergo sum*, because *cogitare* (think) is extensional with regard to its subject term.

In fact, when the logic is properly intensionalized, as it should be, the F-class will never be null, because the thought underlying any properly contextually and situationally integrated utterance by definition creates intensional objects, which allow for reference and quantification as naturally as actually existing extensional objects do. There will, therefore, always be a nonnull intensional F-class to fall back on for reference or quantification. All that remains in a properly intensionalized predicate logic is a precondition of actual existence for extensional argument positions. The problem of UEI has thus been generalized to preconditions of predicates.

One notes, in particular, that we do not follow the advice, usually given by well-meaning standard logicians (see Section 4.1) to presupposition theorists, to define $\forall$ as in (10.69), as if the universal quantifier induced an entailment of actual existence, thereby avoiding truth for cases where $[\![F]\!] = \varnothing$:

(10.69) $[\![\forall]\!] = \{< [\![G]\!],[\![F]\!] > \mid [\![F]\!] \subseteq [\![G]\!] \text{ and } [\![F]\!] \neq \varnothing\}$

One reason for not following this advice is simple: it is not the universal quantifier but the matrix predicate G that is held responsible for the problems arising in connection with the situations where $[\![F]\!] = \varnothing$. In fact, the standard-logicians' advice is a little careless, because following it up would mean that NOT ALL F is G would come to mean 'either some F is not-G or there are no Fs'. And if one then wants to keep the Conversions, SOME F is NOT-G would mean the same, which is absurd (see Section 5.2.4 for a more detailed discussion).

Our solution to the problem of UEI is different. In accordance with the hypothesis that all presuppositions, including those of actual existence, are derived from the preconditions of matrix predicates, we say that the problem of UEI is solved by an appeal to the semantic description of the matrix or G-predicate. The source of existential import is thus located in the existential precondition of the matrix predicate. A sentence like (10.70a) has existential import with respect to the set of all houses because it presupposes the existence of at least one house (or, rather, at least two houses, since ALL is a plural determiner), not because of the semantics of the universal quantifier but because the matrix predicate *be damaged* is semantically (lexically) defined as being extensional with regard to its subject term.

(10.70)   a. All houses were damaged.
           b. All mermaids are a product of some writer's imagination.

By contrast, (10.70b) does not have existential import and does not presuppose the actual existence of mermaids, because the matrix predicate *be a product of some writer's imagination* is nonextensional (intensional) with regard to its subject term. Thus, sentence (10.70a) is radically false when there are no houses, but (10.70b) is not radically false just because there are no mermaids. In the world as it is, (10.70b) is either true or minimally false, depending on whether it is indeed so that all mermaids are a product of some writer's imagination. If some particular mermaid was not thought up by a writer, but, say, by a sculptor, (10.70b) is minimally false.

This system of truth-value assignments is thus not restricted to cases of existential preconditions. It covers all preconditions of any lexical predicate in matrix position. Thus, a sentence like (10.71) is likewise radically false, not because of a failure to satisfy the existential precondition of the predicate *sing*, which requires the actual existence of at least some singer(s), but because of the failure to satisfy some other precondition of the same predicate, in this case the precondition that those who do the singing should be entities capable of making vocal noises—a property one can hardly assign to apples other than in a metaphorical sense.

(10.71)   All apples were happily singing cantatas.

Failure to satisfy the preconditions of the matrix predicate is considered to be the only source of radical falsity. The lexical matrix predicate imposes its preconditions on its terms regardless of whether these terms are universally quantified or definite. If this is a valid principle, as I propose it is, the quantifiers have no bearing on the presuppositional properties of sentences; only the lexical matrix predicate has. The presuppositional variety of predicate logic is thus not only relevant for just the logical constants but has a direct and all-pervasive bearing on the logical analysis of language as a whole, since presuppositional preconditions adhere to almost every predicate in the lexicon of every language. Logic has thus become an integral part of the semantic description of languages, not as a modelling tool, as in model-theoretic formal semantics, but as part of the language machinery itself.

So far, we have only looked at the universal quantifier, which was sufficient to eliminate the problem of UEI. But since we must define the whole of PPredC3, the question now presents itself whether the existential quantifier should likewise be taken to 'inherit' the preconditions of the matrix predicate or whether it should stay as in nonpresuppositional ABPC or SMPC. This is a choice we are facing: either we don't do anything and define ∃ as in standard predicate logic, as in (10.72a), or we add the same precondition as has been added to the universal quantifier, as in (10.72b):

(10.72)   a. $[\![\exists]\!] = \{<[\![G]\!],[\![F]\!]> \mid [\![G]\!] \cap [\![F]\!] \neq \varnothing\}$
(The existential quantifier ∃ denotes the set of all pairs of predicate extensions $[\![G]\!]$ and $[\![F]\!]$ such that the intersection of $[\![G]\!]$ and $[\![F]\!]$ is nonnull.)

   b. $[\![\exists]\!] = \{<[\![G]\!],[\![F]\!]> : [\![F]\!]$ satisfies the preconditions of $G \mid [\![G]\!] \cap [\![F]\!] \neq \varnothing\}$

(The existential quantifier ∃ denotes the set of all pairs of predicate extensions ⟦G⟧ and ⟦F⟧ such that (precondition) all elements of ⟦F⟧ satisfy the preconditions of the predicate G, and (update condition) the intersection of ⟦G⟧ and ⟦F⟧ is nonnull.)

It is hard to decide between the two. The assignment of radical falsity to a sentence like *No mermaid has a bank account* or its paraphrase *There is no mermaid that has a bank account* appears counterintuitive. But if these sentences are considered true and *some* is considered to be preconditionless, which seems to agree with natural intuitions, then *No mermaid does not have a bank account* or its paraphrase *There isn't a mermaid that hasn't a bank account* should also be true, according to Figure 10.9a. But this runs counter to natural intuition, since, for natural intuition, the latter two sentences are equivalent with *All mermaids have a bank account*. According to Figure 10.9b, this equivalence does indeed hold, since, in Figure 10.9b, /**A**/ = /~**I***/. But then *Some mermaid has a bank account* and *No mermaid has a bank account* should both be reckoned to be radically false.

Perhaps we should opt for two varieties of the existential quantifier, one represented by bare *some* and one by *some of the*, whose negation is *none of the*. Bare *some* would then be preconditionless and be defined as in (10.72a), corresponding to the VS-model in Figure 10.9a, while *some of the* would be defined as in (10.72b), corresponding to the VS-model in Figure 10.9b. Minimal falsity would then be assigned to *Some mermaids have a bank account* and truth to *No mermaid has a bank account*. But both *Some of the mermaids have a bank account* and *None of the mermaids has a bank account* would be radically false. If this solution is adopted, the radical falsity of *Some of the mermaids have a bank account* parallels that of *All mermaids have a bank account* and *The mermaids have a bank account*, which has a definite, nonquantified subject term. The Conversion law **A** ≡ ~**I*** would then be restricted to *some of the* and not extend to bare *some*.

It seems sensible, given the still tender state of the theory and in particular our still deficient knowledge of the difference between *some* and *some of the* and between *all* and *all of the*, to leave the question undecided for the time being. Either way, the general principle regarding the source of existential import can be maintained:

Existential import as regards the extension of an argument term *t* of a predicate G derives solely from the fact that G is extensional with

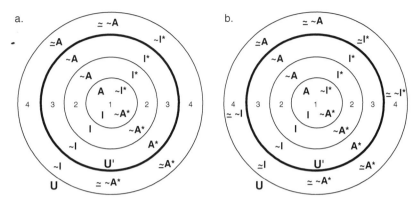

FIGURE 10.9 Two candidates for the VS-modelling of PPredC$_3$

regard to *t*. When **G** is nonextensional (intensional) with regard to *t*, there is no existential import with regard to *t*.

The difference between bare *some* and *some of the* would then be that for bare *some* existential import is a C-entailment whereas for *some of the* it is a P-entailment.

The spaces 1, 2, and 3 form the restricted universe **U**^{R}, the class of situations where all presuppositions are fulfilled: the *presuppositional subuniverse* of **U**^{R}. Space 4 in Figure 10.9b contains only radically negated positive or negative sentences. In Figure 10.9a, by contrast, the radical negations in space 4 are restricted to **A** and **A*** (and their minimal negations) whereas **I** and **I*** are minimally negated, as a result of the fact that (10.72a) specifies no preconditions for ∃ so that **I** and **I*** cannot be radically false. In both cases, **U**^{R} comprises precisely those situations where all presuppositions are satisfied. ABPC (the Square) holds as long as the logic is restricted to **U**^{R}. If this analysis is correct, we have saved the Square from logical disaster: UEI no longer spoils the system. And it does not correspond too badly with natural intuitions. We can thus eat our pudding and have it.

One notes that both the internal and the minimal external negations are otiose when preceded by the external radical negation: $\simeq$**A** $\equiv$ $\simeq$**A*** $\equiv$ $\simeq$~**A**$\equiv$ $\simeq$~**A***. This follows from the fact that the radical negation $\simeq$ merely says that its argument proposition contains a presuppositional error, so that the discourse as built up through prior utterances must be repaired. This analysis is consistent with the observation made above (category **C** in Section 10.4) that negations in the scope of a higher operator are necessarily presupposition-preserving. That being so, the internal negation must be minimal.

Consider the **A**-form ALL F is G and the corresponding **A***-form ALL F is NOT-G. Since NOT in NOT-G is presupposition-preserving, the complement of $[\![G]\!]$ is restricted to **U**^{R}, within which all preconditions of the matrix predicate G are satisfied. Given that under radical negation truth results only when one or more of the preconditions of G are not satisfied, and since the preconditions of G and NOT-G are identical, it follows that the radical negation makes all eight basic sentences types of the calculus not containing the radical negation equivalent.

10.7.2 *The presuppositional version of BNPC*

Let us now see what happens when a presuppositional component is added to the basic-natural predecessor of ABPC, BNPC, resulting in basic-natural PPredC$_3$ or BNPPredC$_3$. As before, when the elements in $[\![F]\!]$ fail to satisfy the preconditions of the G-predicate, radical falsity is assigned to **A** and ~**A** but truth to ~**I** and ~**I***, and also to **N** and **N***. The satisfaction conditions for the quantifiers ALL, SOME, and NO in BNPPredC$_{3>}$ are thus as follows ($[\![F]\!]$ and $[\![G]\!]$ are distinct natural sets):

(10.73) a. $[\![\forall]\!] = \{< [\![G]\!],[\![F]\!]> : [\![F]\!]$ satisfies the preconditions of G $| [\![F]\!] \subset [\![G]\!]\}$
（The universal quantifier $\forall$ denotes the set of all pairs of predicate extensions $[\![G]\!]$ and $[\![F]\!]$ such that (precondition) all elements of $[\![F]\!]$ satisfy the preconditions of the predicate G, and (update condition) $[\![F]\!]$ is properly included in $[\![G]\!]$.)

b. $[\![\exists]\!] = \{< [\![G]\!],[\![F]\!]> | [\![G]\!] \ \text{⓪} \ [\![F]\!]$ or $[\![G]\!] \subset [\![F]\!]\}$
（The existential quantifier $\exists$ denotes the set of all pairs of predicate extensions $[\![G]\!]$ and $[\![F]\!]$ such that $[\![G]\!]$ and $[\![F]\!]$ are in mutual partial intersection or $[\![G]\!]$ is properly included in $[\![F]\!]$.)

c. $[\![N]\!] = \{< [\![G]\!],[\![F]\!]> | [\![F]\!] \ OO \ [\![G]\!]\}$
（The negative existential quantifier N denotes the set of all pairs of predicate extensions $[\![G]\!]$ and $[\![F]\!]$ such that $[\![G]\!]$ and $[\![F]\!]$ are in total mutual exclusion.)

Again, the variables $[\![F]\!]$ and $[\![G]\!]$ do not *have* to be restricted to natural sets: the logic will simply assign a truth value to any given admissible expression keyed to any given situation. One notes that $\forall$ is defined as requiring *proper* inclusion of $[\![F]\!]$ in $[\![G]\!]$, while $\exists$ requires that $[\![F]\!]$ and $[\![G]\!]$ M-partially intersect. This makes /**A**/ and /**I**/ mutually exclusive, so that **A** and **I** are contraries.

a.   b.

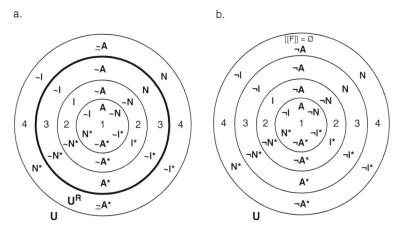

Figure 10.10 VS-model for BNPPredC₃, compared with bivalent BNPC

Figure 10.10a shows the VS-model for BNPPredC$_3$. Figure 10.10b, which represents bivalent basic natural predicate calculus (BNPC) extended to a full logic, is repeated from Figure 3.8b to enable the reader to compare the two. The spaces 1 to 3 in Figure 10.10a,b are reserved for situations where the preconditions of the **G**-predicate are satisfied, while space 4 covers those situations in which they are not (in Figure 10.10b only existential presuppositions are taken into account). As with bivalent BNPC, the spaces 1 to 3 are defined for the following conditions: space 1 for $[\![F]\!] \subset [\![G]\!]$, space 2 for $[\![F]\!]$ ⓪ $[\![G]\!]$ or $[\![G]\!] \subset [\![F]\!]$, space 3 for $[\![F]\!]$ OO $[\![G]\!]$.

Now we can revert to the problem discussed in Section 4.4 of the intuitive equivalence of ~**A** with both **I** and **I*** (intuition 7). If it is assumed that, at least prototypically, NOT ALL **F** is **G** is interpreted as the topic–comment (cleft) structure 'the **F** that is **G** is not all **F**', then NOT ALL **F** is **G** presupposes and thus entails SOME **F** is **G** and also SOME **F** is NOT-**G**, as the two are equivalent. This establishes the entailment from ~**A** to both **I** and **I***. Conversely, both **I** and **I*** entail ~**A** because that is how they are defined in the system of Figure 10.10a: /**I**/ = /**I***/ = {2,4} while /~**A**/ = {2,3,4}, which means that **I**/ **I*** ⊢ ~**A**. We thus have entailment both ways between ~**A** and **I** or **I***, and hence equivalence.

For PpredC$_3$ this result is not attainable. As one can read from Figure 10.9a, the conjunction of ~**A** with its presupposition **I** gives the VS {2}, whereas /~**A**/ = {2,3}, which makes for a one-way entailment from **I** to ~**A**, and no equivalence. Of course, ~**A** and **I*** are equivalent because the Conversions hold in PpredC$_3$ (with minimal negation). Nor is this result attainable for any presuppositional form of AAPC, as is easily checked.

The conclusion is that, provided one lets ~**A** presuppose **I** on account of topic–comment structure, we may add intuition 7 (NOT ALL **F** is **G** ≡ SOME **F** is **G** ≡ SOME **F** is NOT-**G**) to the score of BNPC, now transformed into BNPPredC$_3$, as specified in Section 4.4, which makes BNPPredC$_3$ the clear overall winner of the systems considered. The only intuition still missing is intuition 3 (SOME **F** is **G** ≡ SOME **G** is **F** or **I** ≡ **I**!), but, as has been said, here we have no remedy. All we can say is that this particular intuition is weaker than the others and may be due to the fact that cases where SOME **F** IS **G** is true while ⟦**G**⟧ ⊂ ⟦**F**⟧ are relatively rare and untypical, which may lead intro-specting subjects to overlook them. But even if that is so, we have no explanation for the fact that PNST–5 apparently does not translate directly into BNPC or its presuppositional counterpart BNPPredC$_3$.

10.7.3 *The victorious Square*

The upshot of our trek through the jungle of predicate logic is more or less as follows. The presuppositional variant of BNPC, BNPPredC$_3$, is the richest logic discovered so far, logically sound and empirically the most successful. But it suffers from the fact that it requires full knowledge of the verification domain before existential statements can be valued 'true' or 'false' (since **A** must have been valued before **I** can be). This is not a logical defect but it hampers inductive cognitive processes, and thus the advancement of knowledge.

The presuppositional version PpredC$_3$ of its more advanced sister, ABPC (the Square) is now also logically sound, owing to the added presuppositional component. And it is still next in line as regards empirical success (Section 4.4). This has made it worthwhile to see if the Square cannot be, or should not be, salvaged from the logical scrapheap to which it has been relegated by modern logicians on account of its suffering from UEI. This rescue operation has proved remarkably rewarding, in that presupposition theory appears to be able not only to restore the Square to logical soundness by the addition of a presuppositional component but also to provide an explanatory basis for the fact that utterances fit naturally into specific given contexts and/or situations. In fact, language proves to be tailored to the needs of contingency in that its predicates are, for the most part, purpose-made for specific classes of refer-ence objects and hence of situations. The mere use of a specific predicate may suffice to limit the set of objects one wishes to talk about and the set of situations the utterance in question fits into (as one *composes* music but *writes* a song). The most powerful predicate logic allowing for existential statements without complete situational knowledge, the Square of Opposition, is thus seen to be operative precisely where it needs to be, in the actual, restricted contexts and situations that utterances are used in. Psychologists rightly speak about shared speaker–hearer's knowledge to explain the fact that so much can be left unsaid. Here we have another device that makes language as efficient as it is.

But there is a price to be paid for the logical soundness of the Square. First, it appears necessary to distinguish three truth values for natural language, true (T), minimally false (F1) and radically false (F2), the two varieties of falsity being contingent upon whether or not it is a lexical update condition or a lexical precondition that has remained unsatisfied. Correspondingly, two varieties of natural language negation are distinguished, the minimal negation to repair minimal falsity, and the radical negation to repair radical falsity. Radical falsity is now interpreted as a cry for discourse correction, which explains the metalinguistic 'echo' the radical negation provokes in actual use. The resulting trivalent propositional calculus (which differs from that presented in Kleene 1938, 1952) incorporates standard propositional logic as long as one stays within the boundaries set by presuppositional conditions. Analogously, the resulting new trivalent predicate calculus incorporates the Square as long as there is no presupposition failure. The Square has now been cured of its logical disease while, at the same time, it has been made to fit into a flexible, dynamic system of discourse-restricted linguistic interaction— something no human or superhuman engineer would have thought of, presumably. In this perspective, the trivalence of natural logic is not really a concession to the facts of language and cognition. On the contrary, it is a small investment yielding a huge profit.

A second price to be paid arises from the fact that the logico-semantic system envisaged and partly developed here requires a nonextensional ontology containing 'Meinongian' virtual or intensional objects which derive their being from the fact that they are the product of the cognitive powers of imagination and representation. They have been thought up one way or another and thus combine specific identity with a specification that is not complete on all relevant parameters, as opposed to the complete specification that is a necessary characteristic of actually existing objects. This will perhaps cause some consternation among Anglo-Saxon philosophers trained in the tradition of Russell and Quine. But then, there are plenty of reasons why the purely extensional ontology that is standard in the Western world is anyway hopelessly inadequate if one wants to achieve a proper semantic theory of natural language, regardless of any requirement issuing from a trivalent logical system. Here again, therefore, if there is a price to pay, that price is not a concession to Ockham's principle of minimal assumptions or Quine's (anyway unlovable) 'desert landscape', but much more an investment that is necessary for an adequate insight into the nature of human language and cognition.

10.8 The attempt at equating anaphora with presupposition

In circles associated with Kamp's Discourse Representation Theory (DRT; Kamp 1981, Kamp and Reyle 1994), the notion has spread that presupposition is a form of anaphora. This notion is due in the first instance to Van der Sandt (1992), where it is proposed that there is one single mechanism underlying both anaphora resolution and presupposition projection. Those readers who have seriously worked through Chapters 9 and 10 will be startled at this proposal, as the two do not look as if they had anything in common. And indeed, it is argued here that this identification is just an instance of inexpert, unprofessional botching-up of otherwise good notions.

Rolling anaphora and presupposition into one is *a priori* an extremely unlikely and hazardous enterprise which will require a very solid underpinning indeed for it to be successful. However, Van der Sandt (1992) provides no underpinning at all. On the contrary, he equates anaphora with external, or perhaps with primary, or perhaps even with donkey anaphora, and he equates presupposition with presupposition projection, thus confusing the phenomenon itself with a mechanism associated with it. Having thus blurred the notions concerned, he then claims that the two are identical. This alleged 'identity' can, therefore, only be blurred itself.

DRT-practitioners accepted this all too readily, as they have always felt diffident with regard to presuppositions, either because they consider presuppositions to be of a nonformal, pragmatic nature and thus to be someone else's business or, if presuppositions are formally tractable, because they threaten to drag one down the slope of nonstandard logics and perhaps even of nonstandard mathematics. Van der Sandt's 'solution' thus couldn't have come at a better moment.

Van der Sandt is curiously vague about the nature of presupposition. His paper opens as follows (Van der Sandt 1992: 333): 'The traditional view on presupposition has it that presuppositions are referring expressions.' This is odd, to say the least. Since Strawson (1950)—the starting point of presuppositional studies (see Section 10.1.1)—there have been various approaches or, if one likes, traditions. One can distinguish a tradition that continues the lines drawn by Strawson and is Fregean in nature (Section 10.1.3), a tradition continuing the lines set out in Russell (1905) for the analysis of definite descriptions (Section 10.1.2), a tradition attempting to reduce presuppositions to pragmatic phenomena (Wilson 1975) and a discourse-semantic tradition, defended in the present study, reducing presuppositions to lexical preconditions, together with a trivalent logic and two kinds of falsity (Dummett 1973: 425–6; Seuren 1985, 1988, 2000, and many other publications). Given this diversity of opinions on presuppositional phenomena, one is mystified by Van der Sandt's expression 'the traditional view'.

Moreover, calling presuppositions 'expressions', and 'referring expressions' at that, is something that no current of thought on presuppositions, traditional or not, has, to my knowledge (based on forty years of research in presupposition theory), ever been daring enough to do. It would have helped if Van der Sandt had mentioned some references, to jog his readers' memory or let them find out what could be meant, but, of course, he does not, because there aren't any. Nor does he give any further explanation of this highly original thought. In other words, the first sentence of Van der Sandt's paper is simply bizarre.

But perhaps we shouldn't worry too much about the supposedly 'traditional' but in fact unidentifiable, view, because a few lines down on the same page we read: 'For Frege it is referring expressions that give rise to presuppositions.' In the light of the previous quote, this should be read (in the presumed but unidentifiable 'traditional view') as: 'For Frege it is referring expressions that give rise to referring expressions.' This is an inauspicious start of what is presumably meant to be a serious paper. Since the remainder of the paper hardly adds anything, we can safely let it rest.

Geurts and Beaver (2007), an encyclopedia article on DRT, is equally evasive as regards the notion of presupposition. These authors define, or describe, presupposition as follows (Section 5.2): 'Presuppositions are chunks of information associated with particular lexical items or syntactic constructions.' This is a very different notion from the one put forward by Van der Sandt, but equally unhelpful. An English word like *pal* and an English construction like *ain't* are 'associated with' the 'chunk of information' that a colloquial register is being used. Does that make this information presuppositional? Presumably not. But then, what distinguishes this information from the information conveyed by presuppositions? The answer is not to be found either in this encyclopedia article or anywhere else in the DRT literature. Geurts and Beaver (2007) thus shares the fuzziness with Van der Sandt (1992) but it directs its diffusing bundle of darkness in a different direction.

Yet, despite these notional unclarities, the authors in question maintain that there is one unified mechanism underlying both external-anaphora resolution and presupposition projection. This should entail that where an external anaphor is unresolvable, presupposition projection is blocked and vice versa. *A priori* one is inclined to think that such a view is implausible, because anaphora resolution is a matter of referential identification, whereas presupposition projection is a matter of semantic consistency within a discourse domain and its subdomains. It would be most remarkable if these two processes were to be seen to be subject to the same mechanism. And, of course, they are not.

Geurts and Beaver (2007, Section 2) argue for the same-mechanism position on the strength of examples like (10.74) (the exclamation mark indicates incoherence):

(10.74)   Pedro doesn't own a donkey. !*It* is grey.

In their perspective, a parallel can be drawn with (10.75):

(10.75)   Pedro doesn't own a donkey. !Juanita regrets he does.

Just as (10.75) is incoherent because the (factive) presupposition that Pedro owns a donkey, carried by the second sentence in (10.75), is denied in the first sentence, in the same manner (10.74) is thought to be incoherent because the *it* in the second sentence in (10.74) requires an accessible address to latch on to, which is absent owing to the negation in the first sentence.

In fact, however, the incoherence of (10.74) has nothing to do with anaphora resolution: the anaphoric relation between *it* and *a donkey* is clear enough, as one can see immediately when one replaces *grey* with, for example, *a fiction of his mind*. On the contrary, it has everything to do with the fact that the predicate *grey* induces a presupposition of actual existence. *Grey* is *extensional* with regard to its subject term, which means that, for truth to arise, this term must refer to an actually existing entity: for something to be grey it must first exist (see Section 3.5 in Volume I).

Since extensionality or intensionality of a given predicate with respect to some term position is a matter of lexical preconditions and hence of presuppositions, the incoherence of (10.74) is not a matter of anaphora but of presupposition. The anaphora aspect of (10.74) is unproblematic. The Principle of Maximal Unity for discourse domains (Section 7.2.2) says that entity representations (addresses) in any (sub)domain are retrievable from any (sub)domain. Therefore, the anaphor *it* has free access to any other domain or subdomain in **D**, including the subdomain under negation created by the first sentence in (10.74).

The often heard claim that definite determiners, including those thought to be present in definite pronouns, induce existential presuppositions is false. As has been amply shown in Seuren (1985, 1988, 1994, 2000) and again in Section 3.5.1 of Volume I and Section 10.7 of the present volume, existential presuppositions originate from the extensional character of argument positions and not from definite determiners. Yet Geurts and Beaver (2007, Section 5.2) still claim that existential presuppositions derive from definite determiners, even though they are fully aware of the arguments put forward in many publications by me over the past thirty years showing that this position is untenable. But much as one may try to ignore arguments or theories out of existence, it doesn't necessarily make them go away.

Since the first sentence in (10.74) denies the actual existence of a donkey owned by Pedro, the sequence as a whole is semantically incoherent, though with a perfectly straightforward anaphora resolution. In (10.76a–d), there is again no problem as regards anaphora resolution (although, according to Geurts and Beaver, there should be one in (10.76a)), but they differ from (10.74) in that they are all fully consistent. Their consistency derives from the fact that not all predicates involved in the second clauses of (10.76a–d) are fully extensional with regard to their object-term positions or with regard to the subdomains they introduce:

(10.76)   a. John doesn't own a Ferrari$_i$. $\sqrt{}$ He has simply invented *it$_i$*.
   b. John may own a Ferrari$_i$, but I have never seen *it$_i$*.
   c. John may own a Ferrari$_i$ but he may also have simply invented *it$_i$*.
   d. Geert has announced that he is going to make an anti-Islam film$_i$ but I doubt that *it$_i$* will ever materialize.

Example (10.76a) illustrates the fact that anaphora resolution does not require an antecedent address in the main or truth domain of the discourse at hand. All it requires is the presence of an appropriate antecedent address in *any* domain or subdomain (in this case, the extensional subdomain under negation). This is quite different from presupposition projection, which is restricted by conditions of overall semantic consistency. That no clash arises in (10.76a) is simply due to the fact that the predicate *invent* (in the sense of 'pretend there to be') is intensional with respect to its object term, so that it does not need an antecedent for *it$_i$* in the extensional truth domain. Analogous analyses apply to (10.76b,c,d).

Of course, this analysis requires an ontology that allows for nonexisting, virtual entities, which is something most Western philosophers, burdened as they are with the legacy left by Russell and Quine, have great difficulty with. They ought, however, to consider that this is apparently the way humans naturally construct their ontologies, as appears from the fact that humans refer to and quantify over virtual entities with the same ease and naturalness as they do with regard to actually existing ones (see Chapter 2 of Volume I for extensive discussion). Refusing to admit an intensional ontology means *inter alia* the inability to explain the coherence of sentences like (10.76a–d).

Closer inspection quickly reveals that there are many cases where anaphora resolution proceeds without a hitch but where incoherence arises owing to the blocking of presupposition projection. Consider the following examples:

(10.77)   a. ! John$_i$ pretends that he has left but he$_i$ has come back.
          b. ! I know John$_i$ hasn't left, so he$_i$ must have come back.
          c. ! John never had a wife$_i$. He simply divorced her$_i$.
          d. ! If John$_i$ pretends to have children$_j$, they$_j$ must be staying with his$_i$ sister.

The first clauses in (10.77a,b) entail that John hasn't left while the second clauses presuppose that he has. This clash of entailments blocks the obligatory upward projection of the embedded presupposition of the second clause and thus causes the incoherence of (10.77a,b). Yet there is no problem with the resolution of the anaphor *he$_i$* in the second clauses of (10.77a,b), which is an external anaphor with *John* as its antecedent.

Similarly in (10.77c), where the first clause denies a presupposition of the second. Yet there is no problem with the anaphoric pronoun *her$_i$*, which resolves (by primary or donkey anaphora) into *a wife* in the first clause. In (10.77d), the first clause entails that John has no children, whereas the second presupposes that he has, owing to the fact that the predicate *stay with one's sister* is extensional with regard to its subject term and *must* is a 'hole', giving rise to existential import. But the resolution of the (donkey) anaphor *they$_j$* is entirely unproblematic.

Further examples illustrating free anaphoric access across subdomains are:

(10.78)   a. John has no children. So *they* (*the poor creatures*) can't be on vacation.
          b. If Juan had any children, *they* (*the poor creatures*) would speak Spanish.
          c. A farmer who has no donkey can't feed *it* (*the animal*).
          d. A farmer who has no donkey can still dream about *it* (*the animal*).

(The possibility of epithet anaphora (Section 9.2) shows that these are anyway cases of external and not of bound-variable anaphora, which precludes an analysis in terms of Geach (1969, 1972); see Section 9.4.1.)

This suffices to show the untenability of the position defended by Van der Sandt, Geurts and Beaver, and all too easily adopted by other adherents of DRT. But there is more. Presuppositions are recoverable from their carrier sentences on account of the lexical meanings of the predicates inducing them, while no such help is available for anaphors. Thus, while (10.79a) allows for the conclusion *So he was married*, no corresponding counterpart is available for (10.79b):

(10.79)   a. Harold wanted to get divorced. (So he was married!)
          b. Harold wanted to see her. (Who?)

Van der Sandt's reply to this argument is that (Van der Sandt 1992: 341)

... unlike pronouns, <presuppositions> contain descriptive content which enables them to accommodate an antecedent in case discourse does not provide one.

But this won't do. The difference is that presuppositions consist of *propositional* content while definite descriptions have *descriptive* content. Epithet pronouns, as has been shown, also have descriptive content, yet such descriptive content does not suffice to provide an antecedent:

(10.80)   Harold wanted to see the old girl. (Who?)

We must conclude that Van der Sandt's claim that (Van der Sandt 1992: 341):

... presuppositions are just anaphors. They can be treated by basically the same mechanism that handles the resolution of pronominal and anaphoric expressions.

is confused and bizarre. Not only does it require notional obfuscation for it to be palatable to outsiders such as the school of DRT-practitioners, it also confuses the phenomenon itself with a mechanism associated with it. In the end, DRT still lacks an account of presupposition. Anaphora is anaphora and presupposition is presupposition. The twain meet only in so far as they link arms in context-driven utterance interpretation.

11

Topic–comment modulation

11.1 What is topic–comment modulation?

11.1.1 *The Aristotelian origin of topic–comment modulation*

To understand what is meant by topic–comment modulation, also known as topic–comment structure or information structure, one can hardly do better than go back to Aristotle's definition of the notion of proposition as explained in Section 3.1.2 of Volume I, because the Aristotelian notion of proposition is, in fact, the notion of topic–comment structure, even though this was not discovered until the nineteenth century. One recalls that Aristotle defines a proposition as (*PrAn* 24a16):

> A proposition (prótasis) is an affirmative or negative expression that says something of something.

What matters here is that what Aristotle had in mind was the attribution of a *specific* property to some *specific* entity, as in for example, 'Mr. G. has the property of being obnoxious'. This notion of proposition is schematically rendered in Figure 11.1 (where one notices that Aristotle had no term for what we now take to be the subject term in a propositional structure).

This analysis implies that the something of which something is said—the reference object of what was later to be called the subject term—must be *given* for a proposition to be conceived, uttered, and interpreted. And there are precious few ways in which an object can be *given*—that is, intentionally focused on by the speaker and identifiable by the listener.

A traditional view holds that reference objects are identified in linguistic interaction through the meaning of the predicate embedded in the referring expression (mostly a noun phrase). Husserl writes (1900: 49):

> ...daß es also mit Recht heißt, der Ausdruck bezeichne (nenne) den Gegenstand mittels seiner Bedeutung.
> (...that it is, therefore, correct to say that the expression denotes (names) the object by means of its meaning).

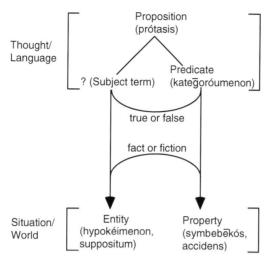

FIGURE 11.1 The Aristotelian notion of proposition

But if this is intended to imply that the meaning of the predicate embedded in a definite NP *suffices* to identify the reference object (ρ-value), it is wrong and, in fact, rather naïve. The meaning of the embedded predicate in a definite NP suffices to identify the reference object only if the object in question is unique in the speaker–hearer world of experience, such as the sun or the moon. But such cases are rare compared with those where the reference object needs ad hoc situational and/or contextual information to be identified. Pointing is, of course, one device, possibly combined with the use of a pronoun, but in the vast majority of cases ρ-values are established in that the cognitive-linguistic context of utterance enables speaker and listener to home in on the intended reference object. (One recalls from Section 9.5 that in some cases of primary anaphora the truth of the utterance in question makes for the fixing of reference.)

An Aristotelian proposition is thus the mental assignment of a specific property to one or more objects that have been given enough salience to act as reference object. When such a proposition is expressed linguistically, the property is expressed by means of a *predicate*, while that to which the property is assigned is expressed by what is now known as the *subject term*. This analysis was adopted, uncritically one has to admit, by the earliest grammarians in the Greek world and mistaken for what we now know as the grammatical or syntactic analysis of sentences. Thus, the first syntactic analysis of sentential structure consisted of a distinction between a *subject term* and a *predicate*, which were seen as the linguistic counterparts of the Aristotelian *something* of which *something* was said, respectively. Luckily for the earliest grammarians, what they discovered was real, since there can be no doubt that syntactic structure, with a subject term (along with a main verb and other argument terms plus any number of adverbial modifiers), is real. But they were less lucky in that they remained fixated on subject-predicate structure, failing to see the roles of further subdivisions within what they considered the 'predicate'.

11.1.2 *The discovery of the problem in the nineteenth century*

As amply demonstrated in Section 3.2 of Volume I, it was not until well into the nineteenth century, when the difference between syntactic structure and topic–comment modulation was discovered, that syntactic analysis was un-shackled and became free to explore those aspects of syntactic structure that had remained hidden for twenty or so centuries. Critical and inquisitive investigators began to see the discrepancy between the original Aristotelian notion of proposition and what had been made of it by the grammarians. And this discrepancy or, as some authors called it, incongruity gave rise to a terrible theoretical predicament that has not found a final solution till the present day. Syntactic structure was the object of fruitful investigation and many positive results have been chalked up (despite the many changes of direction that have taken place over the past fifty years), but the topic–comment counterpart was entirely forgotten by the mainstream theorists and stayed in the remit only of pragmatically oriented investigators, who, on the whole, have little sympathy for the more formally oriented work of syntacticians, semanticists, or linguistic theoreticians.

As a result, there is a lively research area with many practitioners occupying themselves with questions of what is called *information structure*. Yet, apart from notable and important exceptions, such as the work done by the Prague school of linguistics ever since World War II (see below) and the work by Carlos Gussenhoven of Nijmegen University (see, for example, Gussenhoven 1984, 2005), questions regarding the relation between sentence structure and topic–comment modulation are, on the whole, dealt with in more pragmati-cally oriented circles, which, unfortunately, means that foundational ques-tions regarding the semantic status of topic–comment modulation are not or hardly envisaged. It is, therefore, well worth our time to delve a little into the history and the essence of the problem.

The first observations around the incongruity between syntactic structure and the providing of new information regarding given concrete or abstract entities were made around 1850, mostly by German philosophers of language and philologists. Heymann Steinthal observes (1855: 199) that in a sentence like *The patient slept well* the grammatical subject is *the patient* and the grammatical predicate is *slept well*. But if the sentence is interpreted simply as the attribution of the property of sleeping well to the individual described as *the patient*, an important fact is overlooked, namely that often, 'what one wants to say is that the patient's sleep was good'. Therefore, an analysis is wanted, different from the syntactic surface structure, in which the patient's sleep is the reference object of the subject term (Aristotle's *hypokeímenon*) and what has come out in the syntactic structure as the adverb *well* is the underlying predicate.

Somewhat later Georg von der Gabelentz observed (1869: 378):[1]

What does one wish to achieve when one speaks to another person? The answer is that one wants to arouse a thought in him. In my view this implies two aspects: first, one has to direct the interlocutor's attention (his thinking) to something, and secondly, one makes him think this or that about it. I call that of or about which I want my addressee to think the *psychological subject*, and that which he should think about it the *psychological predicate*. In the sequel it will become clear how much these categories often deviate from their grammatical counterparts.

In his ($1891^{1}/1901^{2}$), he defended the view that the grammatical subject expresses what should be considered the hypokeímenon in a *logical* analysis (though he does not indicate what logic he has in mind), while the *psychological* subject consists in a mental representation of that which comes to mind first when one is in the middle of the speech process. This psychological subject will normally also come first in the spoken or written utterance. Thus, in the sentence (1901^{2}: 370) *Mit Speck fängt man Mäuse* (with bacon one catches mice) the psychological subject is *mit Speck* (with bacon), and the psychological predicate is what one does with bacon, namely catch mice. He does, however, point at the difficulty of providing observational support for his thesis (Von der Gabelentz 1901^{2}: 370):

But if one wants to give the inductive proof for all this, one has to be careful with examples. For the phenomena to do with positions in the sentences of different languages are not unambiguous or equivalent.

Around the same time we find Wilhelm Meyer-Lübke, a prominent Romance philologist, reacting to Von der Gabelentz, confusingly using the term *logical* for what Von der Gabelentz had called *psychological* and not for

---

[1] All translations are my own.

what Von der Gabelentz had called *logical*, which for him was the *grammatical* structure of the sentence (Meyer-Lübke 1899: 352):

I want to stress that 'subject' is used here in a purely grammatical sense, and designates, therefore, the agent of the action. Admittedly, this goes against the original meaning of this term, which, as one knows, originated in logic. From the point of view of logic there can be no doubt that in the sentence *il arrive deux étrangers* [two foreigners arrive] the subject is *il arrive* while *deux étrangers* is the predicate [. . .]. But from the point of view of grammar the relation between Noun and Verb remains unchanged, no matter which comes first in the sentence.

Interestingly, Meyer-Lübke specifies the grammatical subject of a sentence as designating 'the agent of the action', not unlike many modern attempts at providing a semantics for lexical argument functions in terms of thematic roles.

   Von der Gabelentz's notion of psychological subject was taken up and further developed by a number of scholars, in particular Philipp Wegener (1885: 21):

It is the function of the subject [die Exposition] to state the position [die Situation klar zu stellen], so that the logical predicate becomes intelligible.

He was followed by Theodor Lipps, who introduced the notion that the 'psychological' predicate is in fact the answer to a question about the hypo-keímenon that has arisen in the current context (Lipps 1893: 40):

The grammatical subject and predicate of a sentence now agree now do not agree with those of the judgement. When they do not, the German language has intonation as a means of marking the predicate of the judgement. The subject and predicate of the associated judgement are best recognised when we bring to mind the question to which the sentence is an answer. That which the full and unambiguous question is about is the subject, while the information required is the predicate. The same sentence can, accordingly, serve to express different judgements, and hence different subjects and predicates.

   Meanwhile, in Britain, some philosophers were working along the same lines. The Cambridge philosopher George Stout compares the progress of thought as expressed in language with the steps one takes while walking (Stout 1909[3], Vol. 2: 213–4):

Predication, from this point of view, just consists in the definition and specification of what is, at the outset, indefinite and indeterminate. It is because this process takes place gradually by a successive concentration of attention, that language is divided into sentences. The predicate of a sentence is the determination of what was previously indeterminate. The subject is the previous qualification of the general topic or universe of discourse to which the new qualification is attached. The subject is that product of previous thinking which forms the immediate basis and starting-point of further development. The further development is the predicate. Sentences are in the process of thinking what steps are in the process of walking. The foot on which the weight of the body rests corresponds to the subject. The foot which is moved forward in order to occupy new ground corresponds to the predicate. [...] All answers to questions are, as such, predicates, and all predicates may be regarded as answers to possible questions. If the statement, 'I am hungry' be a reply to the question, 'Who is hungry?' then 'I' is the predicate. If it be the answer to the question, 'Is there anything amiss with you?' then 'hungry' is the predicate. If the question is, 'Are you really hungry?' then 'am' is the predicate. Every fresh step in a train of thought may be regarded as an answer to a question. The subject is, so to speak, the formulation of the question; the predicate is the answer.

Wilhelm Wundt, one of the founding fathers of modern psychology, also took part in this debate. He denies that there is a disparity between 'psychological' and grammatical structure, in whatever terminology. For him, the grammatical subject always expresses the Aristotelian hypokeímenon. Grammatical structure thus faithfully reflects the logical analysis imposed by Aristotle on sentences. This is, for him, the only legitimate use of the terms *subject* and *predicate* (Wundt 1922[4]: 266):

The fact that the judgement consists of subject and predicate results from an analysis of judgements, and this is an insight that has rightly passed untrammelled from Aristotelian logic [...] into the more modern forms of logic. The subject is the thing the proposition is about, that which forms the basis, *hypokeímenon;* the predicate is the content of the proposition, the *katēgórēma*, as Aristotle called it.

Although it is probably correct, he says, to distinguish, as Von der Gablentz did, between that which comes to mind first and that which is added as new information, that should not be labelled as the subject-predicate distinction. Instead, Wundt proposed the term *dominant representation* (dominierende Vorstellung) for what Von der Gablelentz, Lipps, Stout, and others had called the psychological subject, but Wundt's term never gained acceptance (Wundt 1922[4]: 269–70):

Suppose I transform the sentence *Caesar crossed the Rubicon* into *The Rubicon was crossed by Caesar*, does that mean that the subject *Caesar* has become a remote object, and has, conversely, the original object *the Rubicon* now become the subject? And when I say *The crossing of the Rubicon was achieved by Caesar*, has now the original predicate become the subject?

These are the questions that have led, in our new linguistics, to a kind of distinction that has found a rather widespread acceptance, but which, in my eyes, has increased rather than solved the confusion resulting from the mixing of logic, grammar, and psychology. If we are to believe G. von der Gabelentz we should distinguish between a logical, a grammatical and a psychological subject and predicate. The logical subject and predicate keep the function they have in logic. The psychological subject is seen as 'the representational complex that occurs first in the consciousness of speaker and hearer', while 'the content that is added to this prior representation' should be the predicate. Or, as v.d. Gabelentz formulates it from the teleological point of view, the psychological subject is 'that about which the speaker wants the hearer to think, to which he wants to direct his attention, while the psychological predicate consists of that which the hearer should think about the subject'. [. . .]

When one says that the two sentences *Caesar crossed the Rubicon* and *The Rubicon was crossed by Caesar* have the same logical subject but different grammatical subjects, one has already lost sight of the notion of subject in the Aristotelian sense, namely as that on which the assertion is based, and surreptitiously introduced a psychological consideration, namely that the subject must be an agent. Obviously, the agent in both sentences is Caesar. But only in the first sentence, and not in the second, is he the basis on which the proposition is grounded. The former is an assertion about Caesar, the latter about the Rubicon.

Although one may disagree with Wundt on several counts, he makes some important points, such as the difference between the genesis and the substance of a propositional thought, and the necessity to create a separate terminology for the grammatical distinction of subject and predicate on the one hand and the 'psychological' distinction of 'what comes to mind first' on the other.

As one sees from the quotations given, there was a great deal of confusion about this issue around the turn of the century, and the parties involved were unable to settle on an agreed solution. In fact, the confusion was such that Theodor Kalepky exclaimed (1928: 20): 'Such a confusion simply cries out for relief' (Eine derartige Wirrnis schreit förmlich nach Abhilfe).[2] After 1930 the subject-predicate debate, which had dominated linguistic theorizing for almost a century, disappeared from the limelight, mainly due to the lack of empirical support and the general unclarity of the issues concerned, but also because the new structuralism in linguistics had different interests.

---

[2] Kalepky belonged to a group of linguists who felt that a theory of grammar should be set up without any notion of subject and predicate at all. Others belonging to this movement were Svedelius (1897) and Sandmann (1954). This movement, however, petered out without leaving as much as a trace.

The only place where the debate was continued was Prague, largely owing to a tradition of loyalty to good work done by local scholars. Anton Marty, a disciple of the German phenomenologist Franz Brentano and professor of philosophy at Prague by the end of the nineteenth century, made important contributions to the subject-predicate debate. According to him, logic deserves no place in semantics, all semantics being psychological. Besides an abstract propositional meaning, every sentence has an 'inner form' which expresses the way the propositional meaning is to be integrated into running discourse. He follows Lipps, Stout, and others in saying that this 'inner form' is determined in principle by question–answer structure. Unlike Wundt, he maintains that the terms *subject* and *predicate* are most appropriately used at this 'inner form' level, since it is here that the Aristotelian meaning of these terms is immediately applicable. Despite some unclarities, this makes a great deal of sense, as will be clear in a moment.

Marty's work was continued by the Czech scholar Vilém Mathesius, professor of English at Prague University and founder, in 1926, of the Prague Linguistic Circle. Mathesius followed Wundt in wishing to see a separate terminology for subject and predicate on the level of grammatical analysis on the one hand, and the 'known-new' distinction found to exist at a more psychological level by Lipps, Stout and company on the other. Not wishing to upset existing terminology, he felt that the terms *subject* and *predicate* should go on being used in grammar, no matter what confusions had occurred in recent literature, and proposed a new term pair for the Aristotelian distinction, which is realized at the 'psychological' level. For the latter he proposed a Czech term pair that has been rendered variously as *theme* versus *rheme*, *topic* (or *focus*) versus *comment*, the former pair member indicating the Aristotelian hypokeímenon, the latter the Aristotelian predicate. The structure into which both are combined is not called 'proposition' but the *functional sentence perspective* (Mathesius 1939).

Although the question of the disparity between syntactic structure and topic–comment modulation dominated all discussions about the nature of language for well over half a century, it disappeared from the theoretical agenda when the new structuralism made its appearance around 1930. This was no doubt due to the fact that structuralism in linguistics, in particular the American variety, was strongly focused on grammatical form and tried to dispense with meaning as an object of 'scientific' enquiry altogether. In this perspective, introspection-based talk about 'what comes to the mind first' and things like that was considered unscientific and an improper intrusion of phenomenological psychology into the much more 'scientific' arena of linguistics and behaviourist psychology.

Needless to say, after 1960 the psychologists struck back and joined forces with pragmaticists to develop a pragmatically oriented discipline of discourse and text analysis, sometimes called 'conversation analysis', studying questions of 'information packaging' and 'information structure' in the intuitive terms of personal, introspective experiences. It is as if the practitioners of conversation analysis have turned their backs on formal grammar and even more on everything to do with logic and the more formal aspects of meaning. They represent extreme ecologism as described in Section 1.3.3 of Volume I. It is our purpose here, in the context of discourse semantics, to redress the balance somewhat and shed some light on the more formal and theoretical aspects of topic–comment modulation.

11.1.3 *The dynamics of discourse: the question–answer game*

Let us take up the issue where Lipps and Stout left off, accepting that the normal progress of discourse is driven by a 'game' of questions and answers (see also Seuren 1985: 297–304). Questioning is probably a basic and general cognitive activity that far exceeds, but underlies, the question–answer game in topic–comment modulation that is meant to secure textual coherence. Questioning, whether of the specific (WH-) or the polar (yes/no) variety, pervades the whole of cognition and is probably the main guiding principle in acquiring new knowledge and insight. What we see of it in discourse incrementation procedures is but one of the many uses to which the human propensity to be inquisitive and ask questions is put.

Ideally speaking, the discourse **D** is unrestricted at the initial point. The question-answer game may be opened by what in the theatre is called a *feeder*: an utterance meant to set a discourse in motion without there being any anticipation of a question arising in the audience's mind (other than the general question 'What is this person going to tell us?'). Normally, implicit questions are left out from the actually spoken text, as the speaker anticipates the listener's queries. We then speak of an *implicit question*, to which the following assertion (which may be a new sentence or part of an ongoing sentence) is an answer. It also often happens that speakers themselves pronounce the question they think the listener will come up with. This is a typical feature of what is often felt as 'patronizing' speech, as in teaching situations or in official announcements made by authorities of whatever kind.

Normally, sentences or clauses beginning with *and* are not answers to implicit or explicit questions but continuations of answers given (but see Blakemore and Carston 2005 and note 12 in Chapter 8). It seems that sentences starting with *but* (where *but* is not a comment correction, such as German *sondern*) can be reduced to the speaker's assumption of the implicit question 'Is there nothing that diminishes the effect of the previous utterance?', where *but* signals the answer 'Yes, namely . . . .'.[3]

Opening sentences, or feeders, typically occur in the daily news (Van Kuppevelt 1991):

(11.1)   The workers of the Slumbo mattress factory in Bubble-on-Rhine have announced that they will go on strike tomorrow.

This will naturally give rise to a few questions, such as 'Why?', 'Have there been previous negotiations?', 'How does the management react?', and so on. And indeed, one typically finds that subsequent sentences after such a feeding line answer such questions, under the appropriate intonation.[4]

Existential quantification and OR-disjunctions systematically give rise to implicit questions, as in (11.2a), where the question is actually anticipated by the ('patronizing') speaker:[5]

(11.2)   a. Some time before World War I the Titanic sank. When did the Titanic sink? It sank in 1912.
          b. Some time before World War I the Titanic sank. It sank in 1912.
          c. Some time before World War I, in 1912, the Titanic sank.

A less solicitous or 'patronizing' speaker might have said (11.2b) or even (11.2c). One notes that the underlying 'entity' to which the property 'in 1912' is assigned is 'the time of sinking of the Titanic'. We shall not go into the

---

[3] For the contrast between English *and* and *but*, see, for example, Lakoff (1971), Bellert (1972), Blakemore and Carston (2005). For the corresponding German contrast, one may consult Lang (1977), Abraham (1991), Diewald and Fischer (1998), Fischer (2000). For a comparison between English and German, see, for example, Asbach-Schnitker (1979).

[4] An experiment (Van Kuppevelt 1991) showed that when test subjects read aloud the text of a real-life news bulletin, which did not contain the anticipated or implicit questions, the intonation patterns did not differ from readings by the same subjects of the same text but with the implicit questions filled in as anticipated questions.

[5] The existential quantifier FEW appears to do the same and even more (see note 5 of Chapter 9). As reported in Moxey and Sanford (1986/7), the introduction of a plural discourse address under FEW systematically induces the setting-up not only of a plural address for the set delimited by FEW but also for the complement of that set. Moxey and Sanford found that subjects presented with a sentence like (i) would continue a subsequent sentence starting with *They* . . . in ways that made it clear that they were referring to those students that were **not** at the meeting. A typical continuation would be (ii):

(i) Few students were at the meeting.
(ii) They had (all) gone out with their girl friends.

This strongly suggests that FEW systematically gives rise to an implicit question of the form 'How about the others?', which would also naturally be part of the speaker's text (in the 'patronizing' style of speech mentioned above). Moxey and Sanford use the term *complement anaphora* for primary anaphora to the complement address set up in virtue of that question arising.

philosophical question of what kind of 'entity' this is, but simply accept the reification procedure underlying expressions such as *the time of sinking*. The property assigned to this abstract, reified 'entity' is that it was in 1912.[6]

An important corollary of the assumption that TCM-structure mirrors an ongoing question-answering game in discourse is that TCM-structure is a powerful factor in reducing the effort involved in the interpretation of utterances. Since the topic has already been through the interpretive grinder, all that remains to be processed in the interpretation is the comment, which is often just one constituent and sometimes even no more than one single word. It is surprising that this obvious fact is taken into account so little in the literature on parsing and the experiments related to it.

Now consider again the example of the sentence *John sold the car*, discussed in Section 3.2 of Volume I. Suppose this sentence is uttered in a context where the (implicit or explicit) question is *Who sold the car?* Then the answer requires emphatic accent on *John*, as in (11.3c), or the corresponding cleft or pseudocleft, as in (11.3a) and (11.3b), respectively:

(11.3)   a. It is JOHN who sold the car.
          b. The one who sold the car is JOHN.
          c. JOHN sold the car.

We take it (Seuren 1998*b*) that (11.3a,b,c) have a common underlying SEMANTIC ANALYSIS (SA) corresponding to the topic–comment modulation or TCM structure (11.4), which is input to both the grammar of the language in which the sentence is to be expressed and to the discourse-incrementation procedure (more is said about the predicate $Be_{v\text{-ind}}$ below):

(11.4) $Be_{v\text{-ind}}$ JOHN (the x[x sold the car])

In (11.4), the grammatical subject term the x[x sold the car] is the topic and the grammatical predicate $be_{v\text{-ind}}$ JOHN is the comment, as shown in Figure 11.2 (repeated from Figure 7.8 in Chapter 7 of Volume I).

Assume for the moment that, in general, the surface subject term attracts a grade-1 accent and that what is the predicate of a sentence at SA-level attracts

---

[6] It would appear that quantification in the comment, as in *It is not everyone that is granted the gift of tongues*, cannot be handled by the mechanism of underlying cleft structures other than in ways that are formally so complex as to make their occurrence in language unlikely. Other mechanisms seem to be at work here, for example, the mechanism of quotation. This would impose a metalinguistic interpretation on the sentence just quoted, in the sense that *everyone* should be taken as the quoted form 'everyone': 'the use of the word "everyone" is inappropriate in the given context'. Note also that *someone* or *anyone* are hardly usable in the sentence quoted: *It is not someone/anyone that is granted the gift of tongues*.

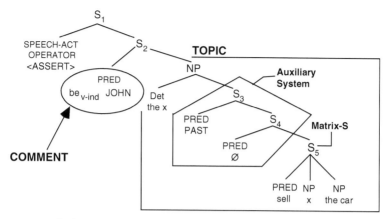

FIGURE 11.2 Underlying SA of *John sold the car*

a coding for sentence-nuclear accent, which is realized as an accenting on the VP-constituent in surface structure, and that the surface-sentential VP-accent settles on the last nominal VP-constituent (Gussenhoven 1984). This makes for an unmarked grade-1 rising intonation on *John* and *the car* in (11.5a) and on *John* and *Mary* in (11.5b) (apart from unmarked grade-1 rising tones on the higher SA-operator *Mónday mórning*):

(11.5)   a. Jóhn sold the cár on Mónday mórning.
         b. Jóhn gave the book to Máry on Mónday mórning.

According to this principle, the SA-predicate Be_{v-ind} JOHN in a TCM structure will receive a coding for grade-1 sentence-nuclear accent. Now assume that sentence (11.3c) results from the LOWERING of the SA-predicate, shortened to just JOHN, to the position of the variable x in the Matrix-S.[7] On that assumption, it makes sense to surmise that the (shortened) lowered

---

[7] Such lowering is, of course, subject to the well-known, possibly universal, ISLAND CONSTRAINTS. One such island constraint forbids the lowering of the comment predicate into a relative clause, as in (i). No constraint prevents such lowering in sentence (ii):

   (i) *Not for JOHN but for BILL are those who work on strike.
   (ii) √Not JOHN's but BILL's workers are on strike.

Since parallel observations can be made for the cleft structures (iii) and (iv), it seems that the island constraints in question should be taken to apply to the relation between lambda-abstracted and non-lambda-extracted pairs at SA-level:

   (iii) *It is not for JOHN but for BILL that those who work are on strike.
   (iv) √It is not JOHN's but BILL's workers that are on strike.

To what extent this might be taken to restrict the cognitive process of questioning in discourse is a matter for further research.

predicate JOHN will carry its coding for grade-1 sentence-nuclear accent along to the new Matrix position of surface subject term and that the grade-1 accent for surface subjecthood is reinforced to a grade-2 accent. This grade-2 accentual peak thus signals the fact that the constituent thus marked is the comment SA-predicate of the corresponding TCM-structure (11.4)—that is, the structure shown in Figure 11.2. The accentual peak is reinforced even further when the comment SA-predicate is contrasted with another such comment predicate.

One consequence of this analysis is that an elegant parallel can be drawn between structures underlying WH-questions such as (11.6) and the corresponding reply (11.4):

(11.6)   Be$_{v\text{-ind}}$ WHO? (the x[x sold the car])

The open-place question predicate 'WHO?' indicates that a value is required in this position. The answer (11.4) provides the value JOHN.

We now define the topic of a sentence as that element in a situation whose specific identity is open to question, or as that parameter in a situation whose value is being requested. The comment then provides the answer by specifying the element (value) in question. Otto Jespersen already saw this parallel, as appears from the following quote (Jespersen 1924: 145):

The subject is sometimes said to be the relatively familiar element, to which the predicate is added as something new. 'The utterer throws into his subject all that he knows the receiver is already willing to grant him, and to this he adds in the predicate what constitutes the new information to be conveyed by the sentence. [...] In "A is B" we say, "I know that you know who A is, perhaps you don't know also that he is the same person as B"' (Baldwin's Dict. of Philosophy and Psychol. 1902, Vol. 2.364). This may be true of most sentences, but not of all, for if in answer to the question 'Who said that?' we say 'Peter said it', *Peter* is the new element, and yet it is undoubtedly the subject.

It thus makes sense to propose a separate structural analysis for the *genesis* of a proposition, as opposed to its actual truth-conditional *substance*. The process of genesis—that is, the progress from what has been established in the discourse to what is added as new information—produces the TCM-structure, which contains, besides the truth-conditional substance, also information about the process that gave rise to the proposition in question.

At this point we need some terminology. Let us call a merely truth-conditionally presented proposition a *flat proposition* (fprop), while its topic–comment modulated variants, each representing a particular history of its genesis, will be called *modulated propositions* (modprop). A flat

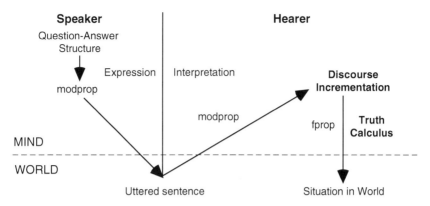

F<small>IGURE</small> 11.3 Discourse-semantic layout of speech process

proposition is like a picture: it represents a mere state of affairs, and cannot express anything like the topicalization found in TCM-structures. A modprop thus consists of an fprop plus a topicalization. Its expression at SA-level is taken to be a TCM-structure as exemplified in (11.4) and in Figure 11.2.

At some stage in the comprehension process, probably immediately upon the incrementation into the current **D**, the hearer must distil the strictly truth-conditional content of an utterance received, the corresponding fprop, from the information incremented to the current **D**, as represented in Figure 11.3. A TCM-structure like (11.4) conveys all the information conveyed by the corresponding flat proposition. In addition, however, it conveys the information requested by the predicate WHO?, as in (11.6), in the flow of discourse. It is this latter fact that guides the incrementation process. It does so by specifying the identity of the element that was the object of querying, in this case the person called *John*. Figure 11.3 gives a schematic survey of the relation between, on the one hand, a modprop of the kind that normally occurs in the flow of speech and the corresponding fprop, whose role has been reduced to the truth calculus with regard to the situation the utterance is keyed to in the world.

11.2 Phonological, grammatical, and semantic evidence for TCM

The empirical evidence for topic–comment modulation is a combination of phonological, grammatical, and semantic observations. More strictly phono-logical evidence is adduced in, for example, Bolinger (1972) and Gussenhoven (1984, 2005). Here we look at certain intonational features in combination with judgements of grammaticality and possible meanings.

Consider first the fully grammatical sentence (11.7a) (also discussed in Section 7.2.2 in Volume I) expressing a flat proposition (fprop) with only grade-1 accentual peaks. This sentence contains the negative polarity item (NPI) *in the least*, licensed, in this case, by the negation *n't*. An answer is now needed to the question why (11.7b) is ungrammatical but (11.7c) is well-formed and meaningful, with grade-2 intonational peaks on both JOHN and PETER and a grade-1 rise on *not*:

(11.7)   a. √John isn't in the least interested.
          b. *JOHN isn't in the least interested, PETER is.

          c. √JOHN isn't in the least interested, nót PETER.

(11.8)   a. *NOT [Be$_{v\text{-ind}}$ JOHN (the x [Be in the least interested(x)])]
          b. √Be$_{v\text{-ind}}$ JOHN (the x [NOT [Be in the least interested(x)]])

The answer lies in the fact that, in the corresponding SA, the NPI *in the least* requires a negation immediately over the S-structure in which it occurs, as in (11.8b), which corresponds to *The one who isn't in the least interested is John,* expressing (11.7c).[8] (11.8a), however, is unwellformed already at SA-level, because there is too much intermediate structure between the negation and *in the least,* causing the ungrammaticality of (11.7b). These facts are thus explained by the two assumptions (a) that the grammatical analysis of TCM is provided by an underlying (SA-level) cleft structure of the type exemplified in (11.4) and (11.8), and (b) that the NPI *in the least* requires a negation immediately over its own clause in SA-structure. (The fact that both assumptions happen to be unpopular in certain schools of linguistics does not diminish their explanatory power.)

Now consider the German examples (11.9) and (11.10) (repeated from note 6 in Section 7.2.1 of Volume I). In German, the use of the conjunction *sondern* (meaning 'but') is strictly limited to comment-correction. It has a metalinguistic flavour in that it says that a comment that was given earlier is to be replaced by a new comment, as in (11.9). It thus requires a *comment negation,* with scope over the whole sentence, and not a negation that belongs

---

[8] It is marginally possible for *in the least* to be separated from the negation by an intervening factive verb taking the clause in which *in the least* occurs as an object complement, as in:

(i) ?She didn't realize that I was in the least interested.

Cases like (ii) are explained by the rule of NEGATIVE RAISING, which takes the negation out of the embedded clause in SA-structure and places it in construction with the commanding verb *believe*:

(ii) √She didn't believe that I was in the least interested.

semantically in the topic-clause, as in (11.7c) and the corresponding (11.8b). Moreover, German, like Dutch, allows for the comment negation to precede the comment, as in (11.9). (In English, this is possible only if the correction follows immediately, as in (11.11a), as against the less grammatical (11.11b).) But German (like Dutch) also allows the comment negation to be incorporated into the Matrix-S, as in (11.10), which then has to rely on the proper intonation contour for the TCM to be expressed—that is, with a grade-2 peak on HERBERT and on SOHN and a grade-1 final rise on *gelacht*. The point is now that with the proper intonation contour for comment negation, as in (11.10a), the use of *sondern* is legitimate, but with the intonation pattern appropriate for negation embedded in the topic, as in (11.10b), which has a grade-1 final fall on *gelacht, sondern* is not allowed:

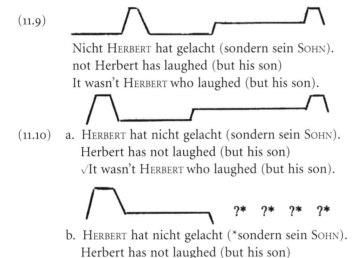

(11.9)

        Nicht HERBERT hat gelacht (sondern sein SOHN).
        not Herbert has laughed (but his son)
        It wasn't HERBERT who laughed (but his son).

(11.10)   a. HERBERT hat nicht gelacht (sondern sein SOHN).
          Herbert has not laughed (but his son)
          √It wasn't HERBERT who laughed (but his son).

                           ?* ?* ?* ?*

       b. HERBERT hat nicht gelacht (*sondern sein SOHN).
          Herbert has not laughed (but his son)
          !!It was HERBERT who didn't laugh (*but his son).

(11.11)   a. Not Herb but his son laughed.
       b. ?*Not Herb laughed but his son.

The argument is, therefore, that the use of *sondern* is sensitive to the scope of the negation in TCM structures of the kind shown in (11.4) and (11.8) and expressed in different intonational contours. Without a TCM analysis, which expresses the scope difference explicitly, the facts shown in (11.9) and (11.10) remain unexplained.

Finally, let us look again at an example quoted in Section 3.2 in Volume I, to do with reflexivization. Consider the little dialogue between a father and his young son, who is crying because he has just hurt his knee:

(11.12)   Father: Well-educated boys don't cry.
         Son: I didn't educate me, YOU did!

It is now widely accepted, and rightly so, that reflexivization is, in principle, an internal lexical process whereby a transitive predicate is applied to the subject: *self-wash*, *self-admire*, and so on. In some languages reflexivization is not expressed at all, but often it is expressed by means of verb morphology or reflexive oblique pronouns, or, iconically, through so-called *body-reflexives*, as in the French-based Creole language of the island Mauritius, where one finds sentences like (Seuren 1995):[9]

(11.13)   Li   pe   lav   so   lecôr.
        he   CONT   wash   his   body
        He is washing himself.

In English, reflexivity is expressed mainly through the suffix *-self* attached to certain pronouns, but is not expressed in, for example, the possessive pronouns *his*, *her*, *their*, unlike Latin or Swedish, which have reflexive forms for reflexive third-person possessive pronouns (*suus* in Latin; *sin* in Swedish). English also allows for a blocking of reflexivization in first-person uses, as in:

(11.14)   a. I hate me.[10]
        b. I don't know me any more.

In such sentences the non-reflexive nature of the predicate is emphasized, so that the *ego* is presented as a third person, which suggests self-alienation. But there is no truth-conditional difference with the corresponding fully reflexivized sentences:

(11.15)   a. I hate myself.
        b. I don't know myself any more.

The point of example (11.12) is that the son's snappy reply does not express any form of self-alienation and that it is truth-conditionally different from:

---

[9] Classical Attic Greek had a special set of (pristine Indo-European) third-person reflexive pronouns (*hou* for the genitive, *hoi* for the dative, and *he* for the accusative) reserved for use in embedded object clauses where an oblique term refers back to the subject of the main clause, as in *Plato$_i$ said that Crito had not listened to him$_i$*.

[10] This form of non-reflexivity is not possible in, for example, Dutch, where *Ik haat mij* is ungrammatical and must be *Ik haat mezelf*, also when one wants to express the kind of self-alienation expressed by (11.14a,b).

(11.16)   **I** didn't educate myself, you did!

I see no other way of providing a principled answer to this fact than to assume, for the son's reply in (11.12), an underlying SA-structure of the form shown in (11.17a), where the verb *educate* is not used reflexively, as opposed to (11.17b), where it is:

(11.17)   a. NOT[$Be_{v\text{-ind}}$ **I** (the x [x educated me])]
           b. NOT[$Be_{v\text{-ind}}$ **I** (the x [x self-educated])]

The lack of reflexivization observed in (11.12) is thus explained by the assumption of an SA-level TCM cleft construction with the predicate $\mathbf{Be}_{v\text{-ind}}$.

Further evidence can no doubt be adduced, but we shall leave it at this.

11.3 The comment-predicate $\mathbf{Be}_v$

We will now say a few words about the specific nature of TCM, in particular about the predicate $\mathbf{Be}_v$ (discussed earlier in Section 3.2 of Volume I), even if it must be admitted that this whole area is fraught with problems, most of which still elude us. With this proviso, we posit that all cleft and pseudocleft sentences (but not all sentences with an emphatic-contrastive accent on one constituent; see Section 11.4) are characterized by the main predicate $\mathbf{Be}_v$, normally realized in English as the verb *be*, as in example (11.4) cited above. The specific use of this predicate is to specify values for function arguments.

That $\mathbf{Be}_v$ is not at all identical with the identity predicate $\mathbf{Be}$ expressing identity ($=$), is not generally recognized. In fact (see Section 5.3.2 in Volume I), Quine (1953: 143–4) mistook the value-assigning predicate $\mathbf{Be}_v$ for the identity predicate $\mathbf{Be}$ in his famous but fallacious argument that (11.18c) is a *non-sequitur* because it is a case of illicit substitution of co-referential terms *salva veritate* (SSV), as a parallel to Frege's even more famous and valid argument that (11.19c) is a *non-sequitur* because it is a case of illicit SSV:

(11.18)   a. The number of planets is nine.
           b. Nine is necessarily greater than seven.
           c. Ergo: !The number of planets is necessarily greater than seven.

(11.19)   a. The Morning Star is the Evening Star.
           b. John believes that the Morning Star is inhabited.
           c. Ergo: !John believes that the Evening Star is inhabited.

Frege was right (a) because the predicate **Believe** introduces an intensional context, where SSV is blocked and (b) because (11.19a) is an identity statement. Quine was wrong (a) because it is not clear that the predicate

Necessarily introduces an intensional context (see Section 7.2.1.3) and (b) above all because (11.18a) is not an identity statement.

Montague (1973: 239), referring to 'a puzzle due to Barbara Hall Partee', discusses the problem of sentences like 'The temperature is ninety and rising', which should carry the absurd entailment that ninety is rising. He seeks a solution in treating nouns like *temperature* or *price* (representing a class of nouns for which he makes an explicit exception) as denoting 'individual concepts', not individuals, but the solution is ad hoc and Montague still treats Be_v as the identity predicate '=', failing to see that Be_v is a value-assigning predicate in its own right. Since Montague (1973), no improvement has been proposed on that faulty analysis.

Meanwhile we distinguish between the two. And we make a further distinction between a value-specifying predicate for *individuals*, written $Be_{v\text{-ind}}$, for *categories*, written $Be_{v\text{-cat}}$, and for *values*, written $Be_{v\text{-val}}$. Thus, for example, the TCM-structure (11.20a), which may be regarded as an answer to the question (11.20b), specifies not an *individual* but the *category* to which the thing that Bert sold belongs. The subscript 'v-cat' makes it clear that what is asked for is not the identification of an individual but of a category of individuals (or of a substance, as when Bert sold milk):

(11.20)   a. $Be_{v\text{-cat}}$ a car the x [Bert sold x]
                 [=Bert sold A CAR]
          b. $Be_{v\text{-cat}}$ WHAT? the x [Bert sold x]
                 [=What did Bert sell?]

It is important to note that the constituent *a car* in (11.20a) does not represent an underlying existential quantifier but denotes a category. We may regard (11.20a) as providing the value for the discourse-determined situation at hand in the function 'what Bert sold' (cf. Scharten 1997: 63).[11]

---

[11] Significantly, Montague wrote (1970: 217):

We have taken the indefinite article 'a' always indicating existential quantification, but in some situations it may also be used universally, and indeed, in precisely the same way as 'any'; such is the case with one reading of the ambiguous sentence 'a woman loves every man such that that man loves that woman'.

That is, Montague held that, apart from cases where it is used generically, the indefinite article *always* expresses existential quantification. This implies, as he admits, that *John is an American* should be analysed as 'There is an x such that x is an American and such that John is identical with x'. Needless to say, this analysis stands in no relation to linguistic reality. It just illustrates again the narrow fixation on quantification at the expense of other, less studied, semantic categories.

Besides $Be_{v\text{-ind}}$ and $Be_{v\text{-cat}}$, we also have $Be_{v\text{-val}}$, which specifies the value of a parameter for other than individuals or categories. For example, a sentence like (11.21a), with the SA (11.21b), specifies the temperature of the room in question, and (11.22a,b) specifies the cardinality of the set of John's children:

(11.21) a. The temperature of the room is twelve degrees.
          b. $Be_{v\text{-val}}$ twelve degrees the x[the temperature of the room is x]

(11.22) a. John has four children. / The number of John's children is four.
          b. $Be_{v\text{-val}}$ four the x[the cardinality of the set of John's children is x]

The temperature parameter in (11.21) involves a function from objects (possibly places) and times to temperature values. The number parameter in (11.22) involves a function from sets to cardinality values. In similar fashion cases can be analysed involving parameters for names, telephone numbers, dates, etc.

As argued in Seuren (1993) and Scharten (1997), this shows the semantic, nonpragmatic, nature of number specifications, generally mistaken for cases of existential quantification. In both the semantic and the pragmatic litera-ture, sentences like (11.22a) are analysed as existentially quantified, and are accordingly taken to have the literal meaning 'John has *at least* four children', which must then be changed into 'John has *precisely* four children' by means of pragmatic principles that are generally too soft and not always justifiable. The much more obvious reading in which, literally, a precise value is assigned to the cardinality function for the set of John's children is entirely neglected, owing no doubt to the general neglect of parameters and value assignments in standard formal semantics.[12]

The same goes for a question like *Which month in the year has 28 days?* The most obvious answer is *February*, in the reading 'the month of the year such that the number of days it has is 28 is February'. But the answer *All months have 28 days* is also justifiable, though clearly less probable. For some strange reason, the latter answer is generally thought to be more 'logical' than the former.

One notes that (11.21a) and (11.22a) are both analysed as TCM-structures. Yet they have no corresponding cleft or pseudocleft surface structures. Sen-tences like (11.23a,b) are highly artificial, if they are grammatical at all:

---

[12] A Be_v-analysis will also help out on the problem, raised in, for example, Donnellan (1966), Kripke (1972, 1980), and Neale (1990), of the reference function for *the Pope* in sentences like *The Pope was Polish in 2000 but is German now*, which does not imply that the Pope has changed nationality. The sentence is now read as 'the *x* such that x was the value of the parameter [$Be_{v\text{-cat}}$ the Pope] in 2000 was Polish but the *x* such that *x* is the value of the parameter [$Be_{v\text{-cat}}$ the Pope] now is German'.

(11.23)   a. ?*It is twelve degrees that the temperature of the room is.
           b. ?*It is four children that John has./?*It is four that the number of
              John's children is.

This is no doubt because sentences like (11.21a) and (11.22a) already possess a
value-assigning topic–comment structure, providing a value on a lexicalized
parameter such as *temperature, price,* or *number* under their SA-predicate
Be$_{v\text{-val}}$. Although it is technically possible to topicalize again an element out
of such structures, leading to 'double topicalization', the result will be felt as
unnatural—though languages may well differ in this respect.

   In general, it must be observed that, but for a few notable exceptions,
existing grammatical as well as formal semantic theories almost totally neglect
constructions involving the assignment of values to given parameters. This
means that the whole area of measurable gradable adjectives like *broad, deep,
high, heavy, far, hot, old,* etc., along with measure predicates like *weigh, cost,
span, contain,* and so on, has been left virtually untouched, which is a serious
handicap for the integration of topic–comment structure into an overall
theory of language.

11.4 *Only, even,* and Neg-Raising[13]

Let us now have a cursory look at the words *only* and *even* (and their
equivalents in other languages). They are usually called 'focus particles',
reflecting the fact that they are intimately related with 'focusing'—that is,
with TCM. We will now try to penetrate a little more deeply into the
semantics and the grammar of these two particles, in the light of the presupposition theory developed in the previous chapter and of what we have
glimpsed so far about TCM.

   Both *only* and *even* require focusing, though in different ways. Both are
treated semantically as sentential operators. They seem to differ in that only
requires the ordinary TCM predicate [Be$_v$ NP] (where 'NP' stands for a
referring expression and takes a marked accent), whereas even requires an
underlying predicate 'contains NP as a member', symbolized as '[∋ NP]', the
inverse of the well-known '∈ C' meaning 'is a member of class C'. More
comment follows in a moment.

---

[13] I am indebted to Larry Horn, THE expert on *only, even,* and Neg-Raising, for useful critiques and
comments.

I follow the standard semantic analysis of the operator only, which says that only presupposes the truth of the argument-S and asserts that no other entity satisfies the main predicate of the argument-S. This analysis appears to provide the best fit to the available facts (*pace* those analyses that propose a laxer, purely existential presupposition 'someone laughed' for (11.24a)). *Only JÓHN laughed*, as in (11.24a) is thus taken to presuppose that John laughed and to assert that nobody else did. Sentence (11.24a) is analysed at SA-level as (11.24b), intuitively paraphrased as (11.24c):[14]

(11.24)   a. Only JÓHN laughed.
          b.

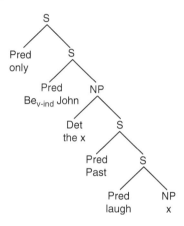

          c. The one who laughed was only JÓHN.

[Be$_{\text{v-ind}}$ NP] is described semantically as nonextensional (or intensional) with regard to its subject term, so that, according to the reference hierarchy discussed in Section 3.5.2 of Volume I, the reference object of the subject term must have *actual existence* when the predicate used (*laugh*) is extensional with regard to the argument term in question, whereas it may have *virtual being* when the predicate in question is intensional with regard to the term at issue. This makes it possible to use an intensional predicate like *imaginary* instead of the extensional predicate *laugh*: *Only JÓHN is imaginary* still presupposes that John is imaginary and asserts that nobody else is. The sentences (11.25a-c) below thus presuppose that someone actually laughed and assert that this person was John, whereas (11.24a) and (11.26a,b) presuppose that John laughed and assert that nobody else did.

---

[14] For details regarding the grammatical theory employed, see Seuren (1996).

(11.25)   a. Who laughed was JÓHN.
           b. It was JÓHN who laughed.
           c. JÓHN laughed.

How does (11.24b) end up as the surface structure (11.24a) or, for that matter, as (11.26a) or (11.26b) below? When we demonstrate this process in terms of the theory of Semantic Syntax (Seuren 1996; see also Section 7.2.1 in Volume I), we see that, leaving **only** out of account for the time being, without Cleft Deletion, the grammar yields either the pseudocleft (11.25a) or the cleft (11.25b). With Cleft Deletion, which is licensed by the predicate **Be$_v$** and lowers the predicate [**Be$_{v\text{-ind}}$ John**] to the position of the variable **x** (the subject term of **laugh**), deleting **Be$_{v\text{-ind}}$** along with $_{Det}$[**the x**] and their immediately dominating nodes **S** and **NP**, the result is (11.25c), where JÓHN has carried with it the sentence-nuclear accent it naturally has in virtue of being the main SA-predicate.

Further lowering of **only** makes **only** land onto **John**, the remainder of the SA matrix predicate, placing it to the left of **John**, according to the general right-branching setting for the syntax of English. This gives either (11.24a) or (11.26a) or (11.26b):

(11.26)   a. Who laughed was only JÓHN.
           b. It was only JÓHN who laughed.

The description is somewhat oversimplified, but further details will be provided in a moment, when the particle *even* is discussed.

First we discuss the ordinary negation of (11.24a):

(11.27)   Not only JÓHN laughed.

As was pointed out in Section 10.4, (11.27) carries the same presupposition as (11.24a): the negation, being in noncanonical position, necessarily preserves the presuppositions of the L-proposition that forms its argument. No particular problem seems to arise here. The negation word *not* in (11.27) clearly represents the sentential (widest possible scope) negation of (11.24a) above. Accordingly, the SA-tree of (11.27) equals that of (11.24a), except that $_S$[$_{Pred}$[**not**]] is added at the top.

So far so good, or so it seems, which does not mean that we have exhausted the treatment of *only*. Thus, we have given no account of the construction *only if*, which we know to be far from trivial. Nor have we explained the connection between the *only* discussed here and the *only* found in sentences like *Only, there is still the problem of what we will do next*, where *only* is roughly equivalent with *but* (the same phenomenon is observed in German (*allein*),

Dutch (*alleen*), French (*seulement*), Italian (*solo, soltanto*), Modern Greek (*móno*), and lots of other languages). And many other difficulties remain.[15] But for the purpose of the present work, we must leave it at this.

Matters stand rather differently with regard to *even*. Semantically, a sentence like (11.28b) is not the negation of (11.28a):[16]

(11.28) a. Even JÓHN laughed.
         b. Not even JÓHN laughed.

In fact, as was observed by Horn (1989: 151), there is no way of negating a sentence like (11.28a) in such a way that (11.28a) and its negation are contradictories. Sentence (11.28b) is anything but the negation of (11.28a). What it is, we shall see in a moment.

Moreover, whereas English has (11.28a,b), these sentences do not have cleft or pseudocleft alternatives, since both (11.29a) and (11.29b) are ungrammatical:

(11.29) a. *It was (not) even JÓHN who laughed.
         b. *Who laughed was (not) even JÓHN.

This we account for by assuming that (11.30a) does not contain, at SA-level, the predicate [$Be_{v\text{-}ind}$ **NP**], but rather the predicate [$\ni$ **NP**] ('contains NP as a member' or 'includes NP'), which does not allow for clefting and requires the incorporation of [$\ni$ **NP**] into its subject-S. (It is assumed that the same SA-predicate [$\ni$ **NP**] also underlies the particles *too* and *also*: *John too laughed* is analysed as 'Apart from others, the class of laughers included John'.) Assuming that [$Be_{v\text{-}ind}$ **NP**] may occur independently of any higher-focusing particle, we can, in principle, explain the ambiguity of JÓHN *laughed*, which is either 'the one who laughed was John' or 'John was among the laughers', perhaps with a slight intonational difference.

The process of incorporation of [$\ni$ **NP**] into the S-structure of the subject-NP is closely akin to Cleft Deletion and consists in placing [$\ni$ **NP**] in (11.30b) (where, as before, the variable $\bar{x}$ ranges over plural objects or sets) in the position of the subject term of **laugh**, thereby deleting $\ni$, leaving only JÓHN (with marked accent inherited from its being the main SA-predicate), and deleting the S-node over $_{Pred}[\ni$ **John**] as well as $_{Det}$[**the $\bar{x}$**] and its dominating

---

[15] We have, it seems, solved the problem of *only some*, which clearly excludes *all*. This is solved by the assumption, made and developed in Chapter 3, that the meaning of *some* is rooted in basic-natural predicate logic, where *some* excludes *all*.

[16] Larry Horn pointed out to me that sentence-initial *not even* constitutes a counterexample (the only one that has come to light so far) to my generalization (Section 10.4) that the negation in noncanonical position is *per se* presupposition-preserving (see note 8 in Chapter 10).

NP-node. This leaves the SA-tree (11.31a), which then undergoes the standard cyclic treatment, whereby the marked accent on JÓHN is preserved throughout.

(11.30)   a. Even JÓHN laughed.
          b.

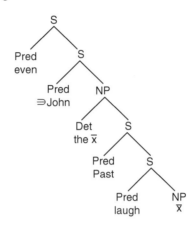

          c. The class of those who laughed contained even JÓHN.

(11.31)   a.

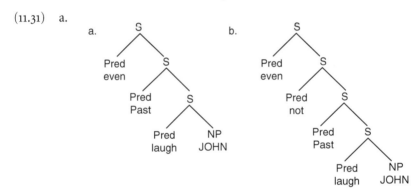

(11.31b) is taken to underlie (11.28b) after the incorporation of [∋ NP] into the subject-S: not negates laugh, not the whole sentence. (11.28b) is to be paraphrased as 'the class of those who did not laugh contained even JÓHN'.

Like [Be_{v-ind} NP], [∋ NP] is described semantically as not requiring actual existence of the reference value of its subject term (see (11.30b)), making it possible to say *(Not) even JÓHN is imaginary* in complete parallelism to *(Not) even JÓHN laughed*. We say that a sentence like *Even JÓHN laughed* presupposes that there is a class of laughers and asserts that John is an unexpected or unlikely member of that class. Analogously, we say that *Even JÓHN did not laugh*, or, perhaps more idiomatically, *Not even JÓHN laughed*, presupposes a class of non-laughers and asserts that John is an unexpected or unlikely member of thát class (cf. Horn 1989: 151). Semantically, therefore, the negation in *Not even JÓHN laughed* belongs in the S-structure of the subject-NP of the predicate [∋ John] and is not a negation creating the contradiction of its nonnegated counterpart.

But how on earth does the negation in *Not even JÓHN laughed* land in that position, while it originates as a negation internal to the subject term of the SA-predicate [∋ John]? What grammatical sorcery has been going on here? Let us note first that English is well-nigh unique in having the negation in sentence-initial position in sentences of this nature. Italian comes close in that it has *anche* or *anzi* for 'even' and *neanche* (also *(nem)manco* or *nemmeno*) for 'not even'. But French says *Même JEAN n'a pas ri*, while German says *Sogar JOHANN hat nicht gelacht* and Dutch has *Zelfs JAN heeft niet gelachen*—all with the negation in construction with the finite verb.

Given a structure like (11.31b), one is tempted to think of what is known as the process of NEG-RAISING (NR), much maligned in the (pragmatically orient- ed) literature yet, in my view, hard to deny as a real grammatical process found in the grammars of many languages.[17] In simple terms, NEG-RAISING is the phenomenon that a negation which semantically belongs in the scope of a predicate ends up in surface structure to the left of that predicate and thus taking scope over it. Well-known examples are sentences like *I don't think he'll make it*, which does not mean, literally, 'it is not the case that I think that he will make it' but rather 'I think that he will not make it'. Likewise for a sentence like *I don't want to die*, which does not mean what it says but rather 'I want not to die'. Nineteenth-century normative grammars told one to avoid such constructions because they ran counter to logic!

It must be observed that NR is less likely to occur in cases where the *that-*clause is the comment in a TCM-structure. For example, when the discourse has given rise to the (implicit or explicit) question 'What does Harry believe?', then the appropriate answer form is rather one without NR, such as *Harry believes that the crisis will not be over next month*. An idiomatic instance, as was once pointed out to me by my Amsterdam colleague Wim Klooster, is *I thought you'd never come*, rather than *I never thought you'd come*.

Horn argues (1971; 1978; 1989: 330–61) extensively that NR-phenomena are the result of pragmatic factors such as politeness strategies, understatement, hedging, or irony. In polite society, one prefers to avoid direct clashes of

---

[17] For an admirable and well-nigh complete survey of the entire complex question of NR and the literature pertaining to it, see Horn (1978; 1989: 308–30).

opinion and thus expresses oneself rather in the weaker terms of 'I don't believe that...' than in the crass terms of 'I believe that not...'. One prefers to say *She is unlikely to come*, rather than *She is likely not to come*, or *This is not good* rather than *This is bad*, etc. etc. (read Horn 1989: it's very well written). I fully agree with Horn to the extent that he seeks a pragmatic origin for NR: it seems to me that his arguments are strong and convincing. I also agree with his conclusion (Horn 1978: 215–16):

> ...that NR originates as a functional device for signalling negative force as early in a negative sentence as possible. [...] NR must be regarded as a rule in the synchronic grammar of English and other languages. NR would thus constitute an example of a pragmatic process which has become grammaticized or syntacticized.[18]

With Horn, I argue that NR has indeed become part of the grammar and lexicon of English and many, perhaps all, natural languages. This appears from a number of facts. First, one sees that NR is, at the level of linguistic description and not at the noncommittal pragmatic level, associated with different verbs in different languages. Thus, English *hope* and its Italian counterpart *sperare* do not induce NR but their French, Dutch, and German cousins do.

Then, as shown in Seuren (2004: 178–81; see also the discussion around examples (7.19–7.22) in Chapter 7 of Volume I), certain Negative Polarity Items (NPIs), such as *in the least* or *yet* or *the slightest*, are licensed only when occurring in the immediate scope of negation:

(11.32) a. √She knows that John hasn't arrived yet.
         b. *She doesn't know that John has arrived yet.

(11.33) a. √Many people are not in the least interested.
         b. *Not many people are in the least interested.

---

[18] The same is often found for grammatical categories that find their origin in natural phenomena but have been extended to becoming autonomous grammatical categories. Grammar often gets 'started up' by what takes place in the world or in communicative situations and then 'takes over' in its own right. Consider, for example, grammatical gender distinctions. To the extent that they correspond with natural gender, the grammatical gender of nouns is almost entirely predictable: *la femme*, *die Frau* (both 'the woman') are predictably feminine (though German also has the neuter nouns *das Weib* ('the woman', used derogatorily) and *das Mädchen* ('the girl'), which is a diminutive). But this natural motivation is no longer valid when these gender distinctions are applied to words denoting objects that simply have no natural gender. Thus French has the masculine *le soleil* for 'the sun', but German has the feminine *die Sonne*, and, ironically, the French and German words for 'moon' are the feminine *la lune* and the masculine *der Mond*, respectively. Speculations about totally different French and German 'popular spirits' were rife in the nineteenth century but have been abandoned now.

(11.34)   a. √Many people don't show the slightest interest.
          b. *Not many people show the slightest interest.

Yet we see that these three NPIs occur naturally and without a hint of ungrammaticality in sentences like:

(11.35)   a. √I don't think John has arrived yet.
          b. √I don't expect John to be in the least interested.
          c. √Don't expect John to take the slightest interest in your work.

Such facts are readily explained when one assumes SA-forms where the negation stands over the embedded clauses and not over the main sentence and one accepts NR as an automatic grammatical process not affecting the semantics of the sentences involved. But they are hard to explain in purely pragmatic terms. One would have to present a purely pragmatic explanation of the occurrence restrictions of NPIs—a feat that has not so far been achieved. As in the case of NR, the very phenomenon of NPIs may have had a pragmatic origin, but their subsequent grammaticalization is hard to deny.

The advantage of the grammaticalization view is that the application range of NR can now be extended to cover less obvious cases. One may think, for example, of the propositional operator AND as a Neg-Raiser, whereby *and* is converted into its counterpart *or*. AND (NOT-P, NOT-Q) thus becomes NOT (OR (P,Q)), as in (11.36a), which becomes (11.36b):

(11.36)   a. He doesn't like planes and he doesn't like trains.
          b. He doesn't like planes or trains.

It has been noted repeatedly in previous chapters that the converse does not work:

(11.37)   a. He doesn't like planes or he doesn't like trains.
          b. !!He doesn't like planes and trains.

This also explains, in principle, the plural *were* in a sentence like (11.38a), derived from an underlying (11.38b). One notes that (11.38c) is ungrammatical:

(11.38)   a. I don't think John or Harry *were* late.
          b. I don't think John was late and I don't think Harry was late.
          c. *John or Harry were late.

In fact, English *so far* appears to be a Neg-Raiser, as we say *not so far achieved*, and not *so far not achieved*, which is what it means. In like manner, we now posit that English *even* is a Neg-Raiser (in accordance with Horn 1971: 132). This allows us to posit that an underlying (11.31b), repeated here as (11.39a), is transformed into (11.39b), after which the syntactic Cycle is free to operate.

(11.39)

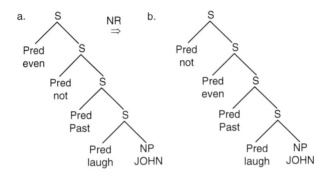

There is, however, an important corollary to this solution: it must be assumed that the syntax of a language does not start with the classic Cycle (which processes each S-cycle successively, starting from the most deeply embedded or lowest S and working its way up till the highest S), but that there is a PRECYCLE that reshuffles SA-trees before the Cycle can start to operate. This is an almost totally unexplored area of research in the theory of grammar, but there are plenty of indications that something like a Precycle must be admitted.[19] Neg-Raising and Cleft Deletion (along with the deletion of its [∋ NP] counterpart) would then have to be taken to be part of the Precycle. On this assumption, the problem of the grammar and the semantics of (11.28b) would be solved.

11.5 Why TCM is a semantic phenomenon: the SSV test

There is one further respect in which TCM-structure has been the victim of myopia in semantic theory. Whereas Frege's discovery of the nonsubstitutivity of co-referring terms in intensional contexts triggered a vast research programme that dominated twentieth-century semantics, no-one seems to have noticed the nonsubstitutivity *salva veritate* of truth-conditionally

---

[19] Larry Horn pointed out that the *it* in *I don't believe that John paid his taxes and Mary is quite sure of it* pronominalizes 'that John didn't pay his taxes' and not 'that John paid his taxes', which would imply that pronominalization must have occurred before NR. Although it is no longer assumed that pronominalization is a syntactic process but is more likely to occur before the syntax starts to operate, in the no-man's land between propositional thought and language, the observation remains relevant and interesting.

equivalent TCM-structures in emotive or evaluative intensional contexts. It was pointed out in Sections 3.2, 6.2.3.2, and 7.2.2 of Volume I and in Section 10.5.2 of the present volume that emotive factive and nonfactive predicates create or continue subdomains where the substitution of otherwise truth-conditionally equivalent TCM-structures makes a truth-conditional differ-ence. Examples are:

(11.40)   a. It surprised Ann that JOHN (and not Kevin) had sold the car.
          b. It surprised Ann that John had sold THE CAR (and not the speedboat).

(11.41)   a. It angered Ann that JOHN (and not Kevin) had sold the car.
          b. It angered Ann that John had sold THE CAR (and not the speedboat).

(11.42)   a. Ann hopes that JOHN (and not Kevin) has sold the car.
          b. Ann hopes that John has sold THE CAR (and not the speedboat).

(11.43)   a. It's a good thing that JOHN (and not Kevin) has sold the car.
          b. It's a good thing that John has sold THE CAR (and not the speedboat).

Clearly, it is possible for the (a)-sentences to be true while the (b)-sentences are false, and vice versa. For example, Ann may hope that John and not Kevin has sold the car because John is her husband and they need the sales commission, while at the same time she regrets that it is the car that has been put up for sale and not, say, the speedboat, as the latter would bring in much more money. Or she may hope that John has sold the car and not the speedboat because the car takes up too much space in the garage, while the speedboat is well away from their home. At the same time, she may regret that John had to do the selling because she knows how bad he is at getting the best price. In fact, a sentence like (11.44) is entirely consistent:

(11.44)   It is fortunate that it is JOHN who has sold the car, but unfortunate that it is the CAR that has been sold.

Substitution *salva veritate* of truth-conditionally equivalent TCM-struc-tures is a fully valid operation in non-emotive intensional contexts, as appears from cases like (11.45a,b), with the non-emotive epistemic intensional verb *believe*:

(11.45)   a. Ann believes that JOHN has sold the car.
          b. Ann believes that John has sold the CAR.

Here it is not possible for the one to be true while the other is false, even though, of course, the two sentences differ as regards their anchoring conditions for given discourse domains.

Yet, as was pointed out in Section 10.4, substitution *salva veritate* of truth-conditionally equivalent TCM-structurings is again blocked under sentential negation. Here, the truth-conditional difference resides in the *presuppositional* truth conditions, as appears from the following examples:

(11.46)   a. JÓHN hasn't sold the car: he is a figment of Ann's mind. PETER did.
           b. !! JÓHN hasn't sold the car: there never wás a car.

(11.47)   a. John hasn't sold the CÁR: there never wás a car. He sold the
              SPEEDBOAT.
           b. !!John hasn't sold the CÁR: he is a figment of Ann's mind.

Clearly, these observations are in full agreement with our analysis, according to which the constituent under a grade-2 accentual peak is the underlying SA-predicate Be$_{v\text{-ind}}$, which induces no existential presupposition with regard to the value specified. But non-accented constituents in the Matrix-S are subject to the normal preconditions holding for the Matrix-predicate.

The conclusion is, therefore, that TCM is not merely a pragmatic phenomenon but does contribute to sentence meaning. This again means that type-level discourse-incremental properties of sentences cannot simply be relegated to pragmatics but must be considered to be part of a *semantic* theory of natural language.

Bibliography

ABRAHAM, W. (1991) 'Discourse particles in German: How does their illocutionary force come about?', in W. Abraham (ed.), *Discourse Particles: Descriptive and Theoretical Investigations on the Logical, Syntactic, and Pragmatic Properties of Discourse Particles in German*. Benjamins, Amsterdam/Philadelphia: 203–52.

ALFORD, M. (1995) 'Isaac Newton: the first physicist'. http://www.physics.wustl.edu/~alford/newton.html

ANDRADE MARTINS, S. (2004) *Fonologia e Gramática Dâw*. 2 vols. LOT, Utrecht.

ASBACH-SCHNITKER, B. (1979) 'Die adversativen Konnektoren *aber, sondern* und *but* nach negierten Sätzen', in H. Weydt (ed.), *Die Partikeln der deutschen Sprache*. De Gruyter, Berlin-New York: 457–68.

BARWISE, J. and R. COOPER (1981) 'Generalized quantifiers and natural language', *Linguistics and Philosophy* 4/2: 159–219.

—— and J. PERRY (1983) *Situations and Attitudes*. MIT Press, Cambridge, MA.

BÄUERLE, R., U. EGLI, and A. VON STECHOW (eds), *Semantics from Different Points of View*. Springer, Berlin-Heidelberg-New York.

BELLERT, I. (1972) 'On certain syntactical properties of the English connectives *and* and *but*', in S. Ploetz (ed.), *Transformationelle Analyse. Die Transformationstheorie von Zellig Harris und ihre Entwicklung*. Athenaeum, Frankfurt: 327–56.

BLAKEMORE, D. and R. CARSTON (2005) 'The pragmatics of sentential coordination with *and*', *Lingua* 115: 569–89.

BLANCHÉ, R. (1966) *Structures intellectuelles*. J. Vrin, Paris.

BOCHEŃSKI, I. M. (1956) *Formale Logik*. Orbis Academicus, Freiburg/Munich.

BOËR, S. E. and W. G. LYCAN (1976) 'The myth of semantic presupposition', Indiana University Linguistics Club.

BOLINGER, D. (1972) 'Accent is predictable (if you're a mind-reader)', *Language* 48/3: 633–44.

BORKOWSKI, L. (1970) *Jan Łukasiewicz: Selected Works*. North-Holland, Amsterdam.

BROUWER, L. E. J. (1966) 'Life, art, and mysticism', *Notre Dame Journal of Formal Logic* 37: 389–429. (Transl. by W. P. van Stigt of L. E. J. Brouwer, *Leven, Kunst en Mystiek*, 1905.)

BROWN, L. and M. S. DRYER (2008) 'The verbs for "and" in Walman, a Torricelli language of Papua New Guinea', *Language* 84/3: 528–65.

BUCKNER, E. (2007) 'The fourth corner', paper read at the international congress 'The Square of Opposition', Montreux, Switzerland, June 1–3, 2007. http://maverickphilosopher.powerblogs.com/posts/1177106402.shtml.

BURLEIGH, W. (1988) *Von der Reinheit der Kunst der Logik. Erster Traktat. Von den Eigenschaften der Termini*. (De puritate artis logicae. De proprietatibus terminorum). Translated and edited by Peter Kunze, with introduction and commentary. Felix Meiner, Hamburg.

BUSSE, A. (ed.) (1897) *Ammonius in Aristotelis* De Interpretatione *Commentarius*. Royal Prussian Academy of Sciences. Georg Reimer, Berlin.

BUTTERWORTH, B. (1999) *The Mathematical Brain*. Macmillan, London.

CARNAP, R. (1956) *Meaning and Necessity. A Study in Semantics and Modal Logic*. Enlarged edition. The University of Chicago Press, Chicago.

CARROLL, L. (= C. L. Dodgson) (1896) *Symbolic Logic. Part I. Elementary*. Fifth Edition. Edited, in 1977, with annotations and an introduction by William Warren Bartley, III. Harvester Press, Hassocks, Sussex, England.

CAVALIERE, F. (2007) 'Sillogismi sfumati, triangolo oppositivo, quadrilatero numerico, inter-bivalenza, con un' appendice storica sulla quantificazione del predicato'. http://www.arrigoamadori.com/lezioni/AngoloDelFilosofo/AngoloDelFilosofo.htm

CLANCHY, M. T. (1997) *Abelard. A Medieval Life*. Blackwell, Oxford.

CLARK, H. H. and D. WILKES-GIBBS (1990) 'Referring as a collaborative process', in P. R. Cohen, J. Morgan, and M. E. Pollack (eds), *Intentions in Communication*. MIT Press, Cambridge, MA: 463–93.

—— (1992) *Arenas of Language Use*. The University of Chicago Press, Chicago.

—— (1996) *Using Language*. Cambridge University Press, Cambridge.

COHEN, L. J. (1971) 'The logical particles of natural language', in Y. Bar-Hillel (ed.), *Pragmatics of Natural Language*. Reidel, Dordrecht: 50–68.

COMRIE, B. (1986) 'Conditionals: a typology', in Traugott et al. (eds): 77–99.

COPI, I. M. (1961) *Introduction to Logic*. Macmillan, New York.

DE MORGAN, A. (1847) *Formal Logic: or, The Calculus of Inference, Necessary and Probable*. Taylor and Walton, London.

—— (1858) 'On the syllogism III, and on logic in general', reprinted in P. Heath (ed.), *On the Syllogism and Other Logical Writings*. Yale University Press, New Haven (1966): 74–146.

DE RIJK, L. M. (1956) *Petrus Abaelardus, Dialectica. First Complete Edition of the Parisian Manuscript*. Van Gorcum/Hak and Prakke, Assen.

—— (1967) *Logica Modernorum. A Contribution to the History of Early Terminist Logic. Vol. II.1: The Origin and Early Development of the Theory of Supposition*. Van Gorcum, Assen.

—— (1972) *Peter of Spain (Petrus Hispanus Portugalensis) Tractatus, called afterwards Summule Logicales*. Van Gorcum, Assen.

—— (1985) 'Walter Burley's tract "De Exclusivis". An edition', *Vivarium* 23: 23–54.

—— (1986) 'Walter Burley's "De Exceptivis". An edition', *Vivarium* 24: 22–49.

—— (1992) *Peter of Spain (Petrus Hispanus Portugalensis) Syncategoreumata*. Brill, Leiden.

—— (2002) *Aristotle: Semantics and Ontology. Vol. I: General Introduction. The Works on Logic*. Brill, Leiden.

DECLERCK, R. and S. REED (2001) *Conditionals. A Comprehensive Empirical Analysis*. Mouton de Gruyter, Berlin.

DEHAENE, S. (1997) *The Number Sense*. Oxford University Press, New York.

—— (2005) 'Evolution of human cortical circuits for reading and arithmetic: the "neuronal recycling" hypothesis', in S. Dehaene, J.-R. Duhamel, M. D. Hauser, and G. Rizzolatti (eds), *From Monkey Brain to Human Brain*. MIT Press, Cambridge, MA: 133–57.

—— V. IZARD, P. PICA, and E. SPELKE (2006) 'Core knowledge of geometry in an Amazonian indigene group', *Science* 11 (January 2006): 381–4.

DIEWALD, G. and K. FISCHER (1998) 'Zur diskursiven und modalen Funktion der Partikeln *aber, auch, doch* und *ja* in Instruktionsdialogen', *Linguistica* 38/1: 75–99.

DONNELLAN, K. (1966) 'Reference and definite descriptions', *Philosophical Review* 75: 281–304.

DOWTY, D. (1979) *Word Meaning and Montague Grammar.* Reidel, Dordrecht.

—— R. E. WALL, and S. R. PETERS (1981) *Introduction to Montague Semantics.* Reidel, Dordrecht.

DUMMETT, M. E. (1973) *Frege. Philosophy of Language.* Duckworth, London.

EBBESEN, S. (1990a) 'Porphyry's legacy to logic: a reconstruction', in Sorabji (ed.): 141–71.

—— (1990b) 'Philoponus, "Alexander" and the origins of medieval logic', in Sorabji (ed.): 445–61.

ECO, U. (1995) *The Search for the Perfect Language.* Blackwell, Oxford.

EVANS, J. St. B. T. and D. OVER (2005) *If.* Oxford University Press, New York.

FAUCONNIER, G. (1985) *Mental Spaces: Aspects of Meaning Construction in Natural Language.* MIT Press, Cambridge, MA.

FILLMORE, Ch. J. and D. T. LANGENDOEN (eds) (1971) *Studies in Linguistic Semantics.* Holt, New York.

FISCHER, K. (2000) *From Cognitive Semantics to Lexical Pragmatics: The Functional Polysemy of Discourse Particles.* Mouton de Gruyter, Berlin.

FODOR, J. A. (1975) *The Language of Thought.* Harvester Press, Hassocks, Sussex.

—— (1983) *The Modularity of Mind. An Essay on Faculty Psychology.* A Bradford Book. MIT Press, Cambridge, MA.

—— (1998) *Concepts: Where Cognitive Science Went Wrong.* Oxford University Press, New York.

FOWLER, TH. (1892) *The Elements of Deductive Logic.* Clarendon Press, Oxford.

FREGE, G. (1884) *Die Grundlagen der Arithmetik: eine logisch-mathematische Untersuchung über den Begriff der Zahl.* W. Koebner, Breslau.

—— (1892) 'Ueber Sinn und Bedeutung', *Zeitschrift für Philosophie und philosophische Kritik* 100: 25–50. (Also in Patzig 1969: 40–65.)

—— (1969) *Nachgelassene Schriften.* Edited by H. Hermes, F. Kambartel, and F. Kaulbach. Felix Meiner, Hamburg.

GAZDAR, G. (1979) *Pragmatics. Implicature, Presupposition, and Logical Form.* Academic Press, New York-San Francisco-London.

GEACH, P. T. (1950) 'Russell's Theory of Descriptions', *Analysis* 10: 84–8.

—— (1962) *Reference and Generality. An Examination of Some Medieval and Modern Theories.* Cornell University Press, Ithaca, New York.

—— (1969) 'Quine's syntactical insights', in D. Davidson and J. Hintikka (eds), *Words and Objections. Essays on the Work of W. V. Quine.* Reidel, Dordrecht: 146–57. (Also in Geach 1972: 115–27.)

—— (1972) *Logic Matters.* Oxford, Blackwell.

GEIS, M. L. and A. M. ZWICKY (1971) 'On invited inferences', *Linguistic Inquiry* 2/4: 561–6.

GEURTS, B. and D. I. BEAVER (2007) 'Discourse Representation Theory', in E. N. Zalta (ed.), *The Stanford Encyclopedia of Philosophy*. http://plato.stanford.edu/entries/discourse-representation-theory/.

GILSON, É. (1978) *Héloïse et Abélard*. J. Vrin, Paris.

GINSBURG, H. P. and B. S. ALLARDICE (1984) 'Children's difficulties with school mathematics', in B. Rogoff and J. Lave (eds), *Everyday Cognition: Its Development in Social Context.* Harvard University Press, Cambridge, MA: 194–219.

GREEN-PEDERSEN, N. J. (1980) 'Walter Burley's "De Consequentiis". An edition', *Franciscan Studies* 40 (annual xviii): 102–66.

GREENBERG, J. H. (1963) 'Some universals of grammar with particular reference to the order of meaningful elements', in J. H. Greenberg (ed.), *Universals of Language*. MIT Press, Cambridge, MA: 73–113.

GROENENDIJK, J. A. G. and M. B. J. STOKHOF (1991) 'Dynamic predicate logic', *Linguistics and Philosophy* 14: 39–100.

GUSSENHOVEN, C. (1984) *On the Grammar and Semantics of Sentence Accents*. Foris, Dordrecht.

—— (2005) 'Semantics of prosody', in K. Brown (ed.), *The Encyclopedia of Language and Linguistics*, second edition. Elsevier, Oxford: 170–3.

HAMBLIN, CH. L. (1970) *Fallacies*. Methuen, London.

HAMILTON, W. (1866) *Lectures on Metaphysics and Logic. Vol. IV* (*Lectures on Logic. Vol. II*, 2nd edition, revised). Edited by H. L. Mansel and J. Veitch. Blackwood and Sons, Edinburgh-London.

HARRIS, M. B. (1986) 'The historical development of SI-clauses in Romance', in Traugott et al. (eds): 265–84.

HEIM, I. R. (1990) 'On the projection problem for presuppositions', in S. Davis (ed.), *Pragmatics. A Reader*. Oxford University Press, Oxford: 397–405.

HOEKSEMA, J. (1999) 'Blocking effects and polarity sensitivity', in J. Gerbrandy, M. Marx, M. de Rijke, and Y. Venema (eds), *JFAK. Essays Dedicated to Johan van Benthem on the Occasion of his 50th Birthday*. Amsterdam University Press, Amsterdam (not available in hard copy). http://www.illc.uva.nl/j50/contribs/hoeksema/hoeksema.pdf

HORN, L. R. (1971) 'Negative transportation: unsafe at any speed?', in *Papers from the Seventh Regional Meeting of the Chicago Linguistic Society 1971*. Chicago Linguistic Society, Chicago Illinois: 120–33.

—— (1972) 'On the Semantic Properties of Logical Operators in English', distributed by Indiana University Linguistics Club 1976.

—— (1978) 'Remarks on Neg-Raising', in P. Cole (ed.), *Syntax and Semantics 9: Pragmatics*. Academic Press, New York-London: 129–220.

—— (1985) 'Metalinguistic negation and pragmatic ambiguity', *Language* 61/1: 121–74.

—— (1989) *A Natural History of Negation*. The University of Chicago Press, Chicago.

—— (1991) '*Duplex Negatio Affirmat...*: The economy of double negation', in *Papers from the 27th Regional Meeting of the Chicago Linguistic Society 1991. Part Two: The Parasession on Negation*. Chicago Linguistic Society, Chicago, Illinois: 80–106.

—— (1997) 'All John's children are as bald as the king of France: existential import and the geometry of opposition', in *Papers from the 33rd Regional Meeting of the Chicago Linguistic Society 1997. Papers from the Main Session*. Chicago Linguistic Society, Chicago, Illinois: 155–79.

—— (2000) 'From *if* to *iff*: conditional perfection or pragmatic strengthening', *Journal of Pragmatics* 32/2: 289–326.

HUSSERL, E. (1900) *Logische Untersuchungen. Vol 2: Untersuchungen zur Phänomenologie und Theorie der Erkenntnis. Teil 1*. Niemeyer, Halle.

ISARD, S. (1975) 'Changing the context', in E. L. Keenan (ed.), *Formal Semantics of Natural Language*. Cambridge University Press, Cambridge: 287–96.

JANSSEN, TH. A. J. M. (1976) Hebben-*konstrukties en indirekt-objektskonstrukties*. HES Publishers, Utrecht.

JASPERS, D. (2005) *Operators in the Lexicon. On the Negative Logic of Natural Language*. LOT, Utrecht.

JESPERSEN, O. (1917) *Negation in English and Other Languages*. Det Kgl. Danske Videnskabernes Selskab, Historisk-filologiske Meddelelser I,5. Andr. Fred. Høst and søn, Copenhagen.

—— (1924) *The Philosophy of Grammar*. Allen and Unwin, London.

JOHNSON-LAIRD, P. N. (1986) 'Conditionals and mental models', in Traugott et al. (eds): 55–75.

KALEPKY, TH. (1928) *Neuaufbau der Grammatik als Grundlegung zu einem wissenschaftlichen System der Sprachbeschreibung*. Teubner, Leipzig.

KAMP, H. (1981) 'A theory of truth and semantic interpretation', in J. A. G. Groenendijk, Th. M. V. Janssen, and M. B. J. Stokhof (eds), *Formal Methods in the Study of Language*. Vol. I. Mathematisch Centrum, Amsterdam: 277–322.

—— and U. REYLE (1993) *From Discourse to Logic. Introduction to Model-Theoretic Semantics of Natural Language, Formal Logic and Discourse Representation Theory*. Kluwer, Dordrecht.

KARTTUNEN, L. (1973) 'Presuppositions of compound sentences', *Linguistic Inquiry* 4/2: 169–93.

KEENAN, E. L. (2003) 'The definiteness effect: semantics or pragmatics?', *Natural Language Semantics* 11: 187–216.

KING, P. (2005) 'Ockham's *Summa Logicae*', in J. Shand (ed.), *Central Works of Philosophy*. Volume I. Acumen Publishing, Chesham: 242–69.

KIPARSKY, P. and C. KIPARSKY (1971) 'Fact', in D. D. Steinberg and L. A. Jakobovits (eds), *Semantics. An Interdisciplinary Reader in Philosophy, Linguistics and Psychology*. Cambridge University Press, Cambridge: 345–69.

KLEENE, S. C. (1938) 'On notation for ordinal numbers', *Journal of Symbolic Logic* 3: 150–5.

—— (1952) *Introduction to Metamathematics*. North-Holland, Amsterdam.

KLIMA, G. (1988) *Ars Artium. Essays in Philosophical Semantics, Mediaeval and Modern*. Doxa Library. Institute of Philosophy, Hungarian Academy of Sciences, Budapest.

KNEALE, W. and M. KNEALE (1962) *The Development of Logic*. Clarendon Press, Oxford.

KRATZER, A. (1979) 'Conditional necessity and possibility', in Bäuerle et al. (eds): 117–47.

KRIPKE, S. (1972) 'Naming and necessity', in D. Davidson and G. Harman (eds), *Semantics of Natural Language*. Reidel, Dordrecht: 253–355.

—— (1980) *Naming and Necessity*. Blackwell, Oxford (= Kripke 1972).

LABOV, W. (1972) *Language in the Inner City. Studies in Black English Vernacular.* University of Pennsylvania Press, Philadelphia.

LAKOFF, R. (1971) 'If's, and's, and but's about conjunctions', in Fillmore and Langendoen (eds): 114–49.

LANG, E. (1977) *Semantik der koordinativen Verknüpfung.* Akademie-Verlag, Berlin.

LANGENDOEN, D. T. and H. B. SAVIN (1971) 'The projection problem for presuppositions', in Fillmore and Langendoen (eds): 55–60.

LENZEN, W. (2008) 'Ploucquet's "refutation" of the traditional Square of Opposition', *Logica Universalis* 2: 43–58.

LEVINSON, S. C. (2000) *Presumptive Meanings. The Theory of Generalized Conversational Implicature.* MIT Press, Cambridge MA.

LEWIS, D. (1979) 'Scorekeeping in a language game', in Bäuerle et al. (eds): 172–87.

LEWIS, G. L. (1984) *Turkish Grammar.* Oxford University Press, Oxford.

LIPPS, TH. (1893) *Grundzüge der Logik.* Dürr, Leipzig.

LÖBNER, S. (1990) *Wahr neben Falsch. Duale Operatoren als die Quantoren natürlicher Sprache.* Niemeyer, Tübingen.

LONDEY, D. and C. JOHANSON (1987) *The Logic of Apuleius: Including a Complete Latin Text and English Translation of the Peri Hermeneias of Apuleius of Madaura.* Brill, Leiden.

ŁUKASIEWICZ, J. J. I. (1934) 'Z historii logiki zdán', *Przegląd Filozoficny* 37: 417–37. [German transl.: 'Zur Geschichte der Aussagenlogik', *Erkenntnis* 5 (1935): 111–31. English transl.: 'On the history of the logic of propositions', in McCall (1967: 66–87); reprinted in: Borkowski (1970: 197–217).]

McCALL, S. (1967) *Polish Logic 1920–1939.* Oxford University Press, Oxford.

McCAWLEY, J. D. (1967) 'Meaning and the description of languages', *Kotoba no Uchu* 2/9: 10–18; 2/10: 38–48; 2/11: 51–7. (Also in McCawley 1973: 99–120.)

—— (1972) 'A program for logic', in D. Davidson and G. Harman (eds), *Semantics of Natural Language*. Reidel, Dordrecht: 498–544.

—— (1973) *Grammar and Meaning. Papers on Syntactic and Semantic Topics.* Taishukan, Tokyo.

—— (1981) *Everything that Linguists have Always Wanted to Know about Logic* *but were ashamed to ask.* Blackwell, Oxford.

McLEOD, E. (1971) *Héloïse. A Biography.* Chatto and Windus, London.

MATHESIUS, V. (1928) 'On linguistic characterology with illustrations from modern English', in *Actes du Premier Congrès International de Linguistes à La Haye*. Reprinted in: J. Vachek (ed.), *A Prague School Reader in Linguistics*. Indiana University Press, Bloomington, Indiana (1964): 59–67.

—— (1939) 'O tak zvaném aktuálnim cleneni vetném' (On the so-called functional sentence perspective), *Slovo a Slovesnost* 5: 171–4.

MEISER, C. (1880) *Anicii Manlii Severini Boetii commentarii in librum Aristotelis Perì Hermēneías.* Pars posterior. Editio secunda. Teubner, Leipzig.

MEYER-LÜBKE, W. (1899) *Romanische Syntax* (Grammatik der romanischen Sprachen III). Reisland, Leipzig.

MIGNUCCI, M. (1983) 'La teoria della quantificazione del predicato nell'antichità classica', *Anuario Filosófico de la Universidad de Navarra* 16: 11–42.

MONTAGUE, R. (1970) 'English as a formal language', in B. Visentini (ed.), *Linguaggi nella società e nella tecnica*. Edizioni di Comunità, Milan: 189–223.

—— (1973) 'The proper treatment of quantification in ordinary English', in K. J. J. Hintikka, J. M. E. Moravcsik, and P. Suppes (eds) *Approaches to Natural Language. Proceedings of the 1970 Stanford Workshop on Grammar and Semantics*. Reidel, Dordrecht: 221–42.

MOODY, A. E. (1953) *Truth and Consequence in Mediæval Logic*. North-Holland, Amsterdam.

MOSTOVSKI, A. (1957) 'On a generalization of quantifiers', *Fundamenta Mathematica* 44: 12–36.

MOXEY, L. M. and A. J. SANFORD (1986/7) 'Quantifiers and focus', *Journal of Semantics* 5: 189–206.

MULLALLY, J. P. (1945) *The* Summulæ Logicales *of Peter of Spain*. (Publications in Medieval Studies VIII) The University of Notre Dame Press, Indiana.

NEALE, S. (1990) *Descriptions*. MIT Press, Cambridge, MA.

NUCHELMANS, G. (1973) *Theories of the Proposition. Ancient and Medieval Conceptions of the Bearers of Truth and Falsity*. North-Holland, Amsterdam.

PARSONS, T. (1997) 'The traditional Square of Opposition. A biography', *Acta Analytica* 18: 23–49.

—— (2006) 'The traditional Square of Opposition', in E. N. Zalta (ed.), *The Stanford Encyclopedia of Philosophy* (October 1, 2006 revision) http://plato.stanford.edu/entries/square/.

—— (2008) 'Things that are right with the traditional Square of Opposition', *Logica Universalis* 2: 3–11.

PEIRCE, CH. S. (1974) *Collected Works. Vol. II: Elements of Logic*. Edited by Charles Hartshorne and Paul Weiss. Harvard University Press, Cambridge, MA.

PETERS, S. and D. WESTERSTÅHL (2007) *Quantifiers in Language and Logic*. Oxford University Press, Oxford.

PICA, P., C. LEMER, V. IZARD, and S. DEHAENE (2004) 'Exact and approximate arithmetic in an Amazonian indigene group', *Science* 306 (October 2004): 499–503.

PICKERING, M. J. and S. C. GARROD (2004) 'Toward a mechanistic psychology of dialogue'. *Behavioral and Brain Sciences*, 27/2: 169–225.

QUINE, W. V. O. (1952) *Methods of Logic*. Routledge and Kegan Paul, London.

—— (1953) *From a Logical Point of View*. Harvard University Press, Cambridge, MA.

—— (1960) *Word and Object*. MIT Press, Cambridge, MA.

REINHART, T. (1983) *Anaphora and Semantic Interpretation*. Croom Helm, London.

RESCHER, N. (1969) *Many-valued Logic*. McGraw-Hill, New York.

ROSCH, E. (1975) 'Cognitive representations of semantic categories', *Journal of Experimental Psychology: General* 104: 192–233.

Rosier-Catach, I. (2003*a*) 'Abélard et les grammairiens : sur le verbe substantif et la prédication', *Vivarium* 41/2: 175–248.

—— (2003*b*) 'Abélard et les grammairiens: sur la définition du verbe et la notion d'inhérence', in P. Lardet (ed.), *La tradition vive. Mélanges d'histoire des textes en l'honneur de Louis Holtz*. Brepols, Paris-Turnhout: 143–59.

—— (2003*c*) 'Priscien, Boèce, les *Glosulae in Priscianum*, Abélard: les enjeux des discussions autour de la notion de consignification', *Histoire Épistémologie Langage* 25/11: 55–84.

Russell, B. (1905) 'On denoting', *Mind* 14: 479–93.

Sandmann, M. (1954) *Subject and Predicate. A Contribution to the Theory of Syntax*. University Press, Edinburgh.

Sanford, A. J., E. J. Dawydiak, and L. M. Moxey (2007) 'A unified account of quantifier perspective effects in discourse', *Discourse Processes* 44/1: 1–32.

Schiller, F. C. S. (1912) *Formal Logic. A Scientific and Social Problem*. Macmillan, London.

Schlenker, Ph. (2007) 'Anti-dynamics: presupposition projection without dynamic semantics', *Journal of Logic, Language and Information* 16: 325–56.

Seuren, P. A. M. (1972) 'Taaluniversalia in de transformationele grammatika', *Leuvense Bijdragen* 61/4: 311–70. (Partially republished in English as Chapter 12 in Seuren 2001.)

—— (1973) 'The comparative', in F. Kiefer and N. Ruwet (eds), *Generative Grammar in Europe*. Reidel, Dordrecht: 528–64.

—— (1974) 'Negative's travels', in P. A. M. Seuren (ed.) *Semantic Syntax*, Oxford Readings in Philosophy. Oxford University Press, Oxford: 183–208. (Reprinted as Chapter 8 in Seuren 2001.)

—— (1975) *Tussen Taal en Denken. Een bijdrage tot de empirische funderingen van de semantiek*. Oosthoek, Scheltema en Holkema, Utrecht.

—— (1977) 'Forme logique et forme sémantique: un argument contre M. Geach', *Logique et Analyse* 79/20: 338–47. (Reprinted in English as Chapter 13 in Seuren 2001.)

—— (1980) 'Dreiwertige Logik und die Semantik natürlicher Sprache', in *Sprache der Gegenwart. Schriften des Instituts für deutsche Sprache, Band L. Grammatik und Logik. Jahrbuch 1979 des Instituts für deutsche Sprache*. Schwann, Düsseldorf: 72–103.

—— (1985) *Discourse Semantics*. Blackwell, Oxford.

—— (1986*a*) 'Formal theory and the ecology of language', *Theoretical Linguistics* 13/1: 1–18.

—— (1986*b*) 'Anaphora resolution', in T. Myers, K. Brown, B. McGonigle (eds), *Reasoning and Discourse Processes*. Academic Press, London: 187–207.

—— (1987) 'Les paradoxes et le langage', *Logique et Analyse* 30 (120): 365–83. (Republished in English as Chapter 6 in Seuren 2001.)

—— (1988) 'Presupposition and negation', *Journal of Semantics* 6/3–4: 175–226. (Reprinted as Chapter 15 in Seuren 2001.)

—— (1993) 'Why does 2 mean "2"? Grist to the anti-Grice mill', in E. Hajičová (ed.), *Proceedings of the Conference on Functional Description of Language, Prague Nov. 24–27, 1992*. Prague: Faculty of Mathematics and Physics, Charles University: 225–35. (Reprinted as Chapter 16 in Seuren 2001.)

—— (1994) 'Presupposition', in R. E. Asher and J. M. Y. Simpson (eds), *The Encyclopedia of Language and Linguistics*. Oxford: Pergamon Press: 3311–20.

—— (1995) 'Notes on the history and the syntax of Mauritian Creole', *Linguistics* 33: 531–77.

—— (1996) *Semantic Syntax*. Blackwell, Oxford.

—— (1998*a*) *Western Linguistics. An Historical Introduction*. Blackwell, Oxford.

—— (1998*b*) 'Towards a discourse-semantic account of donkey anaphora', in S. Botley and T. McEnery (eds), *New Approaches to Discourse Anaphora: Proceedings of the Second Colloquium on Discourse Anaphora and Anaphor Resolution (DAARC2)*. University Centre for Computer Corpus Research on Language, Lancaster University. Technical Papers, Vol. 11, Special Issue: 212–20. (Reprinted as Chapter 17 in Seuren 2001.)

—— (2000) 'Presupposition, negation and trivalence', *Journal of Linguistics* 36/2: 261–97.

—— (2001) *A View of Language*. Oxford University Press, Oxford.

—— (2002) 'The Logic of Thinking', Koninklijke Nederlandse Akademie van Wetenschappen, Mededelingen van de Afdeling Letterkunde, Nieuwe Reeks 65/9.

—— (2004) *Chomsky's Minimalism*. Oxford University Press, New York.

—— (2005) 'Eubulides as a 20th-century semanticist', *Language Sciences* 27/1: 75–95.

—— V. CAPRETTA, and H. GEUVERS (2001) 'The logic and mathematics of occasion sentences', *Linguistics and Philosophy* 24/2: 531–95.

SIGWART, CHR. (1895) *Logic. Vol. I. The Judgment, Concept, and Inference* (authorized translation from the German original by Helen Dendy). Swan Sonnenschein and Co., London/Macmillan and Co., New York.

SORABJI, R. (2004) *The Philosophy of the Commentators, 200–600 AD. A Sourcebook. Vol. 3: Logic and Metaphysics*. Duckworth, London.

—— (ed.) (1990) *Aristotle Transformed. The Ancient Commentators and their Influence*. Duckworth, London.

STALNAKER, R. C. (1978) 'Assertion', in P. Cole (ed.), *Pragmatics*. (Syntax and Semantics 9.) Academic Press, New York-San Francisco-London: 315–32.

STANLEY, J. and Z. SZABÓ (2000) 'On quantifier domain restriction', *Mind and Language* 15/2: 219–61.

STAROBINSKI, J. (1979) *Words upon Words. The Anagrams of Ferdinand de Saussure*. Transl. by Olivia Emmet. Yale University Press, New Haven-London.

STEINTHAL, H. (1855) *Grammatik, Logik und Psychologie, ihre Prinzipien und ihre Verhältnisse zueinander*. Dümmler, Berlin.

—— (1860) *Charakteristik der hauptsächlichsten Typen des Sprachbaues*. (Neubearbeitung von Dr. Franz Misteli.) Dümmler, Berlin.

STOUT, G. F. (1896[1]; 1909[3]) *Analytical Psychology*. 2 vols. Swan Sonnenschein and Co., London/Macmillan and Co., New York.

STRAWSON, P. F. (1950) 'On referring', *Mind* 59: 320–44.

—— (1952) *Introduction to Logical Theory*. Methuen, London.

—— (1954) 'A reply to Mr Sellars', *Philosophical Review* 63/2: 216–31.

—— (1964) 'Identifying reference and truth-values', *Theoria* 30/2: 96–118.

STRAWSON, P. F. (1974) *Subject and Predicate in Logic and Grammar*. Methuen, London.

SULLIVAN, M. W. (1967) *Apuleian Logic. The Nature, Sources, and Influence of Apuleius's Peri Hermeneias.* North-Holland, Amsterdam.

SVEDELIUS, C. (1897) *L'analyse du langage appliquée à la langue française.* Almqvist and Wiksell, Uppsala.

TASMOWSKI-DE RYCK, L. and S. P. VERLUYTEN (1982) 'Linguistic control of pronouns', *Journal of Semantics* 1/4: 323–46.

THOMPSON, M. (1953) 'On Aristotle's Square of Opposition', *The Philosophical Review* 62/2: 251–65.

TRAUGOTT, E. C., A. TER MEULEN, J. SNITZER REILLY, and CH. A. FERGUSON (eds) (1986) *On Conditionals.* Cambridge University Press, Cambridge.

VAN DALEN, D. (1999) *Mystic, Geometer, and Intuitionist: The Life of L. E. J. Brouwer. Vol. 1, The Dawning Revolution.* Oxford University Press, Oxford.

VAN DER AUWERA, J. (1998) 'Pragmatics in the last quarter-century: the case of conditional perfection', *Journal of Pragmatics* 27/3: 261–74.

VAN DER SANDT, R. A. (1992) 'Presupposition projection as anaphora resolution', *Journal of Semantics* 9/4: 333–77.

VAN FRAASSEN, B. (1971) *Formal Semantics and Logic.* Macmillan, New York-London.

VAN KUPPEVELT, J. C. J. (1991) 'Topic en Comment. Expliciete en Impliciete Vraagstelling in Discourse', Ph.D. thesis, Radboud University, Nijmegen.

VAN OIRSOUW, R. R. (1987) *The Syntax of Coordination.* Croom Helm, London.

VELTMAN, F. (1985) 'Logics for Conditionals', Ph.D. thesis, University of Amsterdam.

VON DER GABELENTZ, H. G. C. (1869) 'Ideen zu einer vergleichenden Syntax. Wort- und Satzstellung', *Zeitschrift für Völkerpsychologie und Sprachwissenschaft* 6: 376–84.

—— (1891[1]; 1901[2]) *Die Sprachwissenschaft. Ihre Aufgaben, Methoden und bisherigen Ergebnisse.* Leipzig: Tauchnitz.

WEGENER, C. (2008) *A Grammar of Savosavo, a Papuan Language of the Solomon Islands.* Ph.D. thesis, Radboud University, Nijmegen. (= MPI Series in Psycholinguistics, 51). Max Planck Institute for Psycholinguistics, P.O. Box 310, 6500 AH Nijmegen, The Netherlands.

WEGENER, PH. (1885) *Untersuchungen über die Grundfragen des Sprachlebens.* Niemeyer, Halle. [Reprinted 1991, with an introduction by Clemens Knobloch. Benjamins, Amsterdam-Philadelphia.]

WEIDEMANN, H. (1994) *Aristoteles' Peri Hermeneias. Uebersetzt und erläutert von Herman Weidemann.* Akademie-Verlag, Berlin.

WEIJTERS, A. (1985) 'Presuppositional propositional calculi', Appendix to Seuren (1985: 483–525).

—— (1989) 'Denotation in Discourse: Analysis and Algorithm', Ph.D. thesis, Radboud University, Nijmegen.

WHITEHEAD, A. N. and B. RUSSELL (1910–1913) *Principia Mathematica.* 3 vols. Cambridge University Press, Cambridge.

WIERZBICKA, A. (1996) *Semantics. Primes and Universals.* Oxford University Press, Oxford.

WILSON, D. (1975) *Presuppositions and Non-Truth-Conditional Semantics.* Academic Press, London-New York-San Francisco.

Wundt, W. (1900[1]; 1922[4]) *Völkerpsychologie. Eine Untersuchung der Entwicklungsgesetze von Sprache, Mythus und Sitte. Volume 2, Die Sprache, Part 2.* Kröner, Leipzig.

Zalta, E. N. (1988) *Intensional Logic and the Metaphysics of Intentionality.* A Bradford Book. MIT Press, Cambridge, MA.

Zwicky, A. (1973) 'Linguistics as chemistry: the substance theory of semantic primes', in S. Anderson and P. Kiparsky (eds), *A Festschrift for Morris Halle.* Holt, New York: 467–85.

Index

Printed and bound by CPI Group (UK) Ltd, Croydon, CR0 4YY